THE SOCIALIST OFFENSIVE, 1929–1930

By the same author

THE INDUSTRIALISATION OF SOVIET RUSSIA 2: THE SOVIET COLLECTIVE FARM, 1929–1930

THE INDUSTRIALISATION OF SOVIET RUSSIA 3: THE SOVIET ECONOMY IN TURMOIL, 1929–1930

THE DEVELOPMENT OF THE SOVIET BUDGETARY SYSTEM

FOUNDATIONS OF A PLANNED ECONOMY, 1926–1929, Volume One (with E. H. Carr)

SCIENCE POLICY IN THE USSR (with E. Zaleski and others)

THE SOVIET UNION (editor)

THE TECHNOLOGICAL LEVEL OF SOVIET INDUSTRY (editor with R. Amann and J. M. Cooper)

THE INDUSTRIALISATION OF SOVIET RUSSIA 1

THE SOCIALIST OFFENSIVE

THE COLLECTIVISATION OF SOVIET AGRICULTURE, 1929–1930

R. W. DAVIES
Professor of Soviet Economic Studies
University of Birmingham

M
MACMILLAN
PRESS

First edition 1980
Reprinted 1989

Published by
THE MACMILLAN PRESS LTD
Houndmills, Basingstoke, Hampshire RG21 2XS
and London
Companies and representatives
throughout the world

Printed in China

British Library Cataloguing in Publication Data
Davies, Robert William
The industrialisation of Soviet Russia
1: The socialist offensive, 1929–1930
1: Russia–Industries–History
2. Russia–Economic conditions 1918–1945
I. Title II. Socialist offensive, 1929–1930
338'.0941 HC335.2
ISBN 0–333–26171–2 (hardcover)
ISBN 0–333–46593–8 (paperback)

In memory of my father
WILLIAM DAVIES
1892–1976

CONTENTS

LIST OF TABLES

PREFACE

Between 1929 and 1936, the Soviet Union was transformed into a great industrial power; in its speed and scale, the Soviet industrial revolution has neither precedent nor successor anywhere in the world. This was not intended, exclusively or even primarily, as an economic transformation. The Soviet Communists saw industrialisation as a prerequisite for achieving their central objective—the establishment, in a largely peasant country, isolated in a hostile capitalist world, of a socialist economy and society; and by 1936, with the collectivisation of agriculture, and the elimination of the private hire of labour for profit, a kind of socialist economy had been created.

This formidable and heroic effort of men and women to shape their own destiny by a comprehensive state plan acquired tragic and ironic qualities. The outcome of Soviet policies was neither the systematic economic development nor, in several major respects, the kind of socialist economic system envisaged in the Soviet party at the end of the 1920s. The hopes for higher food production—which would have brought about an improved standard of living in both town and country—were entirely frustrated; the fortunes of agriculture, and the relation between the regime and the peasantry, reached their nadir during the famine of 1932–3. And, although the economy was largely state-owned and centrally planned, Soviet socialism retained or developed unforeseen attributes. Until 1930, it was assumed by Soviet marxists that socialism would be based entirely on moneyless product-exchange. Instead, the Soviet economy remained a monetary economy, with a substantial free peasant market. In place of the expected growing equality of incomes, income differentials greatly increased. The use of forced labour relentlessly expanded. Simultaneously, the political dictatorship, intended as an instrument for advancing the Soviet economy and establishing a free classless society, soon assumed its own mode of behaviour, and followed its own laws of growth.

The final instalment of E. H. Carr's history of Soviet Russia,

Foundations of a Planned Economy, 1926–1929, recounts the background to these events, culminating, in the spring of 1929, in a profound crisis of confidence between the regime and the peasantry, and in the consolidation of Stalin's dictatorship. After collaborating with Dr Carr on the economic volume of *Foundations* with such pleasure and profit, I was unable to resist the temptation to carry forward the story into the 1930s. In the first stages of research it soon became clear that, while the materials available for the study of political decision-making at the centre are wholly inadequate after 1929, and while many gaps in our knowledge of the economy cannot be filled, abundant information on many aspects of economic policy and development is available in Soviet economic and political journals, daily newspapers and statistical publications, and in accounts by Western eye-witnesses. Moreover, since the death of Stalin a great deal of previously unknown material has been reproduced from the archives in Soviet publications, though unfortunately, in common with other Western historians, I have not yet been permitted to use Soviet archives relating to this period.

The focus of interest in the present series of volumes, *The Industrialisation of Soviet Russia*, is the mutual impact of economic policy, economic and political institutions, and the economic and social environment. Two aspects of the study may be of special interest to the general reader. First, I would hope that better understanding of Soviet triumphs and failures in planning economic development might prove relevant to the planned industrialisation on which all developing countries have to a greater or lesser degree embarked. Secondly, improved knowledge of the processes by which the Soviet economic system emerged may assist our understanding of its present operation: the first half of the 1930s was the formative period for the Soviet system, and the main features which it then acquired still remain at the present day.

The series is provisionally planned as five or six volumes. The present volume deals with the relationship between the state, the peasantry and agriculture between June 1929 and the end of 1930. This is the obvious starting point in an economic history of the 1930s: it was the period of the first collectivisation drive, as momentous in its impact on Russian history as the Bolshevik revolution of October 1917, and often described as the third Russian revolution. A second briefer volume, published simultaneously, *The Soviet Collective Farm, 1929–1930*, examines the emergence of the collective farm (kolkhoz) as the predominant economic unit in agriculture (this volume is referred to here as 'vol. 2'). The third volume in the series, now in preparation, will discuss developments in industry and planning during this period. Further volumes will deal with the economic crisis of 1931–3, which turned on the difficulties in agriculture, and with the triumph of planned industrialisation and the consolidation of the economic system from 1934 onwards.

The main narrative in the present volume, concerned with developments from June 1929, is preceded by a long introductory chapter setting the scene (ch. 1). From the autumn of 1927, the market relation between town and country which was at the heart of the New Economic Policy (NEP) was increasingly undermined, and by June 1929 there was a profound crisis of confidence between regime and peasantry. The present volume does not undertake a substantially new investigation of these developments, but in view of their importance to an understanding of collectivisation itself I attempt in chapter 1 to summarise the present state of our knowledge. The grain crisis of the autumn of 1927 was the dramatic moment when the delicate balance of NEP was upset (see pp. 35–40 below). Even more important than the grain crisis itself was the reaction to it of the Soviet authorities. From the beginning of 1928, policy towards the peasantry turned on the profound conviction of a section of the Soviet leadership that industrialisation must be forced ahead at a rapid pace, even at the expense of the abandonment in practice of the market relation with the peasants. The policies pursued were not the only possible industrialisation strategy; the argument that no industrialisation at all was possible within the framework of NEP seems to me untenable. But I would argue, and will try elsewhere to demonstrate, that industrialisation at the extraordinary pace actually achieved in 1929–36 was quite incompatible with a market relation with the peasantry. How did the party come to adopt this breakneck pace of industrialisation in 1928–9? I summarise the existing state of our knowledge of the political, social and economic factors involved on pp. 399–404.

By June 1929, the party leadership had not yet determined how to resolve the crisis. But between the summer of 1929 and February 1930 collectivisation was forced through at an increasing pace, and much of the present volume is concerned with explaining how this came about. Our account begins with the grain collections of the summer and autumn of 1929, the immediate prelude to collectivisation (ch.2). The acceleration of the collectivisation drive in the winter of 1929–30 is then examined in detail (chs 3–5); some conclusions about the causes and nature of this drive are drawn on pp. 405–10. An account of the retreat from collectivisation in February–July 1930, and the crisis in the party associated with it (chs 5–7), is followed by a review of the results of the first harvest after collectivisation, which was remarkably successful (ch. 8, and pp. 410–14). The narrative concludes with the resumption of collectivisation at a more cautious pace in the autumn of 1930 (ch. 9). The problems associated with the mechanisation of agriculture in this period are discussed separately in chapter 10. The party, passionately convinced that modern technology was essential to the construction of socialism, nevertheless embarked on collectivisation prior to mechanisation: this paradox encapsulates the difficulties and the policies of those stormy years. The exciting and fashionable question of the extent to which collectivisation facilitated industrialisation has been reserved for treatment in a later volume.

Many people have provided advice and assistance in the preparation of the first two volumes. I owe a special debt of gratitude to E. H. Carr, who has freely given advice and encouragement over many years; the sections of his history which deal with agriculture in the 1920s have provided much intellectual stimulation and information, and I am proud to be able to continue, however inadequately, one aspect of his work. Moshe Lewin, whose forthcoming social history of the 1930s promises to be a major contribution to our knowledge, has provided similar assistance; his indispensable work, *Russian Peasants and Soviet Power*, which examines developments up to the end of 1929, was a constant source of ideas and information on the first half of the period covered by the present volume. Yuzuru Taniuchi, whose major study of this period is unfortunately available only in Japanese, commented in detail on several chapters, and provided much additional information. I am also conscious of my intellectual debt to other Western scholars: the publications of Baykov, Dobb, Erlich, Fainsod, Jasny, Male, R. F. Miller, Nove, Shanin and others were frequently consulted with much profit.

Stephen Wheatcroft, who has been working with me for the past five years on the economic history of the 1920s and 1930s, has acquired an unparalleled depth of knowledge of Soviet agricultural statistics, their problems and their economic implications, which he has placed freely at my disposal; his ruthless comments and practical advice on my first draft, and particularly on chapters 1 and 8, have been invaluable, and I am most grateful to him. R. A. Lewis provided much useful material for chapter 2. Valuable comments on individual chapters, and other assistance, were received from Donald Filtzer, Mark Harrison, Jonathan Haslam, Teodor Shanin and Leslie Symons.

In the pursuit of material for this and subsequent volumes I visited the USSR on four occasions between 1969 and 1974, attached to the Faculty of Economics of Leningrad University, the Faculty of History of Moscow University and the Institute of History of the USSR of the Academy of Sciences; the Lenin and Saltykov–Shchedrin Libraries were rich sources of material. I was able to have valuable exchanges of views with many Soviet colleagues during my visits; among many others, I must particularly mention Yu. A. Polyakov, V. P. Danilov, V. Z. Drobizhev and I. N. Olegina. On the contentious subject of collectivisation the usual caveat that these Soviet colleagues, and their Western counterparts, bear no responsibility for my conclusions and my errors is patently redundant.

The Baykov Library of the Centre for Russian and East European Studies at Birmingham University provided most of my material, and our indefatigable librarian, Ms J. J. Brine, was an unfailing source of help. The Library of the Glasgow Institute of Soviet and East European Studies and its former librarian, Dr Large, should also be particularly mentioned. Hugh Jenkins undertook the arduous task of preparing the indexes of these two volumes. Jean Fyfe again bore the main burden of accurately transcribing drafts which were in principle indecipherable, often typing at a feverish speed exacted by an impatient author who acquired some of the characteristics of the enthusiastic collectivisers described in his text. Others who typed part of the manuscript included Ruth Ferguson, Olga Griffin, Karen Witherford and Anthea Roth, who as Centre Secretary in 1971–8 also assisted the progress of the work in other ways. My friend Geoffrey Barker, who died tragically in September 1977, selflessly relieved me from administrative burdens over many years; and I am most grateful to Ron Amann, who shouldered the acting Directorship of our Centre at short notice for the session 1977/78, and, supported by John Dunstan and all my other colleagues, provided me with a year of peaceful research. Mr Tim Farmiloe, of Macmillan Press Ltd, offered much encouragement and advice. But the *sine qua non* of these volumes were my wife Frances, and our children Maurice and Cathy, who showed exemplary patience with a nervous author, and provided much comfort, throughout the lengthy gestation of this book.

Work on these volumes has been assisted by the funds provided by the British Social Science Research Council for the Birmingham project on 'The Social and Economic History of the USSR during Industrialisation'. These funds made it possible to employ Mr Wheatcroft (whose work on agricultural statistics is being published separately), supported the purchase of books and microfilms, and travel to the USSR, and enabled me to devote an academic session (1977/78) full-time to these studies.

February 1979 R. W. Davies

On the occasion of the reprinting of the present volume I have taken the opportunity to correct some errors and misprints. The most important changes are on pages 64–65, where Soviet archival data have enabled greater accuracy about the harvest estimates, and on page 375 where I have corrected the date of Syrtsov's critical speech about economic policy from October to 30 August 1930.

January 1988 R.W.D.

TECHNICAL NOTE

This Note summarises some of the conventions used in this volume, and briefly explains the Soviet administrative structure in this period.

(1) The Union of Soviet Socialist Republics was divided at this time into six 'Union republics'; the USSR and the Union republics all had their own government headed by a Council of People's Commissars (Sovnarkom), each with its own People's Commissariats (Narkoms) (i.e. Ministries). Some Narkoms (e.g. for War and Transport) existed only at the USSR, or 'all-Union', level; a second category (e.g. for Finance and Industry) existed at both the 'all-Union' and the 'republican' level; a third category (e.g. for Education) existed only in the republics. Agriculture was served only by republican Commissariats (Narkomzems) until December 1929, when the all-Union Narkomzem was formed: agriculture thus moved from the third to the second category. For brevity, the convention has been adopted in this volume of referring to all-Union commissariats or other agencies without adding 'of the USSR': thus 'Narkomfin' refers to the People's Commissariat of Finance of the USSR, and the equivalent Commissariat for the Russian Republic is referred to as 'Narkomfin of the RSFSR'; the Sovnarkoms of the USSR and the republics are handled similarly. Where no all-Union agency exists, the agency for the Russian republic is referred to in this volume by the short title. Thus, until December 1929 the People's Commissariat for Agriculture of the RSFSR is simply referred to as 'Narkomzem', but after December 1929 'Narkomzem' refers to the all-Union agricultural commissariat, and the agricultural commissariat of the Russian republic is referred to as 'Narkomzem of the RSFSR'.

(2) Traditionally, the main unit of local government in the larger republics was the province (*gubernia*), in turn subdivided into *uezdy* (counties) and *volosti* (rural districts); the *selo* (village) was the lowest administrative unit. By 1929 the transition to a new division was almost complete. The principal unit was the *oblast'* or *krai*; these

both had the same status, and so are both translated here as 'region'. Each region included several former provinces or parts of provinces. The difference between the *oblast'* and the *krai* was simply that the latter had autonomous regions subordinate to it; confusingly, 'autonomous republics' (ASSRs) had approximately the same status as regions (*oblasti* or *krai*), and 'autonomous regions' were subordinate to *krai*. The regions were divided into *okruga* (referred to here simply as okrugs, but in E. H. Carr's history as 'departments'); these were in turn divided into *raiony* (districts); the *selo* (village) remained the lowest administrative unit. Towns fitted into the structure at various levels according to their importance. In the summer and autumn of 1930, okrugs were abolished, so the basic structure was Union republic (SSR) – region (oblast' or krai) – district (raion) – village. Just before the abolition of the okrugs, there were 13 regions, 207 okrugs, 2,811 districts and 71,780 village soviets in the USSR, for a rural population of 120 million or so: thus the population of the average district was over 40,000 persons (about 8,000 households), of the average village soviet about 1,700 persons (about 350 households). There were also 15 ASSRs and 17 autonomous regions.[1]

(3) The party structure was, broadly speaking, parallel to, though effectively superior to, the governmental structure. At the top, the party congress elected a central committee which in turn appointed a Politburo headed by a general secretary (Stalin); in the governmental (soviet) structure, the congress of soviets elected an intermediate Central Executive Committee (TsIK), which in turn appointed Sovnarkom, headed by a chairman (Rykov). The Politburo and Sovnarkom were the effective central working bodies of party and government. Below the all-Union level, every republic had its own Politburo, central committee, TsIK and Sovnarkom; and in every region, okrug, district, town and village the principal officials were the secretary of the party committee and the chairman of the soviet executive committee.

(4) In 1929–30 a soviet congress met only in May 1929 (the fifth); the central executive committee (TsIK) only in December 1929; and the party congress (the sixteenth) only in June–July 1930 (the

[1] PKh, 6, 1930, 94–5; 75 counties and 435 rural districts lingered on from the old system. The Union republics and the regions varied so much in population that an average would be meaningless.

sixteenth party conference met in April 1929); plenums (full meetings) of the central committee were held in April and November 1929, and in July and December 1930 (the July 1930 plenum was formal, associated with the party congress). The Politburo and Sovnarkom met frequently, at least weekly. Resolutions by the Politburo were published as from the 'central committee' of the party, and are described thus in this volume, but it should be borne in mind that normally they were in fact Politburo decisions.

(5) The central committee (in practice, the Politburo) was supported by central committee departments consisting of full-time party officials. In the spring of 1928 a 'department for work in the countryside' was formed, headed at various times by Bauman or Molotov. This department, referred to in the present volume simply as the 'rural department' of the central committee, was abolished in January 1930.

(6) The agricultural year ran from July 1 to June 30 of the succeeding year, and the economic year from October 1 to September 30. The economic year 1929/30 was followed by the 'special quarter', October–December 1930, after which the economic and the calendar year coincided. Following Soviet practice, economic and agricultural years are indicated in this volume by a diagonal line: '1928/29' and '1929/30', not '1928–9', '1929–30', which refer to calendar years.

CHAPTER ONE

THE PEASANT ECONOMY AND THE SOVIET SYSTEM, 1917–29

(A) THE BOLSHEVIKS AND THE PEASANTRY, 1917–21

The victory of the Bolshevik revolution in a predominantly peasant country posed a fundamental dilemma to the makers of Soviet economic policy. In *Anti-Dühring*, written in 1878, Engels had vividly presented the marxist vision of the new social and economic order which would emerge after a socialist revolution:

> The seizure of the means of production by society puts an end to commodity production, and therewith to the domination of the product over the producer. Anarchy in social production is replaced by conscious organisation on a planned basis . . . The laws of his own social activity, which have hitherto confronted him as external, dominating laws of Nature, will then be applied by man with complete understanding . . . It is humanity's leap from the realm of necessity into the realm of freedom.[1]

Marx and Engels exempted the numerous small peasant economies, which persisted even in advanced capitalist countries like France and Germany, from the forcible expropriation to which the factories of the industrialists and the estates of large landowners would be subjected. Instead, the peasants should be converted to collective production and ownership 'by example and by offering social aid for this purpose'.[2]

In Russia after the Bolshevik revolution of 1917 circumstances were not propitious for achieving immediately Engels' 'conscious organisation on a planned basis'. Marx and Engels believed that the world socialist revolution would begin not in a primarily peasant

[1] Engels (London, n.d. [?1939]), 318.
[2] See Carr and Davies (1969), 264n.

country but in countries in which productive forces were already highly developed. While they envisaged that a communist society might emerge in Russia on the basis of the peasant commune, the *mir*, they took it for granted that this would be possible only 'if the Russian revolution serves as a signal for the workers' revolution in the west, so that the two complement each other'.[3]

Engels' vision of the communist future was an integral part of the world outlook of Lenin and the Bolsheviks. In the first few years after the revolution they did not depart from the standpoint that the survival of the Soviet government depended on a successful socialist revolution in an advanced country; and, while they believed that Marx's hopes of the mir had been superseded by the subsequent development of rural capitalism in Russia, they wholly endorsed Engels' rejection of the use of force to socialise the peasant economy.[4] But in 1918–20 they were confronted with widespread civil war; no successful revolution occurred in the West; and they had to manage on their own. Industry was nationalised, and the Soviet government attempted to introduce a system of comprehensive state planning. While the peasants were not forced into collective production or ownership, they were deprived of the results of their labour, forcibly and with almost no compensation, by the requisitioning of grain and other crops. These were emergency measures: Lenin justified the despatch of armed grain detachments to the villages in May 1918 by reference to widespread hunger and imminent catastrophe.[5] But for the Soviet leaders this was not purely an emergency policy. Throughout the Civil War they took the line that all transactions with the peasants should be conducted by the state and its agencies, and that they must be either at fixed prices, or by direct exchange of industrial for agricultural products; market transactions were mere speculation. The grain monopoly, Lenin declared in a telegram dated June 27, 1918, is 'one of the most important methods for gradual transition from capitalist commodity exchange to socialist product-exchange'.[6] With the coming of peace, Lenin insisted at the VIII congress of soviets in December 1920 that grain requisitioning must be maintained. The congress called, with Lenin's support, for the establishment of sowing committees in every rural district which would impose a national

[3] See Carr (1952), 390 (statement by Marx in 1882).

[4] See Carr and Davies (1969), 264–5n.

[5] *Soch.*, xxvii, 354.

[6] *Soch.*, xxvii, 417.

plan for obligatory sowing in the spring of 1921.[7] The forcible socialisation of peasant agriculture continued to be rejected by party doctrine, but obligatory control over the production methods of the peasant, and the forcible seizure of his product, were now regarded as an appropriate and essential feature of the socialist economy.

Widespread disturbances among the peasants, which began in the summer of 1920 and spread to the hungry workers of Petrograd and elsewhere in January 1921, formed the stormy background to the dramatic decision of the X party congress in March 1921 to replace requisitioning by a tax in kind. The peasants were permitted to dispose freely of production in excess of this tax: the crucial feature of the New Economic Policy (NEP), as it emerged during the next few months, was the market relation between the millions of individual peasant households and the rest of the economy. By 1924, a tax in money, the agricultural tax, completely replaced the tax in kind. All shades of party opinion now agreed that coercion could not be used to control either the production activities of the peasants or how they disposed of their products, which should be acquired only at prices which the peasants were prepared to accept voluntarily.

NEP did not involve, however, the abandonment of planning as such. The XII party congress declared in April 1923 that planning now required 'continuous and careful adaptation of the controlling economic machine and its basic objectives, methods and practice to market conditions and relations', the replacement of 'ordering about by government committees (glavkokraticheskoe administrirovanie)' by 'economic manoeuvring'.[8]

Thus an important qualification was added to Engels' notion that the socialisation of the peasant economy would be achieved gradually 'by example and by offering social aid'. The market economy would be retained throughout the period of transition to socialism; the planned development of the economy would be achieved through state management of the peasant market. And in 1925, with proletarian revolution in the more advanced countries no more than a remote prospect, the party concluded that socialism could and would be established in the Soviet Union alone, without the support of other socialist regimes.

[7] Lenin, *Soch.*, xxxi, 471–7, 490–1, 492–8; *Direktivy*, i (1957), 191–6.
[8] *Direktivy*, i (1957), 381–2.

(B) THE PEASANT ECONOMY IN THE MID-1920S

Between 1922 and 1926, the New Economic Policy, by and large, was a brilliant success. Industrial and agricultural production regained their pre-war level more rapidly than anyone had anticipated. The production of the peasant economy in 1926 was equal to that of the whole of agriculture, including the landowners' estates, before the revolution. Grain production reached approximately the pre-war level,[9] and the production of potatoes apparently exceeded that level by as much as 45 per cent (see Table 1). The number of livestock, which fell drastically during the world war and the Civil War, almost regained the 1914 level by 1926, and in 1928 exceeded it by 7–10 per cent in the case of cattle and pigs, and by a considerably higher percentage in the case of sheep (see Table 2).[10] Between 1924 and 1928, the number of livestock rose by 3–4 per cent a year, both more rapidly and more regularly than in the years immediately preceding the First World War, and cattle were heavier and better fed.[11] Some industrial crops provided remarkable examples of the possibilities of adapting peasant economies to specialised production. Before 1914, 79 per cent of sugar beet was grown on estates, and only 21 per cent on 150–200 thousand peasant farms; by 1927, with the same level of production,

[9] It is uncertain whether the pre-war grain figures are comparable with those for the 1920s. The following table shows the range of possibilities (and see Table 1) (1913 was an exceptionally good year, 1926 the best year in the 1920s) (million tons):

1909–1913 (average)		*1913 (highest pre-war harvest)*		*1926–1929 (average)*	*1926 (highest harvest in 1920s)*
Lowest estimate	*Highest estimate*	*Lowest estimate*	*Highest estimate*		
65	80	77	94	74	77

[10] Most sources compare the number of livestock in the 1920s with 1916, and assume that the maximum level before the revolution was attained in this year; they therefore conclude that the pre-revolutionary level was reached as soon as 1925, and exceeded by some 15–20 per cent in 1928. A persuasive article by Vainshtein, in *Ocherki po istorii statistike SSSR* (1960), 86–115, argues, however, that the number of livestock fell substantially between 1914 and 1916; the above statement is based on his calculations for 1914. See also Anfimov (1962), 233–9.

[11] See Danilov (1977), 298; Wheatcroft (1976), 88, n. 3.

68 per cent was grown on as many as 1,200,000 peasant farms, usually on very small sown areas.[12] Cotton growing, always almost entirely a peasant crop,[13] was re-established on even smaller units than before the war. For all these crops the yield (production per hectare) was substantially lower than in 1914.[14] But in 1927 production of cotton and sugar beet reached, and production of oil seeds substantially exceeded, the pre-war level (see Table 1).

As a result of all these developments, the proportion of sown area and of gross agricultural production devoted to grain was lower in 1928 than in 1913[15]—a good general indicator of agricultural progress.

In spite of its successful recovery and development, peasant agriculture in the mid-1920s suffered from major weaknesses from the standpoint of the Bolshevik objective of constructing a planned socialist society and an industrialised economy in the USSR.

First, peasant farming methods and technology, and the resulting level of production, remained extremely backward as compared with the advanced countries which the Soviet government was seeking to emulate.

Secondly, while agricultural production was equal to the pre-war level, the peasant economy participated in the market to a much smaller extent than the agricultural economy of the Russian Empire before 1914. This gave added emphasis to a crucial problem in the industrialisation of a peasant country—how to secure increased supplies of agricultural raw materials for an expanding industry and of food for a rising urban population, while at the same time providing finance for investment in long-term industrial projects.

Thirdly, over the vast and heterogeneous territory of the USSR regional variations in patterns of peasant agriculture were immense. Two major regional problems were a particular source of anxiety. Agriculture in the former tsarist colonies, mainly inhabited by non-Slavic peoples, remained backward, and political and social arguments spoke strongly in favour of developing these regions, though the immense cost held back effective action. A problem of

12 Danilov (1977), 291–4.

13 Anfimov (1969), 220.

14 Compare production figures in Table 1 with figures for sown area in *Sots. str.* (1935), 322–3.

15 *Ezhegodnik khlebooborota*, iii (1931), i, p. viii (Lyashchenko).

more immediate importance was that the recovery of the major grain regions, crucial for feeding the urban population and for the Soviet foreign trade balance, lagged considerably behind most of the other agricultural areas.

Fourthly, the recovery of agriculture involved the re-emergence of capitalistic relations and economic differentiation within the peasantry. The extent of economic differentiation was hotly disputed, but many communists believed that it had gone far enough to constitute a fundamental threat to the social basis of their regime.

Finally, the economic relation between the state and the peasantry, even in the years of recovery, had proved to be extremely unstable.

(i) *Farming and technology*

In the mid-1920s the vast majority of the Soviet population were peasants farming in small family units. The socialised sector of Soviet agriculture, including both sovkhozy (state farms) and kolkhozy (collective farms), was responsible for only 2·2 per cent of gross farm production,[16] the rest being produced by some 25 million individual peasant households. Nine-tenths of the households belonged to a peasant commune (a *mir* or *obshchina*, now known officially as a land society); in the Russian republic on January 1, 1927, only 3·5 per cent of peasant land was cultivated in the form of khutors (fully-enclosed farms) or otrubs (farms on which only the arable land was enclosed).[17]

In the vast majority of the mirs, the arable land was divided into strips. A simple three-field system predominated, with autumn-sown rye or wheat, spring-sown wheat or other grain, and fallow succeeding each other on each field; even more primitive two-field or shifting systems of cultivation were found in many areas. In most places the amount of arable land allotted to each household (the *nadel*) depended on the number of members. Each household was allocated a number of strips in each field, so as to equalise between households the distance to the land from the village and the fertility of the soil. Each household was also allocated a segment of the hayland. Permanent pastures, rivers and lakes were retained by the

[16] *Nar. kh.* (1932), p. xlvii.

[17] *Itogi . . . 1917–1927* (n.d. [?1928], 120–1); 0·9 per cent of land was held as khutors, and 2·6 per cent as otrubs.

mir as a whole for collective use. Cattle, though of course owned by individual households, pastured in common on the fallow, and on the stubble after the harvest;[18] many mirs employed a common herdsman. The only part of peasant activity which was more or less independent of the mir was the cultivation of the household plot—the *usad'ba*—around the cottage, where the household grew fruit and vegetables and kept its animals.

This complex system of communal tenure meant that the general assembly of the commune—the gathering (skhod)—had to decide not only the allocation of land but also what crops should be grown on each field and when the ploughing, sowing and harvesting should take place. Over most of the USSR, the skhod also had the task of redistributing the strips periodically to allow for changes in the membership of each household. Before the revolution, redistribution was becoming less frequent. In the 1920s, a 'general redistribution' of all the land was supposed, according to the Land Code, to take place at most once in nine years. In practice, redistribution took place annually in many areas, and almost everywhere minor adjustments were frequent.[19]

These long-established arrangements were regarded by the peasants as equitable, and were greatly strengthened, by the peasants' own action, after the revolution. But they involved much waste. The peasants had to make long journeys to their numerous scattered strips. Access paths and boundary land could not be cultivated. Where redistribution was frequent, the peasants had little incentive to manure and improve their strips. On the narrower strips not even horse-drawn machinery could be used.

All schools of thought within the Soviet Communist Party in the 1920s—from Trotsky and Preobrazhensky on the Left to Bukharin on the Right—regarded the strip system and communal tenure as inherently inefficient and unprogressive. But no-one expected to be able to entice the peasants from their traditional way of life until machinery could be supplied to the countryside on a large scale. In these circumstances the party leaders were prepared to take advice from non-party experts ('bourgeois specialists') in the People's Commissariat of Agriculture of the RSFSR—Narkomzem—who had faith in modernising agriculture by improvements which did

[18] Danilov (1977), 108–16.

[19] IS, 3, 1958, 101–2; Danilov (1977), 111–22; Male (1971), 57–65. Land was not periodically redistributed in many Ukrainian communes.

not fundamentally change the existing system of land tenure.

Much was achieved by the mid-1920s along three main lines. First, the agencies responsible for improving the allocation of land within and between the mirs (land consolidation—*zemleustroistvo*) and for land improvement made good progress. The intermingling of strips between settlements, and the number of strips per household within individual settlements, were greatly reduced.[20] Multi-field rotations were introduced on 17 per cent of the sown area of the RSFSR by 1927, as compared with 7 per cent in 1924 and less than 1·5 per cent in 1916. The proportion of cleaned and graded seed was raised from 6 per cent in 1924/25 to 14 per cent in 1926/27.[21]

Secondly, the supply of horse-drawn implements and machines greatly increased. By 1926/27, the annual supply, in spite of the decline in imports, was already higher than in 1913.[22]

Thirdly, the pre-revolutionary network of agricultural cooperatives was restored and developed: by October 1, 1926, the total membership of all types of agricultural cooperative was 6·7 million households, over 25 per cent of the total, thus approaching the pre-revolutionary level.[23] In 1926/27, over half the value of implements and machinery purchased by peasants was financed through the agricultural credit cooperatives; and marketing cooperatives already predominated in the purchase of industrial crops from the peasants, and purchased a substantial proportion of dairy products.[24]

Nevertheless, by the end of the 1920s most of the rural economy remained unmodernised, even within the existing system of peasant tenure. By 1929, land consolidation within the mir involved less than 20 per cent of the land area in the RSFSR, and the planning department of Narkomzem estimated that it could be completed in the RSFSR, even within the framework of the strip system, only by resettling 30 per cent of all households.[25]

[20] Latsis and Litvinov, eds. (1929), 273.

[21] Danilov (1977), 278–9.

[22] See Grosskopf (Paris, 1976), 244; stocks of implements and machines, however, were valued at only 60 per cent of the 1917 level (*ibid.* 347); this calculation assumed a high rate of depreciation.

[23] IZ, lxxiv (1963), 5; this figure excludes kolkhozy, but does not allow for double counting.

[24] Danilov (1957), 137; *Istoriya sovetskogo krest'yanstva* (1963), 69–70.

[25] SZo, i–ii, January–February 1930, 72; IS, 3, 1958, 115.

The capital stock of peasant agriculture, in spite of a substantial injection of implements and machinery in the late 1920s, also remained extremely antiquated. Most households owned no horse-drawn machines whatsoever, and therefore hired machines from their neighbours or from state or cooperative agencies—or did not use them at all. Machinery was concentrated in the major grain-growing areas, but even in the Ukraine only 40 per cent of households owned any machinery, and the percentage was only 29 in the North Caucasus, 12·5 in the Lower Volga and 7·5 in the Central Black-Earth region.[26] In 1928, 74 per cent of grain was sown by hand, 44 per cent reaped by sickles and scythes, and 41 per cent threshed by chains or other manual devices.[27] The wooden *sokha* was by this time almost completely replaced by the iron plough, and this was an important achievement, but many households lacked draught animals or ploughs, and hired them from their neighbours or (much more rarely) from the cooperatives. In the RSFSR in 1927, 28·3 per cent of households had no horses or oxen, 31·6 per cent had no ploughing implements.[28] In this respect the situation was worse than before the revolution.

Nor could the agricultural cooperatives claim to have made substantial changes in the activities of the majority of the peasants. In 1929, only 10 per cent of households belonged to the marketing cooperatives. And while cooperative marketing was of major importance in specialised crops, it played only a minor part in grain or livestock marketing until strong administrative pressure was applied by the state from the beginning of 1928; at this point it ceased to be 'cooperation' in any substantial sense. And all the various forms of production cooperatives—including both kolkhozy and unofficial and official producer cooperatives—probably involved only four or five million households by the spring of 1929.

In its level of agricultural production the Soviet Union was substantially in advance of nearly the whole of Asia.[29] In India arable land per person dependent on agriculture was one-third and in China as little as one-seventh of the Soviet level. Although yields

[26] SO, 4, 1929, 11, based on a sample survey; for the concentration of machinery in the grain areas, see *Sdvigi* (1931), 92–3, 109.

[27] *Itogi vypolneniya pervogo pyatiletnego plana* (1933), 135.

[28] Danilov (1957), 53, 58–9.

[29] References for the international comparisons on pp. 9–11 will be provided in a later publication.

were higher in India and China than in the Soviet Union, grain production per head of population in India was only 35 per cent of the Soviet level; and even in the 1950s China, though rich in grain by the standards of Asia and South America, produced only half as much grain per head of population as the Soviet Union of the 1920s. In India and China agriculture supported much smaller numbers of livestock than in the Soviet Union. As a result, the protein consumption of the population was much lower, and a far smaller proportion of it came from meat and animal products.[30]

But while agriculture was more advanced in the Soviet Union than in Asia, it was more backward than in any other major European country, in terms of both yields per hectare and production per person engaged in farming. The wheat and rye yield per hectare, 7–9 tsentners, was only slightly higher than in fourteenth-century English estates, lower than in fourteenth-century French estates.[31] It was no higher than in Spain and Serbia on the eve of the first world war, and substantially lower than in peasant countries such as France and Italy; it was less than half the German level. Historically, Russian agriculture was grain-dominated. Even in the mid-1920s, in spite of the expansion of the area devoted to industrial crops, a far higher proportion of arable land continued to be used for grain production than in any other major European country, or in the United States, and a smaller proportion was sown to industrial crops, root crops and grasses. In this respect the Soviet Union was comparable with the most backward East European countries—Bulgaria, Hungary and Romania.[32]

[30] Protein intake in grams per person per day:

	USSR (1926/27)	*China (1959–61)*
From animal sources	23	3
From all sources	106	48

(for USSR, see Wheatcroft (1976), 95; for China, see *An Economic Profile of Mainland China* (Washington, 1967), i, 265).

[31] Van Bath (London, 1963), 173–4; Van Bath's data have been converted at 1 litre of wheat = 0·75 kg. The estates for which figures are available may, however, have had exceptionally high yields.

[32] Umanskii, ed. (1928), 122–3; in Canada, unlike the United States, the proportion of the sown area occupied by grain was also very high.

Historically, Russia was relatively well-endowed with arable land per head of rural population, but by the 1920s the rapid expansion of the rural population which had taken place since the middle of the nineteenth century had reduced the amount of land per person engaged in agriculture to the level of France and Germany. Yet yields and labour productivity in grain farming remained low. The Soviet Union succeeded in producing more grain per head of total population than France or Germany, but a far higher proportion of the total Soviet population was engaged in agriculture. In the United States, a much smaller percentage of the population was engaged in agriculture, but yields were some 70 per cent higher than in the Soviet Union, labour productivity was much higher, and a larger amount of arable land was available per person engaged in agriculture; in consequence, grain production per head of total population was more than double the Soviet level.

(ii) The peasant and the market

The peasant household in the USSR, as in other peasant countries, was in large part a subsistence economy, which consumed a substantial part of its own production. But it was not a self-sufficient unit, little connected with the town and the market.

Most of the three million rural households whose main occupation was not farming depended on the state or the urban market for their livelihood; this group of peasants had the strongest links with the towns. For each of the 70,000 village soviets, which included on average 1,750 rural inhabitants in 350 families, there were roughly 40 households whose main occupation was not agriculture, though with considerable regional variations. Breadwinners in these households included nine factory workers, ten full-time artisans, two builders, four railwaymen, one private and one state or cooperative trader, 2½ teachers, three persons maintained by the state, 1½ 'declassed' persons, one priest or other religious servitor and one person living on 'non-labour' income. But there was less than one employee in the health services and less than one local soviet official for each village soviet and only one militiaman (policeman) for every five village soviets.

In addition to the four million people engaged in these occupations in the three million 'non-farming' households, in 1926 3·2 million persons in the 23 million 'farming' households were engaged in a non-farming activity as a 'first auxiliary occupation', making 7·2 million persons altogether.[33] Auxiliary occupations other than the first were not recorded in the census, and the number of peasants involved may have been substantial. Surveys in 1927 and 1929 revealed that on average 35·9 per cent of all households in 1927 and 36·9 per cent in 1929, some 9 million households altogether, were engaged in occupations outside their own household, excluding agricultural labour.[34]

Among the peasants engaged in non-agricultural activities, as major and minor sources of income, in 1925/26 at least 3 million persons were *otkhodniki* (literally, 'people going away'), peasants who lived away from the mir for part of the year and worked in such occupations as building, timber-cutting and floating, and peat working, or in mines and factories.[35]

A very substantial proportion of the income of the rural population was received from these various non-farming activities. In 1925/26 37 per cent of all peasant money income was received from artisan production and all kinds of trades (promysly), both local and those involving 'going away'.[36] Even if peasant products consumed by the family producing them are taken into account, the proportion of peasant income in money and kind derived from non-farming activities was still as high as 38·8 per cent.[37]

Peasant households also participated in market relations by working in agriculture outside their own farms. Two categories of agricultural labour were distinguished in the statistics: contract (srokovye) workers (hired for periods of more than a month) and day (podennye) workers (hired for shorter periods). In 1927, at least 2,400,000 contract workers and 2,500,000 day workers were employed in peasant agriculture, some 5 million persons in all.[38] In addition to this employment in the individual sector, 143,000

[33] The above figures are all calculated from data in *Vsesoyuznaya perepis'*, xxxiv (1930).

[34] Calculated from data in *Sdvigi* (1931), 80–1; unweighted average for 13 regions and republics; these figures were for households which existed in both years, and had not merged or divided in the period.

[35] See IZ, xciv (1974), 80 (Danilov).

[36] *KTs . . . na 1929/30* (1930), 536–7.

[37] VF, 2, 1929, 28.

[38] Danilov (1957), 73; *Sdvigi* (1931), 134; the figure for day workers refers only to those employed in the month of August 1927, and excludes the Transcaucasus and Uzbekistan—the true figure must be over 3 million.

contract workers, half of them permanent, and 420,000 temporary workers were employed by sovkhozy in July 1927, and a small number of temporary and permanent workers were employed by kolkhozy.[39]

The economic activity of the peasants in addition to farming in their own households was thus substantial. In 25 or 26 million rural households, over 7 million people were engaged in non-agricultural activities as either their main or their first auxiliary occupation, and about 6 million were employed as contract or temporary farm labourers, some 13 million people altogether. A very large number of peasants also participated in the market by hiring-out and renting equipment and land.

Most peasant money income, however, 53·2 per cent of the total in 1925/26, was earned by the sale of farm products on the market. The extent of participation in the market varied greatly among different products. Of the 77 million tons of grain produced in 1926, 26 million tons at most were sold either on the market or direct to other peasants.[40] Even if grain used by peasants for seed is deducted from total production, this means that no more than 40 per cent of net grain production was sold,[41] and most of this (16½ million tons) was ultimately consumed by peasants or their livestock. Industrial crops participated in the market to a far greater extent: nearly all cotton, sugar beet, tobacco and *makhorka* (cheap tobacco) were sold on the market.

The extent to which the market was in state hands varied considerably from product to product. With industrial crops, purchases by state and cooperative agencies at fixed prices overwhelmingly predominated. With grain, 49 per cent of all sales in 1926/27 were made to state and cooperative agencies at fixed prices: these covered almost all grain for the army, industry and export, most grain consumed in the towns and part of the grain sold to peasants in grain-deficit areas. A further 34 per cent was sold direct

[39] *Sdvigi* (1931), 134–7; in 1928/29 12,082 kolkhozy employed workers for a total of 112,105 man-months.

[40] SS, xxi (1969–70), 324; xxii (1970–71), 293; the figure of 26 million tons may exaggerate the amount of grain sold or bartered direct by peasant to peasant (8·8 million tons) (see also p. 18 below).

[41] This percentage may be somewhat too high: seed grain amounted to 12 million tons, but some of this was purchased by peasants who were short of grain, and should not therefore be deducted from total production.

from peasant to peasant, and 3½ per cent direct to the urban population; the remaining 14 per cent was mainly purchased by private traders.[42] With livestock, sales to private traders and direct to peasants predominated: on average in the first three-quarters of 1927, only 10 per cent of livestock sales were to state and cooperative agencies; the prices of livestock were virtually entirely determined by the free market. In peasant sales of farming products as a whole the free market also predominated.[43]

No precise assessment is possible of the level of peasant market activities in the mid-1920s as compared with the eve of the first world war, but the evidence that a substantial decline took place is overwhelming.

The number of otkhodniki before the revolution can be assessed only by indirect data, particularly the figures for internal passports issued for periods of less than a year. In 1906–10, these amounted to 8,772,000 a year in 43 provinces of European Russia; it is estimated that 40–45 per cent were agricultural workers, the remaining 55–60 per cent being engaged on various non-agricultural occupations.[44] In 1925/26, the number of agricultural labourers working outside their volost' (small rural district) was only 9–10 per cent, and of non-agricultural otkhodniki 51–56 per cent, of this level.[45] The decline in agricultural workers resulted both from the elimination of the agricultural estates, which hired a considerable amount of seasonal labour, and from the decline in the use of hired labour by more prosperous peasant economies.[46] The extent to which a real decline took place in the number of otkhodniki engaged in non-agricultural work is less clear: in some provinces before the revolution permanent factory workers of peasant origin had to obtain a passport, and to that extent the pre-revolutionary figure was exaggerated.[47] But in several important occupations of otkhodniki the demand for

[42] SO, 5, 1930, 140–1 (Mikhailovskii). These calculations are in physical terms; in value terms the proportion sold to private traders and direct to peasants, being at higher market prices, would be higher, especially from the autumn of 1927 onwards.

[43] See SO, 3, 1929, 17; for alternative livestock figures, see p. 49, n. 145, below.

[44] L. E. Mints, cited in IZ, xciv (1974), 70–1, 119; Rashin (1958), 322–43.

[45] IZ, xciv (1974), 80.

[46] IZ, xciv (1974), 81–3; the number of otkhodniki employed as agricultural labourers by peasant households reached a maximum of 584,000 in 1924/25 and fell to 231,000 in 1925/26.

[47] Rashin (1958), 325–6.

labour had certainly declined in the mid-1920s: the building and lumber industries had not recovered to their pre-war level, and far fewer persons were employed in domestic service.

The number of rural inhabitants engaged in small-scale, mainly artisan, industry is also estimated to have declined sharply, from 3·8 million persons in 1913 to 3·04 million in 1926/27.[48] These figures are surprising, as the domestic use of agricultural raw materials for rural artisan production was undoubtedly greater in the 1920s than in 1913 (see pp. 17–18 below). But much of this production was consumed by the household, and does not appear in the statistics; and industrial raw materials, especially metal, were in short supply.[49]

The number of persons engaged in private trade in the countryside, presumably mainly rural inhabitants, was also lower than before the revolution: in 1926/27 the number of private trading units was only 51·7 per cent of the number in 1912, and the average unit was much smaller. The development of rural state and cooperative trade was not sufficient to compensate for this decline.[50] It is not known, however, whether the number of peasants selling their own products on the free market in the towns or direct to other peasants increased or declined as compared with 1913.

Many of the statistics we have cited are not very reliable: the number of otkhodniki and rural artisans before the revolution, in particular, cannot be established with certainty, and peasant budgets in the 1920s may have understated peasant economic activity, particularly of the more prosperous. But it is significant that they all point to a decline. It is striking that the number of peasants reported as engaging in non-agricultural auxiliary activities in the census of 1897, 5·03 million for 50 provinces of European Russia, was much larger than the number of rural inhabitants reported as engaging in non-agricultural auxiliary occupations, 3·22 millions, in the whole USSR in 1926.[51]

[48] PKh, 6, 1924, 87 (Gukhman); *St. spr. 1928* (1929), 494–5; see also Kaufman (Washington, D.C., 1962), 18–27. The average number of weeks per year worked for person engaged in small-scale industry (both urban and rural) was estimated to have fallen from 27·0 in 1913 (Popov, ed. (1926), 196) to 16·1 in the economic year 1928/29; in the latter year the average number of weeks worked in rural small-scale industry was only 13·0 (*Nar. kh.* (1932), 110–11).

[49] For these shortages, see Carr and Davies (1969), 396; EZh, May 6, 1926; TPG, November 11, 1926; Valentinov (Stanford, 1971), 121–2.

[50] *Materialy*, vii (1959), 121–5; see also p. 16 below.

[51] Rashin (1958), 342–3; *Vsesoyuznaya perepis'*, xxxiv (1930), 121.

Conditions for the marketing of agricultural products also substantially deteriorated. The terms of trade were less favourable in the mid-1920s than in 1913: the 'scissors' (the ratio of industrial retail prices to the agricultural prices received by the producer) was calculated at 139·2 for 1925/26 and 140·6 for 1926/27 (1911–14 (average) = 100).[52] Whether a shift in the terms of trade against the peasants is likely to reduce the supply of their products to the market has recently been much discussed. It has been argued that peasant demand for industrial goods is inelastic, and that family labour on the peasant farm is treated as an overhead, so an unfavourable general shift in the terms of trade against the peasants is likely to induce them to put more products on sale at the lower price.[53] So far little evidence is available to test this assumption.

In the 1920s several other factors apart from the prices they were offered also tended to discourage peasants from marketing their products. They did not have such easy access to industrial goods in the 1920s as before the war, a factor which was not reflected in the price index. Throughout the 1920s industrial goods were scarce, except at rare moments, such as the autumn of 1926, when supply and demand were close to equilibrium. And the peasants had far fewer opportunities to purchase industrial goods than before the war: substantially fewer trading outlets existed in rural areas than in 1912, and a far higher proportion of them were 'mobile trading points'—petty trading from temporary stalls, kiosks, carts or trays—rather than retail shops.[54] Both the terms and conditions of trade were thus less favourable to the agricultural producer.

Much importance was attached by Soviet politicians and economists to the 'fragmentation' (razdroblennost') of peasant holdings as a factor encouraging low productivity and low marketability. During the revolution of 1917, the large estates were seized by the peasants and redistributed. Many landless peasant households received land; many new households were created by partitioning. By the spring of 1927, the number of peasant households reached 24 million or more as compared with 19½ million ten years earlier, the

[52] *KTs . . . na 1929/30* (1930), 579; it should be recalled, however, that prices moved in favour of agricultural products between the 1890s and 1914, so that relative agricultural prices in the mid-1920s were very roughly at the same level as in the 1890s.

[53] J. Millar, in *Economic Development and Cultural Change*, January 1970, 218–19; the discussion is reviewed in Harrison (1977).

[54] *Materialy*, vii (1959), 121–5.

average number of persons per household declining from 6·1 to 5·3. But, owing to the land redistribution, the land available per household was approximately the same as before the revolution. The effects of fragmentation of holdings were often exaggerated in Soviet publications. But the elimination of the private estates, the reduction in the land cultivated by kulaks and well-to-do peasants (see p. 24 below) and the reduction in the number of enclosed farms undoubtedly tended to reduce the level of marketings: these sectors of pre-revolutionary agriculture were more oriented to the market. At the same time some peasants who had been landless labourers before the revolution were now growing food for themselves on land which had previously yielded marketed production.[55]

A further factor which tended to reduce the level of marketings was that peasant payments of direct tax and rent were substantially lower than before the revolution: this reduced the pressure on the peasants to take their products to market to raise cash.

While precise data are not available, economists and politicians of all shades of thought agreed that marketed production was lower in the mid-1920s than in 1913. The term 'marketed production' or 'marketability' (tovarnost'), meaning the proportion of agricultural production sold on the market, was sometimes used to refer to all sales on the market, sometimes only to sales on the extra-rural or extra-peasant market; sales on the extra-rural market in their turn sometimes included food products which were sold back to the peasant and sometimes excluded them. According to Gosplan calculations in 1927, sales to the extra-peasant market were only 69 per cent of the 1913 level in 1925/26 and 73·2 per cent in 1926/27: both the *Konjunktur* Institute of Narkomfin and the émigré economist Prokopovich considered that this underestimated the decline.[56] All groups of products were affected, even livestock, for

[55] These topics will be examined in more detail in a later publication.

[56] BP (Prague), lxix (May 1929), 7; *Byulleten' Kon''yunkturnogo Instituta*, 11–12, 1927, 52. The Gosplan figures were as follows (marketed production as percentage of total production):

	1913	*1925/26*	*1926/27*
Grain	20·3	14·1	14·7
Industrial crops	73·1	50·0	53·1
Livestock	30·9	23·2	25·0
All agricultural production	22·2	16·5	16·9

which prices, being determined primarily by the private market, were exceptionally favourable. Some industrial crops, notably cotton, could not easily be put to an alternative use by the peasants, and in these cases, as before the revolution, virtually the whole crop was marketed, though output was strongly affected by the price paid by the state and cooperative agencies which controlled their sales. But a much smaller proportion of flax and hemp was placed on the extra-rural market than before the revolution, the remainder being retained for domestic or local use. The proportion was also much lower for animal products which could be used by the peasants themselves, such as wool and the hides of small animals (for leather goods).[57]

The decline in grain marketings was the most serious manifestation of the general decline in the level of marketing. Grain for the towns, the army, industry and export in 1926/27 amounted to only 10 million tons as compared with 18·8 million tons in 1909–13 (average).[58] No reliable figures are available on the total amount of grain marketed before the first world war, including intra-rural sales. Transport statistics indicate that sales of grain between agricultural areas were at approximately the same level as before the war; if so, total marketings, including exports, were about nine million tons lower than in 1909–13, for a harvest which was at least as large, and may have been larger.[59]

(iii) Regional problems

Regional variations in the type and extent of peasant participation in the market were considerable, and reflected different levels and patterns of economic development.

In a Soviet population of 147 million in 1926, over 20 million lived in the Transcaucasus, Kazakhstan, and Central Asia, all

---

According to a Soviet calculation based on recent official statistics, commodity production fell by 30 per cent between 1913 and 1928, while all agricultural production increased by 24 per cent (Barsov (1969), 22).

[57] For a comparison of 1926/27 and 1913, see data from Soviet sources in BP (Prague), lxvi (February 1929), 11.

[58] See Table 9, and SS, xxi (1969–70), 319.

[59] See p. 13 above and SS, xxi (1969–70), 319; the transport statistics do not include grain transported by cart or by passengers on the railways, which may have been higher than before the war, and do not indicate how much grain was transferred from peasant to peasant within each agricultural area.

colonies of the tsarist Empire which were largely inhabited by non-Slavic peoples. Very different levels of economic development existed side-by-side within each of these three ex-colonial territories. But they all contained substantial areas in which economic and educational development were at a low level, and which, together with large pockets of backwardness in Siberia and in European Russia, constituted a vast hinterland in which industry was even less developed, and agriculture even more backward, than in the main Slavic areas.

The most advanced and urbanised of the three ex-colonial areas was the Transcaucasian Soviet Federated Socialist Republic, comprising the three republics of Georgia, Azerbaidzhan and Armenia. The Transcaucasus was distinguished by the variety of its terrain and its generally sub-tropical climate. Over the lower-lying part of its territory the cultivation of milk, tea, tobacco, wine and fruit for sale in the European USSR was strongly developed. But side-by-side with this intensive and prosperous agricultural sector, a large number of Transcaucasian peasants lived in great poverty, and, in spite of the small amount of arable land per head, shifting cultivation was widely practised. In consequence, output of grain and meat per household was low; and the Republic was a net consumer of grain and meat, mainly from the North Caucasus.

Kazakhstan included two contrasting areas: settled grain farming was carried on largely by Russian immigrants, using shifting cultivation on abundant land; native Kazakhs continued their traditional nomadic cattle and sheep farming on the abundant pasturelands. Kazakhstan was a net seller of grain and livestock; and in 1927/28 it supplied 46 per cent of the coarse wool consumed by Soviet industry.[60] Thirty years later, the Kazakh lands, together with part of Siberia, became Khrushchev's 'virgin and long-fallow lands' which provided the first substantial increase in Soviet grain production above the pre-revolutionary level. Some cotton was grown in Southern Kazakhstan in the 1920s, but 75 per cent of all cotton was grown in our third ex-colonial area, Central Asia. Central Asia consisted of the Uzbek and Turkmen Soviet Socialist Republics, the Kirgiz Autonomous SSR (in the Russian republic) and the Tadzhik ASSR (in Uzbekistan). Central Asian agriculture included a great variety of patterns of production. As well as intensive cotton growing on irrigated lands, nomadic sheep farming

[60] *Pyatiletnii plan*, iii (1930), 327.

was extensively practised, as in Kazakhstan, and both Kazakhstan and Central Asia were industrially and culturally extremely backward. Central Asia, unlike Kazakhstan, was a net consumer of grain. Its characteristics were graphically, if somewhat despairingly, described by the authors of the first five-year plan:

> The main features which characterise the Central Asian republics are: failure to utilise vast natural resources; a traditional crop-raising and livestock farming technique, established over centuries in conditions of a complex irrigated economy of an Asiatic type; an undeveloped factory industry, and a population unaccustomed to factory and industrial labour in large-scale production; traditional forms of artisan and handicraft production, resting on a primitive empirical technology; separation and isolation of oases and districts, as a result of the historical past and of natural conditions (ravines, deserts, high mountains); general poverty of life, with tribal, feudal, national and religious prejudices continuing in places. Tsarist colonies and Eastern despotisms in their recent pre-revolutionary past, the Central Asian republics suffer from an insufficient development of mass popular education and from primitive sanitary and hygienic conditions, and are on a very low cultural level.[61]

In the European part of the USSR, the most important distinction, vital for the support required from agriculture for industrial development, was between the grain-deficit zone and the grain-surplus areas. The grain-deficit zone included the Belorussian republic and, in the RSFSR, the North, the North-west (around Leningrad), the Central Industrial area (around Moscow) and the Western region. The level of economic development in different parts of this zone varied considerably, from the urbanised and relatively densely-populated area around Moscow and Leningrad to the sparsely-populated Northern forest region and the marshy and impoverished Belorussian republic. Throughout the zone the land was less fertile than further south. The whole zone had been part of the Russian state for several centuries, with a settled and growing agricultural population; in consequence, the amount of arable land per head of rural population throughout the zone was

[61] *Pyatiletnii plan*, iii (1930), 330.

relatively small by the generous standards of the Russian Empire. In response to land shortage, three-field agriculture had almost everywhere replaced shifting cultivation, and multi-crop rotations had been introduced on a higher proportion of the arable land than elsewhere in the Soviet Union. Belorussia and the Western region were major flax-growing areas, and the high demand for vegetables and potatoes from the large urban population of Moscow and Leningrad resulted in the development of market gardening in the countryside around these cities. The peasantry near these towns also supplied artisan products to the urban population and labour to the factories in substantial quantities, and as a result the peasantry of the Central Industrial region in particular had relatively high money incomes. In the remainder of the grain-deficit zone—the Northern and Western regions and Belorussia—non-agricultural activities were less significant, and both money and total incomes were lower than the average. But the whole zone depended on the supply of large quantities of grain from the rest of the USSR.

The various grain-surplus regions, producing grain in large quantities for the market, included the southern steppe region of the Ukraine and the Lower Volga region, especially the lands east of the Volga, the North Caucasus and (outside Europe) Siberia. These regions fed the industrial areas of the USSR and supplied what grain was available for export. Non-agricultural activities were much less important than in most other regions. These were areas of relatively recent settlement, where land was relatively abundant. In Siberia, the Lower Volga and the North Caucasus shifting agriculture was still important: after cultivation land was left unused (zalezh') for a period until it had recovered. The three-field system was introduced only in the more populated parts of the Volga regions; multi-crop rotations, and the planting of specialised crops, were hardly known. But serious problems existed. These regions were subject to drought and soil erosion, and extreme variations occurred from year to year in the size of crop. Over a substantial part of the area, land was no longer abundant. According to a careful estimate, in the North Caucasus over 60 per cent and in the Central Volga region over one-third of the arable land was over-cultivated (the land available was insufficient for it to be left fallow long enough to recover); the introduction of a three-field or more advanced crop rotation was overdue.[62]

62 *Statistika i narodnoe khozyaistvo*, 7, 1929, 89–92 (Tarasov).

Intermediate between the grain-deficit and grain-surplus zones was the long-settled Central Agricultural area, the historical centre of Russian agriculture; this included the Central Black-Earth region and the contiguous areas in the Northern Ukraine and on the right bank of the Volga. These are areas of rich agricultural land—mainly a mixture of forest and steppe. But the growth of population greatly reduced the land available per head of population. The three-field system had long since replaced shifting cultivation almost everywhere, and arable was extended at the expense of pasture; sugar beet (especially in the Northern Ukraine), flax and potatoes were introduced into the rotation. In spite of these improvements, this was the classic area of over-cultivation of the soil and of rural over-population, from which large number of otkhodniki made their way to other regions in search of work.

The most important change in the regional pattern of marketings since the pre-war years was the drastic decline in grain marketings from the major grain-surplus regions, only partly compensated for by the increased supply from Siberia. Farming in all the grain-surplus zones was gravely damaged by the Civil War, especially in the North Caucasus, where the Cossack peasants were one of the principal supports for counter-revolution. The Volga regions suffered greatly from the famine of 1921–2. Even by 1928, sown area in the North Caucasus and the Lower Volga was substantially below, and the number of draught animals catastrophically below, the pre-war level.[63] The decline in these regions was primarily responsible for the low level of grain marketings in the USSR as a

[63] See *KTs . . . na 1928/29* (1929), 221 (different, somewhat lower figures are given *ibid.*, 576–7):

	Area sown to grain (1913 = 100)	*Working animals (1916 = 100)*
Whole USSR	87·9	87·8
Central Volga	92·9	81·4
Lower Volga	72·2	72·6
North Caucasus	63·3	75·1
Ukraine	83·6	92·0

The area sown to grain is probably underestimated, and the number of animals overestimated, as compared with before the revolution (see p. 4, nn. 9 and 10, above), but the relation between regions is likely to be correct.

whole, which was a major political and economic problem throughout the 1920s. Increased grain production—or, at any rate, increased grain supplies—from the main grain-surplus areas was essential for the sustenance of the increased urban population which would result from industrialisation.

(iv) Economic differentiation

In marxist studies of the Russian peasantry, three major groups were generally distinguished: kulaks, middle peasants (serednyaks) and poor peasants (bednyaks).[64] The term 'kulak' (literally meaning 'tight fist') was originally reserved for rural usurers and traders as distinct from rural capitalist producers. In the mid-1920s it was sometimes still used in this sense,[65] but now generally referred to all peasant producers who hired labour or exploited their neighbours in some other way. The 'poor peasants', who depended on hiring out their labour as well as on their own family farm for their survival, were also known as 'semi-proletarians', as distinct from the 'proletarians'—the agricultural labourers or 'batraks', who had no land of their own, or for whom their farm was only a minor source of income, and were thus no longer peasants in the strict sense of the term. The middle peasants were supposed to be economically more independent than the poor peasants, primarily cultivating their own land with their own labour. The number of middle peasant households was much disputed before the revolution. Lenin claimed that owing to the development of capitalism in the countryside they were already only a small minority of all peasants; but this assessment was strongly challenged by the Socialist Revolutionaries and others.

The evidence is overwhelming of the emergence in pre-revolutionary Russia of a stratum of wealthier peasants, who rented or purchased land from private landowners to supplement their allotment from the mir, and of a larger stratum of landless

[64] See, for example, Lenin, *Soch.*, xviii, 39 (August 1918).

[65] See Lewin, in SS, xviii (1966–7), 189, 191 (citing Bukharin and A. P. Smirnov); in 1899 Lenin, while using the term 'kulak' to refer to rural usurers and traders, rejected the popular view that such 'kulaks' and the rural peasant producers who hired labour were 'contradictory types of phenomena which were not linked with each other', and insisted that they were 'two forms of the same economic phenomenon' (*Soch.*, iii, 333, 152).

peasants.[66] Much less evidence is available about the extent to which the batraks and the poor peasants were 'exploited' by the kulaks in a marxist sense, by depending on them for capital and for earnings from labour.

The revolution and Civil War considerably reduced economic differentiation in the countryside. Most of the land of the private estates, including the large amount rented to more prosperous peasants, was redistributed among the peasants on a more or less equal basis. Most khutors and otrubs, which were often prosperous, were reabsorbed into the mir. Many formerly landless peasants acquired land, and sometimes implements and draught animals as well. In the early years of NEP, however, some economic differentiation again took place, especially in 1924–5 when restrictions on rural capitalism were at a minimum. But the degree of petty capitalism in the countryside certainly remained far less than before the revolution. Everyone agreed that 'middle-peasantisation' (oserednyachenie) had taken place as a result of the revolution, and that the majority of the peasants were now middle peasants; and most people considered that this was an important factor in the decline of marketed production.

The economic relations within the peasantry in the mid-1920s were confused and complicated.[67] A high proportion of peasant households changed their economic group in the course of a lifetime; the lowest and highest sown-area groups were particularly mobile. This tended to blur the boundaries between classes. And in the lowest groups, whether measured by sown area or by value of means of production, many peasants who were 'proletarians' or 'poor peasants' in their agricultural economy received substantial earnings from a variety of non-agricultural activities, especially from the sale of their labour to the state, while their earnings from selling labour or land to their more prosperous neighbours were relatively small. Peasants who were in the lower groups from the point of view of agriculture could therefore often escape from penury by becoming dependent on the state rather than on the richer peasants.

Nevertheless, a substantial degree of economic differentiation remained, or re-emerged, in the 1920s. The most abundant data are

[66] See Jasny (Stanford, 1949), 145, 149–50; Shanin (1972), 53–4; Harrison (1974), ch. 5.

[67] This question will be examined in more detail in a forthcoming publication.

provided by the analysis of the 1927 sample census of peasant households, supervised by V. S. Nemchinov, a 33-year-old marxist statistician, who grouped households into seven groups by the value of the means of production (buildings, implements and animals) which they possessed. The census showed a considerable degree of differentiation between groups: the top group, containing 3·2 per cent of households, owned on average 2·3 draught animals and 2·5 cows, as compared with the average of 1·0 and 1·1 for all households, while in the bottom three groups, containing 24 per cent of all households, 80 per cent possessed no draught animals, and 57 per cent possessed no cows. The degree of differentiation was even greater for agricultural implements and machinery.[68]

How far, then, was there a distinctive group of petty capitalist peasant households, for which the exploitation of the labour of others, directly or indirectly, was a substantial economic activity? Of the 800,000 households in the top group by value of means of production, about 150,000 were hiring labour for more than 75 days a year. As the average number of days worked in agriculture by an adult member of a peasant household was only 97, it seems reasonable to suppose that for all this sub-group hired labour was an important supplement to family labour. A further 35,000 households in the top group were registered as engaging in 'entrepreneurial non-agricultural occupations' as their main means of existence or their first source of money income, while continuing to operate as a farming economy. These occupations included: those requiring the hire of labour to use together with the means of production belonging to the household for at least three months a year; money-lending; the leasing of barns and stores; trade and sub-contracting; and industrial and other production in which the means of production were substantial.[69] With all these 185,000 households in the top group (150,000 + 35,000), petty capitalist activities were substantial; and to them might be added the equivalent sub-groups in the next group, owning less means of production, a further 320,000 households. These sub-groups, half a million households in all, two per cent of all households, were the core of what might be regarded as a kulak class. A much wider definition, embracing 950,000 households, 3·8 per cent of house-

[68] For statistical tables from this census, see *St. spr. 1928* (1929), 88–134, 144–55; Jasny (1949), 163–82, 780–3. For the principles of classification employed, see Nemchinov, i (1967), 44–127 (a reprint of articles published in 1926–30).

[69] Nemchinov, i (1967), 47–8.

holds, was proposed by Nemchinov early in 1928, and a similar scheme was used by the authorities both for the summary analysis of the census data of the Central Statistical Administration and for analysing the income and tax data collected by Narkomfin.[70] The main additional category included in Nemchinov's definition was all the remaining households in the top two groups which hired labour and hired out means of production, however small the quantity; this added 325,000 households, but many of these could hardly be regarded as exploitative. But the important qualification should be made, affecting all these figures, that the survey may have underestimated the activities of the upper peasant groups, in spite of all the precautions of the Soviet statisticians, owing to the vigorous efforts by these groups to conceal their wealth, and particularly to conceal those activities which were regarded as capitalistic. A detailed examination of the results of the 1927 census was carried out for three large clusters (gnezda) of peasants in the Ukraine, under the supervision of statisticians, by commissions elected by the *aktiv* (activists) in the villages concerned; this revealed that, in the opinion of the commissions, 6·7 per cent of households in these clusters should have been classified as 'petty capitalists' rather than the 3·2 per cent in the official survey.[71]

The most important practical issue for the Soviet authorities—though they usually failed to grasp this point—was not the economic power of the kulaks as such but the wider question of the extent to which the state, the towns and the grain-deficit zone depended on particular groups within the peasantry, whether petty capitalists or not, for marketed production. For several years the issue was obscured by the anxiety of the party majority to conceal the extent of economic differentiation in the countryside. The main trends, however, emerged clearly from the surveys of peasant budgets and the analysis of grain sales and purchases carried out by the Central Statistical Administration. When peasant households were classified by sown area, a reasonable indicator of their strength as grain farmers, the lower sown-area groups in every area were found to have purchased much more grain than they sold. In the grain-surplus areas, only upper and middle groups by sown area, including 55 per cent of the peasant population in these areas, were net sellers of grain in 1927/28; for sown-area groups covering 25 per

[70] See Nemchinov, i (1967), 117–18, iv (1967), 366; *St. spr. 1928* (1929), 940.
[71] *Vestnik statistiki*, 3–4, 1929, 214–18.

cent of the population, sales and purchases were roughly in balance; and 20 per cent were net purchasers of grain. In the grain-deficit zone, on the other hand, only 68 per cent of the peasant population were purchasing grain, and a substantial minority of peasants were selling it. When these transactions between peasants are omitted, net marketings were overwhelmingly dominated in the USSR as a whole by the upper sown-area groups in the grain-surplus areas: 22 per cent of the peasant population in these areas, some 16 per cent of their households, and a mere 10–11 per cent of all households in the European USSR supplied 56 per cent of all net sales of grain in the European USSR in 1927/28, and the percentage was higher in earlier years. Peasants in these upper sown-area groups were not necessarily the most prosperous; peasants in lower sown-area groups might earn more from industrial crops, or from non-agricultural activities. Nevertheless, on this evidence, about 2 million households in the grain-surplus areas, with a sown area in excess of eight hectares per household, were crucial for Soviet grain supplies. Evidence is lacking, however, on whether this minority of 'grain-surplus' households was concentrated in certain 'well-to-do' districts or villages where conditions or traditions were particularly favourable to grain production and marketings, and where peasants selling a substantial amount of grain were a majority of the population. One 'well-to-do' grain region certainly existed: the North Caucasus, with its generous land areas and its Cossack majority, where as many as 43 per cent of the population came within the upper sown-area groups.[72]

Sales of livestock, and of meat and dairy products, were also larger in the upper groups by sown area or by means of production, which tended to have more fodder available, and hence more, or better-fed, animals. But, except in some specialised areas, the upper groups were responsible for a smaller percentage of total marketings than in the case of grain; and in most regions all sown-area groups sold more livestock, and meat and dairy products, than they purchased. Thus the urban market depended on a larger number of peasants for meat than for grain, though the 'kulak' and 'well-to-do' peasants remained important.

Soviet publications and political speeches frequently referred in the 1920s to the 'strong' (krepkii) and the 'well-to-do' (zazhitochnyi)

[72] These calculations are based on the 1927/28 survey of marketed grain, published in SO, 5, 1930, 13–49, 142–7 (Mikhailovskii).

peasant, which was an upper section of the middle peasants distinct from the kulaks,[73] hiring little or no labour and not engaging to a great extent in other capitalistic activities, but market-oriented and economically successful. This term, which modified the simple division into proletarian, poor peasant, middle peasant and kulak, admitted to the marxist analysis some important features of the economic differentiation of the peasant economy of the 1920s. But it provided no guidance about policy. Should the emergence of the large minority of 'well-to-do' peasants within the middle peasantry be treated as a healthy development to be encouraged in the interests of agricultural progress? Or should 'well-to-do' middle peasants be treated as potential kulaks or allies of the kulaks, a symptom of the recrudescence of rural capitalism? The party was divided.

(v) The unstable link

The New Economic Policy presumed that the link between the state and the peasantry through the market would provide a stable basis for the development of both state industry and the peasant economy. In practice, stability on the market was extremely difficult to achieve. Only two of the nine harvests of the 1920s—those of 1922 and 1926—proceeded without a major crisis in economic policy.

After the harvest of 1921, famine was widespread; grain collections for the tax in kind were still the main source of food supply for the towns; the methods used for grain requisitioning were in large part continued.[74]

After the substantial 1922 harvest, the first untroubled harvest of NEP, the tax in kind was collected easily, and the relative price of grain fell in the course of the agricultural year 1922/23.[75] But in April 1923 Trotsky warned that the deterioration in the terms of trade for the peasants was a potential danger, and made his famous comparison of the decline in the prices received by the peasants relative to those they paid for industrial products to the opening of the blades of a pair of scissors.[76] This warning soon proved to be

[73] See SS, xviii (1966–67), 191, 197 (Lewin).

[74] See *Ekonomicheskii vestnik*, i (Berlin, 1923), 56; Polyakov (1967), 247–330.

[75] Dmitrenko (1971), 168–9.

[76] See Carr (1954), 20–2; for a more precise definition of the 'scissors', see p. 16 above.

justified. After the reasonably good 1923 harvest, industrial prices remained very high, owing to the use by state industry of its oligopolistic position on the market to keep prices up, encouraged by a generous state credit policy towards industry. In the resulting 'scissors' crisis' of the autumn of 1923, the peasants did not refuse to sell grain, but they were apparently reluctant to purchase industrial goods, and industrial turnover fell drastically. Equilibrium was restored by the reduction of credit to industry and by forcing down industrial prices on the instructions of the economic agencies of the state.[77]

The use of administrative measures to reduce prices during the scissors' crisis was a significant act. It was henceforth recognised that direct administrative intervention by the general economic agencies of the state might be required in order to maintain a stable market relationship between state industry and the individual peasantry. This first major intervention by the state in the market protected the peasants against the power of state industry, but it also provided a precedent for later attempts to over-ride their economic preferences in the interests of state industry. In 1923—and even in 1926—no-one believed that the peasants should be forced to sell their products at lower prices than they were prepared to accept voluntarily. But legislation by the state relating to the prices of agricultural as well as industrial products was regarded from 1923 onwards as a legitimate, and indeed essential, feature of the New Economic Policy.

After the 1924 harvest, the relation between industry and the peasant was reversed. The harvest was poor, attempts by the state to purchase grain at relatively low 'maximum prices (limitnye tseny)' failed, and the private market in grain expanded (kulaks, well-to-do peasants and private traders purchased grain at free market prices in the autumn of 1924 in the expectation of price increases in the following spring and summer). Some restrictions on grain sales were introduced, primarily directed against private traders. Eventually the crisis was resolved only by abandoning the maximum prices; in May 1925 the prices offered by the state for grain were double those of December 1924.[78] While the state had managed to bring down the prices of industrial goods after the 1923 harvest, after the 1924

[77] See *Khozyaistvennye itogi v 1923–1924 g.* (1925), 29–37 (A. L. Vainshtein); Yurovskii (1928), 228–33; Dmitrenko (1971), 177–8.

[78] *Russkii ekonomicheskii sbornik* (Berlin), i (1925), 99–103, 108–9; Carr (1958), 189–95; the low price paid for grain and the high prices of industrial goods were an immediate cause of an uprising in Georgia at the end of August 1924 (*ibid.* 198–9).

harvest the peasants, particularly the well-to-do and kulak peasants in the grain-surplus areas, proved able to insist on a higher price for grain than the state was willing to pay.

In 1925, the harvest was much better than in 1924, by far the best since the revolution. Immediately after the harvest, the prices paid by the state and cooperative collection agencies, now renamed 'directive prices', fell to half the level of the spring of 1925. But the government attempted to accelerate grain purchases, issuing generous credits to rival collection agencies, and in July–September 1925 collection prices remained substantially higher than planned. Moreover, in the summer of 1925, a substantially new element was introduced into the economic relation between the regime and the peasantry. The summer building season was the first since the revolution in which a substantial amount of new capital construction took place; and this resulted in a considerable increase in urban, and to a lesser extent in rural, demand. But by now firm controls over most industrial prices had been established by the authorities. In consequence, industrial prices did not rise to meet the increase in demand; instead, serious shortages of goods resulted. The peasants, confronted by empty shelves in the shops, reduced their sales of grain: in October–December 1925, grain collections, though higher than after the poor harvest of 1924, were much lower than in October–December 1923. The authorities held to the axiom that the peasant should not be coerced to supply grain, mindful of the failure of the limited administrative restrictions introduced after the harvest of 1924. Instead, plans for the other sectors of the economy were cut back. Plans to export grain in 1925 were abandoned, and plans to import industrial equipment reduced; credits to industry, and its production and investment plans, were also cut.[79]

The three successive crises of 1923–5 were followed in 1926–7 by almost a year of unexpected calm on the grain front, characterised by Gosplan as a period of 'smooth and stable growth'. The 1926 grain harvest was good. As a result of restrictions on the expansion of capital investment, and on the increase in urban demand generally, demand and supply were in equilibrium, and industrial goods were readily available at the official prices. In consequence the grain collection agencies obtained a substantially increased quantity of

[79] See Carr (1958), 290–7, 305–8; Yurovskii (1928), 350–60; for grain collections and grain-collection prices in this period, see Mendel'son, ed. (1930), 51, 70.

grain at much lower prices. One blemish remained. Grain prices rose in the winter of 1925–26, and the prices of livestock and dairy products (sold almost exclusively in the market) were also high. But the prices of industrial crops, such as sugar beet, flax, cotton and oil seeds, which were fixed by state collection agencies acting on behalf of state industry, were somewhat reduced. In consequence, peasants cultivating these crops reduced, or only slightly increased, their sowings in the spring of 1926; yields were also low in that year, and a poor harvest followed (see Table 1). But to the party leaders this seemed a minor fault, and easily remedied. The lower grain prices after the 1926 harvest were partly intended to put this right.[80] With the restoration of the production of industry and agriculture approximately to their pre-war level, the uneasy relationship between the regime and the peasants appeared in the autumn of 1926 and the early months of 1927 to have acquired a novel stability. Was this a new phase, as the party leaders hoped, or a temporary lull before a storm, as their opponents insisted? Which was the typical situation: 1925, or 1926?

(C) THE BOLSHEVIKS AND THE PEASANTRY IN THE MID-1920S

Much of the account of the problems of Soviet agriculture in the previous section would have been accepted by all the major groups in the party and among economists in the mid-1920s. Everyone agreed that agriculture was technologically backward and should be modernised, and that marketings were lower than before the war, and should be increased. Although the extent of economic differentiation among the peasants was heatedly debated, no-one denied that it was less than before the revolution. And it was obvious to everyone that the maintenance of market equilibrium between industry and agriculture was a difficult and crisis-ridden task. But in spite of this partial agreement on the nature of the problems, there was little agreement among rival groups of politicians and economists about the way forward for Soviet agriculture.

The majority of the Politburo, dominated at this time by Bukharin and Stalin, believed that the success of the New Economic Policy could be maintained. They argued that industrialisation

[80] On the economic situation after the 1926 harvest, see Carr and Davies (1969), 7–17, 288–90; Yurovskii (1928), 366–70.

could be achieved by developing the internal market, by improving the standard of living of both workers and peasants, and by 'smoothing and overcoming internal contradictions, not sharpening them'; resources for industrialisation should be accumulated primarily within the state sector itself.[81] In agriculture gradualness should remain the watchword. The technical level of individual peasant agriculture should be steadily raised, and simultaneously cooperation among individual peasant households should be encouraged.[82]

Within the Politburo majority, different shades of opinion existed, which were soon to become important. Bukharin enthusiastically and passionately stressed the importance of moving towards socialism via market relations;[83] in two famous phrases in 1925 he called upon 'all the peasants', including the well-to-do and kulak peasants, to '*enrich themselves*', and admitted that 'we shall move forward at a snail's pace'.[84] Stalin in a letter unpublished at the time declared that the slogan 'enrich yourself' 'is not ours, it is wrong . . . Our slogan is socialist accumulation',[85] and in a speech to a party audience in January 1925 he displayed a certain contempt for the peasantry:

> It is at our side, we are living with it, we are building a new life together with it, whether that's bad or good, together with it. This ally, you know yourselves, is not a very strong one, the peasantry is not as reliable an ally as the proletariat of the developed capitalist countries. But all the same it is an ally, and of all the available allies, it is the only one that is providing and will provide us with direct assistance, receiving our assistance in exchange.[86]

In his writings of 1925 and 1926, Stalin also paid much less attention to the market relation with the peasantry, and displayed less understanding of it, than Bukharin.[87] But all the Politburo majority

[81] Stalin, *Soch.*, vii, 286–7 (November 1926), 122–9 (April 1926).
[82] Stalin, *Soch.*, vii, 315–16, 339–40 (December 1925).
[83] See for example Bukharin (New York, 1967), 288–90 (written 1925).
[84] See Carr (1958), 260, 352 (speeches of April and December 1925).
[85] *Soch.*, vii, 153 (dated June 2, 1925).
[86] *Soch.*, vii, 28.
[87] For evidence that Stalin's approach at this time, unlike Bukharin's, was '*revolutionary rather than evolutionary*', see Tucker (1973), 398–402.

shared a confidence—or a complacency—about the present and future course of economic policy, which was reinforced by the healthy economic climate after the 1926 harvest.

The minority in the party—the Left Opposition headed by Trotsky in 1923–4, the Leningrad Opposition of Zinoviev and Kamenev at the end of 1925, and the United Opposition of both groups in 1926–7—rejected these optimistic conclusions. They shared a common conviction that the party was suffering a 'bureaucratic degeneration', and that the confidence of the leaders in the possibility of completing the construction of a socialist society in the isolated Soviet Union was leading them to adapt their policies to the petty-bourgeois environment in which they were located. The Left held that in economic policies the party was making dangerous concessions to the private traders, and above all to the kulaks. Much more emphasis must be placed on the development of industry; the transformation of agriculture required the prior development of industry, to supply machinery and consumer goods to the peasants. But a policy of industrialisation could not succeed without the restoration of party, workers' and soviet democracy, and the construction of socialism could not be completed without the support of a successful revolution in an advanced country.

The 'bourgeois economists' who were associated with Bukharin, and the party economic specialists who were associated with the Left Opposition, took more extreme positions than the political leaders. Kondratiev, the most influential economist both in Narkomzem and in the People's Commissariat for Finance, Narkomfin, openly if guardedly advocated further economic differentiation in the countryside,[88] and called for a reduction in the '*insupportable* rate of development of industry', a wage-freeze in industry, a switch of resources from capital goods to consumer goods industries, a reduction in the 'excessively heavy burden' of taxation on the 'developing strata of peasant farms', and an increase in imports of consumer goods to meet peasant demand.[89]

In contrast to Kondratiev, Chayanov, the head of the 'Organisation and Production School' of agricultural economists, the so-called 'neo-narodniks', which was the other main focus of 'bourgeois' economic influence in Narkomzem, attached little

[88] *Puti sel'skogo khozyaistva*, 5, 1927, 139–40.

[89] Kondratiev's theses on agriculture and industrialisation are extensively cited, without a precise date, by Zinoviev in B, 13, July 15, 1927, 33–47.

significance to economic differentiation in the countryside. According to Chayanov, the way forward to socialism was to develop 'vertical cooperatives', first in marketing and then in agricultural processing, rather than make an immediate attempt to establish 'horizontal' producer cooperatives—i.e. kolkhozy.[90] If Kondratiev and his colleagues provided Bukharin in 1925 with the arguments which led the authorities to relax the restrictions on the hiring of labour and renting of land in the countryside, Chayanov bolstered Bukharin's view, expressed in February 1925, that 'the high road leads along the cooperative line'; 'collective farms are not the main line, not the high road, not the chief path by which the peasant will come to socialism'.[91]

No bourgeois economists provided such direct inspiration for Trotsky. But Preobrazhensky, a prominent member of the Left Opposition, was an outstanding economist. In his famous work *New Economics* he declared that the Soviet Union must pass through a stage of 'primary socialist accumulation', analogous to the 'primary accumulation' postulated by Marx in his analysis of the rise of capitalism. According to Preobrazhensky, industry could not rely only or mainly on accumulation within the state sector for its expansion, particularly in view of the political and social need (neglected by the Politburo majority) to pay high wages to the industrial workers. Instead, the peasant economy must play a role analogous to that played by the exploitation of pre-capitalist forms of production, including the colonies, in the stage of primary capitalist accumulation: part of the product or incomes of the small-scale peasant economies, and particularly of the kulaks, must be exploited or 'alienated' by the state. Preobrazhensky, like Trotsky, stipulated that this activity would remain within the framework of the market economy: the peasants' product would be obtained through taxation or price policy, not by the forcible methods of war communism, or by the plunder characteristic of primary capitalist accumulation.[92] Neither Preobrazhensky nor Trotsky anticipated that agriculture would be collectivised in the near future.

But a significant disagreement between Preobrazhensky and his

[90] Chayanov (1966), 264–9 (first published in 1925).

[91] See Carr (1958), 220–1; Carr and Davies (1969), 921–2; for passages in Bukharin which directly echo Chayanov's approach to the agricultural cooperatives see Bukharin (New York, 1967), 266–7 (written in 1925).

[92] See Preobrazhensky (Oxford, 1965), *passim* (first published in 1924–6); his reply to the charge that he favoured 'colonial' exploitation is on pp. 227–31.

opponents in the party majority about the role of the market appeared in a doctrinal dispute about the operation of the NEP economy. Preobrazhensky argued that the two laws or regulators of the economy, the 'law of value' (roughly equivalent to the law of supply and demand) and the 'law of socialist accumulation', were in conflict, and could be resolved only by the victory of one regulator or another. His opponents, including Bukharin, argued that while two 'principles' existed, the 'principle of spontaneity' and the 'planning principle', these principles struggled and cooperated within the framework of the law of value, which would be gradually transformed into a 'law of labour outlays' as planning become predominant.[93] The significance of the dispute was that Preobrazhensky treated the regulatory power of the state exercised through the law of socialist accumulation as in principle independent of the market forces exercised through the law of value rather than operating only through the market.

Preobrazhensky was not alone in seeing the market as secondary to the larger goals of state planning. In 1924, Krzhizhanovsky, chief author of the Goelro plan for the electrification of Russia and chairman of the state planning commission Gosplan for most of the 1920s, stressed that commodity exchange and currency circulation must be subordinate to the plan.[94] In 1925 Strumilin, a leading economist in Gosplan, insisted on the need 'to *adapt* the market environment consciously to our planning efforts';[95] and at the beginning of 1927 he argued, in an introduction to a draft of the five-year plan, that 'as the initial coordinates in constructing our plans we can and must take not what can be forecast by a prognosis but what can be programmed by positing it as a goal'.[96] Strumilin was in effect refusing to think within the terms of the market economy, or of the principles of planning adopted by the XII party congress in 1923 (see p. 3 above). His plans were only loosely tied in with any possibility of equilibrium on the market, and were correctly castigated by Narkomfin as risking 'a break in the link with the peasantry'.[97]

Several other significant events in the course of the economic year

[93] See the long discussion in VKA, xiv (1926), 3–254, and in Preobrazhensky (1965), 8–41, 224–67.
[94] EZh, January 13, 1924.
[95] Strumilin (1958), 225.
[96] PKh, 7–8, 1927, 14.
[97] See Carr and Davies (1969), 856–61.

1926/27 revealed the spread of the tendency to relax the axiom that planning should take place through and not against the market. In February 1927, the party central committee ordered that retail prices of industrial consumer goods should be reduced by 10 per cent. On the prevailing assumption that terms of trade for the peasantry should not deteriorate, the decision was a logical consequence of the reduction in grain prices in the summer of 1926.[98] But the success of the price reduction campaign, carried out under the leadership of Mikoyan, the People's Commissar for Trade, at a time when purchasing power was rising rapidly owing to the further expansion of capital investment in the course of 1927, brought prices below the equilibrium position. From the autumn of 1927 onwards, serious shortages of industrial goods resulted. A substantial number of private shops were forcibly closed and some private traders were arrested for speculation. Kuibyshev, chairman of Vesenkha, the commissariat in charge of industry, declared in August 1927 that 'to reduce prices when there is a goods shortage' was 'a very great achievement of the planning principle'.[99] In the same month Vesenkha successfully put great pressure on the Politburo to increase the already substantial capital investment plan for industry for the economic year 1927/28; on August 25, the Politburo increased the planned allocation to capital investment from the state budget.[100] Thus at the time of the 1927 harvest, an influential group in the party and in the economic agencies of the state secured the adoption of plans for industrialisation which were incompatible with market equilibrium and involved overcoming the market by administrative instructions of a kind which had not been adopted since the end of war communism.

This fundamental shift in approach was veiled by loud denials that the framework of policy had changed. Strumilin insisted that his five-year plan targets were compatible with financial stability and would not put a strain on relations with the peasantry. Mikoyan declared that price reduction had strengthened the ruble and provided 'a powerful lever for increasing the agricultural surplus disposed of by the peasantry'.[101] The increases in investment in

[98] On September 16, 1926, the Politburo resolved that the reduction of grain prices made it necessary to reduce industrial prices (*Industrializatsiya SSSR, 1926–1928 gg.* (1969), 510).

[99] TPG, August 14, 1927.

[100] *Industrializatsiya SSSR, 1926–1928 gg.* (1969), 510.

[101] Mikoyan (1927), 3.

industry and in other state expenditures in 1927/28 were implausibly planned to take place without currency inflation.[102] Wishful thinking—sometimes amounting to deliberate deception—was much more prominent in Soviet plans and policies than in the immediate past.

The complex and controversial question of the causes of the fundamental shift in approach in 1927 lies outside the chronological framework of the present volume. Part of the explanation certainly lies in the intractability of the obstacles in the way of raising resources for industrialisation in a predominantly peasant country. But this is not a sufficient explanation: it does not fully explain, for example, the price reductions of 1927, which did not raise resources for industry and harmed relations with the peasants. Factors other than the needs of industrialisation as such pressed the leaders towards using administrative measures to achieve a quick solution to their difficulties. The defeat of the Chinese revolution and the rupture of diplomatic relations with the USSR by the British Conservative government both occurred in the spring of 1927, and revealed the extreme isolation of the USSR, thus imparting a sense of urgency to the plans for industrialisation. The hopes for a rapid transformation of society which are inherent in revolutionary marxism led the section of the party majority headed by Stalin to be impatient with the results achieved by the cautious policies of 1925 and 1926. This section of the party leadership was certainly also influenced in a radical direction by the repeatedly stated fears of the United Opposition that current moderate policies were endangering the basis of the gains achieved by the revolution: it was in October 1926 that Trotsky called Stalin at a Politburo meeting 'the grave-digger of the revolution'.[103] The one-party system, and the monolithic regime within the party, which was being consolidated by 1927, in themselves encouraged administrative solutions, as did the outlook and methods of work of a large number of party members, acquired in the Civil War and not entirely abandoned afterwards (the apparatus and methods of grain requisition, for example, ceased to be used only in the spring of 1924). Paradoxically, it was before the grain crisis of 1927–8, at a time when the efforts to guide the peasant economy through the market seemed to be succeeding, that the pressures towards administrative

[102] *KTs . . . na 1927/28* (1928), 326–7.
[103] See Carr (1971), 16–17.

methods proved sufficiently strong to begin to overturn the apparently deep-rooted commitment to the market relationship with the peasantry.

These changes in approach were still a world apart from the forced collectivisation drive of 1929–30. But several significant changes in agricultural policy occurred in the autumn of 1927. First, the People's Commissariat for Workers' and Peasants' Inspection (Rabkrin) headed by Ordzhonikidze, which was in effect an agency of the party, advocated, though without official endorsement as yet, an extremely ambitious plan to double grain yields within ten years.[104] These plans, while still assuming that the individual peasant economies would continue to dominate agriculture, greatly encouraged confidence that agriculture need not prove a fundamental obstacle to industrialisation. Secondly, the policy of conciliating the kulaks and the well-to-do peasants was finally abandoned: the party committed itself to a 'reinforced offensive against the kulak'. Henceforth, efforts to wage a class struggle against the kulaks, with the support of the poor peasants and in alliance with the middle peasants, coloured every aspect of party policy in the countryside.[105] Thirdly, greater attention was devoted to the kolkhozy. A Politburo commission on the kolkhozy established in 1927 under Molotov's chairmanship was later said by Kalinin to have brought about a 'mental revolution'.[106] At the XV party congress in December 1927 an addendum to the resolution on work in the countryside, apparently supported by the Politburo and criticised by Bukharin and others, emphasised that 'at the present period the task of unifying and transforming small individual households into large collectives must be posed as *main task* (osnovnaya zadacha) of the party in the countryside'.[107] This appears to be the first recorded disagreement between Bukharin and the majority of the Politburo in the winter of 1927–8.

[104] See Wheatcroft (1974), 112–15. No permanent increase in grain yields occurred in Stalin's lifetime.

[105] See Carr and Davies (1969), 32–6.

[106] *XVI konf.* (1962), 293.

[107] *XV s"ezd*, ii (1962), 1419–21; *KPSS v rez.*, ii (1954), 475–8; *Istoriya KPSS*, iv, i (1970), 524–5. Owing to the absence of the definite and indefinite article in Russian, the phrase could equally accurately be translated 'a main task' or 'the main task'.

(D) THE GRAIN CRISIS OF 1927–8

The conflict between the rival approaches of 'planning through the market' and 'planning by overcoming the market' was soon put to a decisive test. In October–December 1927, peasants sold the official collection agencies only half as much grain as in the same months of 1926. With this amount of grain the towns and the army could not be fed.

The peasants were reluctant to sell grain to the official agencies for several reasons. First, the grain harvest in 1927 was several million tons lower than in the previous year, when the weather was more favourable and the yield was high (see p. 42 below). Hence the peasants had less grain at their disposal. Secondly, the price offered for grain by the official agencies was low relative to those of industrial crops and meat and dairy products, so it was more advantageous for the peasants to acquire the cash they needed by selling these other products. Moreover, in view of the rapid growth of the urban economy they also had more opportunity to earn money on seasonal work in the towns. Thirdly, many industrial consumer goods were in short supply, so the peasants were reluctant to convert their grain, which could easily be stored, into cash which they could not use to buy the goods they wanted. Finally, the peasants were in a stronger position than in previous years to resist changes in the terms of trade which were to their disadvantage. Their stocks of cash were higher, and by 1927 they had acquired sufficient basic consumer goods to be prepared to wait for the variety or quality they preferred.[108]

The crisis could have been mitigated if the Soviet leaders and their immediate advisers had been more perceptive in the months before the harvest. The shortage of consumer goods was largely due to the substantial reduction in their prices in the spring of 1927 (see p. 36 above), which was a deliberate decision of the Politburo. Other remedies were also available: an increase in agricultural taxation in 1927 would have compelled the peasants to sell more products in order to obtain more cash. The successful outcome of the harvest of 1926 had induced a dangerous complacency in the authorities.

But some factors in the situation could have been brought under

[108] See Carr and Davies (1969), 44–6, which also discusses other contributory factors.

control only if the authorities had backed down from their industrialisation plans. The shortage of consumer goods was partly due to the increase in purchasing power which resulted from the expansion of industry and of capital construction generally. In other respects, too, the state had much less freedom of manoeuvre. According to a contemporary survey, the most important factor in peasant reluctance to sell grain was its price relative to those of other agricultural products.[109] This was also the most intractable problem for the authorities. A complicated story lies behind the low official price of grain. In 1925, the official agencies increased the price of grain when peasants were reluctant to sell it; while this solved the grain crisis, it also led in the following year to a decline in the production of industrial crops (see p. 31 above). In 1926, the official agencies therefore again reduced the price offered for grain. During the course of these manipulations the prices of meat and dairy products rose steadily; meat and dairy products were mainly sold on the free market and their prices were therefore outside state control. By 1927 it was clearly to the advantage of the peasants to concentrate on the production and sale of livestock products. A less crude price policy in 1926 might have mitigated these difficulties. But at the end of 1927 the only way in which the state could hope to persuade the peasants to sell more grain to the official agencies was by substantially increasing its official price.

This course was rejected. During the similar crisis in the autumn of 1925 the Soviet authorities increased the price of grain and cut their plans for industrialisation; now they kept the price of grain stable and pressed ahead with industrialisation. At the beginning of 1928, compulsion was used to obtain grain from the peasants for the first time since 1924, and on a greater scale. Grain was seized with the aid of the so-called 'extraordinary measures', and, as in 1918–20, the authorities unsuccessfully endeavoured to win the support of the mass of the peasantry against the more prosperous peasants,

[109] In a survey of 800 voluntary correspondents in the grain regions of the RSFSR, the main factors mentioned as hindering the grain collections were as follows (percentage of correspondents mentioning the factor in brackets): low yield in 1927 (54), low grain collection price (57), more profitable to sell livestock (51), shortage of industrial goods (25), rumours of war and famine (23), unpreparedness of grain collection agencies (21), growth of non-agricultural work (11) (*Statistika i narodnoe khozyaistvo*, 2, 1928, 146). I am indebted to Mr S. G. Wheatcroft for drawing my attention to this source.

many of whom were put on trial for hoarding grain and profiteering from its sale.

This was the beginning of the end of NEP. The 'Right wing' of the party, headed by Bukharin, Rykov, the chairman of Sovnarkom, and Tomsky, the head of the trade unions, drew the lesson from the grain crisis that the policy errors which led to it must be avoided at all costs in the future; equilibrium on the market must be restored, and industrialisation must again fit into the NEP framework. Nearly all the non-party economists supported these conclusions. But other party leaders, such as Kuibyshev, Politburo member in charge of industry, and Kaganovich, a close associate of Stalin at party headquarters, took an entirely different view. For them, the policies of 1927 which preceded the grain crisis were not errors, but bold attempts to subordinate market forces to the will of the state; the grain crisis occurred because controls over market spontaneity were not yet adequate; and the 'extraordinary measures' were not a regrettable temporary necessity but a convincing demonstration of the efficacy of 'administrative methods'. 'The will of the state opposed itself to the *Konjunktur* [i.e. to market trends]', Kuibyshev declared, 'and, thanks to all the levers at the disposal of the proletarian state, this *Konjunktur* was broken.'[110] In the machinery of government, the balance of forces which existed until 1926 was reversed; henceforth bold administrative decisions took precedence over delicate adjustments in financial and price policy. Industrialisation proceeded at a pace entirely incompatible with a market relationship with the peasantry, and coercion of the peasantry became a permanent feature of Soviet policy.

(E) THE CRISIS OF THE PEASANT ECONOMY, 1928–9

The 1928 harvest, like that of 1927, was about five million tons less than the post-revolutionary record harvest of 1926. In 1928, the size of the harvest was, as usual, somewhat uncertain: at the time it was reported as slightly below, and in the revised figures as slightly above, that of 1927 (see Table 1). At all events the growth of grain production had come to a halt. The harvest of the two main food grains, wheat and rye, was particularly poor: according to the

[110] See Carr and Davies (1969), 307–10; this statement was made on February 2, 1928.

revised figures, it amounted to 41·3 million tons against 45·9 in 1927 and 48·6 in 1926.

The causes of the poor grain harvests of 1927 and 1928 were complicated. The poor harvest in 1927 was partly a result of the switch of peasant attention away from grain, which was in turn partly a result of the decision of the Soviet authorities to increase the prices of industrial crops relative to those of grain (see p. 31 above). The area sown to grain, which rose about five per cent a year in 1924–6, increased by only one per cent in 1927, while the area sown to industrial crops rose substantially.[111] This slow rate of increase in the sown area was partly, perhaps mainly, a result of the unfavourable price for grain. But it was also due to bad weather which hindered ploughing in the autumn of 1926.[112] Moreover, the absolute decline in the harvest was a result of the low grain yield, which in turn was mainly a consequence of the unfavourable weather conditions during the summer of 1927.[113]

In the following year 1928, while the grain yield was higher than in 1927,[114] the area sown to grain fell by 2·5 million hectares (2·6 per cent).[115] On this occasion the decline in sown area seems to have been entirely due to the exceptionally unfavourable weather conditions in the autumn and winter of 1927–8, which destroyed 5·5 million hectares of the autumn sowings in the Ukraine, North Caucasus and the Central Black-Earth region: 'such catastrophic years for the autumn sowings', the authors of the control figures pointed out, 'have been shown by meteorologists to occur only once every 30–40 years'.[116] If these 'winter killings' of autúmn-sown grain had not occurred, the area sown to grain and the level of grain production in 1928 would have been higher than in the previous year. Autumn-sown grain consists entirely of wheat and rye, so the winter killings were also responsible for the decline in food crops in 1928.

The effect of government policy on peasant behaviour was thus remarkably ambiguous. While the low grain prices of 1926

[111] See Wheatcroft (1977(2)), 9; Carr and Davies (1969), 940.
[112] *KTs . . . na 1927/28* (1928), 106.
[113] See Wheatcroft (1977(1)), 45.
[114] *Ibid.* 45.
[115] See Wheatcroft (1977(2)), 9.
[116] *KTs . . . na 1928/29* (1929), 218, 220; for the unexpected repetition of these conditions in the winter of 1928–9, see pp. 63, 104 below. These conditions recurred in the autumn of 1971 before the bad harvest of 1972.

undoubtedly checked the growth of the area sown to grain in 1927, it is not clear whether the grain difficulties which began in the autumn of 1927 at first discouraged or encouraged the interest of the peasantry as a whole in grain farming. While forced collections at low prices in the grain-surplus areas certainly in themselves tended to discourage production, the large increase in the free-market price of grain may have acted in the opposite direction, and encouraged peasants to sow grain in the hope of selling part of their product on the free market. Peasants in the grain-deficit zone, who now had difficulty in acquiring grain at reasonable prices for their own consumption, were undoubtedly also under economic pressure to grow more of their own grain. The net effect was uncertain, at least as long as a substantial amount of grain could still be sold on the free market. In the spring of 1928 the area sown to industrial crops increased much more rapidly than the area sown to grain (by 18·6 per cent against 5·7 per cent). But the substantial increase in the area sown to grain in the spring of 1928, after the small increase in the spring of 1927, indicates that peasant interest in grain production had not markedly declined.[117]

The poor harvest of 1928 was the occasion for a sharp exchange between the Politburo majority and the emerging Right opposition. In the autumn of 1928, Bukharin in his 'Notes of an Economist' referred to the 'stability and even *regress of grain crops and the weak development of agriculture in general*',[118] and Frumkin wrote, in an unpublished letter circulated to the central committee, of 'stagnation' in the countryside and 'degeneration (degradatsiya)' in agriculture generally.[119] Bukharin's 'Notes' firmly attributed the main responsibility for the agricultural difficulties to excessive industrialisation. The control figures for 1928/29, without mentioning Bukharin or Frumkin by name, sharply commented that in view of the unfavourable weather conditions 'the reduction in the growth of sown area and gross output in the past year or two cannot be interpreted as degeneration', and drew attention to the continuing growth of draught animals, agricultural machines and high-grade

[117] For the figures for spring sowings, see *KTs . . . na 1929/30* (1930), 528. According to later figures, the area sown to grain increased by as much as 8·3 per cent in the spring of 1928, while the area sown to industrial crops rose by only 6·8 per cent (*Posevnye ploshchadi 1935*, i (1936), 6).

[118] P, September 30, 1928; Bukharin used the transliterated word 'regress' in Russian.

[119] See Carr and Davies (1969), 92.

seed. Moreover, according to the control figures, the increase of marketable crops such as wheat and oats at the expense of crops consumed by the peasant economy itself, such as rye and millet, had now continued for several years, and was an unmistakable sign of progress:

> It would only be possible to speak of degeneration if the means of production in agriculture and their quality had declined, if the methods of cultivation had deteriorated, and the ratio of different crops had shifted towards *naturalizatsiya*—i.e. towards the reduction of the proportion of market crops and the increase of the proportion of consumption crops.[120]

In April 1929 Stalin also insisted that party policy could not be blamed for the low harvest of rye and wheat in 1928, which was due to 'the bad harvest failure in the steppe zone of the Ukraine (frost and drought) and the partial failure in the North Caucasus, the Central Black-Earth region and the North-west region'.[121] As an account of the immediate reasons for the low harvest of 1928 these excuses seem to be justified. But the occurrence of bad harvests in particular years was not an unlucky accident, but a result of the inherently unstable natural conditions of Russian agriculture (see p. 21 above). The policy of the Soviet government, which gambled every year that the harvest in the year concerned would be a good one, was inherently unrealistic.[122]

Moreover, the official onslaught on those who claimed that agriculture was degenerating was undertaken at the very moment when unmistakable signs of degeneration were beginning to appear. The number of all types of farm animals increased impressively throughout the 1920s until the spring of 1928. But between the summer of 1928 and the summer of 1929, for the first time since the Civil War, the number of cattle and pigs declined substantially, the number of sheep and goats ceased to increase, and the number of horses, still substantially below the pre-war level, increased much more slowly than in previous years (see Table 2). While the winter of 1928–9 was exceptionally severe, this was certainly not the main cause of the decline. Whether the amount of fodder declined in this period was disputed. A Narkomtorg specialist claimed that the

120 *KTs . . . na 1928/29* (1929), 217.
121 *Soch.*, xii, 86.
122 See Wheatcroft (1977(1)), 12–13.

amount of fodder increased in 1928 and did not deteriorate, except in certain areas, even in 1929/30.[123] A study by the Central Statistical Administration published in 1930 estimated that the amount of fodder per animal declined in the agricultural year 1927/28, but did not change significantly in 1928/29 and 1929/30.[124] A later study by the Central Statistical Administration, however, estimated that fodder consumption per animal, except in the case of pigs, declined in 1927/28 and 1928/29.[125] The balance of the evidence seems to be on the side of these later estimates. While the consumption of potatoes, root crops and oil-cake for fodder sharply increased in 1928/29,[126] the production of some major fodders was inadequate in several major agricultural areas,[127] and in the USSR as a whole the consumption of grain fodder almost certainly declined in both 1928/29 and 1929/30;[128] moreover, the amount of mill feed declined as the extraction rates were increased to cope with the bread shortage. Owing to the shortage of grain, and its continuously rising price, the most prosperous peasants in the grain-surplus areas stored it rather than feeding it to their animals, while peasants in the grain-deficit zone could not obtain enough grain. Some peasants, lacking adequate fodder, or in need of income which they could not obtain from grain, killed and sold their animals.[129]

Other factors also led peasants to dispose of their animals from the summer of 1928 onwards. With the intensification of the drive against well-to-do and kulak peasants, households which possessed several cows suffered various disadvantages: the rates of agricultural and other taxes were substantially increased,[130] and even peasants

[123] VT, 7–8, 1930, 26 (Visherov).

[124] Gaister, ed. (1930), 58.

[125] Nifontov (1932), 127, 147; this refers to peasant animals only. This work was published by the Central Administration for National Economic Records, TsUNKhU; TsUNKhU, the successor to the Central Statistical Administration, was a semi-autonomous organisation within Gosplan.

[126] Nifontov (1932), 127.

[127] It was reported that in 1928 the grass harvest was poor in the Ukraine and the Crimea, and the potato and coarse fodder harvest in the whole grain-deficit zone (EO, 9, 1929, 34).

[128] Gaister, ed. (1930), 58; Nifontov (1932), 127; a writer in the Narkomtorg journal, however, claimed that the decline in grain marketings in 1928 must have led to an increase in the use of grain for fodder (VT, 7–8, 1930, 26 (Visherov)).

[129] EO, 9, 1929, 34; 10, 1929, 34.

[130] EO, 9, 1929, 34.

with two cows were treated less favourably when manufactured and other goods were supplied in return for the sale of milk and dairy products to collection agencies.[131] Well-to-do peasants reduced the amount of land they rented from other peasants, in fear of being labelled as kulaks and therefore subject to individual tax assessment; with less land, they had less fodder, and at the same time less need for draught animals to cultivate the land.[132] All this led to the slaughter of animals or their sale to less prosperous peasants. By the end of the economic year 1928/29 a Narkomtorg official frankly admitted that 'the upper well-to-do groups of the peasantry are reducing the number of their animals, and the poor and middle peasants are increasing their holdings, but cannot so far wholly compensate for the declining livestock of the kulak'.[133] The decline in animals occurred both in areas where fodder was in short supply, and in areas where it was not.[134] In the economic year 1928/29 investment in animals fell by almost 50 per cent. While implements and machinery made available to agriculture substantially increased in quantity, in consequence of the substantial decline in livestock total gross investment in agriculture also fell absolutely.[135]

But the crisis of the peasant economy in 1928–9 was above all a crisis of the market economy, a crisis due to the increased demand for agricultural products, primarily resulting from increases in state expenditure due to the growing pace of industrialisation. In spite of

[131] VT, 7–8, 1930, 28–9.
[132] EO, 9, 1929, 34.
[133] I, September 22, 1929 (I. I. Pankratov).
[134] EZh, August 14, 1929 (Lositskii).
[135] *KTs . . . na 1929/30* (1930), 446–9; the main figures are as follows (million rubles at 1926/27 prices):

	1926/27	*1927/28*	*1928/29 (preliminary)*
Implements and machines	185	210	289
Transport and other equipment	274	299	292
Farm buildings	611	628	699
Housing	1015	973	1054
Animals	1142	1013	548
Other investment	54	64	95
Total agricultural investment	3281	3187	2977

the increases in demand, and the administrative pressure applied by the state to obtain grain, total extra-rural marketings of grain declined in the agricultural year 1928/29.[136] Moreover, the harbingers of future difficulties due to the decline in livestock were already appearing. The amount of milk marketed declined in 1928/29 after rising steadily until that year; marketed production of butter failed to increase, and exports were reduced. Some increase took place in total food supplies to the market. As a result of the abnormally high slaughter of animals, the amount of meat marketed substantially increased in both 1927/28 and 1928/29, as did the number of hides for the manufacture of leather goods. But the capital stock of this sector of farming was literally being eaten up. For the moment, however, marketed agricultural production, measured in fixed prices, rose by 7·0 per cent in 1927/28 and 9·6 per cent in 1928/29, primarily owing to increased sales of meat and industrial crops.[137]

These increases in supply were quite insufficient to meet the rapidly growing demand; and in the course of 1928 and 1929 rationing was introduced in the towns for all staple foods. Bread rationing in the winter of 1928–9 was followed by sugar and tea rationing during the summer and, beginning with Moscow, by meat rationing in the autumn of 1929.[138]

In consequence of the widespread shortages, the general index of the retail prices of agricultural products rose by 8·6 per cent between October 1, 1927, and October 1, 1928, and by a further 16·1 per cent in the following year, 25·9 per cent in all in the course of two years; prices in the socialised sector rose in this period by 16·2 per cent, while those in the private sector rose by as much as 117·2 per cent.[139] Of all the major foodstuffs, grain was the most scarce. The 'bazaar price' (free-market price) for wheat in the grain-surplus areas rose much faster than bazaar agricultural prices as a whole, by as much as 289 per cent between September 1, 1927, and September 1, 1929, and the price of rye flour on the private market

[136] According to *Sdvigi* (1931), 157, marketings were 15·1 million tons in 1927/28 and 13·8 million tons in 1928/29.

[137] For figures of marketed production, see *KTs . . . na 1929/30* (1930), 538–54; SO, 3–4, 1930, 57; these figures are for net marketings on the extra-rural market.

[138] SO, 3–4, 1930, 59; I, September 21, 1929; see also Carr and Davies (1969), 702–4; for bread rationing, see p. 60 below.

[139] See Carr and Davies (1969), 964–5, and Mendel'son, ed. (1930), 100–16, 157.

in the grain-deficit zone increased by 354 per cent.[140] The prices paid to the peasant by the collection agencies rose much more slowly: the price of grain increased by only 24·3 per cent between May 1927 and May 1929, and that of all farming products by only 12·1 per cent.[141] A huge gap had opened up between the price of grain on the market and the price the peasant received in the official collections.

The rise in state expenditure also resulted in a substantial increase in the demand for peasant labour for non-agricultural purposes from state institutions and enterprises. Between 1927/28 and 1928/29, according to Narkomtrud figures, the total number of otkhodniki (excluding those going to agriculture) rose by 14·4 per cent from 3,437,000 to 3,932,000.[142] The number of otkhodniki working in forestry, building and mining increased particularly rapidly; the number working in industry as such declined, however, partly because of the decline in some of the small-scale artisan industries manufacturing consumer goods in which the otkhodniki mainly worked, and partly because some of the otkhodniki transferred to permanent work in the towns. The dynamic censuses for 1927 and 1929 also showed that both the proportion of peasant households engaged in non-agricultural activities in general and the proportion sending labour to work in non-agricultural occupations substantially increased.[143]

These developments resulted in a substantial rise in peasant incomes from non-agricultural activities. The proportion of peasant money incomes derived from this source rose only slightly, however, as peasant money incomes from the sale of agricultural products also rose substantially owing to the rise in prices on the free market. Paradoxically, as a result of the rise in state expenditure, rural demand rose more rapidly than urban demand. All peasant extra-rural earnings rose by 12·0 per cent in 1927/28 and 16·6 per cent in 1928/29, while urban incomes rose by 9·5 and 10·0 per cent.[144]

140 Mendel'son, ed. (1930), 112–13.

141 Mendel'son, ed. (1930), 69–70.

142 VTr, 7–8, 1930, 137; IZ, xciv (1974), 108–11. These figures are not directly comparable with those for 1925/26 on p. 12 above: from 1927/28 onwards otkhodniki working within the same volost' were included in the returns, provided that they did not live at home during their period of seasonal labour.

143 *Sdvigi* (1931), 80–1 (for these censuses see p. 12, n. 34, above). The proportion engaged in non-agricultural activities rose from 52·0 to 58·3 per cent.

144 *KTs . . . na 1929/30* (1930), 476–81.

The Soviet authorities attempted to cope with the crisis on the agricultural market by greatly increasing control by the state. The use of administrative measures to obtain grain continued throughout the agricultural year 1928/29, and is discussed on pp. 56–60 below. Control by the state was also extended to other agricultural products. Until 1927, most meat was purchased by private traders, or sold directly by peasants to consumers at the bazaars. Between 1927 and 1929, the role of the socialised sector in meat and other agricultural purchases greatly increased.[145] The coercion used against the peasants for the grain collections was not yet applied to meat and other products. But by the spring of 1929 'meat collections' were beginning to appear on the agenda of party committees together with the grain collections. At the XVI party conference, Eikhe, the Siberian party secretary, reported that Siberia supplied 19,000 tons of meat in March 1929 as compared with only 700 tons in March 1928, but 'comrade Mikoyan incessantly demands that we should collect in more and more'.[146] Administrative control over peasant production was developing into a system.

Simultaneously, private retail outlets for the sale of foodstuffs and manufactured goods in the countryside were closed or transferred to the state in large numbers. Owing to the disappearance of private shops, the total number of retail outlets declined in both town and country.[147] Private retail trade, measured in current prices, fell from 36·9 per cent of all trade in 1926/27 to 13·5 per cent in 1928/29.[148]

Discriminatory taxation, high grain collection quotas, and other state measures were used to restrict the agricultural activities of the most prosperous peasant households. From the beginning of 1928

145 SO, 3–4, 1930, 54; the role of the socialised sector in the meat and dairy trade increased as follows (as a percentage of all purchases, the remainder being undertaken either by private traders or at the bazaars):

	1925/26	*1926/27*	*1927/28*	*1928/29*
Meat	17·7	30·6	53·7	64·9
Butter	36·3	45·3	47·9	57·4
Eggs	38·0	50·0	59·0	66·1

146 *XVI konf.* (1962), 90.

147 SO, 3–4, 1930, 56.

148 Carr and Davies (1969), 962; these figures do not include direct sales by peasants.

the removal of 'excess' land from kulak households was authorised, and was frequently practised in the North Caucasus and some other areas.[149] As a result of all these measures, and the consequent lack of any incentive to improve their economies, the upper peasant groups declined both in numbers and in economic strength. The number of households in the grain-surplus areas sowing more than 17·6 hectares declined from 381,000 (2·9 per cent of all households) in 1927 to 257,000 (1·8 per cent) in 1929, while their gross grain production fell from 10·2 per cent of the total grain supplied in these areas to 5·8 per cent, and their marketed grain production from 25·1 to 14·0 per cent.[150] The amount of livestock held by the upper groups also sharply declined (see p. 46 above).

A further consequence of the pressure by the state on the more prosperous peasants was that between 1927 and 1929 the number of contract workers employed by individual peasant households fell sharply, from 1,067,000 to 649,000.[151] The number of day workers somewhat increased,[152] but the number of days worked per person declined substantially.[153] If these figures are at all accurate, the total amount of labour hired by individual households substantially declined.

Growing restrictions on the more prosperous individual peasants were matched by measures to encourage the expansion of the socialised sector of agriculture through the establishment of sov-

[149] See IS, 3, 1958, 124–6; NAF, 8, 1928, 4–5 (Larin); for the expropriation of the *bai* in Kazakhstan, see pp. 140–1 below.

[150] *Sdvigi* (1931), 13–14. In the RSFSR as a whole, according to the dynamic census, the percentage of petty-capitalist households fell from 3·9 to 2·2 per cent between 1927 and 1929; the compilers of the statistics claim, however, that these figures exaggerate the decline in these households, because 'well-to-do and kulak strata of the peasantry deliberately underestimated the value of their means of production, and also concealed the amount of labour they hired, means of production they hired out, etc.' (*Sdvigi* (1931), 66–7, 204).

[151] *Sdvigi* (1931), 134; the number working for mirs increased slightly from 685,000 to 720,000; these figures exclude the Transcaucasian and Uzbek republics. The figures for 1929 include workers hired by the fortnight as well as for a month or more, so to this extent the decline may be underestimated (*ibid.* 209); on the other hand, the number is likely to have been under-reported in 1929, owing to the fear that households hiring labour for substantial periods might be classified as 'kulak'.

[152] *Sdvigi* (1931), 134; this includes day workers hired by mirs and other peasant groups.

[153] See *Sdvigi* (1931), 80–1.

khozy, primarily on unused or little-used land, and the organisation of individual peasant households into kolkhozy. Grain production by the socialised sector rose from 1·4 million tons in 1927 to 1·8 million tons in 1928, and its capital investment rose dramatically, from 4·1 per cent of total agricultural investment in 1926/27 to 6·2 per cent in 1927/28 and 12·7 per cent in 1928/29.[154] Loans made to the socialised sector of agriculture to assist production ('production credits') rose from 345 million rubles in 1927/28 to 437 millions in 1928/29, while those to individual peasant households declined from 274 to 215 million.[155] These first steps in the heroic effort to solve the crisis by developing socialist agriculture are further discussed on pp. 109–12 below.

(F) THE REGIME AND THE COUNTRYSIDE

The new policies of 1928–9 involved an unprecedented degree of intervention by the party and state authorities in the affairs of the countryside. Even during the Civil War, the authorities were mainly concerned with obtaining grain and other agricultural products from the peasants, and made little attempt to reorganise agriculture, but in 1928–9 they sought both to obtain agricultural products and simultaneously to begin the socialisation of the peasant economy. This section considers how far a political and administrative basis for these endeavours had been established by the end of the 1920s.

The pre-revolutionary Bolshevik party was overwhelmingly an urban organisation. On the eve of the revolution, only 494 peasants belonged to the Bolshevik party, and before 1917 only four rural party cells existed![156] Much progress was made in the first decade after the revolution, but the party remained overwhelmingly urban. On October 1, 1928, out of 1,360,000 party members or candidate members, 198,000 (14·5 per cent) were peasants or agricultural workers by present occupation.[157] In all, the rural cells included

[154] *KTs . . . na 1929/30* (1930), 550–1, 448–9; capital investment includes additions to livestock and housing; the figures for 1928/29 are preliminary.

[155] *Sdvigi* (1931), 86; these figures are for the Russian, Ukrainian, Belorussian and Transcaucasian republics.

[156] Sharapov (1961), 174.

[157] *St. spr. 1928* (1929), 56–7; 35,000 of the 198,000 peasants combined agricultural work with administrative work, work as artisans, or labour for hire.

293,000 members and candidates on July 1, 1928;[158] those members who were not peasants were primarily government employees or industrial workers.[159] In 1928 there was thus only one peasant party member in every 125 peasant households, and one rural party member per 420 rural inhabitants; the comparable figures were one in ten for urban workers and one in 25 for urban inhabitants. Only 20,700 rural party cells existed on July 1, 1928; while over 90 per cent of these were in the villages, there was only one cell for every four village soviets, and each village soviet included several rural settlements (see vol. 2, pp. 34–5). As Carr remarked, 'many villages can never have seen a communist except in the guise of an occasional visiting official'.[160]

In addition to the 293,000 party members, 1 million peasants and other young persons living in the countryside belonged to the Komsomol.[161] The Young Communists were thus the most substantial group of rural citizens frankly acknowledging support for the regime. Records for Komsomol membership in the countryside were not reliable, and membership was unstable and often ill-educated; but even according to the official statistics only one rural inhabitant in every 100 belonged to the party or Komsomol, on average two persons in every rural settlement. Moreover, membership of the party and the Komsomol did not imply unhesitating support for the new party policies. A year after the launching of the campaign against 'Right-wing' influences in rural party organisations which followed the Smolensk scandal in 1928, the central party authorities still frequently complained of the unreliability of rural party members:

> It is precisely among rural communists most subject to the influence of petty-bourgeois spontaneity [wrote *Pravda* in May 1929] that it is often possible to meet opponents of the rapid development of kolkhozy and sovkhozy, 'principled' supporters of the 'free development of peasant economy', defenders of

158 *St. spr. 1928* (1929), 55; these figures are not entirely complete.

159 For the social composition of rural party cells in January 1927, see Carr (1971), 481; in the 'October enrolment' at the end of 1927 and beginning of 1928 a substantial number of peasants were admitted to the party, and about two-thirds of the members and candidates in rural party cells were peasants by occupation.

160 Carr (1971), 179.

161 See Carr (1959), 99; this figure is for January 1926; later figures have not been traced.

peaceful coexistence with the kulak, people who do not see classes in the countryside.[162]

Other sources of support for the regime in the countryside are less tangible. Support was probably strongest among the half a million rural inhabitants employed in factories and the 300,000 employed on the railways. Half a million employees of governmental and other establishments also lived in the countryside, and party membership among this group was relatively high.[163] The incomes of all state employees depended upon their service to the regime; nevertheless, their attitude was not unambiguous. According to a survey in 1929, the majority of rural teachers, the largest single group of rural employees, were of peasant origin; the author complained that 'a considerable part are standing aside' from the new policies in the countryside.[164] Ex-Red Army men were an important influence in favour of the regime. These were a substantial group: apart from those who served in the Red Army during the Civil War, some 180,000 peasants were conscripted into the Red Army annually. During their period of service, they were subject to systematic political education; many joined the party or the Komsomol; and many ex-Red Army men occupied leading positions in volost' and village soviets.[165]

Nevertheless, the regime did not succeed during the 1920s in establishing in the villages themselves a party or soviet organisation capable of acting as an effective counterweight to the mir. Party cells, as we have seen, did not exist in most villages. And in spite of considerable efforts, the village soviet remained a weak organisation, with less influence with the peasants than the mir, and with small financial powers; even in 1929/30, less than half the village soviets had their own budget, the remainder being dependent on the district (or volost' where this still existed) for their funds.[166]

Culturally, too, the influence of the Soviet regime in the countryside was weak. Newspapers and periodicals were sent into the countryside in increasing quantities in the 1920s, and great efforts were made to adapt them to the interests and understanding

[162] P, May 23, 1929. For the ambiguous position of party members in the countryside, see Carr (1971), 179–89; Lewin (1968), 119–26.

[163] *Vsesoyuznaya perepis'*, xxxiv (1930).

[164] P, September 13, 1929.

[165] See Shanin (1972), 190–2.

[166] See Carr (1971), 236–62.

of the peasants. But many peasants were illiterate; most, perhaps, did not read easily. Circulation was in any case small in comparison with the magnitude of the problem.[167] Kaganovich complained that at the end of 1929 there were only 13,000 reading huts in the RSFSR, and five times as many churches.[168] According to the population census of December 1926, over 60,000 full-time priests and other religious servitors were still employed in the countryside at that time, nearly one for every village soviet; and religious holidays, including as many as 65 days in the course of the summer, were still observed everywhere.[169] The private rural tea-room (chainaya) (not to mention the illicit still), was certainly a more regular meeting place than the reading hut: an impassioned article in the peasant newspaper castigated the tea-rooms as 'real clubs for kulak agitprop', where decisions were taken to disrupt rural meetings.[170]

Thus in the late 1920s the Soviet regime was for most peasants still an alien and external force. It had established rural soviets, and rural party organisations, which began to exercise some influence on the peasants, supported by the rural Komsomol and the ex-Red Army men, and, sometimes half-heartedly, by the million or so workers and employees of state enterprises and institutions in the countryside; but it had not seriously undermined the influence of the traditional organisations in the countryside. It had also developed land consolidation agencies, agricultural cooperatives and other organisations, mainly based in the towns, which worked with the mir and gradually improved the organisation and efficiency of the peasant economy within the framework of market incentives. But the organisations established by the Soviet regime in the villages were utterly inadequate, in numbers, in the quality of their personnel, and in the material resources at their disposal, to persuade the peasants to accept voluntarily the replacement of the market by grain collections at fixed prices, and the replacement of

[167] The circulation of the most popular peasant newspaper, *Krest'yanskaya gazeta*, was 1·2 million in January and 1·5 million in December 1929 (KG, 1, January 1, 104, December 30, 1929).

[168] P, January 20, 1930; according to *St. spr. 1928* (1929), 879, there were 21,876 reading huts in the USSR in 1927/28; according to another account, however, there were as many as 100,000 reading huts, Red corners, etc. in the USSR (P, October 15, 1929).

[169] See KG, 64, August 13, 1929.

[170] KG, 61, August 2, 1929 (S. Uritskii).

their family farm by the kolkhoz. The new policies launched in 1928 and 1929 could be carried out only by reinforcing rural soviet and party organisations with a massive influx from the towns of officials, industrial workers and young people, and of soldiers and police.

CHAPTER TWO

THE GRAIN COLLECTIONS OF 1929

(A) THE GRAIN CRISIS OF 1928/29

The grain collections following the 1928 harvest were a failure. In the agricultural year July 1928–June 1929, total grain collected amounted to 10·8 million tons, less than in each of the previous two years (see Table 8(a)). The decline in 'centralised' collections was even greater: only 8·3 million tons were received as compared with 10·1 in 1927/28. Centralised collections were particularly small in 1928/29 because part of the responsibility for the collections was transferred to local authorities, who were permitted to undertake larger 'decentralised' collections than in the previous year.[1] But even the reduced plan for centralised collections was not fully carried out.[2] The most serious shortage was of food grains: total collections declined by 20 per cent (see Table 8(b)).

The decline was partly due to the bad harvest in the southern part of the European USSR in 1928. Grain collections in the Ukraine and the North Caucasus in 1928/29 were less than half those in the previous year, and the gap was filled only by an enormous increase in collections from elsewhere, particularly from the Urals and Siberia.[3] But the overriding problem was the absence of adequate material incentives to the peasant to part with his grain. The average price paid for grain by the private purchaser over the year 1928/29 as a whole was double that paid by the official collection agencies.[4] Only strong action by the authorities enabled even the smaller collections of 1928/29 to be obtained at official prices. In the

[1] See Table 8(a); comparisons based solely on the centralised collections for 1927/28 and 1928/29 by Kalinin and Molotov are misleading (P, July 19, 20, 1929) (and see Carr and Davies (1969), 103).

[2] Only 90·9 per cent of the final plan of centralised collections was achieved (*Ezhegodnik khlebooborota*, iii, i (1931), p. xv).

[3] *Ezhegodnik khlebooborota*, iii (1931), i, p. xvi.

[4] Malafeev (1964), 119.

'Ural–Siberian method' of grain collections, launched early in 1929, the general village assembly of peasants (the skhod) was persuaded to agree that all grain 'surpluses' in the village should be sold to the official agencies; specific firm individual quotas (tverdye zadaniya) were imposed on kulaks by the skhod, with sanctions if they refused.[5] The Ural–Siberian method thus aimed at obtaining mass support from poor and middle peasants for the additional grain collections and for struggle against the kulak. The skhods sometimes lasted all day or finished late at night,[6] but there is little evidence of solid peasant support, much of peasant resistance: some mass peasant protest demonstrations took place in Siberia at this time.[7] Rykov voted against the Ural–Siberian method at the Politburo, condemning it as 'extraordinary measures of the worst type'.[8]

These methods of social pressure were intensified in the spring of 1929. The majority of the Politburo, after what Kalinin described as 'very heated discussion', rejected proposals from Rykov to import grain, and decided instead to obtain additional grain from the 'kulaks'; Kalinin explained that not even the import of 200,000 tons undertaken in 1928 could be repeated in 1929, as all available foreign currency was needed for the purchase of capital equipment.[9] To obtain additional grain in the last few months of the agricultural year skhods were encouraged to allocate quotas to households based on their wealth. The courts imposed fines on recalcitrant peasants for failure to deliver grain, including the '*pyatikratka*', a fine equal to up to five times the value of the grain not supplied. Those who refused to hand over their grain were frequently 'boycotted': culprits were banned from making purchases at the village

[5] See Lewin (1968), 386–7; Carr and Davies (1969), 101.

[6] EZh, June 26, 1929.

[7] Carr and Davies (1969), 101; Syrtsov, in *XVI konf.* (1962), 320–2.

[8] Vaganov (1970), 127, citing the archives.

[9] P, July 19, 1929; for Stalin's account at the April plenum of proposals to import grain made 'on several occasions' by 'Rykov and his closest friends', see *Soch.*, xii, 92–5. Stalin argued at the plenum that offers made by several capitalist powers of three–six months' credits for grain purchases were intended to test out Soviet financial stability; according to other accounts, Sheinman, the Right-wing chairman of the State Bank, failed to obtain grain credits in the United States, and himself objected to instructions to seek such credits (presumably emanating from Rykov) on the grounds that this would weaken American confidence in the Soviet Union (PRO, FO 371/14029/N 2454, FO 371/14038/N 2419).

cooperative and expelled from machine associations.[10] Grain collection commissions appointed by the skhod, in which poorer peasants were supposed to predominate, were nominally responsible for undertaking all these measures.[11]

The notorious art. 107 of the criminal code of the RSFSR was widely applied against hoarders of grain at this time.[12] This provided that those guilty of deliberate increases in the prices of commodities by 'buying them up, concealing them or not putting them on the market' could be sentenced to up to three years' deprivation of freedom with full or partial confiscation of property.[13] Some 'kulaks' were arrested as disruptive elements: about 1,500 were affected by a decision of the Central Volga regional party committee on May 20, 1929, that kulak counter-revolutionary elements should be removed.[14] On June 19, 1929, the North Caucasus regional committee, seeking the last remnants of grain from the 1928 harvest, ruled that recalcitrant kulaks were to be exiled from their villages and deprived of their land allotments. This brutal measure, frankly described by the committee as an 'exemplary curb on the kulak (primernoe obuzdanie kulaka)', was veiled in democratic form and due legal process. The appropriate resolution was 'to be put through meetings of poor peasants and skhods on the basis of initiative from below'. The kulak was then to be exiled by the court on the basis of art. 107 and to be deprived of his land by the land society (the mir) and the land commission on the grounds that he had 'cultivated the land badly, and failed to carry out the agrominimum and an obligatory resolution' (the last phrase presumably referred to the failure of a kulak to hand over grain to the authorities as required by the resolution of the skhod). For the moment the scope of the action was restricted: only kulaks who had been caught with concealed grain were to be exiled, and the numbers involved were not to exceed one or two per *stanitsa*.[15]

[10] See, for example, EZh, March 29, 1929; KG, 27, April 2, 37, May 10, 49, June 21, 56, July 16, 1929; KG, 27, April 2, 1929, reported a demand that those who went into the village shop to make purchases on behalf of those banned from using it should themselves be banned.

[11] P, June 26, 1929 (Ya. Yanson).

[12] See Carr and Davies (1969), 50–1.

[13] *Ugolovnyi kodeks RSFSR* (1929), 67, cited by R. Beermann in *Soviet Studies*, xix (1967–8), 127.

[14] IZ, lxxx (1967), 89.

[15] *Kollektivizatsiya* (Krasnodar, 1972), 150–1, cited from the local archives; this

While the press accounts usually referred to those punished as 'kulaks', they were often simply described as 'deliberate concealers of grain'.[16] An important feature of the collection campaign of 1928/29 was that the village community as a whole was increasingly assumed to be collectively responsible for the supply of grain. Contracts, already widely used for industrial crops (see p. 13 above), were used for grain for the first time in 1928. In the collections after the 1928 harvest, only 6·6 per cent of grain was obtained through contracts.[17] Contracts for the 1929 harvest were signed for the autumn sowings of 1928 and the spring sowings of 1929 while the collections from the 1928 harvest were proceeding. They covered as much as a fifth of the whole area sown to grain; and considerable efforts were made, from the summer of 1928 onwards, to sign them with territorially contiguous households, 'primarily for continuous land masses, including sown areas for particular crops, in whole settlements and settlement groups'.[18] By the spring of 1929, contracts were usually signed with groups of peasants, either with simple production associations formed specially for contract purposes, or with the mirs themselves.[19] While the contracts did not formally affect the collections from the 1928 harvest, they undoubtedly served, in the villages where the campaign was effective, as a powerful reinforcement of the Ural–Siberian method, which was also directed towards involving the mir and the skhod in responsibility for the grain collections. In the grain collections of the spring of 1929, sanctions were sometimes employed against a whole village: in Siberia consumer cooperative societies were threatened that their supplies would be cut off if the collections from the village as a whole did not improve.[20]

The grain crisis both reflected and reinforced the tensions produced on the market by the repressed inflation which accom-

---

directive was proposed by Andreev, the regional party secretary, and approved by the bureau of the regional committee.

[16] See sources cited on p. 58, n. 10, above.

[17] EO, 1, 1930, 31.

[18] SU, 1928, art. 705 (decree of RSFSR Sovnarkom, August 2, 1928).

[19] Moshkov (1966), 141, n. 2; DK, 11, June 12, 1929, 13; EZh June 28, 1929. For the relationship between the method of contracts and collectivisation, see p. 113 below.

[20] See, the example, EZh, March 29, 1929 (Irkutsk).

panied the rapid expansion of the producer goods' industries and of capital construction. The reduction in the amount of grain collected in 1928/29 was accompanied by a continuous rise in the price of grain, primarily due to the increasing purchasing power both of the urban population and of peasant consumers of grain and its products. To cope with the shortage, bread rationing was introduced, first in Leningrad and Moscow, then in provincial towns; barley and maize were mixed with the wheat and rye; and the milling standard was lowered.[21]

(B) THE COLLECTION PLAN FOR THE 1929 HARVEST

On the eve of the harvest of 1929 most published comments by party leaders about the grain situation acknowledged its gravity. Mikoyan pointed out to the Moscow party committee that the problem of supplying food to the urban workers had already continued for two years, moving from season to season and product to product.[22] Syrtsov, recently appointed as chairman of the Sovnarkom of the RSFSR in place of Rykov, warned an RSFSR conference of kolkhozy that the grain problem would continue for 'a number of break-through years, in which difficulties and disproportions will appear in the process of growth'.[23] In contrast, Kalinin alone among the party leaders at this time played down the extent of the difficulties. Extolling the success of the authorities in cutting grain consumption and of the sovkhozy and kolkhozy in increasing their deliveries, he rashly declared 'we have enough grain . . . the question of grain collections is already solved'; the worst to be expected was an occasional famine year.[24] Kalinin was careful to explain that this was his personal view, and 'not yet the official opinion of the government', and a fortnight later Syrtsov, without explicitly mentioning Kalinin, rejected such complacency: 'It would of course be completely wrong to think and hope that grain difficulties have now finished and that in future everything will go smoothly'.[25]

[21] Carr and Davies (1969), 700–2; Mikoyan in P, June 27, 1929; SO, 3–4, 1930, 56–7; VT, 14, November 1929, 13, 17 (Ts. Kron).

[22] P, June 27, 1929.

[23] P, July 7, 1929; for Syrtsov see Carr (1971), 194, and p. 375, n. 10, below.

[24] P, July 19, 1929 (speech to Ivanovo industrial region congress of soviets).

[25] P, August 13, 1929 (speech of August 5 to Nizhnyi Novgorod regional party congress).

Frankness about present difficulties did not inhibit complacent optimism about the future. All public statements concurred that in the longer term the expanding socialised sector of agriculture would supply a stable and rapidly increasing amount of grain.[26] And the Soviet leaders were confident—at least in their public statements—that the immediate difficulties could be dealt with by rallying the poor and middle peasants against the kulaks. Growing resistance by kulaks was seen as the heart of the grain problem. At the central committee plenum in April 1929 Stalin claimed that a series of good harvests had enabled the kulak to accumulate enough capital by 1927 to be able to manoeuvre on the market and to hold grain in reserve; kulak resistance to the grain collections formed part of the general resistance of the capitalist elements to the socialist offensive against them. According to Stalin, 500 million puds (8·2 million tons) were required annually by the towns, industry, the Red Army and by areas specialising in industrial crops, and of these 300–350 million (4·9–5·7 million tons) were provided by 'spontaneous flow (samotek)'. The remaining 150 million (2·5 million tons) had to be obtained by 'organised pressure on the kulaks and the well-to-do strata', by 'mobilising the poor and middle peasant masses against the kulak class and organising their voluntary support for the measures of Soviet power to increase the grain collections', following the example of the Ural–Siberian method.[27] Stalin's view that a large part of marketed grain was supplied by a minority of peasant households seems to have been justified (see p. 27 above). But he underplayed the awkward fact that much of this grain came not from kulaks but from well-to-do middle peasants; and his assumption that the majority of poor and middle peasants could be mobilised to cooperate voluntarily with the grain collections, insofar as it was not a smokescreen to disguise a general offensive against the economic interests of the peasantry as a whole, was a grave miscalculation. In his speech at the plenum Stalin implicitly admitted that reluctance to supply grain to the state was not confined to the kulak and the well-to-do peasant: he drew attention to the 'dual nature' of the middle peasant, aptly citing Lenin from the period of war communism:

The peasant as a toiler is pulled towards socialism, preferring the

[26] For the turn towards rapid collectivisation at this time, see pp. 117–28 below.

[27] *Soch.*, xii, 12–16, 87–8 (speech of April 22).

> dictatorship of the workers to the dictatorship of the bourgeoisie. The peasant as a seller of grain is pulled towards the bourgeoise, towards free trade, i.e. back to 'normal', old, 'primordial' capitalism.[28]

Stalin praised the 'method of contracts', as a result of which the direct supply of industrial products and machinery to the middle and poor peasants by the state in return for grain and other agricultural products was replacing trade at free prices.[29] But, as will be shown later (see pp. 79–81 below), these arrangements were largely ineffective; and Stalin made no attempt to estimate or even consider the losses suffered by the peasant from the system of compulsory grain collections at nominal prices.

Much evidence had already accumulated that as a result of the grain collections the middle peasant was being pulled not towards the state, but towards the kulak. In March 1929 Mikoyan admitted at a North Caucasian party conference:

> In spite of the political authority of the party in the countryside the kulak in the economic sphere is more authoritative: his farm is better, his horse is better, his machines are better and he is listened to on economic matters. The middle peasant, walking through the village, sees that the kulak has a well-furnished home, good horses, a good harvest, a cattleshed, a well-fed and healthy family. Then he sees the poor peasant farm: a poor hut, bad land, useless horses. And it is understandable that the middle peasant leans towards the economic authority of the kulak. And his authority will be strong as long as we have no large kolkhozy.[30]

In the following month, at the XVI party conference, Syrtsov reported that campaigns for grain contracts had encountered 'strong resistance from the kulak, sometimes supported by part of the poor and middle peasantry', and had resulted in 'one of the most serious mass excesses', including demonstrations and protest meetings.[31] A few weeks later he referred to the 'stagnation, lack of

[28] Stalin, *Soch.*, xii, 42, citing Lenin, *Soch.*, xxix, 359 (article of May 27, 1919).
[29] Stalin, *Soch.*, xii, 43–9.
[30] Chernopitskii (1965), 40–1, citing the archives.
[31] *XVI konf.* (1962), 323–4.

understanding and prejudices of particular strata of the peasantry' and to 'insufficient understanding and lack of confidence in the plans of the proletariat' on the part of the mass of batraks, poor peasants and middle peasants: 'Only gradually will the iron logic of facts do its job and transform the conservative thought of the peasantry'.[32] In the rural party journal, Bauman, a central committee secretary particularly concerned with peasant questions, admitted that the grain question was 'at the centre of the attention of the worker and peasant masses', dominated all political discussions in factories and villages, and resulted in 'a number of confusions, waverings and vacillations' among peasants and some workers and party members.[33] In the same journal a party spokesman on the grain collections admitted that since 1928 '*the kulak has begun to hold on to the grain more tenaciously* and has used every possibility of inciting even groups of the peasant population which are non-kulak, but are close to the kulak, to do the same'.[34] For Stalin and his close associates, however, it was axiomatic that firmness and good organisation could overcome kulak resistance and win over the mass of poor and middle peasants. 'In those places where we broke kulak resistance after demonstrations', Syrtsov reported from Siberia, 'we observed that a strong flow of grain immediately began, as if a cork had been removed.'[35]

In preparing the grain collection plan for 1929, the party leadership thus acted on the assumption that the 'Ural–Siberian method' and the 'method of contracts', which would make the mir collectively responsible for supplying grain, would rally the poor and middle peasants against the kulak, secure larger grain collections and strengthen the position of the regime in the countryside.

The confidence of the leaders in their policy towards the peasants was encouraged by optimistic forecasts of the 1929 harvest; or it is more accurate to say that optimistic forecasts were made of the harvest because they were essential to the confidence of the leaders. In June, Mikoyan reported that the total area sown for the 1929 harvest was 5–6 per cent higher than that of the previous year; the increase in sowings in the spring of 1929 had more than made up for the decline of sowings in the previous winter, so the harvest should

[32] P, July 7, 1929 (speech of July 3).
[33] DK, 8, April 25, 1929, 7–8.
[34] DK, 11, June 12, 1929, 5 (A. L'vov).
[35] *XVI konf.* (1962), 323.

be satisfactory.[36] According to statements by the party leaders, the area sown by sovkhozy and kolkhozy increased by as much as 130 per cent, and, contrary to expectations, even the area sown by individual peasants increased by 3 or 4 per cent; the additional sowings by poor and middle peasants more than compensated for the reduction in sowings by kulaks.[37] This optimism was confirmed by the first announcements of the expected harvest from Soviet politicians.[38] On August 2, an unpublished report from the Central Statistical Administration estimated that the 1929 harvest would amount to 76·5 million tons, as against 72·3 millions in 1928. This increase of 5·8 per cent was derived, after an adjustment downwards, from an increase in yield by 1·1 per cent and in sown area by as much as 5·5 per cent. In the Russian Republic the yield was expected to decline by 6·3 per cent; but this was more than compensated by an estimated increase of over 30 per cent in the Ukraine, where the weather was much more favourable than in 1928.[39]

A harvest of this magnitude would certainly have been a significant achievement: the target set for the 1929 harvest in the previous autumn, and believed by many to be extravagantly optimistic, was an increase of 10 per cent to 81·4 million tons.[40] But the reliability of the harvest estimates was challenged behind the scenes. Groman apparently forecast a low harvest in a report to the Central Statistical Administration in the spring of 1929, and later objected to the official claim that yields had increased.[41] The yield estimate for the RSFSR predicted by its Central Statistical

[36] P, June 27, 1929; these figures were repeated by Syrtsov in P, August 13, 1929.

[37] Syrtsov, in P, August 13, 1929; according to Mikoyan, in B, 15, August 15, 1929, 20, individual sowings increased by 2·9 per cent; according to *KTs . . . na 1929/30* (1930), 120, grain-sown area by individual households increased by 2 per cent in 1928/29, and total sown area increased by 5 per cent; according to Gaister, the increase in sown area by households with no working animals was three times as great as the reduction in sowing by households with three or more working animals (NAF, 1, 1930, 31); see also Carr and Davies (1969), 260, n. 4.

[38] See P, July 30, 1929 (editorial) and Mikoyan in B, 15, August 15, 1929, 17.

[39] TsGANKh, 5240/9/358, 125–8 (data kindly supplied by S. G. Wheatcroft); the estimates were presented by Nemchinov to a joint session of the collegia of Narkomtorg and the Central Statistical Administration.

[40] *KTs . . . na 1928/29* (1929), 414.

[41] SKhG, September 22 (Milyutin), 28 (Groman and Milyutin), 1929. For Groman, a leading ex-Menshevik economist in Gosplan, who at this time was a member both of the presidium of Gosplan and of the Collegium of the Central Statistical Administration (P, November 10, 1929), see Jasny (Cambridge, 1972), 97–123.

Administration on the basis of reports from peasant correspondents on August 1, 1929, was 13 per cent lower than on the same date in 1928.[42] According to Chernov, who was in general charge of the collections, the grain-fodder balance prepared by the expert council of the Central Statistical Administration at the beginning of September 1929, with Groman's participation, and presumably based on these predictions, also took a pessimistic view of the harvest prospects, and was rejected by the central party authorities.[43] It was particularly criticised for its estimate that the 1929 harvest of food grains would be lower than that of 1928.[44] The pessimism of Groman and the expert council eventually proved to be justified. On September 22, the annual control figures presented by Gosplan to Sovnarkom estimated the harvest at 76·3 million tons[45]; this did not differ substantially from the August 2 estimate. But in due course this figure was revised downwards, first to 73·3 and then to 71·7 million tons; the 1929 harvest was therefore finally assessed not at 5·8 per cent higher than in 1928, but at 2 per cent lower![46] The output of food grains fell even more, and was some 5 per cent lower than in 1928.[47]

The over-optimistic official assessment of the prospects for the harvest which prevailed until late in September 1929 was not an accidental error. Ever since 1921, the size of past, present and future grain harvests had been the subject of bitter debate. The Central Statistical Administration and Narkomzem, whose harvest estimates were more cautious, tended to the view that agriculture

[42] *Statistika i narodnoe khozyaistvo*, 5, 1929, 60; for these reports see p. 67 below.

[43] VT, 1, 1930, 6; for the date of the preparation of the balance, see Groman's letter in P, November 10, 1929. M. A. Chernov (1891–1938) was a former Menshevik, who joined the Bolshevik party in 1920; he was People's Commissar for Trade of the Ukrainian SSR before becoming a deputy People's Commissar of Trade of the USSR in 1929 and People's Commissar for Agriculture of the USSR in 1933; he was sentenced to death in the Bukharin trial of March 1938.

[44] Mikoyan, in P, December 7, 1929; the estimate of August 2 anticipated a slight increase in the harvest of food grains.

[45] EZh, September 29, 1929; sown area was said to have risen by 4 per cent, so yield was taken to have increased by less than 1 per cent; for further details see Wheatcroft (1974), 168. Final figures for grain-sown area showed an increase of 4·1 per cent (see Wheatcroft (1977(2)), 29).

[46] A 1929 harvest of 72 million tons was implied by the statement that the 1930 harvest of 88 million tons was 22 per cent higher than that of 1929 in P, October 24, 1930. For the other figures, see *Sdvigi* (1st edn, 1930), 192; *Nar. kh.* (1932), 162–3; in the same sources, the figure for the previous year, 1928, was revised upwards to 75·3 million tons (in 1930) and down again to 73·3 (in 1932)!

[47] *Nar. kh.* (1932), 162–3.

would grow slowly and that the rapid development of industry was impossible. Gosplan, whose harvest estimates were more optimistic, tended to argue that agriculture was not a serious obstacle to industrialisation, which must proceed at a rapid pace. In the early 1920s, the Central Statistical Administration consistently underestimated present and future grain production. By 1926, however, the official harvest estimates, made under strong Gosplan influence, were consistently exaggerated. A year later, at the end of 1927, Gosplan was itself outflanked by the party-dominated Rabkrin, the People's Commissariat for Workers' and Peasants' Inspection, headed by Ordzhonikidze and supported by Stalin. Rabkrin claimed that a rapid increase in yields and sown area was possible, and in December 1928 secured the approval of TsIK and Sovnarkom for a plan to increase grain yields by 35 per cent in the course of five years.[48] The optimum version of the first five-year plan approved in the spring of 1929 proposed that grain production should be as much as 106 million tons in 1933, as compared with 73 million tons in 1928, while extra-rural marketed production would be 19·6 against 8 million tons.[49]

In the summer of 1929 the party leaders insisted that the bourgeois experts and Right-wing communists who resisted their optimistic calculations and plans were reflecting the interests of social classes hostile to socialism—an argument used against opposition ever since Lenin's attack on the Workers' Opposition in March 1921. After the dispute about the 1929 harvest, Molotov condemned 'Menshevik-SR influences' in grain statistics, attributing them to 'bourgeois-kulak ideologists in the centre and the localities'.[50] Molotov particularly condemned Groman, one of the principal defenders of the rejected grain-fodder balance; and at the same conference Ordzhonikidze also attacked Groman more politely, but equally vigorously, for his '*most dangerous and harmful*' ideology.[51] These criticisms were followed by an outright condemnation of the methods used for compiling the grain-fodder balances on which calculations of grain surpluses were supposed to depend. Milyutin, chairman of the Central Statistical Administration, rejected Groman's 'bankrupt predictions' on the grounds that they

[48] The controversy about grain statistics in the 1920s discussed in detail in Wheatcroft (1974), *passim*.

[49] *Pyatiletnii plan*, i (1930), 144–5.

[50] P, September 20, 1929, speech of September 14.

[51] Ordzhonikidze (1957), ii, 177.

underestimated both the yield and the gross production of the 1929 harvest.[52] Estimates of grain yields by voluntary peasant correspondents were held to be generally much too low: checks by threshing and milling on the spot in five okrugs were reported to have revealed a yield of winter wheat between 18 and 54 per cent above that reported by their statistical departments.[53] The peasant correspondents were condemned as 'to a considerable extent socially alien elements',[54] and it was urged that they should be replaced by peasants from the activists, and by former Red Army men.[55]

The harvest was expected to be not only substantially larger in quantity in 1929 than in 1928, but also more favourably located geographically from the point of view of the grain collections. In 1928, the harvest was bad in the major grain-surplus areas; in 1929, the forecasts for these areas were particularly good.[56]

Buttressed by these optimistic assessments of the harvest, in the summer of 1929 the Soviet leaders were confident that they could curb the kulak and win the support—or at least the acquiescence—of the mass of the peasantry. In this atmosphere they proceeded to force through an ambitious grain collection plan. The plan was not published until the campaign was almost complete (they were not confident enough to do that), but partial plans published in June indicated that centralised collections, including the milling levy, would amount in all to about 12½ million tons, 30 per cent higher than in the previous year.[57] This figure was evidently maintained

[52] SKhG, September 22, 28, 1929.

[53] P, September 24, 1929 (Gaister); a more detailed account in SO, 3–4, 1930, 96–103, showed, however, that the corrections made by the Central Statistical Administration usually allowed adequately for these underestimates.

[54] P, October 9, 1929.

[55] P, October 30, 1929 (K. Shaposhnikov); the decision of the Central Statistical Administration of the RSFSR of March 15, 1929, to exclude kulaks, priests and other alien elements from the network of correspondents was criticised on the grounds that the purges were not thorough enough.

[56] See *KTs . . . na 1929/30* (1930), 223, for the influence of this factor on the grain collection plan.

[57] EZh, June 26, 1929 (Chernov), stated that 'organised collections' would be 60 per cent of the total (for 'organised collections', see p. 68 below). It was announced at this time that separate local decentralised collections would not be made in future; instead, part of the centralised collections would be transferred to the local agencies (EZh, June 26, 1929 (Chernov)). The directives of Sovnarkom, P, June 18, 1929, still referred, however, to a 'centralised' fund to supply large

unchanged for some time;[58] but on August 20, 1929, a further unpublished decision of STO approved a higher figure of 13·3 million tons;[59] some time later, the plan was further increased to 13·923 million tons.[60] This substantial increase in the grain collections as compared with 1928/29 was to be obtained without any increase in the general level of prices paid to the peasant by the collection agencies.[61]

The authorities found particular grounds for satisfaction in the high level of what were termed the 'organised' collections. These were to provide 60 per cent of the total collection, as compared with 28 per cent in 1928/29, and included the items shown in the table below (in million tons):

Milling levy (centralised collection from grain-surplus areas)		>1·837[a]
Sovkhozy		0·656[a]
Contracts with kolkhozy	1·6[b]	
Contracts with individual peasants	3·3[c]	
Total from contracts		4·920[a]
Total organised collections		7·413[a]

[a] Mikoyan, P, June 27, 1929; the total is mistakenly given as 'about 7·378'. In EZh, July 26, 1929, the figure for sovkhozy was given as 0·68 million tons, of which 0·11 was to go to the State Special Seed Fund (Gossortfond); but Mikoyan in P, August 25, 1929, gave 0·5 and P, November 4, 1929, 0·48 million tons.
[b] EZh, June 30, 1929 (Ya. Gol'din), reported that this amount was to be provided to the agricultural cooperatives by the 'collective sector'; this figure was repeated by Mikoyan in P, August 25, 1929.
[c] Residual.

Collections under each of these heads were to be much larger than in the previous campaign. The largest increase was in contracts with individual peasants, which were planned at 26·4 per cent of all

towns and individual centres and a 'decentralised' fund to supply the local needs of the grain-surplus regions; and added that small towns of a non-industrial type should continue to be supplied not from either of these funds but from local market turnover.

58 This is indicated by the report in EZh, August 20, 1929, that non-contract grain collections from individual peasants were 40 per cent of the plan.

59 Moshkov (1966), 67.

60 P, December 7, 1929 (Mikoyan).

61 P, June 18, 1929 (directives of Sovnarkom).

collections as compared with only 6·6 per cent in 1928/29.[62] In the contracts for the 1929 harvest, the obligations of the peasant to supply grain were much more stringent than the counter-obligations of the authorities to the peasant. Money advances, the main material inducement to the peasant, were no longer automatically included in the contract: in the spring of 1929, contracts relating to 6·5 out of the total contracted land of 15 million hectares involved no money advances.[63] The contracts no longer restricted the authorities to taking a fixed amount of grain: in August, Mikoyan reported that in some regions whole villages and districts had agreed to hand over not merely stipulated quantities of grain, but all marketed grain, within two months of the harvest.[64]

Encouraged by confidence in their own increasing powers, spurred on by their anxiety to overcome the grain crisis, the authorities endeavoured to carry out this much more ambitious plan in a much briefer period. In the two previous years, grain collections continued throughout the agricultural year. In 1929, the sense of urgency of the authorities grew throughout the summer. Sovnarkom directives on June 18 called for 'maximum fulfilment' in the first six months of the campaign, July–December;[65] six weeks later, a central committee resolution called for the completion of the campaign in the southern part of the USSR by January 1930 and elsewhere by February.[66] On September 1, an editorial in *Pravda*, perhaps repeating the unpublished STO decision of August 20, called for the completion of the entire campaign by January 1.[67] By speeding up the collections, the authorities evidently intended to secure the grain before it could be sold on the free market in substantial quantities, and to prevent the more prosperous peasants from holding on to their grain till the spring in the expectation of even higher free-market prices. From the beginning of the campaign, the party press stressed the importance of freeing the local authorities from the troublesome business of the collections well in time for the spring sowing campaign;[68] and a *Pravda* editorial of

[62] For the 1928/29 figure, see p. 59 above.

[63] EZh, June 20, 1929; the total grain-sown area contracted for the 1929 harvest, including the autumn sowings of 1928, was 19 million hectares (*KTs . . . na 1929/30* (1930), 543).

[64] B, 15, August 15, 1929, 20.

[65] P, June 18, 1929.

[66] P, August 7, 1929 (resolution of July 29).

[67] P, September 1, 1929.

[68] See, for example, DK, 11, June 12, 1929, 6 (A. L'vov).

September 15 explained that with the completion of the collections in January, the party, soviet and cooperative organisations, and the numerous volunteers who were conducting the campaign would be transferred to assisting the drive for collectivisation.[69]

These ambitious plans were not accepted without some active resistance from the agencies and officials concerned with the campaign. At the level of the Politburo, opposition was effectively silenced. At the plenum of the party central committee in November 1929 Mikoyan emphasised the 'clear and unhesitating line of conduct in the leadership of the grain collections', which he contrasted with the situation in the previous year, when 'the hands of the party were tied to some extent by the vacillation and opposition of Right-wing members of the Politburo'.[70] Among the central government agencies, only the expert council of the Central Statistical Administration openly resisted the collections plan: they apparently argued, in line with their assessment of the harvest, that total collections in 1929/30 should be lower than in 1928/29.[71] Scepticism was more widely expressed by local party committees and government agencies in the course of fixing the local grain plans, which were often referred to as quotas (zadaniya). *Pravda* reported that when they received the monthly breakdown of the plans the 'local authorities declared in unison that both the annual and the monthly plans were exaggerated'; such declarations 'are still to be heard now'. The Ukraine in particular 'objected to its annual plan and demonstrated that the monthly plan is also exaggerated, especially for food crops'.[72] In the Urals, the regional

[69] The relation between the grain campaign and the collectivisation drive is further discussed on pp. 132–3, 150, 164 and 206 below.

[70] Cited from the archives by Moshkov (1966), 71.

[71] Moshkov (1966), 68, who gives no specific source for this statement. In his speech of September 14, 1929 (P, September 20, 1929), Molotov stated that the calculations by 'bourgeois-kulak ideologists in the centre and in the localities' *would have led* to a reduction in the grain collection plan if they had been accepted, and the control figures for 1929/30 later reported that the Central Statistical Administration had estimated that the net grain available from the village (*sal'do sela*) in the RSFSR would be only 4·38 million tons as compared with the Gosplan figure of 6·4 million tons (*KTs . . . na 1929/30* (1930), 223); the *sal'do sela* was the crucial figure on the basis of which the plan for grain collections was compiled. For the assessment of the 1929 harvest by the Central Statistical Administration, see pp. 64–5 above.

[72] P, September 5, 1929 (editorial). For the procedure for fixing the quotas, see p. 73 below.

grain-fodder balance drawn up by the local statistical administration purported to show that insufficient grain surpluses were available.[73] Some okrugs also objected to their quotas: in Zaporozh'e in the Ukraine the bureau of the okrug party committee told both the Ukrainian central committee and its own district committees that 70–75 per cent of the quota would have to come from poor and middle peasants, and that this might leave them without sufficient seed and would not leave 'a single kilogram' of grain for sale to the local population.[74] In the North Caucasus, the Terek okrug party committee kept up its objections to the quota for three months.[75]

Resistance was put down very firmly. At the top level, no vacillation was permitted to show itself: Molotov later reported with pride that none of the Right-wing leaders was sent to the countryside as a plenipotentiary of the central committee during the campaign.[76] Statisticians and economic experts who were unwilling to produce grain-fodder balances which would accommodate a high level of grain collections were ferociously condemned. Leading statisticians and agricultural experts, both nationally and locally, were systematically excluded from office: in October the malleable Milyutin was appointed chairman of the expert council of the Central Statistical Administration, Groman was excluded, and several Rabkrin officials were appointed.[77] This phase of the process culminated in the subordination of the Central Statistical Administration to Gosplan at the end of 1929.[78] Similar treatment was meted out to local party officials. Thus after the Zaporozh'e okrug party bureau objected to its grain quota, the Ukrainian central committee removed both the okrug party secretary and the chairman of the okrug trade department.[79]

(C) THE CAMPAIGN

(i) The organisation of the campaign

A barrage of decrees and instructions sought to secure efficient

[73] P, October 9, 30 (K. Shaposhnikov), 1929.
[74] P, October 6, 1929.
[75] P, October 15, 1929.
[76] B, 2, January 31, 1930, 21.
[77] See Wheatcroft (1974), 169, citing EZh, October 8, 1929.
[78] These events will be discussed further in a later volume; for the arrest of leading figures, including Groman, in the autumn of 1930, see pp. 373–4 below.
[79] P, October 6, 1929.

management of the campaign. Narkomtorg, and Mikoyan as People's Commissar for Trade, continued to be in charge of the whole campaign, and no major change was made in the formal division of responsibilities between the various grain collection agencies, which was considered generally satisfactory.[80] Soyuzkhleb, the grain collecting agency of Narkomtorg, collected grain from the sovkhozy and the milling levy from everybody; the grain cooperatives under Khlebotsentr (Vukospilka in the Ukraine) were primarily responsible for collecting grain due under contracts from the kolkhozy and from the production associations of the individual peasants, but also had the right to collect grain from peasants not under contract in the vicinity of its own elevators and mills; the consumer cooperatives under Tsentrosoyuz (Sel'gospodar' in the Ukraine) collected primarily from the 'unorganised' individual peasants, particularly those in remoter places.[81] The responsibilities of the three major agencies were streamlined. With the intention of eliminating competition, Soyuzkhleb was designated as the sole ultimate recipient of all the grain collected by the other agencies,[82] and the remoter collection points of Soyuzkhleb and the centralised collection points of the agricultural and consumer cooperatives were closed down.[83] On July 29, 1929, an elaborate resolution of the central committee called for increased and more systematic participation in the campaign by the party and other organisations. Exhorting them to 'strain their efforts to the maximum', it authorised party organisations to play a direct part in preparing local quotas and checking local grain-fodder balances, and also announced that the 'necessary number of comrades' would be allocated to permanent work in local collection agencies in the main grain areas, and that special groups of senior party officials would check the work of the agencies. The resolution also called for more active participation by the Komsomol and the trade unions.[84]

[80] EO, 7, 1929, 9 (Chernov).

[81] Directives of Sovnarkom in P, June 18, 1929, and of Narkomtorg in EZh, June 13, 1929. In 1929/30 there were 13,811 collection points, 768 under Soyuzkhleb, 5,975 under the agricultural cooperatives and 7,068 under the consumer cnoperatives; these figures do not include the Ukraine (*Spravochnik po khlebnomu delu* (1932), 66).

[82] Narkomtorg decision of August 26, 1929, and Sovnarkom decree of October 31, 1929 (SZ, 1929, art. 652), reported in *Spravochnik po khlebnomu delu* (1932), 60.

[83] EZh, June 13, 1929.

[84] P, August 7, 1929.

The authorities called for a determined effort to provide every village with a specific grain quota.[85] This had already been attempted during the previous campaign, but in practice villages did not as a rule actually receive precise quotas until the end of the calendar year.[86] In 1929, arrangements were accelerated. In July, Narkomtorg set about providing a precise monthly quota for every sovkhoz and kolkhoz, and for those groups of individual peasants which had signed grain contracts.[87] In the following month, the plans for the 'organised' sector were incorporated into the general grain collection plan, approved by STO on August 20 (see p. 68 above), which set specific quotas for each of the main grain regions.[88] Great efforts were made, through both Narkomtorg and party channels, to ensure that the regions quickly divided up these quotas among their okrugs, the okrugs among the districts, and the districts among the villages.[89] A telegram from Mikoyan, published on September 3, instructed the trade departments in the main grain areas to make sure that the plans reached the villages by September 10.[90] While the quotas were an absolute minimum requirement, local authorities were not expected to treat the quota as a maximum. The obligation on kolkhozy, and on some peasants under contract, to supply all their grain 'surpluses' to the authorities was soon extended, at least in principle, to all individual peasants. A circular of VTsIK of the RSFSR dated September 9, 1929, instructed regional executive committees to achieve 'the full inclusion of all marketable surpluses of the grain of peasant households' in the campaign:[91] this implied that peasants had no right to sell any grain on the market even if they had met their quota.

The various decrees and instructions also insisted that the mass of the peasantry was to be persuaded to participate actively in the discussion of the grain quotas. The central committee resolution of July 29, 1929, declared that 'the rural population (obshchestvennost') must from the very beginning of the campaign be mobilised round the planned quotas for particular districts and villages, and to

[85] EO, 7, 1929, 7 (Chernov); P, July 30, 1929 (editorial).
[86] *Spravochnik po khlebnomu delu* (1932), 27.
[87] KG, 56, July 16, 1929.
[88] Moshkov (1966), 67, citing the archives; P, August 25, 1929 (Mikoyan).
[89] Mikoyan in P, August 25, 1929.
[90] EZh, September 3, 1929.
[91] SU, 1929, art. 681.

do this it is necessary among other measures to adopt the approach that the grain collection plan of the village is discussed by general meetings of citizens' (i.e. by the skhod).[92] The systematic effort to secure approval of the village grain quota by the skhod became a major feature of the campaign. This was supplemented by the establishment in the RSFSR of 'commissions to assist the grain collections' (komsods), with wide powers, made up of peasant members elected at the skhods and attached to the village soviets.[93] All this systematised the 'Ural–Siberian method' of the previous campaign on a national scale, with the aim of conferring legitimacy on the collections and unifying the mass of the peasantry against the kulak.

Even the most enthusiastic supporters of the campaign did not suppose that improved planning and management would be sufficient in themselves to prise the grain from the peasants. Strong material incentives were needed, and in particular the generous supply of industrial goods in return for grain. In the previous campaign, substantial quantities of industrial goods were distributed in the countryside, but until the second half of the agricultural year the supply of goods was not directly dependent on the delivery of grain.[94] The central committee resolution of July 29 announced that in July–September 1929 the state would increase the supply of industrial goods and agricultural implements by as much as 38 per cent above the July–September 1928 level.[95] In addition, supplies to the countryside from local industry and from artisan cooperatives would be increased. The narrowing of the gap between supply and demand was intended to eliminate 'one of the most serious obstacles to the successful and prompt carrying out of the grain collections'.[96] But in view of the continuing scarcity of industrial goods, it was clearly crucial to link the supply of goods by the state directly with the supply of grain by the peasant. The central committee resolution of July 29 insisted that 'the allocation of industrial commodities which are sent to the grain collection areas must be directly related to the fulfilment of the grain collection plans of particular districts and villages, and must be used to reward the

[92] P, August 8, 1929.
[93] SU, 1929, art. 681 (decree of September 9, 1929).
[94] EZh, June 26, 1929 (Chernov); EO, 7, 1929, 4 (Chernov).
[95] P, August 7, 1929.
[96] P, July 30, 1929 (editorial).

suppliers of grain'.[97] These arrangements were the direct links between the state and the peasantry applauded by Stalin at the April plenum as 'a major step forward in the strengthening of the planned socialist leadership of the economy' (see p. 62 above); Mikoyan later described them as 'opening the way to planned product-exchange between town and country, gradually reducing the role of market spontaneity'.[98] But the firm principle of reciprocity emphasised by the resolution of July 29 was undermined by the equally firm policy of discriminating against the kulaks and in favour of the middle and above all the poor peasants. According to a ruling of Narkomtorg, kulaks and well-to-do peasants were not to receive any goods, whether scarce or not, unless they carried out their obligations to provide grain; middle peasants were to be provided with scarce goods only if they sold their grain to the authorities, but should in any case be allowed to purchase goods which were not scarce; but poor peasants who actively helped the authorities were to be supplied with goods independently of the quantity of grain collected from them.[99]

Existing provisions for the imposition of penalties on recalcitrant peasants were greatly strengthened in preparation for the 1929 campaign. The use of the notorious art. 107 of the criminal code against grain hoarders was to continue: a circular from the NKVD instructed its local departments and the militia to pay special attention to such offenders.[100] On June 28, 1929, art. 107 was supplemented by an important new decree of VTsIK and Sovnarkom of the RSFSR, which gave legal recognition to decisions by 'a general meeting of citizens (a village skhod) that the grain collection plan should be carried out as a voluntary obligation by the whole village' and to the consequent division of the quota among households. The decree authorised village soviets to impose penalties on households which failed to fulfil these obligations. While art. 107 could in law only be applied to hoarders or those who speculated in grain, penalties could be imposed under the new decree for refusal to supply grain even if it could not be shown that the peasant possessed any. Penalties included the notorious *pyatikratka*, which could now be applied by the village soviet adminis-

[97] P, August 7, 1929.
[98] P, December 7, 1929.
[99] EO, 1, 1930, 33 (Chernov).
[100] P, September 20, 1929.

tratively (that is, without going through court procedures); if the fine was not paid, personal property could be confiscated. In addition, if a group of households refused to deliver grain and resisted the grain allocations, they could be prosecuted through the courts under a new article of the criminal code, art. 61³.[101] This article, promulgated on the same day (June 28), referred sweepingly to the offence of 'failure to carry out general state instructions'. It listed an increasing scale of penalties: the pyatikratka for a first refusal (this could thus now be imposed both by the village soviet and by the court); deprivation of liberty or compulsory labour up to one year for a second refusal; and, for refusal by a 'concerted group', deprivation of liberty for up to two years with full or partial confiscation of property, and banishment.[102] The militia were instructed by NKVD to assist the village soviets to collect fines imposed administratively for failure to deliver grain.[103] It is significant that in both the VTsIK decree and in art. 61³ failure of a household to supply grain was treated as punishable without reference to the socio-economic class of the offender.

This legislation was supplemented by a recommendation of the People's Commissariat of Justice of the RSFSR, Narkomyust, to the procuracy that the existing code should be applied more strictly. In addition to applying art. 107 to 'kulaks and speculators', grain collection officials should themselves be removed from work and put on trial if they had failed to prepare the campaign properly, or had allowed price discipline to relax, or even if they failed to take '*measures of firm compulsion*' against those who refused to carry out contracts; their offences were to be treated as crimes 'committed in the course of their duties', which carried heavier penalties. Chairmen of kolkhozy were to be treated as state officials.[104]

The various improvements in the planning and organisation of the campaign were only partly effective in practice. The grain quota reached the village earlier and in a more definite form than in the previous two years. But it was still belated. In spite of strenuous attempts to fix a precise quota for each village early in the

[101] SU, 1929, art. 589 (decree of June 28); this decree was not published until July 29. According to a further decree of August 5, 25 per cent of the sum received in fines were to be allocated to a 'fund for the collectivised and cooperativised rural poor', the rest to the local budget (SU, 1929, art. 596).

[102] SU, 1929, art. 591.

[103] P, September 20, 1929.

[104] KG, 71, September 6, 1929; for the latter provision, see also pp. 100–1 below.

campaign, in many districts quotas were not allocated to the villages by September 10 as scheduled;[105] even as late as the beginning of October it was merely stated that in most districts 'plans have reached or are reaching the village'.[106] By this time, over 45 per cent of the grain had already been collected (see Table 8(d)). Moreover, in consequence of the late approval of the national collection plan, the plan for each village was not a single plan, but several inter-related overlapping plans. Groups of peasants under contract received their contract plan in August; their village, which might or might not include 'unorganised' peasants in addition to those under contract, then received a quota for the village sometime in September or early October. Coordination was imperfect: the contract plan often stipulated a larger quantity of grain than the total plan of which it supposedly formed a part.[107] The delay in fixing the quota and the uncertainty about its size meant that from the outset the grain campaign, like the previous two campaigns, appeared to the peasant as an exercise of arbitrary power.

In spite of the streamlining of the arrangements between the three main grain collection agencies, the press abounded in complaints about inter-departmental competition throughout the autumn. Mikoyan castigated the competition as 'disorganising grain supplies';[108] in the Lower Volga region, it reached 'unprecedented levels', in the Central Black-Earth region, it was 'frantic'.[109] Each organisation, under relentless pressure to complete its own plan, used the resources at its disposal in a desperate endeavour to acquire as much grain as possible. The considerable ambiguities in the official demarcation of responsibilities were taken advantage of, and the rules were often simply ignored. Soyuzkhleb purchased well beyond its prescribed geographical limits, employing special staff not on its own establishment and offering money bonuses.[110] Agricultural cooperatives endeavoured to take over all surpluses on

[105] P, September 15, 1929 (editorial).

[106] P, October 3, 1929 (editorial).

[107] P, October 13, 1929.

[108] KG, 70, September 3, 1929.

[109] EZh, September 11, P, October 16, 1929.

[110] EZh, August 15, 22, September 11, 1929 (North Caucasus); in one district in the Ukraine, Soyuzkhleb offered sums in excess of the fixed price, and threatened to arrest peasants who would not sell to its agents, even though they were under contract to the agricultural cooperatives (EZh, August 28, 1929); elsewhere in the Ukraine, it claimed an exclusive right to collect grain (EZh, September 13, 1929).

the territory on which they had made contracts, offering credit and machinery as a bait,[111] and even bought up grain unthreshed in order to get hold of it.[112] Consumer cooperatives used their command over manufactured goods to acquire grain: they threatened to cut off supplies of tobacco and matches from villages which handed over grain to Soyuzkhleb, and held back goods in the hope of acquiring grain contracted to the agricultural cooperatives.[113] An official of the consumer cooperatives in the Central Volga region summed up the situation early in the campaign:

> Oh yes! Soyuzkhleb challenges us with a kopek? We block them with a metre of cotton! They want to do us in with a ruble? We shall answer them with roofing iron![114]

In the light of such evidence, Mikoyan's assertion at the end of the campaign that competition between the three collection agencies had been avoided[115] seems more statesmanlike than realistic.

The authorities undoubtedly made strenuous efforts in practice as well as on paper to improve material incentives to the peasant; but the incentives had little impact because they were totally inadequate to deal with the magnitude of the problem. Credits advanced to the peasants on spring grain under contract increased between October 1, 1928, and October 1, 1929, from 5 to 49 million rubles,[116] but this was a very small sum indeed in relation to the amount the peasants could receive from grain on the market. Supplies of industrial consumer goods to the peasants increased substantially. Seven major commodities were directly distributed by Narkomtorg: cotton and woollen fabrics, leather goods, leather footwear, finished clothing, metals and window glass. Supplies to the countryside of this group of particularly scarce goods were 43 per cent above the 1928 level in July–December 1929 while supplies

[111] EZh, October 25, 1929 (Ukraine).

[112] EZh, September 11, 1929 (Lower Volga).

[113] EZh, August 17 (Ukraine), 22 (North Caucasus), 31 (Ukraine), September 11 (North Caucasus), 13 (Ukraine), October 9 (Lower Volga), 1929; P, October 13, 1929.

[114] P, September 8, 1929.

[115] P, December 7, 1929.

[116] VT, 1, 1930, 106; this figure is for the net debt to Gosbank.

to the towns fell in absolute terms.[117] More detailed figures for October–December 1929 (in million rubles, see the table below) show that supplies were overwhelmingly concentrated in the grain-surplus areas:

	1928	*1929*
Distributed in towns	167	140
Distributed to villages in grain-surplus areas	231	341
Distributed to villages in grain-deficit areas	70	85
Distributed elsewhere (including Central Asia)	43	66
Total	510	632

In the grain-surplus areas, supplies per head of rural population in October–December 1929 amounted to 4r 29k as compared with only 2r 08k in the grain-deficit areas; supplies were thus nearly as high to the grain-surplus areas as to the towns (4r 90k).[118] This dramatic transfer of consumer goods to the countryside resulted in what a Narkomtorg official described as 'a considerable denuding of the towns'.[119] Supplies to the countryside of the further major category of consumer goods planned by the consumer cooperatives also increased very considerably, so that total supplies of all 'planned' commodities to the countryside in July–December 1929 were also 43 per cent above the July–December 1928 level.[120] Efforts were also made to channel the products of local and artisan industry to the countryside,[121] after complaints earlier in the campaign that they were mainly being sold in the towns.[122] Statistics about the distribution of local and artisan products between urban and rural areas do not seem to be available; our general picture of the state of supplies to rural areas during the grain

[117] SO, 6, 1930, 74.

[118] SO, 6, 1930, 75–6; the figures for 1929 are for the final plan, but are stated to 'indicate actual supplies reasonably precisely'.

[119] EO, 1, 1930, 33 (Chernov).

[120] TPG, December 29, 1929; supplies by the consumer cooperatives were also concentrated in the grain-surplus areas (SO, 6, 1930, 78–9).

[121] Local trade departments were instructed by Narkomtorg to check the stocks of these industries and send all suitable goods to the countryside (EZh, October 5, 1929).

[122] See, for example, EZh, August 11, 1929 (complaint from Saratov).

campaign is therefore incomplete. Supplies to the countryside were greatly reduced once the grain collections were completed. In the year 1929/30 as a whole, the supply of consumer goods to the countryside was only 9·0 per cent above that in the previous year.[123]

The conflict in distributing industrial goods between economic need and social policy, already revealed in the instructions issued before the collections began (see p. 75 above), continued to be acute throughout the campaign. The grain collection agencies, apparently following the precepts of the central committee resolution of July 29, often offered goods in direct exchange for grain. But such attempts at 'product-exchange' were strongly criticised because they resulted in industrial goods being allocated to kulaks or to well-to-do peasants, or because they deprived poor peasants who could not deliver grain from access to goods; on occasion any direct exchange of goods for grain was declared to be counter to party policy.[124] In one area, as a compromise between economic need and social policy, poor peasants were entitled to purchase goods valued at 40 per cent of the price of the grain, middle peasants at 30 per cent, and kulaks at 20 per cent, but even this degree of differentiation was said to be too favourable to the kulak.[125] In other areas, however, goods were distributed equally among the population,[126] and this arrangement, more acceptable in terms of social policy, failed to bring forth the grain. A delicate balance, in which poor peasants received goods without supplying grain, kulaks received no goods, and middle peasants received goods according to the amount of grain they supplied, would have accorded with social policy, but was difficult to achieve, particularly as much of the grain was supplied by peasants whose status on the borderline between middle peasant and kulak was unclear. As a result of this confusion of aims, no clear system emerged for using industrial goods as an incentive to individual households.

Much more was done to carry out the injunction in the resolution of July 29 that the allocation of consumer goods to a particular area should depend on its performance in the grain collections. In the Lower Volga region, prizes in the form of scarce goods valued at

[123] NPF, 9–10, 1930, 17; in 1928/29 the supply was 17·8 per cent higher than in 1927/28.

[124] EZh, August 21, 1929 (Ukraine); P, September 14, 1929 (North Caucasus); EZh, October 9, 1929 (Kherson).

[125] P, October 18, 1929 (Tula okrug).

[126] EZh, October 29, 1929; TPG, December 29, 1929.

50,000 rubles were offered to village soviets which did best in the grain collection campaign.[127] Elsewhere, additional manufactured goods were sent to districts and villages which had overfulfilled their plan,[128] and others were allocated monetary grants for cultural purposes.[129] Such awards made after the event were presumably a much less effective means of encouraging the supply of grain than bonuses announced in advance. All these measures involved much improvisation; and throughout the autumn of 1929 frequent complaints appeared in the press about delays in transport and inefficiencies in organisation which held up the sale of goods or resulted in poor distribution.[130] At the end of the agricultural year, a leading official of Narkomtorg admitted that grain collection plans and the plans for the supply of industrial goods had not been properly coordinated.[131]

The fundamental difficulty, however, lay not in the lack of cohesion of the plans or in the poor organisation of the distribution of manufactured goods, but in the inadequacy of supply in face of the tremendous rise in rural and urban demand. The acceleration and increased volume of the grain collections in the second half of 1929 automatically entailed a substantial increase in the money income of the peasantry, who also earned much more from sales on the private market and from work outside the village (see Table 7). At the same time urban incomes also rose rapidly, so that the available supply of goods in the towns was quickly taken up, and the peasant could not rely on the town as an alternative source of consumer goods. In the summer of 1929, it was intended that the shortage of goods in the countryside should diminish in the course of the campaign; instead, it substantially increased.

127 P, October 11, 1929 (Balashov okrug).

128 P, October 11 (North Caucasus), 12 (North Caucasus; and Chuvash ASSR), 1929.

129 P, September 29, 1929 (Central Volga).

130 See, for example, EZh, August 11 (Kazan'), 25 (Novosibirsk), September 21 (delays in transport of textiles), October 9 (Samara), 1929; P, October 5, 1929 (unsuitable goods sent to Ryazan'). In September, an expanded meeting of Narkomtorg agreed that the shipment of manufactured goods was satisfactory (EZh, September 24, 1929), but this degree of contentment was a rare oddity. In October inefficiencies in shipments and supplies were extensively aired at Narkomtorg meetings (EZh, October 5, 17, 1929), and in the same month Tsentrosoyuz complained to Sovnarkom of the RSFSR and Narkomput' about delays in goods transport (EZh, October 18, 1929).

131 PKh, 6, 1930, 19 (Chernov).

(ii) The reaction of the peasantry

In the absence of adequate incentives the peasants eagerly sought to evade the depredations of the collectors. Resistance was evidently more stubborn on the part of kulak and well-to-do peasants required to hand over a substantial quantity of their grain, but it is clear even from the press reports that every section of the peasantry was affected.

Grain was buried in concealed pits, at first on the peasant's own land, and then, when this became risky, in bogs, in stacks of straw or in the local church;[132] in the Central Volga region, 'thousands' of 'kulaks' were reported to have concealed grain, and it was found in pits out in the steppe, in ravines and in the forest.[133] Kulaks and well-to-do peasants transferred their grain to their relatives,[134] or took it to different mills in the names of different relatives, so that the extent of their stocks was concealed from the authorities;[135] in one Kuban' village, by the time of the official inventory, no kulak had more than 50 kilograms of grain.[136] Reports frequently appeared in the press that kulaks sold grain to poor peasants in their village at less than the market price rather than hand it to the authorities.[137] Grain was sold at official prices to those lacking grain in the village;[138] poor peasants buying this grain sold it on the free market,[139] and it was not unknown for kulaks to make cash loans to poor peasants so that they could hold on to their grain in the hope of receiving higher prices in the spring.[140] Kulaks who had previously paid batraks in money now paid them in grain.[141] These arrangements were to the mutual economic advantage of the more prosperous and the poorer peasants; and provided a powerful practical impulse towards the cohesion of the village.

Grain which could not be concealed was supplied in as small a quantity as possible.[142] Often the collection agencies provided a

[132] EZh, September 13, 1929 (Siberia); P, October 27 (North Caucasus), 1929.
[133] EZh, November 19, 1929.
[134] EZh, October 11, 1929 (North Caucasus).
[135] P, October 18, 1929 (Far East).
[136] P, September 5, 1929.
[137] For example, EZh, November 19, 1929.
[138] KG, 71, September 6, 1929; P, October 15, 1929 (North Caucasus).
[139] KG, November 1, 1929 (Central Volga).
[140] EZh, October 25, 1929 (Urals).
[141] KG, 71, September 6, 1929.
[142] See EZh, October 9, 1929 (Ukraine).

receipt entitling the peasant to make purchases in the local cooperative whatever the amount of grain supplied, and naturally full advantage was taken of this.[143] Wherever possible, peasants made their deliveries in barley or other secondary grains rather than in wheat or rye.[144] Now that the average market price of grain was nearly five times the official delivery price,[145] it was sometimes to the advantage of the peasant to pay a fine for non-delivery, especially when they were charged double or treble the delivery price rather than the full pyatikratka.[146]

Grain which was not handed over to the authorities or consumed by the peasants was infiltrated into the market through every available channel. In the first few weeks after the harvest, some peasants took their grain to the market quickly so as to minimise their stocks before the authorities fixed the quota for the village.[147] Poor and middle peasants as well as kulaks sold grain on the market.[148]

The status of free trade in grain in the autumn of 1929 was ambiguous. Speculation was prohibited, so the acquisition of grain for re-sale was forbidden, and treated as an offence under art. 107 (see p. 58 above). And while participation by peasants in 'local trade turnover' was permitted, and indeed required if small towns were to be supplied with grain at all (see p. 67, n. 57, above), the line between 'speculation' and 'trade' was difficult to draw.[149] 'Kulaks' who engaged in private sales of grain were clearly liable to prosecution, and the peasantry as a whole was discouraged but not legally barred from selling grain on the free market. In practice, transport of grain by rail was fairly strictly controlled,[150] though some grain was sent by rail in baskets and boxes disguised as artisan

[143] EZh, October 9, 1929; P, October 18, 1929.

[144] P, October 10, 1929 (Ukraine).

[145] In September 1929, the bazaar price for wheat in the grain-surplus areas averaged 326 rubles per ton as compared with the delivery price of 70–80 rubles (Mendel'son, ed. (1930), 112; *Nar. kh.* (1932), 352–3).

[146] EZh, October 29, 1929 (Kazakhstan); P, November 27 (Central Volga), 1929.

[147] P, September 21, 28, October 2, 1929 (North Caucasus), September 17, 1929 (Ukraine).

[148] EZh, October 11, 1929 (Kuban'); KG, 87, November 1, 1929 (Central Volga).

[149] An editorial in P, September 1, 1929, complained that local authorities had not succeeded in separating the two.

[150] P, September 1, 1929 (editorial).

products or household articles.[151] At first little attempt was made to restrict the transport of grain by river, on foot and by road.[152] The press frequently reported that peasant carts were openly taking grain to the towns; groups of these were dubbed 'black waggon-trains' (chernye obozy), in contrast to the 'red waggon-trains' organised by activists and by the authorities.[153] Grain was sometimes moved from one region to another by cart in small quantities at night.[154] Along the Volga, described in the local press as 'a major speculative artery', 'dozens and hundreds' of rafts and boats were loaded with grain, concealed under a thin layer of melons.[155] 'Kulaks' milled their own wheat and sent small parcels of high-grade flour through the post;[156] private millers, evading the legislation against them, sent flour to the market;[157] private or artisan bakers, sometimes backed by an authorisation from the trading department of their local soviet, bought up grain from peasants and speculators.[158] According to the press reports, peasants frequently sold grain to 'bag-traders' (mesochniki) and other intermediaries,[159] who would come to the villages or stop the peasants on the road and offer high prices or manufactured goods in return for grain, sometimes pretending to be official collection agents.[160] Elsewhere kulaks openly purchased grain from other peasants, saying 'Don't give grain to the state; sell it to me, and in the future I will look after you'.[161] They in turn sold the grain to private traders, who sold it in 'quiet streets on the outskirts of the towns'.[162]

The extent of all this trade in grain is difficult to assess. Some reports claimed it was very extensive: in the Tambov district, bazaars were packed with grain;[163] in Azerbaidzhan, the harbour

[151] EZh, September 27, 1929 (Tula okrug).
[152] P, September 1, 1929 (editorial).
[153] EZh, September 27 (Tula okrug), October 9 (Smolensk region), October 11 (Stalingrad okrug), 16 (Moscow region), 29 (Stalingrad okrug), 1929.
[154] EZh, October 3 (Smolensk region), 11 (Stalingrad okrug).
[155] *Povol'zhskaya pravda*, August 29, 1929.
[156] EZh, October 11, 1929 (Stalingrad okrug).
[157] EZh, September 14, 1929 (Odessa okrug).
[158] P, September 21, 1929 (Ukraine); EZh, October 5, 1929 (Ukraine).
[159] See, for example, P, September 13, 1929 (Belorussia).
[160] P, September 21, 1929 (Ukraine).
[161] EZh, September 13, 1929 (Central Black-Earth region).
[162] P, September 21, 1929 (Ukraine).
[163] P, October 18, 1929.

stores were full of private grain.[164] The extent of private trade was undoubtedly exaggerated by the authorities during the campaign. In November 1929, an unpublished resolution of the Ukrainian Politburo recorded that supplies of grain to the Donbass and Krivoi Rog, the coal and iron districts, were extremely unsatisfactory owing to the fall in bazaar sales and the sharp decline in the small-scale retail private market; by the first few weeks of 1930, the markets had all been closed in many areas.[165] But the conclusion of the émigré economist Prokopovich that private trade in grain had almost completely vanished[166] was undoubtedly an exaggeration, and the drift of grain to the peasant bazaar or to the illegal private trader threatened the success of the ambitious official collection plans.

When peasants were unable to conceal their grain, to dispose of it to others or to sell it on the market, in extreme cases they made cereal crops into hay,[167] set fire to them or threw them into the river rather than hand them over.[168] 'Self-dekulakisation' by peasants who sold up and moved to the town, already widely practised, became much more frequent with the growing danger for the better-off that their property would be sold up compulsorily by the authorities in view of their unwillingness or inability to provide the full amount due in grain and taxes.[169] From Aktyubinsk okrug, in Kazakhstan, kulaks departed during the autumn for Tashkent, Andizhan and Bukhara.[170] In one village in the Tatar republic, after rumours that 'communists will arrive tonight to plunder the poor and the rich' for the five-year plan, the whole population moved out for the night, leaving their cottages nailed up; in another village a similar evacuation occurred after a rumour that 'the Komsomol will cut the throats of the middle peasants'.[171]

During the course of the campaign, active peasant resistance to

[164] KG, 81, October 11, 1929.
[165] Moshkov (1966), 121–3; on the closing of markets see also vol. 2, pp. 159–60.
[166] BP (Prague), lxxiv (December 1929), 2.
[167] EZh, August 7, 1929 (Ukraine).
[168] EZh, September 13, 1929 (Siberia).
[169] P, September 17 (Ukraine), October 30 (Central Black-Earth region), 1929; EZh, November 14, 1929 (Kazakhstan); for earlier examples of 'self-dekulakisation', see p. 46 above.
[170] EZh, November 14, 1929. For an estimate of the extent of 'self-dekulakisation' see pp. 247, n. 194, and 250 below.
[171] P, September 21, 1929.

the regime and its representatives appears to have sharply increased, though this was in part a response to the forcing of the pace of collectivisation in the major grain-surplus regions. No reliable national figures have been available.[172] In the Central Volga region, the number of mass demonstrations recorded by the procuracy increased from 93 in January–June to 103 in July–December 1929.[173] In the same region, recorded 'terrorist acts' numbered 37 per month in July–December against 22 per month in January–June 1929,[174] and only 15 per month in 1928.[175] They were at their peak in September–October, the height of the grain campaign, when they reached 96 per month.[176] In the Siberian region, it was reported that 'the hostile activity of the kulak is considerably greater this year'.[177] The region was officially classified as having 'an unfavourable level of banditism' in an unpublished decree of Sovnarkom of the RSFSR; in July–December 1929 some 1,500 members of 'kulak organisations', 'counter-revolutionary groupings' and 'political gangs' were arrested.[178] Figures given in the Smolensk archives show an increase of 'terrorist acts' in the Western region from 17 per month in July–August to 25 in September and 47 in October 1929.[179] But all these figures for 'terrorist acts' are subject to a considerable margin of error. The term normally covered murder, injury, beatings-up and arson; but fisticuffs and fires were common in the Russian countryside, and in the atmosphere of the autumn of 1929 a quarrel between neigh-

[172] Reports in secondary sources that there were 30,000 terrorist acts in the RSFSR alone in 1929 (*Istoriya KPSS*, iv, i (1970), 607) and approximately 10,000 'sacrifices to kulak terror' in the whole USSR in that year (Kukushkin, in IS, 1, 1966, 98) appear to lack any firm basis, as does the similar assertion in a hostile source that in the course of 1929 10,000 communist agents and their supporters were killed, and at least 12,000 of their opponents (mainly peasants) executed (*Vestnik krest'yanskoi Rossii* (Prague), 5(17), May 1930, 18).

[173] There were 33 in January–April, 60 in May–June (IZ, lxxix (1967), 44) and 196 in the whole year (IZ, lxxx (1967), 89); thus the peak months were May–June, when pressure was being exercised to obtain additional grain from the 1928 harvest.

[174] Calculated from IA, 2, 1962, 198.

[175] Calculated from Ivnitskii (1972), 119.

[176] Calculated from IZ, lxxx (1967), 89; *Istoriya KPSS*, iv, i (1970), 607, however, gives a figure of 353 for September–October, which is clearly incompatible with the other figures.

[177] EZh, October 29, 1929.

[178] *Sotsial'naya struktura* (Novosibirsk, 1970), 122 (N. Gushchin).

[179] Fainsod (1958), 241.

bours, or an accidental fire in the cottage of a village soviet official or a party member, could easily have been classified as a 'terrorist act'.

Even if the figures for terrorist acts and peasant demonstrations are taken at their face value, this did not amount to the 'peasant war' or 'rebellion' which one historian claims to have detected in the autumn of 1929.[180] No reports appeared, either at the time or in recent publications from the archives, of general disorder or large-scale demonstrations.[181] But discontent and disaffection were certainly widespread, and were extensively recorded in the contemporary press. Thus incidents reported in three national daily newspapers in a six-day period at the height of the grain campaign included:

(i) agitation against grain deliveries, on one occasion described as 'savage agitation'; this included several cases in which meetings to discuss the grain quotas, including sessions of the skhod and a session of a village soviet, were broken up (five reports);

(ii) arson against the hay, grain, barns and other buildings of peasants active in the grain campaign (six reports); breaking of windows and driving of an axe into the door of a member of a village commission to assist grain collections who had helped to disclose grain surpluses at a meeting of the skhod;

(iii) organisation of a 'detachment' against poor peasant activists;

(iv) serious wounding of a village correspondent who was helping the collections; an activist beaten up and a grain official killed; a batrak killed and seven officials wounded; a member of the village soviet shot; the plenipotentiary of a credit society working on grain collections killed and his throat cut; a member of the Komsomol killed. Thus in six days the murder of five activists was reported.[182]

These were biased reports. They almost invariably attributed the

180 O. Narkiewicz, in SS, xviii (1966–7), 30–1; the only direct authority cited for the 'rebellion' is an account by Avtorkhanov, which may refer to a later period.

181 For reports of such general disorder during the collectivisation drive in February 1930, see pp. 255–60 below.

182 P and EZh, October 20, 22, 23, 24, 25; KG, 84 and 85, October 22, 25, 1929.

unrest to 'kulaks', sometimes to their 'henchmen', and they described meetings as broken up by kulaks which may merely have spontaneously dispersed when the peasants would not accept the proposed quota. But a clear impression none the less remains of widespread resentment and resistance. The various kinds of resistance were graphically described in the peasants' newspaper, though of course attributed to the kulak alone among the peasants:

> He tries to disrupt the joint threshing of grain, organises a kind of grain strike and desperately struggles against acceptance by the peasant of self-obligations for the organised hand-over of surpluses. When this fails, he tries to avoid handing over the amount due from him according to the allocation of the land association, he divides up the grain among his neighbouring poor peasants, buries it in pits, gets the support of his fellow villagers. And in places he goes over to open struggle, beats up the organisers of the collective delivery of grain and the participants in red convoys, burns down barns with grain collected in them, and organises attacks on the most active grain collection officials.[183]

Resistance to the grain collections was not confined to the individual peasant. While the kolkhozy were materially and financially favoured by the authorities, they were required in turn to hand over a higher proportion of their harvest to the authorities than was the individual peasant. In 1928/29 kolkhozy supplied 43 per cent and individual peasants only 12.0 per cent of their harvest.[184] In the plan for the 1929 collections this proportion was increased to 56.4 against 12.3 per cent.[185] Moreover, the kolkhozy were required to complete their deliveries extremely promptly: according to the plan of Kolkhoztsentr, two-thirds of all deliveries were to be complete by the end of September;[186] a *Pravda* editorial

[183] KG, 75, September 20, 1929; for other aspects of this editorial see p. 94 below.

[184] Calculated from *KTs . . . na 1929/30* (1930), 122, 124; the figure for kolkhozy includes all marketed production.

[185] Planned production of kolkhozy was 2·91 million tons (*KTs . . . na 1929/30* (1930), 124), planned collections 1·6 million (see p. 68 above); planned production of individual peasants was 74·7 million tons (79 (see p. 64 above) less production of socialised sector of 4·26 millions (*KTs . . . na 1929/30* (1930), 126)), planned collections 9·2 millions (13·3 less milling levy and socialised sector—see p. 68 above).

[186] *Materialy*, vii (1959), 266–7 (report of Kolkhoztsentr dated September 7).

on September 1 even insisted that all collections from kolkhozy should be completed in that month.[187] Many reports published in the course of the campaign accused kolkhozy of attempting to evade their responsibilities. They distributed more grain to their members than was required for consumption, justifying this by inaccurate calculations in their grain-fodder balances, stored grain unnecessarily, and sold it illegitimately on the private market.[188]

(iii) *The enforcement of the grain plan*

The authorities reacted to the passive and active resistance of the peasantry by determined use of their administrative powers. The despatch of large numbers of party members and officials to the countryside as 'plenipotentiaries' to enforce the grain collections was already a major feature of the 1928/29 campaign. On the eve of the 1929 campaign, the activities of the network of plenipotentiaries were graphically described by an anonymous party official in the rural party journal:

> Side-by-side with the normal organisations in the village an unusual and almost independent *apparat* has come into existence. The plenipotentiary, directly subordinate to the okrug or even regional centre, frequently does not work through the lower rural organisations to the slightest extent. He commands, issues orders and orders people about, both when he is competent to do so and even when he is completely incompetent to do so; the rural party cell and its leading cadres, who are the main people supposed to be responsible for the way the tasks placed before the area are carried out, feel themselves at best to be an 'auxiliary unit' and sometimes simply guests and critics from outside.

The author of this passage did not, however, propose the abolition of the plenipotentiaries, whom he regarded as essential in the view of the weakness of the rural authorities, but merely advocated a change in their attitude, together with an increase in the number of

[187] An article by Mikoyan published at this time, however, merely urged that collections from the socialised sector should be 'concentrated' in August and September (P, August 25, 1929).

[188] See for example EZh, September 21 (North Caucasus), October 1 (Ukraine), 3 (North Caucasus), 15 (Ukraine), November 6 (Central Volga), 1929; P, September 8 (North Caucasus), 1929.

'workers' brigades' despatched to the countryside at the expense of seconded higher officials.[189] In the summer of 1929 very large numbers of officials and activists were again sent from the towns to the villages by the republican, regional, okrug and district party and government organisations. One hundred thousand party members were sent by the regions and republics to the countryside to assist the grain collections;[190] these included 2,719 leading okrug party officials.[191] Those sent from the towns included officials from the local soviets and from the agricultural and consumer cooperatives, young communists and factory workers, some of whom were sent from the big cities such as Leningrad and Moscow to the grain-surplus regions.[192] Many of those sent were not party members: a total of nearly 15,000 townsmen descended on the villages in the North Caucasus alone,[193] and a total of over 200,000 people may well have been sent from the towns in the USSR as a whole. But even this vast number was far less than one person for every settlement, no more than one person for every 100 households; and in practice the visitors frequently spent only a short period—a few hours or a day or two—in each settlement, rushing in to attend meetings of the skhod or to supervise the collections, and then rushing on to the next settlement.[194] As the campaign entered its later stages, the visitors were transferred to districts and settlements where collections were lagging behind the plan.[195]

Most prominent of the tourists was Mikoyan himself, who bore the main responsibility for the collections. In September and October, the decisive months, he visited the Ukraine, the North Caucasus and the Central Black-Earth region, and his speeches at regional and okrug party committees, and at trade departments, were widely reported in the press.[196] Mikoyan upbraided grain collection agencies for insufficient activity,[197] and persuaded unfortunate local agencies that they should exceed the collection plan or

[189] DK, 14, July 26, 1929, 12–13 (the article was signed 'Mikhail').
[190] *Istoriya KPSS*, iv, i (1970), 608.
[191] Ivnitskii (1972), 112.
[192] For examples, see P, October 8 (Ukraine), 24 (North Caucasus), 1929.
[193] Ivnitskii (1972), 112.
[194] See, for example, the accounts for the North Caucasus in P, September 13, 17, 1929.
[195] EZh, October 29, 1929 (proposed by Mikoyan in North Caucasus).
[196] See, for example, P, September 14, 20, October 6, 8, 10, 15, 22, 1929.
[197] EZh, September 17, 1929.

adopt a larger quota than that proposed by their superior authorities.[198] He called for much stronger measures against the kulak;[199] and against 'deliberate withholders of grain' generally.[200]

The effect of the visits by Mikoyan and other leading officials, and of the decrees, instructions and editorials showered upon the local authorities, was to impress on them the supreme necessity of acquiring the maximum amount of grain as soon after the harvest as possible. Local officials who did not adopt a firm and uncompromising attitude towards peasant recalcitrance could expect to be firmly dealt with themselves. An editorial in *Pravda* of September 22 castigated 'the formal attitude of the petty officials (chinovniki) of the collection agencies and the local soviet authorities' and the 'sleepiness' of investigation agencies and the militia; a few days later the local press was also criticised for insufficient militancy.[201] Secretaries and leading officials of a number of district party committees were dismissed for insufficient activity in support of the quotas or against the kulak.[202] In some cases entire district party committees were dismissed and occasionally all the party cells in a district were dissolved.[203] Similar measures were adopted to deal with officials of Soyuzkhleb and the cooperatives.[204]

In this atmosphere the smooth procedures approved at the beginning of the campaign were hardly followed in practice. Grain quotas were frequently imposed on the villages without even a pretence at formal consultation with the skhod.[205] But such cases, though frequent, were probably not typical. Very strenuous efforts were made to secure the endorsement of the quota at meetings of the skhod and of the activists, and to persuade the skhod to divide the quota among households as a 'self-obligation', and to impose high

198 P, September 20, October 6, 1929.

199 P, September 14, 20, 1929.

200 P, October 8, 15, 1929.

201 Article by G. Z. (Zinoviev?) in P, September 25, 1929.

202 See, for example, P, October 9 and 24 (Ukraine), October 6 (North Caucasus), 1929.

203 See, for example, P, October 29, November 15, 1929.

204 See, for example, EZh, August 18 (Volga-German ASSR), November 1 (Tver' okrug), 1929.

205 EZh, October 9, 1929; characteristically this report from the North Caucasus appeared only after Mikoyan's criticisms of the grain collection methods pursued in the region.

individual assessments on kulak households.[206] But the 'participation' of the village community in the approval of the quotas was inherently one-sided. The skhod was almost invariably expected to accept the quota it was allocated;[207] and normally did so.[208] Where skhod meetings were disrupted, or refused to accept the quota, which was not infrequent, the skhod was later reconvened in order to reverse the decision. Thus in the Kiev area, the only two skhods which rejected their grain quota later accepted it by a majority vote when visited by okrug representatives.[209] Sometimes the agitators at village level, following the example of Mikoyan at the higher level, succeeded in persuading the village to increase its quota.[210] In some areas peasant meetings were even reported to have agreed to sell all grain surpluses to the state. 'From our societies', two settlements in the Ukraine are reported to have declared, 'not a single kilogram of grain must go to the free market'. But such decisions seem to have been adopted before definite grain quotas had reached villages, and in any case were certainly infrequent.[211] The more typical village accepted the grain quota only with considerable reluctance, or at best passively.

The acceptance of the quota was only the beginning. Collecting in the grain required much further pressure on the peasants by the authorities. A letter from two industrial workers sent to assist in the grain collections summed up their view of the situation in the countryside:

> They sent us to carry out grain collections in Kozlovskii district, Kaluga okrug.

[206] Reports of skhod and activists' meetings in the Ukraine, for example, may be found in EZh, August 7, September 27, 1929; P, September 7, 26, 1929; KG, 66, August 20, 1929.

[207] Exceptionally, Narkomtorg of the RSFSR told three okrug trade departments that village plans could be reduced where they were 'incontrovertibly too high' (EZh, November 5, 1929); but the annual plans for these okrugs had evidently already been fulfilled!

[208] EO, 1, 1930, 36 (Chernov).

[209] P, September 26, 1929.

[210] After a 'most detailed' explanation of the grain position in the USSR, a village in the Central Volga region increased the target proposed by the Syzran' district from 57·3 to 60·6 tons (KG, 81, October 11, 1929).

[211] KG, 66, August 20, 1929; see also KG, 56, July 16, 1929, and EZh, August 7, 1929 (both these reports are from the Ukraine).

We arrived. The picture is an unhappy one. Grain collections are going badly.

The commission of assistance is not at work: it is afraid of the kulaks. The villages cannot be seen or heard.

We got started. We shook them all up. We rallied the poor peasants. At first the kulaks tried to put pressure on us, to break up the meetings. We set about them. We hit at kulak Grishin with a voluntary boycott. We arrested Zaitsev for harmful agitation. The kulaks held their tongues. The carts with grain moved to the collection point. Grain collection boomed, and the collection plan was carried out.[212]

The effort to obtain a high proportion of the collections from the kulaks, and to weaken their authority among their neighbours in the village, was crucial to the campaign. As in previous years, the authorities fervently hoped that the poor and middle peasants would recognise that, in this respect at least, their interests were identical with those of the state: the more grain collected from the kulaks, the lower the burden on the rest of the village. The anti-kulak campaign had been a distinguishing feature of the 'Ural–Siberian method' in the winter of 1928–9, and it was waged with particular vigour during the drive to obtain additional grain from the 1928 harvest in the last months of the campaign, April–June 1929 (see p. 59 above). In preparing for the campaign following the 1929 harvest, the resolution of the party central committee of July 29, 1929, called for 'pressure on the kulak—the large holder of grain'. On the following day, July 30, a *Pravda* editorial called for individual taxation and self-taxation of 'kulak and well-to-do elements' where the collections were resisted. In the Lower Volga region, and possibly more generally, the amount to be collected in each village in the form of firm individual quotas from kulaks, as well as the quota for the village as a whole, was scheduled to be fixed by September 10.[213] In the course of August 1929, specific quotas were imposed on kulak households in some areas; and the practice of successively fining them, valuing their property and finally auctioning it was sometimes used during these early weeks of the campaign.[214] These arrangements were systematised

212 KG, 91, November 15, 1929.
213 P, November 13, 1929.
214 See, for example, report from Kuban' okrug in P, September 5, 1929.

by the RSFSR decree of September 9, 1929 (see p. 74 above), which instructed the komsody to fix specific quotas for well-to-do (not merely kulak) households; these quotas were to be submitted to the skhod for approval. In the same month, with the stepping up of the grain campaign generally, official attacks on the kulaks greatly increased in ferocity. In a speech upbraiding the Nikolaev okrug in the Ukraine for a declining rate of grain collection, Mikoyan insisted that the '*agitation period in regard to the kulak has finished*'—he should be given a firm date for his deliveries and a warning, and then administrative measures should be taken against him.[215] On September 20, the peasant newspaper published an obviously inspired editorial, 'Break the Resistance of the Kulak', which blamed 'frantic agitation' by the kulaks for failures in the campaign, and called for the imposition of firm quotas and dates on kulak households by the skhod on the advice of the komsod.[216] On September 22, *Pravda* in an editorial attacked the 'toleration of the kulak, and even in some cases the "link" with the kulak' which was found among local authorities, warned its readers that the Right-wing deviation was 'disclosed most clearly of all in the grain collections', and called for firm grain quotas to be imposed as a 'decisive blow against the kulak'. A fortnight later, *Pravda* again called for the imposition of firm quotas on the 'kulak and the well-to-do upper peasant (verkhushka)' with the requirement that the grain must be delivered in the course of October.[217]

During the next few weeks, the campaign for firm quotas received a great deal of public attention. Impressionistic evidence indicates an unwillingness on the part of many peasants to support the campaign against their better-off neighbours. In many villages, the grain quota, in spite of the objections of the authorities, was divided equally among all households, or on a per-eater basis.[218] When the individual firm quotas were imposed, they often covered a smaller percentage of households and called for a smaller amount of grain than the authorities thought desirable. To demonstrate the existence of class division in the village, and to fan the flames of class

215 P, September 14, 1929.

216 KG, 75, September 20, 1929; for this editorial see also p. 88 above.

217 P, October 3, 1929.

218 See KG, November 1, EZh, October 29, November 24, 1929 (Central Volga); P, September 26, 1929 (Lower Volga); EZh, November 24, 1929 (Siberia); *Kollektivizatsiya* (Ryazan', 1971), 241–2 (Kaluga okrug, Moscow region).

hostility, the authorities were anxious to obtain a substantial part of the grain collections from a clearly visible exploiting class. But this strategy, as well as being based on an erroneous assessment of the political heterogeneity of the countryside, also ignored two important aspects of the rural economy. First, strictly kulak households, subjected to administrative and economic pressure for over three years, were now economically weaker. Secondly, if the evidence presented above (pp. 26–7) is at all correct, most marketed grain came from a minority of households, but a much larger minority than the authorities were prepared to admit—as many as 16 per cent of households in the grain-surplus regions in 1927/28. These stubborn facts compelled both central and local authorities to widen considerably their definition of the kulak class, and to bring in the 'well-to-do'. Traditionally kulak households were assumed to amount to 1 or 2 per cent of peasant households. In November 1928 the central committee called for the imposition of individual taxation on 'the richest section of the kulak households', fixing the number at a maximum of 3 per cent of all households; this implied that considerably more than 3 per cent of households were kulaks.[219] The decree of September 9 spoke of imposing specific quotas on the 'well-to-do' peasants (see p. 94 above). During the autumn of 1929 the imposition of firm grain quotas on 3 per cent of peasant households was often treated as insufficient,[220] and cases were reported in which a much higher percentage of households received firm quotas.[221] Information about firm quotas does not appear to have been collected systematically: a Soviet historian, remarking that 'not even approximate total figures have been found' in the archives, estimated that as many as 7–10 per cent of all rural households were allocated firm quotas, and reported that 14 per cent of grain in the Urals and 24 per cent in the Lower Volga region was obtained in this way.[222] A Soviet statistical publication of 1931, however, estimated that households with a sown area in excess of 17·6 hectares in the grain-surplus areas of the USSR, amounting to only 1·8 per cent of all peasant households in these areas, supplied 14 per cent of net marketed grain from these

[219] *KPSS v rez.*, ii (1954), 534.

[220] See for example, KG, 86, October 29, 1929.

[221] In Balashov okrug, Lower Volga region, the figure was 7·8 per cent (P, November 13, 1929).

[222] Moshkov (1966), 72–3.

areas.[223] No evidence seems to have been published on how much grain was collected from the 11 or 12 per cent of well-to-do peasants in these areas. But evidently firm quotas were not imposed on the whole of the group; so, with the equal allocation of quotas which took place in many villages, it is not impossible that the lower sown-area groups supplied a higher proportion of the collections than in previous years.

During the course of the campaign, fines, prison sentences and other penalties were imposed by the village soviets and the courts on a substantial number of 'kulak' households, as Table 11 shows in relation to the main grain regions. The total number of households fined or taken to court must have amounted to a quarter of a million, or over 1 per cent of all peasant households.

Other strong measures were also adopted. As in the previous spring, 'deliberate concealers' of grain were again banned from using the consumer cooperatives.[224] Prison sentences, usually of one to three years, were imposed under art. 107 on peasants and others who concealed, hoarded or speculated in grain.[225] In one village in the Lower Volga region, 15 kulaks out of 41 failed to hand over their 'firm quota': five of these, who actively opposed the collections, were arrested, seven were boycotted, and three were fined.[226] Categories of persons imprisoned for speculating in grain included private millers, workers in cooperative mills and grain collection officials, as well as traders who bought up grain at the market.[227] Peasants who disrupted meetings called to discuss the grain collection plan were also imprisoned.[228] In one dramatic case in the Central Volga region, after a priest and a group of 'kulaks' disrupted grain collection meetings, the village soviet seized their property to auction it, but in protest the middle peasants also ceased to sell their grain. After a woman member of the village soviet had been beaten up by an angry crowd, a visiting court sentenced the

[223] *Sdvigi* (1931), 14; in Siberia, as much as 26·2 per cent of all grain came from 'kulaks' (*Sotsial'naya struktura* (Novosibirsk, 1970), 141 (Gushchin)).

[224] KG, October 22, 1929 (Ukraine); P, October 22, 29 (North Caucasus), 1929.

[225] See for example P, September 29 (Ural), October 10 (Western region), November 2 (Ukraine), 1929; KG, 71, September 6 (Siberia), November 27 (Lower Volga), 1929.

[226] KG, 90, November 12, 1929.

[227] P, September 29, October 10, 1929; KG, 84, October 22, 1929.

[228] See for example P, November 22, 1929.

priest to death and a number of kulaks to prison terms ranging from two to eight years.[229]

Finally, the authorities exiled kulaks for failure to cooperate in the grain campaign, in far larger numbers than in the spring of 1929. Such cases were occasionally reported in the press from September onwards. In a village in Biisk okrug, in West Siberia, a kulak and his two sons were sentenced to two years' deprivation of freedom and exile outside the okrug for three years for refusing to accept the skhod decision to sell only to the state.[230] In the Ukraine:

> In individual places in Odessa district and Pervomaishchina, village KNS [*komitety nezamozhnykh selyan*—committees of poor peasants] have already taken decisions to secure the exile of individual kulak groups, exposed as speculating in grain and agitating against the campaign. These measures have a very sobering effect.[231]

In a village in the North Caucasus which supplied its whole grain collection quota by October 6, 'many' kulaks were boycotted or fined, and the 'most stubborn' were exiled beyond the boundaries of the region.[232] This was not yet a general campaign to eliminate the kulaks from the countryside, but, as a contemporary Soviet historian has remarked, 'all these measures of pressure on kulak households marked the beginning of the elimination of the kulaks as a class'.[233] The Ukrainian Politburo on October 18, 1929, condemned cases where quite unrealistic quotas had been imposed on kulak and well-to-do households, 'with a clear tendency to dekulakisation'.[234]

Reports in the press frequently claimed mass support in the villages for the campaign against the kulak. In a Siberian village, when three kulaks were exiled for selling grain on the free market, the poor and middle peasants were reported as 'very satisfied' with the sentence.[235] In a village in the Central Volga region, when a kulak was given three months' compulsory labour for hoarding 1·2

229 EZh, October 5, 1929.
230 KG, 71, September 6, 1929.
231 P, September 17, 1929.
232 P, October 29, 1929.
233 Moshkov (1966), 72.
234 *Ibid.*, 72.
235 KG, 71, September 6, 1929.

tons of grain, '"That's not much," say the peasants, "He should have been expelled from the district."'[236] In villages in the Central Volga, Lower Volga, North Caucasus and elsewhere meetings of poor peasants were said to have demanded that kulaks resisting the collections should be put on trial; other meetings approved sentences previously passed on kulaks by the courts.[237] But in spite of such enthusiastic accounts of conformity to stereotype, anxiety about village solidarity leaked into the press. Reports sometimes complained that no-one would bid for the property of kulaks when it was sold at public auction;[238] on other occasions kulak henchmen bought up their property and then sold it back to them.[239] The local authorities, unable to collect in grain by other means, frequently applied regulations indiscriminately to the ordinary peasant as well as the more prosperous, thus undermining any hope that they would identify themselves with the state against their kulak neighbour. Early in the campaign, Syrtsov declared that 'we had (and still have) sometimes certain revivals of methods of the period of war communism, as a result of which entirely correct measures, directed against the kulak, in some places are turned against the poor and middle peasant'.[240] These practices were inherent in the nature of the campaign. Persuasion and democratic organisation could not obtain from the poor and middle peasants the 75 per cent or so of the collection plan which they were required to provide, and administrative measures therefore had to be applied against the peasantry as a whole. The terms 'kulak' and 'kulak henchmen' were increasingly used to refer to peasants who were not demonstrably kulaks by their economic position, but who resisted official policy. A village in the North Caucasus at which members of the soviet would attend meetings about the grain collections only if compelled to do so by the militia was even described as a 'kulak village'.[241]

In this situation it is not surprising that the local authorities were frequently accused of treating kulaks too leniently and the mass of the peasants too harshly. The authorities insisted that 'imposing firm quotas on middle peasant elements is absolutely imper-

[236] KG, 71, September 6, 1929.

[237] KG, 80, October 8, 83, October 18, 84, October 22, 1929; P, October 22, 1929.

[238] For example, EZh, October 5, 1929 (Central Volga).

[239] For example, KG, 85, October 25, 1929 (Central Volga).

[240] EZh, September 25, 1929.

[241] EZh, October 9, 1929.

missible'.[242] But 'firm quotas' were imposed very extensively (see p. 95 above) and many households previously regarded as 'middle peasant' were now treated as 'kulak'.[243] Moreover, while the imposition of a firm quota, or a specific plan, on poor and middle peasant households, was supposedly forbidden, the local authorities were encouraged to persuade the skhods and the poor and middle peasants to take on 'self-obligations'.[244] In face of the pressures of the campaign, this was a distinction without a difference. In the North Caucasus the imposition of specific quotas on poor and middle peasants was said to have 'frightened off the vast mass of poor peasants from the grain collections', while well-to-do peasants had been treated with 'an utterly incomprehensible softness'.[245] As the campaign proceeded, local authorities apparently imposed firm individual quotas very extensively in villages which failed to meet their quota. A revealing decree of the Lower Volga regional soviet executive committee banned 'those not fulfilling their firm quota' from joining kolkhozy 'as well as' kulaks, clearly indicating that firm quotas were often imposed on non-kulak households.[246] From Kirgizia, a 'most alarming distortion of party policy' was reported. All the grain of poor and middle peasants was seized, except that deemed to be required for food and seed, and fines were imposed on middle peasants who objected. In consequence, as the reporter delicately put it, the middle peasant 'has begun to lend an ear to kulak agitation'.[247]

All kinds of penalties were imposed on recalcitrant middle peasants. A report from the Central Volga region cited many cases in which art. 61 was applied to poor and middle peasants, and their property, homes and animals were sold up; the author of the report added, 'How many other unpublicised cases must there be which have not come to the attention of the higher authorities?'[248] In retrospect, Krylenko complained at the XVI party congress in June 1930 that 'in practice art. 61 was applied to the middle peasant, and

[242] P, October 3, 1929 (editorial).
[243] See, for example, EZh, November 24, 1929 (Siberia).
[244] See for example the circular letter from Kaluga okrug Soviet executive committee, Moscow region, October 15, 1929, in *Kollektivizatsiya* (Ryazan', 1971), 241–2.
[245] P, November 6, 1929.
[246] *Nizhnee Povol'zhe* (Saratov), 1, 1930, 113 (decree of December 18, 1929).
[247] P, November 16, 1929.
[248] EZh, November 24, 1929.

without the preliminary administrative imposition of a pyatikratka as the law required'—a Siberian procurator who protested against this practice was accused of Right-wing deviation and dismissed.[249] Middle peasants who disrupted the campaign were also imprisoned. In the Moscow region, two middle peasants were sentenced to three years' imprisonment after their opposition had held up the collections; they argued at a skhod that grain sales should be voluntary and that anyway Moscow was not a grain-growing area (one of them also 'created a scandal' together with 'hooligan youth' at a meeting of the komsod). A woman middle peasant was sentenced to one year and a man to two years' imprisonment in strict isolation because a skhod had broken up in confusion after they criticised the grain collections.[250] And whole villages of Crimean settlers were treated as if they were 'malicious kulaks' when they failed to provide very high quotas which often exceeded their entire harvest:

> The settlements were declared under boycott: nothing was sold in the cooperatives; no post was issued or accepted; they were not allowed to travel anywhere; an inventory of property was taken and some settlers were arrested. A panic among the settlers.[251]

These were of course exceptional cases. But an unsigned article in *Pravda* published at the height of the campaign bluntly stated that many local authorities had been '*unable to mobilise the masses in the struggle for grain against the kulak*', and had taken measures against the middle peasants which were intended for the kulaks; mass political work had been replaced by 'naked ordering-about (administrirovanie)'.[252]

The failure of the authorities to solve the grain problem by fanning class struggle in the countryside was particularly obvious in their relation with the kolkhozy. Kolkhozy which failed to deliver their grain were considered to be under kulak influence and were treated accordingly. Early in September the People's Commissariat of Justice ruled that chairmen of kolkhozy who sold grain on the side

[249] *XVIs"ezd* (1931), 352; Krylenko was People's Commissar for Justice of the RSFSR.

[250] P, November 22, 1929.

[251] P, October 9, 1929; an earlier report praised the boycott declared by its neighbouring villages on a village 'under kulak influence'; the reluctant village handed over 150 tons of grain within 48 hours (P, September 17, 1929).

[252] P, October 15, 1929.

or retained it in their barns should be prosecuted as if they were government officials committing crimes in the course of their duties.[253] In the course of his visit to the Ukraine Mikoyan castigated kolkhozy which retained their grain or sold it on the side as working with the kulaks; such kolkhozy were 'not a kolkhoz, but an enemy of the working class, a speculator under the name of the kolkhoz'.[254] In the same month Narkomtorg instructed its local departments that kolkhozy which had not supplied 75 per cent of their quota by October 1 should be deprived of credit and agricultural machines, and their leaders should be put on trial.[255] As only 32 per cent of the kolkhoz plan was reported to have been achieved by this time in the RSFSR,[256] this was a severe injunction. A few days later, an editorial in *Pravda* again urged that when 'bogus kolkhozy' sold grain on the side they should be deprived of state assistance and their 'kulak controllers' should be arrested.[257] In the Kuban' in the North Caucasus, 15 heads of kolkhozy were arrested, three kolkhozy were dissolved and two required to return all loans from the state.[258] Similar actions were reported from the Ukraine and the Central Volga region.[259] Leaders of sovkhozy who failed to deliver grain were also prosecuted.[260]

The campaign was more confused and more arbitrary than the present account has so far indicated. More confused, because the authorities found it extremely difficult to cope with the greatly increased volume of grain as compared with previous collections. Long queues at the collection points were frequent; in some cases, peasant carts were kept waiting for days, and 'red waggon-trains', arriving in triumph, were unable to hand over their grain.[261] The authorities lacked sacks and storage space; by taking over every available spare building, capacity was increased from 5 to 9 million

[253] KG, 71, September 6, 1929; see also p. 76 above.
[254] EZh, September 20, 1929.
[255] P, September 28, 1929.
[256] EZh, September 27, 1929; this refers to the period up to September 20. By the end of September, 50 per cent of the USSR plan for kolkhozy was achieved (0·8 million tons—*Ezhegodnik khlebooborota*, iv–v (1932), 90; for the plan see p. 68 above).
[257] P, October 3, 1929.
[258] P, October 3, 9, 1929; see also EZh, October 3, 1929.
[259] P, October 3, 1929; EZh, November 6, 1929.
[260] EZh, October 10, 1929.
[261] See, for example, EZh, September 13, October 10, 1929; P, September 26, October 16, 1929; KG, 80, October 8, 83, October 18, 1929.

tons, but not before much grain was left in the open air.[262] The railways had difficulties in transporting the grain, and sufficient goods wagons were made available only after emergency measures which included working normally during the November 7–8 holidays under threat of intervention by the OGPU.[263]

The arbitrariness of the campaign derived primarily from the arbitrary changes made in the quotas. The authorities at every level were under great pressure to collect an unprecedentedly large amount of grain at an unprecedented rate. If a region, an okrug, a district or a village achieved its quota, the organisations superior to them usually tried to squeeze even more from them. In launching the campaign Mikoyan insisted that after the quota for a district or village had been fixed at the beginning of the campaign it would '*not, as a rule, be liable to be changed*'.[264] But a precedent for ignoring this rule was set by Mikoyan himself, who, even before planned quotas had been reached, told a meeting of trade departments in the Ukraine that 'the Ukraine can significantly exceed its annual plan'[265] and persuaded the party bureau in Kuban' okrug to accept a higher plan even though it had not met its previous plan on schedule.[266] The Stalingrad okrug enthusiastically increased its annual quota by as much as 24 per cent above the level fixed by the regional authorities.[267] The Maikop okrug overfulfilled its annual quota for wheat as early as September, and '*the appropriate agencies in connection with this passed a decree increasing the wheat collections*'.[268] The plans for four regions in the grain-deficit zone were increased by Narkomtorg of the RSFSR after they had exceeded their plans for the first ten days of October.[269] Collections in excess of the quota were organised on various pretexts. In an okrug in the Western region, eight districts, assisted by 20 worker correspondents and 200 agitators, organised a grain train in excess of the plan as a gift to Moscow workers.[270] When a rural correspondent was killed by

262 EO, 1, 1930, 38–9; EZh, September 13, 20, 22, 27, October 3, 1929.

263 EO, 1, 1930, 38; EZh, September 21, 1929; P, November 2, 1929.

264 B, 15, August 15, 1929, 28.

265 EZh, September 20, 1929.

266 P, October 6, 1929.

267 EZh, November 12, 1929.

268 P, October 10, 1929; see also EZh, October 10, 1929.

269 EZh, October 17, 1929; it is not clear whether this increase refers to the annual plan or a partial plan.

270 P, October 10, 1929.

kulaks in a village near Tambov, the village despatched an additional 'red waggon-train' which resulted in the overfulfilment of its annual quota.[271] In the North Caucasus, many villages substantially exceeded their quota and were rewarded with supplies of manufactured goods.[272]

As a result of this policy, quotas were overfulfilled in many areas. By November 10 the Ukraine had exceeded its quota by 8·8 per cent;[273] by November 20, the Urals had exceeded its quota by 2·4 per cent.[274] As many areas within each region did not reach their quota, these figures conceal a considerable degree of overfulfilment in particular areas: thus Odessa okrug in the Ukraine had exceeded its annual quota by 12 per cent as early as mid-October.[275] Behind the general overfulfilment of the plan must lie increases in the quota in tens of thousands of villages and hundreds of okrugs.

Towards the end of the campaign, the authorities endeavoured to bring this arbitrariness to an end. As early as the end of October, Narkomtorg ruled that trade departments must not permit any increase in the plans for okrugs, districts and villages where the annual plan had already been reached.[276] At this stage such rulings had little effect. A month later a leading Narkomtorg official stressed that such increases in quota were 'categorically forbidden', though grain could continue to be collected from kulaks and well-to-do peasants who had not met their firm quotas;[277] Mikoyan also stated that in successful districts 'it is necessary to go over to *samotek*'.[278] There is some evidence that, equipped with these rulings, the local authorities relaxed. Some grain continued to be collected in regions which had already fulfilled their plan. In the Ukraine, 112,000 tons were collected in December as compared with 454,000 in November; in the Urals, 14,000 as compared with 80,000 tons. The decline in these regions in December 1929 was, however, much greater than that in the country as a whole.[279] But this was very late in the campaign; and the arbitrariness displayed

[271] EZh, October 12, 1929.
[272] P, October 11, 12, 1929.
[273] P, November 15, 1929; EZh, November 16, 1929.
[274] EZh, November 26, 1929.
[275] EZh, October 23, 1929.
[276] P, October 30, 1929.
[277] EZh, November 30, 1929 (Chernov).
[278] P, December 7, 1929; for the term '*samotek*' see p. 61 above.
[279] *Ezhegodnik khleboobrorota*, iv–v (1932), ii, 83.

in the collections from the 1929 harvest was to recur, to the indignation and despair of the peasants, in many future campaigns.

(D) THE RESULTS OF THE COLLECTIONS

Grain was collected much more rapidly and in much larger quantities than in previous years. In each of the months July–October, over twice as much grain was collected as in the equivalent months of 1928, 9·0 million tons being collected in the two months September–October alone (see Table 8(d)). In December, Mikoyan was able to report, in an enthusiastic article entitled 'The Line of the Party has Triumphed', that by December 1, 12·81 million tons had been collected; this was 92·1 per cent of the annual plan, and 99·3 per cent of the annual plan excluding the milling levy.[280] In the agricultural year July 1929–June 1930 the centralised collections amounted to 14·9 million tons as compared with the plan of 13·9 million; the total grain collected was 16·08 million tons (see Table 8(a)).

Within this total, the collection of food grains was less successful: they amounted to 55·2 per cent of the total, as compared with 58·9 per cent in the annual plan and 64·4 per cent in 1928/29 (see Table 8(b)). Moreover, the increase in the total food grains collected from 6·93 million tons in 1928/29 to 8·88 million in 1929/30 was entirely due to the increased collection of rye, the less valuable grain; the collection of wheat slightly declined.[281] The relatively small wheat collections were a result partly of the poor wheat harvest, due to the bad weather which killed off the winter sowings, and partly of the natural preference of the peasants, given the opportunity to surrender rye rather than wheat.

The proportion of grain collected from the 'socialised' and 'organised' sectors of agriculture greatly increased. By January 1, 1930, sovkhozy and kolkhozy supplied 12·7 per cent of the total collections as compared with 9·5 per cent in 1928/29, and individual peasants under contract 21·8 per cent as compared with 6·6 per

[280] P, December 7, 1929; the final figure for December 1, including the milling levy, was 13·52 million tons (see Table 8(d)).

[281] *Ezhegodnik khlebooborota*, iv–v (1932), i, 26; rye increased from 1·60 to 3·80 million tons while wheat declined from 5·33 to 5·08 millions.

cent.[282] Nevertheless the socialised sector failed to fulfil its plan. The performance of sovkhozy was particularly disappointing, as they delivered only 391,000 as compared with the original plan of 660,000 tons.[283] Kolkhozy, supplying 1·51 million tons, did much better, but did not quite reach their plan of 1·64 million.[284] The overfulfilment of the plan was thus achieved entirely through additional collections from individual peasants, who supplied 11·9 million tons as compared with the plan of 9·3 million tons (see Table 8(c)). The socialisation of agriculture did not automatically guarantee increased supplies of grain to the state. This was a harbinger of the future.

The role played by different regions in the collections changed markedly in 1929/30 (see Table 8(e)). Poor harvests in the Central Volga region and in the Urals and Siberia resulted in a decline in collections from these three regions from 4·0 million tons in 1928/29 to 3·1 million in 1929/30. But in the Ukraine, where the harvest was very poor in 1928, collections increased from 1·9 to as much as 5·3 million tons. Mikoyan praised the Ukrainian organisations for their 'triumph on the grain front'.[285] The harvest was also good in the Central Black-Earth region, where grain collections increased from 0·7 to 1·8 million tons.[286] Plans for particular regions were to some extent adjusted to the estimated size of their harvest, but the adjustment was evidently insufficient: peasants in the Ukraine and the Central Black-Earth region retained a higher proportion of their total harvest than those in the regions with poor harvests, and more grain was collected from the Lower Volga region, in spite of a bad harvest, than in the previous year. The North Caucasus and Siberia had the greatest difficulty in reaching their quotas.[287]

An important new departure in 1929/30 was the collection of grain in the grain-deficit regions, which supplied 1·09 million tons, 6·9 per cent of the total, more than double the plan (see Table 8(e)).

[282] EO, 1, 1930, 31; comparable figures for contracted grain for the whole year 1929/30 have not been traced.

[283] See Table 8(c) below and p. 68 above; the grain output of sovkhozy increased only slightly from 1,134,000 tons in 1928 to 1,327,000 in 1929 (*Nar. kh.* (1932), 172–3; for alternative figures, see p. 148 below.

[284] See Table 8(c) below and p. 68 above.

[285] EZh, November 23, 1929.

[286] *Nar. kh.* (1932), 332–9.

[287] See, for example, the reports of the results for different regions in EZh, November 26, 1929.

As a result of the substantial increase in grain collected, the amount at the disposal of the authorities was approximately 5·7 million tons higher than in 1928/29. This additional grain was allocated to three major purposes (see Table 9(a); the figures given in the table below exclude allocations to the armed services):

Stocks	+1·0
Exports	+1·5
Internal market	+3·4
	+5·9

Centralised stocks of grain, which fell after the grain crisis of 1927 to the dangerously low figure of 486,000 tons on July 1, 1928, had increased to 786,000 tons on July 1, 1929. By July 1, 1930, as a result of a deliberate policy of stockpiling, they reached the record figure of 2,084,000 tons.

The 1929 harvest was also the first in three years to yield a substantial amount of grain for export. In the summer of 1928 about 250,000 tons of wheat were imported; in the agricultural year 1929/30 1,334,000 tons of grain were exported, and earned nearly the whole of the increase in export earnings in 1929 and 1930.[288] An unusual feature was that most of the grain exported in the first half of 1929/30 was not wheat but barley: as has been shown (see pp. 65, 104 above), the harvest and the official collections of non-food grains were relatively much higher than those of food grains, and the collections of non-food grains took place earlier in the year. But the rise in grain exports, together with the rise in stocks of food grains, were regarded by the authorities as a convincing demonstration of the success of the grain collections. Two serious losses marred this triumph on the export front. The first, a price paid for victory, was an unintended consequence of Soviet policy. Because of the shortage of food grain at home some meat and dairy products were withheld from export and placed on the home market; and the decline in livestock numbers, itself largely due to Soviet agricultural policy, resulted by 1930 in an absolute reduction of the production of eggs, milk and other products. The volume of animal products exported fell by 9 per cent in 1929 and by a further 28 per cent in

[288] See data in *Vneshnyaya torgovlya SSSR za 1918–1940 gg.* (1960), 264; *Nar. kh.* (1932), 388–91.

1930.[289] The second loss was wrested from the Soviet Union by the world depression: grain prices on the world market fell by 6 per cent in 1929 and as much as 49 per cent in 1930, while the prices of machinery, the most rapidly-growing Soviet import group, remained stable, and those of industrial raw materials, the other major Soviet import group, fell by only 20 per cent over the two years. Ironically, the price of grain fell much more than the prices of most other agricultural products.[290] By 1930 twice as much grain had to be exported per unit of machinery imported as in 1928.

Increased grain collections were above all intended to provide more grain on the internal market, to satisfy the growing urban demand for food resulting from industrialisation. The amount of additional grain allocated for this purpose in 1929/30 was surprisingly small. The total increase in grain allocated to the internal market was about 3·4 million tons. Of this 500,000 tons were allocated to industry, mainly for vodka production; and a further 450,000 tons was used for additional supplies of seed. Of the remaining 2½ million tons, a substantial part was allocated as so-called 'special-purpose supplies'. These were mainly food grains for the cotton-growing areas, to encourage the peasants to grow cotton rather than grain, and fodder for horses and food for seasonal workers in the lumber industry. These increases, the exact amount of which is not known,[291] assisted an important aspect of industrialisation policy. The increase in Soviet cotton production was regarded as essential to Soviet economic independence, and provided an immediate saving in foreign currency. Increased timber supplies were required both for the rapidly expanding construction industry, and for export. But 'special-purpose' grain was, in large part, merely providing state supplies as a substitute for the free market, from which these special areas had previously obtained much of their grain, but which had now greatly declined. Moreover, in 1929/30, some towns in the grain-surplus areas,

[289] *Slavic Review*, xxxv (1976), 617–19 (Dohan). Between 1928 and 1930, exports of animals and animal products fell from 135 to 63 million rubles (in current prices), while exports of grain and grain products rose from 36 to 229 million rubles (these figures are for the calendar year 1930, and so include substantial exports of grain in July–December 1930 from the 1930 harvest) (calculated from data in *Nar. kh.* (1932), 388).

[290] *Slavic Review*, xxxv (1976), 615–16.

[291] The statistics for 1928/29 and 1929/30 are not comparable in this respect (*Ezhegodnik khleboborota*, iv–v (1932), i, 28).

previously supplied from the market, were transferred to state supply. Once all these allocations had been made, very little remained for additional supplies to the urban population. Exact figures are not available. But it is significant that the *total* amount of rye and wheat supplied to the population from the state collections, including special supplies, increased by only 250,000 tons. Supplies to the Central Industrial region, where the major towns were already on state supplies in 1928/29, actually declined from 2·00 to 1·76 million tons, and supplies to Leningrad region remained constant.

The result, then, was paradoxical. Although the increases in special supplies, exports and stocks were obviously all related to the wider goals of industrialisation and national security, they did not contribute directly towards relieving the food shortages in the towns, even though these shortages were in the summer of 1929 one of the major problems which inspired both the grain campaign of 1929 and forcible collectivisation.

CHAPTER THREE

THE EVE OF MASS COLLECTIVISATION, JUNE–SEPTEMBER 1929

(A) THE BACKGROUND

While the kolkhozy received increasing attention from the end of 1926 onwards,[1] the much greater efforts of the authorities to expand the sovkhozy and the kolkhozy in the course of 1928 and 1929 were a direct response to the grain crisis in the winter of 1927–8. In January 1928 Stalin told a party audience in Siberia 'we cannot allow our industry to depend on kulak whims'; kolkhozy and sovkhozy must be 'developed to the full, not sparing our efforts and resources', so that within three or four years (i. e. by 1931 or 1932) they would supply at least one-third of all the grain requirements of the state; moreover, in the long run socialist construction required 'socialisation of the whole of agriculture'.[2]

After the grain crisis, the membership of kolkhozy increased at an unprecedented rate, from a mere 286,000 out of 25 million households on October 1, 1927, to 596,000 on October 1, 1928 and 1,008,000 on June 1, 1929.[3] Collectivisation was more advanced in most of the grain-surplus regions than in the rest of the USSR. By June 1929, 7·3 per cent of households were collectivised in the North Caucasus, 5·9 per cent in the Lower Volga region and 5·6 per cent in the Ukraine, as compared with 3·9 per cent in the USSR as a whole and with only 1·8 per cent in the Moscow region (see Table 17). The rapid advance of collectivisation in these areas in 1927–9 was undoubtedly partly due to the attention devoted to them in the grain campaigns by the central authorities. But this was not the whole story. Even in June 1927, before the grain crisis, when only 0·8 per cent of households were collectivised in the USSR as a

[1] See Carr and Davies (1969), 158–60. [2] *Soch.*, xi, 5–6.

[3] See Table 16, and Carr and Davies (1969), 944.

whole, 1·6 per cent were already collectivised in these three grain-surplus areas. According to Soviet accounts, economic differentiation within the peasantry had proceeded furthest in these areas, so that the poor peasant had most to gain by joining the kolkhozy.[4] The position of the poor peasants was said to be particularly unfavourable in the North Caucasus and the steppe area of the Ukraine, where landless peasants had received some land after the 1917 revolution, but lacked means of production.[5] In more northerly regions, on the other hand, particularly in the industrial areas round Leningrad and Moscow, and in the Central Black-Earth region, peasants who were 'poor peasants' from the point of view of agriculture had considerable opportunities to work as otkhodniki and in other non-agricultural activities, and therefore little incentive to join the kolkhozy.[6]

The first kolkhozy established after the grain crisis tended to be even smaller than their predecessors, and to take the form mainly of the more loosely organised Association for the Joint Cultivation of Land (the TOZ or SOZ), rather than the more socialised artel or commune. But this pattern was reversed from the summer of 1928. The average number of households per kolkhoz increased from 12·5 on June 1, 1928, to 17·7 on June 1, 1929 (see vol. 2, Table 3); about one-seventh of all kolkhozy combined into groups (kusty) for joint cultivation or services, and the proportion of artels and communes increased (see vol. 2, p. 70).

In spite of these changes the average kolkhoz remained a fairly small farming unit with little impact on most peasants: in June 1929, only one household in 25 belonged to a kolkhoz. The kolkhozy were far more mechanised than the individual peasant economies. They owned directly 14,000 tractors and several thousand more were made available to them by the agricultural cooperatives: as much as 43·2 per cent of kolkhoz land was said to have been worked by tractors in 1929.[7] In contrast, only a couple of thousand tractors were owned by the 24 million individual peasant households.[8] But these summary figures exaggerate the technological superiority of

[4] Gaister, ed. (1929), 13 (Vlasov).

[5] NAF, 7–8, 1930, 53–4 (A. Libkind).

[6] *Ibid.* 52–3; and see pp. 20–1 above.

[7] *KTs . . . na 1929/30* (1930), 123; for an alternative calculation, see p. 122, n. 80, below.

[8] Tractors owned by individual peasants declined from 6,309 on October 1, 1927, to 2,487 on October 1, 1928, and by October 1, 1929, individual peasants,

the kolkhozy. The average kolkhoz was too small for effective mechanisation: most kolkhozy had no tractor of their own, and those which possessed a tractor were unable to maintain it efficiently. Matters were made worse by the fact that half the land area of the kolkhozy was not consolidated,[9] but scattered among the strips worked by individual peasant farmers; more advanced crop rotation was therefore impossible unless undertaken jointly with individual peasants by agreement with the mir. The kolkhozy lacked skilled agronomists, vets or mechanics. While they contained a much higher proportion of party members than the individual peasant economies, the proportion was still small: in June 1929 there were 81,957 party members and candidates in 57,000 kolkhozy, 4·3 per cent of all able-bodied adult collective farmers.[10] The members of the kolkhozy were mainly former poor peasants and batraks, who lacked capital, so that most kolkhozy seemed unattractive and poverty-stricken to the individual peasants. In July 1929, Püschel, a German agricultural specialist working in Siberia, summed up the case against the mass of the existing kolkhozy in strong terms:

> The majority of the present kolkhozy—don't deceive yourselves—are candidates for death . . . Inadequate grants on the one hand, and big errors in management on the other, have discredited the whole process of collectivisation and very often have even taken away confidence in the correctness of the principle of collectivisation.
>
> The majority of kolkhozy do not as yet have organisation plans or plans for the location of the personal plot, there is no proper division into fields or crop rotation, and buildings are being put up which don't correspond or correspond very little to their function: in kolkhozy it is still not known what crops should be sown and how they should be sown. Crude mistakes are made in the method of cultivating the soil, they argue about elementary principles and waste time in endless talk about various Utopias instead of getting down to practical work. The land is still used in

according to the official records, owned no tractors at all (*Nar. kh.* (1932), 145).

9 B, 21, November 15, 1929, 55.

10 *Kolkhozy v 1929 godu* (1931), 152–3. The vagueness of information about kolkhoz affairs at this time was reflected in an article in P, May 23, 1929, which claimed that only 13,000 party members belonged to kolkhozy.

a barbarous fashion and the soil continues to deteriorate; this does not help to increase yields or to prevent harvest failure.[11]

The rapid expansion of the membership of the kolkhozy after the XV party congress resulted in a deterioration in their technical level. Although over 4,000 new tractors were supplied to the kolkhozy between mid-1928 and mid-1929, the number of tractors per 1,000 hectares of sown land fell drastically from 7·7 to 3·3.[12]

By the spring of 1929 plans for the socialised sector of agriculture had been greatly increased. The optimum version of the first five-year plan, approved by the XVI party conference in April 1929, proposed that 15·5 per cent of gross grain production and as much as 43 per cent of extra-rural marketed grain from the harvest of 1932 should come from sovkhozy and kolkhozy. As a result of the development of giant highly mechanised sovkhozy, under the grain trust Zernotrest, sovkhozy would produce 4·4 million tons in the 1932 harvest, and as much as 3·4 million tons of this would be marketed.[13] In the same year 5 million tons of marketed grain would come from the kolkhozy (see Table 5). Kolkhozy would include 9·6 per cent of the rural population in 1932/33 and 13·6 per cent in 1933/34[14] (about 3¾ million households). Other variants of the five-year plan for the kolkhozy prepared in the spring of 1929 proposed that they should provide somewhat more marketed grain (5·7–6·0 million tons from the 1932 and over 8 million tons from the 1933 harvest), and that the number of households collectivised should also be somewhat larger (4–6½ million households).[15] All these plans still assumed that 75 per cent or more of the peasantry would remain in individual households at the end of the five-year plan, and that

[11] ZKK (1929), 100–4.

[12] Calculated from figures in *KTs . . . na 1929/30* (1930), 123–4.

[13] For the plans for the expansion of sovkhozy see Carr and Davies (1969), 186–91.

[14] *Pyatiletnii plan* (1930), ii, i, 328–9.

[15] See *Zadachi i perspektivy kolkhoznogo stroitel'stva: proekt pyatiletnego plana* (1929), 255 (prepared by the All-Union Council of Kolkhozy for the XVI party conference in April 1929), and *Perspektivy razvitiya sel'skokhozyaistvennoi kooperatsii v SSSR: pyatiletnii plan na 1928/29–1932/33 gg.* (1929), 120, 127 (prepared by the All-Union Council of Agricultural Cooperation for the V congress of soviets in May 1929). The level of gross production planned for kolkhozy in 1933 in the Gosplan optimum draft of the five-year plan would have resulted in marketed grain production from kolkhozy in 1933/34 of 8 million tons if the proportion of marketed to gross grain production remained the same as in the previous year.

grain production by the individual sector would continue to increase. But the proposal that the socialised sector should supply over 40 per cent of the greatly increased quantity of marketed grain by 1932, and most of it by 1933, was none the less revolutionary. Even in the basic variant of the five-year plan the socialised sector was intended to supply as much marketed grain in 1932 as that supplied in 1927 not merely by the kulaks, but also by the well-to-do households, 10 per cent of households in all.[16] Collectivisation, and the development of the sovkhozy, would simultaneously solve the grain problem and destroy the economic power of the well-to-do peasants.

Throughout 1928 and 1929 new and more ambitious methods of collectivisation received increasing attention. From the end of 1927 onwards Markevich was encouraged by the authorities in his efforts to persuade whole villages to cultivate their land collectively in association with Machine-Tractor Stations (see vol. 2, pp. 16–19); and as early as November 1927 Bauman suggested at a Moscow party conference that whole rural settlements and even districts should be collectivised.[17] In May 1928, the party central committee referred favourably to 'the organised transfer of whole peasant settlements to joint cultivation of the land';[18] and, in the course of 1928, legislation on contracts for grain and industrial crops between the agricultural cooperatives and the peasants stressed the importance of signing contracts with groups of peasants and whole land societies with a view to encouraging joint land cultivation and collectivisation.[19]

At the end of 1928 Kolkhoztsentr, at the prompting of the central committee, launched a campaign for the establishment of 'large kolkhozy' (krupnye kolkhozy). Large kolkhozy were defined as having a sown area of at least 2,000 hectares (in most regions two or three times as large as a traditional village), and were expected to include a total area of 775,000 hectares.[20] Large kolkhozy did not necessarily involve the collectivisation of all the households in an existing group of villages, as they were intended to be established

[16] *Pyatiletnii plan* (1930), ii, i, 276; on grain supplied by well-to-do households, see pp. 26–7 above.

[17] See *XVI konf.* (1962), 367, 805–6.

[18] *Kollektivizatsiya . . . 1927–1935* (1957), 50–2 (dated May 15, 1928).

[19] SZ, 1928, art. 412 (dated July 21); SZ, 1929, art. 29 (dated December 14, 1929); *Neposredstvennaya podgotovka* (Ashkhabad, 1972), 215–17.

[20] *Materialy*, vii (1959), 229; ZKK (1929), 140.

primarily on virgin lands.[21] But in the spring of 1929 a much more ambitious scheme was launched for the establishment of a few 'districts of comprehensive collectivisation' (raiony sploshnoi kollektivizatsii—RSKs) in which all or the majority of households were collectivised; an administrative district contained on average about 8,000 peasant households. Henceforth the advantages were frequently proclaimed of both *massovaya kollektivizatsiya* (mass collectivisation) and *sploshnaya kollektivizatsiya* ('comprehensive', or 'unbroken', collectivisation; both senses are present in the Russian word). The meaning attached to these phrases varied, but they both implied that substantial land masses, a whole village or group of villages, would be collectivised, rather than groups of households within a village.[22] While the voluntary nature of these

[21] Carr and Davies (1969), 173–4.

[22] 'Mass collectivisation' was generally used as a vaguer term than 'comprehensive collectivisation' and unlike the latter term did not necessarily imply that the land of the collectivised households was continuous. The term 'comprehensive collectivisation' was defined and redefined on many occasions. At the conference of large kolkhozy in July 1929 a representative of a district in the Central Industrial Region stated that 'by comprehensive collectivisation we generally mean that kolkhozy are being organised in villages and include the majority of the population of the village' (ZKK (1929), 429–50). At the plenum of the party central committee in November 1929, Molotov, in the context of a discussion of comprehensive collectivisation, also suggested that a region was collectivised 'in the main' if more than 50 per cent of its households belonged to kolkhozy (B, 22, November 30, 1929, 11); but this was a political statement rather than a serious definition. At the conference of agrarian marxists in the following month, I. Nazimov, one of the principal speakers, made the fairly obvious distinction between a 'comprehensively collectivised district' and a 'district of comprehensive collectivisation'. In the former, collectivisation was already complete; in the latter, 'a set of concentrated measures is being carried out to collectivise all the poor and middle peasants and reconstruct their economies by a planned date into a collective farm' (*Trudy . . . agrarnikov-marksistov* (1930), ii, i, 87; see also Ratner in NAF, 10, 1929, 52); the assumption here, frequently made at this time, was that for 'comprehensive collectivisation' 100 per cent of the peasant households (excluding the kulaks) should be collectivised. At the time of the XVI party congress in July 1930, a study of kolkhozy prepared in Gosplan treated 75 per cent collectivisation in a district as indicating that comprehensive collectivisation had been achieved (Minaev, ed. (1930), 234). In December 1930, the central committee plenum stated that collectivisation of 'on average not less than 80 per cent of peasant households' in a region meant 'the completion of comprehensive collectivisation in the main' (*KPSS v rez.*, iii (1954), 78). On August 2, 1931, a further central committee resolution ruled that comprehensive collectivisation of a district or region was 'complete in the main' if 68–70 per cent of peasant households and 75–80 per cent of the sown area were collectivised (*Kollektivizatsiya . . . 1927–1935* (1957), 398–9).

new forms of collectivisation continued to be stressed, they carried with them the unstated implication that the formation and growth of kolkhozy was becoming a planned and organised activity in which the local or central authorities would play a larger part, and in which collectivisation would advance village by village rather than household by household.

These new approaches to collectivisation predominated in the speeches of the party leaders in the spring of 1929. At the plenum of the central committee in April 1929 Stalin hailed the 'serious movement of the mass of millions of peasants in favour of kolkhozy and sovkhozy', but without referring to comprehensive collectivisation.[23] But at the XVI party conference in the same month Kaminsky, chairman of Kolkhoztsentr, after describing the year 1927/28 as a 'break-through year' in collectivisation, claimed that as a result of the further developments in 1928/29 'the middle peasant has begun to go into the kolkhozy'; from this 'impetus (tyaga) of the middle peasants towards the kolkhozy', 'truly mass collectivisation' would result, with the establishment of complete districts of comprehensive collectivisation in 2–3 years.[24] The importance of the movement for comprehensive collectivisation was strongly stressed by other speakers at the conference. Belenky praised the collectivisation of whole villages both because it enabled kolkhozy to be brought under firm control, avoiding the danger of 'capitalist degeneration', and because it would facilitate basic agricultural technical improvements,[25] while Shatskin claimed that it was 'no longer a rare exception, but a fairly widespread phenomenon'.[26]

Collectivisation was believed to have substantial advantages even if it did not entail the introduction of tractors and agricultural machinery. At the party conference, Kalinin, while placing his main emphasis on the great advantages of mechanisation, declared that while the small kolkhoz represented 'manufacture' 'it is still a

[23] *Soch.*, xii, 67.

[24] *XVI konf.* (1962), 391–3; as early as January 1929, A. Yakovlev referred to the 'mass impetus of the batrak – middle peasant masses into the kolkhozy' (DK, 2, January 22, 1930, 9) (this Yakovlev, while also an official of Rabkrin (*XVI konf.* (1962), 719), was not the famous Ya. Yakovlev who became People's Commissar of Agriculture in December 1929).

[25] *Ibid.* 404–5; this was Z. M. Belenky (Rabkrin), not N. M. Belenky of Khlebotsentr.

[26] *Ibid.* 409; Shatskin represented a Leftist trend within the supporters of the Politburo majority (see p. 118 below).

step forward, it is still an association which can be counterposed to the kulak economy in the sphere of production'.[27] But all those who strongly supported collectivisation clearly believed that the supply of machinery to the kolkhozy would be the decisive factor in their success. At the April plenum Stalin insisted that an industrial basis for agricultural development existed, and declared: 'just supply machines and tractors and the cause of the kolkhozy will advance more quickly.'[28] At the party conference Kaminsky bluntly declared that in the new stage of collectivisation, involving the establishment of large kolkhozy, 'the tractor must be the basis'.[29] A speaker from the Kuban' area of the North Caucasus declared that 'although the middle peasants are attracted to the kolkhozy, only a few of them are joining'; and argued that they would remain unwilling to join unless kolkhozy were formed which embraced a whole land society or even a whole *stanitsa* (a thousand or more households) and were served by tractors.[30] Two months after the XVI party conference, Kolkhoztsentr complained to Sovnarkom that 'tractor supply is extremely retarded, and continues to lag behind the rate of growth of the kolkhozy, thus applying a powerful brake on the normal development of large-scale collective agricultural production'.[31] The conflict between the rapid increase in the membership of the kolkhozy and the slower increase in the supply of machinery remained for the moment unresolved.

(B) THE FIRST PHASE OF MASS COLLECTIVISATION

Following the approval of the optimum variant of the five-year plan by the XVI party conference in April and the V congress of soviets in May 1929, enthusiasm for the rapid economic and social transformation of the USSR, coupled with a sense of urgency, mounted among the party leaders and their supporters throughout the summer. This mood was not, as in the summer of 1927, a reaction to

[27] *XVI konf.* (1962), 296; a similar line was taken by Kubyak, People's Commissar for Agriculture of the RSFSR (*ibid.* 421). In Marx's historical analysis of capitalist production, the stage of 'manufacture', organised production using hand-tools, was followed by the stage of 'machinofacture'.

[28] *Soch.*, xii, 67–8.

[29] *XVI konf.* (1962), 392.

[30] *Ibid.* 362–3 (Bulatov).

[31] Cited in IZ, lxxix (1967), 76; the report was dated July 3.

a sudden deterioration in the international situation. The crisis resulting from the Chinese seizure of the Chinese Eastern railway in Manchuria on July 10 was less significant than the defeat of the British Conservatives, the arch-enemy of the Soviet Union, in the election of May 30 and the subsequent appointment of the Labour government, which paved the way to the restoration of Soviet–British diplomatic relations in November.[32] The Soviet assessment at this time seems to have been that they had gained a temporary respite from capitalist attack (see p. 164 below). But at the X plenum of the Comintern executive committee in July, where Molotov was the most prominent Soviet representative, this respite was placed in the context of a period of growing crisis and tension in the capitalist world; in a new revolutionary wave, the majority of the proletariat of the capitalist countries would be won over to the Communist parties, and in this period of intensified class struggle on a world scale the danger of war against the USSR would increase.[33] The Soviet leaders were convinced that the respite must be used to build up Soviet economic and military power; and that this made it essential to find a permanent solution to the agricultural problem.

Within the USSR, a more vigorous offensive was conducted against bourgeois specialists and the Right wing of the party. In May, several prominent non-party engineers, including Palchinsky and von Meck, were executed after a secret trial.[34] In June, seven 'counter-revolutionaries' were executed in Belorussia; their crimes included not only arson but also agitation against collectivisation.[35] In July, 16 'Whiteguards' were executed in the Far East.[36] Throughout the summer and autumn, systematic purges were explicitly directed towards removing those hostile to Soviet power from government institutions and expelling from the party 'non-communist elements'; this phrase referred both to those in opposition to the leadership, and to those who had been corrupted by kulaks and Nepmen.[37] A campaign was launched against the close association of some local party organisations with Nepmen, the corruption of party officials in Astrakhan by private fisheries being

[32] See Carr (1976), 35, (1978), 899–910.

[33] See Kuusinen's and Molotov's reports, published in P, July 31, August 4, 1929.

[34] P, May 23, 1929.

[35] P, June 30, 1929.

[36] P, July 25, 1929.

[37] Arrangements for these purges, approved in principle by the XVI party conference, were announced in P, June 1, 2, 1929; see Carr (1971), 142–7, 311.

held up as an example.[38] An anti-religious campaign, which began in the summer of 1928, and involved the closing down of monasteries and the exile of their monks, reached a new peak in June 1929 with the convening of the all-Union congress of the 'militant godless', addressed by Bukharin on behalf of the central committee.[39] For the next nine months, a vigorous campaign against religion henceforth formed a major part of party activity in the countryside.

The leaders of the 'Right deviation', still not yet named as such in print, were carefully and relentlessly removed from all positions of influence. In June, a plenum of the trade union central council endorsed the decision of the April plenum of the party central committee to remove Tomsky from his trade union posts.[40] In July, the plenum of the Comintern executive committee endorsed the decision to remove Bukharin from Comintern work.[41] In August, a new party cell was formed in *Pravda*, previously edited by Bukharin; the cell consisted 'only of comrades who have fought for the line of the central committee most firmly and in a Bolshevik fashion'.[42]

All other signs of opposition in the party were also firmly suppressed. The 'Leftists' Shatskin and Sten, prominent members of the group of Komsomol leaders who had pressed hard during 1928 and the early part of 1929 for stronger action against kulaks and Nepmen, were now condemned for urging Komsomol members to think more independently.[43] Preobrazhensky, Radek and Smilga, former leaders of the United Opposition, announced that they had broken with Trotsky, and declared their support for the 'Leninist' policy of the central committee.[44] Stalin and the party majority seemed to many of their opponents to be mustering their strength for a decisive struggle against capitalism in difficult circumstances; this was a time to swallow one's disagreements and rally to the cause.[45] Even the large group in exile within the USSR which remained

[38] See Carr (1971), 146n.

[39] P, June 12, 1929; on the anti-religious campaign generally, see R. Medvedev in Tucker, ed. (1977), 208–10.

[40] P, June 2, 1929.

[41] P, July 21, August 21, 1929; the latter issue launched the first public attack on Bukharin.

[42] P, August 4, 1929.

[43] P, August 9, 1929; significantly, the 'general line' of the Komsomol newspaper was explicitly stated to be correct.

[44] P, July 13, 1929 (declaration of July 10).

[45] See, for example, Smilga's and I. N. Smirnov's statements cited in Serge (1967), 252–3, 258.

faithful to Trotsky declared their support for the five-year plan, called for the purging from the party of those who held Right-wing theories, admitted that the Right-wing danger 'must soften the sharpness of the relationship between the Leninist opposition and the party leadership', and expressed willingness in principle to renounce factional activity.[46]

The struggle against the Right wing was closely linked with the struggle for industrialisation and collectivisation. The Lower Volga regional party committee, in a statement endorsed by the central control commission, called for the establishment in Astrakhan okrug of 'large kolkhozy, primarily in sea fishing', and for the increased recruitment of middle peasants into kolkhozy.[47] The statement by Preobrazhensky, Radek and Smilga declared their support for industrialisation, for the struggle against the kulaks, and for the development of sovkhozy and kolkhozy, which they described as 'levers for the socialist transformation of the countryside'.

The first public occasion after the V congress of soviets at which collectivisation was discussed by party leaders was a plenum of the Moscow party committee convened in June 1929. Bauman assured the plenum that 'we are entering the phase of the last decisive struggles between socialism and capitalism in our country'; collectivisation was becoming a movement of middle peasants as well as poor peasants, involving the 'transfer to collectives of whole settlements and even districts, using tractors and complex agricultural machines'; the pace was such that collectivisation in the Moscow province would be completed 'not in a hundred years, but in a decade or two'.[48] This proposed pace of social change, in an agriculturally insignificant province where only 1·5 per cent of peasant households were collectivised, represented a remarkable acceleration. At the plenum Mikoyan repeated the claim that there was a 'serious impetus of the middle peasant towards the kolkhozy'. Assertions that the social basis of the kolkhoz movement now

[46] BO (Paris), vi (October 1929), 3–7; the statement, dated August 22, was signed by 500 oppositionists including V. Kosior, Rakovsky, N. I. Muralov and Sosnovsky; it was endorsed, with reservations, by Trotsky on September 25 (*ibid.* 7–8); see also Deutscher (1963), 78–81.

[47] *Izv. TsK*, 16, June 14, 1929, 14–15.

[48] P, June 16, 1929.

extended well beyond the batrak and the poor peasant would become a familiar theme in propaganda for rapid collectivisation later in the year (see p. 156 below). At the Moscow plenum, in a rare burst of frankness, Mikoyan admitted that the pressure of the authorities for immediate collectivisation was a direct result of the grain crisis:

> I fear my statement will be considered heretical, but I am convinced that if there were no grain difficulties, the question of strong kolkhozy and of the MTS would not have been posed *at this moment* with such vigour, scope and breadth. Of course we would inevitably have come to this task sometime, but it is *a question of timing*. If grain were abundant, we would not at the present time have set ourselves the problems of kolkhoz and sovkhoz construction in such a broad way.[49]

On June 21, 1929, while the plenum of the Moscow committee was in progress, a decree of TsIK and Sovnarkom, 'On Measures to Strengthen the Kolkhoz System', recommended that the republican, regional and okrug kolkozsoyuzy, which were previously advisory in nature, should be given executive powers (pravo operativno-khozyaistvennoi deyatel'nosti), including the right to distribute among the kolkhozy subordinate to them government credits, tractors and other physical resources; particular importance was attached to the large kolkhozy, which were to be directly subordinated to the republican Kolkhoztsentry.[50] This was a significant decision; although the kolkhozy had received a considerable degree of priority in practice, the kolkhoz sector was not previously allocated specific quotas of machines, and the Kolkhoztsentry had no direct influence over their distribution.[51]

Collectivisation campaigns were now undertaken by regional and local party organisations more vigorously than before. In the Western region, where only 1·0 per cent of households were collectivised by June 1, 1929, a long letter from the regional party authorities to district party committees and to rural party cells claimed that 'a tremendous impetus of poor and middle peasants to the kolkhozy' was shown by the fact that over 500 kolkhozy had

[49] P, June 27, 1929.
[50] SZ, 1929, art. 359.
[51] SKhG, July 11, 1929.

been established during the spring, and called for the establishment of 300 more, plus 500 production and cooperative associations, during the autumn.[52] In the North Caucasus, Stavropol' okrug resolved that 32 per cent of its households should be collectivised by May 1930.[53] A few weeks later, on July 4, 1929, Andreev, party secretary in the North Caucasus region, translated the new atmosphere into specific plans for his region in a report to the central committee. Optimistically asserting that 11·8 per cent of households in the North Caucasus were already collectivised, he proposed that the proportion should be increased to 22 per cent in 1929/30; collectivisation would cease to be a spontaneous development, and would take place according to a definite plan involving the establishment of large kolkhozy and the collectivisation of 'whole land societies or at least a considerable part of them'.[54] This proposal clearly required a much more active approach to collectivisation by the authorities than in previous years; 'voluntary' collectivisation would be transformed, even according to the official view, from collectivisation initiated by the peasants into collectivisation initiated from above and merely supported by the peasants.

The first Russian conference of large kolkhozy, which met in Moscow from July 1 to July 10, 1929, registered important changes in collectivisation policy.[55] The proceedings of the conference reveal that progress in the six months since the Kolkhoztsentr decision of December 1928 (see p. 113 above) was significant rather than substantial. A report by Kolkhoztsentr claimed that by June 1929 147 large kolkhozy had been established in the RSFSR, with a sown area of some 240,000 hectares.[56] But this figure was obtained only by sleight-of-hand. In the definition approved by Sovnarkom in December 1928 and endorsed by the organisational section of the conference of large kolkhozy, a 'large' kolkhoz was required to have

[52] *Kollektivizatsiya* (Smolensk, 1968), 143–52.

[53] Turchaninova (Dushanbe, 1963), 159–60.

[54] P, July 7, 1929; a later report by Kolkhoztsentr to the party central committee, dated September 7, 1929, estimated that only 9·2 per cent of households would be collectivised in the North Caucasus on October 1, 1929 (*Materialy*, vii (1959), 217), and the final official figure for June 1929 was only 7·3 per cent (see Table 17).

[55] The proceedings were published as *Za krupnye kolkhozy: materialy 1-go Vserossiiskogo soveshchaniya krupnykh kolkhozov* (1929), referred to here as ZKK.

[56] ZKK (1929), 140, 470–7; their sown area amounted to 220,000 hectares excluding the Central Black-Earth region, for which figures were not available.

a sown area of at least 2,000 hectares.[57] In June 1929, only 39 kolkhozy with a sown area of 121,000 hectares came within this definition; and the higher figure was obtained by defining a large kolkhoz as one with a *total* area of 2,000 hectares.[58]

Even on the official claim, the large kolkhozy included only about 4 per cent of all collective farmers in the RSFSR,[59] and this was less than one in 600 of all peasant households. Nor were the large kolkhozy particularly favoured in the allocation of resources: only a third or a quarter of their draught power was supplied by tractors, roughly the same proportion as for the rest of the kolkhozy.[60] No specific agency was responsible for the large kolkhozy, and a Kolkhoztsentr official explained to the conference that they had emerged on local initiative without any definite central plan, largely by fusing or grouping existing kolkhozy—'we did not know their addresses even in April of this year'.[61]

In spite of this slender progress the conference, backed by Kolkhoztsentr, elevated the large kolkhozy to a key position in the general movement for collectivisation. Kaminsky, who spoke twice at the conference, reiterated his familiar view that large kolkhozy, together with the MTS, would be the nucleus of technological

[57] *Materialy*, vii (1959), 229; ZKK (1929), 123.

[58] ZKK (1929), 140. The appropriate definition was ferociously debated in the organisational section of the conference: speakers suggested that gross production, marketed production, capital employed, and number of households, should also be taken into account. No satisfactory conclusion was reached (*ibid.* 130–2). During the summer, the Central Statistical Administration, Narkomzem, the All-Union Kolkhoz Council and Gosplan worked out a definition for different types of economy and different regions of the RSFSR, based primarily on a minimum of 2,000 hectares of area sown to grain (hence more stringent than the original definition), but also taking into account gross and marketed production. This decision, though mentioned in the report by Kolkhoztsentr of September 7, 1929, was again ignored in its statistical material, which continued to use the definition of 2,000 hectares total area (*Materialy*, vii (1959), 229–30, 222).

[59] On June 1, 1929, there were 659,000 households in kolkhozy in the RSFSR (*Nar. kh.* (1932), 130).

[60] ZKK (1929), 141, gives a figure of 22·5 per cent; the method of calculating it is not stated. According to *KTs . . . na 1929/30* (1930), 123, mechanical power in all kolkhozy amounted to 36·1 per cent in 1929: this ratio is calculated by comparing the ratio of tractor horse-power to animal power, taking one tractor as equal to ten units of animal power. Calculated in this way, the ratio for large kolkhozy would be about 37 per cent (in regions for which data are available, there were 808 tractors, as against 10,319 horses, 3,216 oxen and 158 camels—calculated from ZKK (1929), 470–7).

[61] ZKK (1929), 314.

advance in the countryside. While admitting, in contrast to his statement at the XVI party conference (see p. 116 above), that they must make temporary use of animal power, he again stressed that 'their future lies with combine harvesters and large powerful tractors'.[62] The advanced large kolkhoz would act as the nucleus for the large mass of small kolkhozy which would be formed simultaneously, and which would rely on the collective use of horses and horse-drawn agricultural machines which formerly belonged to individual peasants.[63] Kaminsky predicted a 'stormy development of the large kolkhoz economy, beginning as early as this autumn',[64] and reported that their sown area in 1930 for the USSR as a whole was planned at 3 million out of a total kolkhoz sown area of 8 million hectares. To lend plausibility to the plan, he compared this figure with the *total* area occupied in the RSFSR in June 1929 by large kolkhozy, 750,000 – 1 million hectares; this was a double sleight-of-hand, as large kolkhozy were estimated in terms of the new, less stringent definition.[65]

The need for greater central control of a much expanded campaign for large kolkhozy was stressed both by official spokesmen from the kolkhoz agencies and by delegates from the large kolkhozy; and a resolution was carried urging that large kolkhozy should be allocated the 'main organisational and physical resources of the kolkhoz system'.[66] In the course of the conference, a Kolkhoztsentr official reported an important step in this direction: Kolkhoztsentr

62 ZKK (1929), 7.

63 ZKK (1929), 282–3.

64 ZKK (1929), 5.

65 ZKK (1929), 5, 288. It was presumably this presentation which led the authors of the 1929/30 control figures to give the proportion of kolkhoz sown area for which large kolkhozy were responsible in 1929 as 12 per cent when the true figure was probably less than six per cent, even using the less stringent definition (*KTs . . . na 1929/30* (1930), 555).

66 ZKK (1929), 318–30. A minor but lengthy dispute at the conference concerned the agency which should control the large kolkhozy; several delegates objected to the decision to place them directly under the republican Kolkhoztsentry (see p. 120 above), and argued that they should be placed under regional or okrug kolkhozsoyuzy (ZKK (1929), 291–7, 312–14; eventually Kolkhoztsentr resolved that they should be members of the okrug kolkhozsoyuzy, but that agencies for their management should also be established at republican and regional level (decision of July 25, 1929, reported in ZKK (1929), 465); it is not clear whether these agencies were ever established, and in any case in the autumn the campaign for large kolkhozy was subsumed in the general drive for collectivisation.

and Narkomzem would allocate tractors and large agricultural machines exclusively to large kolkhozy or to groups of kolkhozy.[67]

Two additional conferences held at the time of the conference of large kolkhozy, and reported in the published volume of its proceedings, reinforced the impression of a new and much less restrained phase in collectivisation policy.

On July 4, 1929, an 'inter-kolkhoz conference' held in the small district town of Yelan', in the Urals, resolved that 84 kolkhozy from three adjacent administrative districts should be amalgamated into a single large kolkhoz with a total land area of 135,000 hectares, appropriately known as 'Gigant' (Giant).[68] This development was unprecedented in scale and scope. At the moment of the decision to set up Gigant, its constituent kolkhozy already included 3,800 of the 7,000 rural households in the three districts; and in nine of the 22 village soviets, and 33 of the 102 hamlets, 85 per cent or more of households were members of the kolkhoz. Gigant claimed a much wider range of membership than most kolkhozy, as it was to include some 40 per cent of all the middle peasants in the three districts. But in spite of this unusually broad social base, advanced forms of organisation, which until then had been supposed to be less acceptable to the middle peasant, nevertheless predominated: the proportion of communes was much higher, and of TOZy lower, than for kolkhozy generally at this time (see vol. 2, p. 73).

Some kolkhozy had existed in this area since 1920, but most of the constituent kolkhozy in Gigant appear to have been established after the XV party congress in December 1927. In the publicity attendant on the formation of Gigant, the organisers were concerned to stress the voluntary nature of this expansion. They asserted that it had been due to propaganda by existing successful kolkhozy among a peasantry which had actively supported the regime during the Civil War and which was willing to improve its agriculture:

> When we collectivised, we did not promise tractors, we did not promise rivers of milk with banks of cream. The peasantry collectivised itself.

[67] ZKK (1929), 124.

[68] The conference is reported in ZKK (1929), 433–9; other material on Gigant appeared *ibid.* 28–42, 428.

The organisers admitted that collectivisation had been met by many women peasants ('a darker, more backward and for the most part illiterate element'), with opposition so strong that in 'dozens of cases' it had resulted, at least temporarily, in the break-up of the family. The organisers also claimed that collectivisation was bitterly resisted by 'kulaks', who tried to persuade peasants to leave kolkhoz, burned down cattle-sheds, and wounded kolkhoz horses with knives and axes. A policy of refusing to admit kulaks into the kolkhoz was firmly adhered to, even when, seeing the success of the kolkhoz, and fearing to be isolated from the rest of the population, they had pleaded 'on their knees and with tears in their eyes'.

The extent to which collectivisation in these districts of the Urals was willingly accepted by the peasants in the early months of 1929 cannot now be guessed. An important part was played by land consolidation measures. During the spring sowing of 1929, previously scattered kolkhozy were brought together into unified groups; and this must obviously have led to the displacement of some individual peasants from their existing holdings. It was reported that on one occasion the 'kulaks refused to sow their land', presumably as a protest against these developments. Voluntary or not, this does not seem to have been a movement initiated by the regional or even by the okrug authorities, who apparently were hesitant and cautious throughout: the initiative was said to have been taken by the Komsomol cells and the activists of some of the kolkhozy, with the subsequent support of the okrug Komsomol committee, and to have been opposed by the kolkhozsoyuzy at okrug and regional level. But although the central authorities in Moscow do not appear to have initiated this ambitious scheme, the turning point was the support it received from Kaminsky at the congress of soviets of the RSFSR in May 1929. This official backing was reflected in the attendance at the inaugural meeting on July 4 of a representative of the rural department of the party central committee and of regional, okrug and district government and party officials.

With its massive and broadly-based membership, its element of spontaneity, at least on the part of some of the kolkhoz activists, and its high degree of socialisation, Gigant was a striking example both of a very large kolkhoz and of a district, or group of districts,[69] which

[69] The three districts which contributed to Gigant, though vast in area, were sparsely populated: their total rural population, given at figures varying between 7,000 and 11,000 households, was somewhat larger than that of one average district

had made substantial strides towards comprehensive collectivisation.

The second conference to be held at the time of the conference of large kolkhozy concerned the new movement for 'districts of comprehensive collectivisation' (RSKs), and was convened in Moscow on July 9, at the end of the main conference; according to the official report, it was held 'at the request of individual delegates'.[70] By this time eleven districts in the RSFSR were already officially recognised as RSKs (see Table 18). The districts varied considerably in level of collectivisation, type of kolkhoz and method of approach. Some, like Gigant, were primarily a fusion of existing small kolkhozy into groups or associations; some, like the Tiginsk combine in the Northern region, were based on extensive past involvement in marketing cooperatives or looked towards the establishment of inter-kolkhoz industrial enterprises processing agricultural products on a district scale; some, including three districts in the Volga regions, were built up round a machine-tractor column or station and intended to proceed rapidly to well-developed mechanisation. There was no standard pattern of organisation. Only two or three districts were being organised as a single kolkhoz along the lines of Gigant; at the other extreme, the Tiginsk combine was a loose confederation of kolkhozy in which individual peasant households were also represented; most of the districts included a number of kolkhozy, sometimes grouped together, but retaining their separate identities. The degree of collectivisation also varied considerably. Only the Armizon district in the Urals, with 71 per cent or 2,600 of its households already in kolkhozy, was collectivised to a greater extent than Gigant; in at least six of the districts, less than 40 per cent of peasant households belonged to the kolkhozy. No clear principle was followed in including districts in the approved list, though it is evident from contemporary accounts that Kolkhoztsentr treated requests for inclusion with some circumspection, and that considerable local pressure, or some special reason for central interest, was required before a district was officially recognised.[71]

---

in the USSR at this date. During the summer of 1929, the three districts were combined into a single Krasnopolyanskii ('Red Field') district (P, October 1, 13, 1929).

[70] The conference is reported in ZKK (1929), 421–32.

[71] An example of a district treated with special favour by the centre is the Mineral'nye Vody district in the North Caucasus, containing health resorts

Nor was there yet an agreed definition of the stage at which these designated districts could be said to have achieved 'comprehensive' collectivisation (see p. 114, n. 22, above).[72]

The tentative and contradictory aspects of the movement for comprehensive collectivisation should not, however, depreciate its significance. Whole districts, each embracing several thousand households, were proceeding towards joint cultivation of whole settlements, villages and groups of villages, involving the break-up of the traditional land system and economic and social order of the Russian peasantry. The experience of the few more advanced districts provided a basis for other districts to adopt more ambitious plans. A speaker from Volovo district, Tula okrug, reported to the meeting on July 9:

> When we told the research institute that we intended to collectivise our whole district in five years, they said this was Utopian. But Yelan' district [in the Urals] was extremely significant in this respect: in two or three months the kolkhozy took in nearly 10–15 per cent of the whole territory. After the experience of Yelan' the question of comprehensive collectivisation became clear and the figures of our five-year plan appeared more realistic.[73]

A speaker from an agricultural newspaper summed up the optimistic spirit of the conference:

> I believe there is no more important happening in our Soviet life than this meeting in this room, as the question of comprehensive

---

popular with members of the government; the decision to recognise it as an RSK was greeted by many people with a 'crooked smile' (EZh, October 13, 1929). The claims of the Svitskii Mokh district in the Western region, although it had an unpromising history of unsuccessful kolkhozy, were successfully pressed by the agronomist V. R. Vil'yams, who wanted to undertake large experiments in marshland cultivation (ZKK (1929), 65–73).

72 The representative of Volovo district in the Central Industrial region drew attention to the difference between merely 'making over a district with kolkhozy of one kind and another', which could be done fairly quickly, and the 'full reconstruction of the agriculture of a district', which would take some years, and would require substantial resources (ZKK (1929), 429–30).

73 ZKK (1929), 429.

collectivisation is the foundation of a world revolution (perevorot) in farming.[74]

The movement for RSKs, apparently without any special planning, thus emerged from and formed part of the wider movement for large kolkhozy launched by Kolkhoztsentr at the prompting of the central committee at the end of 1928. By June 1929, it had already begun to overshadow it.

These new trends in policy were consolidated with the adoption of more ambitious plans for 1929/30. In June, Kolkhoztsentr announced that one million households would be collectivised in the RSFSR in 1929/30, implying about 1½ million for the whole USSR; this corresponded to the planned sown area for the kolkhozy in 1929/30, 8 million hectares, announced by Kaminsky at the conference of large kolkhozy.[75] In August, the Gosplan control figures for 1929/30 proposed that the kolkhozy should include a sown area of 13 million hectares;[76] this would correspond to some 2½ million households. This was a very considerable increase as compared with the optimum variant of the five-year plan adopted in the spring of 1929, which envisaged that even by the spring of 1933 only 3·7 million households would be collectivised, with a sown area of 25 million hectares.[77] On September 12, an article by Kaminsky declared that the figure of 13 million hectares for 1929/30 was a minimum which would be 'exceeded considerably', and envisaged the collectivisation of at least 50 per cent of peasant households in the main grain-surplus areas, and 60 per cent of the sown area of the USSR by the last year of the five-year plan, 1932/33.[78] The collectivisation of agriculture would thus require not a decade or so but merely a few years.

Simultaneously with this revision of collectivisation plans, much public attention was devoted to more advanced forms of collectivisation, and during August and September expectations mounted rapidly. On August 7, an editorial in *Pravda*, 'On the Road

[74] ZKK (1929), 431.
[75] ZKK (1929), 288.
[76] EZh, August 18, 1929.
[77] According to *Pyatiletnii plan*, ii, i (1930), 329, 18·6 million persons (i.e. about 3·7 million households) would be in kolkhozy by 1933/34; it is clear from the text (*ibid.* 300) that these figures refer to the harvest of 1933, and therefore presumably to households collectivised by the spring of that year.
[78] P, September 12, 1929.

to Mass Collectivisation', condemned the Right opposition for attempting to confine the kolkhoz movement 'within the framework of an entertaining social experiment', and praised the large kolkhozy and the RSKs; it admitted, however, that 'comprehensive collectivisation is unthinkable without the large machine'. On August 12, a special conference on kolkhoz construction held in the rural department of the party central committee approved the principle of the comprehensive collectivisation of whole districts.[79] On August 16, a less restrained editorial in *Pravda*, evidently inspired by the conference, praised the emergence of new kolkhozy covering tens of villages and suggested that RSKs, based on MTS, could be formed not in five or six years as originally planned but within one or two years. The Politburo itself was, as usual, more restrained in its official pronouncements: in the only relevant published resolution at this time, on the work of the party organisation in Atkarsk (Saratov) okrug in the Lower Volga region, dated August 26, the central committee merely called for 'special attention to the leadership of the kolkhoz movement, increasing the involvement of the poor peasant, production cooperation and the comprehensive collectivisation of whole villages'.[80] But the campaign developed rapidly: on September 5, a further editorial in *Pravda* reported that as many as 100 RSKs associated with MTS were now planned. A week later, in his article of September 12, Kaminsky claimed that as much as two-thirds of the sown area to be collectivised during the five-year plan would form part of large kolkhozy or RSKs.[81] A general report on the state of the kolkhoz movement submitted by Kolkhoztsentr to the party central committee at this time devoted most of its space to the large kolkhozy and the RSK, and launched an even more ambitious scheme: the comprehensive collectivisation of 35–40 okrugs.[82] An okrug, the intermediate administrative unit between the district and the region, contained something like 100,000 households, as compared with some 8,000 in a district, so this was a further major stride towards the full achievement of collectivisation within the space of a few years.

The call for the comprehensive collectivisation of okrugs was

79 VI, 5, 1963, 21.

80 *Izv. TsK*, 26–7, September 20, 1929, 24–5.

81 P, September 12, 1929.

82 *Materialy*, vii (1959), 234; the report was dated September 7, and forwarded to the central committee on September 12 (*ibid.* 206, 211).

prompted by a resolution of the party bureau of Khoper okrug in the Lower Volga region on August 27, 1929, in which it proposed the comprehensive collectivisation of the whole okrug during the course of the five-year plan.[83] The okrug, though described by Kolkhoztsentr as not 'particularly outstanding in its rate of collectivisation and its economic significance',[84] had been under the special aegis of the central authorities for some time,[85] and the extent to which the proposal of August 27 was made independently by the local authorities is not clear. The okrug party bureau and the dominant group in the kolkhozsoyuz strongly advocated rapid collectivisation and pressed the central authorities to supply more tractors;[86] and the soviet executive committee prepared plans in advance for comprehensive collectivisation of the okrug.[87] But the local Khoper newspaper later described comprehensive collectivisation of the okrug as a 'sudden decision of the regional and central agencies'. Local support for the scheme was certainly not unanimous. Several weeks after the decision, the okrug land department was 'ossified and immobile' and the grain cooperatives regarded comprehensive collectivisation as 'not our affair', while in the district organisations, preoccupied with the grain collections and the autumn sowing, 'not a sound or a word' about comprehensive collectivisation had yet been heard.[88] The newspaper also remarked that 'not so long ago a considerable section of the rural communists' also regarded the proposal with 'a certain scepticism'.[89] It was also

[83] The okrug resolution, the date of which is reported in *Krasnyi Khoper*, September 28, 1929, was published *ibid.*, September 17, 1929; Kolkhoztsentr described the okrug as 'the first to pose the question' (*Materialy*, vii (1959), 234). *Kollektivizatsiya* (Krasnodar, 1972), 133–4, reproduces an instruction to the delegates at the 'first congress on comprehensive collectivisation' in Stavropol' okrug, prepared by a village soviet, and proposing that the congress should 'try to obtain a decision in favour of the collectivisation of the whole okrug'; the document is dated April 22, 1929, but this seems far too early a date for a proposal of this kind.

[84] *Materialy*, vii (1959), 234.

[85] An open letter from the Khoper okrug kolkhozsoyuz, published in *Krasnyi Khoper*, August 29, 1929, and SKhG, August 31, 1929, referred to earlier 'directives of the party and government on the maximum development of kolkhoz construction in Khoper okrug'. Kolkhozy in the okrug were visited by Kaminsky and a group of Soviet and foreign journalists in August (*Krasnyi Khoper*, August 24, 1929); see P. Scheffer, *Seven Years in Soviet Russia* (New York, 1932), 76–81.

[86] *Krasnyi Khoper*, August 29, 1929.

[87] *Ibid.*, September 28, 1929.

[88] *Ibid.*, September 28, 1929.

[89] *Ibid.*, September 17, 1929 (editorial).

greeted with scepticism in Kolkhoztsentr in Moscow. According to a Soviet account the board of Kolkhoztsentr sent a telegram to the Lower Volga regional party committee complaining about 'high-handedness (svoevolie)' in the okrug, and on September 4 the okrug was recognised by Kolkhoztsentr as the first okrug of comprehensive collectivisation only after the intervention of the party central committee[90] (i.e. of the central party authorities). At the meeting of Kolkhoztsentr on September 4, Kaminsky somewhat disingenuously argued that it should agree to the comprehensive collectivisation of the okrug because 'we must support the initiative of the localities'.[91] The truth was rather that the party authorities in Moscow were seizing on every possibility of pressing forward collectivisation, against the advice of leading Kolkhoztsentr officials and the resistance of some local party and state officials.

Even at this time no firm decision had yet been reached at the top in the party about the scale and pace of the forthcoming collectivisation drive. On September 18, 1929, Ordzhonikidze, perhaps the most vigorous advocate of rapid industrialisation in the Politburo, referred to collectivisation in moderate terms:

> To complete this work years are needed, we will need to spend years and years in stubborn and consistent work to organise the 25 million scattered peasant economies around the tractor, the kolkhoz, the commune, the artel.[92]

As late as October 2, Andreev still claimed that 'in this Five Year Plan, we can *in no case* count on the complete passage to collective farming'; 'collectivisation is a long-term policy and still demands a great deal of time'.[93] Stalin remained silent: he did not make any public statement about agriculture between April and the beginning of November. Nor was the kolkhoz movement equipped with a strong and well-designed structure of command. Kolkhoztsentr complained in its report of September 7 to the central committee that the decree of June 21, 1929, giving executive authority to the kolkhozsoyuzy (see p. 120 above) had been resisted

[90] Medvedev (Saratov, 1961), 71; the Kolkhoztsentr decision was reported in SKhG, September 8, 1929.

[91] SKhG, September 8, 1929.

[92] Ordzhonikidze, ii (1957), 175 (speech to Moscow provincial party conference).

[93] *Molot*, October 4, 1929, *cit.* Halpern (1965), 165.

by the agricultural cooperatives, and was largely ineffective.[94] But the general political atmosphere undoubtedly encouraged every move from anywhere in the central or local apparatus towards increased collectivisation. On August 21, 1929, *Pravda* published its first open attack on Bukharin by name; and this was followed by a concerted campaign against the Right opposition which included frequent attacks on its pusillanimity about agriculture in general and sovkhozy and kolkhozy in particular. Enthusiastic accounts of the successful formation of kolkhozy appeared frequently at this time in the national press. In the Western region, August 19, a religious holiday, was celebrated as a 'collectivisation day', following a proposal first made, apparently spontaneously, by a regional kolkhoz congress.[95] Strenuous efforts were made to persuade peasants to join the kolkhozy.[96] 'Collectivisation day' was taken up in other parts of the USSR: in Stavropol' okrug it became a 'collectivisation fortnight' and then a 'collectivisation month'.[97] This 'collectivisation day' was not sponsored or endorsed by the central party authorities, but on August 23 the party central committee announced that October 14, another religious holiday, would be celebrated throughout the USSR as a 'Day of Harvest and Collectivisation'.[98]

During the summer of 1929 the procedures for winning over the peasants to collectivisation were regulated and systematised, and this provided a further impetus to collectivisation. Local authorities were urged to collectivise through what was in effect a version of the 'Ural–Siberian method' of grain collections (see p. 57 above), adapted to the social transformation of the Soviet countryside. A significant article in the agricultural newspaper by a Kolkhoztsentr official urged okrug kolkhoz agencies to select specific settlements suitable for putting through comprehensive collectivisation (on the basis, for instance, that cooperation was already reasonably advanced), and then systematically persuade the peasants to join

[94] *Materialy*, vii (1959), 268–9.

[95] The congress took place on July 10–12; the regional party committee endorsed the proposal on August 1 (*Kollektivizatsiya* (Smolensk, 1968), 656).

[96] See *ibid.* 163–5.

[97] Turchaninova (1963), 162–3.

[98] P, July 12, 26, 1929; KG, 57, July 19, 65, August 16, 72, September 10, 1929; for the central committee resolution see *Kollektivizatsiya . . . 1927–1935* (1957), 195; a TsIK resolution on the same subject, dated September 18, appears in SZ, 1929, art. 555.

the kolkhozy, using the combined forces of okrug and district party, soviet and cooperative organisations. Party and Komsomol members, who were obliged to join the kolkhoz, should be approached first; and then, as in the case of the grain collections, separate meetings of the village soviet, of poor peasant groups and of women should precede the convening of general village meetings.[99] This article was in due course reproduced in the local press.[100] It was also at this time that the authorities, fired by the success of the initial stage of the grain campaign, envisaged that the agencies responsible for it could move on to a collectivisation drive similar to the grain campaign in scope and speed: it was announced that the grain collections would be completed by January 1, so that 'from the new year the forces of the party, the Soviet administration, the cooperatives and of all voluntary organisations can be transferred to carrying out the tasks of agricultural reconstruction, to assisting the broad masses of the poor and middle peasants to organise their economy on collective and industrial principles'.[101]

The systematisation of procedures, the campaign against the Right, the general enthusiasm for collectivisation in the national press, and the specific support from the central party administration such as that given to the RSKs and to the collectivisation of Khoper okrug, all encouraged okrug and district party officials to adopt more ambitious plans. It was in these special circumstances that the central authorities were confronted 'from below' with plans which exceeded their own expectations, so that Kaminsky was able to claim that '*reality is overtaking the plans*'.[102]

The new orientation and atmosphere resulted in impressive increases in the membership of kolkhozy. In the four months June–September 1929 the kolkhozy expanded rapidly, from 1 million households, 3·9 per cent of all households, on June 1 to 1·9 million, 7·5 per cent, on October 1, 1929 (see Tables 16 and 17). In the main grain-surplus regions the proportion was much higher: 19 per cent in the North Caucasus, 18 per cent in the Lower Volga, 9 per cent in the Central Volga.[103] This unprecedented expansion undoubtedly encouraged the authorities in their growing belief that

[99] SKhG, August 16, 1929 (G. Dotsenko, head of Moscow kolkhozsoyuz).

[100] For example, in *Krasnyi Khoper*, September 26, 1929.

[101] P, September 15, 1929 (editorial).

[102] SKhG, August 17, 1929.

[103] See Table 17; the percentages on June 1, 1929 were 7, 6 and 4 respectively. Figures cited in different sources vary considerably; see note to Table 17.

collectivisation would provide an immediate solution to their difficulties.

While the new kolkhozy were being formed, the autumn sowings of rye, wheat and barley for the 1930 harvest took place.[104] The autumn-sown area in 1929 was 6·5 per cent higher than in 1928, and somewhat higher than in any previous year. The increase in the three major grain-surplus regions of the RSFSR, where collectivisation was particularly rapid, was as much as 11 per cent.[105] For the first time, substantial areas of the major grain regions were included in the kolkhozy, and were sown collectively; this sowing was of course primarily undertaken without the use of tractors.[106]

In a few model areas even more substantial strides were made

[104] The autumn sowings took place in most years in August and September, immediately after the harvest; in the south, including the Southern Ukraine and the North Caucasus, they were completed in October (*St. spr. 1928* (1929), 174).

[105] The autumn-sown area was as follows (million hectares, including winter killings):

		Autumn 1928 for 1929 harvest	*Autumn 1929 for 1930 harvest*
USSR		36·9	39·3
including:	Ukraine	9·1	9·8
	North Caucasus	3·1	3·9
	Lower Volga	2·0	2·2
	Central Volga	2·5	2·7

(*Ezhegodnik po sel. kh. 1931* (1933), 243–5).

[106] Figures for the kolkhoz autumn-sown area vary considerably, as the following table shows (million hectares, excluding winter killings) (column *A* is from the kolkhoz census of May 1930 (*Kolkhozy v 1930 g.* (1931), 149), column *B* from *Ezhegodnik po sel. kh. 1931* (1933), 252–315):

	By kolkhozy A	*B*	*Total by all sectors*
USSR	4·20	5·43	38·89
Ukraine	1·58	2·11	9·74
North Caucasus	1·05	1·43	3·81
Lower Volga	0·39	0·44	2·19
Central Volga	0·21	0·24	2·72

Both columns apparently refer to collective sowings, but in each case sowings by individual peasants subsequently transferred to the kolkhoz upon joining may have been included.

towards comprehensive collectivisation. Thus in Khoper okrug, where only 2·2 per cent of households were collectivised in June 1929,[107] the proportion had risen to 12·6 per cent on August 1,[108] and by October 1 was stated to have reached 30,[109] or even 38 per cent;[110] in certain districts of the okrug, 70 per cent of households were already collectivised.[111] In the Chapaev RSK, the percentage of collectivised households increased from 25 in July to 63 in September.[112] The press at this time frequently referred to the 'impetus' of middle peasants towards the kolkhoz, but the membership of kolkhozy still consisted primarily of poor peasants. According to the Kolkhoztsentr report of September 7, former poor peasants or batraks constituted between 63 and 80 per cent of kolkhoz households in different parts of the North Caucasus, middle peasants between 18 and 36 per cent; similar proportions were reported from the Urals. The proportion of middle peasants in kolkhozy was not recorded as having increased substantially in the course of 1928/29.[113]

Zealous party and soviet officials employed threats and force as well as blandishments in order to bring the peasants into the kolkhozy as early as March 1929.[114] By June–September 1929 such 'administrative pressure' was evidently already widely employed. The Chapaev district in the Central Volga region, named after the Soviet civil war hero, provides an instructive example. Comprehensive collectivisation of the district was originally proposed by district officials in the spring of 1929.[115] Progress was rapid; and in August a meeting in the rural department of the party central committee resolved that collectivisation in the district should be

[107] *Krasnyi Khoper*, June 6, 1929.

[108] SKhG, September 8, 1929; this figure is given as referring to July 1 in *Krasnyi Khoper*, September 17, 1929.

[109] P, December 29, 1929.

[110] *Povol'zhskaya pravda*, November 7, 1929; for an even higher figure, see p. 152 below.

[111] *Krasnyi Khoper*, October 5, 1929.

[112] ZKK (1929), 427; P, October 1, 1929.

[113] *Materialy*, vii (1959), 239–41; the report claimed to observe 'a process of some increase in the proportion of middle peasants', but the increases shown in its tables were very slight, and it later noted that 'the number of middle peasants attracted into kolkhozy is still low even in districts of mass collectivisation' (p. 268).

[114] For a striking example from the Siberian region in March 1929 see Lewin (1968), 431–2.

[115] SKhG, November 15, 1929.

further accelerated in preparation for September 5, the tenth anniversary of Chapaev's death.[116] Collectivisation was immediately carried out at 'dizzy speed' by officials who rushed from village to village, promising tractors to those who hesitated and sometimes threatening to take away their land if they refused to join.[117] In one village in the Central Black-Earth region a kolkhoz of 50 households was organised only by 'crude ordering-about'; in another, a quarter of the peasants were individually assessed for the agricultural tax, a measure intended only for kulaks, and a quarter of the poor peasants were deprived of electoral rights.[118] In the Ukraine, Shlikhter criticised land consolidation officials who had used 'administrative arguments and mechanically increased their "achievements" in collectivising the population'.[119] Much opposition was aroused. In one district of Khoper okrug, rumours flourished for two months that a 'St Bartholomew's night' of the peasantry was about to occur, and attempts were made to burn down poor peasant houses in which meetings had been held.[120] According to the Kolkhoztsentr report of September 7, 'the class struggle in the countryside became much more acute with the organisation of large kolkhozy' so that the reports from some places where comprehensive collectivisation was being introduced 'literally remind one of a battle-front'. Thus agitation against the authorities, rumours, arson and killing of cattle were frequently reported from the Chapaev district; and a letter from Gigant kolkhoz in the Urals described secret meetings, rumours that antichrist had arrived and that the world would soon come to an end, and the burning down of a settlement which supported collectivisation while its inhabitants were taking part in an antireligious carnival.[121] From the Ukraine, the well-known journalist Zaslavsky reported that while armed banditry, which continued until 1927, had now ceased, slander about the kolkhozy was widespread, including allegations that serfdom was being introduced. Opposition was particularly widespread among women,

[116] SKhG, August 25, 1929.

[117] SKhG, November 15, 1929, in a report referring to this earlier period.

[118] Shuvaev (1937), 40–1.

[119] SKhG, October 2, 1929; Shlikhter was People's Commissar for Agriculture of the Ukraine.

[120] *Krasnyi Khoper*, September 26, 1929.

[121] *Materialy*, vii (1959), 242–5; see Carr and Davies (1969), 175; the letter was dated October 1, 1929, evidently a misprint for September 1, as the Kolkhoztsentr report reached the central committee on September 12 (see p. 129, n. 82, above).

stirred up by the kulaks, though in general there was a 'substantial stratum of vacillators'. In one village where collectivisation had been introduced at silent peasant meetings (Zaslavsky commented wryly 'it is well known that silence means consent'), a large crowd of women who subsequently blocked the road when tractors arrived yelled out 'the Chinese have seized half of Siberia, the Bolsheviks will soon be finished, the Soviet government is bringing back serfdom.'[122] When peasant enthusiasm for the kolkhoz was reported in the press in other than general terms, it was usually associated with anticipation of the benefits to be brought by the tractor. In the Novo-Nikolaevskaya 'model district' in Khoper okrug, 'the presence of a relatively large number of machines facilitated the broad movement to collectivisation'.[123] In a very large kolkhoz in the North Caucasus, where collectivisation was originally strongly resisted, women were reported to have burst into tears of joy on seeing the tractor columns.[124] In Chapaev district, middle peasants who were asked 'Are you for the kulak or for Soviet power?' replied, 'Neither for the kulak nor for Soviet power, but for the tractor'.[125]

(C) THE PROBLEM OF THE KULAK

The grain campaign of 1928/29 was accompanied by an intensified struggle against the kulaks, who were condemned not only for failing to hand over grain themselves but also for inciting middle peasants to similar resistance (see pp. 93–8 above). The controversial question of the relationship of the kulak to the kolkhozy, made more urgent with the rapid development of collectivisation, was discussed in an atmosphere of increasing hostility to the kulaks. Opinion was sharply divided at the XVI party conference in April 1929;[126] no agreement was reached, and the matter was referred first to the central committee, and then to its rural department.[127]

[122] P, September 11, 1929; on the same day the newspaper briefly reported that when at an earlier date peasants in this village had criticised the kolkhoz at meetings the authorities 'threatened them and even resorted to arrests'.

[123] *Krasnyi Khoper*, August 6, 1929.

[124] KG, 77, September 27, 1929.

[125] *Materialy*, vii (1959), 243; for further material on peasant attitudes to mechanisation see pp. 384–6 below.

[126] See Carr and Davies (1969), 177–9.

[127] ZKK (1929), 375.

An article in *Pravda* condemned 'dekulakisation' and the use of 'terror' against kulaks. The seizure of kulak dwellings and property in the course of collectivisation would increase the supporters of the kulaks among middle peasants, and the murder of kulaks by poor peasants was a 'non-proletarian method of struggle with the class enemy'.[128] Later in the same month, an important discussion article by Karpinsky in the party journal accepted the widely-held view that kulaks should not as a rule be admitted to the vast majority of existing kolkhozy, which consisted of a group of households within an existing village: the only exception would be kulaks who handed over all their means of production to the socialised fund of the kolkhoz, preferably to its Indivisible Fund (which would not be returned to them if they left or were expelled). Karpinsky pointed out, however, that collectivisation of whole settlements or groups of settlements raised a new set of problems. If the kulak was not admitted, he would need to be resettled, and as there were no proposals to send him to 'remote areas or a desert island', resettlement would have to be on the village lands. He could move to a separate farm outside the kolkhoz either in a khutor or as part of a separate 'kulak settlement'; or he could be left in the main village and provided with an otrub. All these solutions, according to Karpinsky, left the kulak in a strong position: the one most favoured, the otrub, would enable the kulak to retain his influence in the village and his own production, and would cause serious agro-technical difficulties. Karpinsky therefore proposed that in areas of comprehensive collectivisation the kulak should be permitted to join the kolkhoz. Even if he retained his own horses, cows and buildings, he would be deprived of his land; he would no longer be able to rent out implements and horses; and he would have fewer possibilities of speculating in grain.[129]

Karpinsky's proposal was endorsed by Kaminsky at a session of the All-Union Kolkhoz Council;[130] and on July 4, 1929, at a conference of the rural department of the party central committee, a spokesman for the department also endorsed the view that when a whole settlement joined the kolkhoz kulaks could be admitted, on condition that their property was transferred to the Indivisible Fund and that they did not participate in general meetings of the

[128] P, June 2, 1929.
[129] B, 11, June 15, 1929, 26–35.
[130] EZh, June 16, 1929.

kolkhoz.[131] At the conference a delegate from the Black-Earth region claimed that practical experience demonstrated that the kulak could be kept under control better if he belonged to the kolkhoz; kulak otrubs were 'a Soviet version of the Stolypin reform'.[132] But the conference revealed a strong current of opinion among local party officials against the policy of the central committee department: the majority of delegates at the conference were said to be 'decisively opposed' to the admission of kulaks to kolkhozy.[133] Some delegates even called for the expulsion of kulaks altogether from the villages:

> If he is a kulak deprived of electoral rights [a delegate from the Lower Volga region declared] . . . I think our Soviet government will find it possible to isolate such a kulak somewhere or other in a special area. Something must be done about this: if he gets into the kolkhoz somehow or other he will turn an association for the joint working of the land into an association for working over Soviet power.[134]

A delegate from a Central Volga kolkhoz, whose kulaks had been despatched to other villages and then sent back again, appealed to the authorities to 'find a place further off, so they do not come here again'.[135] In his summing-up, the spokesman for the rural department of the central committee argued defensively that 'for practical work' it was sufficient to accept the general opinion of the kolkhozy that kulaks 'who are hindering or who may do harm' should not be admitted.[136]

The relative moderation advocated by the responsible central committee department accorded with the policy followed in some major areas. In February 1929 the bureau of the Lower Volga regional committee resolved that 'when whole settlements join the

[131] ZKK (1929), 375–6 (M. Vareikis, not to be confused with I. M. Vareikis, party secretary in the Central Black-Earth region, *pace* Carr (1971), 187n, Lewin (1968), 434).

[132] ZKK (1929), 370–1.

[133] ZKK (1929), 375; delegates at a special conference convened by Kolkhoztsentr were reported to have taken a similar attitude.

[134] ZKK (1929), 360–1 (A. Andreev).

[135] ZKK (1929), 369 (Zheleznikov).

[136] ZKK (1929), 376–7 (Meshcheryakov).

kolkhozy it is possible to admit kulaks to them provided that their main means of production (working animals, machines, etc.) are socialised and transferred to the indivisible capital'.[137] In June 1929, at a Central Volga conference, Khataevich resisted the proposal made by some delegates that kulaks and even well-to-do peasants should be excluded from the kolkhozy, and the plenum of the regional party committee in the following month resolved that 'individual kulak elements may be admitted to collective associations if they completely renounce their personal ownership of means of production, if the kolkhozy have a solid poor-peasant and middle-peasant nucleus and if correct leadership is assured'.[138]

Elsewhere in the party a firmer policy towards the kulaks had already been accepted. In August 1928 the TsIK and Sovnarkom of the Kazakh republic resolved that the property of the richest nomad farmers, the *bai*, should be confiscated and the *bai* themselves should be exiled. The measure was directed against farmers who were very much more prosperous than kulaks elsewhere in the USSR: only 700 families, described as '*bai*-semifeudal lords', were affected. Political as well as economic criteria were used to select those subject to exile: *bai* were exiled either if they owned more than 100, 300 or 400 animals (depending on the area), or if they 'belonged earlier to privileged groups by their position'. The operation was carried out between September and November 1928 by a central commission under the chairmanship of the chairman of the Kazakh TsIK or his deputy, which included the chairman of the Kazakh Sovnarkom or his deputy, and representatives of Narkomzem, the OGPU, the Kazakh peasants' union and the agricultural workers' trade union; the procurator was also in attendance. Similar commissions were established in the okrugs, and sent plenipotentiaries to the auls (Kazakh villages) to carry out the expropriation. Committees to assist the expropriation were established in the auls, and meetings of poor peasants, and of some middle peasants, were called in its support. While these procedures and institutions differed in detail from those adopted for the mass expropriation of the kulaks throughout the USSR early in 1930, they were clearly their precursor: both the expropriations of 1928 and those of 1930 had in common the use of political as well as economic criteria to select the victims, the establishment of special commissions in which

[137] *Saratovskaya* (Saratov, 1960), 268.

[138] IZ, lxxx (1967), 90–1; Ivnitskii (1972), 160; Khataevich was regional party secretary.

the OGPU was directly involved, the despatch of plenipotentiaries to the villages and the summoning of peasant meetings to provide some popular authorisation for the measures. Above all, the Kazakh expropriations, like those of 1930, were intimately connected with the collectivisation of agriculture. While 60 per cent of the confiscated animals were distributed to batraks and poor peasants, efforts were made to persuade the beneficiaries to join cooperatives, and 20 per cent of the confiscated animals were distributed to existing kolkhozy and to 293 kolkhozy which were established on the basis of those confiscated herds.[139]

These measures were defended in the decree of August 1928 on the grounds that 'in the Kazakh republic, which contains culturally-backward nationalities, the measures carried out until now have not changed the old pre-revolutionary relationships to a sufficient extent'.[140] Until the autumn of 1929 such measures were taken against kulaks elsewhere only if they were considered to be required by their resistance to the grain collections (see p. 58 above). But in some regions a harder line was adopted towards the admission of kulaks into kolkhozy long before any central party decision about their fate. In February 1929 a Siberian regional party conference resolved that 'when simple production associations are organised (machine, settlement, livestock, seed, etc. associations) . . . the kulaks must not be admitted'.[141] In the North Caucasus, where hostility to Soviet power was traditional among many of the Cossacks, particularly vigorous action was taken by the authorities in June 1929, in the last stages of the 1928/29 grain campaign, against kulaks who failed to hand over their grain (see p. 58 above). Simultaneously, on June 21, 1929, the bureau of the North Caucasus regional party committee resolved that 'it is considered inexpedient to admit kulak households to kolkhoz membership at the present stage, and it is considered necessary to carry out a consistent struggle to purge existing kolkhozy of hostile kulak elements'.[142] This decision was reported to the central

[139] *Kollektivizatsiya*, i (Alma-Ata, 1967), 169–74 (decree of August 27), 190–8, 211–22 (reports of result of measures); see also P, September 11, I, September 15, 1928.

[140] *Kollektivizatsiya*, i (Alma-Ata, 1967), 169–70.

[141] Cited in *XVI konf.* (1962), 802 (the conference was held from February 25 to March 2).

[142] Cited from the archives in *Kollektivizatsiya* (Krasnodar, 1972), 773, n. 39.

committee by Andreev on July 4,[143] and endorsed by the committee on July 18.[144]

In spite of this authoritative declaration of July 18, doubts about how the kulaks should be treated continued to be expressed among party leaders. On August 15, Bauman told a session of the Moscow party committee that the position of kulaks in places where comprehensive collectivisation had been carried out was 'a fairly interesting question not yet finally resolved by the party', and argued that in RSKs tractorisation could be accompanied by admitting kulaks into the kolkhozy while at the same time 'expropriating kulak implements and all their means of production into the socialised fund of the kolkhoz'; this would be 'a kind of local dekulakisation'. Kulaks who continued to oppose kolkhoz construction could be expelled from the kolkhoz and exiled later.[145] But this already seemed a counsel of extreme moderation. On August 14 the Central Black-Earth region followed the example of the North Caucasus and banned kulaks completely from the kolkhozy.[146] By now Kolkhoztsentr itself was now taking a firmer line: the article recommending procedures for collectivisation to local officials warned that even when kulaks handed over all their means of production to kolkhozy attached to MTS they should be admitted only 'as an exception';[147] and Kaminsky called for more attention to the danger from kulaks crawling into the kolkhozy.[148] In its report to the central committee of the party of September 7, 1929, Kolkhoztsentr called for 'a firm directive on the impermissibility of admitting into kolkhozy kulaks and those deprived of civil rights' in the case of RSKs, as well as small kolkhozy, and for the purging of kulaks from large kolkhozy. It also proposed that a decree should be prepared on 'severe measures against kulaks disrupting kolkhoz

[143] P, July 7, 1929.

[144] P, July 19, 1929.

[145] P, August 20, 1929; P, July 17, 1929, explained that the 'decisive attack on the kulak' which was taking place on the basis of NEP was not 'dekulakisation', a term from the period of the Committees of Poor Peasants in 1918, which implied the 'direct expropriation of the kulak as the *main* method of struggle against capitalist elements in the countryside'; a later author pointed out, however, that in 1918 dekulakised peasants were not exiled but compulsorily included in the commune (NAF, 6, 1930, 86); for the Committees of Poor Peasants of 1918, see Carr (1952), 53–5.

[146] Sharova (1963), 123–4.

[147] SKhG, August 16, 1929; for this article see also p. 133 above.

[148] SKhG, August 17, 1929.

construction and terrorising collective farmers', and that two or three show trials of kulaks should be held.[149]

Local practices varied greatly. During the summer of 1929, kulaks were still admitted to kolkhozy in some RSKs in the Ukraine,[150] and, on condition that their property was fully socialised, in both the Central and Lower Volga regions.[151] In some Ukrainian villages, however, kulaks were exiled to the most distant parts of the village, often close to ravines, to settlements popularly known as 'Kamchatka'.[152] Similarly in the Gigant kolkhoz in the Urals, even in the early stages of its formation, kulaks were generally not admitted.[153] Moreover, even though indecision continued at the top, kulaks were usually treated severely when comprehensive collectivisation was being carried out. In the Khoper okrug, in the previously fairly lenient Lower Volga region, 572 kulaks were expelled from kolkhozy; and kulaks who did not agree to the socialisation of all their property were warned that they would be resettled outside the okrug.[154] Substantial numbers of kulaks were expelled from Gigant kolkhoz in the Urals in those villages where they had previously been admitted.[155] The Chapaev RSK drew up plans to expel kulaks from its kolkhozy to remote parts of each village.[156] The increasingly desperate situation of the kulak was reflected in accounts which appeared with increasing frequency at this time of kulaks who, fearing that they would be cast out of their villages, begged to join the kolkhozy, and offered to hand over all their property to kolkhoz funds.[157]

In the second half of September an extremely vigorous campaign was launched to compel kulaks to hand over all their grain surpluses (see p. 94 above); and the attempt to stir up hostility to the kulak in the mir during the grain campaign encouraged the tougher line towards the kulaks in connection with collectivisation. The grain campaign also resulted in stronger action being taken against

149 *Materialy*, vii (1959), 246.

150 P, September 18, 1929.

151 VIK, 4, 1958, 75; IZ, lxxx (1967), 91.

152 P, September 9, 1929; Kamchatka is a remote and inhospitable peninsula in the Soviet Far East.

153 ZKK (1929), 33; see also p. 125 above.

154 *Povol'zhskaya pravda*, September 11, 1929.

155 P, September 12, 1929.

156 *Materialy*, vii (1959), 242.

157 For example, *Materialy*, vii (1959), 242; P, September 11, 1929 (Ukraine).

kulaks, or alleged kulaks, in existing kolkhozy. Kolkhozy which failed to hand over their grain promptly were treated as 'bogus' and accused of being under kulak influence (see pp. 100–1 above). Simultaneously, a more general campaign was launched against bogus kolkhozy; the authorities evidently concluded from their experience of the first few weeks of the grain collections that the kolkhoz could not be relied on automatically to subordinate itself to the needs of the socialist state, but must be led by reliable supporters of the regime. In September VTsIK and Sovnarkom of the RSFSR imposed criminal penalties for participating in bogus kolkhozy for financial gain, for organising them, or for assisting their activities.[158] On September 17, *Pravda*, over three full columns, charged the 'Krasnyi Meliorator' (Red Land Improver) kolkhoz, in the Lower Volga region, with being dominated by kulaks. The *Pravda* material was based on an extensive Rabkrin survey, undertaken in the summer of 1929 after a strike of tractor drivers in the kolkhoz in the previous May.[159] The kolkhoz was established in 1924, was well supplied with tractors and was generally regarded as a model. The investigation purported to have shown, however, that while the kolkhoz had received state credits of 300,000 rubles, its socialised property amounted to only 1800 rubles. Kolkhoz property had been embezzled, land had been rented out to a kulak and batraks had been hired by subterfuge and treated contemptuously; the state credits had been used for personal gain; and the personal economies of the collective farmers had been subsidised by the kolkhoz. The leaders of the kolkhoz were expelled and arrested, and replaced by a strong group of party members sent in from outside: the kolkhoz chairman, a member of VTsIK of the RSFSR and of the All-Union Kolkhoz Council, was a former SR and its board included former traders, the son of a priest and four other former SRs.[160] This may have been a corrupt kolkhoz, but the published evidence did not show that its leaders were or had been kulaks in any economic sense. Rabkrin nevertheless concluded from the investigation that throughout the USSR the cleansing of the kolkhozy by expelling former kulaks must now be a major task.[161] On the following day, September 18, a further article in *Pravda* strongly criticised RSKs in

[158] SU, 1929, art. 705 (decree of September 9).
[159] VIK, 4, 1958, 77.
[160] P, September 17, October 5, 22, 1929; *Kolkhoztsentr: informatsionnyi byulleten'*, 22, 1929, 14–16, *cit.* Ivnitskii (1972), 125.
[161] P, September 17, 1929.

the Ukraine which had admitted kulaks, and even condemned one district for planning to collectivise 'kulak villages' (by which was meant villages under kulak domination).[162] Many reports linked the activities of kulaks in the kolkhozy with attempts by kolkhozy to resist the grain collections or to distribute more grain to their members.[163]

At the Moscow regional party conference, Molotov drew the necessary lesson from the 'Krasnyi Meliorator' affair that 'kulak-SR elements will often hide behind the kolkhoz smokescreen' unless there was a 'merciless struggle' against the kulak while at the same time the poor peasants, and the alliance of poor and middle peasants, were better organised within every kolkhoz.[164] Criteria drawn up by Kolkhoztsentr for recognising 'bogus kolkhozy' were obviously influenced by the 'Krasnyi Meliorator' experience,[165] and it was directly as a result of these revelations that on September 30 the bureau of the Lower Volga regional party committee resolved that 'it is impermissible to admit kulaks and others deprived of electoral rights into kolkhozy; expel kulaks from the kolkhozy'.[166] A report based on material of the rural department of the party central committee distinguished four ways in which kulaks sought to undermine kolkhozy: outright criticism, including criticism via henchmen; '*entry into the kolkhoz with the objective of disrupting it*'; '*organisation of bogus kolkhozy*'; and '*developing exploitation of others within the kolkhoz*'.[167]

In spite of this powerful campaign against the kulaks, unanimity had not even yet been achieved. In the Central Volga region kulaks continued to be admitted into 'strongly organised' large kolkhozy, providing they handed over all their property to the Indivisible Fund: the author of the article reporting this repeated the familiar point that the alternative course of resettling kulaks on the outskirts of a village or group of villages would run the risk of creating '"kulak" kolkhozy'.[168] Within their own terms of reference, the authorities were caught in their own trap, and to escape from it

162 P, September 18, 1929 (M. Kantor).

163 For example, KG, 76, September 24, 1929 (Volga-German republic).

164 SKhG, October 6, 1929.

165 See Ivnitskii (1972), 126.

166 P, October 5, 1929; VIK, 4, 1958, 77. The Georgian central committee took a similar decision at its session of October 18–20 (VI, 3, 1965, 15–16).

167 NAF, 10, 1929, 67–8 (Karavaev).

168 SKhG, October 12, 1929.

required unprecedented ruthlessness and inhumanity. For the time being no central party or government directive was issued. Kulaks and others were already being deprived of their property and expelled from their village for failure to surrender their full quota of grain (see p. 97 above). But exile of the kulaks beyond the boundaries of their own village in connection with collectivisation was still apparently a rare occurrence.

CHAPTER FOUR

THE NEW STAGE OF COLLECTIVISATION, OCTOBER 1929–JANUARY 5, 1930

(A) TOWARDS THE NEW STAGE, OCTOBER 1929

The impressive increases in kolkhoz membership in June–September 1929 did not immediately result in any major change in official plans, and agriculture did not play a prominent part in the discussions on the control figures for 1929/30 at Gosplan and Sovnarkom in October 1929.[1] On the eve of the Day of the Harvest and Collectivisation, a Kolkhoztsentr report cautiously estimated the number of households in kolkhozy at 'over one million', and proposed that by the end of 1929/30 3·1 million households should be collectivised in 103,000 kolkhozy, with a sown area of 15 million hectares.[2] This proposal, only a slight increase above the plan announced in the previous month (see p. 128 above) was included without change in the volume of control figures approved by Sovnarkom and published early in 1930.[3] The proposal in the control figures that the sown area of large kolkhozy should amount to 3·3 million hectares at the end of 1929/30 was also relatively moderate; this was a smaller proportion of the total planned sown area of kolkhozy than in the plans prepared in the previous July.[4] In other respects, however, the control figures were much bolder, proposing that the number of RSKs should increase from 25 to 60–80 in 1929/30, and that a high percentage of the livestock of peasants joining kolkhozy should be socialised (see vol. 2, p. 76).

The sovkhozy also received much attention at this time. The

[1] The control figures for 1929/30 will be discussed in a later volume.

[2] P, EZh, October 13, 1929.

[3] *KTs . . . na 1929/30* (1930), 124.

[4] According to ZKK (1929), 187, the sown area of large kolkhozy was planned at 1·96 million hectares at a time when the total sown area of kolkhozy was planned at 8 millions.

results of the 1929 harvest were at first sight disappointing: production increased only slightly from 917 thousand tons in 1928 to 1,076,000 tons in 1929.[5] But most of the new highly mechanised sovkhozy of Zernotrest were still in process of formation. In September, the new model 'Gigant' sovkhoz in Sal'sk okrug in the North Caucasus celebrated a satisfactory harvest of 60,000 tons in a festival addressed by Maxim Gorky;[6] and the control figures for 1929/30 planned an increase in the sovkhoz harvest to 2·8 million tons in 1930.[7] Kalmanovich, head of Zernotrest, who had recently returned from a visit to the United States, claimed that the experience of Gigant already showed that 'we have overtaken the technically-advanced countries'.[8] On October 26, a *Pravda* editorial 'On Grain Factories' urged that the allocation of land to sovkhozy should be accelerated, and drew attention to the 'revolutionary effect' of sovkhozy on neighbouring peasants.

During October, the enthusiasm for collectivisation expressed by the political leaders far outstripped the proposals of the control figures. In an impassioned speech at Sovnarkom, Pyatakov, formerly a close associate of Trotsky in the Left Opposition, now persuaded that the new policies of the Politburo would take the Soviet Union forward into socialism, assured Sovnarkom that 'there is no solution to the problem of agriculture within the framework of individual farming, and therefore *we are obliged to adopt extreme rates of collectivisation of agriculture*':

> In our work we must adopt the *rates of the Civil War*. Of course I am not saying we must adopt the methods of the Civil War, but that each of us . . . is obliged to work with the same tension with which we worked in the time of armed struggle with our class enemy. *The heroic period of our socialist construction has arrived*.[9]

This was an obvious reference to the most famous book on war communism, *The Heroic Period of the Russian Revolution*.[10] Kaminsky more laconically, but equally dramatically, told the Sovnarkom of

[5] *Sdvigi* (1931), 157; these figures exclude auxiliary agricultural enterprises of various government departments; for alternative figures, see p. 105, n. 283, above.
[6] P, September 3, 1929.
[7] *KTs . . . na 1929/30* (1930), 122.
[8] P, October 1, 1929; EZh, October 3, 13, 1929.
[9] TPG, October 5, 1929; this is the 'revised stenogram' of his speech of October 3; for other aspects of this speech see p. 388 below.
[10] L. Kritsman, *Geroicheskii period Russkoi revolyutsii* (n.d. [?1924]).

the RSFSR that every peasant household was asking itself whether to join the kolkhoz or not, so that the pace of collectivisation bore '*a progressively accelerating character*'.[11] Syrtsov in a discussion article warned that the quantitative growth of kolkhozy was not enough, for a tractor covered by a kolkhoz flag was often turned into a 'tool of capitalism'; but he drew the conclusion not that a halt should be called to quantitative growth but that the level of socialisation in the kolkhozy should be increased, and that it was essential to resist 'the pressure of petty-bourgeois spontaneity', very strong in some parts of the kolkhoz system.[12]

During October, the campaign against the admission of kulaks to kolkhozy was intensified. The plenum of the Georgian party central committee resolved that kulaks should not be admitted to the kolkhozy; so, when land consolidation took place, they should be allocated land outside the kolkhozy.[13] Articles in *Pravda* expatiated upon the grave dangers which would result from admitting kulaks into the kolkhozy.[14] A village soviet chairman in Belorussia who was unwise enough to suggest that one section of the kulaks was '*not harmful*' and could therefore be admitted to the kolkhoz, was denounced for 'a clear manifestation of the Right deviation';[15] and an RSK in the Ukraine, criticised in the previous month for admitting kulaks to the kolkhozy, was now praised for its emphatic rejection of hundreds of applications for membership in which kulaks offered to hand over all their implements and animals.[16] In a despairing letter to Kolkhoztsentr a commune complained that it had been accused by the district party committee of Right deviation simply because it wanted to admit a peasant who had inherited a mill from his uncle, and had offered to hand over both his mill and his land allotment to the commune, and to join it as an ordinary member without holding office. The deputy chairman of Kolkhoztsentr replied sternly that kulaks preferred not to hold office but to influence the kolkhoz through their henchmen: 'the kulak is a wolf in sheep's clothing'; 'it is wrong to divide kulaks into good and bad'.[17]

11 EZh, October 9, 1929.
12 SKhG, October 15, 1929.
13 VI, 3, 1965, 15–16, citing the archives.
14 See for example P, October 22, 1929 (A. Karavaev, A. Mil'rud).
15 KG, 85, October 25, 1929.
16 P, October 27, 1929.
17 SKhG, November 6, 1929 (Odintsov).

In spite of these very firm statements, no clear advice was given on what was to be done with the kulaks. A resolution of the Tatar party committee described exile of kulaks and well-to-do peasants and seizure of part or all of their land allotment as 'one of the extreme methods for isolating kulak elements, which should be applied when kulak elements organise resistance to major measures of the party and government'. The resolution stipulated that kulaks could be admitted to simple production associations covering whole villages, but not to kolkhozy; but it provided no instructions about how the local authorities should deal with kulaks who did not 'organise resistance' when comprehensive collectivisation was carried out.[18] Three RSKs in the North Caucasus launched a 'storm attack on individual farming' on October 13, and decided to resettle their kulaks outside the kolkhoz land, but did not know whether they should be in one place or scattered.[19] In another part of the North Caucasus a member of a district party committee, enquiring ironically 'What shall we do with the kulaks? Kill them or organise them in collectives?' advocated the latter course, and denounced his opponents as Leftists.[20] Meanwhile the arrest of 'counter-revolutionary' kulak groups continued: on October 30, *Pravda* reported that in Dagestan a 'Russian farmers' party of agrarians' had been discovered and eliminated by the OGPU; according to the report, it had underground cells in a number of settlements, consisting mainly of former landowning sheep farmers who were now kulaks, and had worked out a plan for an armed uprising.

In this atmosphere of mounting tension October saw the successful climax of the grain collection campaign (see p. 104 above). At the end of the month, an editorial in *Pravda* called in stronger terms than some weeks previously for the transfer to the collectivisation drive of the large numbers of people engaged in the grain collections:

> *All the care, all the effort, hurled into the grain collections must be just as intensively used on another front of extreme importance, the front of collectivisation and of assistance to the poor and medium farms to improve and reconstruct agriculture.*[21]

[18] *Kollektivizatsiya* (Kazan', 1968), 111–12.
[19] EZh, October 13, 1929.
[20] P, October 29, 1929.
[21] P, October 31, 1929; for the earlier editorial of September 15, see p. 133 above.

On the following day Shlikhter, in an article entitled 'How to Revise the Five-Year Plan' proposed a striking reversal of priorities: the presumption that 'individual, scattered, small-scale peasant economy will continue to be the main base of agriculture for *many* years' should be abandoned in favour of a new theorem, 'the individual economy will be subordinate to (pri) the socialist sector'.[22] Kuibyshev also forcefully presented the now familiar argument that a remarkable change in the outlook of the peasantry made possible 'full collectivisation' in 'units of years':

> Instead of indecisiveness and sometimes even a hostile attitude to collectivisation from the peasant masses, we see this year a completely opposite phenomenon. *A historical shift (sdvig) has taken place, which in a fundamental and decisive manner has changed the feelings of the peasant masses and has driven them in a mighty wave to collective socialist forms of agriculture.*[23]

Grounds for this optimism were found in reports received by the authorities from the main grain areas. The available figures are confused and contradictory, but indicate a substantial increase in kolkhoz membership: thus the proportion of peasants in kolkhozy rose between October 1 and November 1 from 14 to 25 per cent in the Central Volga region,[24] and from 19 to 25 per cent in the North Caucasus.[25] In Khoper okrug, the enormous increase of the previous months (see p. 135 above) was exceeded in October; the number of households collectivised was reported as 53,000 (54 per cent) in a conservative estimate and 67,000 (68 per cent) in a more optimistic estimate.[26] This was not simply collectivisation on paper. Press reports claimed that immediately after the kolkhozy were formed in Khoper okrug the peasants threshed their grain at socialised threshing points, and then carried out sowing of winter

[22] P, November 1, 1929.

[23] SKhG, November 2, 1929 (speech of November 1).

[24] Report of regional party committee to central committee of December 1929, published from the archives in *Kollektivizatsiya* (Kuibyshev, 1970), 133. For much lower figures, also showing a substantial increase (from 7·5 to 14 per cent), see IZ, lxxx (1967), 89; see also Table 17.

[25] See p. 133 above and resolution of regional party committee of November 27, 1929, in *Kollektivizatsiya* (Krasnodar, 1972), 191.

[26] *Krasnyi Khoper*, November 16, SKhG, November 5, 1929; *Krasnyi Khoper*, November 21, 1929, however, more modestly stated that collectivisation had reached over 50 per cent in 'advanced districts' of the okrug.

crops and autumn ploughing collectively.[27] Even non-collectivised villages and individual peasants ploughed their land jointly, ignoring boundary marks;[28] and kulaks who had not been admitted to the kolkhozy insisted on taking part in joint ploughing, even though they were not paid.[29] As a result of joint cultivation, the area ploughed in the autumn of 1929 was said to be more than double that in 1928.[30]

The developments in Khoper okrug led to a clash between Kolkhoztsentr and the local authorities. Kolkhoztsentr earlier resisted the scheme to make Khoper an okrug of comprehensive collectivisation (see p. 131 above). At the end of September the special Kolkhoztsentr commission travelled from Moscow to the okrug, and was shocked to learn that 55 per cent of households had already joined the kolkhozy; this was the figure planned for the autumn of 1930. A member of the commission 'almost screamed' at an official of the okrug kolkhozsoyuz:

> That's incredible! You will have an exodus. Such collectivisation is impossible. It's an unhealthy drive for mere numbers of large kolkhozy.

He alleged that a considerable number of peasants joined because they felt obliged to, encouraged by 'methods of ordering about and pressure'.[31] Baranov, deputy chairman of the commission, and an official of Kolkhoztsentr, prepared a report which deserves to be quoted at length:

> The local authorities are operating a system of shock-work and a campaign approach. All the work of setting up kolkhozy is carried out under the slogan 'The more the better!' The directives of the okrug are sometimes twisted into the slogan 'Those who do not join the kolkhoz are enemies of Soviet power'. There has been no extensive activity among the masses. In one

[27] See, for example, *Povol'zhskaya pravda*, November 2, 1929 (Sheboldaev); according to KGN, 2, January 7, 1930, 60 per cent of the grain was threshed collectively in the okrug in 1929.

[28] *Krasnyi Khoper*, November 2, 1929; a photograph in KGN, 2, January 7, 1930, shows the boundaries between peasant strips being removed.

[29] *Povol'zhskaya pravda*, November 12, 1929.

[30] SZo, i–ii, January–February, 1930, 127.

[31] Reported in P, December 29, 1929.

case a kolkhoz was set up on the basis of a resolution by the skhod, and those who did not wish to enter were asked to make a special statement about why they did not wish to join. In some cases sweeping promises of tractors and loans were made—'You'll get everything—join the kolkhoz'.

These factors, taken together, have formally produced 60 per cent of collectivisation so far, and perhaps 70 per cent while I'm writing this letter . . .

If measures are not taken at once to strengthen these kolkhozy the cause may be compromised. The kolkhozy are beginning to break up. It must be borne in mind that large numbers of animals are being sold up in the okrug.[32]

The commission found widespread 'naked undisguised ordering-about', crude excesses and window-dressing; and one of its leading members (Brudnoi, from the Institute of Economics of the Communist Academy) recommended that the okrug should concentrate on the quality of the work of existing kolkhozy.[33] According to a later report, the chairman of the regional kolkhoz-soyuz, who had at one time been in charge of the kolkhozy in Khoper okrug, also failed to recognise that comprehensive collectivisation of the okrug was possible, while an official of the agricultural cooperatives, surprised at the rate of collectivisation, ingenuously asked: 'Aren't they all frightened by the OGPU?'[34]

Assailed by criticisms from the Moscow commission, and confronted with hostility or indifference from the regional agricultural agencies, on October 17 the okrug party newspaper, in an editorial entitled 'For the Quality of Kolkhozy' attacked the 'unhealthy tendency to quantity', and called on all party and Soviet officials to turn their attention to improving the internal organisation and efficiency of existing kolkhozy; the voluntary principle must be fully maintained by insisting that personal requests from peasants to join the kolkhozy should accompany the collective decisions of the skhods.[35] This shift back in policy was half-hearted and momentary.

[32] Cited from the archives in VIK, 4, 1962, 64–5.

[33] This summary of the commission's findings has been pieced together from later reports in *Krasnyi Khoper*, November 26, 1929; I, April 19, 1930; IZ, lxxvi (1965), 20.

[34] *Povol'zhskaya pravda*, November 7, 1929.

[35] *Krasnyi Khoper*, October 17, 1929; for other aspects of this editorial see vol. 2, pp. 77–8.

On the same day, the newspaper reported the formation of new kolkhozy; and two days later a headline, 'When Establishing New Communes and Kolkhozy, Think Seriously about their Quality', in itself indicated that the editorial of October 17 had not been taken too much to heart; the news items under this heading concerned either new kolkhozy or 'improvements in quality' which had been achieved by the expulsion of kulaks.[36] Within a few days of the editorial, Sheboldaev, Lower Volga party secretary, intervened with a letter to *Pravda* in which he extolled the rapid expansion of collectivisation in Khoper okrug, hailed the 'tremendous uplift and enthusiasm' of collective ploughing, and declared that normally only 5 or 10 per cent in each village opposed collectivisation. Local party committees had become 'general staffs of collectivisation', sending out dozens of people, receiving messages on horseback. This was 'a big mass movement, going far beyond the framework of our notions of work on collectivisation', and could be expected to spread to other okrugs. Sheboldaev admitted that there was some talk of 'pressure' being used to get peasants to join. But the overwhelming thrust of his argument was clearly directed against the Kolkhoztsentr commission, in support of the okrug party officials.[37] A few days later, it was reported that a 'commission of five' had arrived in Khoper okrug to work with the Kolkhoztsentr commission, and that another commission had arrived in Saratov from Moscow headed by Ryskulov, deputy chairman of Sovnarkom of the RSFSR, who was soon to become a key figure in the pressure for more rapid collectivisation.[38] The Khoper newspaper soon abandoned its more cautious line. On October 31, a further article again called for attention to the quality of kolkhozy, but its use of the term 'quality' was now more ambiguous than a fortnight previously, indicating the extent of the socialisation of the means of production as well as efficiency. Two days later, the newspaper displayed its split personality. An editorial praised collective ploughing in enthusiastic terms, and the formation of new kolkhozy was again extensively reported. But in the same issue a report from the rural

[36] *Krasnyi Khoper*, October 19, 1929; at the end of October, however, news items about new kolkhozy were less frequent.

[37] P, October 22, 1929; the letter was signed 'Sh———v'.

[38] *Krasnyi Khoper*, October 24, 26, 1929; *Povol'zhskaya pravda*, October 20, 22, 1929, first reported that the Ryskulov commission was to look into the ore resources of the okrug and then that it was investigating sovkhozy and kolkhozy, including the question of land disputed by two sovkhoz organisations.

department of the okrug party committee drew attention to cases of hasty collectivisation, involving threats to seize peasants' land if they did not join the kolkhoz, and also criticised attempts to form artels and communes when the peasants preferred the TOZ; a further article on the same day fancifully suggested that in many places kulaks had themselves initiated a hasty movement of a whole village into a kolkhoz or even a commune so as to discredit collectivisation.[39] Up in Saratov an article by Sheboldaev, published on the same day, unambiguously announced the opinion of the regional party. The article repeated much of his *Pravda* letter, declared that the 'party cannot occupy the position of "holding back" this movement', and reported that a counter-revolutionary organisation had been apprehended in Khoper okrug, consisting of 142 ex-tsarist officers, kulaks, traders and priests.[40] Thus in Khoper okrug, in which collectivisation was proceeding at an unprecedented speed, the higher party authorities again intervened on the side of the practitioners of unrestrained collectivisation; and the publication of Sheboldaev's letter in *Pravda* of October 22 made it clear that such local initiatives were favoured in high places.

(B) THE NOVEMBER PLENUM

The publication on November 7, the twelfth anniversary of the revolution, of Stalin's article 'The Year of the Great Break-through', was designed to dispel all doubts.[41] The article was published on page 2 of *Pravda*, not the most prominent position, but its impact was considerable: a hostile witness wrote 'It both reflected and deepened the sombre tone of the national life. Its every sentence became a war cry. Sycophants and bigots read into it a wisdom beyond the compass of a merely mortal mind.'[42] According to Stalin, the main feature of the break-through, which had occurred in the course of the economic year 1928/29, was 'the decisive *offensive* of socialism against the capitalist elements of town and country', which resulted in improved labour productivity, in

[39] *Krasnyi Khoper*, November 2, 1929.

[40] *Povol'zhskaya pravda*, November 2, 1929; the article also appeared in *Kommunisticheskii put'* (Saratov), 20, 1929.

[41] P, November 7, 1929; the article was undated in *Pravda*, but was dated November 3 in Stalin, *Soch.*, xii, 118–35, published in 1949.

[42] Lyons (1938), 266.

the solution of the problem of accumulation for capital construction in heavy industry and in 'a *fundamental break-through* in the development of agriculture from small backward *individual* economy to large-scale progressive *collective* agriculture'. As a result 400 million puds (6·6 million tons) of marketed grain, more than 50 per cent of all extra-rural turnover, would come from the kolkhozy and sovkhozy in 1930 (here Stalin based himself on the control figures of early October). The future for agriculture was bright:

> If the development of kolkhozy and sovkhozy proceeds at an accelerated pace, there are no grounds for doubting that in three years or so our country will become a leading grain producer, if not the world's leading grain producer.

The article strongly emphasised the change of mood among the peasants. They were pouring into the kolkhozy in 'whole villages, volosts and districts', indicating that the '*middle peasant has entered the kolkhoz*'. While Stalin condemned '"Leftist" phrasemongers' who wanted to introduce kolkhozy by decree, he reserved his main fire for the Right, and insisted that the only source of serious peasant dissatisfaction was the inadequate supply of machines and tractors. The shift of the middle peasants to the side of the kolkhozy was a decisive achievement, which explained the recent frantic hostility of class enemies within the country and of the lackeys of capital abroad.

Stalin's article, with its confident tone, formed part of a concerted campaign to encourage the enthusiasm of the party cadres and prepare the way for the plenum of the party central committee which was about to assemble in Moscow. In the first few days of November, the press carried numerous reports of resolutions from local party meetings attacking the Right wing.[43] Those followers of Bukharin who had not come to heel, such as Slepkov and Goldenberg, were castigated in the press,[44] and long reports were published in *Pravda* of the exposure of a Right-wing group in the Industrial Academy.[45] A *Pravda* editorial called for 'iron unity and

[43] See, for example, P, November 2, 10, 1929.

[44] See, for example, P, November 3, 4, 1929.

[45] P, November 3, 4, 5, 6, 1929; for the Industrial Academy see Carr and Davies (1969), 598; Khrushchev was a student at the Academy and after further struggles against the Right wing in 1930 eventually became secretary of its party cell (for a very confused account, see *Khrushchev Remembers* (1971), 36–41).

discipline'.[46] Shatskin admitted his 'serious political mistake' in appearing to lack confidence in the party leadership, and condemned his own activities and those of his associates as manifesting 'a certain divergence (osoblennost')' leading to 'elements of group behaviour (gruppovshchina)'. Sten insisted on the importance of the 'iron solidarity of party ranks' at a time when, 'transforming the foundations of the economy, we are at every step colliding with a most terrible force—the strength of the habits of millions and tens of millions'.[47] To a greater extent than ever before in party history, undeviating unity and loyalty was presented as essential to the victory of socialism in the USSR.

The plenum, which met from November 10 to November 17, 1929, was the first since the previous April.[48] The first three days were taken up with the directives on the control figures for 1929/30, introduced by reports from Krzhizhanovsky and Kuibyshev. The importance of collectivisation was emphasised throughout the proceedings. On the first day, Kuibyshev assured delegates that the 'middle peasant has moved in a huge avalanche' into the kolkhozy;[49] he then set the tone for the debate by vigorously condemning the Right for their 'infamous accusation' in the previous February that the party and the central committee were responsible for the 'feudal exploitation' of the peasantry: 'history

[46] P, November 3, 1929.

[47] P, November 12, 2, 1929; a declaration by Lominadze on similar lines followed on November 14 (P, November 19, 1929); both Shatskin and Lominadze now explicitly withdrew their proposal at the XVI conference to establish a national organisation of poor peasant groups. For Shatskin and Sten, see p. 118 above.

[48] At the time the only part of the proceedings to be published were the resolutions (P, November 18, 19, 21 and 29, 1929) (except the resolution on the Bukharin group, which was eventually published from the archives in *KPSS v rez*., ii (1954), 662–3), the speeches by Molotov on the Bukharin group on November 13 (B, 2, January 31, 1930, 7–25) and on the discussion on kolkhoz construction on November 15 (B, 22, November 30, 1929, 10–23) (both these speeches were published 'with some cuts'), the report by Kaganovich on cadres (B, 23–24, December 31, 1929, 50–68), the statements at the plenum by the Right-wingers Kotov and Mikhailov on November 12 and 13 and the written statement by Uglanov and Kulikov of November 17 (P, November 18, 1929); according to IA, 2, 1962, 195, Andreev's speech was also published. The present account of the plenum is based on these published sources unless otherwise stated; the references to recent Soviet publications are to their citations from a two-volume edition of the proceedings available only in Soviet archives and so far inaccessible to Western scholars.

[49] Chigrinov (1970), 41.

will laugh at these croaking prophets, who proved bankrupts within a few months of their croaking'.[50] During the subsequent discussion, according to one Soviet historian, 'the sharpness of the struggle with the Right grew', many speeches being entirely devoted to their delinquency.[51] Mikoyan reproached them with in essence favouring a capitalist development of agriculture while concealing this line by advocating the development of trade turnover and the normalisation of the market; as a result, they had of course underestimated the significance of sovkhozy and kolkhozy.[52] Other speakers attacking the Right included Goloshchekin (Kazakhstan party secretary), Eikhe, Chubar', Khataevich, Vareikis (Central Black-Earth region party secretary) and Gamarnik. An unexpectedly discordant note was struck by Syrtsov, who read out at length Baranov's memorandum criticising the imposition of collectivisation in Khoper okrug: Stalin called out reprovingly 'Do you think that everything can be "organised in advance"?'[53]

At the end of the debate on the control figures, on the evening of November 12, Rykov read out a statement from himself, Bukharin and Tomsky conceding that the past year could be considered a 'break-through' year and announcing the 'withdrawal of disagreements' with the majority. The statement also admitted that 'we mistakenly underestimated to a certain extent the powerful levers of influence (vozdeistvie) on the countryside which in the last analysis have begun to outweigh the negative sides of the extraordinary measures'. The group still insisted, however, that they had not objected to the existing rates of industrialisation and collectivisation, or the policy of a 'decisive offensive' against the kulak, but merely to the methods of achieving these policies, and they boldly asserted that the alternative methods which they had proposed at the April plenum 'could have attained the desired results by a less painful path'.[54] The failure of the statement to condemn the past attitudes of the group angered the majority of the committee, and was immediately followed on the morning of November 13 by

[50] Nemakov (1966), 82.

[51] Chigrinov (1970), 49.

[52] Nemakov (1966), 82; other citations from the speech will be found in Chigrinov (1970), 45, 49, and Moshkov (1966), 71–2.

[53] For Baranov's memorandum see pp. 152–3 above; Stalin's interjection is reported in IA, 2, 1962, 194. Chubar' was chairman of the Ukrainian Sovnarkom.

[54] Vaganov (1970), 246–7; VIK, 4, 1962, 58; passages from the document were quoted at the time by Molotov in B, 2, January 31, 1930, 7–9.

speeches against the Right from Ordzhonikidze, Postyshev, Yakovlev, Yaroslavsky and others.[55] Stalin denounced the statement as merely a retreat in order to prepare a new attack, praised the grain campaign as a 'mass offensive of poor peasants and middle peasants against the kulak' and declared that 'even the blind can see that the kolkhozy and sovkhozy are growing at an accelerated pace'.[56] Molotov criticised the Right for their 'clear lack of confidence' in the growth of sovkhozy and kolkhozy and described the recent stage, in which the '*middle peasant has moved into the kolkhozy*', as 'a new period of our revolution': the choice now was either 'attack the capitalist elements on the whole front, not failing in necessary cases to use extraordinary measures' or 'fold up one's line opportunistically under the furious counter-attack of the class enemy'. The Right were heading a move to 'the camp of bourgeois liberalism'.

After these bitter and protracted attacks on the Right, Kaminsky presented his report on 'The Results and Further Tasks of Kolkhoz Construction'. The keynote of the report was the change in the pace of collectivisation resulting from the movement of the middle peasants into the kolkhoz; he dismissed reports of compulsion and administrative pressure in Khoper and elsewhere—'it may have been used in some places, but it is of minimum significance'.[57] In the course of the report he referred with approval to successes in collectivisation not only in the main grain regions, but also in the North and in Bashkiria; thus this part of his report in effect endorsed an immediate movement towards comprehensive collectivisation in grain-deficit areas and in the national republics. He also pressed for the rapid completion of comprehensive collectivisation in the grain areas, arguing that in those areas in which 50 per cent of households were already collectivised, the remainder could be expected to join not in years, but in months. If agricultural machinery were supplied on a substantial scale, the overwhelming majority of poor and middle peasant households in the main areas producing grain and industrial crops would be collectivised in 1½–2 years (i.e. by the middle or end of 1931).[58] This was a much more dramatic

[55] VIK, 4, 1962, 58.

[56] VIK, 4, 1962, 67; Danilov, ed. (1963), 97; Vaganov (1970), 248; Stalin, *Soch.*, xii, 389; the expression 'even the blind can see...' was favoured by Stalin at this time.

[57] Nemakov (1966), 78, 83.

[58] Ivnitskii (1972), 88.

foreshortening of the prospects for collectivisation than had previously been indicated by any official spokesman. Kaminsky argued that, in spite of the weaknesses of this stormily developing movement, no 'obstructive' measures must be put in its way. He also gave strong backing to large and giant kolkhozy, and to further socialisation (see vol. 2, pp. 40, 78).[59] Kaminsky summed up the aspirations behind mass collectivisation in a quotation from a poor peasant from the Black-Earth region, offered perhaps to counter Syrtsov:

> I have lived my whole life among the batraks. The October revolution gave me land, I got credit from year to year, I got a poor horse, I can't work the land, my children are ragged and hungry, I simply can't manage to improve my farm in spite of the help of the Soviet authorities. I think there's only one way out: join a tractor column, back it up and get it going.[60]

As in his report to the central committee in September, Kaminsky argued that kulaks should be excluded from all kolkhozy and that measures of legal repression against them should be stepped up.[61] The brief accounts available of the sections of his report dealing with kolkhoz organisation indicate that he was by no means uncritical of the existing situation: the supply of machinery was insufficient, labour discipline was poor, there was too much egalitarianism and too much personal consumption.[62] But none of these deficiencies led him to conclude that the pace of collectivisation should be restrained: in the autumn of 1929, it seemed to the leaders that improved organisation and greater effort could solve all problems.

In the discussion which followed, Andreev reported that in the North Caucasus 25–30 per cent of households were already collectivised; comprehensive collectivisation had already been achieved in whole villages and even districts.[63] The 'main middle-peasant mass' were 'on the threshold' or 'with one foot over the

[59] VIK, 4, 1962, 59; VI, 3, 1965, 3; Chigrinov (1970), 47–8; Danilov, ed. (1963), 97.

[60] VIK, 4, 1962, 56.

[61] VIK, 4, 1962, 67.

[62] VIK, 4, 1962, 59–60.

[63] Nemakov (1966), 78–9.

threshold' of collectivisation.[64] In the North Caucasus about 50 per cent of households could be collectivised in 1929/30 and it would be very difficult but possible to complete collectivisation in the main by the summer of 1931.[65] While the expression 'complete in the main' is somewhat ambiguous, Andreev's proposal represents a considerable advance on his previous statements. While proposing to accelerate the pace of collectivisation, Andreev revealed a certain hesitancy about the consequences of the June decision to exclude kulaks from all kolkhozy in the North Caucasus. He explained that while the kulaks would be 'isolated' at first, they would in the future be allowed to play a part within the socialised economy.[66] Mikoyan, in a later speech to the plenum, warned that it would be 'extremely dangerous to admit kulaks to kolkhozy in the early stages of organisation', but also argued that 'when we have organised the kolkhozy firmly and strengthened them we will perhaps admit the kulak, because where are we to put him?'[67]

Speaking after Andreev on November 14 or 15, Kubyak, People's Commissar for Agriculture of the RSFSR, criticised some party organisations which tended to introduce collectivisation everywhere simultaneously, and complained that collectivisation was badly organised even when it took place on a voluntary basis.[68] From the brief published accounts of his speech, it is impossible to judge how far, if at all, it was substantially critical of Kaminsky's report. Sheboldaev, who spoke after Kubyak, evidently displayed no hesitation about the pace of collectivisation advocated by Kaminsky. While only a brief extract from Sheboldaev's speech has been published, a long article in *Pravda* presented his views. In the article he extolled the virtues of Khoper okrug, including its experience with 'horse columns'; in the absence of sufficient tractors 'simple unification and aggregation of farms' would increase labour productivity' even without tractors. He asserted that collectivisation in Khoper okrug was 'a spontaneous movement of the masses of poor and middle peasants', though he now spoke of 'no more than 10–12 per cent' voting against or abstaining from the proposals of collectivisation, as compared with the figure of 5–10 per cent

[64] Moshkov (1966), 57–8.
[65] VI, 3, 1965, 5.
[66] VI, 4, 1958, 79; VIK, 2, 1964, 67; this passage is cited in full in Lewin (1968), 474.
[67] Ivnitskii (1972), 163.
[68] VIK, 1, 1964, 33.

opposition which he gave three weeks previously. General conclusions could be drawn from the Khoper experience:

> Evidently the acceleration of the kolkhoz movement, about which until recently we only dreamed, has become a fact. Under the Leninist leadership of the party, correct relations with the middle peasant were preserved, and this peasantry now, by entering the kolkhozy, is making it clear that it has firmly chosen the path of the proletariat, constructing a socialist society.

The 'tremendous potential of socialising the main agricultural processes' would be best realised in 'large kolkhozy of 30–40,000 hectares and more' (this would mean only a few kolkhozy in each district, and would thus fit in with Kaminsky's ambitious conception). Sheboldaev anticipated the collectivisation of the whole Lower Volga region in '1½–2 years' (i.e. by the spring or autumn of 1931), adding 'this will evidently not be confined to the Lower Volga'. There was a danger that the selling up of animals and inefficiency would at first lead to a decline in the productive forces of the countryside, but in spite of this

> the party cannot take the attitude of 'restraining' this movement. This would be wrong from a political and an economic point of view. The party must do everything possible to put itself at the head of this movement and lead it into organised channels. At present this mass movement has undoubtedly overwhelmed the local authorities, and hence there is a danger that it will be discredited.[69]

In his speech at the plenum, he reported that 25 per cent of households were now collectivised in the Lower Volga as compared with 8 per cent three months previously, and declared that the Lower Volga region would also be an area of comprehensive collectivisation 'in a year or a year-and-a-half' (i.e. by the end of 1930 or middle of 1931);[70] it was unclear whether this meant that the establishment of comprehensive collectivisation would merely be under way in the whole region, or be completed. He also urged that, as the party was not yet prepared to cope with the kolkhoz

[69] P, November 15, 1929.
[70] Nemakov (1966), 79; Ivnitskii (1972), 89.

movement, a special permanent commission should be established in the central committee as a collective organ, with the remit of solving the major questions of the transition to socialism of the countryside and providing daily guidance to the kolkhoz movement.[71] This proposal has been interpreted by both Soviet and Western historians as an attempt to restrain the pace of collectivisation.[72] It is clear from his *Pravda* article, however, that Sheboldaev was one of the most vigorous advocates of more rapid collectivisation. His proposal reflected the disquiet of regional party secretaries at the woolliness or complete absence of directives on key issues from the central party authorities; such complaints recurred frequently in the next few months.

A long speech by Molotov on November 15 was published in the party journal a fortnight later, and exercised a substantial influence on the further development of the kolkhoz movement.[73] He began by citing Lenin's *Left-wing Communism* in defence of the view that the transformation of the petty commodity producers requires 'strictest centralisation and discipline within the party of the proletariat' in order to prevent the proletariat from relapsing, under pressure from petty-bourgeois spontaneity, into 'petty-bourgeois spinelessness, disintegration, individualism and alternate moods of exaltation and dejection'. Turning to 'questions of the present day', he claimed that in collectivisation as in other matters the authorities were too bureaucratic and in consequence were lagging behind the poor and middle peasants. The pace of collectivisation, according to Molotov, was 'really frantic'. The North Caucasus would obviously achieve more than 50 per cent collectivisation in the course of next year, so that 'in the main it will already have been collectivised during 1930'; the Lower Volga was keeping up with this, and the other major grain regions were not far behind. This constituted a substantial modification of Andreev's proposal, startling enough in

[71] Danilov, ed. (1963), 98; VIK, 1, 1964, 33; according to the latter source, 'this proposal was accepted', but, if so, nothing appears to have eventuated except the temporary Politburo commission (see p. 185 below).

[72] For example Abramov in Danilov, ed. (1963), 98; Lewin (1968), 461.

[73] It appears from recent Soviet articles that Molotov made two speeches on agriculture at the plenum: one on November 15, the other a report on the proposal to form an all-Union Narkomzem (Nemakov (1966), 84, gives references to pp. 50–2 and VI, 3, 1965, to p. 90 of the second volume of the archive copy of the proceedings, and speeches by other delegates occur on intervening pages; Danilov, ed. (1963), 97, refers to the report by Molotov on Narkomzem). It is unclear which part of the *Bol'shevik* article was delivered when.

itself, to complete the collectivisation of the North Caucasus in the main by the summer of 1931 and of Sheboldaev's to collectivise all the Lower Volga region by the spring or autumn of 1931. Molotov also insisted that 'next autumn [i.e. in the autumn of 1930] we shall probably already be able to see that collectivisation will be completed in the main not only in a single region, not only in the North Caucasus', which was a clear advance on Andreev, and he added for good measure 'it seems to me that in the near future, and as soon as next year, we shall be able to talk not only of collectivised regions but also of collectivised republics'.[74] In later passages in his speech Molotov eschewed all caution. He argued that the five-year plan must be ignored for all the main agricultural districts and regions:

> What five-year plan can now embrace the kolkhoz movement, when the countryside is turning everything upside-down and has really turned into a bubbling sea?

The organisational forces which achieved the grain collections could now concentrate on the spring sowing campaign, in which 'the question of comprehensive collectivisation of a number of very large agricultural areas will also be decided, and the question of collectivisation for the USSR as a whole will develop in a completely new fashion':

> We must think not about the five-year plan but about the remaining few months of the winter of 1929/30. November, December, January, February and March—this is what remains for us to prepare for the spring sowing campaign. In these 4½ months we must carry out tremendous work . . . Inasmuch as messrs. the imperialists have not so far decided to attack us directly, we must utilise this moment for a decisive advance in the economic development and collectivisation of millions of peasant households. Therefore, if we are not to fall down on the job, we must utilise the next months, weeks and days on the new tasks which now face us in their full magnitude.

[74] The latter passage, which does not appear in such strong terms in the published version, is cited in Danilov, ed. (1963), 97, and is attributed to the report on the all-Union Narkomzem.

The remainder of the speech dealt with questions of kolkhoz organisation, and was much vaguer: significantly it called upon the kolkhozy to model themselves on sovkhozy, and urged a huge increase in their socialised funds (see vol. 2, pp. 3, 78). He warned emphatically against the danger of kulaks penetrating the kolkhoz, and, in a passage which was later frequently quoted, discussed the future of the kulak in terms more ruthless than any yet heard from a Politburo member: 'Treat the kulak as a most cunning and still undefeated enemy'.

Molotov's speeches at the plenum were undoubtedly designed to persuade the leading local party officials to press ahead with collectivisation at breakneck speed; and recent Soviet historians have placed the major blame on Molotov, together with Kaminsky and the silent but evidently assenting Stalin, for the developments which followed in the next few months.[75] A member of the central committee, reporting back after the plenum to the Ivanovo-Voznesensk party aktiv, remarked, in evident reference to the atmosphere created by Molotov's speech, 'at this plenum of the central committee we felt entirely that really a terribly small amount of time is available for collectivisation, that we almost have no chance of preparing properly for it: only this winter is at our disposal, because the spring sowing campaign will be of decisive significance as a basic turning point of the main masses into the collectives'.[76]

At a further sitting of the plenum Kosior presented a report on the development of agriculture and work in the countryside in the Ukraine, arguing that the only way to progress in agriculture was through the kolkhoz.[77] He frankly admitted that in reports from dozens of villages comprehensive collectivisation was 'blown up and artificially created; the population did not participate in it and knew nothing about it',[78] but argued that only by 'completely turning one's brains inside out' could the 'very many dark sides' block from view the general picture of collectivisation as a whole.[79] Kosior's specific proposals about collectivisation in the Ukraine are not known, and an article by Shlikhter published in *Pravda* at this

[75] See for example Chigrinov (1970), 48–50; VIK, 4, 1962, 64–5 (Ivnitskii).

[76] A. V. Artyukhina, on December 2, 1929, cited in Nemakov (1966), 85; Artyukhina was a member of the central committee and of the party secretariat.

[77] Moshkov (1966), 58; VIK, 4, 1962, 60; Kosior was Ukrainian party secretary.

[78] Danilov, ed. (1963), 96.

[79] VI, 3, 1965, 5.

time, while enthusiastically applauding plans to increase socialisation in kolkhozy, also failed to give specific dates for collectivisation.[80] It is reported that both Shlikhter and I. A. Gavrilov, chairman of the Ukrainian Kolkhoztsentr, stated somewhat modestly that collectivisation in the Ukraine would be completed in its general features by the end of the first five-year plan (i.e. by the autumn of 1933),[81] but in relation to the main grain area of the Ukraine Gavrilov went a long way to meet the ambitious goals proposed by Kaminsky and Molotov:

> The Politburo of the CC of the [Ukrainian Communist Party] has resolved in relation to the steppe part of the Ukraine to complete the matter in the next two years, i.e. about the same target as that stated by comrade Andreev; perhaps not by the early spring, but by the autumn, perhaps in spring of 1931 in the steppe part of the Ukraine the collectivisation of agriculture will in the main be completed.[82]

The uncertain locution was a reaction to the strong pressure to force the pace to which the representatives of the grain areas were subjected at the plenum.

Six resolutions were adopted by the plenum.[83] They included a resolution on the Bukharin group which condemned them for failing to renounce their past views, removed Bukharin from the Politburo, and sternly warned Rykov and Tomsky.[84] The resolution on the control figures, praising the 'spontaneous impetus of the mass of poor and middle peasants to collective forms of agriculture' insisted that 'the decisive success of the policy of the offensive of socialism against the capitalist elements is ensured and *the cause of building socialism in the country of proletarian dictatorship can be secured in an historically minimum period*'. It was optimistic about the grain problem: 50 per cent of extra-rural grain would be obtained from the socialised sector after the harvest of 1930, and this, with the further extension of the contract system, 'should result in the

[80] P, November 16, 1929; for this article see vol. 2, p. 81.
[81] VI, 3, 1965, 5.
[82] Ivnitskii (1972), 89.
[83] Apart from the resolutions discussed in the present volume, the plenum also adopted a resolution 'On Cadres of the National Economy', following a report by Kaganovich (*KPSS v rez.*, ii (1954), 632–42).
[84] *KPSS v rez.*, ii (1954), 662–3.

elimination of grain difficulties'.[85] The resolution on Kaminsky's report on the kolkhozy declared that 'the *middle peasant masses* have followed the poor peasant into the kolkhozy', drew attention to the 'transition to comprehensive collectivisation of districts and okrugs' and stated that the 'collective farm movement is already posing the objective of comprehensive collectivisation of individual regions'; moreover, the basis existed for a '*new movement forward*' in the reconstruction of the countryside during the spring sowing campaign. The resolution on the kolkhozy did not, however, commit itself to specific dates and percentages, and the resolution on the control figures retained their proposal that a sown area of 15 million hectares should be collectivised by the end of 1929/30. This was modest in comparison with Molotov's proposal at the plenum; the element of urgency conveyed by Kaminsky's report and Molotov's speeches, and by the tone of the proceedings in general, was muted.[86] The resolution on Ukrainian agriculture noted that the whole working agricultural population of the steppe regions would be collectivised within two or three years (i.e. by 1931 or 1932); this again was a relatively cautious proposition, especially as the resolution elsewhere declared that the Ukraine had all objective conditions throughout its territory for a faster rate of collectivisation than the other republics.[87]

The resolution on Kaminsky's report was also somewhat more cautious on the question of the kulak than might have been expected from the tone of Molotov's speech. It declared that the 'sharpening of the class struggle in the countryside' was taking the form both of an increase in open struggle, including terror in the form of murder, arson and wrecking, and of concealed disruption by kulaks who as members and even administrators of the kolkhoz were endeavouring to dismember it from within. The resolution called for a 'decisive offensive against the kulak, obstructing and cutting off attempts of kulaks to penetrate the kolkhozy'. There was no reference, however, to the expropriation of the kulak from his individual farm, still less to his expulsion from the village.[88]

Given the rapid expansion of the kolkhozy and the impossibility of making immediate use of the most experienced peasants, the

[85] *Ibid.* ii (1954), 627, 630.
[86] *Ibid.* ii (1954), 627, 643, 653.
[87] *Ibid.* ii (1954), 657, 659.
[88] *Ibid.* ii (1954), 643–4.

kulaks, the resolution on Kaminsky's report was greatly concerned with the shortage of trained personnel in the kolkhozy. Its most important proposal was 'to send out to the countryside, in the course of the next few months, at least 25,000 workers with adequate experience of political organisation'; these '25,000-ers', as they became known, were additional to leading party members who were due to be sent to the kolkhozy.[89]

A further resolution of the plenum, 'On an All-Union Narkomzem', noted that 'it is high time for the concentration of the leadership of agricultural production in a single all-Union centre', and called for the immediate establishment of a Narkomzem for the USSR so as to 'bring about unity in the development of large sovkhozy, kolkhozy and machine-tractor stations, strengthen the management of machinery supplies and electrification, agricultural credit and the training of cadres, and also strengthen work on developing enterprises to rework agricultural production'. It hopefully added that the initiative and independence of national regions and republics should be maintained.[90] As this was to be a 'unified' Narkomzem, the Narkomzems of the republics would continue to exist. The absence of a Narkomzem for the whole USSR was a long-standing anomaly, due partly to the desire of the party authorities to limit the influence of the agricultural interest at the top level of Soviet government, partly to the desire of the republics to retain their autonomy in the light of their very varied conditions. With the growth first of planning and then of state farming and collective farming, *ad hoc* organisations responsible for units engaged in production had already been set up at an all-Union level before Narkomzem of the USSR was established. These included Zernotrest and Traktorotsentr, and also Kolkhoztsentr, which had recently been transformed into an organisation for the whole USSR.[91] The management of agriculture was divided awkwardly between the Narkomzems of the republics, the various all-Union production organisations, Narkomtorg (responsible for the grain

[89] *Ibid.* ii (1954), 648.

[90] *Ibid.* ii (1954), 653–6.

[91] The establishment of Kolkhoztsentr of the USSR was referred to as a past event in the resolutions of the November plenum (*KPSS v rez.*, ii (1954), 646, 654), but, oddly, no decree promulgating its formation appears in *Sobranie zakonov*. Kaminsky was appointed chairman of Kolkhoztsentr of the USSR while remaining chairman of Kolkhoztsentr of the RSFSR, and the two organisations had a common staff. For Zernotrest see Carr and Davies (1969), 189; for Traktorotsentr see vol. 2, p. 19.

and flax collections) and Vesenkha (responsible for the cotton and sugar beet collections).[92] 'What would the position of industry be', one agricultural expert plaintively enquired, 'if it was all torn into pieces, if coal was managed by the Vesenkha of one republic, metal by another, and if it was impossible to transfer engineers from one network to another?'[93]

On December 7, the session of TsIK which followed the plenum formally approved the establishment of Narkomzem of the USSR;[94] and on December 8 Yakovlev was appointed as its first People's Commissar.[95] The appointment of Yakovlev guaranteed the subordination of the interests of agriculture to the needs of industrialisation; Yakovlev, as deputy People's Commissar for Workers' and Peasants' Inspection, had led the campaign for higher agricultural plans,[96] and Rabkrin was now at the forefront of the drive to increase the five-year plan in various industries. Four formidable deputy People's Commissars reinforced Yakovlev: Grin'ko (former deputy chairman of Gosplan and enthusiastic advocate of industrialisation), Kalmanovich (chairman of Zernotrest, a food commissar during the Civil War), Klimenko (chairman of Traktorotsentr, former Ukrainian agricultural and party official) and Yezhov (former member of the Cheka, and since 1927 deputy head of Orgraspred, the personnel allocation department of the central committee, which came directly under Stalin).[97] Shortly afterwards Kubyak was replaced by A. I. Muralov as People's Commissar for Agriculture of the RSFSR.[98] This was not a team of 'yes-men', for Grin'ko was noted for the independence of his approach, and Klimenko is recorded as resisting unrealistic grain

[92] P, November 4, 1929.

[93] P, October 6, 1929.

[94] SZ, 1929, art. 718.

[95] SZ, 1929, part ii, art. 278. A decree of January 6, 1930, laid down the major tasks of the new commissariat (SZ, 1930, art. 44), but a further decree of January 13 postponed the approval of its Statute to January 1, 1931 (SZ, 1930, art. 38); this presumably means that Zernotrest, Kolkhoztsentr and Traktorotsentr were not formally subordinated to it.

[96] See Wheatcroft (1974), 114–15, 134, 148; for a critical biography of Yakovlev see BP (Prague), lxxv (January 1930), 2.

[97] SZ, 1929, ii, art. 292, dated December 16; for brief biographies see SKhG, December 16, 1929.

[98] KG, 104, December 30, 1929; Muralov was an old Bolshevik and professional agronomist from a peasant family, whose competence later impressed visiting foreign agriculturalists (private communication).

plans in September 1928.[99] But the balance was overwhelmingly in favour of a radical policy towards agriculture.

The November plenum thus registered and announced a profound shift in party policy from the attempt at gradual social reconstruction which had prevailed throughout the 1920s to the establishment of whole villages, districts, okrugs and even regions in which collectivisation was complete, and in which the kulak had no place. The absence of precise dates in the resolutions was less significant than the endorsement of the view that socialism could be constructed within '*an historically minimum period*' and that considerable progress could be made with the reconstruction of the countryside during the spring sowing campaign of 1930. From the November plenum onwards, it was undisputed doctrine—though nowhere stated in the resolutions—that individual agriculture had broken down and that all hopes for the future expansion of agriculture must rest on the kolkhozy and the sovkhozy. This marked a drastic shift of approach from that taken by Stalin and the April plenum; he clearly assumed at that time that individual agriculture would continue to predominate for a number of years, even though the market relationship with the individual peasant was being replaced by direct exchange through contracts. Andreev at the November plenum recognised 'something like a state of breakdown in the individual peasant economy, especially in the North Caucasus'; 'however hard we might try now to provide incentives to improve it, this cannot now give a decisive result', and the individual peasant economy would not solve the grain and especially the livestock problem.[100] From the standpoint of the party leadership this diagnosis was patently realistic: whatever the latent possibilities for individual peasant farming in the past, by November 1929 inflation had progressed so far that only a drastic revision of the whole economic programme could have restored to the peasant his willingness to produce and sell to the state in increasing quantities. With the abandonment of the attempt to link the peasant with the state sector through the market and economic incentives, cynicism about individual peasant farming prevailed in official thinking. 'Every peasant', a Narkomzem official told Hindus in 1929 or 1930, 'has his own five-year plan, at the end of which he wants to attain to the position of a *koolack*'; and at the other

[99] See Wheatcroft (1974), 143.
[100] Moshkov (1966), 57–8.

end of the state machine a student acting as a plenipotentiary in a kolkhoz remarked to the same visitor, 'Do you know what the chief trouble is with our *muzhiks*? . . . They all want to become *kool-acks*.'[101] With surprising frankness, Vareikis wrote in *Pravda*, a few weeks after the plenum:

> There is nothing surprising in the fact that the peasant, living for centuries as a small individual master (khozyaichik) is often subject to petty-bourgeois tendencies to grab, wreck and plunder. This is indeed the nature of the petty proprietor, that his personal interest always comes out on top, and dominates over the social interest.[102]

Nor would the peasant economy advance technologically. Kosior argued at the plenum that the pre-war level of marketed production could not be restored within the framework of individual agriculture in the Ukraine, where 2·1 of its 5·3 million households possessed neither a horse nor a pair of oxen.[103] Stalin assured the conference of marxist agrarians a few weeks later that 'everyone knows that individual labour, equipped with old and already useless tools of production, does not give the profit which is required to be able to live tolerably, and consistently improve one's material position, develop one's culture and come out on to the broad road of socialist consturction'; tens of millions of hectares of land were available, but could not be cultivated by the peasant with his 'pitiable tools'.[104]

While the individual peasant economy was thought to be in a blind alley, the events of the past few months seemed to the party leaders to have demonstrated that the power and influence of the regime in the countryside was now sufficient to mould the peasantry to these new purposes. Even without full-scale collectivisation, a well-organised campaign, using the full authority of the state, together with such support in the countryside as could be mustered, had obtained grain from the peasants in unprecedented quantities. The result of the experiment of introducing comprehensive collectivisation in the course of a few weeks in such districts as Chapaev in the Central Volga, and above all in Khoper okrug,

[101] Hindus (1934), 70, 177. Hindus was an American journalist who retained close ties with his native Central Russian village.

[102] P, December 31, 1929.

[103] Moshkov (1966), 58; VIK, 4, 1962, 60.

[104] *Soch.*, xii, 159, 155.

seemed to demonstrate that the methods of the grain collections could be successfully applied to collectivisation.[105] On a very favourable interpretation the events in these areas seemed to indicate that the middle peasant, recognising the impossibility of developing his own economy satisfactorily, allured by the prospects of mechanisation, would succumb to the arguments of the workers' brigades and the other plenipotentiaries and sign up for the kolkhoz: this optimistic diagnosis of the situation in the countryside, based on slender evidence, lay behind the brazen assertions about the 'impetus' of middle peasants towards the kolkhozy.

Although the policy of immediate collectivisation was a hasty improvisation in face of a serious crisis, it was not seen by the leaders or their supporters as a desperate remedy for a mortal sickness. On the contrary, this was for them a time of great hope. The substantial industrial progress of the past three years and the burgeoning capital construction in industry in the summer of 1929 provided a basis for believing that the vast programmes of the revised five-year plans might be achieved. The successful development of industry would in turn make possible within a very few years the supply of agricultural machinery and fertilisers which would transform agricultural production (see pp. 392–4 below). Meanwhile, to those imbued with an optimistic revolutionary faith, the apparently favourable outcome of joint autumn ploughing with oxen in the Khoper okrug seemed to provide adequate evidence that in the next year or two the kolkhozy could achieve some improvement in production while awaiting the massive supply of tractors, and the success of the autumn sowing campaign generally seemed to indicate that comprehensive collectivisation could be undertaken without damage to agricultural production.

This broad programme of advance was not seriously challenged at the November plenum. Nor was there any objection to the important corollary that a condition for success was the isolation of the kulaks and their supporters, whose increased hostility to the policies of the regime seemed to have been demonstrated in the course of the grain collections and the initial efforts to collectivise. All accepted and perhaps most shared the common faith that within a few years industrialisation could be achieved, agriculture could be

[105] Informative and fairly frank articles describing the collectivisation of Chapaev district appeared in the agricultural newspaper at the time of the plenum (SKhG, November 7, 15, 20, 1929).

transformed; this sharply distinguished them from the Right wing in the party and from the vast majority of the non-party specialists. It was by now assumed by everyone, in practice, if not in principle, that in the next year or two the growth of the kolkhozy would outstrip the supply of tractors. What was not yet agreed, within this common framework, was the pace of development and the tactics of the offensive. The critical remarks of Syrtsov and Kubyak and the caution of Andreev and the Ukrainian leaders turned on whether collectivisation in the major grain-surplus areas should take three years or be pressed ahead in the next few months, and completed in the next eighteen months, as Kaminsky and Molotov insisted. Thus the less ambitious proposals still envisaged a revolutionary pace of change. Similar disagreements about the form of the kolkhoz and the degree of socialisation also remained unresolved.

It was now generally accepted that the power of the kulaks in the countryside must be destroyed, but much confusion remained about the nature of the offensive that should be undertaken against them. For Stalin, Molotov and Kaganovich this was an all-out war. At the plenum Molotov castigated the Right wing on the grounds that 'disorganisers in any army are not necessary, especially not in the army staff';[106] and Kaganovich reported enthusiastically to a meeting of Moscow party activists that the class struggle in the Ural Gigant kolkhoz was 'just like at the front'.[107] This approach to collectivisation reflected and encouraged the tension among local officials in the countryside. A *Pravda* report described the atmosphere in Khoper okrug:

> We are in Uryupinsk. It is a couple of paces from here to the front positions. The breathing of the front is clearly felt. At meetings, there are laconic and specific speeches, as in conditions of military tension.[108]

'This was war, and is war', a student working in a kolkhoz told Hindus in 1930. 'The *koolack* had to be got out of the way as completely as an enemy at the front. He is the enemy at the front. He is the enemy of the kolkhoz.'[109] Molotov recommended to a

[106] B, 2, January 31, 1930, 17.
[107] P, November 26, 1929.
[108] P, December 29, 1929.
[109] Hindus (1934), 175.

conference convened by the central committee that in the growing class struggle of the first few months of 1930 the correct tactics for victory was 'to break the enemy at the very beginning and deprive him of any wish to make any attempt to resist'.[110] Those at the November plenum who were less uncompromising than Molotov did not deny that the kulaks were an enemy, but, given the ease with which they could be captured, were concerned (though they did not draw this analogy) to provide proper working arrangements for their prisoners of war, and to ensure that they did not destroy their equipment before surrendering.

The November plenum thus drastically changed the framework of the discussion, or rather finally confirmed the change which was maturing in the previous few months. The completion of collectivisation was not a matter of decades but of a few years, and much could be undertaken immediately. The kulak was an enemy who could not, at least until the war was won, be allowed any terms but unconditional surrender.

(C) THE DRIVE FOR COMPREHENSIVE COLLECTIVISATION, NOVEMBER–DECEMBER 1929

The November plenum created an atmosphere in which the policies of the party leadership could no longer—at least for the moment—be challenged, even within the party. In a further statement, Bukharin, Rykov and Tomsky, more obediently than on November 12, but still with some ambiguity of wording, announced that 'we consider it our duty to declare' that in the dispute of the past 18 months 'the party and its CC have proved right', and promised to support the struggle against 'the Right-wing deviation and appeasement of it'.[111] This statement provided the basis for similar apologies from Bukharin's most prominent followers.[112] From the former extreme Left, Shlyapnikov, leader of the Workers' Opposition in 1920–2, reproved those communist groups who, 'tortured by a "worm of doubt"', believed that the period set by the party for achieving its programme was too short, and condemned 'rumours'

110 P, January 21, 1930; for this conference see p. 216 below.

111 P, November 26, 1929; the statement was dated November 25.

112 P, November 27 (Matveev), 28 (Maretsky and Astrov), 28 (Aikhenval'd), 1929; see Cohen (1974), 334–5.

of 'administrative pressure on the poor and middle peasants, allegedly "driven" into the kolkhozy'.[113] The climax of the campaign for party unity was reached on Stalin's fiftieth birthday, December 21, 1929; six and a half of the eight pages of *Pravda* were taken up with encomiums by Soviet and foreign communist leaders, unprecedented in their homage and enthusiasm. An article by Pyatakov, entitled 'For the Leadership', welcomed the birthday celebrations as 'a fact of great political significance', in which the party 'again demonstrated its unity, its solidarity, its readiness to fight decisively and firmly for the general line and support its leadership, elected and warmly supported by the party'; 'it is now already completely clear that it is wrong to be for the party and against the *existing* Central Committee, to be for the Central Committee and against Stalin'.[114]

Simultaneously with these appeals for party unity, the campaign against bourgeois specialists became much more strident. On November 10, the day on which the central committee plenum opened, the editors of *Pravda*, following the controversy about the size of the 1929 harvest (see pp. 64–5 above), condemned Groman's 'menshevik socialism' as 'the ideology of capitalist restoration', and a few days later Vaisberg, an active party member in Gosplan, attacking Groman, declared that 'the real danger of bourgeois miasmas and petty bourgeois bacilli still remains—disinfection is necessary!'[115] At the session of TsIK on November 29, Krzhizhanovsky insisted that 'there can be no apoliticism in our country; *he who is not for us is against us*'.[116] The principal non-party specialists on agriculture, including Chayanov, Makarov and Kondratiev's former deputy A. L. Vainshtein, published statements renouncing their earlier views and declaring their support for industrialisation and collectivisation.[117] But these declarations did not satisfy their accusers. At two special meetings of Gosplan specialists, the principal non-party specialists in Gosplan were bitterly attacked by Vaisberg, Strumilin and others; and the declarations by agricul-

[113] P, December 16, 1929; in a letter published in *Pravda* on December 26 he also withdrew his earlier criticisms of the state of party life.

[114] P, December 23, 1929; see also Lewin (1968), 450–2.

[115] EZh, November 13, 1929.

[116] *TsIK 2/V*, No. 1, 6–7.

[117] SKhG, December 12, 1929 (Chayanov and Makarov); VT, 1, 1930, 126–7 (Vainshtein, letter dated December 18).

tural specialists such as Chayanov were condemned as insincere.[118] At the second Gosplan meeting Grin'ko claimed that wrecking activity had increased since 1926/27, and that 'there is not a single leader of parts of our state administration who has not known one, two or three wreckers working beside him for years'. He made fervent appeal for unity:

> In the process of carrying out the five-year plan we physically sense, we feel with every fibre of our being, how essential it is for us to organise a social and political mechanism which leads 150 million people to act together, guided by a unified plan, a unified concept, a unified will, a unified effort to accomplish what is laid down in the plan.[119]

This was the atmosphere in which the drive for collectivisation was intensified at every level of the Soviet administration. While the plenum was still in progress, a *Pravda* editorial entitled 'On the New Stage of Collectivisation' called for 'further development of collectivisation at a reinforced rate'.[120] The agricultural newspaper repeated in the most urgent language the call for the immediate transfer of everyone previously engaged in the grain collections, which were now virtually completed, to the spring sowing campaign and collectivisation: 'not a single agronomist, technician or public official must stop in his office'; in the most important districts of the grain areas all poor and middle peasants must be collectivised by the spring.[121] Kaganovich rhapsodised about the future of the kolkhozy in his report on the plenum, presenting the Urals Gigant as his main example.[122] Kaminsky at this time went further than others in presenting the work of the party in the countryside in terms of a military campaign:

> The nub of the matter is to carry out all work in a military fashion, as if at the front. This means that after discussing an issue

[118] EZh, December 18, 26, 1929; one of Chayanov's principal critics was Vol'f, head of the agricultural section of Gosplan, later himself executed as a wrecker.

[119] EZh, December 26, 1929; the developments in Gosplan at this time will be discussed in vol. 3; for the campaign against Chayanov see vol. 2, pp. 40–1.

[120] P, November 16, 1929; for the term 'reinforced' (forsirovannyi) see Carr and Davies (1969), 32–3, 277.

[121] SKhG, November 17, 1929.

[122] P, November 26, 1929 (report of November 21); see also vol. 2, p. 40.

it must be put into effect immediately, all forces must be mobilised immediately to put it into effect.[123]

In the main grain-surplus areas sessions of the regional party committees responded to the proceedings of the central committee by adopting revised plans for collectivisation. In the North Caucasus a meeting of the party bureau on November 27 retrospectively approved Andreev's statement to the central committee and at the same time made some concession to the counter-proposal from Molotov. While Andreev had stated that collectivisation could *with difficulty* be completed *in the main* by the summer of 1931 (see p. 161 above), the bureau now dropped the qualifications, resolving 'to complete collectivisation *not later than* the summer of 1931' (my italics—RWD); it set up a commission on collectivisation, including Andreev, to arrange the details.[124] On December 4, the regional soviet executive committee advanced completion to the spring of 1931.[125] On December 12, the North Caucasus party bureau appeared to step back a little. It warned its national minority regions not to try to keep up with the general rate of collectivisation, and local party organisations elsewhere in the North Caucasus not to 'rush formally ahead in rates, or engage in phrasemongering, or in a formalistic bureaucratic approach to collectivisation', but to stick to the rates of collectivisation approved by the regional party committee. But it simultaneously announced a further acceleration, recommending them to 'develop immediately a frantic preparation of all forces, so that they base themselves on 100 per cent collectivisation by the spring sowing campaign [of 1930] of the best prepared districts and okrugs'; and endorsed a recommendation from its commission on collectivisation listing nine okrugs (including the whole of the Don area) and two national regions to be collectivised in this period.[126] The decisive push in the weeks before the spring sowing of 1930 recommended by Molotov

[123] NFK, 3, December 15, 1929, 66 (speech of November 28).

[124] *Kollektivizatsiya* (Krasnodar, 1972), 191–2.

[125] KG, 98, December 10, 1929; the date of the decision is given in *Kollektivizatsiya* (Krasnodar, 1972), 191n.

[126] *Kollektivizatsiya* (Krasnodar, 1972), 197–9, 735, n. 45; further material from the archives will be found in Chernopitskii (Rostov, 1965), 89–91; a recommendation in relation to eight okrugs was made on December 9, and the full list was proposed on December 11.

was clearly now established as the programme for the North Caucasus.

In the Central Volga, Khataevich reported to a plenum of the regional party committee and control commission on November 26 that at the November plenum of the central committee the party had posed to the three major grain-surplus regions of the RSFSR the problem of achieving comprehensive collectivisation during the sowing campaigns of the spring and autumn of 1930 and the spring of 1931 (this is a reference to the exhortations of Kaminsky and Molotov, as no such proposal appears in the resolutions of the November plenum), and commented 'we are, generally speaking, making for that goal'.[127] The Central Volga plenum resolved that comprehensive collectivisation could be achieved in the next 18 months (i.e. by June 1931), that it was 'a completely realistic objective' to collectivise at least 50 per cent of peasant households in the region 'in the forthcoming spring agricultural campaign (approximately by July 1)' and to go considerably further in three okrugs.[128]

In the Lower Volga region, the 'government commission' headed by Ryskulov (see p. 154 above) visited twenty kolkhozy and some non-collectivised settlements in the Khoper okrug. After these visits Ryskulov forthrightly condemned the view that the pace of collectivisation in the okrug was due to the use of 'naked ordering-about', and reproached 'certain comrades' with 'complete confusion':

> Some comrades are inclined to restrain this growth, and try to slow down the kolkhoz movement; others think that haste in the construction of kolkhozy is superfluous. In contrast to these opinions, which incidentally are without foundation, we must place before ourselves a precise and clear task: develop the rate of kolkhoz construction still further, and pull up districts which are backward in this respect to the level of the advanced districts in which comprehensive collectivisation has reached over 50 per cent.[129]

[127] Nemakov (1966), 85, citing *Bednota*, December 7, 1929.

[128] *Kollektivizatsiya* (Kuibyshev, 1970), 119–20; the plenum met from November 23–7.

[129] *Krasnyi Khoper*, November 21, 1929; the commission was reported to have been in Uryupinsk on November 16–17 (*ibid.* November 19, 1929), and to have left for Saratov before November 26 (*ibid.* November 26, 1929).

It was announced at this time that the okrug had proved to be one of the best suppliers of grain in the region, having delivered ten per cent more than its quota by November 20; in recognition of this success Mikoyan presented it with a motor-car.[130] Rapid collectivisation and ability to meet the grain quota appeared to go hand in hand. After the visit of the Ryskulov commission, the unfortunate Khoper party newspaper condemned its own now notorious editorial of October 17 (see p. 153 above), attacked Brudnoi, the member of the Kolkhoztsentr commission who took the same line, as a Right opportunist, and called in a headline for 'Complete Collectivisation of the Whole Okrug in 1929/30'. This was already a counsel of moderation, as 64·7 per cent of all households were reported to have been collectivised by November 15.[131] On December 12, a full page in the newspaper urged the completion of collectivisation in the okrug by January 1, 1930. Meanwhile back in Saratov the Ryskulov commission drew more general conclusions about collectivisation in the whole of the Lower Volga region: it was reported that 'comrade Ryskulov categorically stated that, having met face-to-face both the peasants who have joined and the peasants who have not joined the kolkhoz, he has not had a single complaint about compulsory involvement in kolkhozy, and peasants on the contrary complained of delays in establishing the kolkhozy in due form'.[132] The Ryskulov commission proposed that collectivisation in the grain districts should be completed by the end of 1930.[133] The regional collectivisation commission and agricultural department soon outbid these proposals, recommending that 80 per cent of all peasant households could be collectivised during the spring of 1930,[134] and the presidium of the regional soviet executive committee called for the whole region to be collectivised in 1930. Some resistance to these developments was evidently encountered. The presidium condemned 'certain individuals and groups who, fearing the unprecedented scale of the kolkhoz

130 SKhG, November 28, 1929.

131 *Krasnyi Khoper*, November 26, 28, 1929.

132 P, November 24, 1929.

133 *Krasnyi Khoper*, November 26, 1929; *TsIK, 2/V*, No. 6, 1; according to P, November 24, 1929, the commission proposed that collectivisation in the region, not specifying only the grain-surplus districts, would be completed by the end of 1930; according to KG, 96, December 4, 1929, it proposed that it would take two years, i.e. to the end of 1931.

134 P, November 29, 1929; EZh, December 4, 1929.

movement, claim that it is virtually a consequence of "administrative measures" and attempt to reduce the planned rate of collectivisation'.[135] A few days later a plenum of the regional party committee resolved that all poor and middle peasant households should be collectivised in 1929/30—i.e. by the end of September 1930.[136]

Thus by the beginning of December 1929 plans had been approved in each of the main grain-surplus regions of the RSFSR to complete collectivisation throughout their region by the middle of 1931 (by the end of 1930 in the Lower Volga region), and to complete collectivisation in a substantial number of their districts in the spring of 1930. Other regions also adopted more ambitious plans at this time. In the Central Black-Earth region, at least half the sown area was to be collectivised in 1929/30 and the whole region was to be collectivised by the end of 1930/31.[137] Comprehensive collectivisation of the Ryazan' okrug of the Moscow region was to be carried out by the spring of 1931.[138] In Kazakhstan 30 per cent of households were to be collectivised during 1929/30.[139]

The high reported level of collectivisation achieved at this time in some regions was as remarkable as the plans: by the beginning of December reports claimed that 30 per cent of all peasant households were collectivised in the Central Volga,[140] 50–60 per cent in the Lower Volga,[141] and by January 1, 1930, these figures had risen to 42 and 70 per cent; 48 per cent of households in the North Caucasus were also reported as collectivised by this time (see Table 17).[142] In the Lower Volga region, the main drive for comprehensive collectivisation was thus completed in 1929; and in the Central

135 EZh, December 6, 1929; *Krasnyi Khoper*, December 7, 1929.

136 Session of December 11–14, 1929, reported in P, April 27, 1930.

137 Plenum of regional party committee, December 6–13, *cit.* Sharova (1963), 124.

138 *Kollektivizatsiya* (Ryazan', 1971), 301–2 (decision of bureau of Moscow party committee dated December 11).

139 *Kollektivizatsiya*, i (Alma-Ata, 1967), 273 (resolution of plenum of Kazakhstan party committee, December 11–16, 1929).

140 SKhG, December 13, 1929; IZ, lxxx (1967), 89–90.

141 P, November 24, 1929, gives 50 per cent; Khlopyankin in *TsIK 2/V*, No. 6, 2, gives 50–60 per cent on December 2; Nemakov (1966), 92, reports from the archives the obviously exaggerated figure of 72 per cent for December 10.

142 Different sources give percentages ranging from 58 to 72 per cent for the Lower Volga region (*Nizhnee Povol'zhe*, 2–3, 1930, 184; I, January 5, 1930 (Ryskulov); EZh, January 12, 1930; and see Table 17, note [b]).

Volga and the North Caucasus, collectivisation was very advanced in many districts. In 124 districts, almost all in the grain regions, more than 70 per cent of households were collectivised as early as December 15.[143] Only three months before, the proposal to collectivise 100 RSKs during the course of the five-year plan seemed remarkably bold. According to the monthly reports by Kolkhoztsentr to Narkomzem, in the USSR as a whole, over 5 million households were collectivised by January 1, 1930 (see Table 16); this compares with 2 million on October 1, 1929, and perhaps 3 million at the beginning of December.

These impressive statistics are extremely unreliable. At this time of rapid change, when over most of the USSR the snow had already fallen, 'joining the collective' could merely mean a decision of the skhod which had no immediate practical consequences. At the session of TsIK in December Petrovsky aptly if despairingly commented that 'with the present general movement to collectivisation it is difficult to estimate the number of kolkhozy and the state of organisation they are in at the present moment'.[144] But even on a sceptical view they indicated a movement of vast scope,

[143] According to a report to the Politburo commission on collectivisation (see p. 185 below), the districts in which more than 50 per cent of households belonged to kolkhozy were as follows:

	Total number of districts in region	*Number of districts collectivised*	
		50–70%	*70% and over*
Lower Volga	96	16	51
Central Volga	97	11	8
North Caucasus	117	13	4
Central Black-Earth	147	11	16
Siberia	205	5	2
Urals	168	11	15
Moscow	117	1	2
Western	82	—	3
Ukraine	510	24	14
Other	834	25	9
USSR	2373	117	124

(IISO, [i] (1964), 270–1; information was not available for a number of districts).

[144] *TsIK 2/V*, No. 17, 16; see also note to Table 17 below.

and played their part in encouraging further increases in other regions.

These increases in plan and achievement led the chairman of the Lower Volga soviet executive committee to argue at the session of TsIK on December 2 for the abandonment of the slogan that the five-year plan for collectivisation for the whole USSR (20 per cent of all households) would be achieved in 1929/30; instead, the formula should be that the comprehensive collectivisation of the whole USSR would be achieved in 1929/30 and 1930/31![145] A little more moderately, Yakovlev, at the conference of TsIK members on December 6, estimated that 30–40 per cent of households in the RSFSR, as compared with the existing plan of 11 per cent, would be collectivised by the end of 1929/30.[146] The RSFSR plan for the spring sowing campaign approved on December 11 provided for the collectivisation of a sown area of 24 million hectares (including 6·6 million households) as compared with the previous figure of 15 million hectares: this was to include 300 RSKs covering a sown area of 12 million hectares, in which 75–90 per cent of poor and middle peasant households were to be collectivised by the end of 1930.[147] This corresponded to the sown area of 30 million hectares (over 8 million households), now planned for the whole USSR.

(D) THE DRIVE AGAINST THE KULAKS, NOVEMBER–DECEMBER 1929

The intensification of the collectivisation drive after the November plenum posed even more sharply the unresolved problem of how the kulaks were to be dealt with when whole villages or districts were collectivised. While the plenum was in progress *Pravda* published an article by Shlikhter which was harsh and uncompromising towards the kulak, and adumbrated, if still in somewhat vague terms, the emerging shape of party policy:

> We cannot re-educate the kulak, and moreover no educational tasks at all in relation to the kulak—apart from 'educating' him

145 *TsIK 2/V*, No. 6, 4.

146 P, December 7, 1929.

147 SU, 1929, art. 910; and see *Plan kollektivizatsii v vesennyuyu sel'skokhozyaistvennuyu kampaniyu 1930 g.* (1930), based on this decree.

by methods of undeviating and decisive class struggle with him—can be the subject of our solicitude and experimentation. Economic isolation, and, if it is needed in a particular case, the use also of administrative measures against the kulak—this is the line along which we will be able to find the specific forms of the most suitable solution to the problem of the kulak in a given place and conditions.[148]

In the same issue of *Pravda* an authoritative article by the agricultural journalist Azizyan, an abridged version of two substantial articles shortly to appear in the party journal, elaborated the case against admitting kulaks into the kolkhozy.[149] According to Azizyan, the motives of the kulaks in joining the kolkhoz were: to avoid the pressure of the Soviet state for taxes and grain; to hold on, either individually in his household plot or through the kolkhoz, to the best land, which he would otherwise lose; to hold on to his implements and machines, for which he might still be responsible through the kolkhoz when otherwise they would be sold at auction; and to enable his children to retain the right to education. To secure admission, kulaks pretended to be poor peasants or joined kolkhozy in other areas. Kulaks also urged resistance to the grain collections: 'the grain collections of 1929 were the litmus paper which defined the real social physiognomy of the kolkhoz'. Kolkhozy which were dominated by kulaks must be dealt with by a 'punitive policy (karatel'naya politika)', because of their political influence on the surrounding countryside. In the course of collectivisation the 'punitive policy' pursued against the kulaks at large must bring in poor peasant and batrak organisations to cooperate with 'our punitive agencies' so that the poor peasant was placed at the head of the 'organised rebuff to the kulak'. Azizyan's approach to the kulaks was a world away from Karpinsky's of five months previously (see p. 138 above). Karpinsky proposed that in villages which were completely collectivised the kulaks should be admitted to the kolkhoz on certain quite strict conditions; now the kulak was treated

148 P, November 11, 1929.

149 P, November 11, 1929; B, 21, November 15, 1929, 51–9; B, 22, November 30, 1929, 56–64; the account which follows is based on both the *Pravda* and the *Bol'shevik* articles (for other aspects of these articles see vol. 2, p. 79). According to Gershberg, (1971), 50, 144, Atyk Azizyan, who was head of the agricultural department of *Pravda*, was a tall and passionate Armenian with a loud voice.

as an incorrigible enemy, and increasingly severe measures against him were advocated and applied.

The struggle against kulak influence was now carried into the kolkhoz, and a determined effort was made to remould the kolkhozy for the new tasks of socialist construction. Kolkhozy which failed to carry out their obligations to the state were treated as under kulak domination (see pp. 100–1 above). The influence of the kulak was blamed for resistance to the socialisation of livestock in the kolkhozy and to the remuneration of the work of collective farmers strictly according to the quantity and skill of their work; this effectively undermined opposition to ventures which were later denounced by the party leaders themselves as extravagant and premature. Even the resistance by kolkhozy in Siberia to proposals from the okrug authorities for their amalgamation was attributed to kulaks who feared that the leadership of the kolkhoz might be undermined, while elsewhere in Siberia resistance of the okrug authorities to similar proposals from the lower district authorities was blamed on the influence of the pro-kulak theories of Chayanov![150] In the atmosphere following the November plenum the Central Volga region, which had long held out for a flexible policy of limited admissions of kulaks to kolkhozy, now fell into line: the plenum of its party committee ruled that kulaks should be expelled from the kolkhozy.[151]

Press reports about the struggle against the kulak became increasingly strident in tone. In Khoper okrug, according to the head of its kolkhozsoyuz, 'at least 15 per cent of households were deprived of the right to join the kolkhozy'; a correspondent reported that while 'the weak half of the human race' sympathised with the kulaks, collective farmers in conversation with the correspondent and the chairman of the okrug kolkhozsoyuz had been quite uncompromising, saying 'send them out of the village into the steppe' and 'put them in quarantine for fifty years'.[152] Reports continued to appear from time to time that kulaks were being displaced to the outskirts of their village. Thus in a village in the Black-Earth region during land consolidation 'the kulaks are put on the clay, far outside the village, and the collective farms and the

[150] P, November 29, 1929 (article by B. Petrov and others); for Chayanov's theories on the size of agricultural unit see vol. 2, p. 240.

[151] SKhG, December 13, 1929 (I. Shapiro); the plenum met November 23–27.

[152] *Povol'zhskaya pravda*, November 12, 1929.

poor peasant get the black earth near the vegetable plots'; a visiting commission also ejected kulaks from existing kolkhozy and put them out 'into the clay'.[153] The distinction of making the first major official decision to exile kulaks from their villages in large numbers is held by the Siberian party committee, which resolved on December 5: 'exile the most active kulaks from the districts of kolkhoz associations into Siberian districts which (in an agricultural respect) are uninhabited'.[154]

(E) THE POLITBURO COMMISSION, DECEMBER 1929

On December 5, 1929, against this background of feverish collectivisation, feverish preparation of plans for further collectivisation, and increasingly brutal hostility to the kulaks, the Politburo established a commission under the chairmanship of Yakovlev with the remit of preparing a draft decree on the rate of collectivisation in various areas of the USSR; it was given only two weeks to complete its work.[155] The establishment of the commission was not publicly announced at the time, and its proceedings are known only from articles based on the archives published by Soviet historians from 1962 onwards. No full member of the Politburo was appointed to the commission, but it included nearly all the key people involved in decisions about agriculture immediately below the Politburo level. Its chairman was Yakovlev, and its 21 members included party secretaries from important grain-surplus regions or republics (Andreev or his deputy Ivanov, Khataevich, Sheboldaev or his deputy M. Khloplyankin, F. Goloshchekin (Kazakhstan), Vareikis and Kosior), and (in Cyrillic alphabetical order), Bauman (secretary of the Moscow region and former head of the central committee department on work in the countryside), Belenky (Khlebotsentr?), Vol'f (Gosplan), M. Golendo, Grin'ko, Kaminsky, M. Katsenelenbogen (central committee staff), Klimokhin, I. Klimenko (Narkomzem RSFSR), Maksimov,

[153] KG, 96, December 4, 1929.

[154] *Sotsial'naya struktura* (Novosibirsk, 1970), 127.

[155] VIK, 1, 1964, 33–4; Ivnitskii (1972), 166; the commission's official title in its minutes was 'commission on districts of comprehensive collectivisation' (VI, 5, 1963, 25).

Mal'tsev (central committee staff), N. Patrikeev, Ryskulov, Stetsky and Syrtsov.[156] It was permitted to interpret its remit very widely. At its first meeting, on December 8, it established eight subcommissions on: (1) the rate of collectivisation (chairman: Kaminsky); (2) the type of economy of collectivised areas (Grin'ko) (see vol. 2, pp. 84–5); (3) organisational questions (Katsenelenbogen); (4) the distribution of material resources (Patrikeev); (5) cadres; (6) the mobilisation of peasant resources (Golendo); (7) policy towards the kulak (Bauman); and (8) cultural and political services in the RSKs (Stetsky).[157] These met between December 9 and 13 to prepare recommendations for the main commission, so this stage of the proceedings was particularly characterised by very great haste.

The rate of collectivisation, the degree of socialisation within the kolkhozy (with which the subcommission on the type of economy was almost exclusively occupied) and policy towards the kulak were at the centre of attention: Soviet articles based on the archives do not indicate that any substantial discussion took place about the internal organisation of the kolkhoz, forms of remuneration and other matters crucial to agricultural efficiency (the subcommission on organisation primarily dealt with the relationship of the kolkhozy to government and other agencies).

The discussion on rates of collectivisation was delegated to the board of Kolkhoztsentr itself, headed by Kaminsky,[158] which for this purpose was recognised as a subcommission. At its initial meeting on December 8, the main commission recommended that 'comprehensive collectivisation in the main grain areas must be completed in 2–3 years [i.e. by the end of 1931 or 1932] and in other areas in the main at the end of the five-year plan [i.e. September 1933]' or somewhat later.[159] This was considerably less bold than

[156] VIK, 1, 1964, 34; *Istoriya SSSR*, viii (1967), 548–9; Ivnitskii (1972), 166–7; for a possible twenty-second member, see n. 157 below. In practice Ivanov represented Andreev (VI, 5, 1963, 25). Andreev, Bauman and Kosior were candidate members of the Politburo.

[157] IISO [i] (1964), 266–7; VIK, 1, 1964, 34; *Istoriya SSSR*, viii (1967), 548–9. The name of the chairman of the subcommission on cadres is not given: it is likely to have been Yezhov, who wrote about the subject at this time, and was likely to have been a member of the Politburo commission, as deputy People's Commissar for Agriculture of the USSR (see p. 169 above; Kalmanovich, the only deputy chairman who was definitely not a member of the commission, was in charge of sovkhozy).

[158] IISO, [i] (1964), 266.

[159] IISO, [i] (1964), 266.

the proposals made by both Kaminsky and Molotov at the November plenum of the central committee, which envisaged the completion or near-completion of collectivisation in these areas at the latest by the end of 1931. Since the November plenum the three main grain-surplus regions of the RSFSR had adopted plans to complete collectivisation by the middle of 1931 or even the end of 1930; and collectivisation had in practice been pressed forward rapidly and determinedly in all these regions. In an article published in *Pravda* on December 9, which must have been written, at the latest, on December 8 when the main commission first met, Ryskulov, generally thought to have been close to Stalin at this time, appeared to agree with this proposal, as he suggested that 100 per cent collectivisation should be completed in the 'leading agricultural areas' in 2–3 years. But 'leading agricultural areas' need not be merely the grain areas; and Ryskulov, claiming that rates of collectivisation 'exceed the boldest assumptions', reported plans to collectivise the 'agricultural districts' in Nizhnii-Novgorod, primarily a grain-deficit region, by the end of 1930. He also strongly attacked those who, 'frightened by the unusual scale of the kolkhoz movement, try to explain it as a consequence of "ordering-about"—i.e. of the compulsory involvement of peasants in kolkhozy'. Ryskulov repeated his claim that in all the visits of his commission to okrugs and villages, no peasant had complained about compulsion (see p. 179 above), and added for good measure that there was no settlement on which the peasants did not intend to enter the kolkhoz.[160]

The recommendation of the main commission was not treated as binding in the course of the deliberations. The subcommission chaired by Kaminsky is said to have commented with an air of moderation that 'it is better for the central committee to have reserves than to adopt a decree which proves unrealistic'.[161] Nevertheless, as might have been expected with the enthusiastic Kaminsky in the chair, the subcommission recommended a considerable further speed-up. It agreed that collectivisation in the remoter areas need not be completed even by the autumn of 1933, but recommended that complete collectivisation, and it was made clear that this meant 100 per cent collectivisation of non-kulak

[160] For other aspects of this article see vol. 2, p. 84.

[161] According to Nemakov (1966), 93; but he may have confused the main commission and the subcommission (see n. 163 below).

households, should be scheduled for the autumn of 1930 in the Crimea and the Lower Volga region, the spring of 1931 in Central Volga and the North Caucasus (all these proposals merely reflected decisions already approved by the regional authorities), the autumn of 1931 in the Central Black-Earth region, the Urals and the steppe areas of the Ukraine, and the spring of 1932 in Siberia, in Moscow and Nizhnii-Novgorod regions, which were grain-deficit regions,[162] and in the rest of the Ukraine; most of the remaining areas of the USSR should be completely collectivised by the autumn of 1933. It also proposed that as many as 400 RSKs, including 30 okrugs of comprehensive collectivisation, should be established in 1929/30, including up to 300 in the RSFSR.[163] As far as the RSFSR was concerned, the proposal on the number of RSKs corresponded to a decree adopted and published while the subcommission was in progress.[164] The subcommission on the type of kolkhoz, under Grin'ko, took a similarly enthusiastic line about socialisation in the kolkhozy, with strong support from Ryskulov and Syrtsov (see vol. 2, pp. 82, 84).

The subcommission on policy towards the kulak, under the chairmanship of Bauman, included Klimenko, Ryskulov and Kaminsky; its recommendations were also signed by Belenky.[165] The subcommission resolved that 'the time is ripe for the question of the elimination of the kulak class to be posed in a specific form';[166] this statement was no doubt agreed with Stalin. The political prerequisite for the elimination of the kulaks as a class now existed; they had been politically isolated owing to the turn of the middle peasant towards the kolkhozy. The material prerequisite now existed: sovkhoz and kolkhoz grain had replaced kulak grain. At the same time the increased struggle of the kulaks against the kolkhoz

[162] The source gives the spring of 1931 for these three regions, but from the context this is evidently a misprint.

[163] VIK, 4, 1962, 62. According to VIK, 1, 1964, 34–5, these proposals all came from the main *commission* on December 14–15, but this appears to be an error; according to Nemakov (1966), 93, in the commission (*sic*) chaired by Kaminsky 'the opinion predominated that the grain areas should be collectivised in 2–3 years, and in five years and a bit for the whole USSR', but this was clearly the recommendation of the main commission on December 8, not the opinion of the Kaminsky subcommission.

[164] SU, 1929, art. 910 (decree of December 11): the decree was first published in P, December 13, 1929.

[165] IISO, [i] (1964), 273–4.

[166] VIK, 1, 1964, 34; VIK, 4, 1958, 80.

movement and Soviet power, through terror and counter-revolutionary conspiracy, made decisive action against them imperative.[167] The subcommission proposed that in RSKs 'a process of dekulakisation' should be carried out: means of production of the kulaks should be expropriated and transferred forthwith to the Indivisible Funds of the kolkhozy.[168] So far this was quite uncompromising. Its other recommendations combined unprecedented harshness with a more judicious approach than might have been expected in view of the tone which prevailed at the November plenum and in the press. Boldly arguing that 'it is obviously hopeless to try to solve the "kulak problem" by exiling the whole mass of the kulak population to distant areas or measures of that kind', the subcommission recommended that the tactics for limiting the influence of the expropriated kulaks on hesitant peasants should differentiate between three different groups of kulaks according to their attitude to collectivisation. The first group, actively opposing the socialist system and engaging in counter-revolutionary disruption, should be arrested and their families exiled to distant areas,[169] and according to some reports it was agreed that 'all measures of state compulsion' should be used against them (this implied both imprisonment and the death penalty).[170] The second group, kulaks who refuse to submit to comprehensive collectivisation, should be exiled to, or resettled in, distant areas.[171] These arrangements went further in systematically harsh treatment for hostile kulaks than anything previously proposed. But for the third group, on the other hand, anachronistically moderate treatment was suggested. They should be permitted to work in the kolkhoz for a probationary period of 3–5 years, without rights, after which, if they worked conscientiously, they could become full members of the kolkhoz.[172] Moreover, while no precise

[167] VIK, 4, 1958, 80–1 (P. V. Semernin); how much of the above account actually appears in the recommendations of the subcommission is not made clear in the source, which is in indirect speech throughout. The style is Stalin's.
[168] Ivnitskii (1972), 170.
[169] VIK, 4, 1958, 81: IISO, [i] (1964), 273.
[170] Khataevich's report to the bureau of the Central Volga regional committee, December 21, 1929 (IZ, lxxx (1967), 93 and Nemakov (1966), 99); this clause may have been added by the main commission.
[171] IISO, [i] (1964), 273; VIK, 4, 1962, 68; Nemakov (1966), 99; the reference to the distant areas may have been added by the main commission.
[172] IISO, [i] (1964), 273; Khataevich referred to a probationary period of only 2–3 years (IZ, lxxx (1967), 93).

proposals were made on how many kulaks should be in each group, it was stated that the majority of what were estimated, with their families, at 5–6 million persons, would be in the more leniently treated third group.[173] The published accounts of the subcommission do not mention whether the kulaks were to have land allocated to them for cultivation in addition to their work for the kolkhoz or whether they would receive payment from the kolkhoz. Two members of the subcommission, Ryskulov and Kaminsky, were vigorous proponents of extreme policies, but its chairman, Bauman, may have pressed for a more moderate approach.[174]

The proposals of the various subcommissions were discussed at a meeting of chairmen of subcommissions on December 14 and 15 and at a meeting of the full commission on December 16 and 17; the latter meeting was attended by representatives of various areas including Khoper okrug.[175] The commission appointed a further commission of nine members to prepare the final text of the draft central committee resolution: this was approved on December 18 and sent to the Politburo on December 22.[176] The recommendations of the three major subcommissions were all hotly disputed at the sittings of December 14–15 and 16–17. On both the pace of collectivisation and the degree of socialisation in the kolkhozy, Yakovlev, who does not appear to have been a member of any of the subcommissions, exercised a moderating influence (on socialisation see vol. 2, p. 84). At the session of December 14–15,

[173] IISO, [i] (1964), 273; Ivnitskii (1972), 171; at the main commission Yakovlev is said to have estimated that 5 per cent of peasants were kulaks, or 1·5 million households with a population of 7–8 million (Nemakov (1966), 99); 1·5 should evidently be 1·25 million—there were 25 million peasant households with five persons per household, and well-to-do households were larger than average (see p. 27 above).

[174] On Bauman's earlier attitude to the kulak see p. 142 above. The above account is based on IISO, [i] (1964), 272–3, VIK, 4, 1958, 80–1 and 4, 1962, 68, except where otherwise stated; the last-named source purports to describe the proposals of the *commission* of the Politburo but evidently refers to the subcommission.

[175] IISO, [i] (1964), 268; VIK, 4, 1962, 61; Danilov, ed. (1963), 34–5.

[176] IISO, [i] (1964), 277; VIK, 1, 1964, 35; the members of the commission were Yakovlev, Grin'ko, Sheboldaev, Bauman, Kaminsky, Belenky, Ivanov, Katsenelenbogen and Klimenko. The draft resolution was described by the main commission on December 17 as being on 'the question of okrugs of comprehensive collectivisation' (VIK, 1, 1964, 35); its title when it was sent to the Politburo on December 22 was 'On the Plan of Collectivisation and on Measures of Assistance on the Part of the State to Kolkhoz Construction' (IISO, [i] (1964), 277–8).

while accepting that there must be no lagging behind the 'spontaneous growth' of collectivisation, he also warned that it would be extremely dangerous to engage in 'any kind of ecstasy of ordering about, galloping ahead or excessive impatience; if this became widespread on a more or less substantial scale, it would threaten the movement with bureaucratisation, would run the risk of frightening-off certain strata of the poor and middle peasants from collectivisation, and of substituting parade collectivisation, formal collectivisation, for real collectivisation'; he also criticised organisations for a 'sporting approach' to collectivisation in which they tried to reach 100 per cent first. He was criticised in his turn by Sheboldaev and others, who denied that collectivisation was being forced artificially and insisted on more ambitious plans.[177] Eventually the commission approved and sent forward to the central committee a draft resolution which claimed that 'at least one-third of the sown area will be cultivated collectively by the spring of 1930', and proposed that the overwhelming majority of the peasantry should be collectivised during the five-year plan. '*Collectivisation of the main grain areas* should be completed in 2–3 years [i.e. by the end of 1931 to the end of 1932] (and perhaps more rapidly in certain okrugs and regions) and collectivisation of the non-grain areas in 3–4 years [i.e. by the end of 1932 to the end of 1933]'.[178] While these proposals were extremely ambitious, they were less extreme than those of the subcommission or than those which prevailed in the main grain-surplus regions; and they were accompanied by a proposed paragraph of the resolution which warned, using Yakovlev's phrases, both against restraining the development of the movement and against 'an ecstasy of ordering-about'; it specifically criticised the practice of establishing RSKs in districts where a high proportion of households were not yet collectivised.[179] Under Yakovlev's influence the proposals of the subcommission on socialisation were also replaced by somewhat more moderate recommendations in the draft sent to the central committee (see vol. 2, p. 85).

The course of the deliberations about the kulaks was more complicated. Policy towards the kulaks was raised at a discussion on

[177] IISO, [i] (1964), 269–72; VIK, 4, 1962, 63; Yakovlev's criticism of the 'sporting approach', presumably made on this occasion, is reported in Nemakov (1966), 92.

[178] VI, 5, 1963, 25–6; VIK, 1, 1964, 36.

[179] VIK, 1, 1964, 37.

land consolidation at the collegium of Narkomzem of the RSFSR held on December 13, the day before the meeting of the chairmen of the subcommissions. Unlike the proceedings of the Bauman subcommission, the proceedings at the Narkomzem of the RSFSR were partly reported in the press. If anyone proposed at the collegium that kulaks should be allowed to work as probationers in kolkhozy, as the Bauman subcommission had suggested, this was not mentioned in the press. But some members of the collegium proposed that the most stubborn and actively hostile opponents of collectivisation should be settled right outside the RSKs, and that other kulaks should be scattered in separate inconvenient allotments, rather than settled in groups (gnezda).[180] Kubyak, People's Commissar for Agriculture of the RSFSR, was even more uncompromising, and 'categorically rejected proposals to resettle kulaks within the limits of inhabited districts', adding:

> Let them take over new lands in distant districts of Yakutia and Kamchatka. Kulaks remaining locally can be put at the boundaries of the former land societies.[181]

The recommendation of the Bauman subcommission that the majority of kulaks should be allowed to work in the kolkhoz for a probationary period was also implicitly challenged by Vareikis in a report to the main commission about comprehensive collectivisation in the Central Black-Earth region dated December 15. He argued that kulaks should not be admitted *in any form* into new kolkhozy, or into areas where comprehensive collectivisation was complete or where MTS were operating; instead they should be sent out of the area or resettled on the most distant and worst lands outside the lands of kolkhozy: malicious kulaks and those not working the land themselves should be deprived of land altogether.[182] On the other hand, a report to the central committee from Khataevich, presumably submitted to the main commission, presented the situation in the Central Volga region, where the kulak was more leniently treated than in other grain areas, in more ambiguous terms, merely stating without comment:

[180] EZh, December 15, 1929.

[181] SKhG, December 15, 1929; Kubyak was replaced as People's Commissar for Agriculture of the RSFSR a few days later (see p. 169 above).

[182] IISO, [i] (1964), 274.

Practical work indicates the following proposals:

1. Provide the kulak with lands at the end of the fields of the rotation without sending him out of the village.
2. Provide the worst lands and land outside the fields and consolidate them in scattered farms which are not contiguous in order not to form kulak villages.
3. In individual cases—a proposal to resettle the kulak households beyond the boundaries of the region on uninhabited land set aside for colonisation.[183]

Some members of the main commission are reported to have opposed the view of the subcommission that the means of production of the kulaks should be expropriated immediately, on the grounds that this should await the completion of collectivisation.[184] According to Khataevich, the commission failed to reach agreement or to adopt a definite decision.[185]

The draft resolution eventually submitted to the central committee on December 22 closely followed the relatively moderate recommendations of the Bauman subcommission.[186] All means of production of kulaks in areas of comprehensive collectivisation were to be confiscated and transferred to the Indivisible Funds of the kolkhozy, and by the decisions of skhods and local congresses of soviets the kulaks were to be allocated distant land of the worst quality. After this, kulaks actively opposing collectivisation were to be expelled and exiled: the draft apparently did not divide them into two groups, and hence did not specifically provide for the exile of the most hostile to remote areas. Those of the expropriated kulaks who were obedient and carried out kolkhoz decisions conscientiously would be permitted to work in the kolkhoz without being given the right to participate in its affairs during the next few years (the period was not apparently specified).[187] The draft resolution, like the recommendations of the subcommission, apparently did not stipulate whether kulaks working for the kolkhoz would also retain

[183] *Kollektivizatsiya* (Krasnodar, 1970), 140.

[184] Ivnitskii (1972), 173.

[185] Ivnitskii (1972), 172–3.

[186] VIK, 1, 1964, 37–8; Ivnitskii (1972), 173.

[187] According to Ivnitskii (1972), 173, and VI, 5, 1963, 31 (Bogdenko), this provision applied to 'that part of the kulak family' which was well-behaved; according to VIK, 1, 1964, 38 (Abramov), the draft resolution simply referred to 'kulaks' who were well-behaved (both accounts were in indirect speech).

land for their own use or receive payment. This was a remarkable attempt by Bauman, evidently with the support of Yakovlev and Khataevich, to find a way of dealing with the kulaks which might eventually bring the majority of them within the framework of the kolkhozy; and, in the Central Volga region, which had only recently relinquished its policy of limited admission of kulaks to the kolkhozy (see p. 184 above), Khataevich hastened to state in the local press that kulaks could be admitted as probationers if they showed no opposition.[188] But an article about the Central Volga region published in the central agricultural newspaper at this time advised that 'it is not necessary to hold back from exiling individual kulak households beyond the particular district or even okrug',[189] and elsewhere the decision to exclude kulaks altogether from the kolkhozy was pressed forward unremittingly. On December 18, the presidium of the Lower Volga soviet executive committee extended the categories which were not to be admitted to the kolkhoz to all those fined or prosecuted under art. 61 for failure to deliver grain, and ruled that those not admitted to the kolkhoz should be allocated land of the worst quality which was distant and not continuous.[190] On December 31, Vareikis declared that the kulak, a 'malicious wrecker and grabber', must not be admitted to the kolkhoz, and the anger of the poor and middle peasants must be raised against him.[191]

(F) THE COLLECTIVISATION RESOLUTION OF JANUARY 5, 1930

During these final stages of the proceedings of the Politburo commission the first All-Union Conference of Marxist Agrarians assembled in Moscow. The conference was held from December 20 to December 27 under the auspices of the Communist Academy; it was primarily attended by academic agricultural specialists, but party and government officials, including Kalinin and Shlikhter, also played an active part; and at the end of the final session Stalin appeared unexpectedly and made his first public speech since his fiftieth birthday on December 21. At the conference the older

188 *Vol'zhskaya kommuna*, December 29, 1929, *cit.* IZ, lxxx (1967), 93.
189 SKhG, December 19, 1929 (P. Rubinov).
190 *Nizhnee Povol'zhe*, 1, 1930, 113.
191 P, December 31, 1929.

generation of agricultural specialists, and their attachment to the small family farm, were derided and denounced at length; and rapporteurs and delegates elaborated upon the virtues of socialised farming, and particularly of the giant kolkhoz with a high degree of socialisation (see vol. 2, pp. 41–2, 85–7).

In his opening statement Milyutin foresaw the 'most complete collectivisation' of the North Caucasus, the Lower Volga and the Ukraine within one or two years, and thus identified himself with the Kaminsky subcommission rather than with the main commission of the Politburo. In the next few years mechanisation, including mechanisation of livestock farming, would enable farming to become a branch of industry; at a later stage 'comprehensive collectivisation' would give way to 'comprehensive electrification of agriculture'.[192] In the debate which followed the advantages of socialist over capitalist agriculture were strongly stressed. Safarov argued that only socialist agriculture would be able to move forward from mechanisation to 'the widespread application of electricity to arable farming'[193] (this was one of the fantasies of the moment). Another speaker predicted that Soviet agriculture would be more successful than Soviet industry in overtaking the United States and Western Europe owing to the great disadvantages of private property to agricultural development.[194] The alluring prospects for socialist mechanised agriculture were not to be allowed, however, to inhibit immediate collectivisation: Stalin brushed aside lingering doubts with his firm insistence that collective farming had great advantages over individual farming even when machinery was not available (see pp. 391–2 below).

On the unresolved issue of what to do with the kulak, opinions were again divided. Larin was co-rapporteur with Milyutin at the conference, and discussed the question at length. He reiterated his long-held view that the kulak should not be admitted to the kolkhoz, but also pointed out that there were several million kulaks, and, as 'we do not hold the view that all kulaks and their descendants should immediately be shot', they would have to be re-educated. At first they should be allocated a separate isolated piece of land, cut down to a certain norm; but when it appeared that they were inclined to collaborate, all their means of production should be

192 *Trudy . . . agrarnikov-marksistov*, i (1930), 51–3.
193 *Ibid.* i (1930), 134–5.
194 *Ibid.* 205.

confiscated, and they should be required to undertake compulsory work in a commune under observation, later being admitted to membership. Larin thus broadly followed the line of the Politburo commission, but he added three important qualifications. First, pursuing his advocacy of a rapid transition to state farming as the only truly socialist form of organisation, he proposed that kulak implements and animals should be transferred not to the kolkhoz but to the state. Secondly, their probationary labour should be undertaken in a commune, where the socialisation of all means of production and of consumption would guard against their return to old habits. Thirdly, and here he was harsher than the commission, the kulaks should be resettled outside their own district for their probationary labour, because otherwise their influence and connections would make it extremely doubtful whether they would sincerely and permanently go over to non-exploitative labour.[195] During the conference, several agricultural officials expressed bewilderment about what should be done with the kulak in the absence of clear guidance: one intervened in a lengthy argument about agrarian theory between Dubrovsky and the supporters of Kritsman to urge that such practical guidance would be better than abstract polemics.[196] Karpinsky withdrew from the lenient position of his earlier article in the party journal (see p. 138 above), but argued that if the kulaks were not admitted to the kolkhoz the question of '*human material*' still remained: 'the question of some kind of "reworking", of some kind of "mastering" of the remnants of human material from the defeated capitalist classes in socialist society was posed by Vl. Ilich [Lenin] on the day after the revolution'.[197] But no other delegate supported Larin's proposal for the re-education of the kulak. Two delegates objected to the allocation of land to the kulak without payment.[198] Another delegate suggested that an earlier proposal by Larin that private traders should be sent to the Far East should apply to the kulak now that 'the question of the gradual elimination of the kulak is on the agenda'.[199] In his reply to the discussion, Milyutin, who was adept at the timely expression of opinions held at the highest level in the

[195] *Ibid.* i (1930), 75–6.

[196] *Ibid.* i (1930), 140–1 (B. Karklin, Belorussia), 376.

[197] *Ibid.* i (1930), 159.

[198] *Ibid.* i (1930), 339, 378.

[199] *Ibid.* i (1930), 140; this appears to be the only use of the phrase 'elimination of the kulak' at the conference prior to Stalin's speech.

party, declared that 'the heart of the matter is that comrade Larin is working out forms of contract with the kulak instead of forms of struggle', and reproached him for 'caring about the fate of the kulak and seeking to work out methods for his re-education'; this 'apparent radicalism' had 'nothing in common with a Bolshevik approach'.[200] Larin, for many years the heretical scourge of the Nepman and the kulak, now found his proposal to resettle 5 million persons for probationary labour outside their own districts treated as an heretical advocacy of leniency towards his old enemy.

In his remarks at the end of the conference Stalin strongly identified himself with the proponents of a tough line towards the kulak.[201] He described it as 'a fact of immense importance that the kolkhoz movement, taking the character of a powerful, growing *anti-kulak* wave', was clearing the way for socialism in the countryside. The party had 'launched an offensive along the whole front against the capitalist elements of the countryside', and this had given very good results:

> This means that we have gone over from a policy of *limiting* the exploiting tendencies of the kulak to a policy of *eliminating* the kulak as a class (likvidatsiya kulachestva, kak klassa).

This was 'one of the most decisive turns in our whole policy'. Until recently, the policy of merely limiting the kulak was entirely correct: in 1926/27, when there was no broad network of sovkhozy and kolkhozy, the policy of an immediate offensive against the kulak advocated by the Zinoviev–Trotskyist opposition would have been a dangerous adventure. The offensive against the kulak class meant breaking it, 'striking a blow against it so that it cannot stand up again'. The kolkhozy and sovkhozy would produce 700 million puds of grain in 1930 (11·5 million tons) and hence supply 200 million (3·3 million tons) to the state: as this was 'much more than by the kulak in 1927', it would more than replace what the kulak class had produced in 1927.[202] This made its elimination possible:

[200] *Ibid*. i (1930), 271; P, December 25, 1929.

[201] *Soch*., xii, 141, 166–70; the speech first appeared in P, December 29, 1929; for other aspects of the speech see pp. 391–2 below and vol. 2, p. 87.

[202] Here Stalin made a curious error. The figures he cited were out-of-date and much too low, and on the following day, December 30, he hastily published in

The question is asked on all sides: what about the policy of dekulakisation, is dekulakisation permissible in districts of comprehensive collectivisation? A ridiculous question! . . . Dekulakisation is now an essential element in forming and developing the kolkhozy. Therefore to keep on discussing dekulakisation is ridiculous and not serious. When the head is cut off, you do not weep about the hair.

Another question seems no less ridiculous: can the kulak be admitted into the kolkhoz? Of course it is wrong to admit the kulak into the kolkhoz. It is wrong because he is an accursed enemy of the kolkhoz movement.

Stalin had deliberately refrained from any specific recommendations about the fate of the kulak, but the harshness of his language made it clear that no compromise of the Bauman or Larin variety would be tolerated.[203] Forty years later, one of the principal participants in the conference described the effect of Stalin's announcement that the kulaks were to be eliminated as a class as 'electrifying'.[204]

While the conference of marxist agrarians was taking place, the draft resolution of December 22 prepared by the Yakovlev commission was considered by members of the Politburo. Molotov described it as unsuccessful, especially in relation to the rate of collectivisation and the degree of socialisation within the kol-

Pravda the corrected figures for the plans of sovkhozy and kolkhozy in 1930: 900 million puds gross production (14·7 million tons) and 400 million puds of marketed grain (6·6 million tons); the latter figure was now described as '*incomparably* more than by the kulak in 1927'. This error is particularly odd because the correct figures were apparently given in the statement of the Bauman subcommission from which Stalin seems to have derived much of his argument (VIK, 4, 1958, 80).

[203] Larin, in a version of his speech which appeared as an article in EO, 1, 1930, took a harsher line than at the conference: 'after confiscation, kulaks must be sent to the northern timber workings, be turned into workers in the kolkhoz under supervision, etc.—by a *long* period of useful work let them earn themselves forgiveness' (p. 44), but he was denounced in the same number by N. Anisimov on the grounds that 'to trouble about the kulak, how to make him a working person, an ally of the proletariat, is not the business of a proletarian party' and is 'a vegetarian, "Christian" point of view' (p. 66). Larin's further attempt to defend himself in NAF, 3, 1930, 156–8, was also rebuffed, on this occasion for combining 'naked dekulakisation' with 'negotiating with the kulaks as a class'.

[204] S. M. Dubrovsky, in an interview with S. G. Solomon, an American scholar (see Fitzpatrick, ed. (Bloomington, Indiana, 1978), 148, 285).

khozy.[205] Stalin, according to Soviet historians, returned the draft to Yakovlev, proposing that the periods for collectivisation of the leading grain areas should be reduced, and that the resolution should be considerably shortened: matters relating to the kolkhoz Statute or coming directly within the competence of Narkomzem should be excluded, and a Model Statute for the agricultural artel should be drawn up jointly by Narkomzem and Kolkhoztsentr.[206] A note sent to the Politburo by the ubiquitous Ryskulov violently attacked the commission and criticised the draft of December 22. He called for an increase in the pace of collectivisation in areas specialising in industrial crops and livestock, claiming to have found 'a great impetus' to the kolkhozy in Central Asia: the new cotton areas in North Caucasus and the Crimea would be collectivised 100 per cent in the course of 1930. This was a vast extension of comprehensive collectivisation beyond the main grain areas, already hinted at in his earlier phrase 'leading agricultural areas' (see p. 187 above). In his note to the Politburo Ryskulov accused the commission of wanting to 'replace the revolutionary character of the kolkhozy by an overemphasis on the voluntary principle', strongly criticised its approach to the socialisation of livestock, and rejected its proposal that peasants who left the kolkhozy should have the right to take all or part of their property with them.[207] The date of Ryskulov's note is not clear; but according to Soviet historians its main points were approved by Stalin and Molotov.[208]

In the light of Molotov's and Stalin's comments, the Politburo sent the draft back on December 25, and Yakovlev submitted a revised draft on January 3.[209] The draft was a third to half the length of the draft of December 22, and the numerous cuts seem,

[205] VI, 3, 1965, 6.

[206] IISO, [i] (1964), 278; VIK, 1, 1964, 40. A decree of Sovnarkom dated December 1, 1929, insisted in strong terms that draft decrees of all kinds must not in future be overloaded with instructions which could be adopted departmentally or interdepartmentally (SZ, 1929, art. 711), and this was one of the first occasions on which Stalin had the opportunity to put this principle into practice on a major matter.

[207] IISO, [i] (1964), 278–82; for his views on socialisation see vol. 2, pp. 87–8.

[208] IISO, [i] (1964), 282. The note is said to have gone to Stalin and the Politburo on January 5 (*ibid.* 283), but this may merely mean that it was included in the papers of the Politburo sitting of that date; a copy went to Ordzhonikidze on January 3 (*ibid.* 278), and Yakovlev's revised draft of January 3 already appears to take it into account.

[209] VIK, 1, 1964, 40.

from the incomplete version available to Western historians, to have removed or modified passages tending to restrain enthusiasm for collectivisation. Thus according to the draft of December 22 the central committee would judge success in collectivisation 'not only on the basis of the growth of the number of households unified in collectives but primarily on the basis of the extent to which a particular district is able in practice, on the basis of collective organisation of the means of production and labour, to increase sown area, raise yield and improve livestock breeding'. This attempt to give primacy to the productive forces was completely excluded from the draft of January 3.[210] Modifications to the section about socialisation in the kolkhoz partly reverted to the more ambitious standpoint of the Grin'ko subcommission (see vol. 2, pp. 87–9). But the most important change in the draft was that the proposed period for collectivisation of the three main grain regions was reduced to 1–2 years (i.e. end-1930 to end-1931) instead of the 2–3 years (i.e. end-1931 to end-1932) in the draft of December 22. This was substantially a reversion to the position of the Kaminsky subcommission (see pp. 187–8 above). In the draft of January 3, the period of 3–4 years (end-1932 to end-1933) for the collectivisation of the grain deficit and national minority areas was retained.[211] The new draft also omitted the proposal to permit certain kulaks, or members of kulak families, to work in kolkhozy on a probationary basis, stating much more uncompromisingly:

> Kulaks shall not be admitted to kolkhozy; kulak means of production shall be confiscated and transferred to the Indivisible Funds of kolkhozy in districts of comprehensive collectivisation in accordance with the decisions of poor and middle peasants combining together in kolkhozy, and of local soviets; kulaks shall be allocated distant land and the worst land; malicious kulak elements shall be exiled from the districts.[212]

On January 4, the revised draft was edited by Stalin and Yakovlev; it was then finally approved by the Politburo at its session of January 5.[213] Now renamed 'On the Rate of Collectivisation and

[210] VIK, 1, 1964, 40.

[211] IISO, [i] (1964), 286–7.

[212] VI, 5, 1963, 31.

[213] IISO, [i] (1964), 283–5; the Politburo session was attended by ten members of the commission (listed in VIK, 1, 1964, 42). The text of the resolution was first published in P, January 6, 1930, and may be found in *KPSS v rez.*, ii (1954), 664–7.

on Measures of Assistance by the State to Kolkhoz Construction' (for its earlier titles see p. 190, n. 176 above), it strongly emphasised the assistance to be rendered by the state. Credits to kolkhozy were increased in 1929/30 from 270 to 500 million rubles at the expense of other sectors (this proposal was apparently not included in any of the previous drafts),[214] and the resolution also stated that land consolidation and other services must give over-riding priority to the kolkhozy. The resolution, while insisting that collectivisation must not be held back because tractors were not available, included in a briefer form the warning against collectivisation by compulsion in Yakovlev's draft of December 22:

> The central committee in full seriousness warns party organisations against any 'decreeing' from above of the kolkhoz movement, which could create a danger of replacing real socialist emulation in organising the kolkhozy by playing at collectivisation.

On the crucial issue of the rate of collectivisation the resolution approved on January 5 followed the draft of January 3. It accepted that the socialised sown area would 'considerably exceed 30 million hectares' in the spring of 1930 (30 million hectares was the current figure in Narkomzem plans). It also proposed that rapid collectivisation should continue after that:

> It can be established without doubt that within the five-year period instead of the collectivisation of 20 per cent of the sown area proposed in the five-year plan we will be able to resolve the task of collectivising the overwhelming majority of peasant households, and the collectivisation of such major grain areas as the Lower Volga, Central Volga and North Caucasus can in the main be completed in the autumn of 1930 or in any case in the spring of 1931; the collectivisation of other grain areas can in the main be completed in the autumn of 1931 or in any case in the spring of 1932.

For the major grain areas, apart from the saving clause 'in the main', this was as fast a pace as that proposed by the Kaminsky subcommission; and the explicit statement in previous drafts that

[214] IISO, [i] (1964), 285.

grain-deficit and national minority areas should take three–four years was now dropped.[215] At its session of January 5, the Politburo also approved, in an unpublished decision, Syrtsov's proposal, based on a report by Ryskulov to the Sovnarkom of the RSFSR, that the rate of collectivisation should be increased in areas specialising in livestock and industrial crops.[216]

As for the kulak, the resolution of January 5 showed little trace of the deliberations of the main Politburo commission or the Bauman subcommission. It merely stated in its first section that the emergence of the basis for replacing the large-scale kulak economy by large-scale kolkhoz production 'has provided the party with a complete foundation for going over in its practical work from the policy of limiting the exploiting tendencies of the kulak to the policy of eliminating the kulaks as a class'. These phrases were taken from Stalin's speech of December 27, and implicitly rejected the proposal by the Bauman subcommission that kulaks should be permitted on certain conditions to work in the kolkhozy. But no official decision about the fate of the kulak had yet been taken.

[215] In his article of April 3, 1930, Stalin stated that the resolution of January 5 divided the regions of the USSR into three groups: the first completing collectivisation in the main by the spring of 1931, the second by the spring of 1932, and the third 'can extend collectivisation to the end of the five-year plan, i.e. to 1933' (*Soch.*, xii, 208). The dates for the first two groups were here subtly changed and the third group resuscitated from previous drafts (see VI, 3, 1965, 13). The resolution of January 5 merely stated that individual land consolidation could continue in 'certain national areas and individual areas of the grain-deficit zone where collectivisation has not yet developed on a wide scale'.

[216] IISO, [i] (1964), 288; Ivnitskii (1972), 176; VIK, 1, 1964, 41. For the clause on socialisation in the resolution, see vol. 2, pp. 88–9.

CHAPTER FIVE

THE ALL-OUT DRIVE, JANUARY–FEBRUARY 1930

(A) THE PROCESS OF COLLECTIVISATION

The resolution of January 5 was not a precise programme. Its function was rather to sanction and offer encouragement, in somewhat vague terms, to the officially-inspired collectivisation drive. But the avalanche began well before the adoption of the resolution. The number of households in kolkhozy increased by 1 million in the four months June–September 1929 and by a further 2½ million in the three months October–December (see Table 16 below and pp. 180–1 above). Collectivisation continued to gather momentum during January and February 1930. By March 10, 1930, the date on which it reached its peak in almost all regions, 79 per cent of households were reported as collectivised in the North Caucasus, 64 per cent in the Ukraine, and 57 per cent in the Central Volga region.[1] Rapid increases also took place in other grain-surplus regions, including the Urals, Siberia and the Central Black-Earth region, which scored a record 83 per cent. In many of the grain-deficit regions, intended for a much slower rate, collectivisation was even more rapid.[2] The most astonishing rate of growth took place in the Moscow region, where the percentage rose from 14 on January 1 to 74 on March 1 (see Table 17). In the USSR as a whole, the number of households recorded as collectivised rose from about 5 million on January 1 to 8·1 million on February 1, 14·3 or 14·6 million on March 1 and a peak of 15·0 million on March 10.[3]

[1] In the Lower Volga region, where about 70 per cent of households were already reported as collectivised on January 1 (see p. 180 above), the percentage was approximately the same at the beginning of March (SZe, March 9, 1930; PKh, 5, 1930, 78).

[2] IZ, lxxvi (1965), 31; somewhat higher percentages for all these regions are given in PKh, 5, 1930, 77.

[3] I, March 9, 1930; IZ, lxxvi (1965), 31; and see p. 181 above and Table 16 below.

No substantial study has been made of the activities of the townsmen who were sent into the countryside in the last weeks of 1929 and the first two months of 1930, or who remained there after the grain collections. At the XVI party congress in July 1930 Bauman compared this invasion with the 'going to the people' movement in the 1870s, when several thousand student revolutionaries attempted to convince the peasants that they should support them in their struggle for a new social order:

> One involuntarily recalls the time when individual revolutionary populists, like Zhelyabov in the seventies, went to the countryside and got a very small result, and in those conditions they could not achieve more; but now, comrades, a whole class of proletarians, hundreds of thousands of *proletarian* Zhelyabovs, together with the poor peasant and middle peasant activists, have embarked on the transformation of the countryside on socialist lines.[4]

Bauman's comparison contained an element of validity: like the populists, the collectivisation brigades and plenipotentiaries hoped to win over the peasants to the transformation of society by bringing them revolutionary ideas from the towns. But his image of the collectivisation brigades was incomplete. The large number of factory workers sent into the countryside were accompanied by an equally large number of local party and government officials seconded to the campaign. In the Ukraine, for example, 23,500 okrug and district officials as well as more than 23,000 industrial workers organised into 5,088 brigades had descended on the countryside before the end of February.[5] Red Army units were sent in to the villages in large numbers to support the drive.[6] OGPU troops were responsible for arresting and exiling kulaks and recalcitrant peasants. And the functions of the plenipotentiaries were quite different from those of the populists. While the populists intended to retain the traditional peasant community and use it to destroy the state, the plenipotentiaries were agents of the state in its

[4] *XVI s"ezd* (1931), 216. In the spring of 1918 Lenin declared that in the food detachments scouring the countryside for kulak grain the industrial workers were leading the poor peasants and had thus '"gone to the people"'; he also, perhaps more accurately, referred to them as a 'crusade' (P, May 24, 1918, reprinted in Lenin, *Soch.*, xxvii, 355–62).

[5] SZe, March 12, 1930.

[6] See for example *Kollektivizatsiya* (Kuibyshev, 1970), 625.

efforts to destroy the peasant community and replace it by a collective economy subordinate to the state. Collectivisation was later officially designated as a revolution 'accomplished *from above*, on the initiative of the state, and directly supported *from below* by the millions of peasants, who were fighting to throw off kulak bondage and to live in freedom in the collective farms'.[7] In this strange revolution a quarter of a million or more voluntary or conscripted agents of the authorities were sent out from the towns to cajole or bully 25 million peasant households into transforming their way of life, armed with the instruction that a million of these households were implacable enemies, confronted with the unacceptable reality that only a small minority of peasants were willing to offer them voluntary support. This was a crusade as much as a revolution.

The collectivisation plenipotentiaries or brigades despatched to the countryside usually worked under a 'headquarters' (shtab) especially appointed in both the okrug and the district: thus in Tambov okrug in the Black-Earth region, the 'okrug headquarters of the agricultural campaign' (*okruzhnoi shtab agropokhoda*—the terms were entirely military) consisted of 19 officials under the command of the chairman of the soviet executive committee.[8] The okrug and district headquarters were themselves often advised by officials sent to them by the regional or even the central party authorities.[9] This emergency structure was superimposed upon the complex established hierarchy of local soviets and agricultural cooperatives, and from the beginning of the campaign its extraordinary powers were made explicit. Thus the Central Volga regional party committee ruled that organising groups sent to the localities 'are subordinate only to the instructions of the party committee despatching them and must take all the steps they can to obtain full cooperation with the local party organisation'.[10] 'Special head-

[7] *History of the Communist Party of the Soviet Union (Bolsheviks): Short Course* (Moscow, 1945), 305. This is the official history, first published in 1938, in the preparation of which Stalin was very active; authorship of the history was sometimes attributed to him.

[8] *Materialy*, i (1955), 325; the headquarters was established early in December 1929.

[9] Thus an 'organising group (orggruppa) of the central committee' consisting of seven persons worked in Vologda okrug from the end of 1929 (*Kollektivizatsiya* (Vologda, 1964), 283, 677, n. 29); organising groups were despatched to sovkhozy and kolkhozy early in January 1930 by the Central Volga regional party committee (*Kollektivizatsiya* (Kuibyshev, 1970), 146–7).

[10] *Kollektivizatsiya* (Kuibyshev, 1970), 147.

quarters' often prepared the plans for collectivisation, issu important instructions to districts and villages, sent out plenipote tiaries and brigades, and compiled reports of what had happened

The preparations for departure to the countryside, bearing mind the haste with which they were undertaken, were often caref and elaborate. In Tambov okrug, plenipotentiaries attend briefing conferences and short courses in the okrug town, a further meetings in the district town, before leaving for t countryside; they were supplied with pamphlets and leaflets, a with copies of the Statutes (not yet revised) of the kolkhoz.[12] T instructions with which they were issued insisted that they shou follow 'methods of mass work': the procedures, clearly based on t 'Ural–Siberian method' of grain collection (see p. 57 above involved the successive persuasion of the local activists, the villa soviet and meetings of poor peasants. The plenipotentiaries we warned that they should at first meet only small groups of po peasants, as 'it is unwise to call meetings of poor peasants of t whole village at the beginning, as they do not always succeed'. Th should then meet small, mixed groups of poor and middle peasan and only subsequently venture to summon a general meeting of t whole village (excluding, of course, the kulaks). A firm warning w given that 'administrative compulsion must not be used to get t middle peasants to join the kolkhoz'; if a minority wished to rema outside they should be allowed to do so, and be offered land at t ends of the kolkhoz fields.[13] These arrangements and instructio are similar to those prepared by Kolkhoztsentr in August 1929 (s pp. 132–3 above), and appear to have been a particular variatio on a standard pattern.

Simultaneously, intensive efforts were made to train enormo numbers of peasants for the tasks which the large-scale kolkh economy would impose upon them. In the Ukraine, during t early weeks of 1930, 3,877 short courses were provided for 275,0 peasants.[14] In the Central Black-Earth region, over 65,000 peasan and others attended courses in preparation for the spring sowin and another 40,000 collective farmers attended courses arranged b trade unions and by factories and other sponsors of kolkhozy;[15]

[11] NAF, 5, 1930, 39.
[12] *Materialy*, i (1955), 326, 335, 337.
[13] *Materialy*, i (1955), 338–42; these instructions were drawn up in January 19
[14] SZe, March 12, 1930.
[15] Sharova (1963), 179.

the Tambov okrug of this region, conferences and courses lasting from two to ten days were planned in the winter of 1929–30 for over 10,000 collective farmers, women collective farmers, poor peasants, chairmen of village soviets and teachers.[16] In these brief training programmes, particular emphasis was placed on the retraining of the 'agro-plenipotentiaries'; these were peasants appointed to secure the achievement of the 'agrominimum', a minimum standard for good farming. In the RSFSR alone there were over a quarter of a million 'agro-plenipotentiaries' by the beginning of February 1930.[17]

Such efforts to educate the peasants to the complex tasks of collectivisation were supplemented by the transfer of Red Army men, industrial workers and others to permanent work in the kolkhozy. If the collectivisation brigades were a modern form of the 'going to the people' movement of 1874, these permanent migrants corresponded perhaps to the attempts, partly successful, of populist doctors, teachers and others to settle among the peasants in 1877. The most numerous category were probably the demobilised Red Army men. Former Red Army men, often themselves originating from the countryside, had been an important channel for Bolshevik influence in the villages ever since their demobilisation after the Civil War. By November 1929, an article in the agricultural newspaper could claim that as a result of Red Army men returning to the countryside in earlier years 'you will undoubtedly find a former Red Army man as leader and organiser in every reading hut, cooperative, land association and kolkhoz'.[18] Thirty thousand further activists, trained on Sundays and in their free time, were released by the army to the kolkhozy in the autumn of 1929, and the training of a further 100,000 was undertaken during the first few months of 1930.[19] The Red Army trained substantial numbers of tractor drivers, lower- and middle-level agricultural specialists, officials of the agricultural cooperatives, cinema operators and radio men.[20] Far-reaching plans for the crash training of agricul-

[16] *Materialy*, i (1955), 333–6.

[17] SZe, February 8, 1930; for the agrominimum, see Carr and Davies (1969), 242–3.

[18] SKhG, November 23, 1929.

[19] SZe, November 23, 1929; P, December 19, 20, 1929; SZe, May 23, 1930; the training of the latter group was not completed in time for the collectivisation drive of January and February 1930.

[20] SKhG, January 5, 29, 1930; P, December 20, 1929, February 23, 1930; an

tural cadres, prepared by the Politburo commission on collectivisation, were approved by the central committee in December 1929. By speeding up the training of specialists and by retraining thousands of agricultural officials and specialists and transferring them to kolkhozy, the RSKs were to be provided with 8,000 specialists and 14,500 kolkhoz officials by the spring of 1930.[21] Many batches of officials were transferred to the countryside in the succeeding weeks. On February 16, 1930, a decree of the presidium of TsIK ordered the mobilisation of 7,200 members of urban soviets to work for a minimum of one year in village soviets and district executive committees in RSKs.[22]

The most far-reaching and best-publicised scheme, approved by the central committee plenum in November 1929, planned to send 25,000 politically experienced industrial workers to permanent work in the countryside (see p. 168 above). Over 70,000 workers volunteered, and by the end of 1929 some 27,000 had been selected by special party commissions; 70 per cent of them were party members, nearly half of them had been working in industry for more than ten years, and four-fifths of them came from the main industrial regions. After attending a fortnight's course in January 1930, they had nearly all reached the countryside by the middle of February: most of them were sent to the main grain regions.[23] At the time of the census of kolkhozy in May 1930, 19,581 of the '25,000-ers' were working in the kolkhozy, primarily as chairmen or in other leading posts,[24] the living embodiment of the 'link' between the proletariat and the peasantry.

Thus collectivisation was to be accomplished by a massive incursion into the countryside of plenipotentiaries and brigades who would win over the peasants to large-scale socialist production. They would be accompanied and followed by a large number of newly trained industrial workers, Red Army men and others who would

---

article in SZe, May 23, 1930, complained that inadequate financial assistance was given to these Red Army courses, even though they cost a fraction of the normal civilian ones. A decree of the Revolutionary Military Council signed by Voroshilov, dated January 30, 1930, set out the arrangements for training Red Army men for release into the kolkhozy in the autumn of 1930 (P, February 1, 1930).

[21] VIK, 1, 1964, 39–40.

[22] SZ, 1930, art. 140; on the transfer of book-keepers, see vol. 2, p. 138.

[23] *Materialy*, i (1955), 395, 463, 489–90; Selunskaya (1964), 67, 76–7.

[24] *Kolkhozy v 1930 g.* (1931), 224.

settle in the countryside, and work with the much larger number of retrained collective farmers to manage the kolkhozy on modern lines. Simultaneously, tractors and agricultural machinery would flood into the countryside and begin the technological transformation of agriculture. This was the intended framework for the all-out drive of December 1929–February 1930. Stalin assured the conference of marxist agrarians in December 1929 that these developments were 'transforming the psychology of the peasant and turning his face towards the town':

> There is nothing surprising in this, as the peasant is now receiving from the towns machines, tractors, agronomists, organisers and direct help to struggle with and overcome the kulak class. The peasant of the old type, with his primitive lack of trust in the town as a robber, is retreating into the background. He is being replaced by a new peasant, the peasant collective farmer, who looks at the town as a source of real *production* assistance. The peasant of the old type . . . is being replaced by a new peasant with a new perspective—join the kolkhoz and get out of poverty and darkness onto the broad road of economic and cultural advance.[25]

Stalin's description of the changing psychology of the peasants is not supported by the evidence of independent observers. Peasant attitudes to the kolkhozy on the eve of collectivisation were described by Hindus, who spent the summer of 1929 in his native village in Central Russia. The peasants told him that 'all but the young folks were afraid of it, even the *bedniaks* [poor peasants], in spite of all the promises made to them'. It would involve giving up one's land and implements and working with other families, under orders, not temporarily, as in the army, but for ever—'it means barracks for life':

> These peasants never believed in anybody's words; they had always mistrusted the whole world. None of them had ever bought a *bulka* in the bazaar without first picking up the white roll and feeling it to make sure that it was not hollow inside; they never bought a scythe or a sickle without eyeing it carefully from every angle, feeling it with their hard hands, striking it against

[25] *Soch.*, xii, 160.

their boots, snapping their fingers on it and listening to the resulting sound, or even biting upon it with their teeth to make sure that they were not being fooled by the metal. And now they were to give up their individual land, their horses, their cows, their farm buildings—the things that had given them bread, protection against starvation, the very security they needed to hold body and soul together—all on the mere promise of a youthful agitator that this would enrich their lives![26]

The verbal and material inducements offered to the peasants in the winter of 1929–30 were wholly insufficient to change their attitude to the kolkhozy. The supply of machinery and tractors, though vastly increased, failed to keep pace with the expansion of the kolkhozy. Even at the level of collectivisation to which the countryside returned during the spring of 1930, a much smaller proportion of kolkhoz land was worked by tractors than in the previous year. At the conference of marxist agrarians Stalin frankly recognised that this was a 'manufacturing period' for the kolkhoz system, in which draught animals and implements would be supplied to the kolkhoz by the former individual peasant (see pp. 391–2 below). Peasants who joined the kolkhoz expecting to give up exhausting manual labour were soon disillusioned. And in spite of the vast training programme, the peasant scrutinising his local kolkhoz at the beginning of 1930 would rarely have discerned an improvement in the quantity or quality of its agronomists and organisers. Even by May 1930, there were agronomists in only 8·8 per cent of the kolkhozy.[27] Between May 1929 and May 1930, owing to the expansion of the kolkhozy, the proportion of party members in their working population declined from 4·3 to 2·3 per cent, even though membership quadrupled in absolute terms.[28] The most enthusiastic and well-disciplined group of new arrivals, the 25,000-ers, provided less than one organiser for every four kolkhozy, and even the three main grain regions of the RSFSR received only 6,300 of the 25,000-ers for 8,500 kolkhozy, each of which had on average 180 households.[29] Yet the 25,000-ers included a high proportion of the party members permanently transferred to the countryside at this

[26] Hindus (1934), 31, 33–4, 43.
[27] *Kolkhozy v 1930 g.* (1931), 247; figures for 1929 do not appear to be available.
[28] *Kolkhozy v 1929 godu* (1931), 152–3; *Kolkhozy v 1930 g.* (1931), 224; these figures include candidate members.
[29] Selunskaya (1964), 76–7; *Ezhegodnik po sel. kh. za 1931* (1933), 444–5.

time: between January 1 and April 1 the number of party members in the countryside increased by 38,500, and 18,000 of these were 25,000-ers.[30] And the peasants could not fail to observe that many of the former industrial workers, officials and students sent to the countryside both in the collectivisation drive and for permanent work lacked any practical experience of agriculture. Many tales were told of the ignorance of the townsmen: a plenipotentiary inspecting a suspected kulak household insisted that it had two cows, although one was a heifer.[31] Even workers from peasant families who had agricultural experience, and those peasants who had attended brief training courses, were not properly equipped to cope with the changed conditions of large-scale farming; and the knowledge and experience of veteran collective farmers, gained in the small kolkhozy with a few households which predominated until the end of 1929, were of limited value for the new circumstances in which the authorities were trying to persuade whole villages to join the kolkhoz.

Moreover, at the beginning of 1930 the peasants were not being urged to join the TOZ, in which a substantial part of their individual economy could continue untouched, or even the type of artel in which socialisation stopped half-way. The collectivisation brigades—who were clearly even less knowledgeable about agriculture than those sent to work permanently in the countryside—acting under instructions from Kolkhoztsentr and the regional party authorities, and supported by a national press campaign, urged the peasants to hand over their cows and even their poultry to the kolkhozy, and were unable to assure the collective farmers that they had a right to cultivate their household plots. This was particularly alarming to the peasants because they had become increasingly dependent in the past two years on their animals and vegetables for food and for earnings on the market owing to the shortage of grain and the restrictions on its sale. The campaign to socialise animals and poultry particularly antagonised the women, who tended the farm animals and were anxious that their children should continue to get milk. Finally, the collectivisation brigades often informed the peasants that they would soon be members of a giant kolkhoz, embracing a whole administrative district (see vol. 2, pp. 42–50, 95–8). The cultural amenities and welfare services of

30 Selunskaya (1964), 114—15; PS, 11–12, 1930, 18, 44.
31 Hindus (1934), 162–3.

such an enterprise were almost everywhere merely dreams for the future, and dreams for which the collective farmers would themselves be expected to find the resources.[32] The impression that the kolkhoz would be a remote and alien force placed above the village was greatly strengthened. Nor could the peasant on joining the kolkhoz hope to be spared the pressure of the grain collector and the tax agent: the grain campaign of the autumn of 1929 demonstrated that the authorities would require the kolkhozy to transfer all their grain 'surpluses' to the state (see pp. 100–1 above), and in February 1930 this was followed by a campaign to obtain tax arrears and debts from peasants joining the kolkhozy, and to persuade them to pay substantial membership fees (see vol. 2, pp. 120–3).

These disadvantages of the kolkhoz did not apply equally to all peasants. A family which lacked a horse or a pair of oxen could hope to be no longer dependent upon neighbours; a family which had few or no animals of its own might receive a greater share of the income of the village as a result of the high degree of socialisation of livestock favoured in the early weeks of 1930; batraks and poor peasants, who were given priority in the appointments to leading positions in the kolkhoz, might find this a time of great opportunity, and they might materially benefit from the expropriation of the kulak. No Soviet investigations of collectivisation have satisfactorily demonstrated that these advantages were sufficient to overcome on any substantial scale the social cohesion of the village and bring large numbers of batraks and poor peasants to join the kolkhozy of their own free will. It seems likely that among the peasants who remained in the kolkhoz in the summer of 1930 many may have joined it voluntarily (see, however, p. 286 below). But in the winter of 1929–30 the majority of peasants undoubtedly preferred to remain outside the kolkhoz, and a great deal of well-thought-out argument and material encouragement would have been required to persuade them to join.

The reaction of many peasants to the kolkhozy was expressed in the myths and rumours circulating in the countryside, freely reported in the press and often attributed to kulak machinations. One very widespread tale was that women would be socialised, and all members of the kolkhoz would have to sleep under a common

[32] According to the surveys of kolkhozy in May 1929 and May 1930, the percentage of kolkhozy with any social and cultural amenities such as kindergartens and reading rooms considerably increased, but they remained a minority (*Kolkhozy v 1929 godu* (1931), 118; *Kolkhozy v 1930 g.* (1931), 247).

blanket in a single hut.[33] Rumours were heard that a special machine would burn up all the old people, so that they would not eat the grain,[34] that the children would be sent away to a crèche or to China,[35] and that the devil's seal would be put on the kolkhoz.[36] Fears of China and of war were widely reported: 4,000 young women were being sent to China to pay for the Chinese Eastern Railway;[37] the Whites would soon come; the world would end within two or three years;[38] collective farmers would be the first to be taken off to the war.[39]

Obviously the instructions to the collectivisation brigades to bring very large numbers of peasants into the kolkhozy before the spring sowing, but not to use compulsion, were incompatible. In the first few weeks of 1930, a note of caution and restraint was occasionally heard among the clarion calls of leading politicians and in the press. At a discussion in the Sovnarkom of the RSFSR about the Lower Volga, the region where the percentage of households collectivised was by far the highest, Syrtsov, while insisting that '*nothing must hold up the growth of the kolkhoz movement*' also argued that '*in the sphere of collectivisation we must now place our main emphasis not on the quantitative aspect*', and again warned against 'a kind of sporting contest in relation to the quantitative growth of the kolkhozy'; '*Potemkin kolkhozy are not necessary to us*'.[40] A handful of news items criticised officials and brigades who used threats and force in order to bully peasants into joining the kolkhozy;[41] a substantial article in the agricultural newspaper about the use of force in Siberia was very sharply worded (but also declared that the

[33] P, December 12, 1929 (Khoper okrug); SZe, February 1, 1930 (North Caucasus); B, 6, March 31, 1930, 21 (North Caucasus); *Kollektivizatsiya* (Ryazan', 1971), 899 (Kaluga okrug, Moscow region)—in one version the blanket was 10 m × 10 m, in another 70 m × 70 m, in a third (perhaps for a giant kolkhoz!) 700 m × 700 m.

[34] B, 6, March 31, 1930, 25.

[35] P, January 13, 1930 (Khoper okrug).

[36] KG, 15, February 23, 1930 (Khoper okrug).

[37] B, 6, March 31, 1930, 25.

[38] KG, 15, February 23, 1930 (Khoper okrug).

[39] NAF, 7–8, 1930, 89 (Gigant kolkhoz, Urals).

[40] I, January 5, 1930; SKhG, January 5, 1930; in 1787, during Catherine the Great's visit to New Russia, her favourite Count Potemkin erected bogus villages in order to impress her. This phrase was frequently quoted against Syrtsov during the campaign against him at the end of 1930 (see p. 376 below).

[41] P, January 6, 1930 (Ivanovo-Voznesensk); SKhG, January 8, 1930.

plan to collectivise only 28·1 per cent of households in 1930 was too modest).[42] In decisions of December 30, 1929, and January 11, 1930, which do not appear to have been published at the time, the Lower Volga regional party committee warned that 'actions bordering on administrative pressure' which had been reported were a distortion of the party line, and removed the party leadership in Kamishin okrug for '*a sporting-contest approach* (sportsmenstvo) *and the use of compulsion*'.[43] But for the first four weeks of 1930 a few items of this kind are all that can be found in the press; and a diligent search of the party archives by those Soviet historians who are anxious to demonstrate the irreproachability of the central committee has not yielded anything further.

The overwhelming thrust was towards all-out collectivisation. Immediately after the central committee resolution of January 5, Andreev admitted at a congress on comprehensive collectivisation in the North Caucasus that the proposal of the regional party bureau in December that collectivisation should be completed by mid-1931 (see p. 177 above) was too modest. Collectivisation would instead be completed by the spring of 1930 in the steppe areas and the end of 1930 elsewhere:

> No force in the world, and especially no threats or howls from our opponents and the enemies of collectivisation (especially from the opponents of collectivisation who are nearest to us, the kulaks) can now stop or temporarily restrain this victorious advance of the collectivisation of agriculture.[44]

A session of the Lower Volga soviet executive committee, meeting from January 6 to January 10, resolved that the region should be collectivised by the spring of 1930.[45] By this time the fever had spread to the grain-deficit regions. Kirov is reported by his biographer to have returned to Leningrad from Stalin's birthday celebrations with 'Stalin's directive to increase the rate of collectivisation'.[46] A joint plenum of the Moscow party committee and control commission, which met from January 6 to January 10,

[42] SKhG, January 16, 1930.

[43] P, April 27, 1930.

[44] P, January 15, 1930; according to P, January 10, 1930, this speech was made on January 9.

[45] IZ, lxxvi (1965), 20.

[46] Krasnikov (1964), 174; this statement may be unreliable: no source is given for

resolved that 40–50 per cent of households should be collectivised in 1930, and Bauman, in spite of Syrtsov's warnings, called for a collectivisation competition between different local authorities:

> Ryazan' proposed to collectivise 60 per cent or even 75 per cent of peasant households by the time of this spring sowing campaign. When I was in Tula, I pointed out the successes of Ryazan'. The Tulans are now entering into socialist emulation with the Ryazanians.[47]

The Tula okrug party bureau resolved to collectivise a number of districts in the course of 1930, and within a few weeks the Ryazan' authorities decided to complete collectivisation throughout their okrug by March 15.[48] On January 11, following such meetings in various regions, an all-Union conference of representatives of RSKs opened in Moscow. Significantly, the two main reports were delivered by representatives of the advanced Lower Volga region, and of the Gigant kolkhoz in the Urals, where collectivisation was almost complete. The report from the Lower Volga insisted that administrative pressure had not been used against the peasants and urged the fullest possible socialisation of peasant animals. The Gigant kolkhoz announced triumphantly that all the resources of its middle peasants were being transferred to its Indivisible Fund, that all the church bells in the district had been removed for scrap, and that during Christmas large numbers of ikons had been collected and burnt. The grain-deficit areas publicly announced at their conference their intention of pressing forward rapidly. A delegate from the remote Northern region, previously placed in the slowest group for collectivisation, reported local plans to collectivise 80 per cent of households during the spring sowing. No word of caution appears anywhere in the extensive press accounts of the conference; and at the conference the official spokesmen from Narkomzem and Kolkhoztsentr seem to have tacitly accepted all these proposals.[49] Kaminsky assured the delegates, in a remark apparently unpublished at the time:

---

it, and the biography was written at a time when Stalin's personal responsibility for excesses was strongly emphasised.

47 Kozlova (1971), 189, 191, citing the report of the plenum.

48 *Ibid.* 191–2.

49 P, January 12, 13, 14, 15, 1930; SKhG, January 12, 14, 1930; ZI, January 14, 1930; for other aspects of the conference see vol. 2, pp. 191–2.

If in some matter you go too far and you are arrested, remember that you have been arrested for a revolutionary cause.[50]

Simultaneously with the conference two long articles in *Pravda* enthusiastically recounted the experiences of collectivisation, socialisation and dekulakisation in Khoper okrug, where in the autumn the percentage of households in kolkhozy increased from 13 to 60 in six weeks.[51] A few days later Yakovlev assured a meeting of 25,000-ers who were about to depart for the kolkhozy that they could concentrate their efforts on the proper organisation of production, as the need to persuade the peasants of the merits of collectivisation was no longer a real issue; 'it would be like freezing ice or heating hot water, as the peasants who are coming together in collectives are *already* persuaded of the advantages of collectivisation'.[52] Laconic endorsement of further increases in the rate of collectivisation was a feature of the speeches of party leaders at this time. On January 13, Molotov, without any hint of caution, told a conference of representatives of local party committees that 'comprehensive collectivisation of individual districts and okrugs' had been joined by the beginning of the 'comprehensive collectivisation of whole regions and republics'.[53]

At this conference, a major reorganisation of the central party apparatus was announced, affecting all its departments. Following the establishment of Narkomzem of the USSR, the rural department of the central committee was abolished as redundant, and its functions in respect of collectivisation were transferred to a new 'department of agitation and mass campaigns'.[54] Kaminsky was appointed head of the new department, and removed from the chairmanship of Kolkhoztsentr.[55] Nothing is known about the reasons for Kaminsky's removal; while he nominally remained responsible in the party for the collectivisation campaign, henceforth he never made a substantial pronouncement on agricultural

[50] Cited from the archives in VI, 3, 1965, 7.

[51] P, January 13 (G. Makharadze, okrug party secretary), 15 (I. Bakhtanov), 1930.

[52] I, January 24, 1930; for other aspects of this speech see vol. 2, p. 90.

[53] P, January 21, 1930.

[54] P, January 17 (central committee resolution), 21 (Kaganovich's report of January 13), 1930; the main purpose of the reorganisation was to introduce 'functional' principles into the division of responsibilities.

[55] P, January 15, 1930; leading officials were also removed (private communication).

questions. Perhaps his enthusiasm was too obtrusive. But his removal did not imply any slackening of the collectivisation drive. He was replaced by Yurkin, the manager of 'Gigant' sovkhoz in the North Caucasus, who could be expected to sympathise with efforts to establish large kolkhozy along sovkhoz lines.[56] A few days after Kaminsky's removal, Stalin, in his only published statement in January 1930, tacitly endorsed the enormous increase in RSKs with the complacent remark that their 'sphere of influence is growing not day by day but hour by hour'.[57]

Higher planned rates of collectivisation continued to be reported in the last few days of January. On January 27, Eikhe, pointing out that in the main grain regions of the USSR '100 per cent of the poor peasants, batraks and middle peasants will achieve collectivisation this spring or at any rate during the autumn sowing campaign', announced that at least 50 or 60 per cent of the peasants would join kolkhozy in Siberia in the course of 1930, and urged the well-organised Novosibirsk okrug to proceed even faster than this:

> We must decisively put pressure on our *apparat* so that now, when poor peasants and middle peasants have moved into the kolkhozy *en masse*, the period for the completion of the comprehensive collectivisation of Siberia should be reduced to a minimum. This acceleration of the rate of collectivisation will enable us to reduce considerably the overheads which accompany such a radical break in economic organisation and in the way of life.[58]

The party committee of the Black-Earth region, meeting on January 26–27, also, according to the vague phrase of a Soviet historian, 'began to orient' its party organisations to the completion of comprehensive collectivisation in the first six months of 1930.[59]

[56] T. A. Yurkin, a metal worker in Moscow and Leningrad until 1919, was on 'food work' during the Civil War; in 1921 he was appointed head of the organisation department of Narkomzem; from 1922 he was director of various sovkhozy, being appointed head of Gigant sovkhoz in 1928; the short biography published on his appointment as head of the Kolkhoztsentry of the USSR and RSFSR drew attention to the fact that Gigant had 180,000 hectares (P, January 15, 1930).

[57] *Krasnaya zvezda* and P, January 21, 1930; for this statement see p. 233 below.

[58] Eikhe (Novosibirsk, 1930), 4–5.

[59] Sharova (1963), 137; the text of the decision is not cited.

Finally, the movement for comprehensive collectivisation spread into Central Asia. On January 30, the Central Asian party bureau resolved that 36 RSKs should be set up in Central Asia, and that the kulaks in them should be expropriated. This decision was immediately communicated to the press,[60] and by telegram to the central committee in Moscow.[61] The movement for comprehensive collectivisation had thus spread far beyond the vague limits set by the resolution of January 5.

In the atmosphere of optimism and enthusiasm of these weeks, more ambitious plans for collectivisation were thus frequently proposed at every level, and criticism of them was inhibited by unwillingness to restrain initiative at the lower levels, or simply by fear of being labelled Right wing. The Politburo exercised no restraint; and at the republican and regional level, as Kosior later explained, the party authorities were unwilling to fix a maximum percentage of collectivisation for each district.[62] A contemporary Soviet commentator drew attention to 'the increase in plans of collectivisation on the route from the centre to the periphery'—'if the centre intended to include 15 per cent of households, the region raised the plan to 25 per cent, the okrug to 40 per cent and the district posed the task of reaching 60 per cent';[63] okrug officials, visiting the soviets and plenipotentiaries in a village, demanded that they should get 10–15 per cent ahead of their plan in readiness for a forthcoming report to the region.[64] An okrug official in the Black-Earth region is reported to have told his subordinates: 'remember, comrades, our approach is that it is better to overstep the mark than to fall short . . . remember that we won't condemn you for an excess, but if you fall short—watch out!'[65] A similar uncontrolled mechanism caught the planners in industry in its grip at this time, until it was halted by the highest authorities, with the important difference that while over-ambitious plans for industrial production do not necessarily produce bricks and steel, over-ambitious plans for collectivisation did thrust peasants into the kolkhozy.

These imperative demands for immediate collectivisation did not leave much room for patient propaganda and explanation in the

[60] SZe, January 31, 1930.
[61] IZ, lxxvi (1965), 22, which refers, however, only to 32 RSKs.
[62] P, April 26, 1930.
[63] PKh, 5, 1930, 79; *Na novom etape* (1930), i, 158 (Kraev).
[64] Chernopitskii (Rostov, 1965), 107.
[65] SZe, May 7, 1930.

villages. As in Khoper okrug and other areas of advanced collectivisation in the autumn of 1929 (see pp. 136, 152–3 above), the collectivisation brigades generally had little time to spend in each settlement. A report published in a party agricultural journal later in the year claimed that 'in the majority of cases' the plenipotentiaries merely called a general meeting of the peasants, prepared a resolution on the establishment of the kolkhoz, and selected its board of management.[66] Brief sorties into the countryside of this kind were certainly very frequent in these weeks. In some districts of Moscow region, they were officially known as 'cavalry charges', and were sometimes followed by the issue of reports resembling military communiqués.[67] In a district in Tver' okrug, a 'three-day shock attack for comprehensive collectivisation' was undertaken early in January to coincide with the Orthodox Christmas. Ten brigades of between 30 and 50 workers and students, each supported by a brigade of collective farmers, went to the villages, talked to groups and assemblies of poor peasants, women and youth, and raised the percentage of collectivisation from 40 to 80 in 19 days, while at the same time trying to persuade the villagers to remove the church bells and ikons and close the churches.[68] In an RSK in Central Asia 'each official set himself the rule "do not return to the district centre without a kolkhoz" '.[69] In Nizhnii Novgorod region collectivisation was agreed at peasant meetings in one or two hours.[70]

Elsewhere the pace was not quite so hasty. In reports from workers' brigades in Tambov okrug published from the archives, the plenipotentiaries spent periods from two days to six weeks in each village or group of settlements, and several of them diligently followed their instructions and addressed enormous numbers of meetings of different groups of peasants: one brigade spent five weeks in a village of 413 households, and held 67 meetings attended in all by 2,174 peasants, at the end of which 80 households joined the kolkhoz.[71] But, even in this okrug, turnover of personnel in the brigades was very high: of the 259 plenipotentiaries in the villages in December, only 74 remained by the end of January, the rest having

66 NAF, 5, 1930, 39 (Tsil'ko).

67 Kozlova (1971), 187–8; B, 5, March 15, 1930, 41.

68 SZe, February 2, 1930.

69 SZe, January 29, 1930.

70 SZo, iii–iv, March–May 1930, 58.

71 *Materialy*, i (1955), 346–89, especially 370–3.

been replaced by 338 new arrivals.[72] In one district in the North Caucasus, an average of 38 different plenipotentiaries visited each village between October 1929 and May 1930.[73] The overwhelming impression from scattered sources is of feverish activity in which a variety of brigades launched themselves on the villages for periods from a day or two to a couple of months. Hindus summed up the position in his native village in Central Russia:

> Why, asked person after person, had I not come in the winter, when the village, aye the whole countryside, boiled with excitement? *Akh*, what things had happened—meetings, debates, quarrels, fights, denunciations, and everybody wondering what would come of the effort to make people join the kolkhoz whether they wanted to or not.[74]

A serious attempt to persuade the peasants of the virtues of the kolkhoz was certainly an important aspect of the activities of the brigades. What happened in one district of Moscow region was later bitterly summed up in a propagandist magazine issued by Kolkhoztsentr:

> They promised golden mountains. They said that Kashira district would get 40 million rubles, every kind of machine, tractors, combine-harvesters, etc. They said that women would be freed from doing the washing, from milking and cleaning the animals, weeding the garden, etc. Electricity can do all that, they said. And as none of these promises could be met, the women, naturally enough, were very disillusioned and therefore easily fell under kulak influence.[75]

Such glittering images of the benefits which the new agricultural economy would quickly secure were very prominent in the conferences and publications of these weeks, and were undoubtedly half-believed by their exponents; but they did not impress the peasants. Frequently the collectivisation brigades were confronted with noisy opposition, which they could refute only in the most

[72] *Materialy*, i (1955), 323–30.
[73] Chernopitskii (Rostov, 1965), 107.
[74] Hindus (1934), 146.
[75] *Kollektivist*, 7–8, April 15–30, 1930, 35.

general terms. Thus according to a workers' brigade in Tambov okrug:

> They [the kulaks and well-to-do peasants] organised around themselves groups of loud-mouths, who shouted out at meetings 'they robbed us during the grain collections, they ruined us peasants and now they want to ruin us completely, to take our last horse and cow; setting up the kolkhozy is a kind of serf labour (barshchina) where the peasant will again have to work under the rod'; here they nod towards the women and say that they will have to give up all their work as housewives and run to work in the kolkhoz; a manager will be appointed in the kolkhozy, who will force us to work beyond our strength, and so on. All that the well-to-do peasants say is that the Soviet government should enrich the peasants first and then push through the establishment of kolkhozy, and not do what it is doing now, which is to try to make a rich farm out of ruined farms which have no grain, and so on.
>
> We replied to them along the lines that our country is socialist, we are building socialism, and the peasant economy is capitalist because it is looked after by an individual peasant, and therefore we must give up private property for ever, hand it over to the community and strengthen and improve our economy by our joint efforts.[76]

After such unequal exchanges many of the plenipotentiaries soon found themselves resorting to threats and force, both in the major grain regions where collectivisation was already far advanced and in the grain-deficit regions and national minority areas. In a village in Leningrad region the chairman of the village soviet told those who did not join that they would be taxed by individual assessment, like kulaks.[77] In a village in Ivanovo-Voznesensk region, the peasants were told that collectivisation was compulsory and that those who failed to join would be exiled from the village.[78] In the Lower Volga region, 'in one settlement the community voted against establishing a kolkhoz and organisers of the meeting then asked "*Who is against Soviet power?*"; as no-one declared themselves

[76] *Materialy*, i (1955), 357–8.

[77] *Neizvedannymi putyami* (Leningrad, 1967), 252 (reminiscences of a 25,000-er).

[78] P, January 6, 1930; see also SZe, February 11, 1930.

to be *against Soviet power*, a resolution was recorded that the question of collectivisation was decided "unanimously"'. In this region, the normal procedure was that the kolkhoz was declared to be established immediately a peasant meeting had voted to establish it, without any personal application from the future collective farmers being required; those who did not wish to join were required to opt out in writing, and were treated as being members while their statements were being considered.[79] When no statements opting out were received, the local authorities reported that 100 per cent collectivisation had been achieved.[80] When such statements were received, they were sometimes shelved for months; in one case the majority of households in a village signed statements opting out, but the establishment of a kolkhoz for the whole village was still approved.[81] In Nizhnii Novgorod region, decisions to join the kolkhoz were taken by a simple vote binding on the participants.[82]

Peasants reluctant to join the kolkhoz were harassed and victimised. Even where normal procedures were followed, a household remaining outside the kolkhoz could expect an unfavourable allocation of land. In the Lower Volga region a leading party official made fun of a middle peasant who complained that he had been compelled to join the kolkhoz by the decision to allocate him remote land outside its boundaries; the official insisted that where the kolkhoz was in a dominant position (which by this time was almost everywhere in the region) its land must not be divided.[83] For the USSR as a whole, a simplified procedure for land consolidation was adopted, with the objective of reallocating the land in all those districts which had a 'considerable growth of kolkhozy and sovkhozy'.[84] In many districts land consolidators were sent out of skis to mark up the snow ready for the spring sowing.[85] The normal procedure at this stage was apparently to leave the individual peasants in their cottages with their household plot (usad'ba) in the

[79] I, April 19, 1930 (Kiselev); this is a retrospective survey of developments in the region at the end of 1929 and beginning of 1930.

[80] VI, 3, 1965, 7 (speech by Kalinin in Lower Volga region in June 1930; it is not clear whether this statement refers specifically to this region).

[81] I, April 19, 1930 (Kiselev).

[82] SZo, iii–iv, March–May 1930, 58.

[83] SKhG, January 4, 1930 (Gusti, a secretary of the regional party committee).

[84] SKhG, January 7, 1930 (decree of Narkomzem).

[85] SKhG, January 3, February 9 (North Caucasus, Western region), SZe, February 15 (Central Volga), 1930.

centre of the village, but to transfer their main arable land beyond the kolkhoz lands. In some districts it was already assumed that 100 per cent collectivisation had been achieved, so that any individual peasant not in the kolkhoz received no arable land.[86] In a village in Ivanovo-Voznesensk region, the party secretary went round listing land to be seized, buildings to be destroyed and peasants to be exiled.[87] Peasants not joining the kolkhoz were pressed to pay arrears of taxes, or extra taxes,[88] or were simply fined.[89] In the Novosibirsk okrug, heads of households who wanted to consult their families were abused as 'parasites who should be wiped off the face of the earth', and peasants refusing to join were locked up in cold bath-houses for two or three days and exiled with their families to the outskirts of the village.[90] Poor and middle peasants were arrested for disrupting meetings,[91] for expressing their opposition to collectivisation,[92] or simply for refusing to join the kolkhozy.[93] When, in spite of all the pressure exerted on them, village meetings rejected the proposal to join the kolkhoz, the plenipotentiaries sometimes threatened to exile the whole village from the district;[94] and whole settlements were 'boycotted' (deprived of consumer goods, etc.) for refusing to join.[95]

Such forms of pressure were evidently widespread at this time. In Tambov okrug, where the workers' brigades seem to have acted with relative moderation, reports from six out of twelve villages in which kolkhozy were established between the middle of December 1929 and the end of January 1930 refer to the use at key stages of the campaign of what were later condemned as administrative methods. These included the boycott of a settlement, the collection for the use of the kolkhoz of seed stored by individual peasants, the dismissal and imposition of extra taxes on members of a village soviet, and five separate cases of arresting recalcitrant peasants or

[86] SKhG, February 9, 1930 (Central Volga).

[87] P, January 6, 1930; see also SKhG, January 16, 1930 (Novosibirsk), SZe, February 11, 1930.

[88] NAF, 7–8, 1930, 91 (Gigant kolkhoz, Urals).

[89] SKhG, January 16, 1930 (Novosibirsk).

[90] SKhG, January 16, 1930; SZe, February 11, 1930.

[91] SZe, January 30, 1930 (Poltava).

[92] SZe, February 2 (Tver' okrug), 4 (Bobruisk okrug), 1930.

[93] SKhG, January 16, 1930 (Novosibirsk); I, April 19, 1930 (Lower Volga—article by Kiselev); Chernopitskii (Rostov, 1965), 101.

[94] *Kollektivist*, 6, March 31, 1930 (Tula okrug).

[95] I, April 19, 1930 (Lower Volga); *Materialy*, i (1955) (Tambov).

reporting them to the district soviet for disrupting village meetings and similar activities. In several cases the reports do not even attempt to stigmatise those arrested as kulaks.[96] Accounts from all parts of the USSR published in the Soviet press in 1930 in the aftermath of the campaign concurred that such forms of pressure were very widely used during the first few weeks of the year; they differed only about whether peasants joining the kolkhozy in the autumn of 1929 were also responding to threats rather than blandishments. Accounts of collectivisation in the Lower Volga and part of the Central Volga regions dated back the switch to administrative methods to the beginning of the autumn.[97] An article on the Gigant kolkhoz in the Urals, however, claimed that the 'period of distortions' began only in November, after the local authorities had expanded the kolkhoz to incorporate five former administrative districts and decided that collectivisation could be completed in all of them by the spring of 1930.[98]

The collectivisation campaign by-passed or subsumed the local agencies of Soviet power in the villages. The plenipotentiaries, feverishly trying to persuade the peasants to join the kolkhoz, frequently found that the village soviet was uncooperative and ineffective, sometimes that it was hostile. Molotov reported to a conference of local party officials held under the auspices of the central committee that both village soviets and district executive committees of soviets 'have been standing aloof from the kolkhoz movement';[99] and a later survey showed they had played 'an insignificant part' in collectivisation.[100] In the North Caucasus, according to a study by a Soviet historian based on the archives, 'their role as mass organisations of the working people was replaced by the plenipotentiaries'.[101] In many villages, a small party cell was effectively responsible for all aspects of administration. An okrug party secretary reported at the conference of party officials:

[96] *Materialy*, i (1955), 346–89; the editor of the documents claims, without adducing any evidence, that the brigades were sent to the most backward villages (pp. 326–7).

[97] I, April 19, 1930 (Kiselev); P, April 10, 1930; on Khoper okrug in the Lower Volga see pp. 152–3 above.

[98] NAF, 7–8, 1930, 86–7, 90–1; for earlier developments in this kolkhoz see pp. 124–5, 136 above.

[99] P, January 21, 1930.

[100] B, 6, March 31, 1930, 18 (A. Angarov).

[101] Chernopitskii (Rostov, 1965), 107.

> Comrade Kaganovich correctly pointed out that all guidance and all activity on collectivisation is carried out by the village activists and the okrug party officials. In the villages the activists merely amount to the secretary of the cell and the person responsible for agitation and propaganda. These two people carry the burden day and night: they hold meetings to collect kulak debts (*Voice*: And deal with individual taxation)—and deal with everything else (*Voice*: And are divided into twenty sectors) . . . Running about like squirrels in a cage, they are quite unable to read even the leading articles in *Pravda*.[102]

Yet even this degree of party organisation existed only in a minority of villages. Kaganovich pointed out at the conference that party cells existed in only 23,458 out of 70,849 village soviets, so that '*if we formulate it sharply and strongly, in essence we have to create a party organisation in the countryside*, capable of managing the great movement for collectivisation'; this required the recruitment of poor peasants and batraks, and the influx of workers from the town.[103] According to another speaker at the conference, however, in many villages these party cells were so weak that the movement for collectivisation had by-passed them.[104]

This situation was not greatly changed in the weeks which followed. Suggestions that in RSKs the village soviet should be abolished, and the kolkhoz transformed into the lowest organ of soviet power, were firmly rejected. At the party conference in January, Molotov argued that the kolkhoz should deal with production, and the soviets with schools, libraries, roads and telephones;[105] a later article in the party journal condemned attempts to recognise the kolkhozy as organs of state power on the grounds that they ignored the class division within the kolkhozy and would result in establishing 'kolkhozy without communists'.[106] These arguments are hardly persuasive; there seems to be no reason why the party cell could not dominate the elected board of management of the kolkhoz as effectively as it could dominate the

[102] P, January 19, 1930 (Kostroma okrug); for this conference see p. 216 above.

[103] P, January 20, 1930 (report of January 13).

[104] P, January 19, 1930 (Bulat, a secretary of the Moscow party committee).

[105] P, January 21, 1930 (report of January 13).

[106] B, 2, January 31, 1930, 64–6; according to the Soviet version of the history of the Kronstadt rebellion in March 1921, the main slogan of the rebels was 'soviets without communists'.

elected village soviets. The attitude of the Soviet authorities was evidently based partly on a sense of the impropriety of state authority in the village being managed by a supposedly voluntary organisation, partly on their unease about the permanence and reliability of the kolkhozy.[107] Certainly the village soviets had not shown themselves to be entirely reliable. At the party conference Molotov called for immediate new elections to village soviets where they were not coping with their tasks, and especially in RSKs.[108] During the next few weeks many village soviets were re-elected: in the Don okrugs of the North Caucasus region 23·4 per cent of all village soviets were dissolved between February 15 and March 15, 1930;[109] in the Central Volga region, Khataevich declared that '*an overwhelming majority of village soviets and a considerable number of district soviets have proved to be not at the level of their new tasks*' and that some village soviets had even been 'a direct agency of the kulaks'; in consequence, a half to two-thirds of all village soviets should be re-elected.[110] Many village soviets now eagerly embarked on actions to secure the expropriation of the kulaks and immediate collectivisation which were later declared to be impermissible pressure.[111] According to a Soviet historian, however, only 10 per cent of soviets

[107] The case for abolishing the village soviet was argued in articles by A. L'vov and B. Kavraiskii in I, August 31, and by M. Ryakhov in I, September 11, 1929; the latter suggested that 'the kolkhoz village may be the beginning of the dying out of individual links of state power in the Soviet Union', and that the functions of the district soviet should also be re-examined. A draft decree on the functions of the village soviet, prepared by TsIK, was extensively discussed in the peasant newspaper on the assumption that the village soviet would continue (KG, 75, September 20, 76, September 24, 77, September 27, 78, October 1, 1929). On December 13, 1929, TsIK approved a decree 'On the Significance and Work of the Village Soviets in Districts of Comprehensive Collectivisation' (SZ, 1930, art. 40) in which the transfer of the functions of the soviets to the boards of the kolkhozy was stated to be 'incorrect and completely impermissible'. The element of uncertainty about the matter was indicated by the failure to publish the decree until a month later (I, January 12, 1930); according to Soviet historians a clause insisting on the importance of village soviets in RSKs was struck out of the resolution of January 5 in the final stages of drafting (VIK, 1, 1964, 41–2), but perhaps this was merely part of Stalin's struggle to reduce the length of the resolution (see p. 199, n. 206, above).

[108] P, January 21, 1930 (report of January 13).

[109] Chernopitskii (Rostov, 1965), 110; on the disturbances in this area see pp. 258–9 below.

[110] SZe, February 20, 1930.

[111] B, 6, March 31, 1930, 18–25.

were in fact re-elected at this time;[112] and in the RSFSR regions were authorised to delay re-elections by the presidium of VTsIK.[113] Generally the village soviets were ignored or treated as unimportant by the higher authorities throughout these stormy weeks of rapid collectivisation. Even after the collectivisation drive had been brought to an end, a writer in the party newspaper still complained that in the Central Volga region the plenipotentiaries and brigades constituted 'a second organ of power in the village', costing much more to maintain than the village soviet, and often working independently of it.[114]

The development of comprehensive collectivisation entailed, at least formally, the disappearance of the mir (the land society) and its skhod in the villages in which collectivisation was complete, and the absorption of its economic functions by the kolkhoz or the agricultural cooperatives, and its other functions, including its power to impose self-taxation on the peasants, by the village soviet. In November 1929, Shlikhter pointed out that the skhod was now becoming redundant.[115] In January 1930 the Ukrainian Narkomzem abolished land societies throughout the republic; an article accompanying this announcement denounced them as 'outlived', as tending to hold up collectivisation and as 'the last refuge for the kulak' (kulaks were not permitted to belong to the kolkhoz or the cooperatives, and were often disenfranchised).[116] The abolition of land societies in the RSFSR awaited a decree of VTsIK and Sovnarkom of the RSFSR of July 30, 1930; the decree was restricted to RSKs, and applied to all villages in which at least 75 per cent of households were already collectivised.[117] In a further decree on August 16, the collection and disbursement of self-taxation, while remaining nominally voluntary, was formally transferred completely to the village soviets throughout the USSR; the maximum permissible rate was increased, but members of

[112] Kukushkin (1968), 248.

[113] *Vlast' sovetov*, 10, March 9, 1930, 24.

[114] P, May 25, 1930, disk. listok 2 (I. Bogovói); for a vivid description of these practices during the collectivisation drive, see *Vlast' sovetov*, 22–23, June 9, 1930, 20.

[115] P, November 16, 1929.

[116] SKhG, January 26, 1930; the article, by a certain L. Okrainchuk, is marked 'for discussion'.

[117] SU, 1930, art. 621; the decree was not published until October (I, October 22, 1930).

communes and artels were exempted from all payment.[118] The collectivisation drive of the winter of 1929–30 had thus, in spite of all vicissitudes, greatly weakened the position of the mir and strengthened the administrative authority of the party in the countryside, working partly through plenipotentiaries, to a lesser extent through the village soviet.

(B) 'SPONTANEOUS DEKULAKISATION', JANUARY 1930

The collectivisation drive was intimately associated with the campaign against the kulak. The party authorities at every level stressed that during the offensive against the capitalist elements in the countryside the class struggle was bound to be intensified. Stalin characterised the struggle with the kulak as 'a struggle to the death',[119] Molotov warned that 'in certain districts the class struggle may acquire in the next few months a sharpness against which the facts of the preceding period look pale'.[120] An editorial in the party journal described the elimination of the kulak as a class as 'the last decisive struggle with internal capitalism, which must be carried out to the end; *nothing* must stand in the way; the kulaks as a class will not leave the historical stage without the most savage opposition'.[121] The movement to expropriate the kulaks was strongly encouraged by the authorities: Kosior, describing it as 'a broad mass movement of poor peasants, middle peasants and batraks', called upon party organisations not to restrain it but to organise it to 'deliver a really crushing blow against the political influence, and particularly against the economic prospects, of the kulak stratum of the village'.[122] Kulaks were increasingly treated in the press as a category of mankind which should not be given human consideration. Thus in Khoper okrug 'every honest collective farmer avoids the kulak when he sees him in the distance; no-one wants to meet people with whom the whole collective has refused to deal'.[123] All opposition to the kolkhozy, like earlier oppo-

[118] SZ, 1930, art. 451; for the earlier history of self-taxation, see Carr (1971), 464–8.

[119] *Soch.*, xii, 164; speech of December 27, 1929.

[120] P, January 21, 1930; report of January 13.

[121] B, 2, January 31, 1930, 4.

[122] *Kommunist* (Kharkov?), January 28, 1930, *cit.* Danilov, ed. (1963), 182, and Slin'ko (Kiev, 1961), 188.

[123] P, January 15, 1930.

sition to the grain campaigns (see pp. 87–8 above), was attributed to the kulaks and to their influence. In the Lower Volga region, kulaks were responsible for 'anti-kolkhoz agitation on an unprecedentedly broad scale'.[124] When middle peasants hesitated about belonging to the kolkhoz or about handing over their cows to it, their vacillations were attributed to kulak influence,[125] and when priests opposed collectivisation this was because 'the church is the kulaks' *agitprop*'.[126] According to the Soviet press, the kulak was cunning and resourceful: he was able to use his powers of 'economic and political mimicry' to disguise his aims and ambitions.[127]

This attitude to the kulaks, though now often taking extravagant forms, was deeply rooted in the Bolshevik analysis of the relationship between the regime and the countryside. The Soviet countryside was seen as polarised into an exploiting class of kulaks at one extreme and a mass of exploited poor peasants and batraks at the other, with a large number of middle peasants placed between the two. It was acknowledged that the revolution and civil war had diminished the economic strength of the kulaks and moved many poor peasants into the ranks of the middle peasants (see p. 24 above), but this was not believed to have fundamentally changed this picture of class conflict in the countryside. The strategy of the regime throughout the 1920s, except for a few months in 1925, was to isolate the kulaks by supporting the poor peasants against them and winning over the middle peasants as an ally. Some hostility towards the well-to-do and kulak peasants, particularly on the part of poor peasants and batraks, undoubtedly existed; and the numerous reports in the press that some poor peasants and batraks supported the campaign against the kulaks may not have been entirely fanciful. But the Bolshevik analysis underestimated the mobility between economic groups in the countryside and the cohesion of the village community (see p. 24 above); and the regime was never very successful in its strategy even in the more leisurely years of NEP. The policy of immediate collectivisation in fact required the abandonment in practice of the strategy of winning over the middle peasant; but it was unthinkable that the regime could admit that it was pursuing a policy which was resisted by the middle peasants, the majority of the whole Soviet population.

124 SKhG, January 4, 1930.
125 P, January 13, 1930 (Khoper okrug).
126 SKhG, January 4, 1930 (Khoper okrug).
127 SKhG, January 19, 1930.

Hence in face of all the evidence the authorities at every level continued to insist that the middle peasant had swung over to the kolkhoz. According to a *Pravda* editorial of January 11, 'the poor peasant—the bastion of the proletariat—is for the kolkhoz, the middle peasant—the ally of the proletariat—is also going into the kolkhoz'; once the middle peasant had joined the kolkhoz, he was placed in a position of irreconcilable struggle with the kulak, and this position must be consolidated by a policy of socialisation within the kolkhoz which would diminish the economic differences between the former poor and middle peasants. But the core of the struggle against the kulaks, urged a further *Pravda* editorial, must be the batraks and the poor peasants, who should be immediately organised into groups in every kolkhoz in every RSK and also in every village soviet.[128]

The unremitting campaign against the kulaks strongly influenced the mood and the activities of the collectivisation brigades. They justified the actions they were compelled to take against poor and middle peasants as being directed against 'henchmen' of the kulaks and 'those who were singing the kulak's tune'. In 14 out of the 27 reports from workers' brigades in Tambov okrug which have been published from the archives, references are made to the role of the 'kulaks', the 'well-to-do' (mentioned as frequently as the kulaks), the 'big-wigs', 'the kulak henchmen' and the 'loudmouths' who spread rumours, agitated and disrupted meetings. Even poor peasants opposed to the kolkhoz were described on several occasions as being under control of the kulaks. An unauthorised anti-kolkhoz meeting was said to have been inspired by the kulaks even though no well-to-do peasants or kulaks were there. When the house of a peasant who was prominent in the dances at an anti-religious evening was burnt down, this was seen as 'terrorism' on the part of the kulak and the well-to-do.[129] According to some reports, kulaks even sent round beggars who agitated against the kolkhozy while seeking alms.[130] At a general meeting in a village in Ivanovo region, a party member summed up what must have been the feeling of many plenipotentiaries: 'The kulak's day must come to an end; because of his agitation of every possible kind he must be eliminated, so that he should not get in our way'.[131] In many places

128 P, January 16, 1930.

129 *Materialy*, i (1955), 346–89.

130 SZe, February 6, 1930 (Rzhevsk okrug).

131 *Kollektivizatsiya* (Ryazan', 1971), 337; the meeting was on January 31.

poor or middle peasants were classified as kulaks, and arrested or deprived of their land on the grounds that they were 'singing to the kulaks' tune' or guilty of 'dangerous thoughts'.[132] Officials often argued: '*It's true that he is not economically a kulak, but his ideology is a kulak one*'.[133]

The expropriation of the kulaks which took place in January 1930 was at first supported by no central legislation. It was unplanned, unsystematic, at times even chaotic. It was inspired by the pronouncements of Stalin and the relentless press campaign, but its scope and speed were determined by the local authorities or even by the plenipotentiaries and brigades themselves. Reviewing this situation, Krylenko later told a meeting of the bureau of the party members in VTsIK of the RSFSR that while the new laws about the kulak were being worked out and distributed, 'a spontaneous movement to dekulakisation took place locally; it was properly organised only in a few places'.[134] Actions against the kulaks, already undertaken by some local authorities in the autumn of 1929 when whole villages or groups of villages were being collectivised, multiplied after Stalin's speech of December 27, 1929, and the further encouragement which he offered to the elimination of the kulaks as a class in his letter of January 21 (see p. 233 below). 'Hundreds of the most malicious kulaks' were reported to have been expelled from Khoper okrug.[135]

But the expropriation of the kulaks was not confined even at this stage to those areas where collectivisation was most advanced: in Orel okrug in the Central Black-Earth region, at the moment of receiving the new law on the kulaks at the end of January, dekulakisation was already almost complete in a number of districts.[136] Before the end of January, 50 kulaks were exiled in a district of Tver' okrug for 'malicious propaganda and open opposition to the establishment of kolkhozy';[137] in a village in Armenia, the land, garden, houses and property of 37 kulaks were confiscated and 16 of them were exiled from the district as malicious opponents of collectivisation; in an okrug in Azerbaidzhan, skhods resolved that when kulaks attempted to drive their cattle into Persia

[132] SKhG, January 16, 1930 (Siberia); SZe, March 8, 1930 (Ukraine).
[133] SZe, March 8, 1930.
[134] Kukushkin (1968), 230, citing the archives; the meeting was on February 20.
[135] P, January 26, 1930.
[136] Kukushkin (1968), 230, citing the archives.
[137] SZe, February 3, 1930.

it should be confiscated and they should be exiled to the Transcaspian.[138]

The injunction to base the expropriation of the kulak on support from groups of batraks and poor peasants was imperfectly observed. Sometimes village soviets established commissions to undertake dekulakisation;[139] but sometimes the party members, together with some batraks and poor peasants, expropriated a kulak household without any preliminary explanations.[140] The commissions or brigades frequently seized the personal property of the kulaks, including their hens, buckets, ikons, watches, underwear and boots; sometimes poor peasants and others retained this personal property for themselves.[141] For some people the offensive against the last exploiting class was an occasion for sordid personal profit.

(C) THE LEGISLATION ON THE KULAKS

Following the rejection of the proposals on the kulaks made by the Politburo commission on collectivisation, a new Politburo commission, 'the commission to elaborate measures in relation to the kulaks', was established under Molotov's chairmanship on January 15.[142] The 21 members of the Molotov commission included the party secretaries of all the main grain regions, and also, significantly, of the main regions to which kulaks were exiled—the Northern region, Siberia, the Urals and Kazakhstan; other members were Yagoda (deputy head of the OGPU), Syrtsov, Yakovlev, Muralov, Kalmanovich and Yurkin, the new chairman of Kolkhoztsentr.[143] A commission under the chairmanship of Molotov could be relied upon to be harsh towards the kulak; and when constituted the new commission did not apparently include any of the members of the earlier Bauman subcommission, not even Ryskulov, though Bauman and Kaminsky were among five members added by the Politburo.[144] On the eve of the formation of the commission A. V. Odintsev, a vice-chairman of Kolkhoztsentr of the RSFSR, told the conference of RSKs:

[138] SZe, January 30, 1930.

[139] For example, SKhG, January 25, 1930.

[140] For example, SZe, February 4, 1930 (Orekhovo-Zuevo district, Moscow region).

[141] SZe, February 4, 1930 (Moscow region).

[142] Ivnitskii (1972), 177.

[143] For Yurkin's appointment see p. 217 above.

[144] VI, 3, 1965, 16; Ivnitskii (1972), 177–8; the five members were added

We must deal with the kulak like we dealt with the bourgeoisie in 1918. The malicious kulak, actively opposing our construction, must be cast into Solovki. In other cases resettle on the worst land.[145]

The conference called for 'decisive aggressive measures in relation to kulaks actively opposing the kolkhozy', including expropriation of their means of production and dwellings, and exile or allocation of the worst lands outside the kolkhoz.[146] No mention was made in the published records of the conference of the proposal of the Bauman subcommission that some kulaks might work in the kolkhoz for a probationary period. While the Molotov commission was in progress, Stalin again adopted an uncompromising attitude to the kulaks in a letter to the Red Army newspaper *Krasnaya zvezda*, criticising it for failing to distinguish sufficiently sharply between the previous policy of 'squeezing out' the kulaks and the new policy of eliminating them as a class. Stalin welcomed the setting-aside of the laws permitting the rent of land and the hire of labour in RSKs, and insisted that 'the opposition of this class must be *broken* in open battle'.[147] The only hint which appeared in the press at this time that the probationary membership proposal was not entirely dead was a vague phrase by Yakovlev, who told the 25,000-ers that when the kulaks were expropriated and deprived of land or given it outside the kolkhoz '*they are deprived of the possibility in the collective of becoming a full member of the new socialised economy*'.[148]

The commission sent a draft resolution to the Politburo on January 26, and the final resolution of the central committee, 'On Measures for the Elimination of Kulak Households in Districts of Comprehensive Collectivisation', was approved by the Politburo on January 30 and telegraphed to all local party organisations on the

---

between January 16 and 23. Krylenko, the People's Commissar for Justice of the RSFSR, was not a member of the commission, though he apparently participated in its work (Ivnitskii (1972), 178; VI, 5, 1963, 31; VI, 3, 1965, 16).

[145] SKhG, January 14, 1930; Solovki is a reference to the notorious prison camp on Solovki islands in the Far North.

[146] IZ, lxxx (1967), 93; ZI, January 14, 1930.

[147] *Krasnaya zvezda* and P, January 21, 1930, reprinted in *Soch.*, xii, 178–83; on the same day the former Right-winger Ryutin, who was deputy editor in charge of the newspaper, replied accepting Stalin's criticisms.

[148] I, January 24, 1930.

same day.[149] Nothing is known of the proceedings of the commission, though its spirit was reflected in a speech delivered in Novosibirsk on January 27, immediately after its work was complete, by Eikhe, Siberian party secretary, and a member of the commission:

> It is necessary to apply sharp measures to the most hostile reactionary part of the kulaks immediately. In our opinion these kulaks should be resettled in the distant areas of the North, say in Narym, Turukhansk, in a concentration camp. The other part of the kulak class can be used for work in labour colonies. We must resort to this, we must prepare for this now, because if, after the expropriation of the means of production, we leave all the kulaks in the same settlement, in the same village, turned into a comprehensive collective farm, the kulak will try to wreak his revenge on it . . .
>
> We are now going to build the Tomsk–Yeniseisk road, build in uninhabited districts of the *taiga*, in distant forests. Let the kulaks go there and work, spend a few years at a working life, and then we shall see what a particular kulak is like.[150]

The proposals of Bauman and Larin that the kulak should undertake a probationary period of labour in a kolkhoz had thus undergone a brutal transformation.

Neither the resolution of January 30 nor the detailed instruction from TsIK and Sovnarkom which followed it on February 4 have been published.[151] A pale reflection of the resolution of January 30 appeared in a decree of TsIK and Sovnarkom of February 1, which was immediately published in the press. This abolished the right to rent land and hire labour in RSKs, and authorised regional executive committees to 'apply necessary measures of struggle with the kulak class up to and including full confiscation of kulak property and exile beyond the boundaries of particular districts or

[149] Ivnitskii (1972), 178.

[150] Eikhe (Novosibirsk, 1930), 8–9; the *taiga* is the coniferous forest zone.

[151] The account below is based on a resolution of the bureau of the Western region dated February 2, which appears to follow closely the original text (see *Kollektivizatsiya* (Smolensk, 1968), 246–50, 657–8), and on the following publications of Soviet historians based on the archives: Ivnitskii (1972), 178–84, who refers to the instruction of February 4 on p. 183; Danilov *et al.*, eds. (1970), 234–9; Sharova (1963), 135–6; *Sotsial'naya struktura* (Novosibirsk, 1970), 128–9.

regions'.[152] The resolution of January 30 divided kulaks into three categories, stipulating that the total number of kulak households in all three categories was not to exceed 3–5 per cent in grain areas and 2–3 per cent in non-grain areas:

(I) 'The counter-revolutionary *aktiv*'. Whether a kulak belonged to this category was to be determined by the OGPU, within a limit of 63,000 for the whole USSR fixed by the resolution. Their means of production and personal property were to be confiscated; the heads of families were to be sentenced on the spot to imprisonment or confinement in a concentration camp; those among them who were 'organisers of terrorist acts, counter-revolutionary demonstrations and insurrectionary organisations' could be sentenced to death. Members of their families were to be exiled as for Category II.

(II) 'The remaining elements of the kulak *aktiv*', especially the richest kulaks, large-scale kulaks and former semi-landowners. According to one account, kulaks placed in this category 'manifested less active opposition to the Soviet state but were arch-exploiters and naturally supported the counter-revolutionaries'; according to another account, they 'actively opposed collectivisation'. Lists of kulak households in this category were to be prepared by district soviets and approved by okrug executive committees on the basis of decisions by meetings of collective farmers and of groups of poor peasants and batraks; these meetings were to be guided by instructions from village soviets elaborated on the basis of directives from regional, okrug and district party organisations, which fixed quotas within an upper limit for the whole USSR of 150,000 households. The means of production and part of the property of the families on these lists were to be confiscated; they could retain the most essential domestic goods, some means of production, a minimum amount of food and up to 500 rubles per family. They were then to be exiled to remote areas of the Northern region, Siberia, the Urals and Kazakhstan, or to remote districts of their own region.

[152] SZ, 1930, art. 105.

(III) The remainder of the kulaks, described in one source as kulaks 'reliable (loyal'no) in their attitude to Soviet power'. It is not clear how many households came into Category III: at the very least 396,000 households, possibly 852,000.[153]

Part of the means of production of the households in Category III was to be confiscated, and they were to be resettled on new land specially allocated to them outside the limits of the kolkhoz lands but within the administrative district (according to one account, probably erroneous, within the region). The procedures for resettling households in this category were to be determined by the okrug, but Eikhe's speech of January 27 made it clear that it was not envisaged in Siberia at any rate that the kulaks should remain in their own village. In the Western region kulaks were to be removed altogether from districts in which collectivisation was on a mass scale, and they were to be resettled in small groups administered by *troiki* (committees of three) or by plenipotentiaries; some or all of them were to be used 'in special labour detachments (*druzhiny*) and colonies on forestry, road, land improvement and other work'.

Confiscated means of production and property were to be transferred to the Indivisible Funds of the kolkhozy and considered as being in lieu of the payment of entry fees by poor peasants and batraks; confiscated kulak dwellings were to be used as clubs, schools, kolkhoz offices or for other social purposes, or else as communal dwellings for former batraks (in practice they were sometimes allocated to poor peasants). If a kulak was in debt to the state or to the cooperatives, part of his property was to be used to cover this. No provision was made in the regulations for the property of the expropriated kulaks to be retained by other individuals.

Members of soldiers' families were to be exempted from all these

[153] According to one account 10 per cent of all kulaks were to be in Category I and almost a quarter in Category II (Danilov *et al.*, eds. (1970), 235–6 (Borisov)); as there were 213,000 households in these two categories, there would therefore be about 396,000 in Category III, and 609,000 in all. But according to another account, in the main areas of the RSFSR there were 52,000 families in Category I and 112,000 in Category II, while 'four-fifths' were in Category III (Danilov, ed. (1963), 105 (Abramov)); this would give 656,000 in Category III in the main areas of the RSFSR alone. If 'four-fifths' is applied to Category III for the whole USSR, we get 852,000 in Category III and 1,065,000 in all, which seems much more likely.

provisions, and kulaks whose immediate relatives had worked in industry over a long period were to be given special consideration. In the Western region at least, young members of kulak families who opposed the majority of the kulaks were also to be given special consideration.

The whole operation was supposed to be carried out as an integral part of the process of collectivisation: with the exception of kulaks in Category I, who were to be arrested whatever the level of collectivisation, kulak households were to be expropriated only in RSKs. A letter from the central committee, also despatched on January 30, insisted that local organisations should concentrate on collectivisation and refrain from 'naked dekulakisation' without simultaneous collectivisation.[154] But the resolution stipulated that the whole operation was to be carried out with great urgency: 50 per cent of the number of kulaks stipulated for Categories I and II were to be expropriated and exiled by April 15 and all of them by the end of May (at this time the authorities were expecting collectivisation in the main agricultural areas to be virtually complete during the spring sowing).

In the major grain regions, in all of which collectivisation was far advanced, spontaneous dekulakisation (see pp. 230–2 above) was already taking place on a large scale in January. In these circumstances, even before the decree of January 30 was approved by the Politburo, the local party authorities, who were aware from their representatives on the Molotov commission of the line it was taking, issued their own instructions in an endeavour to regulate dekulakisation. On January 20, the Central Volga party committee resolved that the anti-Soviet kulak *aktiv* (i.e. Category I) should be eliminated by February 5 and that 10,000 kulak families in Category II should be exiled between February 5 and 15. Before January 30, similar decisions followed in the other major grain regions.[155] The national legislation was therefore superimposed upon regional legislation which had already been transmitted to the okrugs and the districts, and was in some districts already being acted upon.

154 IZ, lxxvi (1965), 21; *Leninskii kooperativnyi plan* (1969), 109.

155 Lower Volga (January 24), Central Black-Earth (January 27), Ukraine (January 28), North Caucasus (January 29 and February 2) (VI, 5, 1963, 33 (Bogdenko)). A confidential circular on dekulakisation from the Ukrainian central committee is reported to have been acted on in one district as early as January 25 (Slin'ko (Kiev, 1961), 187–8).

(D) POLICY VACILLATIONS, JANUARY 30 – FEBRUARY 10, 1930

While the legislation on the kulaks was being prepared, the attention of the Soviet authorities at every level was turning increasingly to the problems of the spring sowing campaign. Plans for the campaign had already been approved by the Sovnarkoms of the RSFSR and the USSR in December 1929;[156] the RSFSR decree stressed the importance of the campaign by appointing Syrtsov as the 'plenipotentiary' responsible for it throughout the republic. The plan for the USSR envisaged an ambitious increase in the spring sown area for all crops by 'at least 11 per cent' to 93 million hectares, over 30 million hectares of which would be sown by the kolkhozy. While the total planned sown area was not increased in subsequent weeks, the unplanned expansion of the kolkhozy meant that in February the arrangements for the spring sowing had to be reconsidered: by the middle of the month the authorities estimated that the sown area of the kolkhozy would amount to 60–70 million hectares.[157] This was an urgent matter for several of the major regions: sowing was due to begin in the periods March 10–20 in the Crimea, March 20–30 in the North Caucasus and the steppe area of the Ukraine and April 10–20 in the Lower Volga region.[158]

By the end of January, these issues became more prominent in the orders and instructions of Narkomzem, and in the public statements of its officials, while continuing to be intertwined with exhortations to increase collectivisation and to socialise more livestock. As early as January 24, Yakovlev entitled his report to the 25,000-ers 'The Battle for the Organisation of Real Collective Production', and after warning that 'in the spring the kolkhoz movement will be submitted to the greatest of examinations in the presence of the working class and peasantry of our country, watched by the whole world', dealt at length with land consolidation, draught power, labour organisation and seed.[159] In January Narkomzem required every village soviet and kolkhoz to report the progress of preparations for the sowing campaign, including the collection of seed, every ten days by telegraph to the district; summaries were to be telegraphed by the

[156] SU 1929, art. 910; this RSFSR decree, dated December 11, was first published in P, December 13, 1929; the USSR decree, dated December 23, 1929, is in SZ, 1930, art. 4.

[157] P, February 18, 1930.

[158] BP (Prague), lxxx (June–July 1930), 4; see also *Stat. spr. za 1928* (1929), 174–5.

[159] I, January 24, 1930.

districts to the okrugs, and hence via the regions to Narkomzem.[160] Many reports were published in January to the effect that peasants joining kolkhozy were selling up their stocks of seed rather than handing them over to the kolkhozy.[161] According to plan, all kolkhoz seed for collective sowing should have been collected by January 15; yet only 189,000 tons out of the original plan of over 2 million tons was collected by that date, and 412,000 tons by January 20 (see p. 253 below). Meanwhile, owing to the expansion of the kolkhozy beyond the original plan, the seed collection plan had to be revised upwards to 3·34 million tons.[162] This was a serious emergency. A telegram from Kalinin as president of TsIK, instructing all regional soviets to make sure that the grain was collected by February 15,[163] was followed by a central committee decision that the Politburo should hear a summary Narkomzem report on preparations for the sowing campaign at every meeting, i.e. every five days; the central committee also prudently instructed Narkomzem not to allow peasant wheat to be ground at its mills until after all the seed was collected in.[164]

At the end of January and beginning of February 1930 a series of decisions by the Politburo indicated a certain unease in the highest party circles. Following the resolution of January 5, during almost the whole of January no published statement by leading members of the Politburo, and no decisions of the party central committee, attempted in any way to restrain the rapidly expanding kolkhoz movement in the grain regions and its further spread to grain-deficit and national minority areas. On January 31, however, the day after the far-reaching resolution on dekulakisation was approved by the Politburo, a telegram from Stalin and Molotov to the Central Asian party bureau replied to their request to undertake the comprehensive collectivisation of 32 districts with the warning that 'we consider mistaken transfer of accelerated rates of collectivisation from centre of USSR to districts of Central Asia', and instructed the bureau 'advance cause of collectivisation to extent that masses

160 SKhG, January 4, 1930; I, January 26, 1930; these were substantial reports: the village telegram included 31 indicators and the district summary telegram was the equivalent of over 60 lines of newsprint.

161 See Moshkov (1966), 76n.

162 I, February 6, 1930; these figures exclude the Transcaucasus and the Central Asian republics, but include the Ukraine and Belorussia.

163 P, February 5, 1930.

164 *Kollektivizatsiya . . . 1927–1935* (1957), 275–6 (resolution of February 5).

really involved'.[165] Similar telegrams were sent to the Transcaucasus.[166] On February 4, the central committee decided that conferences of the heads of party organisations in the national republics and the grain-deficit areas should be convened later in the month.[167] The central committee also sent telegrams or letters to a number of regions, including the Central Volga, warning them against undertaking 'naked dekulakisation' separately from collectivisation.[168] These telegrams (which have not even now been published in full) appear to have criticised the use of administrative methods in collectivisation: on February 4 a letter from the Central Volga regional party committee to local organisations, presumably a response to the telegrams from the central committee, insisted that 'collectivisation must be carried out on the basis of the development of broad mass work among poor peasants and middle peasants, with a decisive struggle against the slightest attempts to drive the middle and poor peasants into the kolkhozy by the use of administrative methods'.[169] On February 3, Andreev, who was a candidate member of the Politburo, signed a resolution of the bureau of the North Caucasus party committee which stressed the turn towards consolidation:

> . . . mass establishment of kolkhozy, i.e. the first stage of accepting and registering their Statutes, is coming to an end. Now the main attention of all organisations, the whole stress in work on collectivisation, must be concentrated on organisational work within the kolkhozy and on strengthening the economy of the kolkhoz.[170]

At this time, too, Sheboldaev, at the first Lower Volga conference of batrak and poor peasant groups, condemned in a published

[165] *Leninskii kooperativnyi plan* (1969), 109–10; IZ, lxxxvi (1969), 22; for the Central Asian request or decision see p. 218 above.

[166] *Leninskii kooperativnyi plan* (1969), 110.

[167] Trapeznikov, ii (1967), 256–7; the conferences were to be on February 12 and 21.

[168] VIK, 6, 1968, 116; Trapeznikov, ii (1967), 256. Following a Central Volga party decision of January 20 to exile the most dangerous kulaks within two weeks, a central committee telegram to Khataevich on January 31 declared, 'your haste on the kulak issue has nothing in common with party policy' (*Slavic Review*, xiv (1986), 515 (Viola)).

[169] IZ, lxxx (1967), 99.

[170] *Kollektivizatsiya* (Krasnodar, 1972), 236–7.

statement the use of administrative measures against the middle peasants 'to drive them by force into the kolkhoz':

> We have never and nowhere stated that there must be obligatory, immediate 100 per cent inclusion of poor and middle peasant economies in the kolkhozy. If we have 70–80 per cent of households in the kolkhozy, the question is decided.[171]

In the Western region a representative of Kolkhoztsentr found that '*the rate of collectivisation has been artificially forced and kolkhozy have often been organised compulsorily*'.[172]

It is tempting to conclude that the slowness of the preparations for the spring sowing, particularly the failure of the kolkhozy to collect in seed on any substantial scale, had imposed a policy of prudence on the Politburo. But the telegrams and decisions at the end of January and beginning of February were strictly limited in their scope. They endeavoured to restrain somewhat the pace of collectivisation in certain national areas, and to bring about a certain consolidation in the Central Volga region and possibly in some of the other major grain-surplus regions. The telegrams to the national areas do appear to have constituted a definite attempt to set some limits to the collectivisation drive; but as these areas were insignificant as suppliers of grain Stalin and Molotov could not have been motivated by fears for the success of the sowing campaign, except insofar as collectivisation in these areas was seen as a diversion from the main tasks confronting the regime. And while the policy for the major grain-surplus regions, at least as it was interpreted by the regional party secretaries, had switched towards consolidation of the kolkhozy, the consolidation envisaged by the Politburo was to be achieved by the rapid elimination of the kulaks and the use of the methods of the grain collections to bring about better organisation. No attempt was made by the Politburo at this time to discourage the widespread campaigns for the socialisation of all animals, the merging of kolkhozy into 'giants', and their transformation into communes (see vol. 2, pp. 42–7, 92–4).

Moreover, moves to restrain the pace of collectivisation were half-hearted. Almost nothing about them appeared in the press; and no serious attempt was made by the Politburo to follow them up. They

171 P, February 7, 1930.
172 ZI, February 5, 1930.

were accompanied and followed by other statements and measures which encouraged the further expansion of collectivisation. On January 30, a central committee letter was despatched to local party committees which, referring to reports received from the localities that 'organisations in a number of districts have discarded the cause of collectivisation and concentrated their efforts on dekulakisation', explained that 'such a policy is fundamentally incorrect'.[173] Following this letter, the press frequently warned against 'naked' dekulakisation, carried out without the participation of the middle and poor peasantry and independently of the campaign for collectivisation; and drew the conclusion not that dekulakisation should be restrained but rather that more attention should be devoted to collectivisation. On February 1, a headline in the agricultural newspaper summarised the prevailing mood: 'Not Naked Dekulakisation, but a Stubborn Bolshevik Struggle for Mass Collectivisation'.[174] As far as is known, proposals made at the end of January and beginning of February to extend collectivisation in the Central Black-Earth region and in Siberia did not meet with any objection from the Politburo.[175] On February 3, a *Pravda* editorial emphatically encouraged further collectivisation with the statement that 'the latest proposal for collectivisation—75 per cent of poor and middle peasant households in 1930/31—is not a maximum one'; according to Soviet historians, this sentence was included on Stalin's instructions.[176] On February 4, Kosior stated that all the steppe okrugs in the Ukraine should be 'completely collectivised in the course of the spring sowing campaign' and that the comprehensive collectivisation of the whole Ukraine should be completed during the autumn sowing campaign.[177] A week later, on February 9, 1930, in his replies to questions from students of the Sverdlov Communist University, Stalin agreed that there was a danger that kulaks in districts without comprehensive collectivisation might engage in 'self-elimination', and drew the emphatic conclusion:

[173] *Leninskii kooperativnyi plan* (1969), 109; IZ, lxxvi (1965), 21.

[174] SZe, February 1, 1930; see also SZe, February 4, 1930.

[175] On January 27, a session of the Central Black-Earth party committee decided to complete comprehensive collectivisation and the elimination of the kulaks as a class in the first six months of 1930 (Sharova (1963), 137); on February 2, the Siberian party committee warned against excesses but called for comprehensive collectivisation in the spring agricultural campaign (IZ, lxxvi (1965), 22).

[176] Danilov, ed. (1963), 44 (chapter by Danilov and Ivnitskii); no source is cited.

[177] Slin'ko (Kiev, 1961), 197; this statement was confirmed by a circular from the Ukrainian central committee to okrugs and districts.

> There is only one way of resisting the 'squandering' of kulak property—strengthen the work on collectivisation in districts which do not have comprehensive collectivisation.[178]

This was open encouragement, immediately before the conference of heads of party organisations in national minority areas, for the further extension of collectivisation.

And the most important consequence of the decisions adopted at the end of January and beginning of February was undoubtedly the enormous impetus which was given to the anti-kulak drive, resulting in the unleashing of what amounted to a reign of terror in large areas of the countryside, and providing a powerful impetus to a further wave of collectivisation.

(E) EXPROPRIATION OF THE KULAKS, FEBRUARY 1930

Following the precedents of the grain collections and the collectivisation drive, *ad hoc* organisations responsible for dekulakisation were established at every level. These overlapped with but were separate from the collectivisation headquarters and plenipotentiaries; their main distinguishing feature was the formal involvement of the OGPU. The arrangements differed considerably from region to region, but had certain common ingredients. In the Western region, about which the available information is most detailed, troiki (groups of three persons) were set up at the regional level, and in every okrug and district; each consisted of the first secretary of the party committee, the chairman of the Soviet executive committee and the head of the local OGPU.[179] In the Lower Volga region a special commission on dekulakisation was established in every district; it was headed by a representative of the okrug soviet executive committee and included representatives of the district soviet executive committee, the district party secretary and a plenipotentiary of the OGPU.[180] In every village in the region, a special commission attached to the village soviet was to be headed by a representative of the district soviet, and to include the chairman of the village soviet, and representatives of the party

178 P, February 10, 1930; *Soch.*, xii (1949), 184–90; for other aspects of Stalin's replies see p. 250 below.

179 *Kollektivizatsiya* (Smolensk, 1968), 246–50; Fainsod (1958), 242.

180 IS, 4, 1958, 22.

organisation and of the poor peasants' group. This special village commission was in turn to be in charge of 'commissions to register and confiscate kulak means of production', including batraks, poor peasants and middle peasants appointed by the village soviet.[181] According to the instructions issued in the Western region, the militia was seconded to assist in dekulakisation, and all participants were armed.[182] The formal procedures by which the mass of the peasantry were supposed to be involved in dekulakisation varied from region to region. The lists for Category I were a matter for the OGPU; they are not mentioned in those local instructions which are available. For the other Categories, the procedure by which lists of victims were approved varied in different regions. In the Central Volga and Western regions, they were to be approved by 'general meetings of collective farmers, and at poor peasant and batrak meetings';[183] in the North Caucasus, by 'decisions of batraks, poor peasants and general assemblies of citizens'.[184] Thus little provision was made for the skhod, and for the middle peasant who had not joined the kolkhoz. In any case the part to be played by the mass of the peasantry was strictly limited. Following what were now standard Soviet planning procedures, in every aspect of the economy from the distribution of steel among factories to the allocation of agricultural tax or grain quotas among the village communities, each region was allocated by the central authorities definite 'control figures' for the numbers of kulaks to be expelled in each of Categories I and II, and these were then divided up by the region among the okrugs, and by the okrugs among the districts and the villages.[185] Dekulakisation was more tightly controlled than collectivisation, the numerical quotas in Categories I and II being more closely adhered to than the planned percentages for collectivisation. Enthusiastic regional party committees sometimes increased the quota set by the central committee: in the Moscow region, the quota for those to be exiled (presumably those in

[181] IS, 4, 1958, 22.

[182] Fainsod (1958), 242.

[183] *Kollektivizatsiya* (Kuibyshev, 1970), 156 (resolution of February 8).

[184] *Kollektivizatsiya* (Krasnodar, 1972), 251 (resolution of February 10).

[185] See pp. 235–6 above, *Kollektivizatsiya* (Smolensk, 1968), 246–50 and *Kollektivizatsiya* (Kuibyshev, 1970), 156; in the Northern region, the okrug figure for Category II was determined by the okrug itself within a maximum of 'an average of 3–5 per cent of households' in each district (*Kollektivizatsiya* (Vologda, 1964), 273; resolution of February 5).

Category II) was increased from 7,000 to 13–16,000, and in the Ivanovo-Voznesensk region from 4,000 to 7–8,000.[186] But the okrugs and districts seem to have adhered to the quotas fixed by the regions. And at the village level, the function of the poor peasant groups and village soviets was not to try to increase or exceed their quota, but to influence or determine the names to be included in the list. Even in this respect their powers were limited, as Category I lists were drawn up or approved by the OGPU, and Category II and III lists had to be approved by the district and okrug soviets or their special commissions.[187] In February 1930 the planning of dekulakisation was more realistic and more closely controlled from the centre than the planning of collectivisation, capital investment or industrial production.

The instructions for dekulakisation issued by the republican and regional authorities were nevertheless in many respects confused and contradictory, and were themselves superimposed upon practices and procedures evolved during the period of 'spontaneous' dekulakisation up to the end of January (see pp. 230–2 above). They provided little guidance about how the kulaks in Categories II and III should be selected. The Siberian regional executive committee stated that lists of taxpayers, in which kulaks were classified separately, should be used, so that middle peasants were not caught up in dekulakisation; but apparently no guidance was given on how kulaks should be divided between Categories II and III.[188] The rural commissions responsible for making the selection were established in villages in most of which there was neither a party cell nor a poor peasants' group, and in which the chairmen of the village soviet were frequently apathetic or inexperienced. The main responsibility for dekulakisation, as for collectivisation, rested in practice on workers' brigades and local officials sent in from the towns, but now actively assisted, and sometimes superseded, by the OGPU and the militia.

What happened in practice in February 1930 has been amply recorded by Western historians.[189] Kulaks, or those classified as kulaks, were expelled in large numbers from their homes, their land and often from their villages. Many, perhaps most, of these were richer households, and many such households, especially those

[186] *Voprosy agrarnoi istorii* (Vologda, 1968), 49–50.

[187] See p. 235 above, and, for the Lower Volga region, IS, 4, 1958, 24.

[188] See Stepichev (Irkutsk, 1966), 465–9.

[189] See for example Lewin (1968), 496–506; Fainsod (1958), 245–6.

arrested or exiled to remote areas, had provided some reason or other for being regarded as hostile to collectivisation. Thus far, dekulakisation accorded with the plans of the authorities: the power of capitalism in the countryside was being broken, and resistance to collectivisation had presumably been undermined. A substantial number of those expropriated, however, were 'ideological' kulaks, middle and poor peasants who resisted collectivisation. The practice of expropriating the merely recalcitrant, already prevalent before the resolution of January 30 (see pp. 230–1 above), though denounced by the authorities, continued unabated during February; and it undoubtedly facilitated the forcing-through of collectivisation.[190] The traditional structure of the village was also further weakened by the deportation of the village priests, which often took place simultaneously with the deportation of kulaks.[191]

The confiscation of the personal property and dwellings of the victims was a prominent feature of dekulakisation. Some poor peasants and batraks, as well as being motivated by the desire to pay off scores against their former exploiters, were also attracted by the possibility of benefiting from a share in the spoils, and this also corrupted some plenipotentiaries. And as it was inherently difficult to distinguish between a kulak and a well-to-do middle peasant, the race for personal gain often resulted in the arbitrary expropriation of middle peasants and the theft of their belongings, and in the theft of kulak property which should have been transferred to the kolkhoz or to the state. In January 1930, these activities already occurred, as a by-product of the confusion of 'spontaneous' dekulakisation. Their continuation and extension in February 1930, after elaborate and stringent arrangements for the central control of dekulakisation had already been approved, again demonstrated the extent to which reliable and competent supporters of the regime were lacking in the countryside in spite of the vast powers of plenipotentiaries from the towns. In the anti-kulak drive of February 1930, the highly

[190] A striking fictional description of the dekulakisation of a 'kulak henchman' who opposed the kolkhozy, written by a participant in dekulakisation, is cited in Tucker, ed. (1977), 210–1.

[191] For an example see Arina *et al.* (1939), 162. The resolution of the bureau of the Western regional party committee on dekulakisation dated February 2, 1930, announced that directives on the anti-religious movement were to be prepared, corresponding to the latest decision of the central committee on this question (*Kollektivizatsiya* (Smolensk, 1968), 246–50); this was presumably a reference to the expulsion of priests. See also Tucker, ed. (1977), 209 (Medvedev).

organised and brutal procedures of mass exile enforced by the disciplined troops of the OGPU were incongruously combined with the vigorous, confused and sometimes corrupt activities of ill-informed plenipotentiaries and deprived peasants. A few months later, the authorities recognised that tens of thousands of peasant families had been dekulakised by mistake (see pp. 280–1 below).

The expulsion of the kulaks took place rapidly and systematically. The statistical evidence published by Soviet historians from the archives is summarised in Table 19. According to the Soviet accounts, by the end of 1930 330,000 households had been expropriated in Categories I–III,[192] over 1½ million persons; the majority of these were expropriated in the first half of 1930, most of them probably between February and April.[193] In addition, an unknown but substantial number of kulaks and their families fled from their villages (the 'self-dekulakised') at this time.[194]

The evidence available about the numbers in each category is far from clear. It seems likely that the plan to imprison or execute the heads of 63,000 households in Category I and to exile their families to remote areas was carried out in full in February and March 1930. In the two regions for which firm figures are available, 14,000 kulaks were arrested under Category I in February 1930, 9,000 in Siberia[195] and 5,000 in the Central Volga region; the latter figure is substantially above the 3,000 originally projected for this category.[196] In each case this amounts to 10 per cent of the estimated number of kulaks in the region, while the planned total of 63,000 is only 6 per cent of the 1 million kulak households deemed to exist in

[192] Danilov, ed. (1963), 105.

[193] According to one source, over 320,000 households had already been dekulakised by July 1930 (VI, 3, 1965, 18); various regional figures place a high number of expropriations in February–April or even in February alone (thus in the Central Volga region 25,000 households had been dekulakised or were about to be dekulakised by February 13, 28,000 had been dekulakised by May 1 (IZ, lxxx (1967), 97–102)).

[194] A Soviet source estimates the total number of 'self-dekulakised' in the four years 1929–32 at 200,000 out of 1 million kulak households (Danilov *et al.*, eds. (1970), 239); this figure seems too low, though it is consistent with the figure in another Soviet source that 5·9 out of about 28·6 thousand kulak households in the central Volga region fled by the beginning of 1931 (IZ, lxxx (1967), 82, 101; the figure for the 'self-dekulakised' refers to 56 out of 86 districts).

[195] Ivnitskii (1972), 230; VI, 7, 1968, 29 (Sidorov); *Sotsial'naya struktura* (Novosibirsk, 1970), 130–2 (Gushchin).

[196] Nemakov (1966), 138–9; IZ, lxxx (1967), 82, 96–102.

the USSR at this time. One Soviet historian estimates, without giving a source, that 'heads and individual members of families of kulaks in the first category (that is, the representatives of about 100,000 households)' were arrested and tried on the spot by the end of 1931.[197]

Two alternative figures are given for the number of families exiled to distant areas in Category II in 1930: 77,975 for 1930,[198] and 115,231 by October 1930 from RSKs in the RSFSR, the Ukraine and Belorussia.[199] According to one Soviet historian, the latter figure includes some alleged kulaks who were rehabilitated and sent back, and involves some double-counting, as both the head of the family arrested under Category I and the family members exiled under Category II are treated as separate units; it may also include some kulaks resettled within their own area.[200] Whichever figure, 78,000 or 115,000, is correct, it remains unclear whether it includes families of persons arrested under Category I, and thus covers both Category I and Category II. Within Category II, kulaks whose homes were in the Urals, Siberia and the North, regions to which kulaks from Categories I and II were being exiled from elsewhere, remained within their region but were sent to the remote and uninhabited or poorly populated northern districts; they were transferred to the OGPU as were all other households expropriated under Categories I and II.[201]

The number of households expropriated under Category III in the calendar years 1929 and 1930 is given in Soviet sources as 250,000; this is presumably obtained as a residual from Categories I and II; if a higher number of families than 78,000 were in fact exiled under the first two categories, then the number remaining in Category III should be reduced accordingly. Local reports in the spring of 1930 frequently refer in relation to Category III to resettlement outside the village. Thus in the North Caucasus some kulaks in Category III were resettled on distant and difficult land

[197] Danilov *et al.*, eds. (1970), 239 (this chapter was written by Yu. Borisov).

[198] VI, 3, 1965, 19 (Vyltsan, Ivnitskii and Polyakov); no archival source is given.

[199] *Leninskii kooperativnyi plan* (1969), 108 (Abramov); no archival source is given.

[200] Ivnitskii (1972), 299; this is denied by Abramov and Kocharli in VIK, 5, 1975, 140, who claim that the figure was obtained by a careful check of the number of kulak families in the areas of exile, and from information supplied by 'the organs which carried out the exiling'.

[201] Ivnitskii (1972), 226, 228; Nemakov (1966), 143; in the North all kulaks in RSKs were placed in Categories I or II (*Kollektivizatsiya* (Vologda, 1974), 273).

within their own district or okrug, others were transferred to four okrugs in which land was available for settlement; they were resettled in units of 50–100 households under special observation, and had to construct their own dwellings and organise their farms within three months.[202] In an okrug in Western region, kulaks were resettled within the okrug, but evidently outside their own village, on land set aside from eroded areas or swamp-lands in woods, or on other land in need of improvement.[203] In the Northern region a resolution of the bureau of the party committee on February 5 stated that all kulaks in Category III, while remaining within their own district, were to be sent to special settlements.[204] In Siberia, Eikhe warned against the danger of permitting kulaks to remain in their own village and proposed to organise labour battalions under Siberian auspices (see p. 234 above); kulaks in Category III were not permitted to remain within their own village, but seem to have been settled within their own district.[205] Resettlement within the village certainly also continued in some regions in the spring of 1930. An American journalist, revisiting his native village in Central European Russia in the summer of 1930, reported that while some peasants in nearby villages had been sent to the north of Russia, 'the few men in my village who had been "dekoolackized" had one thing to solace them—they were allowed to remain in their native countryside, three of them in the village'.[206] The extent to which this was generally permitted for households in Category III is not known. In the Lower Volga and the Central Black-Earth regions, the normal Category III was subdivided into two further categories: here Category III referred to households resettled outside the village but within the okrug; and Category IV to those remaining in their own village. The evidence available from both regions is insufficient to enable any firm conclusions to be drawn about the break-down between these two categories.[207] But the publication of reports in the press that peasant meetings were demanding the expulsion of all their own kulaks from

[202] SZe, February 12, 1930; *Kollektivizatsiya* (Krasnodar, 1972), 248–52 (decree of presidium of regional executive committee dated February 10).

[203] Smolensk archives, WKP 53, *cit.* Fainsod (1958), 242–3.

[204] Nemakov (1966), 143; *Kollektivizatsiya* (Vologda, 1964), 273, 275.

[205] Stepichev (Irkutsk, 1966), 469–70; Ivnitskii (1972), 229.

[206] Hindus (1934), 235.

[207] IS, 6, 1958, 24; Nemakov (1966), 139–40. In one okrug in the Lower Volga the plan for expropriation was as follows: I 400 households, II 990, III 200, IV

their village or even from the region would seem to indicate a disposition on the part of the local if not the national authorities to remove kulak households from their villages altogether.[208]

The provision that means of production and property confiscated from kulaks were to be transferred to the Indivisible Funds of the kolkhozy was only partly carried out in practice. Ever since 1927, better-off peasants had been getting rid of their livestock and their implements, as well as their personal property, in order to avoid being classified as kulaks, or in order to find the money to cover the rising level of taxation; and middle peasants had refrained from acquiring new capital. According to a Soviet calculation, by 1929 the value of the fixed capital of petty capitalist households had fallen in the three main grain-surplus regions of the RSFSR to only 30 per cent of its 1927 level.[209] During the grain collection campaign of 1929 and the collectivisation drive which succeeded it in the autumn and winter of 1929–30, 'self-dekulakisation' became widespread; and kulaks frequently gave their property away to their relatives or to other peasants to avoid seizure.[210] In his reply to the students of the Sverdlov Communist University published on February 10, 1930, Stalin admitted that 'it is possible and probable that in districts without comprehensive collectivisation a certain part of the kulak class, in anticipation of dekulakisation, will engage in "self-elimination", "will dissipate their property and means of production"'.[211] But kulak property was transferred to the kolkhozy in substantial quantities. Kulak dwellings were used for schools, Red corners, club-houses or kolkhoz headquarters,[212] and were transferred to former poor peasants who had joined the kolkhoz.[213] Substantial numbers of implements, horses and other

---

3,500; in a district in the Central Black-Earth region, the following expropriations had been carried out by the end of February: I 151 households, II 261, III 84, IV 128.

[208] EZh, February 8, KG, 15, February 23, 1930 (Khoper okrug); Ivnitskii (1972), 224 and Sharova (1963), 139, citing the local press from Lower Volga and Central Black-Earth regions.

[209] *Kolkhozy v 1930 g.* (1931), p. L.

[210] See for example the reports in SZe, January 25 (Western region), 30 (Ukraine, and Odessa), February 12 (Belorussia), 19 (Ivanovo region).

[211] *Soch.*, xii, 188.

[212] See, for example, P, January 15, 1930 (Khoper okrug); Hindus (1934), 149–50.

[213] A photograph in KGN, 15, February 23, 1930, shows poor peasants moving from broken-down huts into a smart kulak house.

farm animals were transferred to the Indivisible Funds of the kolkhozy. According to a survey undertaken in May 1930, by which time only 23·6 per cent of peasant households in the USSR remained in kolkhozy, 175 million rubles of the Indivisible Funds of the kolkhozy, which amounted in all to 510 million rubles, had been expropriated from kulak households; and this was 11·5 per cent of the total fixed capital of the kolkhozy. As only half the kolkhozy had by this time received kulak property, a substantially higher proportion of Indivisible Funds and fixed capital was derived from the kulaks in those kolkhozy receiving kulak property.[214] In the main grain areas, where the expropriation of the kulaks was most advanced, the means of production received by kolkhozy amounted to about 50 per cent of the total fixed capital owned by kulak households in 1929.[215]

Dekulakisation was intended to be an integral part of comprehensive collectivisation; while this policy was imperfectly put into practice, there is no doubt that collectivisation was facilitated by dekulakisation. Even in those areas in which general dekulakisation did not take place, kulaks in Category I were arrested. Kulaks in Category II were exiled from their villages in substantial numbers, not only in the three main grain-surplus regions of the RSFSR, where collectivisation was far advanced, but also in such grain areas as the Ukraine and Siberia, where only a minority of households were collectivised, and in such grain-deficit regions as Moscow and Ivanovo-Voznesensk, and even from the Northern region.[216] Dekulakisation was almost everywhere accompanied by a further drive for collectivisation, often following explicit instructions issued by the regional authorities simultaneously with the legislation on dekulakisation (see pp. 237, 240 above). A district party committee in the Ukraine reported that 'immediately after dekulakisation meetings and meetings took place in all villages; they had breaks only for dinner and sleep. The % of households collectivised grew every hour, reaching more than 50, and in 2 more

[214] Calculated from data in *Kolkhozy v 1930 g.* (1931), 200–1; on p. LV, all these sums are stated to be underestimated, but this would not affect the proportions.

[215] Calculated from *Kolkhozy v 1930 g.* (1931), 200–1.

[216] Slin'ko (Kiev, 1961), 189–90; *Sotsial'naya struktura* (Novosibirsk, 1970), 130–2; *Voprosy agrarnoi istorii* (Vologda, 1968), 49–50; Nemakov (1966), 143, 150.

days rose to 68'.[217] In a district of the Uzbek republic, dekulakisation was followed by comprehensive collectivisation, using 'arch-shock methods'.[218]

After the promulgation of the legislation on the kulaks, the number of households reported as collectivised throughout the USSR rose from 8·1 to 14·6 millions in the course of the single month of February 1930; in the Ukraine the number of households in kolkhozy almost doubled, and the increase was much larger than this in most of the grain-deficit regions (see Table 17 below). Throughout February, in most of the USSR, the growing mood of caution among some of the party leaders, and the gentle warnings about excesses communicated to the local organisations, had far less effect on the collectivisation drive than dekulakisation, which was carried out under the close control of the Politburo, and greatly accelerated collectivisation.

(F) THE SITUATION IN THE COUNTRYSIDE, FEBRUARY 1930

On February 10, Stalin's laconic encouragement of the further extension of collectivisation appeared in *Pravda*; on March 2, his article 'Dizzy with Success' insisted on restraint and caution. This reversal of policy evidently took place only after protracted disputes in the party; but only tantalising glimpses of the controversy appeared in the Soviet press at the time or have been afforded us in recent accounts by Soviet historians based on the archives. To attempt to explain what happened it is necessary to look more closely at the relation between the regime and the countryside in February 1930.

At the end of January, almost all the seed for the spring sowing was still in the hands of the peasants (see p. 239 above). In the course of the next few weeks, with the increase in the number of households in kolkhozy, the seed plan was increased from 2·7 to 3·98 million tons.[219] The grain was acquired by the kolkhozy by a repetition on a

[217] Slin'ko (Kiev, 1961), 199; see also *ibid*. 188.

[218] SZe, February 21, 1930; this was described as a 'district of comprehensive mistakes (raion sploshnykh oshibok)', but reports from other districts in the okrug were said to be similar.

[219] See p. 239 above, and Moshkov (1966), 78–9; a plan of 3·81 million tons, excluding Turkestan, Tadzhikistan and Yakutia was reported in I, February 16, 1930.

smaller scale of the methods of the main grain collection campaign. Large numbers of officials were sent to the countryside, including members of the Ukrainian central committee and all the okrug and district officials in the Lower Volga region. In some areas, grain was seized from individual peasant households, and some of them were impelled to join the kolkhozy in consequence.[220] The campaign was successful. Most seed grain was collected during the first three weeks of February, and by March 10 the total reached 4·14 million tons, as the table below shows (in million tons):

January 10	0·16[a]
January 15	0·19[a]
January 20	0·41[b]
February 1	0·91[b]
February 10	1·85[c]
February 20	3·24[d]
March 1	3·92[e]
March 10	4·14[f]

[a] I, January 21, 1930; it is not clear whether these figures refer only to the RSFSR.
[b] I, February 6, 1930; these figures exclude the Transcaucasian and Central Asian republics; the figure for February 1, including Transcaucasia, but excluding Turkestan, Tadzhikistan and Yakutia, was later given as 1·08.
[c] I, February 16, 1930.
[d] SZe, February 26, 1930.
[e] I, March 6, 1930.
[f] P, March 29, 1930; SO, 3–4, 1930, 109.

This was enough, together with state seed loans to areas which had experienced particularly bad climatic conditions in 1929, to sow 48–49 million hectares.[221] The level of collectivisation actually reached at this point corresponded to a planned sown area of about 60 million hectares.[222]

In spite of a substantial decline in the number of horses, a similar campaign secured the transfer of large numbers of draught animals and implements to the kolkhozy (see vol. 2, pp. 98–9). The campaign

[220] See, for example, the report from a village in Tambov okrug, Central Black-Earth region, in *Materialy*, i (1955), 359.
[221] SO, 3–4, 1930, 11.
[222] 55 per cent of households were collectivised and the sown area plan for all households was 93 million hectares (see p. 238 above); the estimate assumes that the kolkhozy had somewhat more land per household than the individual peasants.

for simplified land consolidation, launched early in January (see pp. 222–3 above), and an essential prerequisite for collective sowing, was also vigorously pursued, but with less immediate success. In the North Caucasus, special groups of land consolidators and agronomists were sent out early in February, and were instructed that by February 15 they must estimate the land mass of each kolkhoz and its location, and provide a preliminary indication of the location of the principal fields.[223] In the Central Volga, the land consolidators set out on skis as instructed and were engaged by the middle of February in great efforts to complete the marking out of the snow by March 1.[224] But elsewhere little was accomplished. In the Lower Volga region, the whole of February was taken up with collecting materials, preparing district maps and other preliminary activities, and instructions to the land consolidators about how to proceed were not issued until the beginning of March.[225] In the Khoper okrug of this region, it was assumed that the slogan 'land consolidators on skis' was not meant to be taken literally, and the consolidators sat in their offices getting plans ready for when the snow melted.[226] In many places, the formation of giant kolkhozy containing many settlements, and the frequent changes in the boundaries of the kolkhozy, produced very great confusion. At the Fourth Russian Land Consolidation Conference, which met from February 12 to 18, Shuleikin, in charge of land consolidation in the RSFSR, warned that 'our comrades are being distracted' by such schemes, condemned over-ambitious plans to re-plan land arrangements over vast areas, and insisted on a straightforward approach which would 'indicate the land to the kolkhozy as quickly as possible', while at the same time enabling them to cultivate unused land immediately.[227] But later reports indicated that in many districts elaborate revolutionary schemes, threatening the destruction of existing crop rotations, continued to prevail throughout February;[228] and as a result of the continuous expansion of the kolkhoz area the proportion of kolkhoz land which was consolidated

[223] SZe, February 9, 1930.

[224] SZe, February 15, 1930.

[225] SZo, iii–iv, March–May 1930, 61–2.

[226] SZo, i–ii, January–February 1930, 127; SZe, February 13, 1930, reported that the slogan provoked 'sceptical smiles' in Siberia.

[227] SZo, i–ii, January–February 1930, 85–94; see also vol. 2, p. 43.

[228] SZe, May 30, 1930.

Ironically, it was the expropriation of the kulaks which unified the majority of the peasants in many places against the authorities. In Gigant kolkhoz in the Urals, while the anti-kulak drive was supported by some poor peasants who benefited from it, a substantial section of the middle peasants feared that they would be dekulakised:

> [They] became opponents of collectivisation, Soviet power and the whole policy of the party. All this practice formed a watershed in the district between the middle peasant and the poor peasant, and even abolished to a certain extent the isolation of the kulak.[237]

Frequently peasants were moved by pity for their kulak neighbours and their children.[238] In a village in Belorussia, 300 women gathered at the house of a sectarian priest on the day of dekulakisation, and many kissed his hands and feet; in another village, a crowd defended its 'virtual dictator' from the dekulakisation commission by 'surrounding his house in a complete wall'.[239] Over 2,000 kilometres away in Uzbekistan, at a large meeting inaugurating a kolkhoz, peasants shouted out that 'the *bai* don't need to be exiled from the district, let them work in the kolkhoz'.[240] Articles in the press lamented the 'pity shown for the kulak', the 'opportunist vacillations in certain sections of the party, especially in rural organisations',[241] and the '*opportunism, indecisiveness and appeals to "humanity" in questions of dekulakisation*' which characterised some lower party, cooperative and land agencies.[242] The atmosphere was later cautiously summarised by *Pravda*: 'far from all the middle peasantry were politically prepared, and able to recognise the need for the organisation and development of kolkhozy, the need for the elimination of the kulaks as a class'.[243]

The peasant disturbances of January and February 1930 are naturally incompletely documented. In the Ukraine, according to Soviet historians, 'in individual places, for example in Shepetovka

237 NAF, 7–8, 1930, 92–5.
238 See Lewin (1968), 508–9, and 513, notes 95–96.
239 *Trud i byt v kolkhozakh*, i (Leningrad, 1931), 173–4.
240 SZe, February 21, 1930.
241 P, January 18, 1930.
242 EZh, February 19, 1930.
243 P, March 5, 1930 (M. Garin).

and Tul'chin okrugs, and in some villages of Proskurov, Odessa and other okrugs, the enemy succeeded in provoking anti-Soviet demonstrations'.[244] In Central Asia, 38 demonstrations were reported involving 15 thousand people.[245] In the Central Black-Earth region 2,000 or more people sometimes participated in demonstrations, and according to a Soviet historian some of these 'were half-way to an uprising': in one okrug six 'kulak demonstrations' were suppressed by armed force, and at the end of February 1930 'kulak counter-revolutionary demonstrations seized the northern part' of another okrug.[246] Anti-kolkhoz demonstrations, 'which began to develop into an anti-Soviet movement', also took place in Siberia, the Central Volga region, the Crimea, and the Moscow region.[247] In Siberia, according to a Soviet historian, 'at the end of 1929 the struggle of the kulaks became not only more fierce, but also more organised', and at the beginning of 1930 'terrorist acts' by kulaks increased. One thousand such acts were registered in the first six months of 1930 and, between February 1 and March 10, 19 'insurrectionary counter-revolutionary organisations' and 465 'kulak anti-Soviet groupings', including more than 4,000 kulaks, were exposed.[248] According to Soviet historians, 'in the period from January to March 15, 1930, the kulaks organised in the whole country (excluding the Ukraine) 1,678 armed demonstrations, accompanied by the murder of party and soviet officials and kolkhoz activists, and by the destruction of the property of kolkhozy and collective farmers'.[249]

The most dramatic events occurred in the North Caucasus. According to a Soviet account, based on the archives:

> The most serious events took place in Sal'sk okrug. On February 10, 1930, an armed demonstration took place in the village of Yekaterinovka as a result of distortions in the policy of the party. On subsequent days it spread to the neighbouring villages: Baranniki, Novo-Manych, Srednii Yegorlyk, Novo-Yegorlyk

[244] *Ocherki istorii Kommunisticheskoi partii Ukrainy* (Kiev, 1964), 402.

[245] IZ, lxxvi (1965), 28–9.

[246] Sharova (1963), 156, based on the local archives.

[247] Danilov, ed. (1963), 109–10.

[248] *Sotsial'naya struktura* (Novosibirsk, 1970), 122, 124 (Gushchin).

[249] VIK, 5, 1975, p. 137 (Abramov and Kocharli); no source is given, and these authors are concerned to emphasise the opposition of kulaks in order to justify the scale of their suppression.

> and Sandatu. In Yekaterinovka a crowd of 2,000 demanded that those who had been arrested should be released and their property returned to them, and then destroyed the village soviet, the party cell building and the stores where confiscated property was kept. Former Red partisans, Komsomols and even certain party members took part in the demonstration. At the beginning it was an anti-kolkhoz demonstration . . . But during these days, because the jails were overcrowded, arrested kulaks were sent home from Sal'sk to await exile. Under the influence of the agitation of these most active kulaks the anti-kolkhoz demonstrations began to become anti-Soviet. The slogan appeared: 'For Soviet power, without communists and kolkhozy'. In a number of places elected commissions prepared declarations which demanded that local party cells, committees of assistance (komsods) and kolkhozy should be dissolved, that kulaks under arrest should be released and their confiscated property returned. The seriousness of the position is indicated by the fact that the Sal'sk party organisation was put under martial law, arms were issued to communists and Komsomols, and detachments of them were set up to protect the town. When it began to turn into an anti-Soviet demonstration, the Red partisans, poor peasants, batraks and part of the middle peasants who had previously been passively looking on, began to set up detachments to rebuff the kulaks. After five or six days, the demonstrations were suppressed with the aid of these detachments, and of cavalry units and armoured cars of the Red Army.[250]

Elsewhere in the region a wave of 'women's mutinies (bab'i bunti)' took place, strongest in five villages in the Taganrog district. In Sambek a 'huge crowd' shouted 'Down with the kolkhoz' and 'Long live Lenin and Soviet power', and in another village the slogan was 'We are for Soviet power, but without collectivisation'.[251]

Rumours about popular discontent circulated widely in the capital. A dissident foreign communist who was in Moscow at the time reported that 'more and more echoes were heard of peasant resistance and peasant risings'; he was told by 'a trusty Stalinist, a

250 Chernopitskii (Rostov, 1965), 101–2.

251 Chernopitskii (Rostov, 1965), 101; Chernopitskii states that these demonstrations took place 'in the second half of February', but the chairman of Sambek village soviet was dismissed as early as February 13 (see pp. 263–4 below).

collaborator of the Central Committee' that the party leaders were particularly impressed by the peasant bands in Ryazan' okrug, within reach of the capital.[252] According to a report in the archives of the British Foreign Office, Voroshilov 'warned Stalin early in 1930 that he would not be responsible for the army if the latter persisted in the process of ruthless and indiscriminate collectivisation'.[253] The British Ambassador in Moscow told the Foreign Office that 'certain members' of the Soviet government feared that the military party in Poland would 'promote a quarrel' owing to the latent disaffection in the Red Army: Red Army men, who were often sons of 'better-to-do' peasants, 'registered considerable emotion' when, on returning from the Far East, they found that 'their relatives, whom they were going to impress, had themselves been forcibly removed to the Siberia through which they had just triumphantly returned'.[254]

The peasant demonstrations were certainly taken seriously by the Soviet authorities. Mikoyan later told a party audience that the distortions of policy had been 'extremely dangerous' because 'in a number of areas, owing to these stupidities, distorting and disrupting party policy, we had demonstrations by the peasants'.[255] Stalin later condemned those he blamed for these distortions as 'people who were rushing headlong towards the abyss'.[256] The XVI party congress bluntly stated: 'If these mistakes had not been corrected on time by the central committee . . . this *would have threatened* to disrupt the collectivisation of agriculture, to *undermine* the very *foundation* of the Soviet state—the alliance of the working class with the peasantry'.[257] According to Soviet historians writing over 30 years later, 'In the second half of February 1930 the dissatisfaction of the masses of the peasantry became extremely intense in character, and the central committee of the party was obliged to

[252] Ciliga (London, 1940), 95; in Ryazan' okrug collectivisation was being pressed ahead particularly vigorously (see p. 215 above).

[253] PRO (London), FO 371/14887; this anonymous report is in the Northern Department files on Soviet leaders. I am indebted to Mr Jonathan Haslam for this reference. Voroshilov was People's Commissar for War.

[254] Woodward and Butler, eds. (1958), doc. 77, dated March 28, 1930; this report was written in explanation of Litvinov's anxiety about the danger of war, particularly from Poland, expressed in an interview with the ambassador on February 8 (*ibid.* doc. 64).

[255] SZe, June 3, 1930.

[256] *Soch.*, xii, 213; for this article see pp. 281–3 below.

[257] *KPSS v rez.*, iii (1954), 54.

[*Ryazan' okrug secretary*:] We think we shall complete collectivisation by March 15 (*K. Ya. Bauman*: You can easily complete it by March 10).[263]

A long article by Bukharin on February 19 was the last major defence of unrestrained collectivisation to be published in the national press. The article, 'Great Reconstruction (on the Current Period of the Proletarian Revolution in our Country)' described the current '*anti-kulak revolution*' as an '*abrupt break-through*', which was as significant as the launching of NEP in 1921, and praised giant sovkhozy and kolkhozy:

For the first time in history, the deformities and apathy of agriculture have yielded up their place and gone into a decline: the darkest, most oppressed, most poverty-stricken sector of every previous society is now, not without the torments of the transition period, on new paths. *This is a new page of human history*.[264]

Bukharin was still in some respects less than orthodox, cautiously stating for example that the middle peasant was turning 'in the main' to the kolkhoz but retained 'remnants of disbelief'; but his almost unqualified endorsement of the policy of all-out collectivisation even in its most extreme aspects was evidently cheering to the party leaders, and *Pravda*, rejecting criticisms of the article which appeared in the industrial newspaper, praised it as 'in the main *correct* and following the party line'.[265]

While such expressions of confidence in the existing party line were still prominent in the press, and many regions were pressing ahead with further collectivisation, the first moves in a radical shift in policy were already being made. In the North Caucasus region, following the repression of the disturbances of February 10, higher authorities vigorously condemned the imprudent behaviour of lower authorities. On February 11, the Sal'sk okrug party committee criticised its village soviets for failure to work with the poor peasants and a tendency to descend to naked use of administrative methods.[266] On February 13, the presidium of the regional soviet

[263] Cited from the archives in Kozlova (1971), 194–5.
[264] P, February 19, 1930; see also vol. 2, p. 44.
[265] ZI, February 20, 1930; P, February 21, 1930.
[266] Chernopitskii (Rostov, 1965), 108.

executive committee in turn severely censured the Don and Sal'sk okrug executive committees, removed the chairmen of two district executive committees, and dismissed the chairmen of six village soviets and sent them for trial; they were accused of 'the criminal use of administrative methods, distortion of the class line, completely ignoring directives of the higher organs of power, impermissibly weak work of the soviets and complete absence of mass work, crudeness and a high-handed attitude in dealing with the population'.[267] On February 17, the regional party committee complained that 'all regional committees of the national minorities are forcing ahead comprehensive collectivisation of their regions and even of their mountain districts' without sufficiently working with the poor and middle peasants; this was discrediting comprehensive collectivisation and bureaucratising the movement. It added that workers' brigades and Russian communists sent in to help were often replacing the party organisations of the national minorities:

> The regional committee again warns the regional committees of the national minorities against rushing ahead in the rates of collectivisation . . . It points out that it is not obligatory to establish kolkhozy on the principles of the artel; in certain conditions the establishment of TOZy is entirely permissible.[268]

On the following day, February 18, a further lengthy circular of the regional committee drew attention to a number of major errors committed on a large scale in the region in the course of collectivisation: the 'crude use of administrative measures', which had involved a high-handed attitude to the poor and middle peasants, and especially to women; the all-out and compulsory socialisation of cows, poultry, orchards, nursery gardens; and 'the criminal disobedience of directives in carrying out dekulakisation'. The circular called upon local party organisations to relinquish attempts to obtain 100 per cent collectivisation without adequate preparation, and instead to concentrate on the consolidation of existing kolkhozy in preparation for the spring sowing. It did not anywhere affirm the principle of voluntary membership of kolkhozy, and the right of members of existing kolkhozy to withdraw from them, but in other respects it anticipated in the North

[267] *Kollektivizatsiya* (Krasnodar, 1972), 741, n. 65; the phrases quoted are a recent Soviet summary of the unpublished resolution of the presidium.

[268] *Kollektivizatsiya* (Krasnodar, 1972), 255–9.

Caucasus region the decisions taken by the Politburo in relation to the whole USSR.[269] The circulars of February 17 and 18 were both signed by V. Ivanov, secretary of the regional committee junior to Andreev, and not by Andreev himself; but it seems extremely likely that after such stormy events their main points were approved by Stalin or one of his close colleagues. They indicated a fundamental change in policy.

While these various decisions were being reached in relation to the North Caucasus, the central committee conference of leading party officials from national areas, primarily Central Asia and the Transcaucasus, took place in Moscow between February 11 and 16. At the conference, Molotov warned against 'kolkhozy on paper' and reminded the meeting that the national areas in the East were particularly backward, and had less experience of collectivisation and a poorer technical base than the more advanced areas.[270] Following the conference, on February 20 a central committee resolution condemned the mechanical transfer of high rates of collectivisation to areas which were insufficiently prepared. In Central Asia, efforts should be concentrated on the most developed cotton areas; in the national areas generally, collectivisation was bound to take place at a slower rate. Dekulakisation in these areas was to take place only in RSKs, and even then the percentage of dekulakised households must not exceed 2–3 per cent, and households placed in Category II must be resettled within the republic or region.[271] A further central committee resolution on February 25 condemned administrative methods of collectivisation in certain districts of Uzbekistan and of the Chechen region in the Transcaucasus;[272] this followed an Uzbek decision to introduce 17 RSKs in the republic.[273] The central committee decisions of February 20 and 25 were not reported in the press, but on February 27 an editorial in *Pravda* warned against comprehensive collectivisation and expropriation of the kulak in national areas where insufficient preparation had been undertaken; it would 'substitute administrative measures by the Soviet *apparat* for the activity of the

269 *Kollektivizatsiya* (Krasnodar, 1972), 259–66.

270 Cited in P, June 14, 1930, disk. listok 12 (S. Dimanshtein).

271 Based on reports from the archives in IZ, lxxvi (1965), 23–5; VI, 3, 1965, 17–18; Ivnitskii (1972), 193–4.

272 Ivnitskii (1972), 194; IZ, lxxvi (1965), 24.

273 Danilov, ed. (1963), 239, 242, where the Uzbek resolution is variously dated February 11 and February 17.

masses', antagonise the masses and reduce the marketed production of cotton and wool.

On February 20, the day on which the Politburo approved the main decision on collectivisation in the national areas, an article in *Pravda* by Milyutin gave the first public indication of a substantial change in policy towards socialisation; this article was obviously prompted by higher authorities, and was immediately followed by a series of supporting articles (see vol. 2, pp. 104–5). On the same day Syrtsov, at a meeting of the party cell in the Institute of Red Professors, also condemned excessive socialisation and warned against the 'production apathy and production nihilism which have appeared among a considerable section of the peasantry who have joined the kolkhozy'; the peasant waited for orders, but 'in our organisational chaos and mindlessness' he was left without guidance, and it was now essential to 'develop the initiative of the peasant on a new basis'. Syrtsov called for 'maximum but realistic rates', and condemned the 'artificial inflation of percentages as part of unhealthy competition between districts'; rates of growth on paper were a result not only of revolutionary enthusiasm but also of 'official optimism' with its rose-coloured spectacles. With considerable foresight, he reminded his listeners that the results of the collectivisation drive would be judged by 'the real figures which remain both during the spring sowing campaign and after it'.[274] It was also presumably on February 20 that the Politburo established a new commission, including Kalinin, Syrtsov, Yakovlev and Yurkin, the remit of which was to elaborate measures for the organisation of the spring sowing, for carrying out further collectivisation (*sic*) and for eliminating the kulaks as a class.[275] Reports of excesses in collectivisation now began to appear more frequently in the press.[276] The agricultural newspaper criticised a local Moscow newspaper for failing to mention that membership of the kolkhozy was voluntary;[277] however, nothing about the volun-

[274] B, 5, March 15, 1930, 41–58; the speech was published after Stalin's article of March 2 and the central committee resolution of March 15, so its text could possibly have been adjusted to the new circumstances.

[275] Ivnitskii (1972), 195; IZ, lxxvi (1965), 26; the date on which the commission was set up is not given.

[276] See for example SZe, February 19 (Siberia—report by M. Rogov dated January 30—and Ukraine), 21 (Central Asia), 1930.

[277] SZe, February 22, 1930; the offending newspaper was *Moskovskii rabochii* for February 18.

tary nature of kolkhoz membership yet appeared in *Pravda*.

The second central committee conference planned on February 4, the conference of the secretaries of regional committees of grain-deficit regions, met from February 21 to February 25, and was attended by Stalin and Molotov. While the conference was in progress, various prominent party leaders who had been sent to the provinces to help preparations for the spring sowing returned to Moscow: they included Kalinin (who was in the Central Black-Earth region), Ordzhonikidze (the Ukraine), Kaganovich (Lower Volga region), and Yakovlev (Central Volga region).[278] While in the provinces, these party leaders did not, according to the available evidence, take a very critical line towards local excesses. While Kalinin and Ordzhonikidze criticised in a limited way the excessive socialisation of animals (see vol. 2, pp. 103–5), Kalinin praised the Central Black-Earth region for collectivising at least 73–75 per cent of households, and rejected the notion that the peasant had been driven into the kolkhoz as 'a tale for the kindergarten': 'where could we get the mysterious power to drive millions of peasants into the kolkhozy against their will?'[279] The Ukrainian party central committee, in a letter sent out immediately after a session attended by Ordzhonikidze, approved the collectivisation of the steppe areas in the spring of 1930 and of the rest of the Ukraine, in the main, in the autumn.[280] But, after their return to Moscow, Ordzhonikidze and Kalinin are said to have criticised *Pravda* at the central committee conference on February 24 for baffling local officials with 'statements which are very frequently incorrect'.[281] On the following day, February 25, a central committee resolution about the grain-deficit areas, like the previous resolutions on the national areas, stated that comprehensive collectivisation and dekulakisation were to be carried out only in individual districts where the prerequisites were present; collectivisation was not to be completed

[278] See IISO, [i] (1964), 283; ZI, February 23, 1930; P, March 3, 1930, for references to Kalinin's visit and to his speeches in Borisogleb okrug and Voronezh on February 16 and 18; IZ, lxxvi (1965), 26, for a reference to Ordzhonikidze's presence at the Ukrainian central committee on February 21; SZe, February 20, 1930, for Yakovlev's visit. It is not known whether Kaganovich and Yakovlev returned to Moscow before the end of the conference.

[279] P, March 3, 1930 (speech of February 19—see p. 255, n. 232, above).

[280] P, April 26, 1930; the letter was dated February 24. For Ordzhonikidze's attendance at the central committee session of February 21, see IZ, lxxvi (1965), 26.

[281] IZ, lxxvi (1965), 26; *Istoriya KPSS* (1962), 445.

until the end of the first five-year plan.[282] It was probably on the same day, February 25, that the Politburo entrusted to its commission the task of preparing a further revision of the kolkhoz Statute; it is also said to have invited Stalin to prepare an article for *Pravda*.[283] It is not known whether at this stage the Politburo had explicitly decided to re-emphasise as a general principle the voluntary nature of the kolkhozy. Three days later, on February 28, a resolution of the collegium of Narkomzem of the USSR was published in the agricultural newspaper:

> Instruct Kolkhoztsentr, in all specific cases of compulsory recruitment to kolkhozy, to carry out appropriate inspections immediately, either directly or via the regional kolkhozsoyuzy; inform the press about the results of these investigations and the measures taken to punish persons guilty of distorting the party line.[284]

A final sentence of this resolution did not appear in the newspaper, and was published from the archives over 30 years later:

> Request the editorial board of *Pravda* to publish an article against the cases which have occurred of distorting the party line in relation to collectivisation.[285]

The editorial board of *Pravda* promptly complied.

[282] Ivnitskii (1972), 195; according to this source, the resolution was approved by the new Politburo commission after 'the central committee on February 25 decided to combine the work of the conference and the Politburo commission'.

[283] *Istoriya KPSS* (1962), 445; no archival source is cited for the statement that the Politburo instructed Stalin to write the article; February 25 is the date of the last known Politburo meeting before its publication.

[284] SZe, February 28, 1930.

[285] IZ, lxxx (1967), 99. The resolution will be found in TsGANKh 7486/19/2, 110, which reports that 'the question was decided by correspondence (oprosom) with members of the collegium'.

peasants should be permitted to leave the kolkhozy and, if so, on what terms.

In spite of this caution in its practical recommendations, the article was strongly worded, and its impact on the peasantry was very considerable. According to Hindus, in his native village:

> News came of a letter which Stalin had written, ordering organizers to stop driving people into the *kolkhoz*. At once people braced up. They rushed to the post offices and to the town to buy the newspapers that printed Stalin's letter. They paid, three, four, five roubles for a copy of such a paper, that was how eager they were to see the letter with their own eyes. In the market places peasants gathered in groups and read it aloud and discussed it long and violently, and some of them were so overjoyed that they bought all the vodka they could pay for and got drunk. Others stuck the paper inside their bosom and rushed home to show it to the neighbours and went to the Soviet offices and, flashing it before the officials and the organizers, gave them a piece of their mind.[3]

Another foreign observer reported that it caused a 'tremendous sensation' and as much as 15 roubles was paid for a copy; one peasant said that it was regarded 'as their forefathers had regarded the edict which emancipated the serfs'.[4]

The revised Statute of the agricultural artel was published simultaneously with Stalin's article. In respect of the right of the collective farmer to leave the kolkhoz no change was made in the severe conditions of the Statute of February 6:

> The board shall settle the account of a member who leaves the artel, and return to him his share fee; a person leaving the artel may be provided with a land allotment (nadel) only outside the boundaries of the land area of the artel. As a rule the account shall be settled only at the end of the economic year.[5]

The term 'share fee' was a reference to that part (normally 50–75 per cent) of the socialised property (including animals) of the collective

[3] Hindus (1934), 147.
[4] Hoover (1931), 111–12.
[5] P, February 7, March 2, 1930 (clause 10).

farmer which had not been included in the Indivisible Fund.[6] Thus, if the peasant left, he was to get back only part of his means of production and would not receive even that part until the autumn; and he would have to find land outside the kolkhoz boundaries. On March 7, the agricultural newspaper confirmed these arrangements, and recommended peasants leaving the kolkhoz to ask the local land authorities to provide a land allotment 'from the free lands of the state land fund'.[7] Thus it was evidently supposed that the number of peasants leaving the kolkhoz would not be numerous: this was a consolidation and not a retreat. Immediately after the publication of Stalin's article, a *Pravda* editorial assumed that the kolkhozy would be responsible for more than 50 per cent of the spring sowing.[8] Two days later a report from a Narkomzem official claimed that 59 per cent of households had been collectivised by February 20, as compared with only 17 per cent a month previously, and predicted in a footnote that 'in the period remaining to the spring, and during the spring sowing, the number of collectivised households will continue to increase considerably'.[9] A few days later, a report from the Ukraine in the agricultural newspaper announced that the rate of collectivisation had accelerated in the past 20 or 30 days and claimed that at least 75 per cent of households would be collectivised by the spring sowing, and in the same issue an article by Kosior claimed that comprehensive collectivisation would be completed in the whole of the steppe area of the Ukraine during the spring of 1930 and 'in the main' in the whole of the Ukraine by the autumn.[10] The plan for the Ukraine of the beginning of February (see p. 242 above) was thus unchanged. In the first ten days or so after the publication of Stalin's article, hard-hitting reports in the press criticised giant kolkhozy and the compulsory collectivisation of all farm animals, and many complaints appeared about a subject not mentioned by Stalin—the expropriation of middle peasants and the theft of personal property

[6] P, February 7, March 2, 1930 (art. 9); see vol. 2, p. 121.

[7] SZe, March 7, 1930.

[8] P, March 3, 1930.

[9] P, March 5, 1930 (V. Feigin, who was head of the department of rural construction and industrialisation of Narkomzem of the RSFSR and a member of its collegium—BU NKZ RSFSR, 7, 1930, 2, 23); the report was presumably prepared before March 2, but the editorial staff of *Pravda* must have decided to publish it, and to permit the author to add, or leave in, the footnote.

[10] SZe, March 8, 1930.

in the course of dekulakisation.[11] But very little was said about the compulsory recruitment of peasants to kolkhozy. Between March 1 and 10, the membership of kolkhozy actually increased, though at a slower rate than at any time in the previous three months.[12]

On March 10, a central committee resolution prepared by the secretariat, 'On the Struggle with Distortions in the Party Line in the Kolkhoz Movement', was approved by the Politburo and sent by telegraph to all local organisations.[13] On March 14, the Politburo decided to publish the resolution in the press, strengthening it with a clause which insisted that 'all these distortions are the *main brake* on the further growth of the kolkhoz movement and a *direct help* to our class enemies'.[14] The resolution reiterated Stalin's attacks on compulsory collectivisation and excessive socialisation. Party organisations were now instructed 'to *remove* from their posts officials who are not able or do not wish to carry out a decisive struggle with distortions of the party line and *replace* them by others'. It also condemned the prohibition of markets and bazaars, and, except where the overwhelming majority of peasants approved, the closing of churches. The resolution strongly criticised some of the practices of dekulakisation, linking them with the violations of the 'voluntary principle':

> In a number of districts voluntary collectivisation has been replaced by *compulsion* to join the kolkhozy by threatening dekulakisation, deprivation of the franchise, etc. As a result the 'dekulakised' sometimes include part of the middle and even the poor peasants, and in some districts the percentage of 'dekulakised' has risen to 15 per cent and the percentage of disfranchised to 15–20 per cent. Cases have occurred of extremely crude, shameful and criminal treatment of the population by some lower officials, who are sometimes themselves the victims of

[11] For example, SZe, March 4 and 7 (Siberia), 6 (Khoper okrug), 8 (Ukraine), 1930.

[12] See table in IZ, lxxvi (1965), 31 and Table 16 below.

[13] IZ, lxxvi (1965), 29; the resolution has not been published in the form in which it was approved on March 10.

[14] IZ, lxxvi (1965), 29; the only other known change, apart from a trivial change in the title, is that a list of the areas from which reports of the distortions had been received, including the main grain areas, was omitted from the published version (compare Sharova (1963), 160, on the resolution of March 10 with the text of the resolution of March 14 in *KPSS v rez.*, ii (1954), 668–71).

provocation by counter-revolutionary elements who have joined in (pillaging, share-out of property, arrest of middle and even poor peasants, etc.).

Party organisations were to check the lists of those who had been dekulakised and disfranchised, and to '*correct errors*' in relation to both middle peasants and former Red partisans, to members of the families of village school teachers and Red army men of all ranks. Kulaks and disfranchised persons could be admitted to the kolkhozy if they were vouched for by members of their family who were Red partisans, Red army men or school teachers and 'devoted to Soviet power'.[15]

After the approval of the first resolution (that of March 10), an editorial in *Pravda* assured its readers that only 'helpless cretins writing in bourgeois and Menshevik newspapers abroad' believed that compulsion was the basis of Soviet collectivisation, but conceded for the first time that cows and pigs socialised by compulsion could be returned to collective farmers, and that 'here and there (koe-gde)' collective farmers 'recruited by decree' might decide to leave.[16] But no indication was given even now that this decline would be substantial, or that it might affect the major grain areas. On the same day, March 12, in a full page of the agricultural newspaper devoted to collectivisation in the Ukraine, Chubar' reported that 63 per cent of peasant households in the Ukraine belonged to kolkhozy on March 1, and did not refer at all to a subsequent decline, and Kosior repeated the plans for collectivisation which he had referred to a few days previously (see p. 272 above).[17] Kosior and Chubar' were both candidate members of the Politburo. A few days later Preobrazhensky, in a report of his impressions on a recent visit to RSKs, his first published article since 1927, enthusiastically praised collectivisation:

> The working masses in the countryside have been exploited for centuries. Now, after a chain of bloody defeats beginning with the peasant uprisings of the Middle Ages, their powerful movement for the first time in human history has a chance of victory.

The plan of every district should make the assumption that it would

[15] P, March 15, 1930; *KPSS v rez.*, ii (1954), 668–71.

[16] P, March 12, 1930.

[17] SZe, March 12, 1930.

be fully collectivised, as 'tomorrow life will catch up with the plan': while in many cases half those who joined the kolkhoz reconsidered and left again after a week, most conscious and cultured middle peasants were now won over, and their hesitations were at an end; and 'every poor peasant is now an agent of Soviet power in the countryside'. After a celebratory village meeting in a rural school he had sat up all night discussing with the peasants:

> I said to myself, looking at this new village cemented together by the kolkhoz, 'they will not desert the kolkhoz; a year or two of economic success on the basis of the new system and this welding together of the village economy from below will compel the collective farmers to fight with machine guns like lions against all the forces of world imperialism'.[18]

In the second half of March, party leaders and senior agricultural officials again visited the provinces on the instructions of the Politburo. During a tour of the Ukraine, Ordzhonikidze criticised the use of any compulsion and pressure against those leaving the kolkhozy, and complained to Stalin and Kosior by direct wire about the situation in Krivoi Rog okrug: 'Here distortions atrocious: 100% collectivised. Individuals leaving not given back horse or seed. Explanation: we'll finish sowing, and then talk'. He added that with flexible leadership half the kolkhozy could be retained.[19] This was a remarkable change in orientation by Ordzhonikidze, who is reported to have said a month previously that local officials in the Ukraine were excellent and had no deviations.[20] In the Central Black-Earth region, Kaganovich, according to a report sent in from Kozlov okrug to Narkomzem, stuck to the old methods:

> On March 20, 1930, comrade Kaganovich (CC CPSU(b)) arrived in Kozlov. At the bureau of the okrug committee comrade Kaganovich advised us as follows: you must struggle until the sowing for collective work in the fields, expel those against the kolkhozy from the kolkhozy, cut off some remote land for them, don't give them loans, etc.[21]

[18] P, March 16, 1930.
[19] VI, 3, 1965, 8.
[20] *Ocherki istorii Kommunisticheskoi partii Ukrainy* (Kiev, 1964), 402.
[21] VIK, 4, 1962, 66; Kozlov was later renamed Michurinsk.

In the North Caucasus, Molotov supported a decision of the regional party committee and regional soviet executive committee which implied that collective farmers should not be permitted to leave until after the spring sowing:

> I think that this decision of the regional party committee and regional soviet executive committee is correct and that the CC will not be against it, although it formally contradicts the decision of the CC that the voluntary principle should be introduced systematically and formally . . . Our approach . . . is to manoeuvre, and, by securing a certain level of organisation not entirely voluntarily, consolidate the kolkhozy and strengthen the nucleus of collective farmers during the spring sowing.

He also remarked that he did not 'exclude' the practice that 'the majority may dictate its will to a certain part of the minority on the question of collectivisation as well', and did not regard this as in conflict with 'our Bolshevik proletarian understanding of the voluntary principle'.[22] These brief reports from the archives by Soviet historians may well be biased in favour of Ordzhonikidze and against Kaganovich and Molotov, but they reveal confusion at the highest level, as well as a continued effort to retain as many peasants as possible in the kolkhozy.

The severe provisions of the model Statute for peasants leaving the kolkhoz were not yet modified. As late as March 25, an article in *Pravda* which strongly condemned the excesses of previous weeks also declared that the 'Bolshevik voluntary principle' differed from the 'SR-kulak voluntary principle' which presupposed equality of conditions for the kolkhoz and for individual peasants; the author confirmed that clause 10 of the model Statute was to be applied to those leaving the kolkhoz.[23] Two days later, however, the same author conceded that, if the majority of the members of kolkhoz, or a 'considerable section' wanted to leave, 'in necessary cases, for considerations of political expediency, particular points in the Statute (including clause 10) should not be adhered to as the dead letter of the law'.[24] This appears to be the first occasion on which

[22] Chernopitskii (Rostov, 1965), 124–5; the decision was on March 18, and Molotov's speech was on March 26; the omissions in the quotation were made by Chernopitskii.

[23] P, March 25, 1930 (S. Krylov).

[24] P, March 27, 1930.

any reference was made in *Pravda* to the possibility of relaxing the application of the Statute. By this time millions of peasants had left the kolkhozy, seizing their animals, implements and seed, and demanding land.[25] Between March 10 and April 1, the percentage of households recorded as collectivised fell from 57·6 to 37·3;[26] in the Central Black-Earth region and the grain-deficit regions the enormous increases of January and February melted away (see Table 17).

In the absence of workable instructions from the centre, local authorities went their own way. In the Lower Volga region, as late as March 20–25, the land consolidation officials continued to mark out the land on the assumption that all peasants apart from kulaks belonged to kolkhozy.[27] In the Central Volga region, a directive of the regional party committee recommended on March 21 that the 'share fee' should be returned immediately to all members leaving, but seed, fodder and part of the Indivisible Fund should be returned only if a considerable group left the kolkhoz and the majority of the village did not support the kolkhoz firmly; it advised local organisations to 'try to delay the moment of return of seed until the sowing itself, but don't specifically insist if there are acute, insistent demands from the majority'. Peasants leaving in small groups should be allocated land beyond the boundaries of the kolkhoz, otherwise they should be allocated land at the end of each field of the rotation. This implied, without specifically saying so, that part of the land previously included in the territory of the kolkhoz should be transferred to those leaving.[28] In these recommendations to local organisations, the regional committee was obviously doing its best to retain as many peasants in the kolkhozy as possible. But the departures from the Statute suggested by the committee were not authorised by any legislation of the central authorities, and its authorisation of the return of seed, fodder and part of the Indivisible Fund went beyond the concessions announced in *Pravda* on March 27. In the North Caucasus, after Molotov's visit, the regional party committee emphasised to its local organisations that 'in very many cases an individual peasant leaving the kolkhoz or excluded from it is placed in an even worse position than the

25 See, for example, *Kollektivizatsiya* (Krasnodar, 1972), 286; P, March 14, 1930.

26 IZ, lxxvi (1965), 31; for alternative, slightly higher, figures see Table 17.

27 SZo, iii–iv, March–May 1930, 61–3.

28 *Kollektivizatsiya* (Kuibyshev, 1970), 174–5; this was a directive drafted by Khataevich, to be sent by telegraph to local party organisations.

kulak (deprived of land, draught power and seeds, allocated land of poor quality, etc.)'. But it made no specific recommendations about this, merely remarking unhelpfully that 'the question of allocation of land to individual peasants still remains in disorder'.[29] In those regions where very large numbers of peasants left the kolkhozy the provisions of clause 10 of the model Statute were sometimes quickly rescinded. In the Black-Earth region, Kaganovich's harsh remarks on March 20 contained the concession that land, although 'remote', should be 'cut off' from the kolkhoz land for those leaving (see p. 275 above). In the Moscow region, where the number of households collectivised fell from 74·6 per cent on March 1 to 12·7 per cent on April 1, a district party committee in Tula okrug decided as early as March 3 that the land consolidation agencies should revise all their previous allocations.[30] But confusion in the region was considerable. On March 13 the presidium of the Moscow regional executive committee and the Moscow soviet instructed the okrug authorities: 'When individual peasant households leave the kolkhozy, be guided by new Statute of the agricultural artel as published',[31] though this was obviously impracticable in view of the large numbers leaving.

Everywhere and at every level the forlorn effort continued to keep the peasants in the kolkhozy while simultaneously adhering to the voluntary principle. In the Lower Volga region, the soviet executive committee called for the 'strengthening and developing of kolkhoz construction' in Khoper okrug, and even insisted that a start should be made there on building the first socialist agrogorod in the USSR.[32] In the North Caucasus, Andreev assured a Rostov party meeting on March 18 that 70 or even 80 per cent of the peasants in the region would remain in the kolkhozy;[33] in fact the percentage fell to 67 on April 1 and 63 on May 1 (see Table 17). In the Central Volga region, the directive of March 21, much more flexible than many party instructions issued elsewhere at this time, nevertheless insisted 'it is unconditionally necessary to consolidate actual collectivisation at 50 per cent on average for the region';[34] in

[29] *Kollektivizatsiya* (Krasnodar, 1965), 287; this was a 'directive—letter' sent by Andreev on March 28.

[30] *Kollektivizatsiya* (Ryazan', 1971), 365.

[31] *Kollektivizatsiya* (Ryazan', 1971), 382.

[32] *Nizhnee Povol'zhe*, 4, 1930, 121–2; this statement was probably dated March 18.

[33] Andreev (Rostov, 1930), 3, 21–2.

[34] *Kollektivizatsiya* (Kuibyshev, 1970), 175.

fact the percentage fell to 44 on April 1 and 30 on May 1.[35] At the end of March Milyutin in the party journal still stated that 56 per cent of peasant households in the USSR were members of kolkhozy, with the mild reservation that 'a certain percentage' of these had left.[36] A report in the statistical journal prepared at this time admitted that 'some reduction, purely statistical, however, may be expected in the percentage of collectivisation', but also claimed that 'the measures adopted are in the main securing the strengthening and extension of the successes of collectivisation'.[37] On April 1 a party agricultural expert proclaimed in *Pravda* that 'half the Soviet countryside has gone over from individual to collective production'.[38] In fact 39 per cent of households remained in kolkhozy on April 1 (see Table 17). The most realistic report at this time, in an editorial in the agricultural cooperative journal, variously claimed that collectivisation on March 20 included 'more than 50 per cent' and 'has firmly attracted into its ranks about 40 per cent' of all peasant households.[39]

At the beginning of April, the Politburo, after reviewing the reports from the party leaders and senior officials who had journeyed to the provinces in the second fortnight of March, embarked on further policy changes designed to stabilise the situation in the countryside. On April 2 an Appeal from the central committee to party organisations, entitled 'Tasks of the Kolkhoz Movement in Connection with the Struggle with Distortions in the Party Line', again strongly condemned '*the policy of ordering the middle peasant about, which is entirely inimical to Leninism*'. It called upon local party organisations to admit their errors rather than 'blame everything on to the vacillations of the middle peasants'. They were to take urgent measures to put things right, including the dismissal of officials who were trying to prevent the correction of excesses, and report back within three days.[40] A few days later, probably on April

35 See Table 17; IZ, lxxvi (1965), 31, gives even lower percentages: 41·0 on April 1 and 25·2 on May 1.

36 B, 6, March 31, 1930, 7–8.

37 SO, 3–4, 1930, 5; the report was prepared towards the end of March.

38 P, April 1, 1930 (A. Gaister).

39 NFK, 7–8, March 1, 1930, 3; the editorial included data of March 20, so must have been written a few days before the end of the month at the earliest.

40 This Appeal does not seem to have been published; it was cited in the resolutions of the XVI party congress in *KPSS v rez.*, iii (1954), 54, and in IZ, lxxvi (1965), 33.

5, the Politburo dismissed Bauman, one of the most enthusiastic supporters of hasty collectivisation, from the secretaryship of the Moscow committee. The Moscow committee, a bastion of the Right in October 1928, before Bauman and Molotov replaced Uglanov, was now condemned for 'Leftist' excesses.[41] Kaganovich, who replaced Bauman in April 1930, dismissed 153 senior okrug and district party officials and transferred 74 to other work.[42] After the Appeal of April 2, other regional and okrug party organisations also took firm action against those deemed responsible for excesses. In Balashov okrug, in the Lower Volga region, one of the first districts in the USSR to embark on comprehensive collectivisation, a district party bureau was dissolved, several district party secretaries were dismissed, and 92 people were prosecuted, over half of whom were members of the party or the Komsomol.[43]

Some of the grosser abuses of dekulakisation were also rectified during April by commissions which were established in all okrugs and districts to check the lists of dekulakised and disfranchised.[44] The most important of these was a special commission of the central committee concerned with those exiled to the Northern region, established on April 9. The special commission, under the chairmanship of Bergavinov, party secretary in the region, operated through okrug subcommissions. These reported that mistakes had been made in the case of 10 per cent of the 46,261 kulak families which had been exiled to the region by this time. The special commission, however, reduced this figure to 6 per cent, arguing that the other 4 per cent, though not kulaks in terms of 'social indicators', were counter-revolutionary elements. The treatment of active opponents of collectivisation as though they were kulaks thus continued. Of the 2,800 rehabilitated families some were simply allowed to return home, others were enfranchised but settled in the Northern region.[45] Further commissions checked lists of kulaks exiled or intended to be exiled to other regions, and of kulaks placed in category III by the local authorities. In the course of two or three

[41] For the previous history of the Moscow committee, see Carr and Davies (1969), 90–2, 94–5; Carr (1971), 76–8.

[42] Kozlova (1971), 213–15.

[43] SZe, April 15, 1930.

[44] IZ, lxxvi (1965), 35.

[45] Ivnitskii (1972), 238–9; for a personal account of a family sent to the Far North and then returned, owing to the support of their son, a former Red army man, see Hindus (1934), 235–50.

months 70,000 families were rehabilitated in the five regions about which information is available.[46]

Simultaneously with these measures to correct the excesses of January and February, the Politburo approved a central committee resolution 'Privileges to Kolkhozy', which was immediately enacted into law by a decree of TsIK and Sovnarkom, published on April 3.[47] The decree announced various concessions to the collective farmers in relation to their animals and household plots, allocated the credits of 500 million rubles granted to the kolkhozy for the current year by the decree of January 5 (see p. 201 above), cancelled various debts and payments due from kolkhozy and personally from collective farmers, and announced tax concessions covering the next two years (see vol. 2, pp. 124–5).

A second article by Stalin, 'Answers to Collective Farmer Comrades', also published on April 3, reiterated his earlier criticisms of excesses. Stalin still attempted to gloss over the extent of the decline in the kolkhozy: he brushed aside the huge reduction in membership in the grain-deficit areas and tried to make the decline in the grain areas look smaller by underestimating the earlier figures for kolkhoz membership. But he reported the current position in the grain regions frankly for the first time:

> A month ago we considered that we had over 60 per cent of collectivisation in the grain regions. It is now clear that, if we have in mind real kolkhozy which were at all stable, this figure was obviously exaggerated. If, after the outflow of one section of the peasants, the kolkhoz movement is consolidated at 40 per cent collectivisation in the grain regions—and this can surely be

[46] In 11 okrugs of the Central Black-Earth region, '32,583 incorrectly dekulakised middle peasant households were restored to their rights by May 25' (Sharova (1963), 165–6); in the Lower Volga region the property of 5,500 middle peasant households and in Kazakhstan of 9,356 was restored by the summer of 1930 (IZ, lxxvi (1965), 35); in the Central Volga region property was restored to about 5,000 middle peasants and over 10,000 were enfranchised (IZ, lxxvi (1965), 35; IZ, lxxx (1967), 80); in Siberia 13,100 petitions from dekulakised peasants had been approved by June 1, 1930 (*Sotsial'naya struktura* (Novosibirsk, 1970), 131).

[47] *Kollektivizatsiya . . . 1917–1935* (1957), 290–3; SZ, 1930, art. 230; both decisions were dated April 2. A preliminary version of the central committee resolution was sent to regional party committees, which are reported to have sent back 'important amendments' (IZ, lxxvi (1965), 33–4).

achieved—this will be an outstanding achievement of the kolkhoz movement at the present moment.[48]

Stalin's main objective in the article was to present the decline as a fairly minor matter, and to restore confidence in the policy of the party leadership towards the peasantry. He fully admitted that the danger of a rupture with the mass of the peasantry had been serious, but he treated it as a brief interlude: it 'made itself felt in the second half of February' and had been dealt with immediately by the central committee. Nor was the emphasis by the party on the voluntary principle a retreat: its consistent objective was to undertake a '*real* offensive against our class enemies' on the basis of the resolution of January 5. In accordance with the laws of an offensive it was essential, as in all military campaigns, to consolidate the positions already taken; in accordance with the class nature of the offensive, it was necessary to bring to an end the tendency to attack not the capitalist elements in the countryside but 'our ally the middle peasant'. Moreover, the withdrawal of 'dead souls' from the kolkhozy was an advantage, and was 'not even their withdrawal but the discovery of an emptiness'. It was also advantageous that hostile elements were leaving. The withdrawal of vacillating peasants was admittedly a 'serious but temporary loss' to the kolkhozy, and it was very important to persuade them to return; but these peasants were acting mistakenly, as they would lose the privileges recently granted to collective farmers by the Soviet authorities. 'The kolkhozy are the *only* means by which the peasantry can escape from poverty and darkness.' On the sensitive issue of the kulaks, which Stalin ignored in his article of March 2, he now conceded that the kulak class could not be eliminated 'in one blow', but at the same time castigated the kulaks, with the aid of an apt quotation from Lenin, as 'blood-suckers, spiders and vampires' with whom there could be no peace.

[48] The following are the actual percentages of households collectivised eventually reported for these areas:

	March 1[a]	*April 1*[a]	*May*[b]
Three main grain regions of RSFSR	69·9	54·9	39·4
Ukrainian SSR	60·8	46·5	38·2

[a] Calculated from data in Table 17, and sources there cited.
[b] Calculated from data for number of households in kolkhozy given in *Kolkhozy v 1930 g.* (1931), 3–7 (the kolkhoz census of May 1930), and from number of total peasant households as calculated in my Table 17 (see sources).

Stalin thus maintained intact the twin policies of rapid collectivisation and elimination of the kulaks as a class. On this basis he confidently urged the kolkhozy to pay more attention to their own organisation and to economic affairs. They should involve middle peasants and non-party persons in leading positions in the kolkhozy, pay more attention to women peasants, and 'subordinate all other tasks of the kolkhozy to the task of sowing.'[49]

Ten days later, on April 13, an important 'explanatory note' of Narkomzem and Kolkhoztsentr, approved by TsIK and Sovnarkom, endeavoured to provide incentives for the kolkhozy to undertake the spring sowing wholeheartedly, and also to encourage the collective farmers to remain in the kolkhozy by strictly limiting the amount of grain to be collected from the kolkhozy after the 1930 harvest. The explanatory note stated that for kolkhozy in areas primarily growing grain 'the norm of marketed grain production for transfer (sale) to the collection agencies is fixed at between one-quarter and one-third of the gross harvest, based on a calculation of the average harvest'. Elsewhere, it would not be more than one-eighth of the gross harvest. 'All the remainder of the gross harvest in both grain and non-grain areas remains at the full disposal of the kolkhozy.' The explanatory note of April 13 also announced that grain sown in the autumn of 1929 by individual peasants who had since become collective farmers belonged to them, and was to remain at their personal disposal after they had handed over part to the collection agencies, and part to their kolkhoz to pay for collective harvesting and threshing.[50] These rulings were a major concession to the kolkhozy and the collective farmers, who were strongly pressed after the 1929 harvest to hand over all surplus grain to the collection agencies. Owing to the very high free-market price of grain, the right to dispose of their additional grain on the recently reopened markets was much more valuable to the collective farmers than the financial concessions of April 2.

During April, the press, while more realistic in its accounts of the decline of the kolkhozy, did not abandon its optimism about their future. On April 3, the day on which Stalin's article was published, the agricultural newspaper announced 'a mass flow into the kolkhozy' and that the 'wave of those returning to the kolkhozy is

[49] P, April 3, 1930; *Soch.*, xii, 202–28.

[50] SZ, 1930, art. 256; the MTS already used the system of charging a percentage of the harvest for their services (see vol. 2, p. 18).

growing'.[51] Similar reports appeared later in the month.[52] Nikulikhin, a party publicist specialising in agriculture, in an article criticising 'tendencies towards spontaneous flow', explained that the voluntary principle did not meant that no 'organisational help' should be given to the peasants, and called upon party members to continue to mobilise industrial workers to assist collectivisation. He also claimed that the outflow from the kolkhozy had now finished, and a 'new mass wave' was beginning; the practice of fixing definite time-periods for collectivisation should continue, and 'about half' of all peasant households should be collectivised by the autumn of 1931.[53] A few days later, on April 17, while the sowing was continuing, the bureau of the Central Volga regional committee resolved that as a result of the success of the spring campaign 'the task of achieving comprehensive collectivisation (set on January 5) can in general be carried out by the date proposed—the spring of 1931'—and condemned the tendency to renounce this policy as 'blatant capitulationism'.[54] On April 20, *Pravda* devoted a whole page to the success of the 'Leninskii Put'' ('Lenin's Path') kolkhoz of 1,200 households in Khoper okrug, where after some vacillations 90 per cent of the peasants remained in the kolkhozy. 'Leninskii Put'', in an appeal addressed to all collective farmers in the USSR, declared 'we condemn the quitters, and consider them as deserters from the kolkhoz struggle'. A *Pravda* journalist praised the 'revolutionary daring' of the kolkhoz for launching its appeal. Reports from the kolkhoz described the bitter struggle for its establishment, in the course of which half its animals had been destroyed, and praised its success in the spring sowing.[55] The prominence given to this kolkhoz in *Pravda* was in itself a strong indication that the halt in the collectivisation drive was likely to be purely temporary; and on May 6 an unpublished decree of Narkomzem of the USSR formally divided the USSR into three collectivisation zones for the first time in an official decision, and proposed that in the course of the

[51] SZe, April 3, 1930.

[52] See, for example, SZe, April 10, 1930.

[53] SZe, April 11, 1930; on the same day an article in *Pravda* criticised an earlier article by Nikulikhin (SZe, March 28, 1930) for playing down the extent to which economic and political levers would be used to bring about collectivisation, and particularly objected to his stress on 'mass' collectivisation in contrast to 'comprehensive' collectivisation.

[54] *Kollektivizatsiya* (Kuibyshev, 1970), 185; the resolution is published from the archives.

[55] P, April 20, 1930.

economic year 1930/31 the proportion of households collectivised should reach approximately 70–80 per cent in Zone I, approximately 40–50 per cent in Zone II and 15–20 per cent in Zone III.[56] Henceforth it was an axiom that the drive for collectivisation should be resumed.

A full census of the kolkhozy held in the first fortnight of May, when the main exodus had already taken place, shows clearly that in the spring of 1930 they were much stronger than before the collectivisation drive of the autumn and winter of 1929–30. The kolkhozy now contained 6 million households as compared with 1 million at the time of the census of June 1, 1929, and 1·9 million on October 1, 1929 (see Table 16). Collectivisation was now very advanced in a minority of administrative districts: in 110 out of 2,851 districts covered by the census more than 70 per cent of households belonged to the kolkhozy, and membership exceeded 50 per cent in 372 districts.[57] Such a degree of collectivisation had been reached only in one district by June 1929, and only in a couple by September (see pp. 126, 135 above). The size of the kolkhozy varied considerably between regions, from over 200 households in the North Caucasus and the Lower Volga region to 20–30 households in the grain-deficit regions.[58] In the most advanced districts, most households in almost every village were collectivised; in the least advanced, each village contained only a small minority of kolkhoz households, or none at all. But everywhere the kolkhozy were much larger than a year previously, and the average kolkhoz now contained 70 households, as compared with only 18 households in June 1929. Socialisation within the kolkhozy had increased substantially. Most kolkhozy were now artels, whereas in the previous summer and autumn most had been the simpler TOZy; and a far higher proportion of the draught animals of the collective farmers, and a higher proportion of cattle,

[56] Cited from the archives in VI, 3, 1965, 9. Zone I included the Lower Volga, the trans-Volga part of the Central Volga, the North Caucasus and the Crimean steppe; Zone II Siberia, the Urals, the Kazakhstan steppe, Bashkiria and the Far East; Zone III the grain-deficit zone and the national areas. Zones I and II thus corresponded very roughly to the first and second zones in the resolution of January 5 (see p. 201 above). The Ukraine was not apparently mentioned in this decree.

[57] *Kolkhozy v 1930 g.* (1931), 17; and see p. 287, n. 62 below.

[58] *Ibid.* pp. 15–16.

were in social ownership (see vol. 2, pp. 107–8). Although the number of party members in kolkhozy increased from 81,957 to 313,220 between June 1, 1929, and May 1930, the number per 100 households declined from 8·4 to 5·2.[59] But as the number of the kolkhozy increased much more slowly than kolkhoz membership, so did the number of members of their boards of management; hence 22·2 per cent of board members were party members in May 1930, as compared with only 14·0 per cent in June 1929.[60] Nevertheless, 46·3 per cent of kolkhozy had no party members whatsoever on their board in 1930.

A comparison of the results of the census of May 1930 with the figures available for the beginning of the year reveals that most of the ground gained during the precipitous advance of January and February 1930 was surrendered in the retreat of March and April. For the USSR as a whole, according to current returns, the kolkhoz membership of over 5 million households on January 1, which rose to 14 million at the beginning of March, fell again to 7·1 million on May 1 and 6·3 million on June 1; according to the kolkhoz census it amounted only to 6·0 million in the first half of May (see Tables 16 and 17). The net results of the inflow and outflow of January–April 1930 varied greatly between regions. Two important grain regions in which collectivisation was relatively less developed—Siberia and the Ukraine—retained a substantial proportion of those who joined in January and February, and so, to a lesser extent, did the North Caucasus, where collectivisation was already very advanced by January 1. In the Southern Ukraine and the North Caucasus, the spring sowing begins towards the end of March, so peasants could not withdraw from the kolkhozy in March and April as easily as they could in more northerly regions; and in the North Caucasus, following the grave unrest of February, the authorities seem to have interpreted the 'voluntary principle' less leniently than elsewhere. In Central Asia, including Kazakhstan, and in the Transcaucasus, where little collectivisation took place in 1929, a high proportion of the new recruits of January and February 1930 also remained in the kolkhozy; this was of considerable importance to the authorities, as it meant that a high proportion of the area sown to cotton and tobacco had now been transferred to the socialised sector. In the

[59] *Kolkhozy v 1929 godu* (1931), 152–3; *Kolkhozy v 1930 g.* (1931), 224; these figures include candidate members.

[60] *Kolkhozy v 1929 godu* (1931), 154–5; *Kolkhozy v 1930 g.* (1931), 236; there were 272,416 persons in 'administration' in 1929, 378,869 'members of boards' in 1930.

other major grain areas—the Urals and the two Volga regions—the decline in kolkhoz membership was substantial. A very substantial net decline in kolkhoz membership also took place in regions where sowing took place later and where collectivisation had been pressed ahead particularly rapidly by enthusiastic local authorities, particularly the Moscow and Central Black-Earth regions, and Belorussia.

In all, the net increase between January 1 and May 1930 in the number of collective farm households in those regions in which the kolkhozy expanded was nearly 2½ million; the net decline in the other regions was over 1 million.[61] In the course of this tremendous upheaval, peasants withdrew from kolkhozy in RSKs in which collectivisation was almost or largely complete by the end of 1929: the 110 districts in which more than 70 per cent of households belonged to kolkhozy in May 1930 were fewer than the 123 districts in this category in December 1929, and at least 95 of those 123 districts no longer continued to have 70 per cent of their households collectivised in May 1930.[62]

While the quantitative increase in kolkhoz membership between January 1 and May 1930 was fairly small, and membership

[61] Calculated from data in *Ezhegodnik po sel. kh. 1931* (1933), 440–3.

[62] This is shown by the following table of the number of districts in each region in which more than 70 per cent of households were collectivised in December 1929 and May 1930:

	December 15, 1929	*May 1930*
Western	3	0
Moscow	2	0
Central Black-Earth	16	7
Kazakhstan	3	3
Siberia	2	0
Ural	15	0
Crimea	1	2
Lower Volga	51	0
Central Volga	8	1
North Caucasus	4	32
Ukraine	14	65
Belorussia	4	0

(calculated from data in IISO, [i] (1964), 270–1, and *Kolkhozy v 1930 g.* (1931), 17–77).

fluctuated considerably, the kolkhozy were strengthened in this period in a number of important respects. The number of draught animals in the kolkhozy (both individually and collectively owned) increased from 2·11 millions in January to 4·77 millions in May.[63] The increase in animals was much more rapid than the increase in membership. Some of these extra animals formerly belonged to kulaks; some may not have been withdrawn by peasants when they left the kolkhozy. It is also possible that a higher proportion of former middle peasants belonged to the kolkhozy in May than in January: by May 32·7 per cent of kolkhoz board members were former middle peasants,[64] a much higher proportion than ever previously recorded. But the major factor in the greater strength of the kolkhozy in the spring of 1930 was the acquisition of large quantities of land from kulaks and from the majority of the peasants who did not join, or who withdrew from, the kolkhozy.

The question of the allocation of land between the individual peasants and the kolkhozy was almost completely ignored throughout March; this was a counterpart to the authorities' unwillingness to acknowledge and later to regularise the exodus from the kolkhozy. At the beginning of March the problem of the individual peasants was briefly mentioned in the press. An editorial in *Pravda* pointed out that half the spring sowing would be undertaken by individual peasants, and called for 'mass Bolshevik work' to counter 'kulak agitation' for reduction in spring sowings by poor and middle peasants;[65] the agricultural newspaper pointed out that those who did not join the kolkhoz could not be deprived of membership of the cooperatives or charged additional tax, and would 'receive land outside the boundaries of the socialised land area'.[66] But this was all. No mention was made of arrangements for the individual peasant in Stalin's article of March 2 or in the party resolution of March 14. Although sowing should have already begun by the middle of March in most southern districts, almost nothing about the individual peasant appeared in instructions and statements from the party and Narkomzem in the first fortnight of March. Preparations for sowing

[63] I, March 9, 1930; *Kolkhozy v 1930 g.* (1931), 10; see, however, p. 298 below, for the continued shortage of horses in kolkhozy as compared with individual households.

[64] *Kolkhozy v 1930 g.* (1931), 236; 8·0 per cent were former batraks, 49·4 per cent former poor peasants.

[65] P, March 3, 1930.

[66] SZe, March 7, 1930.

in the individual peasant sector were not even mentioned in the ten-daily reports of Narkomzem of the Ukraine.[67] The agricultural newspaper eventually reported that 'in the Siberian, Leningrad and Western regions the individual peasant, who predominates in agriculture, has fallen out of the vision of the regional and local authorities'.[68] The position was similar in the Lower Volga region; and in Siberia 'we thought attention to the individual peasant would be assessed as an attack on collectivisation'.[69] On March 14, a telegram from Narkomzem of the USSR belatedly called upon republican Narkomzem and regional agricultural authorities to organise sowing by the individual poor and middle peasants immediately.[70] Further telegrams and decrees announced that the tax exemptions for individual poor and middle peasants who extended their sown area remained in force, and that seed collected into the 'insurance fund' for the individual peasant sector could be issued as a loan to poor and middle peasants who lacked seed and agreed to extend their sown area.[71] But no provision was yet made for regularising land arrangements between the kolkhozy and the individual peasants, even though during collectivisation individual peasants had frequently been allocated small amounts of distant and poor quality land, or not been allocated land at all.[72]

On April 12, long after the spring sowing would normally have begun in most areas, the central authorities, faced with clear evidence that 70 or 75 per cent of the peasantry remained or had again become individual peasants, seriously attempted to regularise their position in a decree of TsIK and Sovnarkom entitled 'Measures to Assist the Extension of Sown Area in Individual Peasant Households'. The decree conceded officially for the first time that seed contributed to a kolkhoz by peasants who had left it could now be returned to them if they agreed to fulfil completely the spring sowing plan. It also belatedly explained how land should be provided to the individual peasants:

The basic law on land consolidation and utilisation, which states

[67] I, March 24, 1930.
[68] SZe, March 23, 1930.
[69] SZe, March 23, 1930; I, March 24, 1930.
[70] I, March 14, 1930.
[71] P, March 18, 19, SZe, March 18, 1930.
[72] See SZe, March 22, 23, 1930, and, for further examples cited from the Soviet press, BP (Prague), lxxviii (April 1930), 2.

> that the best and most convenient land shall be allocated to the kolkhozy, must be carried out without any exceptions. But if it is possible to allocate land outside the collective fields which is close at hand and convenient, a complete halt must be called to attempts to allocate unsuitable land to individual households which have left the kolkhoz or are leaving it; a complete halt must also be called to attempts to reduce illegally the size of the land allotment (nadel) of individual peasants.

Individual peasants who increased their sown area would not have to pay extra tax; but those refusing without good reason to sow the land allocated to them would be taxed at the level of 1929 and their land would be taken over by the kolkhozy.[73] This decree was followed by a telegram from Muralov, People's Commissar for Agriculture of the RSFSR, instructing land authorities: 'decisively cease allocation of inconvenient lands to individual farmers', and 'desist from taking their pastures and commons and reducing their land allotments'.[74] Although they did not specifically say so, both the decree and the telegram obviously implied that the land area previously allocated to kolkhozy should be reduced when their membership declined, thus waiving clause 10 of the model Statute: there was no other way, except when unused land was available, in which the allotment of the individual peasant could be maintained. In the middle of April, an extensive campaign in the agricultural newspaper condemned the failure of local authorities to allocate adequate land, or even any land, to individual peasants. In the North Caucasus, the regional organisations were accused of having 'completely forgotten the individual sector'. The allocation of both land and seed was delayed, and the land which was offered was inadequate and of poor quality:

> In the B. Krepkaya *stanitsa* 52 mainly poor peasant households were allocated, in place of their former 250 hectares, 110 hectares of the worst land, which they refused. In Chernigovskaya *stanitsa* seven poor and middle peasant households were allocated land which they had to refuse after breaking four ploughs on it in one day.[75]

[73] SZ, 1930, art. 254.
[74] SZe, April 15, 1930.
[75] SZe, April 16, 18, 1930.

The position was similar both in grain-surplus areas such as the Lower Volga and the Ukraine, and in grain-deficit areas.[76] In Belorussia, where only 20 per cent of the peasantry were collectivised, in some districts the individual peasants had not yet been allocated land, and in others they received land in 'small morsels' or without access to pastureland and water, or 10–15 km from the village; as a result an 'unceasing flow' of written complaints was received by the Belorussian Narkomzem and peasants made their way to Minsk both singly and in groups.[77]

The effort to partly redress the balance in favour of the individual peasant continued throughout the remainder of the spring sowing. On April 27, a further circular from Narkomzem of the RSFSR, while reiterating that kolkhozy should be allocated the 'best, most easily mastered and best placed land, in one unit if possible', also stated that the quantity of land per 'allocation unit' for the kolkhozy and the individual poor and middle peasant households should be equal. This presumably meant that the amount of land per household or per eater should be the same in each case, excluding any former kulak land allocated to the kolkhozy.[78] Coming at a time when the spring sowing would normally be complete in the southern areas and the North Caucasus, and well under way in the Lower Volga and the Black-Earth region, this was a pious hope rather than a proposal capable of fulfilment.[79]

(B) THE SPRING SOWING OF 1930

Preparations for the spring sowing were disrupted, almost rendered futile, by the tremendous changes in the membership of the kolkhozy during the first four months of 1930. In addition to the enormous influx in January and February, and the almost equally substantial exodus in March and April, minor ebbs and flows in membership took place in every district of the USSR. In response to all these changes, the land consolidation officials, who had embarked in January and February on schemes for land reallocation of unprecedented scale and grandeur, were compelled to repeat their work. Shuleikin later reported that 'basic land indicators' had been

[76] SZe, April 16 and 19 (Lower Volga), 17 (Ukraine), 15 (grain-deficit areas).

[77] SZe, April 16, 20, 1930.

[78] SZo, v, June 1930, 79–87; the Russian term is *razverstochnaya edinitsa*.

[79] For normal dates of sowing see *St. spr. za 1928* (1929), 174.

provided for 39,500 of the 51,000 kolkhozy in the RSFSR, and that for 30,800 kolkhozy the work had been carried out twice, and in some cases as often as four times.[80] According to a report from the Lower Volga region, the allocation of land in the region on the assumption of 100 per cent collectivisation continued until March 20–25, but by the second half of March the number of peasants leaving the kolkhozy was so large that the work had to be repeated, and this time it was 'more complicated, painstaking and tense as well as extremely urgent'. Nor was this all: further changes were made necessary by complaints from individual peasants about this first revision, and by 'changes in the composition of the kolkhozy which took place in the Lower Volga region almost on the eve of the field work', with some peasants still leaving the kolkhozy while others returned.[81] The grain-deficit regions, where the decline in membership of the kolkhozy was particularly large, presented even greater problems. In the Western region, where the proportion of households in kolkhozy declined from 38·8 per cent on March 1 to 11·2 per cent on April 10, the regional plans for land consolidation assumed that the whole region would be reorganised into groups of kolkhozy in which each group covered 40–50,000 hectares; and it was frequently assumed that all the land would be allocated to the kolkhozy, so that individual peasants would be left without land. New instructions from the region were not received until the end of March, so land allocations had to be revised without them; the revision was still going on in the middle of April.[82] In several okrugs of the Nizhnii Novgorod region, land allocations which established giant kolkhozy, each tens of thousands of hectares in area, continued to be made until March 15. But kolkhoz membership declined from 49·7 per cent of households on March 1 to 13·5 per cent on April 15, so all this work had to be redone. The land consolidation staff was increased temporarily from 500 to 1,000 by recruiting forestry officials and others. By working without days off, often for 16 hours a day, they were able in the course of two or three weeks to reallocate land to over 4,000 kolkhozy, now based on the land society or the village.[83]

[80] SZo, v, June 1930, 19; this was a report to the party cell of Narkomzem of the RSFSR delivered on June 24, 1930. The figures exclude the Northern region and the Far East.

[81] SZo, iii–iv, May 1930, 61–4.

[82] SZo, iii–iv, May 1930, 66–72.

[83] SZo, iii–iv, May 1930, 56–9.

Everywhere land allocation was hasty and belated, and was frequently completed only on the eve of the spring sowing, or after the spring sowing should have begun. 'Basic land indications' were provided for at least 85·3 per cent of kolkhozy in the RSFSR by April 20. But the work was often merely sufficient to deal with the immediate problem of the spring sowing. In the case of 18·6 out of the 39 million hectares which were allocated, only the land on which the kolkhozy were to sow in the spring of 1930 was indicated, and no decisions were taken about the remaining land.[84] In the Northern region, the land consolidators still continued their work at this time. 'After the collapse of the "paper" kolkhozy', the agricultural newspaper reported from Vologda on April 20, 'neither the individual peasants nor the remaining kolkhozy *know where to sow*'.[85]

The hasty adjustments and readjustments of the first few months of 1930 were superimposed on patterns of land use which varied considerably in different areas, and the land configuration which resulted was extremely complicated. In the North Caucasus, the only region in which the majority of the peasants remained in the kolkhozy, each kolkhoz had already been allocated fields for the spring sowing by March, based on the existing practice in each village. The land consolidators, who at this stage assumed that all peasants would be in the kolkhozy by the spring, divided each field into crops, and each crop area into land sections (uchastki) the right size to be sown by a brigade (in some villages, each brigade received a single section, which was in turn divided into fields). When peasants left the kolkhozy in the course of March and April, different procedures were followed in different villages. By one procedure, those who left were each allocated a strip of land in each of the sections of their former kolkhoz brigade; while this partly restored the strip system, it had the advantage that it would be simple for them to rejoin the kolkhoz. This was one version of the 'open' kolkhoz, in which the individual peasants shared the same fields as the kolkhoz. By a second procedure, all the individual peasants leaving the kolkhoz were provided jointly with one or more complete sections formerly allocated to a kolkhoz brigade, and the collective farmers whose sections were transferred to the individual

[84] SZo, v, June 1930, 19–20 (report to party cell of Narkomzem, June 24); for the North Caucasus, see SZo, ix, October–November 1930, 35.

[85] SZe, April 20, 1930.

peasants were redistributed among other brigades. A 'brigade' of individual peasants was thus placed within the kolkhoz land. By a third procedure, the individual peasants were allocated land outside the kolkhoz boundaries altogether. Both the second and the third procedures kept the kolkhoz land in unbroken units, but made it difficult for individual peasants to rejoin the kolkhoz except as a group.[86]

In the Lower Volga region, the arrangement of land allocations so as to make it easy for the peasant to rejoin the kolkhoz was 'rarely observed as a leading principle'.[87] The 'open' kolkhoz was, however, widely introduced elsewhere, even in areas in which the percentage of collectivised households was smaller. Frequently the 'ring' system was adopted, a form of 'open' kolkhoz in which individual peasants were allocated land at the end of each kolkhoz field; but this often made access to pasture and water difficult for the individual peasants, who had to cross the kolkhoz land to get there, and sometimes involved an increase in the distance to be covered by the individual peasants to reach all their strips of land.[88] Various forms of 'closed' kolkhoz are also described. Sometimes, when a kolkhoz had a few members living in each of several settlements, it was simply allocated the land of one of the settlements;[89] elsewhere kolkhozy were established as a single land area on the borders of several land societies, or allocated the land on one side of the village, the rest being allocated to the individual peasants.[90]

Collectivisation did not automatically involve the abolition of the strip system. In one district in the Central Black-Earth region all the kolkhozy simply received a group of strips in each of the fields of the land society concerned, so that one kolkhoz with 43 members received nine strips for each, a total of 387 strips; they were, however, promised the right to consolidate their land into ten or twenty larger strips.[91] At the other extreme, in certain areas the land of some peasants before collectivisation was allocated in khutors or

[86] SZo, vii–viii, August–September 1930, 99–101; the arrangements made in February 1930 for land allocation in the North Caucasus are also described in SZe, February 9, 1930.

[87] SZo, iii–iv, May 1930, 64.

[88] SZo, iii–iv, May 1930, 59, 66–72 (Nizhnii Novgorod and Western regions); SZe, May 30, 1930.

[89] See, for example, SZo, iii–iv, May 1930, 59 (Nizhnii Novgorod).

[90] SZo, vii–viii, August–September 1930, 131 (Central Black-Earth region), SZe, May 30, 1930.

[91] SZo, vii–viii, August–September 1930, 128–9.

otrubs, which formed a single land area for each household. When part of the village was collectivised, the khutors and otrubs were broken up, and the remaining individual peasants were allocated land in each of the fields of the land society. In the rare cases where all the peasants in a whole village owned separate farms, as in parts of the North Caucasus (the *paikovaya sistema*), land consolidation to form large fields for a kolkhoz was particularly difficult, as the land sown with winter crops was scattered.[92] Over most of Soviet territory, however, collectivisation was greatly facilitated by the existence of communal land tenure, and, in spite of the great variety of land systems, boundaries between strips were usually eradicated on the kolkhoz lands, and the strips were merged.

Everywhere, the individual peasants received land last of all, and were treated much worse than the kolkhozy. Individual peasants sent petitioners (*khodoki*—literally 'those going on foot') or went in groups to complain to their local land agencies; finding they were treated unsympathetically in the district and the okrug, the representatives then made their way in large numbers to the headquarters of the republican Narkomzems in Moscow and Kharkov. Narkomzem of the RSFSR, after receiving no petitioners in January and February, presumably because the peasants were nervous about approaching the central authorities, or thought they would receive no help, was besieged by 630 individuals and groups of peasants in March and April, some 1,500 petitioners altogether, the number of visitors rising to 90 a day; most of them came from the Western, Ivanovo and Nizhnii Novgorod regions, relatively accessible to Moscow. Only 3 per cent of the complaints were considered by the group of specialists dealing with them to be unworthy of attention.[93] Even in May, the Narkomzem of the Ukraine was still receiving every day dozens of group statements and visits from petitioners from all over the Ukraine.[94] A report from Narkomzem of the RSFSR based on peasant complaints concluded that individual peasants were almost always allocated less land than they were entitled to. The kolkhoz legitimately received, in addition to the land to which it was entitled by virtue of its number of members, the land formerly worked by kulaks, land not in use, land freed by the disappearance of households (through

[92] SZo, iii–iv, May 1930, 75 (Western region); SZo, vii–viii, August–September 1930, 101 (North Caucasus).

[93] SZo, iii–iv, May 1930, 73–4.

[94] SZe, May 25, 1930.

the death of their surviving member or through migration) and land refused by individual peasants. Batraks, shepherds and smiths who had joined the kolkhoz were also entitled to a land allotment even if they had not previously received one. But in addition to this, kolkhozy also counted teachers and other rural employees as members for the purpose of receiving land, and kolkhozy were in practice allocated a higher norm per 'allocation unit' than individual peasants.[95]

The land received by the individual peasant was not merely smaller in quantity, but also distant, scattered, marshy and root-infested. Narkomzem of the RSFSR concluded:

> In a number of cases such land allocations for individual farms threatened to disrupt the spring sowing campaign. The individual peasant was completely forgotten and ignored; was not provided with land suitable for spring crops, and no account was taken of the fact that potatoes, oats, buckwheat etc. cannot be sown on every kind of land, particularly on land not prepared for it. In a number of cases kolkhozy were given land so that individual peasants' allotments were 10–15 km away, and they refused them altogether. This situation was widespread (Western and Leningrad regions). Looking at such schemes and listening to the explanation of the peasants, one comes to the conclusion that their authors were trying to create conditions for the individual farmers in which they could not carry on their economy normally; at the same time these conditions did not favour the kolkhoz. The representatives of individual farms were usually not involved in discussing the land consolidation schemes, they were simply ignored and land was allocated exclusively at the wish of the kolkhoz.

Frequently the individual peasants were not provided with access to pastureland and water, and also deprived of vegetable gardens and hayfields.[96] Similar reports were received from districts too remote to send representatives to Moscow. Thus in the Lower Volga region, 'the kolkhoz was allocated lands it chose itself, which it indicated itself, and the leading role of the land consolidation official was extremely weak; he really simply carried out the orders of the

[95] SZo, iii–iv, May 1930, 77–8; for 'allocation unit' see p. 291 above.
[96] SZo, iii–iv, May 1930, 74–6.

kolkhoz'. In consequence, the interests of the individual peasant were not taken into account.[97] No allowance was made in determining the amount of land allocated to the kolkhoz for its superior quality.[98] Frequently individual peasants were displaced unnecessarily from their dwellings.[99] Some peasants, then, were confronted at the time of the spring sowing with the need to construct a new dwelling and a new shed for their animals.

The position of the individual peasant was not fundamentally improved as a result of the belated legislation of April 12 and 27. According to Shuleikin, even at the end of the spring sowing the individual peasants were sometimes still neglected to the point at which farming was almost impossible, and were provided with less land in a 'whole number of districts';[100] the position of the individual peasant was particularly unsatisfactory in the grain-deficit zone. In the summer of 1930 Hindus reported from his native village, where only one-sixth of the households belonged to the kolkhoz, that the kolkhoz had been allocated 'seven hundred hectares of the richest land lying closest to the village with the finest pastures and the best water'.[101] The advantages of the kolkhozy, at the time of the spring sowing, in many areas where collectivisation still included only a minority of the peasants, were summed up by a Narkomzem report:

> The kolkhoz, consisting perhaps of only a few households, has very often received all the best land, and the remaining households, to a considerable extent poor and middle peasants, retain only uncultivated lands, marshes, shrubland, wasteland etc. Such a land distribution evoked the dissatisfaction of the peasants, especially if the percentage of persons not particularly engaged in agriculture, e.g. employees, was high in the kolkhoz.[102]

The kolkhozy and the individual peasants ploughed and sowed their newly allocated lands in the spring of 1930 with a substantially depleted work stock. In the course of January and February 1930,

[97] SZo, iii–iv, May 1930, 63.
[98] SZo, iii–iv, May 1930, 78.
[99] SZe, May 30, 1930.
[100] SZe, May 30, 1930.
[101] Hindus (1934), 212.
[102] SZo, iii–iv, May, 1930, 78.

nearly 8 million horses and oxen, out of a total of 25 million, were transferred to the kolkhozy; in March and April over 3½ million of these were taken away again by peasants leaving the kolkhozy.[103] Many well-to-do peasants got rid of their second horse in the hope of escaping the charge of being a kulak; many middle peasants sold their animals rather than take them into the kolkhoz. Fodder was scarce and expensive. As a result of this upheaval, the number of draught animals declined from 28·1 million in May–June 1929 to 24·9 million in May–June 1930; and, an unhappy augury for the future, the number of foals aged up to one year declined from 3·8 to 2·6 millions.[104] The quality of the animals also greatly deteriorated through poor feeding and minding. Both the individual peasant and the kolkhoz were affected. The number of draught animals per individual peasant household declined from 1·13 to 1·04 between May–June 1929 and May–June 1930.[105] But the kolkhoz, while almost everywhere provided with abundant land of superior quality, suffered from an extremely severe shortage of draught animals. In May 1930, while some 19 or 20 million individual peasant households owned 20·1 million draught animals, or 1·0–1·1 per household, the 6·0 million collective farm households owned only 4·6 million draught animals, or 0·77 per household.[106] The scarcity of horses in the kolkhozy was due to several factors. A high proportion of collective farmers were former batraks or poor peasants without horses, or employees who had not been engaged in agriculture. The kolkhozy had always been more attractive to batraks and poor peasants, and middle peasants predominated among peasants leaving the kolkhozy in March and April 1930: when the large influx of middle peasants into the kolkhozy took place in January and February 1930, the number of draught animals per kolkhoz household, both socialised and individually owned, rose from 0·47 on January 20 to 0·84 on March 1.[107] In the kolkhozy themselves, the socialised animals were badly looked after (see vol. 2, pp. 101–2); and in many cases the kolkhozy, lacking fodder, sold off their horses, assuming that with joint ploughing they

[103] I, March 9, 1930; *Nar. kh.* (1932), 188–9.

[104] *Nar. kh.* (1932), 188–9.

[105] Calculated from data in *Nar. kh.* (1932), 188–9.

[106] Calculated from data in *Nar. kh.* (1932), 130–1, 188–9 and (for number of individual households) Table 17 below; 4·3 million draught animals were in the socialised sector of the kolkhozy and 0·2 millions individually owned by collective farmers.

[107] I, March 9, 1930; see also vol. 2, Table 5.

would not need so many horses, and that tractors would soon be available anyway.[108] In fact the tractors available did not compensate for the lack of draught animals: even on October 1, 1930, the tractor stock owned by MTS and kolkhozy amounted to only 480,500 h.p., equivalent to some 640,000 or 960,000 horses.[109] Only about eight per cent of the spring sowing in the kolkhozy was undertaken by tractors (see vol. 2, p. 28). The authorities still clung to the hope that, following the example of Khoper okrug in the autumn of 1929, the kolkhozy by pooling horses and implements would be able to use them more efficiently to cultivate their abundant land.

Both the individual peasants and the kolkhozy were inadequately prepared for the spring sowing. When the sowing started, the individual peasants in the major grain areas were uncomfortably situated on small amounts of poor land which usually had only just been allocated to them. While they needed to grow grain and other crops in order to survive, they faced an immediate future in which they were uncertain of their position as individual farmers, and certain only that the 1930 harvest would be followed by substantial grain collections. The rise and subsequent decline of the kolkhozy swept away most of the agricultural services established for a minority of the individual peasants in the course of the 1920s. In RSKs during the period of rapid collectivisation, the primary cooperative associations at the level of the rural settlement, of which there were 49,528 with 7,126,000 members on October 1, 1929, were for the most part reorganised into kolkhozy, abolished, or simply ceased to exist. When large numbers of peasants left the kolkhozy in March and April, the primary associations were not re-established: on May 1, 1930, only 18,035 associations with 1,973,000 members remained, with the paradoxical result that the number of households in both agricultural cooperatives and kolkhozy actually declined from 8·9 millions on October 1, 1929 to 6·9 millions on May 1, 1930.[110] As a result, individual peasant

108 See P, May 11, 1930.

109 *Nar. kh.* (1932), 145; for tractor h.p.: horse equivalent, see note to Table 20.

110 NAF, 6, 1930, 18; P, June 12, 1930, disk. listok 11 (F. Tsil'ko), June 30, 1930, disk. listok 25 (A. L'vov); IZ, lxxvi (1965), 34–5. According to NFK, 14–15, June 15, 1930, 135–6, the figures cited may somewhat exaggerate the decline, as the figures for October 1, 1929, *include* and those for May 1, 1930, *exclude* credit cooperatives; moreover, no allowance is made for double-counting resulting from the fact that some peasants belonged to two or more cooperatives, and dual or multiple membership was much more frequent on the former date.

households were left 'outside our organisational and economic pressure and services', and were not supplied with machinery, seeds, or credit.[111] While these resources were in large part diverted to the kolkhozy, in some cooperatives agricultural implements and credits earmarked for the individual peasant remained immobile.[112] The individual peasant could, however, derive some mild encouragement from the support Stalin had given to the voluntary principle in collectivisation and from the strong condemnation, albeit belated, by the authorities of the unfair allocation of land which had taken place.

The kolkhozy were also poorly prepared for the spring sowing. On February 20, Syrtsov spoke of the 'production apathy and production nihilism which have appeared with a considerable section of the peasantry on entering the kolkhozy', and, attacking the 'centralisation and bureaucratism' prevalent in the kolkhoz movement, called for 'developing the initiative of the peasant on a new basis'.[113] The exodus from the kolkhozy in March and April removed those peasants who were least willing to participate in the new economic order. But in April Yurkin, at a Kolkhoztsentr conference, reiterated Syrtsov's earlier cries of alarm: 'the collective farmer has forgotten that he is the master of the kolkhoz, and thinks that it is only the board which needs to worry about the kolkhoz'.[114] No adequate incentives or controls were established in the collective sector of the kolkhoz to replace the motives which impelled the peasants into backbreaking labour when they were entirely responsible for their own economy—the need to feed themselves and their children by their own efforts, the desirability of selling their products for a money income so that they could pay their debts and taxes, and acquire manufactured goods, materials and implements. A shrewd émigré observer, in a review of the kolkhozy entitled 'The Rural Economy without a Master', summed up the crucial problem of collectivised agriculture:

> Whatever one's attitude to bourgeois 'spontaneity' or the socialist 'plan', from time immemorial, not only in Russia, but everywhere, and in all circumstances, the rural economy, like any

[111] NAF, 6, 1930, 18–19; SZe, April 15, 1930.
[112] P, May 23, 1930 (A. L'vov).
[113] B, 5, March 15, 1930, 48.
[114] I, April 15, 1930.

> other economy, is unthinkable *without a master*, and cannot be carried on *without economic accounting*. Whatever one's attitude to the 'huge upheaval' now being carried out by the Bolsheviks in the Russian countryside, whether one approves it or condemns it, one is bound to conclude, with astonishment and alarm, that *at the present moment* a spectacle is unfolding itself before us which has never been seen before: over an immense territory one of the most responsible operations in the rural economy is taking place, but no economic subject is to be seen, *homo economicus* is absent . . . Behind the vast number of extremely varied and extremely contradictory instructions, explanations and declarations which originate from authorities of all ranks and titles, the most attentive examination cannot distinguish the one thing which is most essential—economic accounting.[115]

This harsh judgment was one-sided: in industry what the author condemned as the 'decrees and cavalry charges' of Soviet planning succeeded in achieving rapid development, at a time when 'masters' armed with the latest methods of economic accounting plunged capitalist economies throughout the world into crisis. And in Soviet agriculture, decrees and cavalry charges succeeded—though at a human and economic cost which was entirely unanticipated—in calling forth from agriculture the grain which enabled the development of the industrial economy to be pressed ahead. But there were two important senses in which the kolkhozy lacked the kind of 'master' or guiding principle in the spring of 1930 which proved to be essential even within the framework of the centrally planned economy of the 1930s. First, throughout the spring sowing of 1930 the arrangements for remunerating the collective farmers for their work in the collective sector were unclear in principle and chaotic in practice (see vol. 2, pp. 140–56). 'The collective farmers', according to Andreev, 'to a large extent work because of their trust in the party and the Soviet government, and in kolkhozy'.[116]

Secondly, no clear arrangements existed for controlling the kolkhozy or for issuing instructions to them. In the summer and autumn of 1929, elaborate schemes were launched for regularising

[115] BP (Prague), lxxix (May 1930), 1–2; the Russian terms for 'boss' or 'master' (khozyain) and 'economy' or 'household' (khozyaistvo) have a common root, analogous with 'husband' and 'husbandry' in English.

[116] *Kollektivizatsiya* (Krasnodar, 1972), 288 ('directive letter' of the Central Volga regional party committee, March 28, 1930).

relations between Narkomzem, the interlocking network of different kinds of agricultural cooperatives, the Kolkhoztsentry and their agencies, and the kolkhozy themselves. The intention was to simplify agricultural cooperation and integrate it closely with the kolkhoz movement. To this end, it was decided that in each district one of the six specialised unions of agricultural cooperatives (for grain, flax, sugar, fruit and wines, poultry, and livestock) should be designated as the 'leading cooperative', the regional and okrug unions of the other specialised cooperatives either working through this raikoopsoyuz (district cooperative union) or treating their own district unions as secondary to it. All kolkhozy in a district were supposed to join the leading district cooperative union, in which they could form an autonomous section, if there were sufficient of them; the 'most mechanised' kolkhozy were to directly join the autonomous kolkhoz section of the regional or okrug cooperative union. In RSKs, the leading district cooperative union was to be renamed the 'district kolkhoz cooperative union' (raikolkhozkoopsoyuz), and the same applied at the okrug level. In respect of the kolkhozy, the agricultural cooperative unions at each level were subordinate to the authority of the Kolkhoztsentry and their regional and okrug kolkhozsoyuzy.[117] The subordination of the agricultural cooperatives to the kolkhoz movement was reflected in the appointment of Yurkin, chairman of Kolkhoztsentr, as temporary chairman of the all-Union council of agricultural cooperatives.[118]

During the autumn of 1929 and the first few months of 1930 some progress was made in diminishing the complexity of the cooperative-kolkhoz system. Attempts to establish a leading cooperative union in each district responsible for acting on behalf of all the specialised cooperatives were partly successful. According to a survey covering over 40 per cent of administrative districts, on May 1, 1930, 60·4 per cent of districts in the USSR had a single district cooperative union, 20·2 per cent two, and 19·4 per cent three or more; unification at the district level was almost complete in the

[117] The principal decisions on the agricultural cooperatives and their relationship with the kolkhozy may be found in *Resheniya*, ii (1967), 78–82 (central committee resolution of June 27, 1929), 131–5 (TsIK and Sovnarkom decree of September 18, 1929, also in SZ, 1929, art. 565) and SKhG, December 4, 1929 (decree approved by Kolkhoztsentr of the USSR and RSFSR).

[118] SKhG, January 19, 1930.

Urals, largely complete in the two Volga regions.[119] But the leading organisations almost invariably acted only on behalf of the specialised cooperative to which they were directly responsible, and treated the other branches of agriculture with contempt.[120] In some mixed-farming regions, therefore, several specialised cooperative unions continued to exist in each district: in the Central Black-Earth region, for example, there were over 500 district unions in 173 districts.[121] Even in those districts where a single leading cooperative union was established, representatives from different specialised cooperatives dealt directly not only with the district cooperative union but also with the kolkhozy. Above the district level, in the okrugs and the regions, the various specialised cooperatives continued to exist, together with the kolkhozsoyuz, and their functions were confused and overlapping. At the republican and all-Union level, the cooperative Union of Unions and Kolkhoztsentr duplicated each other's work on a variety of major and minor matters.[122]

Other state agencies also continued to be important. The relation between the kolkhoz-cooperative systems and the land departments of the soviets, which were controlled by Narkomzem and responsible for such important matters as land consolidation, was 'completely unregulated' even at the regional level. Narkomtorg, the consumer cooperatives and Vesenkha retained their responsibilities for the collection of various products. The 25,000-ers were reported to be 'organised by everyone, with insufficient coordination, serious direction and recording of their work'.[123] A journal of Kolkhoztsentr complained of *bezkhozyaistvennost'*, i.e. 'the absence of a master and of economic management'. Too many masters were giving orders ('the kolkhoz, the district soviet executive committee, the district party committee, the kolkhoz union, the group of kolkhozy, the regional executive committee, the regional party committee, agricultural credit, and the cooperatives'); the kolkhoz itself, with its chairman often absent, had a master only on paper;

[119] NFK, 14–15, June 15, 1930, 141–4.
[120] NAF, 6, 1930, 20; P, March 31 (I. Vareikis), June 12, 1930, disk. listok 11 (F. Tsil'ko).
[121] NAF, 6, 1930, 20; P, May 22, 1930, disk. listok 1 (Sarkis).
[122] P, May 22, 1930, disk. listok 1 (Sarkis); NAF, 5, 1930, 85.
[123] NAF, 5, 1930, 85–6; these examples are taken from the North Caucasus. On the 25,000-ers, see also P, June 5, 1930.

'agricultural illiteracy' was general.[124] Within this plethora of organisations, the system of temporary plenipotentiaries predominated; and the okrug and district party organisations emerged as the controllers of the plenipotentiaries. Established for the grain collections and continued for the collectivisation drive, the system of plenipotentiaries was again used for the spring sowing campaign.

The sowing campaign was conducted with all the vigour of the grain collections. The arrangements were similar to those in the spring of 1929: a 'sowing plan' was transmitted through regional and lower soviet authorities to every village.[125] Grin'ko later claimed that a spring sowing plan had for the first time been supplied to every village, kolkhoz and individual household; 'a programme of organised sowing corresponding to the interests of the country as a whole' had replaced the mere 'spontaneous resultant of the combination of the individual wills of petty scattered commodity producers'.[126] However, the process was belated and incomplete. The local authorities were preoccupied with the collectivisation drive; in preparing for the sowing campaign they were instructed to give priority to the seed collections;[127] the continuous changes in the relative sizes of the kolkhoz and individual sectors meant that the division of the plan between the two sectors was always out-of-date. The sowing plan was scheduled to reach every village and kolkhoz by January 15,[128] but the Sovnarkom of the RSFSR complained as late as April 10 that 'although the sowing period has already begun in a whole number of districts, in certain districts the breakdown of production plans to the district, the village and the kolkhoz has not yet been completed'.[129] But the arrangements for checking the progress of sowing were much more elaborate than on any previous occasion. Reports were sent up every five days through the Soviet hierarchy, and between the middle of April and the end of June, with a delay of only a few days, Narkomzem reports summarising the situation in every region of the USSR were prominently displayed in the press at five-daily

[124] *Kollektivist*, 4, February 28, 1930, 17.

[125] See Carr and Davies (1969), 259–60.

[126] PKh, 5, 1930, 12.

[127] *Kollektivizatsiya . . . 1917–1935* (1957), 275 (resolution of central committee dated February 5).

[128] SZ, 1930, art. 4 (decree of December 23, 1929).

[129] SU, 1930, art. 235.

intervals.[130] According to Grin'ko, the reports which were sent up were 'crude, primitive and at times insufficiently accurate', but, as they 'linked centre and periphery by thousands of threads', they were an important factor in the success of the campaign.[131] The progress of the campaign was frequently discussed at Narkomzem conferences,[132] and was reported regularly at sittings of the Politburo.[133] In addition to the visits by the political leaders to the provinces in March, a team of senior officials of Narkomzem of the RSFSR travelled to the Crimea to study the experience of the earliest sowings;[134] and later in the month officials from Narkomzem of the USSR visited other regions in which sowing was already in progress.[135] Large numbers of agronomists and other experts were sent to the villages: a Moscow contingent is reported to have marched through the streets bearing banners reading optimistically but confusingly 'we need not an agrominimum but an agromaximum'.[136] During the spring sowing campaign 10,420 workers' brigades, comprising 72,000 industrial workers and specialists, were despatched to the countryside.[137] The methods popular in production campaigns—socialist emulation between kolkhozy, production conferences, the formation of shock brigades—were also attempted in the sowing campaign.[138] In the 'Leninskii Put'' kolkhoz in Khoper okrug, famous for its Appeal to all collective farmers not to desert the kolkhozy, a 'sowing committee' worked round the clock issuing instructions to the kolkhozy; on one occasion harrowing was carried on at night with the aid of flares, ceasing only when the soil froze.[139] Some successful kolkhozy sent help to the more backward.[140] The sovkhozy, once

[130] I, April 15, 1930 (for April 10), etc.

[131] PKh, 5, 1930, 12.

[132] See, for example, BU NKZ RSFSR, 9, 1930, 2 (decree dated March 11); SKhIB, 2 (11), April 1930, 15–16 (report of Narkomzem USSR conference of April 7).

[133] On February 5, the central committee (i.e. the Politburo) resolved 'to hear at each sitting the results of the summary report of Narkomzem on the course of the preparation for the sowing campaign' (*Kollektivizatsiya . . . 1927–1935* (1957), 276).

[134] BU NKZ RSFSR, 9, 1930, 2.

[135] SKhIB, 2 (11), April 1930, 15.

[136] PKh, 5, 1930, 17.

[137] Danilov *et al.*, eds. (1970), 221; Selunskaya (1964), 81.

[138] Sharova (1963), 169–70; Kozlova (1971), 226; Moshkov (1966), 85–7.

[139] P, April 20, 1930.

[140] See, for example, *Kollektivizatsiya* (Kuibyshev, 1970), 299.

they had completed their own sowing, provided men and machines to the kolkhozy; 1½ million hectares were sown in this way. In one well-publicised incident, tractor columns were sent dramatically but expensively by Zernotrest from the Crimea and the North Caucasus in special trains to the Urals and Siberia.[141] Once the sowing in the kolkhozy was well under way, party organisations were called upon to assist the individual peasants.[142]

In spite of exhortations, sowing was much delayed: a careful study by an émigré economist showed that while it began at more or less the same time as usual, and even earlier than usual in some areas, the sowing was spread over a much longer period: in the period 10–15 days after the normal date for completing 'mass sowing', 20–25 per cent less oats and barley, and 17–20 per cent less wheat, had been sown than in 1926–8 (average).[143] The delay in sowing by kolkhozy was partly attributed to an unusual spell of cold weather.[144] But sowings by individual households were particularly delayed; on April 30, only 11·7 out of a total so far sown of 30·3 million hectares had been sown by individual households. This delay was clearly due to the confusion about land allotments as a result of the increase and decline of the kolkhozy. Individual sowings increased greatly during May; by June 5 individual peasants had sown 40·7 out of 73·2 millions.[145] The spring of 1930 was particularly favourable to an extended period of sowing. At the end of the campaign, the agricultural newspaper declared that 'the weather was on the side of the kolkhozy';[146] and Vol'f later reported that 'nature gave us an extra month of spring, and there was enough time for the individual peasant to quarrel with the kolkhoz and then to reconcile himself with it'.[147] Eventually, Gosplan reported that a total of 89·6 million hectares had been sown to all crops by June 25 as compared with the plan of 93 million hectares.[148] Although the

[141] I, April 8, 23, 1930; SZe, April 22, 23, 1930; PKh, 5, 1930, 12.

[142] See, for example, resolution of bureau of Central Volga regional party committee dated April 17, referring to previous resolutions of March 29 and April 11, in *Kollektivizatsiya* (Kuibyshev, 1970), 184; a Ukrainian Politburo directive of April 18 is cited in Moshkov (1966), 90.

[143] BP (Prague), lxxx (June–July 1930), 1–7; for a similar conclusion by a Soviet historian, see IZ, lxxvi (1965), 37.

[144] In NPF, 9–10, [May] 1930, 74, Golendo blamed the delay on 20 cold days.

[145] BP (Prague), lxxx (June–July 1930), 1–7.

[146] SZe, June 24, 1930.

[147] PKh, 7–8, 1930, 8.

[148] SO, 6, 1930, 13.

plan was not entirely fulfilled, this figure was about 3 million hectares above the spring sowings of 86·7 million hectares in 1929;[149] together with the successful sowings of winter grain in the autumn of 1929, the total sown area for the 1930 harvest on this first estimate amounted to 128·5 million hectares as compared with 118·0 million hectares in the previous year.[150] This preliminary estimate of the spring sowing was slightly reduced in July 1930 to 88·3 and in 1932 to 84·8 million hectares (see Table 4). Thus an increase of 3·3 per cent as compared with 1929 was transformed in the fullness of time to a decline of 2·2 per cent; but even on this more pessimistic reckoning the total sown area for the 1930 harvest was 122·2 million hectares, 3·5 per cent above the previous year.[151] The increases in the area sown to industrial crops, notably cotton (+48 per cent) and sugar beet (+34 per cent) were particularly impressive, and in the case of cotton partly resulted from the substantial increase in the supplies of grain to Central Asia.[152] The

149 *Ezhegodnik po sel. kh. za 1931* (1933), 256.

150 For the sown area for the 1929 harvest, see Table 4; I have calculated the estimated sown area for 1930 by adding the Gosplan figure of 89·6 million hectares to the autumn sowings of 38·9 million hectares reported in *Sdvigi* (1931), 142.

151 The July 1930 Narkomzem estimate of 88·9 million hectares appeared in *Sdvigi* (1931), 142, and was later republished as 88·3 million hectares (*Ezhegodnik po sel. kh. 1931* (1933), 256; the note on p. 256 makes it clear that this is the estimate approved in July 1930). The 1932 TsUNKhU estimate of 84·8 appeared in *Nar. kh.* (1932), 152–3, with a lower figure for the autumn sowings of 37·4 million hectares; a note explained that 'in connection with the preparation of the control figures for 1932, more accurate calculations of the sown area and the output of field farming in 1930, which used additional material, differed from the earlier figures' as published in *Sdvigi* (1931), 'the reduction being a maximum of 5%' (p. 655). In all these figures, the autumn-sown area on which winter killings occurred have been deducted (5·5 million hectares for the 1929 and 0·4 million hectares for the 1930 harvest—*Ezhegodnik po sel. kh. 1931* (1933), 243). The preliminary estimate for 1930 was based on the five-daily reports. In the July 1930 estimate, reports of sovkhozy, kolkhozy and village soviets were corrected by selective 'check measures' (kontrol'nye obmery) of the fields carried out by the local land authorities; this estimate was approved by a special commission of Gosplan in July 1930 (*Ezhegodnik po sel. kh. 1931* (1933), 256n). In the 1932 estimate, in the case of kolkhozy and individual peasants, data from the regional authorities based on taxation records were corrected by a 2 per cent selective measure of the fields (perhaps the same as in the July 1930 estimate?), while the data for sovkhozy were provided by the sovkhoz authorities (*Nar. kh.* (1932), 654).

152 These percentages are based on the revised figures in *Nar. kh.* (1932), 152–3, 176–7; the earlier figures showed larger increases. For the supply of grain to the cotton areas see p. 107 above.

area sown to grain in the spring of 1930 was, however, less than in 1929 by 1·7 million hectares (2·6 per cent) even on the relatively optimistic estimate of July 1930, and by 3·5 million hectares (5·4 per cent) in the 1932 estimate.[153] The total area sown to grain for the 1930 harvest was, however, 6·0 per cent higher than in the previous year in the July 1930 and 2·7 per cent in the 1932 estimate, owing to the large increase in the autumn sowing of 1929 and the small amount of planted seed which perished during the winter.

The most remarkable feature of the spring sowing campaign was the extraordinarily high proportion of the total sown area for which the kolkhozy were responsible. The kolkhozy sowed, on the Gosplan estimate of July 1930, 32·6 million hectares to all crops, excluding the area sown by collective farmers individually. This figure was remarkably, though coincidentally, in line with the sown area 'considerably exceed[ing] 30 million hectares' predicted by the central committee resolution of January 5.[154] The kolkhozy and sovkhozy were together responsible for 40·5 per cent of all spring sowings. As much as 55 per cent of spring wheat and 48 per cent of industrial crops were sown by kolkhozy and sovkhozy, as compared with only 27 per cent of oats and 9·6 per cent of potatoes.[155] The predominance of the socialised sector in marketed crops was partly because the kolkhozy were most developed in the main areas growing wheat and industrial crops, and partly because the kolkhozy themselves concentrated on marketed production.[156] Over 85 per cent of the spring sowings by the socialised sector were by kolkhozy.

Although only 26 per cent of all peasant households and about 23 per cent of the peasant population belonged to kolkhozy, in the spring of 1930 the collective farmers sowed 42·7 per cent on the July 1930 and 36·5 per cent on the 1932 estimate of all the spring crops sown by individual peasants and kolkhozy taken together.[157] On average each collective farm household sowed 4·8 hectares on the July 1930 and 4·2 hectares on the 1932 estimate as compared with only 2·8 sown by the individual peasant household; the discrepancy

[153] *Ezhegodnik po sel. kh. 1931* (1933), 253; *Nar. kh.* (1932), 152–3.

[154] For the revised figure of 1932, 29·6 million hectares, see Table 4.

[155] Calculated from data in *Ezhegodnik po sel. kh. 1931* (1933), 252–6; these figures exclude individual sowings of collective farmers.

[156] *Ezhegodnik khlebooborota*, iv–v (1932), i, 9.

[157] See Table 4; the 1932 estimate does not include individual sowings of collective farmers; allowing for these, the percentage would reach about 38·1.

was similar both for grain and for the major industrial crops (see Table 4). Some 10 or 11 million hectares of land were sown by collective farmers in excess of what they were entitled to in terms of numbers of households; at most 2 million hectares of this was newly ploughed land,[158] the rest having been transferred from kulaks or, in the course of land consolidation, from poor or middle peasants.[159] The favourable position of the kolkhoz was summed up in trenchant terms by an individual peasant in the summer of 1930:

> You have got the best land in the village, the best pasture, the best grain for seeds, the best horses, cows and pigs, raised by decent people with their own sweat and blood in this or other villages. You have wood and lumber from the State forests, tractors, and other machines, credit from the government; everything, all the help, all the advantages. Where then will the miracle be if you succeed in raising better crops than we do?[160]

The case was a little exaggerated, for, as Soviet economists pointed out, the high level of sowings in kolkhozy was undertaken with limited labour and very limited draught power, and seemed to demonstrate that the 'manufacturing stage' of the kolkhozy, when tractors were available for only a small portion of the total sown area, could still bring great economies in the use of man-power, horses and implements.[161] But, in view of the enormous advantages gained by the kolkhozy, particularly in the allocation of land, arguments on the basis of the results of the spring sowing that

158 *Kolkhozy v 1930 g.* (1931), 151; the 2 million hectares include newly ploughed autumn sowings.

159 The additional sown area held by kolkhozy was apparently not a consequence of the fact that collectivisation was concentrated in particular geographical areas: while the spring sown area per household was higher than the average for the USSR in the Lower Volga and the North Caucasus, it was lower than average in the Ukraine. The spring sown area per household was 84 per cent higher for kolkhozy than for the individual sector in the Ukraine, 95 per cent in the North Caucasus and as much as 171 per cent in the Lower Volga region, as compared with the USSR average of 60 per cent (calculated from *Ezhegodnik po sel. kh. 1931* (1933), 252–316, using the number of households in June 1, 1930, calculated as for Table 17; these figures are for the July 1930 estimate in Table 4, and exclude individual sowings by collective farmers).

160 Hindus (1934), 171.

161 See, for example, PKh, 6, 1930, 23 (Minaev).

kolkhozy could produce more per unit of labour and more per horse than the individual peasant lack conviction.[162]

The success of the spring sowing campaign, and the high level of sowings by the kolkhozy, were greeted by the party leaders with considerable enthusiasm. In a report to a Moscow party conference, Mikoyan proclaimed that the party in the space of one or two months put right the errors in collectivisation and achieved complete 'tranquillisation'; this was the word used by the tsarist Prime Minister Stolypin to describe his policy after the 1905 revolution—'first tranquillisation (uspokoenie), and then reforms'. Mikoyan pointed out that the 'sober' spring sowing area in the kolkhozy of 30 million hectares proposed by the resolution of January 5 had been overfulfilled (the phrase was subtly changed from the original 'considerably exceed[ing] 30 million hectares'), and variously predicted that the 1930 harvest would be 'average' or 'considerable', and hailed the results of the campaign as 'leading us to a complete solution of the grain problem':

> We need a maximum of one or two sowing campaigns and we will have nothing to fear from bad weather or a bad harvest, because in a year we shall possess such strength through the kolkhozy and sovkhozy that even a bad harvest will not have decisive significance. One more year, and we shall not only secure ourselves enough grain, but become one of the largest grain producers in the whole world.[163]

Grin'ko, writing in the Gosplan journal, declared that, with the socialist sector successfully responsible for nearly 40 per cent of the spring sowing, 'the Rubicon has been crossed'. The hand of the party and government had been on the pulse of agriculture, and every backward crop and area had been stimulated by their direct intervention. Socialist emulation had replaced the methods of private competition.[164]

[162] For these arguments see for example PKh, 7–8, 1930, 98 (Kindeev).
[163] SZe, June 3, 1930.
[164] PKh, 5, 1930, 11–13; for this article see also p. 304 above.

CHAPTER SEVEN

THE CRISIS IN THE PARTY, MARCH–JULY 1930

(A) THE DIAGNOSIS OF ERROR, MARCH–JUNE 1930

In declaring a halt to the collectivisation drive, Stalin firmly placed the blame for previous excesses on local officials. In his initial article of March 2 he condemned 'tendencies in the ranks of our party' manifested by 'certain of our comrades', and confined his criticisms of party organisations to 'certain districts' in the remote Northern region and in Turkestan (see p. 269 above). The central committee resolution of March 14 condemned the behaviour of 'a number of districts', making no mention of regional or even okrug officials (see p. 273 above). At this time, the authorities believed that only small numbers of peasants would leave the kolkhozy, exclusively in the grain-deficit regions. With the departure of millions of peasants from the kolkhozy in the second half of March, this limited attribution of error became utterly unconvincing. In his 'Answers to Collective Farmer Comrades' of April 3 Stalin widened his criticisms to the Moscow and Central Black-Earth regions and to the Transcaucasus, though significantly still omitted the main grain-surplus zone. He also admitted that dizziness from success had affected 'not only local officials, but also certain regional officials and even certain members of the central committee'; the members of the central committee were not named, but Stalin clearly had Bauman in mind (see p. 280 above). At the same time he vigorously insisted that the central committee as such bore no blame for the excesses, which he attributed solely to failure by others to keep to its resolution of January 5. According to Stalin's account, the central committee dealt with excesses immediately they occurred in the second half of February, 'and did not delay its intervention, authorising Stalin to warn comrades who had gone too far in a special article'. Stalin went out of his way to point out that his article of March 2 was not the result of his personal initiative but a 'reconnaissance in depth by the CC'.[1] Presumably some of hi colleagues on the Politburo protested about its publication over hi signature, which gave the impression that only he was wise enoug to recognise the dangers and pull the regime back from the abyss

There is of course no doubt that Stalin's exemption of himself anc the central committee from criticism was a crude evasion o responsibility. His own remarks, and the speeches of his clos associate Molotov, at the November plenum greatly encouragec regional party committees to press lower organisations for a higl level of collectivisation before the spring sowings of 1930; anc during the campaign of January and February Stalin's only public remarks encouraged the further extension of collectivisation (see pp 217 and 243 above). If Stalin believed that the drive coulc have come to an end spontaneously, without explicit and firm intervention from the Politburo, his understanding of the political mechanism created in the later 1920s was extraordinarily deficient.

Valiant attempts to exempt Stalin and the Politburo from all responsibility for the excesses continued in the ensuing weeks. In an elaborate apologia to a Moscow party conference, Mikoyan attributed the excesses to '*insufficient marxist–leninist preparedness* of part of our cadres and their careless hastiness', and boldly asserted that '*the central committee did not give a single unrealistic or mistaken target for collectivisation*'. He rebuked local organisations for failing to report excesses to the central committee, and claimed that it discovered the facts only when its representatives went to the provinces in the middle of February. He eventually conceded, however, that while all the directives of the central committee were correct, 'we possibly overestimated the marxist–leninist understanding of some local organs'.[2] This image of an upright, moderate and trusting central committee whose clearly stated aims were subverted by stupid and inexperienced local officials could hardly have seemed convincing to a Moscow party audience.

The regional party authorities were at first equally unwilling to admit error. In the first month after the publication of Stalin's article on March 2, all the published statements by regional party committees and their secretaries confined themselves to criticisms of the excesses of their subordinate okrug and district organisations, and refrained from mentioning the pressure to which they had

[1] *Soch.*, xii, 210–13.
[2] SZe, June 3, 1930.

themselves subjected the local authorities. In an article published on March 12 Kosior even blandly excused the excesses: 'in the historical stage in which the party finds itself, difficulties and mistakes are inevitable and must not depreciate the truly grandiose results of our work'.[3] In the Lower Volga region, a statement on March 14 from the bureau of the regional party committee condemned excesses in local organisations, but uttered no word of self-criticism. In the North Caucasus, where peasant disturbances early in February had alerted the authorities to the dangers of the course they were following (see pp. 258–9 above), Andreev was able to claim that 'the regional committee gave fairly categorical instructions to the localities long before the decision of the central committee' of March 14, and he accordingly dismissed that decision rather lightly, as far as the North Caucasus was concerned, as merely 'a confirmation of our policy'. Like the other regional leaders, he strongly criticised okrug and district organisations which had failed to keep the collectivisation drive under control, but he was an amiable man, and his reproof to local officials at the grass roots for having 'forgotten the limits in a great task' was couched in friendly, almost fatherly, tones:

> They are the rank-and-file workers in carrying out collectivisation . . . We have in fact real heroes from the rank-and-file activist in the village and the *stanitsa*; they have carried out the work and directives of the party, often without sleep for several days, without any rest, always fearing kulak revenge.

He attributed those resignations from the kolkhozy which had taken place in the North Caucasus to 'inevitable vacillations by the small property owner' just before the spring sowing.[4] The assumption continued to be made in the grain regions throughout March that most of the peasants would remain in the kolkhozy.

Complacency was not confined to the major grain-surplus regions. During March, regional committees both in the grain-deficit regions of European Russia and in the national republics also issued statements in which they criticised lower party organisations under their control but refrained from criticising their own behaviour, or from modifying the high targets for collectivisation

[3] SZe, March 12, 1930.

[4] Andreev (Rostov, 1930), 11–13; speech to Rostov party of March 18.

which they had themselves authorised in the previous weeks or months.[5] As late as April 1, 1930, the bureau of the Northern regional party committee, while condemning the Vologda and other okrugs and numerous districts in strong terms for 'crude distortions of the party line', administrative methods, and arbitrary dekulakisation, nevertheless still presented these deficiencies as being due to their failure to carry out the directives of the regional committee.[6]

Stalin's article of April 3 opened the way, after the huge exodus from the kolkhozy in the second half of March, for a drastic reduction of collectivisation plans in grain-surplus as well as grain-deficit regions, and for any republic or regional committee of the party, and any individual member of the central committee, to be accused of excesses. It was immediately followed, on April 5, by the dismissal of Bauman from the secretaryship of the Moscow committee (see pp. 279–80 above); at a further session of the Moscow party committee on April 22 Bauman admitted that 'we undoubtedly got too far ahead, undoubtedly got carried away and lost a sense of proportion', and the committee denounced its own errors.[7] Other party committees in the grain-deficit regions and the national republics fell into line. The Belorussian central committee admitted that its appeal in January for full collectivisation by the end of 1931 was a mistake.[8] The Kazakhstan party committee withdrew the ambitious plans for collectivisation which it adopted in December 1929 and criticised its own 'undifferentiated approach' to different regions.[9] The bureau of the central committee of the Turkestan party withdrew its own resolution of January 1, 1930, calling for complete collectivisation by the end of the five-year plan, and the subsequent resolutions in January which called for comprehensive collectivisation in one okrug by the spring of 1931, and for the upgrading of TOZy in Turkestan to artels. It also condemned as a 'particularly crude mistake' its own failure to ensure that local party organisations properly informed the

[5] See, for example, *Pobeda* (Ashkhabad, 1968), 88–96 (resolution of central committee of Turkmen party of March 11); *Kollektivizatsiya*, i (Alma-Ata, 1967), 289–92 (directive of Kazakh regional committee dated March 21); Kozlova (1971), 212–13 (reference to resolution of session of Moscow party committee on March 26–8).

[6] *Kollektivizatsiya* (Vologda, 1964), 311–15.

[7] Kozlova (1971), 213–14.

[8] P, May 19, 1930 (referring to decision of April 17).

[9] *Kollektivizatsiya*, ii (Alma-Ata, 1967), 572 (resolution of April 20).

peasants about both Stalin's article of March 2 and the subsequent central committee decisions.[10] The party secretary in the Northern region admitted that the regional committee had been imprecise about the rate of growth of collectivisation and had proposed an exaggerated degree of socialisation.[11]

Such avowals of error by the regions and the republics were still sometimes made reluctantly and half-heartedly. In the Tatar ASSR, although the party committee recognised on April 6–7 that its earlier call for comprehensive collectivisation by the autumn of 1930 was mistaken,[12] a subsequent resolution of a rural conference in the republic praised 80 per cent collectivisation as a decisive success, and was apparently endorsed by the bureau of the republican committee; and a further republican committee document even claimed that the mass exodus from the kolkhozy was due to the use of administrative measures to keep them in![13] At a conference summoned by the central committee in May, members of the central committee staff condemned these errors of the Tatar republican committee, and also condemned it for failing to recognise that its earlier call for 100 per cent collectivisation was responsible for the behaviour of the localities; a resolution of the central committee reproved the Tatar committee for 'hastiness and pressing for a high percentage of collectivisation'.[14] A fortnight later the republic finally came into line: a Tatar party conference approved the central committee resolution 'wholly and fully'.[15]

In the major grain-surplus regions, the regional authorities were less ready—or perhaps merely less under pressure from the central authorities—to acknowledge error. Only the regional committee of the Central Black-Earth region admitted soon after Stalin's article of April 3 that it had pressed for too much collectivisation;[16] and this

[10] *Pobeda* (Ashkhabad, 1968), 113–15 (resolution of April 26); the original resolutions will be found *ibid.* 19–26, 35–41. The Soviet editors of the collection claim that in the event, as collectivisation was in fact completed in the agricultural districts of Turkmenistan by the end of 1932, 'the correctness of the view taken by the CC of the [Communist Party of Turkestan] on January 1, 1930 was confirmed' after all! (*ibid.* 631, n. 14).

[11] P, June 2, 1930 (S. Bergavinov).

[12] *Kollektivizatsiya* (Kazan', 1968), 146, 330.

[13] PS, 11–12 (13–14), June 1930, 76–7.

[14] PS, 11–12 (13–14), June 1930, 85–6; the resolution was dated May 23.

[15] *Kollektivizatsiya* (Kazan', 1968), 330.

[16] Sharova (1963), 164 (referring to resolution of April 7); this criticism was repeated by a regional party conference held on June 5–8 (*ibid.* 172, 179).

region did not appear in the central committee resolution of January 5 in the priority category of regions due for collectivisation in 'the autumn of 1930 in the main or in any case in the spring of 1931'. In the Central Volga region, a resolution of the party bureau on April 17 reaffirmed the decision of the November 1929 plenum of the regional committee that 50 per cent of households should be collectivised by the spring of 1930;[17] apparently no later decision had approved any higher plan. The party bureau did not go further than conceding that it 'did not take sufficiently firm and severe preventative measures against the drive for quantitative indicators of collectivisation', and against 'bureaucratic ordering-about of peasant-collective farmers'.[18] In the Ukraine, the republican party leaders were even less willing to admit error. Kosior, at a meeting of the Kharkov party activists, claimed that the Ukrainian central committee had made no mistakes of principle: in directives sent to districts as well as okrugs, it had insisted on quality of collectivisation rather than on high percentages, had warned against the socialisation of cows and small animals, and had stressed the voluntary principle. All he was willing to concede was that in February the Ukrainian central committee, accustomed to rely on the lower organisations, had been insufficiently critical in response to reports and figures received from below, and hence had unwisely agreed to more rapid collectivisation—these were 'serious practical mistakes' rather than mistakes in principle.[19] At the XVI party congress in June, a delegate from the Ukraine proudly drew attention to the fact that the Ukraine had adopted a slower pace of collectivisation than many regions in the RSFSR, but had subsequently retained a higher percentage of households in kolkhozy than in any other region except the North Caucasus.[20] In the North Caucasus, Andreev, who had been badgered by Molotov at the central committee plenum in November 1929 to adopt a higher rate of collectivisation, was in a strong position to insist on his irreproachability. At a regional party conference, while admitting that his committee had placed too much confidence in local reports, and had not sufficiently resisted 'the spontaneity of unhealthy emulation', he claimed that it had not made any political mistakes.

17 *Kollektivizatsiya* (Kuibyshev, 1970), 182.

18 *Ibid.* 182–3.

19 P, April 26, 1930.

20 *XVI s"ezd* (1931), 602–3 (N. Demchenko).

The conference 'fully endorsed' the decision of the North Caucasus committee of November 27, 1929, that collectivisation could be completed 'by the summer of 1931 at the latest'.[21] These proceedings quietly ignored the various decisions made in the North Caucasus in December 1929, as well as Andreev's declaration on January 9, 1930, that collectivisation would be completed not in 1931 but by the end of 1930 (see pp. 177 and 214 above).

The Lower Volga region, which led the way for the rest of the USSR throughout the decisive last few months of 1929, was more vulnerable. On April 19, 1930, Kiselev, a central committee member who was a secretary of TsIK of the USSR and inspected the region on its behalf, published a strong attack on the Lower Volga authorities for 'major distortions in the party line', particularly condemning their decision of January 1930 that 100 per cent of poor and middle peasant households should be collectivised by the spring, and calling on them to 'recognise these mistakes openly and fully, in a Bolshevik manner'.[22] Sheboldaev conceded that the decision of January 1930 had been mistaken, but claimed that it was without practical influence, as only 68 per cent of households were collectivised by March 1930 as compared with 62 per cent in December 1929; Kiselev's exaggeration of the degree of error and disorder assisted the Right wing.[23] Subsequently, a plenum of the regional committee declared that the 'party line was correctly carried out, but "dizziness from success" in the organisation was not overcome soon enough'; Kiselev's article was 'clearly Right-wing and gave false information to the party on the position in the Lower Volga'.[24]

Some attempts were made to go beyond merely attributing blame to inexperience and lack of competence on the part of local officials and party members. As we have seen, Kosior conceded that the Ukrainian central committee failed to take a sufficiently critical attitude to reports from the okrug and the distinct, and Mikoyan conceded that in the USSR central committee 'we possibly overestimated the marxist–leninist understanding of some local organs' (see pp. 312 and 316 above). The view that the system of communications between the centre and the village was somehow

[21] P, June 16, 1930; *Kollektivizatsiya* (Krasnodar, 1972), 348; for the decision of November 27, see p. 177 above.

[22] I, April 19, 1930; in 1920 Kiselev had been a leader of the 'Workers' Opposition'.

[23] P, April 27, 1930; see also Sheboldaev in B, 11–12, June 30, 1930, 65.

[24] *Saratovskaya* (Saratov, 1961), 128 (resolution of May 12).

at fault was not resisted by even the most ardent defenders of Stalin and the central committee. Some officials and publicists also tried to place the political upheavals of the previous few months in a social context. The unstable outlook of the middle peasant, with his two 'souls'—that of a small proprietor and that of a proletarian—was frequently adduced: Andreev blamed the first exodus from the kolkhozy onto 'inevitable vacillations by the small property owner' (see p. 313 above), and Yaroslavsky, among others, suggested that the excesses reflected the 'anti-middle-peasant strivings of certain elements of the poor peasants'.[25] This fitted in with the more plausible notion, widely held among officials, and given currency by Yakovlev at the XVI party congress, that the excessive socialisation of January and February had favoured the poor peasant at the expense of the middle peasant, and weakened the alliance of the regime with the latter (see vol. 2, pp. 112–13). Bauman compared the ebbs and flows in collectivisation with the ebbs and flows generally found in a mass revolutionary movement.[26] But such notions of natural 'ebbs and flows' were soon firmly rejected as underestimating the part played in the recent upheavals both by the disruptive activities of the kulaks and by the excesses of local officials.[27]

But the central feature of the official review of previous excesses in March and April 1930 was a stubborn insistence that the central authorities in Moscow were not to blame. The peasants were assured, in articles to which they had fairly ready access, that the responsibility for the treatment to which they had been subjected in the past few months rested fully with those who had meted it out—the local officials and party members, the volunteer workers and others sent into the countryside. All this could be expected to shatter the morale of the lower officials and to arouse their hostility. The increasing penalties on non-conformity greatly inhibited the public expression of this hostility; and the blocking of the channels of information concealed from the disaffected what was happening in other places, and prevented the emergence of any common opposition movement. The increasingly heavy press censorship of 1930 in any case conceals from the present-day historian the extent

[25] Cited in Chernopitskii (Rostov, 1965), 104.

[26] Speech at third plenum of Moscow party committee cited in *XVI s"ezd* (1931), 214; the plenum met from March 28 to March 30 (Kozlova (1971), 212).

[27] P, April 20, 1930 (Krumin); see also Bauman's avowal of error at the party congress (*XVI s"ezd* (1931), 214).

and depth of the disaffection. Nevertheless, there is considerable evidence that discontent among party members and party officials was widespread. A circular letter from the Ukrainian party central committee reported 'panic' and 'disarray (rasteryannost')';[28] a Rabkrin investigation of a Lower Volga district described 'some disarray and lack of confidence in work' among party organisations;[29] in the Smolensk region 'some okrug workers . . . were taken aback, not knowing where to begin and how actually to approach the correction of mistakes';[30] the Vologda okrug in the Northern region also reported 'disarray and a disposition to panic' among officials.[31]

In the first two or three months after the publication of Stalin's article of March 2 the press frequently reported that local officials and party members who had taken an active part in the collectivisation drive regarded the new policy as an unnecessary and harmful retreat. In the model Khoper okrug, 'many local officials were hostile' to Stalin's article;[32] in the North Caucasus, according to Andreev, 'some local officials were somewhat put out by the central committee resolution';[33] in Belorussia both Stalin's article and the central committee directives were criticised at district meetings.[34] The general view of these critics was that Stalin's article was disruptive and reactionary. The secretary of a Komsomol district committee in Siberia protested that 'Stalin's article is incorrect; it will disorganise the work'.[35] 'We are correcting our mistakes by giving up the position', a district official in Ryazan' complained.[36] In a Chimkent district, Stalin's article was treated as a 'retreat to capitalism';[37] a party cell in Tver' okrug resolved that the new kolkhoz Statute and Stalin's article were 'a backward step in the rates and methodology of kolkhoz construction';[38] in the Tatar republic, according to a report from Kolkhoztsentr, 'many officials treated the central committee directives on the correction of

[28] IZ, lxxvi (1965), 28.
[29] IZ, lxxvi (1965), 28.
[30] Fainsod (1958), 257, citing Smolensk archives, WKP 151, 191–6.
[31] *Kollektivizatsiya* (Vologda, 1964), 298, 307.
[32] KGN, 32, April 23, 1930.
[33] Andreev (Rostov, 1930), 10 (speech of March 18).
[34] P, May 19, 1930.
[35] IZ, lxxvi (1965), 28.
[36] *Ibid.* 28.
[37] P, May 13, 1930.
[38] PS, 6(8), March 1930, 3.

excesses as concessions to the kulak'.[39] A party publicist admitted the existence of 'talk' to the effect that the party was 'crawling to the policy of the Right wing'.[40] Local officials argued that Stalin's article should have been concealed from the peasants, and some actually tried to conceal it.[41] 'In order that the kolkhoz should not split up', a party member declared at a cell meeting, 'all newspapers with comrade Stalin's article must be collected in and destroyed, and the article should be discussed only after the harvest'.[42] In the first four weeks after the publication of the article, the belief at the centre that the retreat would be very limited was naturally reflected in the behaviour of the local organisations and individuals responsible for carrying out policy; but even in April and May some district and local organisations still resisted any rehabilitation of dekulakised peasants, opposed the regrading of communes as artels and insisted on the socialisation of animals.[43]

On the eve of the XVI party congress, the official press still complained that some local officials blamed Stalin's article for the decline in collectivisation. At an okrug conference in the Lower Volga region, one indiscreet official is alleged to have claimed that it was Stalin's article which had broken up all the kolkhozy, and to have criticised the absence of collective leadership by 'leaders like Trotsky'.[44] At the Ukrainian party congress in June, some delegates complained privately to Petrovsky that 'Stalin's article destroyed many kolkhozy'.[45] According to one survey article, 'many comrades who travelled to the provinces' reported that it was after Stalin's article and the central committee decision that the kolkhozy dispersed:

> There is sometimes felt a certain moment of regret about this interference, which interrupted a process which had begun so well and was developing so stormily . . . Many local officials are often ready to assume that without this authoritative and firm

[39] PS, 11–12 (13–14), June 1930, 75.

[40] P, April 20, 1930 (Krumin).

[41] SZe, May 7, 1930 (Orsha), P, May 13, 1930 (Chimkent); *Kollektivizatsiya* (Kuibyshev, 1970), 628 (reminiscences dated February 1962).

[42] PS, 6(8), March 1930, 3 (Atkarsk okrug).

[43] P, April 24 (L. Kovalev), May 24 (autonomous region in Azerbaidzhan), 1930.

[44] B, 11–12, June 30, 1930, 46; he was an assistant director of a sovkhoz.

[45] P, June 18, 1930; Petrovsky was president of the Ukrainian TsIK.

'clarion call' everything would have sorted itself out and we would have had far better quantitative results . . . Many many officials have even now not recognised how great the danger was.[46]

The mood lingered on, in spite of harangues and harassment from the centre. Some months later, a poor peasant declared at a Central Volga regional conference:

> I would join the kolkhoz with great pleasure, but there isn't one. When I was sent on a course to Samara, we had a large kolkhoz of six village soviets, things were going well, but when they read Stalin's reply in the newspapers, the kolkhoz broke up, and we can't so far persuade the poor peasants to organise a kolkhoz.[47]

Even among local officials and party members who agreed with or acquiesced in the change of policy, there was widespread indignation with the central and regional authorities for placing the blame for the old policies on those who had tried faithfully to carry them out; perhaps this was the predominant mood. Thus at a conference of rural party cells in the Central Volga region, speakers claimed that they had merely carried out the orders of the plenipotentiaries; any comment on their part had resulted in accusations of deviation, or even in their arrest.[48] In the Ukraine, local officials claimed that it was the okrugs which were responsible for the 'pace-setters' (strelochniki—literally 'pointsmen' on a railway) in the districts.[49] Generally, many officials described the Stalin article as 'unexpected', 'a bolt from the blue'.[50] Khataevich was moved to write to Stalin complaining about the way in which local officials had been handled:

> Many complaints are heard that 'we have all been indiscriminately dubbed blockheads'. In fact directives should have been given to the central press that, in criticising the distortions and excesses of collectivisation, it should not have been only the lower officials who were stigmatised and abused. Many directives on

[46] FP, 5, 1930, 8–9.
[47] *Kollektivizatsiya* (Kuibyshev, 1970), 208 (speech of September 21, 1930).
[48] P, April 10, 1930.
[49] P, April 26, 1930 (speech by Kosior).
[50] P, April 24, 1930.

the socialisation of all animals, including small production animals, and on forcing the pace of collectivisation did in fact come from Kolkhoztsentr, from Narkomzem.[51]

This muted criticism is the only reported objection made to Stalin's policies at this time by one of the group of high party officials active in the collectivisation campaign. Criticisms by local officials at lower levels, briefly reported in the press, went much further than Khataevich indicated. The central committee itself was by no means immune from criticism. The point was frequently made that excesses could have been prevented if a firmer line in favour of voluntary collectivisation had been taken by the central authorities.[52] In Kharkov criticism of the central committee was voiced in the party cells of the Ukrainian Narkomzem, Narkomyust and Rabkrin, and of Artem University and the Agricultural Institute. According to Postyshev, critics in the Ukraine held that the central committee itself suffered from 'dizziness from success' and was insufficiently sensitive to what was going on, and blamed the committee's own errors of leadership both for the excesses, and for the retreat and concessions which resulted in March; he castigated the criticisms as amounting to a 'platform'.[53] At a party meeting at the Timiryazev Agricultural Academy in Moscow, the official speaker was interrupted by shouts from the floor such as 'Where was the CC during the excesses?' (a *Pravda* correspondent compared these interruptions with 'a skhod in a kulak village'); and six people eventually voted for, and 20 or 30 reportedly sympathised with, a 'counter-resolution' criticising the central committee for failing to supervise the implementation of its 'correct' line.[54] At the Trade Academy, a speaker from the floor, supported by several other party members, pointed out that the central committee must have known what was going on because the leading officials in the campaign were members of it and Bauman was even one of its secretaries; and ventured on a bold comparison:

Under Lenin the CC also made mistakes, but comrade Lenin and

[51] IA, 2, 1962, 197, citing the archives (letter of April 6).

[52] P, March 25, 1930 (article by S. Krylov).

[53] P, April 26, 1930 (Kosior), May 8, 1930 (Postyshev).

[54] P, May 31, June 1, 1930.

the CC admitted their mistakes; nowadays the CC doesn't admit its mistakes.[55]

Similar outbursts were reported from the Industrial Academy and the Parostroi and Balakirev works in Moscow; and from both grain-surplus and grain-deficit regions.[56] The total number of dissidents referred to in all these scattered press reports amounted to no more than a few hundred people; these were isolated cries of indignation. But the willingness of even a small number of party members to risk the penalties of expulsion and loss of post now often incurred by such deviation evidently reflected a much more widespread discontent. On May 27, an alarmed *Pravda* editorial, headed 'More Fire Against the Right!', denounced demands that the party leadership should engage in self-criticism as 'hysterical' and condemned as 'demagogy' all attempts to '*discredit the Leninist leadership of the party*' and to criticise the party 'regime'.

Both the ability of the leadership to dispense with regular party procedures and its preoccupation with the problems of agriculture were reflected in the postponement of the XVI party congress. The congress was originally scheduled for May 1930 by the November 1929 plenum (already five months later than the requirements of the party Statute). On April 6, 1930, *Pravda* announced its postponement to June 15, presumably as a result of the confusion following the retreat from collectivisation. On June 7, *Pravda* announced a further postponement to June 26 on the grounds that the spring sowing was not yet completed.

In the publicity for the congress in the weeks before it assembled, the long-term intention of renewing the collectivisation drive was strongly emphasised. On May 18, the Politburo approved the publication of the theses of Yakovlev's report to the congress on 'The Kolkhoz Movement and the Development of Agriculture', and they appeared on the following day.[57] A long section of the theses condemned 'the errors of the spring of 1930' as 'a crime against the dictatorship of the proletariat' and frankly admitted the risks to the stability of the regime which these errors had entailed, and a further section called for careful handling of peasants who remained outside the kolkhozy. But the main emphasis of the theses

[55] P, June 3, 1930.

[56] P, May 24, 27, June 2, 23, 1930 (places mentioned include various Ukrainian okrugs, Belorussia, Tula, Yaroslavl' and the Northern region).

[57] P, May 19, 1930; for other aspects of the theses see vol. 2, pp. 54, 110–11.

was on the present achievements of collectivisation and its future prospects. They designated the period since the previous party congress as 'a very great break-through in agriculture', singled out the collectivisation of 40–50 per cent of peasant households in the main grain areas as having solved the grain problem 'in practice', and reiterated support for the collectivisation plans announced in the central committee resolution of January 5. The theses claimed that the 'considerable section' of the middle peasants in the main grain areas which joined the kolkhozy had done so on a voluntary basis, praised the policy of eliminating the kulaks as a class and asserted that the remaining individual peasants 'will undoubtedly be persuaded by the experience of the kolkhozy, and in a very brief period of time, that it is necessary to take the road of collectivisation'. According to the theses, it was now possible to embark on a substantial programme of livestock breeding both in the sovkhozy and in special livestock units on the kolkhozy, and to plan for a national scheme for regional agricultural specialisation; careful preparation should be made for collectivisation of the non-grain areas. The theses ended by describing collectivisation as 'the second and decisive step' made by the October revolution in the countryside, the first step being the confiscation of the land of the landowners; 'only bureaucrats and petty officials, not revolutionaries, could think that a transformation of such a significance, affecting the very foundations of the economic structure and the life of vast masses, could be carried out without difficulties, without a sharpening of the class struggle and the vacillations of the middle peasant associated with this'. Frantic opposition from the kulaks could still be expected, but the party, by strengthening the alliance of the working class with the middle peasant, would '*complete the process of collectivisation and thus lay the foundation of socialist society*'.

Simultaneously with the publication of the Yakovlev theses the Politburo announced that the theses for all the main reports to the party congress were to be discussed at party meetings and in the press; 'a Discussion Sheet is to appear in *Pravda*, for the publication of critical articles, amendments to the CC theses, specific proposals about the theses, etc.'[58] Thirty discussion sheets appeared between May 22 and July 10. For the most part the contributions dealt with

[58] P, May 19, 1930; the theses for the other major reports were approved at a meeting of the Politburo on May 20 and published on the following day (P, May 21, 1930).

secondary issues. But on June 9 a strong criticism of Yakovlev's theses appeared in Discussion Sheet No. 9 from a certain Mamaev, who was a student or lecturer at the courses for sovkhoz directors run by Zernotrest in Saratov.[59] Mamaev vigorously rejected the assertion in the theses that the middle peasant voluntarily joined the kolkhozy, citing as proof the central committee's own statement that up to 15 per cent of peasants had been dekulakised. Stalin was correct to attack compulsory collectivisation, but 'the question involuntarily arises—whose head got dizzy? . . . one should speak about one's own disease, not teach the lower party masses about it'. Mamaev diagnosed the errors in terms similar to those used by Stalin and the central committee in March and April, but in his account the crisis was treated as much more profound, and much more blame was attached to the authorities:

> As a result of the mass application of repressive measures to the middle and poor peasants, the middle peasant barbarously destroyed not only marketable livestock but also breeding cattle and other types of production of prime necessity. These were still the main sources of supply of the industrial centres. This led at that moment to a food crisis.
>
> Because of leadership which lacked authority and initiative, the lower rural organisations lost authority in the eyes of the mass of the peasants themselves (the middle peasants) and of the lower party organisations. Things got worse because okrug and regional officials sinned themselves and then condemned 'pace-setters' and intimidated all and sundry for 'excesses'. It appears that 'the tsar is good and the local chinovniki are useless'.

According to Mamaev, the outflow of the middle peasants from the kolkhozy took place because conditions were not ripe for collectivisation—comprehensive collectivisation could not take place without mechanisation, which would 'stimulate the poor and middle peasant to go over from primitive working of the land to machines and mechanised economy': in future, collectivisation should be carried out jointly with mechanisation.

Mamaev's criticism of the party leadership and its policy is unlikely to have been published without Stalin's specific sanction, and was evidently printed so as to provide an opportunity for a

59 For Mamaev, see P, June 16 and June 18, 1930, disk. listok 14.

large-scale propaganda campaign against the widespread hostility to the central committee. A huge salvo was immediately fired at the unfortunate Mamaev and his deviation, which soon became known as 'Mamaevism' (Mamaevshchina). An article by Azizyan argued that the article was a slander on the central committee and on Stalin; familiar passages from official documents were cited to demonstrate that the voluntary principle in collectivisation had always been insisted upon. Mamaev had distorted the facts: thus the central committee in its resolution of March 14 said 'up to 15 per cent' of peasants were dekulakised '*in certain districts*', not generally. Mamaev was 'an agent of the kulaks within the party'.[60] Later articles against Mamaev, summarised under the heading 'An Explosion of Indignation', stressed that substantial numbers of peasants remained in the kolkhozy and successfully completed the spring sowing—'the militia can't be used to do the sowing'. Mamaev's claim that collectivisation should await mechanisation was also refuted: one author crushingly reminded him that during the Civil War the party had not told the Red Army to cease its struggle until technical re-equipment was possible.[61] A later issue summarised numerous letters from local officials who generously insisted that their mistakes had been their own and should not be blamed on the central committee. According to the editors of *Pravda*, only four people wrote in defending Mamaev to some extent, and three of them were anonymous.[62]

Only one further article critical of the party authorities was published; this boldly asserted that 'there is no doubt that if comrade Stalin's article "Dizzy from Success" and the CC resolution of April 2 (by analogy) had appeared 1½–2 months earlier, we would not have had so many crude mistakes in the collectivisation of agriculture'.[63] This seems to have been the last occasion on which an article openly critical of Stalin or the party central committee appeared in *Pravda*; the rapid attenuation of the right to criticise was reflected in the presentation of the article, which, unlike Mamaev's, was published in small print and preceded by a refutation in large print. Further sporadic reports appeared of criticisms of the party authorities at the meetings and conferences preceding the party

[60] P, June 10, 1930, disk. listok 10; for Azizyan see p. 183, n. 149, above.

[61] P, June 16, 1930, disk. listok 14.

[62] P, June 28, 1930, disk. listok 23; criticisms of Mamaev also appeared in P, June 12 (disk. listok 11), 16, 18, 1930.

[63] P, June 25, 1930 (I. Mashkov).

congress.[64] Mamaev was apparently unrepentant: at a meeting in Saratov, which spent six hours trying to persuade him of his errors, he continued to criticise what he described as 'comprehensive bureaucratisation' in the party and to condemn 'artificial inflaming of the class struggle'.[65] In Saratov, half-a-dozen people made speeches in his favour.[66]

Little support was obtained for the critics from the leaders of the former Right. Bukharin remained silent, and Tomsky and Rykov publicly defended the central committee and denounced their own past errors.[67] Only Uglanov publicly displayed some sign of what he later described as 'new hesitations, very serious hesitations about the correctness of the line of the party'.[68]

Trotsky, in exile in Turkey, and Rakovsky and a small group of Left oppositionists, in exile in the USSR, forthrightly condemned Stalin's policies. In February 1930, Trotsky condemned precipitate collectivisation and dekulakisation as a 'bureaucratic adventure'. The attempt to establish socialism in one country on the basis of peasant equipment was doomed to failure (see p. 392 below); it had carried the contradictions of petty commodity economy into the kolkhoz, and would eventually result in the re-emergence of capitalist tendencies.[69] In March, he condemned Stalin for failing to admit that the 'utopian reactionary character of "100 per cent collectivisation"' lay in 'the compulsory organisation of huge collective farms without the technological basis that could alone insure their superiority over small ones'; the exploitation of the land in such manufactories could, due to lack of personal initiative, be inferior to that in small peasant holdings.[70] A few weeks later, he

64 See, for example, P, June 16 (Lower Volga), 18 (Ukraine), 26 (Moscow factory), 1930.

65 P, June 16, 1930.

66 P, June 22, 1930.

67 Tomsky's speech at the Transcaucasian party congress was reported in P, June 14, 1930, and criticised for not denouncing the Right sufficiently; for Rykov's speech at a Ural party conference see *XVI s"ezd* (1931), 149.

68 *XVI s"ezd* (1931), 131; for a reference to a critical statement by Uglanov at a party cell in a Moscow factory see Rudzutak in P, June 14, 1930. An article by Bukharin in P, March 7, 1930, attacking the papacy, has been taken as a criticism by analogy of Stalin because it describes the pope as having 'short arms', but this seems fanciful (Cohen (1974), 349; Wolfe (1955), 36–7).

69 BO (Paris), ix (February–March 1930), 3–5 (article dated February 13), x (April 1930), 18 (letter dated February 7).

70 *Writings of Leon Trotsky (1930)* (1975), 138–9 (March 23, 1930); BO (Paris), xi (May 1930), 6–8 (April 25, 1930).

asserted even more firmly that the kolkhozy 'will fall apart while waiting for the technical base'.[71] In April 1930 a statement drawn up by Rakovsky, V. Kosior, N. Muralov and V. Kasparova, the remaining leaders of the Left Opposition in exile within the USSR who had not capitulated, and apparently written without any communication with Trotsky, also condemned comprehensive collectivisation as doomed to failure in the absence of advanced technology. The statement blamed the central committee for the economic and political crisis: no warning was given in its resolution of November 1929 that force should not be used against the middle and poor peasant, or that communes were premature. 'The elimination of the kulak by decree' was curtly rejected as 'economic nonsense'. The general situation in the USSR was more serious than at any time since the Civil War—'every party member feels this, but it is denied by the leadership'. The statement proposed that comprehensive collectivisation should be 'formally renounced' and the expulsion of the kulaks should cease; but it also warned against the danger of a 'Neo-Nep' which could lead to agrarian capitalism. The retreat must not go too far: the rate of growth of industry must be maintained, and kulaks already exiled must not be allowed to return to their villages. But no clear alternative policy was put forward, apart from a brief reference to the importance of greater attention to the sovkhozy as a means of solving the food problem, and a call for the formation of 'unions of poor peasants' as a political basis for the kolkhoz movement.[72] A few weeks later, at the time of the preparations for the party congress, Trotsky drew attention to the condemnation by the party leaders of all attempts, even those made in closed party cells, to criticise mistakes by the central committee in implementing collectivisation; this indicated that 'the bureaucratic regime is well on its way to establishing the principle of the *infallibility of the leadership*, which is the necessary complement to its *actual nonaccountability*'.[73]

In the month preceding the party congress, in spite of the quiescence of the leaders of the Bukharinist Right, and the enforced silence or apostasy within the Soviet Union of the Trotskyist Left, many speeches and much space in the press were devoted to

[71] BO (Paris), xi (May 1930), 24.

[72] BO (Paris), xvii–xviii (November–December 1930), 11–19; for unions of poor peasants see p. 157, n. 47, above.

[73] *Writings of Leon Trotsky (1930)* (1975), 255–7 (May 31, 1930).

denouncing them. But the main emphasis of official propaganda was on the need to renew the drive for collectivisation. In the pre-congress discussion in *Pravda*, the party publicist Nikulikhin, repeating his earlier call for 50 per cent collectivisation in 1930/31, declared 'our wager is on collectivisation; the perspective of the next few years is the comprehensive collectivisation of the USSR'.[74] The phrase 'our wager is on collectivisation' was a reference to earlier descriptions of Soviet concessions to the richer peasants as a 'wager on the kulak',[75] a phrase which in turn echoed Stolypin's famous statement that 'our wager is not on the drunken and the indolent but on the sober and the strong'. At a meeting in the Communist Academy, Grin'ko also called for 50 per cent collectivisation in 1931.[76]

Apart from a general reaffirmation of the resolution of January 5, no specific plans for collectivisation were formally approved by the party at this stage, and the importance of working within the framework of the voluntary principle continued to be stressed. But in June 1930, as in the previous January and February, all opposition to the kolkhozy was firmly attributed to the kulaks. A whole page of the agricultural newspaper was devoted to the need to struggle against the kulak; 'kulak' attacks on kolkhozy and collective farmers were described, and it was alleged that individual peasants were forcibly prevented by kulaks from becoming members of the kolkhozy. The Agrarian Institute of the Communist Academy claimed to have discovered an 'anti-kolkhoz movement' in the North Caucasus (Yeisk), headed by an ex-sergeant from the tsarist army, which disguised its real aims by pretending to support the drive against excesses but treated the kolkhoz as identical with a landowner's estate. The reports complained that in many places the families of departed kulaks tended to be 'surrounded by an atmosphere of sympathy and depicted as innocent sufferers'; 'tearful letters from the exiled kulaks were frequently used for propaganda'

[74] P, June 21, 1930, disk. listok 16; on this occasion Nikulikhin proposed that at least half the sown area should be in the socialised sector; this was slightly less ambitious than his earlier figure, as the average sown area per household in kolkhozy was substantially higher than in the individual sector.

[75] See Carr (1958), 260–1.

[76] P, June 28, 1930, disk. listok 23 (where Grin'ko is cited by Larin); in PKh, 5, 1930, 15, Grin'ko called for collectivisation of two-thirds of the sown area in 1931 (this was roughly equivalent to 50 per cent of households).

in a 'festival of tears' (sleznitsa).[77] All this placed the 'voluntary principle' in a very restricted framework, in which any expression of unwillingness to join the kolkhoz could be condemned as kulak activity.

For the moment this slightly menacing tone in party propaganda was without a practical outcome. In spite of the favourable situation and satisfactory performance of the kolkhozy, some peasants continued to leave the kolkhozy: the number of households in kolkhozy fell by 799,000 in May and 596,000 in June.[78] Over half of those leaving were in the Ukraine and the North Caucasus, where the percentage of households in kolkhozy was still high relative to the other regions at the beginning of May. According to later accounts, some of these households simply postponed their withdrawal until after the spring sowing, because of pressure from the authorities;[79] others were said to have left because they hoped to secure for their own use the abundant harvest to be expected from the substantial sown area per household in the kolkhozy.[80] In the light of these withdrawals, the local authorities in the Ukraine were criticised for having swung from 'crude anti-middle-peasant Trotskyist errors' to the automatic acceptance of resignations from the kolkhozy without discussion; this was castigated as 'trying to form a bloc with the Right-wing opportunists'.[81]

(B) THE XVI PARTY CONGRESS, JUNE 26–JULY 13, 1930

The XVI party congress was the first in Soviet history at which no voice was raised against any major aspect of official party policy. The theses on the report of the central committee condemned Trotskyism, 'which has entirely moved over to a counter-revolutionary Menshevik outlook' and also 'reconciliatory attitudes to Trotskyism, which are primarily expressed in the under-

[77] SZe, June 24, 1930.

[78] See Table 16; the figures in this source for those remaining in kolkhozy are somewhat higher than those of the kolkhoz census of May 1930 (*Kolkhozy v 1930 g.* (1931), 6–7), so the decline may be partly due to an overestimate of the numbers of households in kolkhozy at the beginning of the period.

[79] IZ, lxxvi (1965), 37; and see p. 286 above.

[80] SZe, July 23, 1930 (editorial).

[81] SZe, July 16, 1930 (D. Rul').

estimation of the alliance of the working class with the middle peasantry'. But the theses reserved their fire for the 'main danger in the party', the Right deviationists, who were 'objectively an agency of the kulak class', and whose line would lead to 'capitulation to kulak and capitalist elements in the country'.[82] Opposition to party policy was thus identified with social classes hostile to the regime, as it had been ever since 1921. Defence of the excesses of collectivisation was treated as 'a reconciliatory attitude to Trotskyism', and criticism of the party leadership of the Mamaev kind was treated as Right deviation. The terms were strained, as Trotsky and the Right were in agreement that forced collectivisation and dekulakisation were a dangerous adventure of an irresponsible leadership.

Bukharin was not present at the congress, pleading illness, and submitted no statement to it, but Uglanov, Rykov and Tomsky all made speeches declaring their support for the general line of the party and renouncing past errors.[83] Rykov declared that his own main mistake, 'of tremendous political significance', had been to underestimate the possibility of socialising agriculture; and he strongly condemned Mamaev, whom the official resolution did not deign to mention by name.

The condemnation of the Right provided the background for the congress to endorse enthusiastically the correctness of the general line of the party and to praise the activities of the central committee under Stalin's leadership. From the outset, it was made clear that the onward march of socialism in the countryside was now being resumed after the very brief halt in the spring. In his opening remarks, Kalinin, as chairman, singled out 'comprehensive collectivisation of agriculture and the elimination of the kulaks as a class' as the key formula in the party's success;[84] Stalin's report, which was the first item on the agenda, after contrasting the crisis of world capitalism with the growth of socialism in the USSR, characterised the congress as 'the congress of the *expanded offensive* of socialism *on the whole front*, the elimination of the kulaks as a class and the realisation of comprehensive collectivisation'.[85] In the sections of the report concerned with agriculture, Stalin, while admitting

[82] *KPSS v rez.*, iii (1954), 10–22.
[83] *XVI s"ezd* (1931), 130–2, 142–8, 148–54.
[84] *XVI s"ezd* (1931), 4.
[85] *Soch.*, xii, 235–338, 342.

the grave decline in livestock, insisted that 'the grain problem has been solved in the main' owing to the successes of the sovkhozy and the kolkhozy, and that on this basis the problems of livestock breeding and of the production of industrial crops could also be solved. Stalin praised the central committee resolution of January 5, hardly mentioned the subsequent excesses, and firmly called for further collectivisation; he defended the 'method of comprehensive collectivisation' as 'a necessary method without which the five-year plan to collectivise all regions of the USSR cannot be fulfilled' and condemned its opponents as 'voluntary or involuntary enemies of communism'.[86]

Yakovlev, in his report on the kolkhoz movement and agriculture, offered an enthusiastic account of the technical and organisational advantages of socialist agriculture:

> *In the United States of America tractors are the monopoly of the rich farmer, here they are the monopoly of the sovkhozy and of the kolkhozy, which are an association of small peasants.*
>
> *The rich farmer works on a land area of 100–200 hectares; our kolkhoz is on a land area of 1,000 hectares, and the sovkhozy are on tens of thousands of hectares . . .*
>
> *There tractors are scattered, one per rich farmer; here they are concentrated–dozens of tractors per machine-tractor station or sovkhoz.*
>
> In short, they have capitalist power, and we have working-class power. (*Prolonged applause.*)
>
> *This is why, although we have seated a semi-literate labourer on the tractor, who only yesterday was bending his back for the kulak for 16–18 hours a day, this labourer gives four times as much output per tractor as the civilised American farmer.*
>
> *This is why our rate of creating large-scale farming has no precedent in the history of mankind.*[87]

He added that in 1931 more machinery would be supplied to agriculture in the Soviet Union than in the United States. Armed with this confidence in socialist mechanised agriculture, Yakovlev sketched out a plausible programme for regional agricultural specialisation which would soon outstrip all capitalist farming.[88] As

[86] *Soch.*, xii, 274–90, 333–7.
[87] *XVI s"ezd* (1931), 576–7.
[88] *Ibid.* 577–85.

a preliminary to achieving this programme, collectivisation must of course be completed. The kolkhozy must prepare to open their doors wide to the 'powerful new wave' of peasants who would seek to join them in the autumn; at the same time, now that joining a kolkhoz was a purely voluntary matter, collective farmers must recognise an obligation to work in a disciplined manner, and those 'kulak henchmen', who expected to be able to remove land, horses and implements if they left the kolkhoz, were deserters:

> All pseudo-liberalism, which is even ready to set aside kolkhoz land at any moment for any such deserter, although this is directly forbidden in the Statute, must be seen as of direct assistance to the kulak . . . The artel is not a passage way . . . The unified land fund of the kolkhoz must in no circumstances be divided, those leaving must be allocated land outside the kolkhoz fields (*Voices*: Hear! hear! *Applause*), they must not be paid until after the harvest, and the Indivisible Fund must be left intact.[89]

In the debate on the reports by Stalin and Yakovlev, the excesses of the previous winter were not ignored. Bauman denounced as '"Leftist" errors' both the appeal issued by the Moscow committee while he was its secretary for the elimination of the 'new bourgeoisie' in the towns as a class as well as the kulak in the countryside, and the 'rapid rate of collectivisation, insupportable for us' which the Moscow party committee had adopted. He also withdrew his now notorious attempt to justify 'ebbs and flows' in collectivisation: the outflow from the kolkhozy had no 'regular inevitability', but was 'mainly due to our own mistakes'.[90] Krylenko, People's Commissar for Justice, strongly criticised the widespread undervaluation of 'revolutionary legality' and the casual attitude adopted during the collectivisation drive earlier in the year to norms set by the party and to Soviet legislation. He castigated the indiscriminate application of the laws on the grain collections, on the slaughter of animals and on counter-revolutionary agitation as 'a blow against the middle peasant'; 'the transformation of the party apparatus of the courts and the party apparatus of the procuracy into an appendage of the administrative mechanism and the complete

[89] *Ibid.* 592–5.
[90] *Ibid.* 214–16.

elimination of their political and their party-political presence is a result of the contemptuous attitude displayed by very many people to the laws, and to both revolutionary and party norms'.[91] But such criticisms of the excesses of January–February were carefully circumscribed. Bauman insisted that while he had committed errors he had not followed 'a separate line from the line of the party', and Krylenko, though attempting to create a separate sphere of action for the courts and the procuracy, took it for granted that the laws were entirely at the disposal of the highest party authorities, and that it was entirely proper that party decisions, and even Stalin's statement in December 1929 on the elimination of the kulaks, had immediate legal force even before any specific legislation had been enacted.

The main thrust of the discussions about collectivisation at the congress was towards the new collectivisation drive which would begin in the autumn after the harvest. The first speaker in the debate on Yakovlev's report, the always orthodox Milyutin, envisaged the development in the near future both of 'agro-industrial combines' and of 'industrial–agrarian combines' which would integrate such construction projects as the Ural-Kuznetsk iron and steel combine with agriculture. This presupposed a socialised agriculture; and Milyutin argued that the Right deviation would now take the form of an attempt to hold up further collectivisation and dekulakisation, and criticised those local authorities who 'treat the voluntary principle as implying *non-interference in the process of collectivisation*': collectivisation must be encouraged, planned and organised.[92] A Ukrainian delegate envisaged that, after the new wave of collectivisation which would begin in the autumn, 'next year will be a year of unprecedented development of kolkhozy':

> The XVI congress of our party is examining the results of the first decisive successes in collectivisation, and the XVII congress will examine the results of the comprehensive collectivisation of the USSR.[93]

Khataevich declared that 'in the depths of his soul the middle or

[91] *Ibid.* 351–3.
[92] *Ibid.* 600–2.
[93] *Ibid.* 604–5.

poor peasant who has not yet joined the kolkhoz nevertheless knows that he will have to join sooner or later', and predicted that in the Central Volga region, where 68 per cent of the main grain area on the left bank was sown by kolkhozy in the spring of 1930, the central committee resolution of January 5, 1930, would be fulfilled and comprehensive collectivisation would 'be achieved in the main by the spring of 1931'. But he predicted that, throughout the grain areas, the achievement of the January 5 resolution would require 'a fierce struggle with the Rightist elements in our party'.[94] Other speakers did not refer to specific dates by which collectivisation would be achieved, but the resolution on Yakovlev's report, which reaffirmed the rates of collectivisation laid down in the decree of January 5, was adopted with only minor amendments, and Kalinin concluded the congress with a stirring call for '*the comprehensive collectivisation of the whole Soviet Union*' and the '*complete victory of socialism*'. After the singing of the 'Internationale', delegates cheered Stalin and the 'Leninist CC'.

The XVI congress thus formally ended the widespread criticism of the conduct of the central party authorities during the collectivisation drive. This was the last disagreement with the leadership to be openly expressed at party meetings and given some publicity in the party press in Stalin's lifetime. A few days later, in a letter from abroad written to his remaining Soviet supporters, Trotsky declared that 'the plebiscite regime has been established conclusively within the party'; 'the preparatory work within the party for Bonapartism has been completed'.[95] Rakovsky, in a long analysis of the economic situation written immediately after the congress, condemned the 'ultra-left' policy pursued in the countryside and called for the removal of the 'centrist leadership' headed by Stalin. His diagnosis was now very pessimistic: according to Rakovsky, the kolkhozy remained intact in the spring only because the peasants wanted to retain a share in the sown area; after the harvest the collective farmers would try to divide them up, a united front of the countryside against the state would emerge, and productive forces would decline even if a correct policy was followed. The crisis required the abandonment of the previous policies: the only way forward was to limit the kulak while not fully

[94] *Ibid.* 164; the resolution of January 5 was in fact somewhat bolder than Khataevich: it envisaged that collectivisation in the main grain regions could be 'in the main completed in the autumn of 1930 or in any case in the spring of 1931'.

[95] *Writings of Leon Trotsky (1930)* (1975), 335 (dated July 25, 1930).

depriving him of incentives, and to impose a tax in kind on the middle peasant; industrial goods should be temporarily imported to supplement home-produced supplies to the peasant. Rakovsky abandoned his insistence in his pre-congress statement that the growth of industry must be maintained; he now even described a reduction of industrial production as inevitable. He acknowledged that his new policy resembled the proposals made by the Right wing in the previous year, but somewhat lamely explained that 'the distinction between ourselves and the Rights is the distinction between an army retreating in order and deserters fleeing from the field of battle'. According to Rakovsky, success would be achieved only after the removal of the 'centrist leadership' under Stalin; and even then a sharp class struggle in the countryside over a period of years would be required.[96] To Stalin and the party leadership, on the other hand, it seemed abundantly clear that the successful continuation of collectivisation and industrialisation required the relentless suppression of the remnants of both Right and Left oppositions, and of those who shared, or half-shared, these views.

[96] BO (Paris), xxv–xxvi (November–December 1931), 28–32; this article, dated July–August 1930, will be further discussed in a subsequent volume.

CHAPTER EIGHT

THE HARVEST OF 1930

(A) THE HARVEST

The harvest was a great success, in spite of all the vicissitudes of the previous twelve months. While the spring sowings of grain were somewhat smaller than in 1929, the misfortunes of the previous two winters were not repeated, and grain sown in the autumn of 1929 survived the winter. The total grain area harvested in 1930 was therefore higher than in 1929 and, owing to the favourable weather of the summer of 1930, the yield was also high.[1] First reports put the grain harvest as high as 88 million tons. This figure was later reduced to 83·5, and eventually to 77·2 millions (see Table 1 and p. 349 below). But even the lowest figure was equal to the record post-revolutionary harvest of 1926 and 5 million tons higher than the harvests of 1927–9 (see Table 1). The harvest was successful in all the major grain-surplus regions, and the production of the main food crops, wheat and rye, was some 10 million tons higher than in 1929.[2]

Most other crops also did well. According to the official statistics, the potato harvest was an all-time record (see Table 1), and the total production of potatoes and vegetables was 20 per cent higher than

[1] For the summer weather see *Ezhegodnik khleboborota*, iv–v (1932), i, 19 (Lyashchenko).

[2] According to *Nar. kh.* (1932), 162–3, the output was as follows (million tons):

	1929	*1930*
Rye	20·4	23·6
Wheat	18·9	26·9
Total	39·2	50·5

The figures for 1930 are somewhat exaggerated, as they assume a total harvest of 83·5 million tons.

in 1929 (see Table 3). The gross output of the main vegetable crops was reported as shown in the table below (in million tons):[3]

	1928	*1929*	*1930*
Potatoes	46·4	45·6	47·2
Vegetables	10·5	10·6	17·5/13·9
Melons and other cucurbits	5·2	6·1	6·9
Total	62·1	62·3	71·6/68·0

Industrial crops were supported by the state through favourable prices and special supplies of grain, and total production increased by over 20 per cent; most of the major crops, including cotton and sugar beet, achieved record harvests. Self-sufficiency in cotton production now seemed to be within sight.

In contrast to the successful harvest, all branches of animal husbandry declined in the calendar year 1930. The animal population fell considerably, and this led to reduced production of meat, hides, wool, milk and eggs; the total production of livestock farming fell by over 22 per cent (see Table 3). This was a result both of the decline in fodder crops in 1929 and 1930 (see pp. 44–5 above), and of the slaughter and bad maintenance of animals during the collectivisation drive (see vol. 2, pp. 101–2). 'It will take years to relieve the situation in livestock products', a senior Soviet official frankly admitted in the spring of 1930.[4] The decline in animal products more than cancelled out the increase in crops, and the gross production of all branches of agriculture in 1930 was lower than in 1929 (see Table 3).

The socialised sector was now of major importance: kolkhozy were responsible for 17·5 per cent, and sovkhozy for 3·6 per cent of gross agricultural production as compared with only 3·1 and 1·6 per cent in 1929.[5] In addition, 7·3 per cent of gross production came from the household plots of collective farmers and the small plots cultivated by urban workers;[6] the socialised sector in this wider

[3] *Nar. kh.* (1932), 178–9; the lower figure for vegetables in 1930, which still seems remarkably high, is in *Tekhnicheskie kul'tury: kartofel', ovoshchi* (1936), 85.

[4] Krzhizhanovskii *et al.* (1930), 44 (Kviring).

[5] *Materialy po balansu* (1932), 142.

[6] Their gross production was valued at 1,761 million rubles in current prices out of a gross agricultural production of 24,107 million rubles; the equivalent percentage in 1929 was 2·9 (*Materialy po balansu* (1932), 84, 139); see also vol. 2, Table 8.

sense was responsible for 28·4 per cent of gross agricultural production as compared with 7·6 per cent in 1929.

On their collective lands the kolkhozy were responsible for 27·8 per cent of all grain production, and a further 5·0 per cent was grown by collective farmers individually; most of this was sown in the autumn before they joined the kolkhoz (see Table 4). The share of the kolkhoz sector in the production of different grains varied considerably. It grew only 14·6 per cent of rye, but as much as 45·0 per cent of wheat and 43·2 per cent of barley. This was because the kolkhozy were concentrated in the wheat and barley-growing areas of the Ukraine and the Volga region, and within these areas were more oriented towards production for the market than the individual peasants.[7]

Kolkhozy were also of major importance in the production of cotton, sugar beet and tobacco. The collective production of potatoes and vegetables, however, was relatively small.[8] Only 4·4 per cent of meat and dairy products came from the socialised sector of the kolkhozy.[9] For potatoes, vegetables and meat and dairy products the household plots were of major importance. In livestock farming the kolkhozy were relatively weak even if the household plots of collective farmers are included in the collective sector; taken together, the kolkhozy and the collective farmers, who were predominantly former poor peasants and batraks, possessed fewer animals per household than the individual peasants.

Sovkhozy also expanded very rapidly. The total grain production of all types of sovkhozy, including farms attached to government departments, factories and so on, increased from 1,327,000 to 3,256,000 tons.[10] In their first year of large-scale production, the new grain sovkhozy of Zernotrest produced 773,000 tons as compared with a mere 75,000 tons in 1929.[11] According to Campbell, the American grain farmer, in the Gigant sovkhoz in the North Caucasus an 'untechnical people' had acquired the 'spirit of

[7] *Ezhegodnik khlebooborota*, iv–v (1932), i, 9.

[8] The percentages were as follows (1929 in brackets): cotton 39·1 (5·7), flax 20·4 (3·1), sunflower 56·3 (*sic*) (5·0), tobacco 48·9 (5·7), sugar beet 37·3 (3·4), potatoes 12·8 (1·3), vegetables 20·4 (2·3), livestock 4·4 (0·7) (*Nar. kh.* (1932), 178–9). Figures for the production of individual crops, apart from grain, on the household plots of collective farmers have not been available. For an informative account of the collectivisation of cotton areas, see NAF, 6, 1930, 45–53 (E. Zel'kina).

[9] *Materialy po balansu* (1932), 142.

[10] *Nar. kh.* (1932), 162–3.

[11] Bogdenko (1958), 249.

American energy and progress': 'I have raised wheat throughout my life, but never before had I seen such fields of grain as I saw on that night ride across the Giant Farm'.[12]

The production of the new grain sovkhozy was, however, less than planned;[13] and both the new and the old sovkhozy absorbed large amounts of capital. In 1930, 66·2 per cent of the power used in all sovkhozy, and as much as 98·6 per cent in the grain sovkhozy, was supplied by tractors and other mechanical power, as compared with 20·1 per cent in the kolkhozy;[14] although they produced only 3·9 per cent of the grain, sovkhozy were allocated over 60 per cent of the new tractors in 1929/30, and by October 1, 1930, controlled 48·1 per cent of all tractors.[15] The authorities were nevertheless fortified by the satisfactory level of production, and adhered to the plan that marketed production from the grain sovkhozy should reach 4,500,000 tons in 1931 and over 7,000,000 tons in 1932.[16]

(B) THE GRAIN COLLECTIONS

(i) The contracts campaign

Preparation for the grain collections from the harvest of 1930 began in the summer of 1929. On August 26, 1929, a resolution of the party central committee outlined arrangements for contracts between the state and the peasants covering the areas to be sown to grain in the autumn of 1929 and the spring of 1930. The resolution confirmed that advance payments on future production, originally the main attraction for the peasants in the contract system, and already drastically reduced for the 1929 harvest (see p. 69 above), would be 'reduced and gradually eliminated' in the future. It nevertheless presented the contracts as advantageous to the peasants as well as to the state. The contract system was a key factor in 'planned product-exchange between town and countryside', and contracts must be an 'agreement between two sides'. In the contract 'a definite order

[12] Campbell (1932), 96, 99.
[13] The plan for 1930 was 920,000 tons (P, October 26, 1929).
[14] *Sots. str.* (1934), 152, 167.
[15] See vol. 2, Table 1 (b); these percentages are calculated in terms of tractor horse-power. On the high cost of Gigant sovkhoz see Knickerbocker (1931), 108–12.
[16] SZe, August 14, October 28, 1930; marketed production in 1930 was 475,000 tons (*Sel. kh. 1935* (1936), 715–16).

from the state for the production of agricultural output of a certain quantity and quality' would be set off against 'the acceptance by the cooperatives of an order from the peasants for the supply of means of production and, when possible (po vozmozhnosti), of consumer products'; agrotechnical help and loans would be provided by the state in return for systematic peasant efforts to improve their farming techniques, to cooperate in production and to collectivise.

The phrase 'when possible' with reference to consumer products revealed the one-sidedness of the 'agreement between two sides', and a later clause in the resolution formally stipulated for the first time that 'in order to facilitate the struggle against the kulak class' the contracts, signed as a rule not by individual households but by kolkhozy, simple production associations and land societies, were binding on all members of the association or society; the group concerned must accept 'collective responsibility' to carry out the contract.[17] This restored under a new name the '*krugovaya poruka*' (mutual obligation by members of the mir) which was enforced by the tsarist authorities and relinquished only in 1903. A later decree of the RSFSR empowered village soviets to collect products administratively from peasants who failed to comply with the resolutions of land societies; this was an addition to the provisions of the RSFSR decree of June 28, 1929, and of art.61[3] of the Criminal Code, which were used extensively in the 1929 campaign (see pp. 75–6, 99–100 above) and were now declared to be applicable to breaches by peasants of contracts signed by land societies.[18]

A very considerable increase in the number of contracts was envisaged: for the 1929 harvest the grain contracts covered 19 million hectares; for the 1930 harvest, an initial plan of 36·1 million hectares was expanded first to 44 and then to 81·8 million hectares, four-fifths of the planned sown area.[19]

Further 1929 decisions announced specific obligations to supply grain from the contracted sown area in terms of 'norms per hectare' for different regions and different social groups. Thus in the North Caucasus poor peasants were to supply 0·13 to 0·20 tons per hectare

17 P, August 27, 1929; the text is also in *Kollektivizatsiya . . . 1927–1935* (1957), 196–8. The major points of the resolution were incorporated in a decree of Sovnarkom of October 7, 1929, the collective obligations of peasants appearing in clause 5 (SZ, 1929, art. 610).

18 SU, 1929, art. 900 (Decree of December 30).

19 *KTs . . . na 1929/30* (1930), 543; Moshkov (1966), 143; the date on which the highest figure was approved is not stated.

and middle peasants 0·24 to 0·32 tons (the average yield in the region in 1929 was 0·65 tons, so these were substantial requirements).[20] The average norm for the USSR was a minimum of 0·30 tons per hectare; if all the area planned to be sown to grain were subject to contracts, this very high figure would have resulted in grain collections in 1930 amounting to about 30 million tons. The norms were a blunt instrument. While they were differentiated according to the type of grain, the difference was insufficient to allow for the different uses of crops in different areas: thus peasants in the North Caucasus were expected to supply 0·25 tons of oats per hectare sown to oats, as compared with 0·27 tons for barley and 0·25 tons of spring wheat, even though oats were grown almost entirely for consumption by the peasants' horses, and barley and spring wheat were grown largely for sale on the market.[21] This appears to have been an administrative blunder, as barley and wheat were more valuable to the state than oats. Moreover, the amount which the peasants were expected to supply under the contract was not confined to the stipulated norm per hectare. Narkomtorg ruled that both simple production associations and kolkhozy must treat the norms as a minimum, and hand over all 'commodity surpluses' to the state.[22] This ruling, if obeyed, would prevent the peasants from taking any grain to the market; and, in the event of harvest failure, as the norm was a minimum, it would have to be met even at the expense of the usual consumption of the peasants or of their animals.

During the winter and spring of 1929–30 the upheaval of rapid collectivisation threw the contract system into confusion. In the early stages of the spring sowing campaign, contracts were apparently signed with a large number of kolkhozy; by March 1, 39 per cent of the planned spring sown area was under contract.[23] But the membership of every kolkhoz was in flux; many kolkhozy were about to disappear; and the grain cooperatives, which negotiated and signed all the contracts, were greatly weakened (see p. 299 above). The whole contract procedure was therefore repeated between April and July 1930. In April Khlebotsentr issued instructions that all existing contracts should be checked, and

[20] Moshkov (1966), 144 (Narkomtorg decision of December 23, 1929); for the yield in 1929 see *Ezhegodnik po sel. kh. 1931* (1933), 396.

[21] EZh, July 16, 1930 (N. Vinogradskii).

[22] Moshkov (1966), 144 (Narkomtorg instruction of January 1, 1930).

[23] P, March 20, 1930; the area under contract increased from 19·7 million hectares on February 20 to 45·8 million on March 10 (SO, 3–4, 1930, 109).

Narkomtorg, in view of the disappearance of land societies in many places, restored the earlier arrangement that contracts could be signed with individual peasant households as well as with production associations and land societies.[24] On June 28, a further decree excluded the sown area of kulak households from the contract procedure, and made it subject to separate fixed quotas. Clause 5 of the decree of October 7, 1929, which gave the struggle against the kulak as the reason for obliging all members of a land society to accept its decision to sign a contract (see p. 341, n. 17, above), was obviously no longer appropriate. So in the new decree the phrase about the kulak was removed, but the obligation of members of land societies remained unchanged![25]

New arrangements were also announced for the kolkhozy. As early as April 13, as part of the effort to halt the exodus, Sovnarkom announced that the 'delivery norms' for kolkhozy would amount to one-quarter to one-third of the harvest in grain areas, and to not more than one-eighth of the harvest elsewhere; the remainder would be 'at the full disposal of the kolkhozy'.[26] Three months later, on the eve of the harvest, norms for the kolkhozy in each region were belatedly fixed by Narkomtorg; the spread was from 3 per cent in the Northern region to 35 per cent in the Ukraine; the Ukrainian norm thus slightly exceeded the stipulated maximum of one-third.[27]

Strenuous efforts were made during the summer of 1930 to secure the signing or re-signing of contracts by kolkhozy, by individual peasants and by land societies. Narkomtorg officials admitted in the course of the new campaign that the contracts were often a matter of 'naked administration' or 'simple administrative instructions', with no participation by the peasant or kolkhoz household.[28] Figures for the sown area covered by contracts were conflicting. According to one source, contracts covering 51·5 million hectares were eventually signed, equivalent to well over half the sown area; 25·1 million hectares were in kolkhozy, 26·4 million in individual peasant households.[29] According to another source, however, contracts covered only 37 per cent of the total sown area.[30] The confusion

[24] VT, 5, 1930, 11 (Chernov); Moshkov (1966), 147.
[25] SZ, 1930, art. 374.
[26] SZ, 1930, art. 256.
[27] SZe, July 16, 1930.
[28] VT, 5, 1930, 8 (Chernov); B, 9, May 15, 1930, 28 (Mikoyan).
[29] Moshkov (1966), 147–8, citing the archives.
[30] ST, 5–6, 1931, 25.

reflects, perhaps, the formal nature of the contracts and the relatively slight importance attached to them. By 1930, the grain collections were in practice an obligatory quota for each village, imposed impartially on its peasants whether or not they had signed a contract. The contracts were little more than a legal fiction, concealing the new relation between the state and the peasants in the terminology of NEP. But the authorities clung to the contract system as a device for demonstrating to the peasants that the grain quota had the force of law, and in the forlorn hope of persuading them that they were to receive something more than one-fifth of the market price in return for their grain.

(ii) The collection plan

When the control figures for 1929/30 were complied in the autumn of 1929, the grain harvest for 1930 was planned at 88·9 million tons, 16·7 per cent above the 1929 harvest, then estimated at 76·2 million tons. To achieve this ambitious objective, the sown area was planned to increase by 10 per cent and the yield per hectare by 6 per cent.[31] After the spring sowing of 1930, the total area sown to grain was believed to amount to 6–7 per cent above the 1929 level,[32] the highest since the revolution. If this estimate had been correct (it was later reduced to 2·8 per cent above 1929), it would still have been about 4 per cent less than the plan, so the planned harvest could have been achieved only by a very substantial increase in yield. On June 27, 1930, at the XVI party congress, Stalin, using, as he stated, information supplied by Gosplan and Narkomzem, nevertheless announced that the harvest 'according to all the data' would be 16·5 per cent above that of 1929.[33] If Stalin was still assuming a 1929 harvest of 76·2 million tons, this percentage implied a 1930 harvest of about 89 million tons, the same as in the plan prepared in the previous autumn, requiring an increase in yield of nearly 10 per cent.

All the prospects seemed favourable. At a conference of collective farmers on July 6, 1930, reports from the provinces indicated that the harvest would be extremely good in the south and much better than in 1929 almost everywhere.[34] While Mikoyan at the end of

[31] KTs . . . *na 1929/30* (1930), 118, 127, 139.
[32] See p. 307 above, and Stalin, *Soch.*, xii, 274.
[33] *Soch.*, xii, 275.
[34] SKhIB, 19–20, 1930, 49.

July cautiously predicted a 'not bad or average' harvest,[35] throughout the collection campaign both Narkomtorg and Gosplan assumed that the harvest would be 88 or 89 million tons (see Table 12). In July, Mikoyan explained his expectation of a reasonable harvest by the good weather and the technical assistance provided to agriculture by the state.[36] In September, Minaev, responsible for statistics within Gosplan, claimed that the sown area had increased by 6 per cent and the yield by as much as 15 per cent, so that the harvest was 21·9 per cent above the 1929 level; in this remarkable increase in yield, 'climatic conditions played a definite and considerable role'.[37] By this time the estimate of the 1929 harvest had evidently been reduced to 72 million tons (see footnote 38 below), so Minaev's percentages again imply a 1930 harvest of 88 million tons. On October 24, another Gosplan official reported in the press that the harvest was 88 million tons; this seems to be the first occasion on which a specific figure was published.[38] Finally, the central committee plenum of December 1930 stated that the harvest was 87·4 million tons.[39]

This optimistic estimate of the harvest provided the basis for an extremely ambitious grain collection plan. As early as May 1930, Mikoyan predicted 'the full solution of the grain problem' in the autumn of 1930 and the spring of 1931, which would in turn enable an easier triumph in industrial crops; subsequently, in 'approximately 1931', presumably on the basis of the increased supply of grain for fodder from the 1931 harvest, a successful drive could be undertaken to solve the livestock problem.[40] At this time, no firm plan for the grain collections had yet been approved. While a specific figure for the total grain collection plan was not published until after the campaign was over, it is evident from the various percentages and partial figures which did appear that a plan of about 23 million tons, including the milling levy, as much as 7 million tons above the 1929 level, was approved in July and remained in force throughout the campaign (see Table 13). Now that the major agricultural experts of the 1920s had been removed

[35] P, July 29, 1930.

[36] P, July 29, 1930.

[37] PKh, 7–8, 1930, 50.

[38] P, October 24, 1930 (Maimin); this harvest was said to be 22 per cent higher than that of 1929, implying a 1929 harvest of only 72 million tons.

[39] *KPSS v rez.*, iii (1954), 75.

[40] B, 9, May 15, 1930, 27.

from office, and the Right wing in the party effectively silenced, the bitter dispute of August and September 1929 was not repeated in the summer of 1930 even though the plan was now much higher; in the laconic phrase of the Narkomtorg journal, the centre had 'freed itself' from the grain-fodder balance.[41]

This very high figure assumed that all, or almost all, 'marketed' grain (tovarnaya chast') would be sold to the state; the planned level of 'marketability (tovarnost')' was assumed to be approximately equal to the grain collection plan.[42] The assurance to the kolkhozy in the previous April that all grain in excess of the fixed norm per hectare was to be at their 'full disposal' (see p. 343 above) therefore turned out to have been merely an encouraging statement of the legal position, not to be taken seriously in practice. In an article of May 1930 launching the campaign in the Narkomtorg journal, Chernov insisted that 'sending to the private market surpluses of socialised output in excess of the established delivery norms would discredit the very idea of the kolkhoz movement'.[43] In July he pointed out that the collective farmer had 'not yet discarded his individualist psychology' and would be attracted to the market by 'speculative prices'; the sale of grain on the market by the kolkhoz would be 'direct assistance to the kulak, who struggles against planned product-exchange between town and country, and for the preservation of market spontaneity'.[44] Chernov also insisted that the collection agencies must persuade individual peasants under contract to sell them any 'marketable' grain remaining after they had met their delivery norms, and called for 'a major effort at explanation' to dispel the widespread impression given earlier in the summer that one-third of the harvest was the maximum that the kolkhoz would be required to deliver to the state:

> Grain delivery norms both for collective farmers and for individual households under contract are below the actual marketability. Therefore free marketable surpiuses of grain will remain in every farm, at its disposal. Our task includes persuad-

[41] ST, 2–3 (7–8), April–May 1931, 11.

[42] Thus Chernov in P, August 17, 1930, stated that marketability would be 26 per cent; and 26 per cent of a total harvest of 89 million tons is 23·1 million tons.

[43] VT, 5, 1930, 9.

[44] SZe, July 19, 1930; PKh, 6, 1930, 16; these two articles were evidently written more or less simultaneously, as much of their content, including the statistics, coincides.

> ing them to sell these surpluses to the state as well. It goes without saying that we cannot tolerate a situation in which a kolkhoz, or a household contracting its sown area, sells even part of its grain on the speculative market.

To attract this additional grain, a special fund would be established of industrial consumer goods, agricultural machinery and tractors, in addition to the normal supplies of industrial consumer goods which would be made available to peasants supplying grain to the state.[45]

The preliminary instructions about the campaign also made it clear that individual peasants who had not signed contracts were also to be put under pressure to sell all their grain to the state. While stipulating that only 'social pressure' was to be used in relation to these peasants, Chernov urged that they should be persuaded to take on 'self-obligations' to the village, as in the previous year;[46] and the village komsods were instructed by Narkomtorg to take 'all measures' to ensure the sale to the state of all the market surpluses of households without contracts.[47] Another Narkomtorg official instructed his colleagues to explain to the individual peasants that although the markets were not closed, sales to 'speculators' or at 'speculative' prices should be regarded as 'forbidden fruit' which would lead to 'a break with society, the kolkhoz and the cooperative'.[48]

The total plan of approximately 23 million tons was divided between the main sectors as shown in the table below (and see Table 13):

	Amount (in million tons)	*Percentage of total*
Sovkhozy	1·8	8
Kolkhozy	10·1	44
Individual peasants:		
under contract	5·8	25
not under contract	4·6	20
Kulaks	0·7	3
Total	23·0	100

[45] PKh, 6, 1930, 17–19.
[46] VT, 5, 1930, 12; PKh, 6, 1930, 19; and see p. 99 above.
[47] SKhIB, 23, 1930, 10–15 (instructions dated July 16).
[48] P, August 5, 1930 (A. L'vov).

The figure for kolkhozy included collections from the harvest on land sowed individually by collective farmers in the autumn of 1929 before they joined the kolkhozy; according to a decree of Kolkhoztsentr dated July 13, 1930, these collections were to amount to 2·11 million tons.[49] This plan assumed that the proportion of the kolkhoz harvest to be marketed, though lower than in 1929, would be 32 per cent as compared with only 19 per cent from the harvest of the individual peasants. The kolkhozy and the collective farmers would thus deliver substantially more grain per hectare and over three times as much grain per household as the individual peasant (see Table 15). This was not at all unfair to the kolkhozy. The sown area per household in the kolkhoz sector was 70 per cent higher than in the individual sector, and it was expected to produce more than twice as much grain per household. After the grain quota had been met, the kolkhoz would retain at its own disposal much more grain per household than the individual peasants. Once more the flexibility of the term 'commodity' or 'marketable' grain was demonstrated: the 'non-marketable' or 'non-commodity' grain of the kolkhoz would provide more food grain per person and more fodder grain per animal than the 'non-marketable grain' of the individual peasant. Moreover, even with the bumper harvest which had apparently been achieved, the position of the individual peasants would actually deteriorate: the amount of grain at their disposal after the grain collections was planned to decline slightly, to only 2·16 tons per household as compared with 2·19 tons in 1929.[50]

All these calculations rested, however, on false premises. The grain collection plan was a much heavier burden on both peasants and collective farmers than the authorities appreciated, or were prepared to admit in public. It assumed a harvest of 88 or 89 million tons, which would have left 65 million tons with the collective farms

[49] SKhIB, 22, 1930, 20. This decree gave the total collection from the kolkhozy as 9·59 million tons, thus evidently excluding the milling levy.

[50] For the 1930 plan see Table 15. The 1929 figure is calculated as follows from data in *Nar. kh.* (1932), 162–3, 338–9:

Grain produced by individual peasant households: 1929 harvest: 67·7 million tons.

Grain collected from individual households: 14·0 million tons (11·9 million tons plus 2·1 million tons of the milling levy—the latter figure is an approximation).

Grain remaining at disposal of individual households: 53·7 million tons.

Number of individual peasant households: approximately 24·5 million.

Grain remaining per household: 2·19 tons.

and the peasants, as compared with 56 million tons in 1929, so they would have retained over half the increase in the harvest, all of which would have gone to the kolkhoz sector. The initial harvest estimate was only slightly reduced in the course of the grain campaign (see p. 345 above). The figure announced by the central committee plenum in December 1930, 87·4 million tons, still appeared in an official statistical handbook in 1931.[51] In 1932, however, a later handbook reported that the sown area and crop output for the 1930 harvest had previously been overestimated by up to 5 per cent and accordingly reduced the figure for the grain harvest to 83·5 million tons.[52] Even this revised total was too large: the gross harvest was obtained by multiplying the sown area by the yield per hectare, and in 1930 the yield was calculated by a less reliable method than in 1929.[53] The 1930 harvest appears in the grain-fodder balances preserved in the Soviet archives as only 77·2 million tons.[54] But if this figure is correct, only 54 million tons of grain remained with the peasants after the collections, as compared with the 65 million tons originally envisaged, and 56 million tons in 1929. The whole of the increase in the harvest, plus a further 2 million tons, may thus have been removed from the peasants.

The overestimation of the harvest was particularly large in the case of the kolkhozy. The estimates made in the summer of 1930 assumed a harvest from collective cultivation (excluding individual sowings by collective farmers) of some 27 million tons, which meant that the yield would be about 7 per cent higher than in individual peasant farms, and Yurkin even claimed that the yield was 15–30 per cent higher.[55] In the 1931 handbook, however, the kolkhoz harvest was reduced to 25·2 million tons, and in the 1932 handbook it was further reduced to 23·2 million tons; the harvest from individual households (including individual sowings by collective farmers) was reduced much less, from about 58 to 57 million tons.[56]

51 *Sdvigi* (1931), 200.
52 *Nar. kh.* (1932), 162–3; see Table 12.
53 In 1929 the yield was obtained 'on the basis of communications from voluntary correspondents, corrected according to the data of the autumn sample questionnaire and the peasant budgets'; in 1930 'from the data of statistical plenipotentiaries, corrected by expert commissions on the basis of mass reapings and threshings' (*ibid.* 654–5).
54 Moshkov (1966), 230–1; the same figures may be calculated from *Materialy po balansu* (1932), 312–19.
55 SZe, October 15, 1930.
56 *Sdvigi* (1931), 200; *Nar. kh.* (1932), 162–3.

The yield in the kolkhozy, in spite of their superior land, thus turned out to be not 7 per cent above but 2 per cent below that obtained by individual peasant households (see Table 14). But in the uncertain world of grain statistics this conclusion may be imprudent, as the estimates of the yield on land sown by individual peasants, and of their total harvest, may also have been exaggerated by the statistical plenipotentiaries, and not subjected to a subsequent reduction: as we shall see, the authorities were anxious to demonstrate that the harvest of individual peasants was high, so as to collect more grain from them.

(iii) The campaign

The grain collections followed the procedures established during the 1929 campaign. The 'quota' imposed on every village in 1929 was now elevated to the status of a 'village plan', but continued to be fixed by the district authorities on the basis of a district plan or quota sent to them from the region. At the village level, sub-quotas were fixed for each of the four major groups of peasant households—the kolkhozy; middle and poor peasant households under contract; middle and poor peasant households not under contract; and kulaks. The sub-quota for the kolkhozy was fixed on the basis of the approved delivery norms by a district commission, or by the MTS where this existed, and could not be changed by the village soviet or the komsod; the sub-quotas for the other groups were fixed by the village soviet or the komsod, using the approved delivery norms in the case of households under contract. As in 1929, every kulak household was set a firm individual quota by the village soviet.[57] An estimate of surpluses in excess of quota, which were to be collected from both kolkhozy and individual peasants, was also included by the village soviet as a separate item in its plan.[58] If the sum of the sub-quotas was less than the plan fixed for the village by the district authorities, the delivery norms laid down in the contracts were to be increased.[59] The village plan or quota thus took absolute precedence over all other arrangements with the peasants.

Following the prompt preparation of the collection plan for the USSR as a whole, collection plans reached the villages much earlier

[57] VT, 5, 1930, 12; SKhIB, 23, 1930, 10–15 (instructions to the komsods dated July 16).
[58] *Spravochnik po khlebnomu delu* (1932), 29.
[59] P, July 29, 1930 (Mikoyan).

than in 1929, often by the beginning of the campaign.[60] The chaotic competition between different agencies which was a prominent feature of the 1929 collections was apparently almost completely eliminated in 1930. At long last responsibility for the collections was placed firmly in the hands of a single agency, the grain cooperatives under Khlebotsentr, which were required to transfer all the grain they collected to the state organisation Soyuzkhleb. 'Grain troiki' consisting of representatives of Narkomtorg, Soyuzkhleb and Khlebotsentr were formed centrally and locally to rule on major problems.[61]

Simultaneously, a major reform was carried out in local government. Some 200 okrugs, the level of administration intermediate between the 13 regions and the 2,800 districts, were abolished.[62] In the course of 1929/30, the district party and soviet organisations had already emerged as the principal link between the central authorities and the kolkhoz and the village, and in the second half of 1930 the staff of the district soviets was increased substantially by the addition of staff transferred from the former okrugs: in the average district by the end of 1930 some 40–50 staff were responsible for a population of 50,000, including some 8,000 peasant households.[63]

In the summer of 1930, a further effort was also made to straighten out the great confusion in the administrative agencies responsible for the kolkhozy and the agricultural cooperatives. In each district, the administration of the kolkhozy was now separated from the administration of supplies and sales: the district kolkhoz-koopsoyuz was split into a kolkhozsoyuz, responsible for the organisation of the kolkhozy, and for their activities as producers, and a koopsoyuz, responsible for supplies to and marketings by both

[60] *Spravochnik po khlebnomu delu* (1932), 29; a complaint in SZe, August 31, 1930, that 'in some places' the plan had not yet reached the kolkhoz in itself revealed an improvement as compared with 1929.

[61] *Spravochnik po khlebnomu delu* (1932), 28–9; the consumer cooperatives and the other agricultural cooperatives participated in the collections only in those places, particularly in the grain-deficit regions, where the grain cooperatives were weak. As in 1929, Soyuzkhleb itself collected grain from the kolkhozy, and the milling levy from all those who used the mills.

[62] See p. xx above. For slightly different figures for the number of okrugs, see *XVI s"ezd* (1931), 335; for the number of districts in May 1930 see *Kolkhozy v 1930g.* (1931), 17 (2,851 districts, excluding some minor regions and republics).

[63] For some rather confused statistics on the increase in the staff of the districts, see B, 13, July 15, 1930, 17; *XVI s"ezd* (1931), 335; IZ, lxxvi (1965), 38n.

the kolkhozy and the individual peasants, including the all-important grain and other collections.[64]

In spite of improvements in organisation, this was by no means a smooth campaign, conducted according to the formal rules laid down by the authorities. Before the campaign, the decree of October 7, 1929, strongly condemned as a major weakness the practice that 'contract plans and conditions are changed during their preparation and execution',[65] and in May 1930 Chernov declared that frequent changes in the quotas 'unnerve the lower organisations and harass the peasants'.[66] In practice, however, in 1930 as in 1929, the quotas for the villages were unstable throughout the campaign. The quotas for each region were worked out on the basis of their planned gross harvest and of past figures for the proportion of marketed grain to the total harvest in the region. The planned gross harvest, however, varied considerably from the actual harvest. It depended on the planned sown area and the planned yield, but both of these were uncertain, the planned sown area because the past estimates of sown area on which it was based were inaccurate, the yield because it was affected by unpredictable regional variations in climate.[67] As a result, after the harvest some regional quotas were increased and others reduced: at the extreme, one quota was cut by 27·4 per cent, another increased by 22·5 per cent.[68] In the Ukraine, an initial plan of 7 million tons was first increased by the USSR government to 7·2, then to 7·7 and finally to 8 million tons; according to a Soviet historian, this resulted in 'great confusion' and in 'the dissatisfaction of a considerable section of the peasants, thus making it more difficult to carry out the collections'.[69] In those republics and regions where the quota was increased, similar increases had to take place in every district and village. Moreover, as in 1929, when some districts within a region and some villages within a district failed to reach their quotas, additional quotas were imposed on districts and villages which had already met their initial obligations in full.[70] These changes,

[64] *KPSS v rez.*, iii (1954), 59 (resolution of XVI congress); I, July 15, 1930 (resolution of presidium of central control commission and collegium of Rabkrin, July 9, 1930).

[65] SZ, 1929, art. 610.

[66] VT, 5, 1930, 8.

[67] ST, 2–3 (7–8), April–May 1931, 11.

[68] Calculated from data in ST, 2–3 (7–8), April–May 1931, 11.

[69] Slin'ko (Kiev, 1961), 281–2.

[70] ST, 2–3 (7–8), April–May 1931, 11.

coupled with the pressure on all peasants to hand over all 'marketable' grain to the state, meant that, as in the previous year, the grain quota was not a fixed obligation but one which was subject to unpredictable increases.

As in 1929, industrial consumer goods were not available in sufficient quantities or with sufficient regularity to provide a substantial incentive for the peasants to hand over their grain voluntarily. The supply of textiles, clothing and footwear, the most sought-after consumer goods, was lower than in 1929 owing to the reduction in cotton imports and the decline in the supply of hides.[71] In the first few months of the campaign, little seems to have been done to relate the supply of consumer goods to the fulfilment of the collection plan.[72] Postyshev, who travelled to the Central Black-Earth region on behalf of the Politburo, bluntly told a party meeting that 'it is an opportunist line, and not the line of the party, to make the possibility of realising the harvest dependent on the presence of industrial goods'; more sugar and industrial consumer goods would be available for the peasants in three or four months (after the collections were over).[73] It was not until half-way through the campaign that a Narkomtorg directive signed by Mikoyan belatedly announced that definite quantities of consumer goods would be supplied in exchange for grain delivered: for one-sixth of a tsentner of grain (worth about 1 ruble at delivery prices), goods would be supplied to kolkhozy to the value of 35 kopeks and to individual peasants to the value of 25 kopeks.[74] But even these belated arrangements seem to have been slow to take effect.[75]

An additional disincentive to the peasants emerged during the 1930 campaign. In previous years currency was made available in abundance to pay the low delivery prices to the peasants, but in 1930 the grain campaign coincided with a fierce drive to halt currency issues and reduce the level of inflation. Currency was therefore supplied to the districts in inadequate quantities, and the districts were urged to collect taxes and insurance dues promptly,

[71] Moshkov (1966), 152, states that the supply of these three groups of consumer goods was 14·5 per cent less in the economic year 1929/30 than in 1928/29; no quarterly figures have been traced.

[72] See for example NPF, 6, March 1931, 14 (a survey of a district in the North Caucasus).

[73] SZe, October 18, 1930 (speech of October 8).

[74] EZh, October 12, 1930.

[75] See NPF, 6, March 1931, 14.

and to seek out overdue debts, in order to acquire enough currency to pay the peasants in full for the grain.[76] In the autumn of 1930, it was transparently obvious that the primary concern of the authorities was not to establish an acceptable system of product-exchange between town and country, but to squeeze as much grain as possible out of the peasants.

In these conditions the grain collections retained the character of an emergency campaign. The district koopsoyuz, formally responsible for the grain collections, usually had no organisation at the village level after the decline in the membership of the agricultural cooperatives during the autumn and winter of 1929–30 (see pp. 299–300 above), and once again large numbers of party members and officials were hurled into the countryside. In practice, the campaign was managed by the district committees of the party and their numerous brigades and plenipotentiaries, working, now that the okrugs had been abolished, directly under the regional party committee. Attempts to secure the formal support of the village population for the quota through meetings of the skhod—the 'Ural–Siberian method' to which great importance was attached in the 1929 campaign—were now much more perfunctory, and were rarely mentioned in the press. During the collectivisation drive, the skhod had generally been greatly weakened, or had even disappeared; and for the quarter of the rural population which belonged to the kolkhoz, its board or its chairman now acted as the link with the district authorities. Accordingly, in the autumn of 1930 the plenipotentiaries, assisted by the village soviet and the komsod, dealt with the board or chairman of the kolkhoz and directly with individual peasant households. As a substitute for the mass participation of the village community, the device of 'socialist emulation' was borrowed from industry, and districts, villages and whole regions competed to outdo each other in prompt fulfilment of the collection plan. Reports also occasionally appeared of 'counter-plans' in which kolkhozy offered to provide more grain than their stipulated quota.[77] But most villages and most kolkhozy were evidently not involved in socialist emulation and counter-planning, and the new devices had little influence on the pattern of the campaign as a whole.

[76] SZe, October 18, 1930 (Postyshev on Central Black-Earth region); NP, 11, 1930, 117–19 (Lower Volga); NPF, 6, March 1931, 14–15 (North Caucasus).
[77] For some examples see Moshkov (1966), 152–4.

As in 1929, considerable pressure from the authorities was required to obtain the grain quotas in full. The Ukrainian central committee sent all the members of some of its district committees into the countryside. The 'sowing and grain collection troika' of Kolkhoztsentr resolved that 'leaders of kolkhozy who hold up and disrupt the grain collections must be immediately put on trial, and kolkhozy retaining their grain must be deprived of loans, and the supply of agricultural machinery to them must cease'.[78] Numerous cases were reported in the press of the dissolution of komsods, the arrest of kolkhoz chairmen and 'wrecker brigade leaders' and the dissolution of kolkhozy, for resisting or failing to meet the quotas.[79]

As in 1929, the authorities set out to collect nearly all their grain before the end of the calendar year, and most of it by the end of October. In July–December 1930 much more grain was collected in each month than in the equivalent month of 1929. By the end of October 1930, the total reached 14·8 million tons, almost as much as in the whole of the agricultural year 1929/30 (see Table 8(d)). In terms of the more ambitious plan for 1930, however, progress was slower than in the previous year; by the end of October only 64 per cent of the annual plan had been collected as compared with 70 per cent by the end of October 1929. The quotas for the kolkhozy proved much more difficult to achieve than the quotas for the individual peasant: by the end of October the kolkhozy had provided only 50 per cent, the individual peasants as much as 80 per cent, of their initial annual quota.[80] A major reason for the difficulty was the considerable overestimation of the kolkhoz harvest in the early stages of the campaign (see p. 349 above). If the original collection plan for the kolkhozy had been enforced, the collective farmers would have retained only 2·86 tons per household, including their individually-sown grain, as compared with 3·74 anticipated in the collection plan.[81] It is not known when the authorities realised that the harvest estimates for the kolkhozy were exaggerated; they were not publicly revised until 1931. But as early

[78] Moshkov (1966), 150; SZe, October 26, 1930.

[79] Chernopitskii (Rostov, 1965), 140 (North Caucasus); I, October 18 (Central Volga); SZe, October 19, 22 (North Caucasus), 1930; other examples relating to the Central Volga and the North Caucasus are cited from the Soviet press of October 1930 in BP (Prague), lxxxiii (November 1930), 7–8.

[80] *Ezhegodnik khlebooborota*, iv–v (1932), ii, 90, 103.

[81] 27·4 million tons less original collection plan of 10·1 million tons = 16·3 million tons ÷ 5·7 million households = 2·86 tons.

as September 18, 1930, an important but little publicised decree of Khlebotsentr announced a drastic change in approach, which considerably lessened the demands on the kolkhozy and increased the demands on the individual sector:

> In view of the fact that, according to the data of the Administration for Contracts and Deliveries, and of the regional and republican [cooperative] unions, the delivery norms on contracts for the North Caucasus, Crimea, Lower Volga, Western Siberia, Eastern Siberia, the Ukraine and the Far East are lower than the delivery norms per hectare for the kolkhozy, and also taking into account that for all the main grain areas delivery norms for non-contracted individual households are considerably lower than the delivery norms of contracted individual peasants and kolkhozy, it is proposed to the Administration for Contracts and Deliveries and to all regional unions:
>
> to re-examine accordingly, with the object of increasing them, the delivery norms for contracts (for the areas named), and also, in applying the practice of self-obligations from individual non-contracted households, to act on the assumption that the size of self-obligations of non-contracted individual peasants should be no lower than with collective farmers.[82]

The decree evidently reflected a decision taken at a high level, possibly by Stalin or the Politburo, and presumably followed the Narkomtorg directive which was said to have been issued along the same lines.[83] It recorded a fundamental change in policy. The original grain collection plan assumed that 0·31 tons would be collected per hectare from the kolkhozy as compared with 0·17 tons from individual peasants, and these original figures were still assumed in a detailed article of September 27.[84] If the proposed change were put into effect within the total plan of 23·2 million tons, the collections planned from the kolkhozy would fall from 10·1 to 7·0 and those from the individual peasants would increase from 11 to 14·5 million tons.[85] No immediate change was, however, made in

[82] *Khlebotsentr*, 33, October 1, 1930, 17.

[83] See reference to this directive in EZh, October 7, 1930.

[84] EZh, September 27, 1930.

[85] Calculated from sown area figures in Table 4 (July 1930 estimate); individual surveys of collective farmers are included under kolkhozy, and it is assumed that

the plan for the kolkhozy. On October 15, Yurkin stated that about 10 million tons of grain were to be delivered to the state by the kolkhozy;[86] and early in November an article in the economic newspaper incongruously condemned the failure to carry out the 'government ruling' that the norm per hectare for individual households must not be less than that for kolkhozy, while continuing to cite figures which indicate that the original quotas were still in operation.[87]

Though the plan for the kolkhozy had not yet been formally reduced, pressure on the individual peasants steadily increased. The Khlebotsentr decree of September 18 ruled that 'firm quotas' should be imposed on 'kulak and well-to-do' peasants, 4–5 per cent of all households in each region, and a maximum of 7 per cent in particular districts.[88] These were very high figures, as over 300,000 kulak households had already been expropriated, and many others had fled from the countryside: the grain collection plan assumed that only 6¼ per cent of all the grain from individual peasants would come from kulaks on whom firm quotas had been imposed, and must therefore have assumed that only 2 or 3 per cent of households would be affected.[89] The inclusion of 'well-to-do' households among those subject to a firm individual quota made it a weapon much more easily used against any individual peasant refusing or unable to deliver his grain quota. The point was brought home by *Pravda*, which condemned a statement in the poor peasants' newspaper that 'the kulak has been destroyed', and with surprising frankness rejected the optimistic assertion in an editorial in *Izvestiya* that 'in the USSR the peasant, while still on his own piece of land, can develop his economy with the help of the proletarian state'. According to *Pravda*,

> If the 'peasant' can *develop* his individual economy, why should he join the kolkhoz?[90]

21·4 million tons (including the milling levy) was to be collected from kolkhozy and individual peasants, 1·8 millions from sovkhozy (see Table 13).

[86] SZe, October 15, 1930.

[87] EZh, November 5, 1930 (Z. Zinoviev).

[88] *Khlebotsentr*, 33, October 1, 1930, 17.

[89] PKh, 6, 1930, 12; P, August 17, 1930.

[90] P, October 16, 1930; I and *Bednota*, October 15, 1930.

A few days later, *Pravda* informed its readers that yesterday's middle peasant could soon become today's kulak:

> Even the best activists in the countryside often cannot spot the kulaks, failing to understand that in the circumstances of the present autumn when there has been a good harvest, . . . in the circumstances of high speculative prices for grain, meat and vegetables at the markets, certain middle peasant households are rapidly transformed into well-to-do and kulak households.[91]

The proportion of the grain collections from the individual peasants which was to be obtained from kulaks and well-to-do households was more than doubled, from 6¼ to 13–15 per cent,[92] and peasants failing to meet firm individual quotas were fined or imprisoned, and their property was sold—in the Crimea, penalties were imposed on 77 per cent of households subject to firm quotas in the course of the autumn of 1930.[93]

At some point in the course of November, the division of the quotas between sectors was brought into line with the new policy: the quota for individual households was increased to about 14 million tons, that for kolkhozy reduced to about 7½ million tons. Henceforth, the individual sector, which had met a higher proportion of its plan than the kolkhozy, lagged badly behind its new quota. Although by the end of November individual peasants had more than fulfilled their original quota, and the kolkhozy had not met more than 60 per cent of theirs, the grain collection agencies were now frequently criticised for insufficient attention to the individual peasants. The agricultural newspaper declared that '*fulfilment of the grain collection plan by the individual sector lags far behind the fulfilment of the plan by the kolkhozy* in a number of areas, including Kazakhstan, North Caucasus and the Lower Volga region', and condemned '*opportunistic underestimation of the individual sector*';[94] the journal of the grain cooperatives complained, on the basis of the revised plan, that '*the kolkhoz sector has to compensate for underfulfilment by the individual peasants*'.[95]

[91] P, October 21, 1930.
[92] EZh, November 5, 1930 (Z. Zinoviev).
[93] Moshkov (1966), 155.
[94] SZe, November 27, 1930.
[95] *Khlebotsentr*, 45–6, December 23, 1930, 9.

(iv) The results of the collections

By December 31, 1930, only 87·4 per cent of the total planned collections had been obtained in spite of all the efforts of the authorities, and even by the end of the agricultural year 1930/31 only 22·1 million tons had been collected as compared with the plan of 23·2 millions. In contrast, in 1929/30 the plan for the centralised collections was overfulfilled before the end of 1929 (see Table 8(d)). In the autumn of 1930 the sovkhozy, the kolkhozy and the individual peasants all slightly underfulfilled their revised plans; but the socialised sector supplied only 8·7 million tons (39 per cent of the total), as compared with the original plan of 12 million tons (52 per cent), while the individual sector supplied 13·5 million tons instead of the original plan of 11·1 millions (see Table 13). As a result of the campaign against the kulak and well-to-do households, by March 1, 1931, as much as 1·7 million tons, 13 per cent of the grain collection from individual households, was supplied by peasants with firm individual quotas. According to a Soviet historian, in the first weeks of 1931 in the Ukraine kulaks failing to deliver grain were expropriated and exiled, and 'in many districts of the Ukraine and the North Caucasian and Lower Volga regions and in other places this struggle turned into a new wave of the elimination of the kulak as a class, which was in turn directly associated with the further growth of collectivisation in the winter and spring of 1931'.[96] The relentless pressure against the individual peasant denuded him of grain: even if the harvest was as much as the 83·5 million tons officially claimed, each individual household was left with only 1·95 tons of grain as compared with 2·19 tons in 1929 and 2·16 tons originally planned (see Table 15 and p. 355 above). The kolkhoz households were much more favourably placed; and this must have been an important factor in persuading individual peasants that it was necessary to join or rejoin the kolkhozy.

As the harvest was good throughout the USSR, the regional variations in the collections were less striking than in previous years: the Ukraine, which had a bad harvest and low collections in 1928/29, repeated its good performance of 1929/30, and in the Central Volga region and the Urals, where the harvest and collections were poor in 1929/30, the grain collections more than doubled in 1930/31.

[96] Moshkov (1966), 156–7.

Although the collections were less than required by the plan, the total of 22·1 million tons was over 6 million tons more than in the previous agricultural year 1929/30, and double that of 1928/29; the authorities also obtained a little more grain by reducing the seed loans, on the assumption that peasants could now meet their original requirements, by two-thirds, 0·8 million tons, as compared with 1929/30 (see Table 9(a)). Food grains collected were 14·7 as compared with 8·9 million tons, and thus accounted for the whole of the increase in the collections (see Table 8(b)); the increase in the collection of wheat was particularly large.[97]

Two-thirds of the increase in the grain collections was allocated to exports, which rose from 1·3 million tons in the agricultural year 1929/30 to 5·8 million tons in 1930/31. This was more than twice the previous highest level of grain exports in the post-revolutionary period, 2·7 million tons in 1923/24, and nearly 60 per cent of the pre-revolutionary level;[98] it also proved to be the largest amount of grain ever exported in a period of twelve months in the history of the Soviet Union. But the Soviet economy did not benefit to the extent planned. The world economic crisis was by now in its most acute phase, and the price of wheat obtained by the Soviet government on the world market in January–February 1931 was only 36 per cent of that in January–February 1930;[99] the prices of machinery and other commodities imported by the Soviet Union fell to a much smaller extent.[100]

As in 1929/30, special supplies of grain to the timber and cotton areas, and supplies to industry, also increased substantially; in 1930/31 grain allocated to the production of biscuits and other flour products doubled, and grain allocated for the production of alcohol rose by 50 per cent.

Grain supplies to the towns, which rose only slightly in 1929/30, increased by 21·7 per cent in 1930/31, from 7·47 to 9·09 million tons. Unlike 1929/30, when increases in supplies to the towns were confined to the grain-surplus regions, in 1930/31 supplies increased both in the central industrial regions and in the grain-surplus regions. As in 1929/30, the relative modesty of the total increase in urban supplies is perhaps its most remarkable feature. It was

[97] *Ezhegodnik khlebooborota*, iv–v (1932), i, 26.

[98] See Table 9(a) and *Nar. kh.* (1932), p. xlviii.

[99] *Vneshnyaya torgovlya*, 2 (68), February 1931, 19.

[100] Compare the relative prices of imports purchased by the Soviet Union in the same period, *ibid.* 84–112.

adequate enough to cover the planned increase in the urban population, without a substantial increase in their bread rations. But in 1931 the numbers actually employed in industry, building and other urban occupations increased to a much greater extent than planned, more rapidly than in any other year in Soviet history. In order to relieve the resulting pressure on grain supplies, many smaller towns were taken off rationed supply altogether and in some others only workers in priority industries received rations. In spite of these cuts, the number of persons receiving bread rations rose from 26 to 33 millions, an increase of 27 per cent, so demand was adjusted to supply by transferring some categories of workers to lower rations. Simultaneously the amount of the milling levy retained by the local authorities was cut from 200,000 to 126,000 tons. In consequence, in the rural districts of the Ukraine, where grain allocations were not available from central supplies, only medical personnel, village teachers, and those employed by the police and the OGPU were permitted to receive grain from this source.[101]

In the collections of the autumn of 1930, grain was thus taken from the peasants in unprecedented quantities, and exported at low prices, and supplied in increasing amounts to the cotton and timber areas, in order to make it possible to keep up the supplies of machinery and industrial materials on which the industrial programme depended. In order to free grain for these purposes, supplies to the towns increased more slowly than the urban population. But this was industrialisation in the name of socialism, and the kolkhozy fared much better than the individual peasants; it was industrialisation based on large modern capital goods factories, so workers in these priority projects were allocated higher bread rations than those in industries and towns regarded as less important.

(C) OTHER COLLECTIONS

In 1930, the total wage fund of workers and employees increased by nearly 40 per cent, while the total output of food crops and animal food products declined: food products consumed per head of population were conservatively estimated (in 1928 prices) to have

[101] Moshkov (1966), 126–31; *Ezhegodnik khlebooborota*, iv–v (1932), i, 27–8.

fallen to 79r 00k in 1930 from 80r 80k in 1929.[102] The price of agricultural products on the free market increased rapidly, reaching 525·3 per cent of the 1928 level in 1930 (annual average), more than double the 1929 level.[103] Every type of foodstuff was affected. The authorities, anxious that the urban workers, particularly those in key industries, should obtain adequate food supplies at reasonable prices, and convinced of the efficacy of the system of state collections, rapidly extended it from industrial crops and grain to other food products.

The results are summarised in Table 6. For some products, the official collections were actually smaller in 1930 than in the previous year. Egg collections fell by more than 50 per cent. This was partly due to the substantial reduction in total egg production, in turn a result of the huge fall in the number of hens in the spring of 1930. But this was not the only factor, as the proportion of marketed eggs acquired by the official collections also declined sharply: with the rise in the price of eggs on the free market, egg collections could have been maintained only by the exercise of the kind of pressure used for the collection of grain. The official collections of some other products declined even though production increased. In the case of flax fibre and oil seeds, official collections were predominant, but the collections declined in 1930 as a result of the retention by the peasants for their own use of a higher proportion of total output. This was the 'retreat into self-sufficiency' due to unfavourable market conditions which was feared by all Soviet economists in the 1920s.

But this was not the normal pattern. The official collections took a substantially higher proportion of the potato crop after the 1930 harvest than in the previous year. And in the course of 1930 official collections of vegetables were introduced for the first time, while the method used in the livestock collections came to resemble much more closely those of the grain campaign.

Until 1930 the vegetable trade was overwhelmingly dominated by the private producer and the private trader. Most vegetables were

[102] *Materialy po balansu* (1932), 151; consumption by the agricultural population is valued at rural prices.

[103] Barsov (1969), 107–8; the average price received by the agricultural producer was 117·20 in 1929 and 180·00 in 1930 (1928 = 100).

grown by peasants for their own use on their household plots; some urban workers cultivated vegetable gardens; near the large towns many peasants grew vegetables primarily for the market; some vegetables grown in the south were transported long distances by peasants or private traders for sale in central European Russia.[104] Only 3·6 per cent of vegetables were grown by sovkhozy and kolkhozy in 1929, and almost all vegetables were sold either by private traders or direct from producer to consumer.[105] Many private traders, in vegetables as in other commodities, were forced out of existence in 1929–30, and simultaneously the state made its first efforts to introduce official vegetable collections. The urgent attention now paid to vegetables was partly an attempt to cope with the meat shortage and the imminent decline in meat production, now inevitable in view of the reduction in livestock numbers. An editorial in the Narkomtorg journal condemned notions of vegetarianism, which had some currency at this time, as 'contradicting the principles of nourishment and not corresponding to our social system', but admitted that vegetables must provide a temporary substitute for meat;[106] and an extremely ambitious scheme to treble the production of fruit and vegetables by 1932/33 was approved by Sovnarkom.[107]

The immediate efforts of the authorities in 1930 were directed at encouraging the expansion of the spring sown area and establishing a system of official collections at fixed prices. On March 27, 1930, a decree of Sovnarkom stated that contracts for purchases from the spring sowings of vegetables should be signed by April 15; these should primarily be made with kolkhozy and simple production associations, but contracts with individual market gardeners were 'not excluded'.[108] In the spring of 1930, the total area sown to vegetables apparently expanded considerably: the area sown by collective farmers on their household plots and by individual peasants increased, and the area collectively sown to vegetables in kolkhozy was 15 times as large as in 1929, and amounted to 20·4 per cent of the total vegetable sown area.[109] According to alternative official statistics, the harvest of 1930 was 31 or 65 per cent higher

[104] See SO, 5, 1929, 24–6; EZh, August 14, 1930 (N. Vinogradskii).
[105] *Nar. kh.* (1932), 178–9; EZh, August 14, 1930.
[106] VT, 6, 1930, 7–8.
[107] SZ, 1930, art. 393 (decree of July 16).
[108] SZ, 1930, art. 227.
[109] *Nar. kh.* (1932), 176–7.

than that of 1929 (see Table (6)(a)). Such increases, if they really occurred, must have been due not to state encouragement, which was insignificant and belated, but to the stimulus provided by the high market prices of vegetables, the absence of official collections at low prices and the peasants' own need to find substitutes for grain and meat. The urgent consumption needs of the urban consumers impelled the authorities to seek substantial supplies, and the first vegetable collection plan, announced in August, amounted to as much as 2·5 million tons, more than the total amount marketed in 1929.[110] To enforce this ambitious plan, G. A. Chukhrit was appointed as 'special plenipotentiary of STO', responsible for the 'successful achievement of collections and sales' of fruit, potatoes and vegetables in 1930.[111]

Many reports were published of chaos and confusion in the harvesting and marketing of vegetables. According to Rabkrin of the RSFSR, '*spoilt and perished fruit and vegetables have reached astonishing proportions this year*'.[112] The collections at first went badly, and by October 1 only 5–20 per cent of the collection plan for the main vegetables had been fulfilled.[113] Even when official supplies of vegetables were available, the distribution system was very badly organised.[114] On October 6, Narkomtorg announced that in certain central regions vegetable collections must be given the same status as the grain collections, and as an inducement to the peasants agreed to provide industrial goods in the main vegetable areas to the value of 15 per cent of the collections.[115] The reported final figure for the collections—1·49 million tons—though less than the plan, was astonishingly high, and represented a high proportion of all marketings, though it remained a very small proportion of total production (see Table 6(a)). The consumption of vegetables (including melons and other cucurbits) per head of population in 1930 was estimated to have increased by 18·5 per cent in the case of the agricultural population and 26·9 per cent in the case of the non-agricultural population.[116] If all these statistics are correct, while

[110] EZh, August 14, 1930; it is not clear whether this figure included melons and other cucurbits, but urban consumption of these was in any case not high (it was estimated at about 400,000 tons in 1926/27 (see SO, 4, 1929, 28–9).

[111] SZ, 1930, art. 445 (decree of August 27).

[112] EZh, August 20, 1930.

[113] EZh, October 7, 1930 (decree of Narkomtorg dated October 6).

[114] EZh, August 19, 1930.

[115] EZh, October 7, 1930 (decree of October 6).

[116] *Materialy po balansu* (1932), 168–9.

nearly all purchases of vegetables in the early months of 1930 were made on the free market, over 60 per cent of the vegetables supplied to the non-agricultural population in the agricultural year 1930/31 may have come from the official collections at fixed prices.[117]

Official collections of meat and dairy products began several years before vegetable collections. Between 1926 and 1929, they expanded rapidly at the expense of the private trader, but all purchases were made at market prices, and without contracts with the peasants; no form of compulsion was used. In November 1929, Narkomtorg announced the establishment of a system of centralised collections, based primarily on contracts with individual peasants to sell cattle, pigs and sheep.[118] A month later, the party central committee approved the first 'plan for meat collections and contracts', covering the economic year 1929/30; 'up to' 2,700,000 cattle were to be acquired, 1,200,000 under contracts with individual peasants or simple cooperative associations, up to 1,600,000 under contracts with kolkhozy, and 500,000 from various kinds of sovkhoz. The system of contracts was similar to that introduced for grain collections, including contracts both with and without money advances. Animals were to be acquired at fixed ('convention') prices, and the principal economic incentive to the peasants and the kolkhozy was to be the establishment of a special fund of industrial goods amounting to 10–15 per cent of the value of contracted animals.[119] The machinery of collection was centralised. Slaughter-houses were transferred to Narkomtorg, and Soyuzmyaso, equivalent to Soyuzkhleb, and also forming part of Narkomtorg, was made responsible for all meat collections, Narkomtorg acquiring 'rights of centralised leadership analogous to [its] rights in relation to grain'.[120] Mikoyan later complained or

[117] In 1930 the total consumption of vegetables (including melons and cucurbits) by the non-agricultural population was 2·369 million tons (non-agricultural population, 34·284 millions, multiplied by annual consumption per head, 69·11 kg—*Materialy po balansu* (1932), 168–70) and the total consumption in the agricultural year 1930/31 was presumably approximately the same; official collections in 1930/31 were 1·49 million tons (see Table 6(a)).

[118] VT, 14, November 1929, 6.

[119] *Kollektivizatsiya...1927–1935* (1957), 246–8 (extracts from resolution of December 20; the full resolution was originally published in PS, 1, 1930, 84–7).

[120] SZ, 1929, art. 692 (decree of November 18, 1929); PS, 1, 1930, 84–7; SZ, 1930, art. 181 (decree of February 13, 1930).

admitted that 'in the sphere of meat we lagged about two years behind grain in all respects'.[121]

The introduction of the centralised collection system was temporarily facilitated by the widespread destruction of livestock in the winter of 1929–30. The Narkomtorg journal predicted that collections in October 1929 – March 1930 would be easily achieved owing to the spontaneous slaughter of livestock by the peasants,[122] and in practice large numbers of animals made their way to the collection agencies in this period without any pressure from the authorities; 43·1 per cent of all meat collections in the economic year 1929/30 took place in October–December 1929, and 22·7 per cent in January–March 1930, while in the previous year the percentages were 28·8 and 21·3.[123] According to Mikoyan's later account, the 'supply of animals was huge', market prices were often below the official state prices, and it proved unnecessary to allocate a planned quota to the villages.[124]

In the spring of 1930, the policy of socialising livestock was temporarily abandoned (see vol. 2, pp. 102–11), the slaughter of livestock ceased, and prices on the free market began to rise, reaching two or three times the level of state collection prices by the end of 1930.[125] In the summer, the press reported 'speculation' in the sale of meat and animals. 'Frantic speculation' was reported from Rostov, while in the Ukraine 'whole gangs' were going round the villages, buying up animals, killing them secretly and sending them to Kiev.[126] Peasants and kolkhozy lacked all incentive to sell their animals to the official collection agencies at low prices; without a large rise in the collection prices, only compulsion could now succeed. As early as March 11, a Sovnarkom decree complained that insufficient attention had been given to the signing of contracts for livestock, and called for a contracts campaign.[127] But this was a measure without teeth, and in April–June 1930 collections were only half the level of January–March.[128]

[121] B, 1, January 15, 1931, 14 (report to December 1930 plenum of central committee).

[122] VT, 14, November 1929, 8.

[123] Nifontov (1932), 298–9; Mendel'son, ed. (1930), 68, 153.

[124] B, 1, January 15, 1931, 15.

[125] B, 1, January 15, 1931, 15.

[126] EZh, July 22, August 22, 1930.

[127] SZ, 1930, art. 188.

[128] See Table 10; in previous years collections were usually somewhat higher in April–June than in January–March (see Mendel'son, ed. (1930), 68).

In July, a Narkomtorg decree called for 'unity of action' in the final quarter of 1929/30 under the leadership of Soyuzmyaso, and for a 'decisive struggle' with private capital; on this basis official meat purchases should amount to 300,000 tons (carcass weight) in July–September,[129] the equivalent of about 600,000 tons live weight. The summer of 1930 was the turning point. Mikoyan later frankly reported:

> In the second half-year, coming up against the same difficulties as in the sphere of the grain collections, we began gradually to use in the meat collections the method of the grain collections. The plan for the fourth quarter was already constructed along lines somewhat approaching the grain collections, based on bringing the plan to the villages, relying on the help of local party organisations, involving the Soviet public, etc.[130]

Syrtsov was reported to have condemned these measures, predicting that 'bringing the plan down to the village will mean that a considerable number of peasants will eliminate their last cow'.[131] But in spite of their severity these measures were inadequate. In July–September, collections were almost double those in the previous quarter, but they were lower than in the same quarter of 1929 (see Table 10). Moreover, they were substantially lower than the plan for the quarter, even though collection agencies sometimes succumbed to the temptation to pay market prices for animals.[132] A meeting of the collegium of Narkomtorg blamed the failure on the late compilation of the plan, poor organisation, and appeasement of the kulaks, and called for the appointment of special plenipotentiaries in the main livestock districts, directly responsible to the regional office of Soyuzmyaso; a report in the economic newspaper on the same day condemned wreckers in the collection agencies who used 'gang-like speculative methods to purchase animals at bazaars and fairs'.[133]

At the collegium, Mikoyan, implausibly claiming that livestock was in the best condition when collection plans were carried out in

129 EZh, July 25, 1930 (decree of July 23).
130 B, 1, January 15, 1931, 15.
131 Cited in B, 1, January 15, 1931, 23.
132 EZh, September 30, October 17, 1930.
133 EZh, September 30, 1930; for the arrest and trial of Soyuzmyaso officials, see p. 374 below.

full, called for the stepping-up of the campaign in the last months of 1930.[134] In October and November, a press campaign for higher livestock collections followed the pattern of the grain campaign.[135] The amount collected increased by 23 per cent in October–December 1930 (see Table 10), but this was not an outstanding achievement, as collections in previous years were always substantially higher in October–December, when animals were sold to avoid the high cost of feeding them during the winter months. In spite of all efforts, collections amounted to only 2,041,000 tons in the economic year 1929/30, and 1,739,000 tons in the calendar year 1930, as compared with 1,821,000 tons in the agricultural year 1928/29 (see Table 10); and these figures substantially exaggerate the collections in 1929/30, as they include animals purchased not for meat but for transfer to the herds of sovkhozy and kolkhozy. The sombre background to these figures is the absolute decline both in total and in marketed livestock production in 1930. But, though the livestock collections did not increase in absolute terms in 1930, their share in marketed production rose substantially at the expense of sales by private traders and individual peasants.

Taking the official collections as a whole, the increase in grain, vegetables and other products far outweighed the decline in the collections of such products as oil seeds and flax. In comparable prices, the value of the official collections roughly doubled between the economic year 1928/29 and the calendar year 1930.[136] Marketed agricultural production increased at a much slower rate: it is estimated to have risen by 12·0 per cent in 1929 and 17·7 in 1930.[137] Thus the share of the official collections in marketed production greatly increased, while peasant sales at free-market prices to private traders, and directly on the market, greatly diminished in real terms. Peasant money income from sales at free-market

[134] EZh, October 5, 1930.

[135] For the livestock collection campaign, see for example EZh, October 2, 14, November 18, 1930.

[136] Peasant income from the collections was estimated in current prices at roughly 4,000 million rubles in 1930 as compared with 1,774 millions in 1928/29 (FP, 3–4, 1931, 23; Mendel'son, ed. (1930), 74, 154), but delivery prices rose by only 10·6 per cent in 1929 and 3·3 per cent in 1930.

[137] Barsov (1969), table facing p. 112, referring to 'gross extra-rural alienation of agricultural production', including agricultural products purchased by peasants outside their own village.

prices, however, continued to increase, owing to the enormous rise in prices; it was estimated that peasant sales on the free market in current prices rose from 2,000 million rubles in 1929 to 2,800 million rubles in 1930, although in real terms sales declined by 43 per cent.[138] Peasant income from non-agricultural earnings, notably from otkhodnichestvo, also increased substantially. In all, peasant extra-rural money incomes increased by some 78 per cent between 1928/29 and 1930, the share of incomes from sales to the official collection agencies increasing from about one-quarter to about one-third of the total (see Table 7).

Thus the outcome of the great expansion of the official collections was paradoxical. The state secured essential supplies of agricultural products at prices far below the market level. But, taking collections and market sales together, the prices received by the agricultural producer increased far more rapidly than the prices of industrial goods.[139] The terms of trade turned in favour of agriculture, though this shift in money terms was modified by the complete unavailability of most industrial goods in the countryside, and the consequent large increase in peasant cash holdings. In real terms, the consequence to the agricultural population of all these changes in 1928–30 was that their total purchases of all commodities slightly increased.[140] The consumption of food products per head by the agricultural population declined, but that of industrial goods increased, as shown in the table below (in rubles):[a]

	1928	*1929*	*1930*
Crop products	10·21	10·49	11·22
Livestock products	24·55	26·00	22·22
Grain products (flour and groats)	18·02	17·76	17·28
Industrial food products	7·77	7·70	7·80
Total food products	60·55	61·95	58·52 *(continued)*

[138] Calculated from data in Malafeev (1964), 131; in FP, 3–4, 1931, 23, rural income from non-planned sales of agricultural goods in 1930 was estimated at 3,324 million rubles.

[139] See *Economic Journal*, lxxxv (1975), 849 (Ellman, summarising estimates by Barsov (1969)).

[140] In terms of 1928 prices, purchases rose by 7·0 per cent in 1929 and declined by 3·6 per cent in 1930, the overall increase being 4·2 per cent (*Materialy po balansu* (1932), 143).

	1928	*1929*	*1930*
Drink and tobacco	8·46	8·71	8·93
Industrial goods (excluding food, drink and tobacco)	28·29	32·20	32·33
Housing (amortisation)	4·92	4·89	4·87
Total consumption	102·22	107·75	104·65

[a] *Materialy po balansu* (1932), 159; these figures for annual consumption are calculated in 1928 rubles at rural prices.

Among food products, the consumption of potatoes and vegetables increased; the consumption of bread, meat and vegetable oil, dairy products, eggs, sugar and tea declined. Among industrial goods, increased purchases were principally of made-up clothing and footwear; purchases of cotton fabric by the agricultural population, which overwhelmingly predominated in peasant purchases of clothing, declined by 33·2 per cent between 1928 and 1930; purchases of building materials, roofing iron, cement, window glass and timber also declined considerably.[141]

The relative consumption of the agricultural and non-agricultural (mainly urban) population did not change substantially. According to Soviet estimates, the share of the agricultural population in the total consumption of 'material goods', which increased slightly from 56·5 to 57·4 per cent between 1928 and 1929, declined to 54·4 per cent in 1930.[142] But in view of the more rapid increase in the non-agricultural population, its consumption per head declined between 1928 and 1930, while that of the agricultural population increased slightly or remained constant, as shown in the table below (in rubles):

Consumption per head of population, in 1928 prices (1928 = 100)[a]

	Non-agricultural population	*Agricultural population (estimated in urban prices)*	*Agricultural population (estimated in rural prices)*
1929	97·6	103·3	105·4
1930	97·5	99·0	102·4

[a] *Materialy po balansu* (1932), 157, 160.

[141] *Ibid.* 168–9, 280–5.

[142] *Ibid.* 166. Consumption by the agricultural population is valued at rural prices; when it is valued at urban prices, the percentages became 66·7, 70·1, and 67·2 (*ibid.* 164).

The changes in the two years were in sharp contrast. In 1929, as in previous years, the relative position of the agricultural population substantially improved. In 1930, however, the absolute decline in consumption per head by the agricultural population was accompanied by a temporary stabilisation of consumption per head of the non-agricultural population, even though its numbers increased substantially.[143] The centralised control of agricultural production seemed to have had some success in its primary aim of securing food supplies for the urban population and agricultural raw materials for industry.[144] But the price for this extension of the socialist offensive remained to be paid.

[143] The population was estimated as follows (million):

	1928	*1929*	*1930*
Agricultural	121·7	123·6	123·9
Non-agricultural	29·8	31·3	34·3
Other	1·0	1·1	1·2
Total	152·5	156·0	159·3

(*Ibid.* 170); for slightly lower estimates of total population see *Arkheograficheskii ezhegodnik za 1968 god* (1970), 251 (Danilov).

[144] Other aspects of the relation between agriculture and industry in 1928–30 will be discussed in a later volume; on this subject see *Economic Journal*, lxxxv (1975), 844–64 (Ellman).

CHAPTER NINE

THE RESUMPTION OF COLLECTIVISATION

In the summer and autumn of 1930, after three years in which industrial expansion was accompanied by low harvests and grain crisis, the fortunes of industry and agriculture were unexpectedly—though temporarily—reversed. The harvest of 1930 was good, but the performance of industry was unexpectedly poor. In the last quarter of the economic year, July–September 1930, industrial production declined, and as a result the ambitious annual plan for industry was not fulfilled. The upheaval in agriculture was partly responsible for these difficulties. The supply of labour from the countryside, though still increasing, for the first time was insufficient to satisfy the growing demands of industry. Poor food supplies in the coal-mining areas were partly responsible for a large exodus of miners to their villages; the uncertain situation in the countryside resulting from collectivisation encouraged peasants to remain at home, or to return there, to look after their land and crops; the good harvest in itself attracted otkhodniki back to the villages to cope with it. At the same time the claims of agriculture on industry increased. The effort to mechanise agriculture, made more urgent by the decline in the number of horses, resulted in large increases in capital investment in the tractor industry, agricultural engineering, and in other industries associated with agriculture; and this was a significant factor worsening the shortages and bottlenecks which made the expansion of industry more difficult to achieve. Simultaneously cotton imports were drastically reduced in order to increase the import of tractors, and in consequence textile factories had to close. The industrial crisis was primarily due, however, not to these effects of agriculture upon industry but to the immense problems inherent in imposing a vast programme of capital investment on an industry already working near full capacity.[1]

[1] The industrial crisis will be further discussed in vol. 3.

The Soviet leaders stubbornly insisted that the ambitious increases in the five-year plans for various industries approved at the XVI party congress could not be modified; and October–December 1930 was declared to be a 'special quarter', intermediate between the economic year 1929/30 and the calendar year 1931, in which the gap between plan and reality in industry would be closed. The industrial plan for the special quarter was only partly fulfilled; nevertheless, the economic plan for 1931 adopted by the central committee plenum of December 1930, envisaging an expansion of industrial production by 45 per cent in a single year, fully maintained the revised five-year plans.[2]

Two major consequences for agriculture followed from these events in industry. First, the unrelenting drive for industrial expansion carried with it a determined effort to squeeze agriculture still further. In the autumn of 1930, the state collections were much larger and covered a much wider range of products; and simultaneously taxes and other payments were substantially increased in the case of both the kolkhozy and the individual peasants (see vol. 2, pp. 128–9). Investment in agriculture was limited, both because state credits were restricted and because all kinds of building materials, diverted to the major industrial projects, disappeared from the countryside. All these measures further weakened economic incentives to agricultural production. Secondly, the lag in achieving industrial plans affected the planned expansion of the tractor, lorry and agricultural engineering industries; tractors were not provided in sufficient quantities in the early 1930s to compensate for the reduction in the number of horses. The 'metal link' between the state and the peasants was much weaker than the state intended. The conditions were established for the agricultural disasters of 1931–3.

The further industrialisation drive in the autumn of 1930 was accompanied by a ferocious campaign against bourgeois specialists and Right-wingers who might stand in its way. In the widely-publicised 'Industrial Party' trial of November 1930, major non-party industrial specialists in Vesenkha and Gosplan were found guilty of conspiracy with the French to overthrow the Soviet government. Agricultural economists and specialists were also persecuted. On September 3, the daily newspapers reported that nine prominent specialists had been arrested, accused of participat-

[2] See Zaleski (Chapel Hill, 1971), 148–66.

ing in or leading counter-revolutionary organisations; they included the three most important agricultural economists of the 1920s, Kondratiev, Chayanov and Makarov, as well as Groman and Bazarov.[3] Later in the same month 48 prominent Narkomtorg officials concerned with the food trade were indicted for sabotage of food supplies; two full pages of confessions by the accused appeared in *Pravda* and other newspapers.[4] The accused included Karatygin, deputy chairman of the scientific and technical council for the food and agricultural industry, a former tsarist economic official who was prominent in agricultural planning in Vesenkha in the 1920s.[5] Soyuzmyaso, the Narkomtorg department responsible for meat supplies (see p. 365 above), was particularly singled out as an organisation which had assisted wrecking. A ferocious editorial in *Pravda* accused the high officials under arrest of being '*organisers of famine and agents of imperialism*'; their crimes allegedly included issuing instructions for the killing of horses so as both to upset the urban population, who did not like horse meat, and simultaneously cause damage to agriculture; they were said to have collaborated with Mr Fothergill, of the British Union Cold Storage Company, whose aim had been to disorganise the refrigeration business in Russia as a basis for obtaining a concession.[6] Three days later, it was announced that all 48 accused had been shot.[7] A further *Pravda* editorial, headed 'Blow for Blow', complained that the proletariat of the USSR had shown 'too much forbearance to its accursed enemies'.[8] This abrupt and brutal action underlined the intensity of the economic crisis and the determination of the authorities to maintain the course they had set.[9]

The difficulties of the summer of 1930 led to a re-emergence of

[3] P, September 3, 1930. Groman was prosecuted in the 'Menshevik Trial' of March 1931; the agricultural economists were not brought to trial, but died in custody later in the 1930s; Kondratiev was apparently driven insane.

[4] P, September 22, 1930.

[5] For Ye. S. Karatygin, see Valentinov (1971), 130, 160, 230–1; he edited *Torgovo-promyshlennaya gazeta* and other economic journals before the revolution.

[6] P, September 22, 1930.

[7] P, September 25, 1930. For a rebuttal of these charges by Mr Arthur Fothergill, who last visited Russia in 1928, see *Times* (London), September 24, 25, 26, 1930.

[8] P, September 26, 1930.

[9] This case, and contemporary reactions to it, are discussed in Lyons (1938), 356–9; a dramatic but not obviously inaccurate account of the arrest and execution of the specialists may be found in W. Reswick, *I Dreamt Revolution* (Chicago, 1952), 294–8.

policy conflicts within the party. Only brief glimpses of these disputes appear in the press, and in later reminiscences by survivors. The most far-reaching criticisms of Stalin's policies came from Syrtsov and Lominadze. Syrtsov, chairman of Sovnarkom of the RSFSR, was elected a candidate member of the Politburo immediately after the XVI congress;[10] Lominadze was a former 'Leftist' supporter of Stalin who was now party secretary in the Transcaucasian republic. In the autumn of 1929 Syrtsov was in the forefront of the campaign for collectivisation in general and the socialisation of livestock in particular; in February 1930, however, he was one of the first to criticise the excesses of collectivisation. On August 30, 1930, he made a quite unauthorised two-hour speech on the control figures for 1930/31; in November this speech was violently criticised in the press. The speech was mainly concerned with industry and planning, but its brief passages on agriculture made it clear that he was strongly in favour of caution about further collectivisation.[11] He argued that 1931 should be a 'year of verification' for collectivisation, called for the provision of incentives which would enable collectivisation to be consolidated and proclaimed the heretical doctrine that 'the percentage of kolkhozy is significant only if kolkhozy are organised on new principles and the percentage is backed up by the level of the productive forces' (i.e. by tractors and agricultural machinery).[12]

[10] P, July 14, 1930. S. I. Syrtsov (1893–1938), joined the party in 1913; successively a military commissar and chairman of Rostov soviet during the Civil War; worked in central committee offices in 1921–6, where his posts included head of the personnel department (1922) and of the agitation and propaganda department; subsequently worked as a party official in Siberia, where he is said to have been close to Stalin during the grain campaign of January 1928; appointed chairman of Sovnarkom of the RSFSR in place of Rykov, May 1929; elected candidate member of Politburo, July 1930; expelled from central committee, December 1930; in 1936 was director of the 'Nogin' military chemical works (*XI s"ezd* (1961), 248, 852; Avtorkhanov (Munich, 1959), 18, 190–1). He is said to have supported the Trotsky platform on the trade unions in 1920 (*XI s"ezd* (1961), 852) and to have been on the Right in 1927–8, urging well-to-do peasants to 'accumulate', and arguing that successful industrialisation would be an '*auxiliary outcome* of agricultural reconstruction' (NAF, 11–12, 1930, pp. x–xii).

[11] The text of the speech appeared as a pamphlet; this was not available to me when the present volume was researched, but will be discussed in vol. 3. See also *Soviet Studies*, xxxiii (1981), 29–50 (Davies).

[12] P, December 11, 24, 1930; B, 21 November 15, 1930, 22 (B. Tal'); NAF, 11–12, 1930, p. xiii (B. Tal'); SZe, December 24, 1930 (Karpinskii). Boris Tal', head of the economic department of *Pravda*, and a professor of political economy, who was in

His scepticism about the tractor programme was indicated by his description of the Stalingrad tractor factory, completed in July 1930 but so far working badly, as a 'Potemkin village'.[13] He was even more sceptical about the livestock programme, declaring that it had 'no real backing' and gave rise to 'great doubts about whether we shall succeed in carrying it out'.[14]

A declaration by the republican party committee in the Transcaucasus, drafted by Lominadze, combined support for the party line with comments about both planning and agriculture which fitted in closely with Syrtsov's views. The declaration condemned the 'lordly feudal attitude to the needs and interests of workers and peasants' prevalent in the Transcaucasian soviets, and explained that district and village soviets were generally mere 'policing and taxation points';[15] the latter phrase was particularly strong, as it applied the standard pre-revolutionary radical criticism of the mir to the post-revolutionary soviets. Lominadze, in an heretical outburst, reverted to the question of the social nature of the kolkhoz in a veiled attack on Stalin:

> If the question 'who will defeat whom' is not yet completely resolved within our country (and it is not resolved in the countryside), if ¾ of peasant households are still outside the kolkhozy, if the existing kolkhozy are still not yet enterprises of a consistently socialist type, then it is hardly possible to say that we have already entered the period of socialism.[16]

The critics were pilloried as a 'Rightist–"Leftist" bloc', the Right allegedly being headed by Syrtsov, the Left by Lominadze, and were summarily dealt with: Syrtsov and Lominadze were dismissed

---

the forefront of the press campaign against Syrtsov and Lominadze, was described by a contemporary as 'tall and elegant, wearing a suit of military cut, with the Order of the Red Banner on his dark-blue jacket, black-bearded, with large metal-framed glasses, somewhat professorial'; 'he spoke in a somewhat loud voice, in an agitational and propagandist manner, with smooth gestures of his left hand' (Gershberg (1971), 38, 41–2).

[13] NAF, 11–12, 1930, p. vii; for his earlier use of this phrase see p. 213 above.

[14] NAF, 11–12, 1930, p. xiv; *Kollektivist*, 22, November 30, 1930, 3.

[15] B, 21, November 15, 1930, 39–41; the full text of the declaration has not been available, and its precise date is not known.

[16] Cited in PE, 11–12, 1930, 4–5, and in SZe, December 24, 1930; the date and occasion of this statement are not given; for the earlier discussion on this topic, see vol. 2, pp. 85–7. For Stalin on the 'period of socialism' at the XVI congress, see *Soch.*, xiii, 6.

from their posts during November, together with a number of their supporters, and on December 1 they were both expelled from the party central committee, and Lominadze's associate Shatskin was expelled from the central control commission. The expulsion was carried out by a joint session of the Politburo and the central control commission; this was the first occasion on which a member was expelled from the central committee without the consent of a plenary meeting of the committee, and was thus a further step in the subordination of the central committee to the party machine.[17] Syrtsov and Lominadze received no support from Bukharin and his colleagues, and were condemned by Bukharin in his self-critical statement of November 19.[18] But the former Right deviationists were subjected to further harassment during the autumn of 1930, culminating in the replacement of Rykov as chairman of Sovnarkom by Molotov and his expulsion from the Politburo by the December 1930 plenum of the central committee.[19]

The crushing of the last vestiges of opposition—and the provision of scapegoats for the economic difficulties—was seen by the dominant group of party leaders as the political prerequisite for the renewed socialist offensive, a crucial feature of which was the drive to complete collectivisation in the main agricultural areas. During the harvest period, while the decline in membership of the kolkhozy was much slower than in previous months, it still continued: the net number of households leaving the kolkhozy in July and August 1930 was 242,000 (see Table 16).[20] But from September onwards the campaign for collectivisation was pursued with much greater vigour and determination. On September 3, 1930, an appeal of the central committee stated for the first time in a published document from the highest party authorities that a minimum of 50 per cent of all peasant households was to be collectivised by the end of the economic year 1930/31.[21] The authorities hoped to begin to put this plan into effect during the autumn of 1930. In September, in his report to an all-Union conference of planning officials, the head of

[17] P, November 3, 26, December 2, 1930; Medvedev (London, 1971), 142; Avtorkhanov (Munich, 1959), 192; for Shatskin see p. 43 above. These events will be further discussed in vol. 3.

[18] P, November 20, 1930.

[19] P, December 20, 1930; *KPSS v rez.*, iii (1954), 74.

[20] According to IZ, lxxvi (1965), 40–1 (Bogdenko), however, a net increase in kolkhoz membership had already taken place in August.

[21] P, September 3, 1930.

the agricultural section of Gosplan stressed that the kolkhozy should be expanded during the autumn so as to assist the autumn sowing plans. He also argued that collectivisation should be concentrated into October and November 1930, so as to avoid repeating in the spring of 1931 the upheaval of the spring of 1930. On September 24, a central committee letter called for 'a decisive shift in the organisation of a new powerful upsurge of the collective-farm movement'; a further resolution proclaimed that in 1930 the 'Day of Harvest and Collectivisation' would in fact be an 11-day campaign, from October 15 to October 25, for the recruitment of 'additional millions of poor and middle-peasant households' into the kolkhozy.[23]

The version of the voluntary principle proclaimed at the XVI party congress (see pp. 333–5 above) was assiduously propagated. Considerable emphasis was placed on the need to organise the collectivisation campaign, and all attempts to leave collectivisation to 'spontaneous flow' (samotek) were sternly condemned.[24] A characteristic editorial in the agricultural newspaper, while reiterating that 'the individual peasant knows that no-one will compel him to join the kolkhoz by force', also insisted that '*the present rate of recruitment clearly does not correspond either to the feelings of the poor and middle peasant masses of the peasantry or to the relationship of the class forces in the countryside*', and explained that even though the masses had 'turned towards' collectivisation they would not join the kolkhozy without 'organised pressure on every middle peasant individually':

> *Pressure from the proletarian party and the advanced collective farmers is obligatory: this is a constituent element of the Leninist voluntary principle.*[25]

The exercise of this pressure was undertaken by familiar methods. At the end of August, Yurkin called for systematic propaganda by

[22] PKh, 7–8, 1930, 57–8 (Vol'f).

[23] *Istoriya KPSS*, iv, ii (1971), 158 (September 24); *Kollektivizatsiya . . . 1927–1935* (1957), 322–3 (dated October 6); in the Lower Volga region, a 'collectivisation month' was held from September 15–October 15 (SZe, November 14, 1930), while in the Central Volga region, a 'collectivisation ten days' lasted from September 25 to October 4 (*Kollektivizatsiya* (Kuibyshev, 1970), 213–14).

[24] See, for example, resolution of the North Caucasus party committee of September 5, 1930, in *Kollektivizatsiya* (Krasnodar, 1972), 368.

[25] SZe, October 15, 1930 (V. Nodel').

the kolkhozy among the peasants. The boards of the kolkhozy should give 'frank reports' to general meetings of individual peasants in their villages; special meetings should be held of those who had left the kolkhozy to discuss their reasons for leaving; the kolkhozy should provide agricultural assistance to the individual peasants, and issue wall newspapers jointly with them; 'initiative groups' should be formed of individual peasants intending to join or form a kolkhozy.[26] These arrangements became widespread during the autumn. Initiative groups, already formed in the Central Black-Earth region in July 1930,[27] were supplemented by 'recruitment commissions' of voluntary or elected collective farmers from strong kolkhozy; 5,625 of these recruitment commissions or brigades were in existence in the RSFSR by September 1930.[28] At a district level, brigades were sent from advanced districts to districts with a low proportion of agricultural households ('tug-boat brigades').[29] In some regions individual peasants were invited in large numbers to attend kolkhoz general meetings at which their annual reports were discussed, and reports on the work of the kolkhozy were presented to individual peasants at skhods (where they still existed) or at special meetings; it was claimed that 3½ million peasants attended such meetings of individual peasants in the Central Black-Earth region alone.[30] Simultaneously, further measures were taken against those who resisted collectivisation. Many kulak households were exiled from the Ukraine in the second half of 1930,[31] and in Siberia a substantial number of kulak households in Category III were exiled to special settlements in the summer and autumn of 1930.[32] It is not clear how far these mass exiles were associated directly with the renewed collectivisation drive. On December 25, 1930, however, the West Siberian regional party committee resolved to exile and confiscate the property of the 'most malicious kulaks, who are actively harming collectivisation'; 717 families were affected.[33]

[26] P, August 31, 1930.

[27] Sharova (1963), 210; P, September 26, 1930; SZe, November 20, 1930.

[28] Pogudin (1976), 119; SZe, November 20, 1930; in the Central Volga they were known as 'red match-makers' brigades'.

[29] SZe, November 20, 1930.

[30] Sharova (1963), 208–9.

[31] According to Trifonov (1975), 341, 11,400 households were exiled from 11 okrugs by March 10, 1930, and 75,000 from the whole of the Ukraine by the beginning of 1931.

[32] *Sotsial'naya struktura* (Novosibirsk, 1970), 13.

[33] *Ibid.* 134.

The collectivisation campaign of the autumn of 1930 was clearly not carried out with the vigour of the first collectivisation drive in the previous winter. At every level officials and party members were somewhat chastened by the experience of the previous campaign. The central party authorities refrained from exercising sufficient pressure to overcome this diffidence. It is not known whether the relative restraint at the top was the outcome of a deliberate decision that the time was not yet ripe for an all-out drive, or simply due to preoccupation with the troubles of industry and planning, and with the climax of the campaign against the bourgeois specialists. But certainly warnings that the 'voluntary principle' should be maintained continued to be given throughout the autumn; no specific quotas for collectivisation were set by the central authorities, and attempts by local authorities to adopt firm 'control figures' for the number of households to be collectivised in each district were condemned. A cartoon in the agricultural newspaper showed a man who was grasping a five-day recruitment plan chasing an individual peasant, and shouting 'Stop him! My plan has not been fulfilled'.[34] Nor was there any large-scale central campaign in the autumn of 1930 analogous to that of the first weeks of 1930, to arrest and exile kulaks and their 'henchmen' in districts where collectivisation was being carried out.

In consequence of this careful campaign, the monthly net increase in the number of collectivised households accelerated during the autumn, but remained modest by the standards of the winter of 1929–30:

September	October	November	December
70,000	190,000	410,000	450,000

The increase took place mainly in the grain-growing regions: 645,000 of the 1,120,000 households which joined the kolkhozy in September–December 1930 were in the Ukraine, the two Volga regions, the North Caucasus, the Urals and Western Siberia.[35]

The central committee plenum, meeting from December 17 to December 21, 1930, praised the 'serious achievements in agriculture and the solution of the grain problem in the main' as 'a direct result of the very great successes achieved in kolkhoz and sovkhoz

[34] SZe, October 9, 1930.

[35] See Table 16; and *Ezhegodnik po sel kh. 1931* (1933), 440–7.

construction, and of the elimination of the kulaks as a class on the firm basis of comprehensive collectivisation', and looked forward in terse and self-confident phrases to a major further advance in collectivisation and dekulakisation in 1931:

> Ensure in 1931 that on average no less than 80 per cent of peasant households are collectivised in the Ukraine (steppe), North Caucasus, Lower Volga, Central Volga (Trans-Volga), which means that in these areas comprehensive collectivisation and the elimination of the kulaks as a class shall, in the main, be completed. In the remaining grain areas—the Central Black-Earth region, Siberia, the Urals, Ukraine (forest-steppe), Kazakhstan (grain areas)—ensure 50 per cent collectivisation of peasant households. In the grain-deficit zone, for grain farms—20–25 per cent. In cotton and sugar-beet areas ensure at least 50 per cent collectivisation of the total number of households.
>
> On average in the USSR for all branches of farming ensure that in 1931 at least half of peasant households are collectivised.[36]

[36] *KPSS v rez.*, iii (1954), 78, 81; see also vol. 2, pp. 177–8.

CHAPTER TEN

THE MECHANISATION OF AGRICULTURE

> We are becoming a metal country, a motorised country, a tractorised country. And when we have seated the USSR on an automobile and the peasant on a tractor—let the esteemed capitalists, who boast about their 'civilisation', try to catch us up then. We will then be able to see which countries can then be 'classified' among the backward and which among the advanced.[a]
>
> [a] Stalin, *Soch.*, xii, 135.

The famous passage with which Stalin concluded his article published on November 7, 1929, reflected the spirit and the hopes of the party activists in the second half of 1929. The theme that agriculture no less than industry could be transformed by advanced technology was not a novel one. Lenin declared ten years previously that '100,000 first-class tractors', with petrol and drivers, if only they were available, could win the middle peasantry for communism.[1] In the Goelro plan of 1920, Krzhizhanovsky looked forward to the time when the columns of the proletariat would go into the countryside to show the peasants the great possibilities held out by advanced technology. The theme was common to all wings of the party. In his 'Notes of an Economist' Bukharin praised the tractor columns as 'the fighting battalions (druzhiny) of technical revolution', as a result of which 'the free feather-grass is singing its last song before its death'.[2]

By the time of the XVI party conference in April 1929, Krzhizhanovsky felt able to declare that the time of which he wrote in 1920 was now at hand; the day of the horse was coming to an end, and with the aid of the tractor isolated agriculture would be

[1] Lenin, *Soch.*, xxix, 190.

[2] P, September 30, 1928.

replaced by 'an agricultural industry'.[3] Markevich, the founder of the Shevchenko MTS, firmly asserted in his book on *Inter-village Machine-Tractor Stations* published in 1929 that no difference in principle existed between large-scale agriculture and factory industry. He argued that while individual peasant agriculture had not exhausted all its possibilities, its production was limited: peasant households with tiny parcels of land were bound to use poor implements; they would in any case find it impossible to maintain more complicated machines; and they could not cope with drought, which was always followed by a great decline in numbers of horses. Large-scale tractor economy, on the other hand, using the best world technology, could lead to a vast increase in yields, and in the marketed production of grain. Markevich rejected the argument that mechanisation was unnecessary in view of the abundance of rural labour, envisaging that the introduction of the tractor would be accompanied by a simultaneous increase in labour-intensive crops and in livestock farming. Unlike some leading policy makers in industry, however,[4] he accepted the view that the scarcity and high cost of capital and abundance of labour in the USSR required a combination of '*improved technology with maximum labour intensity*' in agriculture. He therefore strongly supported measures to bring about the use of each tractor for more hours a year, and for more years altogether, than was customary in the United States.[5]

The advantages of modern machinery were incessantly urged upon the peasants. During 1929, this was a central theme of the widely read peasant newspaper published in Moscow by the party central committee.[6] Peasants were taken in large numbers to the most mechanised sovkhozy.[7] It was Soviet policy to support collectivisation in particular areas with the inducement that they

[3] *XVI konf.* (1962), 36.

[4] See Carr and Davies (1969), 416–17.

[5] Markevich (2nd edn, 1929), 170–80, 276–7, 238, 240, 92–3; for a further account of Markevich's views see Miller (1970), 71–4.

[6] A typical issue of *Krest'yanskaya gazeta*, No. 55, July 12, 1929, a six-page tabloid, carried pictures of trainees at a combine-harvester operators' course and a water pipeline under construction (p. 1), an American anti-pest machine and thresher (pp. 2, 3), a new binder being assembled, an American pulveriser and Ukrainian tractor workshop (p. 4) and an American lorry for pouring grain (p. 5). Its circulation in 1929 was 1,208,000–1,400,000 as compared with *Pravda's* 661,000 and *Izvestiya's* 441,000 (*XVI s''ezd* (1931), 74; KG, 1, January 1, 104, December 30, 1929).

[7] Bogdenko (1958), 191–3.

would be generously supplied with tractors and other machinery. A decree of June 5, 1929, explained that Machine-Tractor Stations (MTS) would bring about 'the reconstruction of individual peasant farms into large collective farms', and instructed that districts in which collective farming was most advanced should receive priority in the establishment of MTS.[8] Even before the establishment of MTS, key districts in the collectivisation programme were given priority in tractor supplies. Thus when a meeting called by the rural department of the central committee decided to give immediate priority to the collectivisation of Chapaev district in the Central Volga region, it simultaneously recommended that tractors for the autumn ploughing should immediately be issued to the district.[9] In Khoper okrug in the Lower Volga region, the first 'okrug of comprehensive collectivisation', both the kolkhozsoyuz and the party bureau, when announcing their progress in collectivisation and their future plans, called upon the authorities in Moscow to supply more tractors.[10] Traktorotsentr, the organisation in charge of state MTS (see vol. 2, p. 19), first resolved that two, and then that four of the 100 MTS to be established in the USSR before the spring of 1930 should be in Khoper okrug; and the okrug in turn decided that all poor and middle peasant households within the area covered by these MTS should be collectivised within two months.[11]

The reaction of peasants to the tractor was extremely varied. Numerous accounts appeared of hostility to the tractor, and of cynical reactions to the frequent breakdowns. The press complained that 'kulaks' argued that tractor columns were a return to serfdom.[12] One confused rumour among the peasants asserted that the communists were organising the large kolkhozy on the basis of a treaty with the Chinese, with machinery supplied by America, and that these kolkhozy would be transferred to the landowners, who had already arrived in the guise of MTS directors.[13] On occasion

[8] *Kollektivizatsiya . . . 1935* (1957), 174–80; for other aspects of this decree see vol. 2, p. 19.

[9] SKhG, August 25, 1929; see also pp. 135–6 above. A few days later, the Sovnarkom of the RSFSR asked Narkomzem to send 100 tractors to the district (SKhG, September 6, 1929).

[10] *Krasnyi Khoper*, August 29, September 17, 28, 1929 (open letter of August 21, resolution of August 27).

[11] *Ibid.* September 5, October 1, 5, 1929.

[12] P, July 6, 1929 (Central Black-Earth region); KG, 68–9, August 30, 1929 (Central Volga region).

[13] B, 3–4, February 28, 1930, 57 (Odessa okrug).

stones were thrown at the tractors, and in more than one case crowds of women and children blocked the road to prevent tractors entering the village.[14]

Many reports of favourable reactions by peasants were also published. The promise and, still more, the arrival of tractors was a concrete embodiment of the desire of the town to modernise the countryside, and evidently helped to soften opposition. The main report to the organisation section of the conference of large kolkhozy in July 1929 recorded that 'in all cases everywhere the main incentive, the main lever to collectivisation was the technical basis, i.e. the wish to use mechanised draught power, large complex agricultural machines'.[15] In Chapaev district, after much hostility had been shown to the first tractors in 1928, the ability of the tractor to tackle the virgin steppe was said to have whetted the appetite of the peasants for tractors.[16] In Khoper okrug, promises of tractors were said to have played an important part in encouraging the peasants to support collectivisation.[17] Reports from other areas also described the positive response of peasants to tractors and tractor columns.[18] A positive attitude to the tractor among some peasants would appear to be indicated by the relative success of the campaign for subscriptions to tractors at a time when other appeals for peasant money were unsuccessful (see vol. 2, p. 23).

Official spokesmen were confident in their assertions that large numbers of peasants were persuaded of the advantages of modern technology. In June 1929, Mikoyan informed the Moscow party committee that 'many dozens and hundreds of villages' had sent in requests for the establishment of MTS.[19] In October Molotov assured a Moscow regional party conference that the 'broad middle-peasant mass' was convinced that 'kolkhozy with tractors and large-scale agricultural machines have tremendous advantages

[14] KG, 68–9, August 30, 1929 (North Caucasus); SKhG, January 8, 1930 (Central Black-Earth region). For other examples of hostility to the tractor see Carr and Davies (1969), 211–13.

[15] ZKK (1929), 124; for a modification of this view see pp. 124, 126 above.

[16] SKhG, November 7, 15, 1929 (A. Ozerskii).

[17] *Povol'zhskaya pravda*, November 7, 1929; Sheboldaev claimed that many peasants in Khoper had been influenced by excursions to the Stalingrad tractor factory site (P, November 15, 1929).

[18] P, July 13, October 3 (North Caucasus), 1929.

[19] P, June 27, 1929; P, August 16, 1929, reported that most MTS received mass requests to join from peasants in the surrounding villages.

over small farms'.[20] At the end of the year Rykov told TsIK that 'we have everywhere a mass desire of the peasantry to go over from backward, small-scale, low-productive individual agriculture to large-scale collective farming, based on advanced machine technology'.[21]

But all these hopes and promises rested on a weak foundation. The total draught power of tractors available to the peasantry on October 1, 1929 (excluding those in sovkhozy) was 268,000 horse-power;[22] this was sufficient to work only 2 or 3 million hectares. The control figures for 1929/30 proposed that a further 142,000 horse-power should be added to the stock of tractors in kolkhozy and MTS in 1929/30,[23] but this impressive increment was quite insufficient to bring about a substantial degree of mechanisation in the kolkhozy, even in terms of the relatively moderate collectivisation programmes of the early autumn of 1929. In a report to Sovnarkom of the RSFSR, Kaminsky revealed that while 48 per cent of ploughing in kolkhozy had been carried out by tractors in 1927/28, with the growth of the kolkhozy this figure had fallen to 30 per cent in 1928/29 and was expected to fall to only 14 per cent in 1929/30.[24]

By the time of the conference of large kolkhozy in July 1929, the view was widely accepted that the lag of tractor supply behind the growth of collectivisation made it necessary to concentrate tractors and other resources on the large kolkhozy and the RSKs rather than dispersing them among the small kolkhozy. Until the November plenum of the party central committee the need for large kolkhozy to be highly mechanised was almost taken for granted. 'We will not travel far on horses', a delegate remarked at the conference of large kolkhozy; and the organisation section of the conference resolved that 'the main lever in developing large kolkhozy is the group supply of tractors and complex agricultural machines'.[25] On August 7, 1929, in an editorial entitled 'On the Road to Mass Collectivisation', *Pravda* firmly stated:

[20] SKhG, October 6, 1929.
[21] *TsIK 2/V* (1929), No. 1, 12.
[22] *Nar. kh.* (1932), 145.
[23] *KTs . . . na 1929/30* (1930), 123, 131.
[24] EZh, October 9, 1929. According to other figures, however, 62·3 per cent of draught power in kolkhozy was mechanised in 1929 (see Table 20).
[25] ZKK (1929), 429, 142.

Comprehensive collectivisation is unthinkable without the large machine.

At this stage it was not beyond the bounds of possibility that all the large kolkhozy and RSKs which were planned for the end of 1929/30 could be mechanised during the course of that year. The plan approved by STO in September 1929 assumed that by the end of 1929/30 large kolkhozy would include a sown area of only 3·34 million hectares; in addition the sown area of the 20 districts designated as RSKs would amount to 0·7 million hectares. According to the plan, the large kolkhozy were to receive 7,100 tractors, and at least 50 per cent of their field work would be mechanised.[26] The annual control figures for 1929/30 explained that all the tractors allocated to kolkhozy in 1929/30, 70,000 h.p. in capacity, would be allocated to large kolkhozy with a sown area of more than 2,000 hectares; this would enable the tractors to be used for two or three shifts a day.[27] The 20 RSKs planned at this time were particularly favoured: they would take on average three years to establish, and by that time their fields would be entirely worked by tractors: in these districts, according to a Narkomzem spokesman, 'the central question' was 'the full re-equipment of the whole technical and power basis of the district'.[28] Agricultural officials were so confident that their proposals for the mechanisation of large kolkhozy were realistic that they began to make arrangements for the sale of 'unnecessary means of production', suitable only for peasant farming.[29] A similar confidence about the state-owned MTS led to proposals that the number of horses in the areas served by the MTS should be steadily reduced, the fodder released being fed to productive animals.[30] A spokesman for the tractor columns of the agricultural cooperative Khlebotsentr even claimed that most peasant implements were no longer required in the areas covered by the columns.[31]

These decisions of September–October 1929 marked the high

[26] SKhG, September 17, 1929; this figure was larger than the previous *total* allocation to kolkhozy for 1929/30, given as 6,800 *ibid.* September 2, 1929 (*cit.* Miller (1970), 41).

[27] *KTs . . . na 1929/30* (1930), 123.

[28] EZh, October 13, 1929 (L. Gavrilov).

[29] SKhG, September 17, 1929 (editorial).

[30] EO, 9, 1929, 32 (Gershman), 10, 1929, 51 (M. Golendo).

[31] EZh, September 9, 1929.

point of the policy of carrying out a substantial degree of mechanisation in a favoured minority of kolkhozy. The results could be achieved only by starving the small kolkhozy: although a sown area of 11·7 million hectares in 1929/30 was planned for the small kolkhozy, against only 3·3 millions for the large kolkhozy, the total number of tractors at their disposal was planned at only 3,272 against 13,658 in the large kolkhozy.[32] But by the time the control figures had been formulated and approved, existing plans were being swept aside. In October 1929, a report of Kolkhoztsentr announced that not 20 but 60–80 RSKs would be established in 1929–30;[33] in November, the number was increased to 178.[34] Even before the prospects for mechanising RSKs were swamped by their rapid expansion, RSKs and large kolkhozy were established without any immediate prospect of obtaining tractors. At the conference of large kolkhozy in July 1929, while most of the large kolkhozy firmly insisted that their economies should be based on the tractor, spokesmen for the Ural Gigant kolkhoz, which was both a large kolkhoz and an RSK, boasted of having collectivised without promising tractors (see p. 124 above). In the following months articles in *Pravda* criticised organisations in the Irbit okrug which had resisted the formation of large kolkhozy on the grounds that tractors were not available, and drew favourable attention to another Ural RSK in which 'it is not the tractor which determines the pace of collectivisation'.[35]

In a speech at Sovnarkom on October 3, Pyatakov voiced the paradox which confronted supporters of forced industrialisation: while 'the bare idea of collectivisation without appropriate equipment for socialised farms is fruitless, contradictory and harmful', rapid collectivisation was essential, so the only solution was to push ahead.[36] A few days later Shlikhter, People's Commissar for Agriculture of the Ukraine, rejected as the 'line of least resistance' the restriction of plans for mass collectivisation to areas which could

[32] *KTs . . . na 1929/30* (1930), 125; a substantial proportion of the tractors in the large kolkhozy, which were to receive only 7,100 new tractors in 1929/30 (see p. 387 above), was evidently to come from the existing small kolkhozy by amalgamation or transfer.

[33] P, October 13, 1929 (this was the same day as the publication of the article from Narkomzem which still referred to only 20 RSKs—see p. 387 above).

[34] EZh, November 24, 1929.

[35] P, August 22, October 1, 1929.

[36] TPG, October 5, 1929; for this speech see also p. 148 above.

be served by tractor columns, and drew attention to Ukrainian experience in organising 'machine-horse columns' or 'horse columns', in which, on a credit basis, the agricultural cooperatives provided horses and horse-drawn machinery to assist poor peasants.[37] Sheboldaev reported that in Khoper okrug in some newly collectivised villages autumn ploughing was undertaken jointly by groups of over 100 people using 30–40 ploughs, and that this had given rise to 'tremendous élan and enthusiasm'.[38]

When the central committee plenum met in November, the lag of mechanisation behind collectivisation was one of the major preoccupations of its members.[39] The comprehensive collectivisation of several major grain regions in the course of a few months proposed by Molotov at the plenum (see p. 164 above) ruled out any possibility of a substantial degree of mechanisation. In his report, Kaminsky apparently recommended the establishment of large kolkhozy even where no MTS existed.[40] Molotov more ambiguously called for the implements of the peasants to be pooled, while describing them as both 'completely insignificant' and 'essential'. But he had nothing to say about the role of the horse and its relationship with the tractor.[41] The resolution of the plenum stressed the importance of 'large mechanised kolkhozy' and described the MTS as 'centres for the comprehensive collectivisation of whole districts'; its only specific mention of the need to use 'simpler tools' was made in the context of 'the simplest kolkhozy and cooperative production associations'. It also suggested, however, that small kolkhozy should work together to construct large 'machine stations', partly based on existing machine hiring points; these would use horses or mixed draught power. In the resolution, such combinations of small kolkhozy were also referred to as 'large kolkhozy', thus implying that large kolkhozy might not have a high degree of mechanisation immediately.[42] But even careful readers of

[37] SKhG, October 6, 1929.

[38] P, October 22, 1929.

[39] According to VIK, 4, 1962, 59, it was emphasised by Mikoyan, Andreev, Klimenko and Ryabinin (chairman of the Central Black-Earth regional executive committee).

[40] Chigrinov (1965), 47.

[41] For Molotov's speech see pp. 163–5 above.

[42] *KPSS v rez.*, ii (1954), 646. The plenum resolution on Ukrainian agriculture specifically stated that the whole of the agriculture of the steppe was to be collectivised in two or three years, and that at least half the sown area was by then to be worked by tractors (*ibid.* 657).

the resolution could be forgiven for believing that party policy still assumed that comprehensive collectivisation must always have a firm basis in mechanisation. Such ambiguities provided a basis both for flexibility in policy and for later repudiation of excesses.

The detailed plans at both central and local level had already moved far beyond the terms of the resolution. At the beginning of December, the change of front was openly announced. At a conference of delegates to TsIK, Kaminsky stated

> We hold to the course of full mechanisation of the kolkhozy, but from this it does not follow that if we have not yet got enough tractors we can somewhat weaken our work on the construction of large kolkhozy.[43]

A few days later Ryskulov, who had previously condemned officials in Khoper okrug for their practice of offering to supply a tractor forthwith in order to persuade peasants to set up a kolkhoz,[44] dismissed as 'Right opportunism' the notion that 'the rate of development of kolkhozy must be adjusted to the supply of tractors'.[45] Henceforth the general trend was towards the immediate establishment of giant kolkhozy with a high degree of socialisation, irrespective of whether tractors were available. Even in the optimistic plans of the authorities, only 30 of the over 300 RSKs now planned for 1929/30 were designated as 'model districts' which would be allocated a complete new technical base within two years.[46] Yakovlev estimated at a meeting of the Politburo commission on collectivisation that it would take five or six years to establish a full machine base; peasant implements would accordingly have to be used until then.[47] The vast majority of RSKs, and all the okrugs and regions of comprehensive collectivisation, would have to rely on the collective use of the horse. Much attention was accordingly devoted to peasant implements and horses: an article in *Pravda* asserted that a '*DECISIVE role will be played by the socialisation and organisation of PEASANT IMPLEMENTS*'.[48]

[43] EZh, December 6, 1929.

[44] *Krasnyi Khoper*, November 21, 1929.

[45] P, December 9, 1929.

[46] P, December 13, 1929 (decree of Sovnarkom of the RSFSR dated December 11).

[47] IISO, [i] (1964), 277; for a similar assessment relating to the Ukraine, see KG, 98, December 10, 1929.

[48] P, December 23, 1929 (S. Brike); see also P, December 17, 1929 (editorial).

At the conference of marxist agrarians, which met towards the end of December 1929, opinions about the role of mechanisation in the kolkhozy were still divided. Larin argued that while the horse-drawn plough was a requirement for an individual farm, the small kolkhoz of 10–15 families required a tractor and the large kolkhoz in an RSK required an MTS.[49] A delegate from the Urals provocatively asserted that the peasants' contribution to the kolkhozy was 'an economic zero, and however much the number of these zeroes is increased, they will never turn into a real magnitude'.[50] Other delegates, however, insisted upon the gains to be achieved from bringing peasant implements together in joint work, and Milyutin from the platform condemned Larin's failure to appreciate the gains to be achieved from the socialisation of peasant resources.[51] In his report, Lyashchenko presented what was probably now the general view: use of work teams and horses in RSKs was analogous to the stage in industrial development of 'large-scale manufacture' as compared with factory production, but must be purely transitional, in conditions of comprehensive collectivisation, to large-scale mechanised technology.[52] In his unexpected intervention on the last day of the conference, Stalin emphatically endorsed the viability of collectivisation without mechanisation. According to Stalin, the arguments in favour of large sovkhozy 'wholly and fully' applied not only to developed kolkhozy with a machine-tractor base but also to the 'primary kolkhozy' which were being established in areas of comprehensive collectivisation, and were based on a 'simple putting together of peasant tools of production', 'representing as it were the manufacturing period of kolkhoz construction':

> Take for example the kolkhozy in the area of Khoper in the former Don region. In appearance, these kolkhozy are apparently no different from the point of view of technology from the small peasant economy (few machines, few tractors). But the simple putting together of peasant implements in the heart of the kolkhozy has given a result of which our practical workers have

[49] *Trudy . . . agrarnikov-marksistov* (1930), i, 71.

[50] *Ibid.* i, 90.

[51] *Ibid.* i, 268, 380; ii, 115, 116–17.

[52] *Ibid.* ii, 52–3. For Kalinin's use of the term 'manufacture' in April 1929 see pp. 115–16 above; according to IA, 2, 1962, 202, citing the archives, the expression was also used by Yakovlev at the November 1929 plenum.

never dreamed. What is this result? It is that going over to the kolkhoz has increased the sown area by 30, 40 and 50 per cent.[53]

The central committee resolution of January 5 even more firmly declared that 'the comprehensive replacement of horse-drawn implements by machines cannot be carried out in a short period and requires a number of years', denounced 'tendencies to under-estimate the role of horse draught power at the present stage of the kolkhoz movement' which had led to the selling up of horses, and called for the creation of '*horse-machine bases*' and '*mixed tractor–horse bases*' in the kolkhozy.[54] On the same day as the publication of the resolution, an editorial in *Pravda* denounced as 'simple stupidity' the view that large-scale agriculture was impossible without tractors, and bitingly dismissed plans by 'dizzy-headed communists' to reduce the number of horses as amounting to 'wrecking'.[55] Yakovlev, who estimated that 1½ million tractors would be required for full mechanisation, told a meeting of 25,000-ers that horses and horse-drawn implements would be required in basic agricultural operations for the next three or four years, and called for 'a doubling of the productivity of the horse and the plough'.[56] During January and February draught animals in most kolkhozy were socialised; and strenuous efforts were made by the central authorities, though with little practical outcome, to persuade kolkhozy to establish machine-horse stations (see vol. 2, pp. 43, 99). Writing from exile, Trotsky condemned this change of front on the relationship between mechanisation and collectivisation as a striking demonstration of the absurdities resulting from 'adventurist' policies: 'with the aid of peasant sokhas and peasant nags, even in association, it is not possible to create large-scale agriculture, just as it is not possible to build a steamship out of a collection of fishing boats'.[57]

The change of front was not seen by anyone within the USSR as more than a temporary and transitional development. In his speech at the conference of marxist agrarians, Stalin did not forget the bright developments which mechanisation would bring:

[53] *Soch.*, xii, 154.
[54] *KPSS v rez.*, ii (1954), 665.
[55] P, January 6, 1930.
[56] I, January 24, 1930.
[57] BO (Paris), ix (February–March 1930), 3 (article dated February 13); see also p. 327 above.

> It goes without saying that the advantages of kolkhozy over the individual peasant economy will become still more incontrovertible when our machine-tractor stations and columns come to the aid of the primary kolkhozy in districts of comprehensive collectivisation, when the kolkhozy themselves have the possibility of concentrating tractors and combine harvesters in their hands.[58]

During the autumn of 1929, plans for mechanisation were greatly expanded. At this time the programmes for the major capital goods' industries were all substantially increased; and in the case of tractors and agricultural machinery this general tendency was reinforced by awareness of the pressing needs of newly-established kolkhozy. At this time too, as a result of a number of visits paid by Soviet experts to the United States, enthusiasm for American achievements in agricultural technology mounted, and the Soviet leaders became confident that Soviet socialist agriculture could soon outstrip that of the capitalist West. A *Pravda* editorial proclaimed that the example of the United States had 'compelled bourgeois economists to admit that in 10–15 years agriculture will have reached the level of an extractive industry'.[59] Writing from the United States, Vol'f, the chief agricultural expert in Gosplan, reported on United States achievements and concluded that Soviet plans for agricultural engineering were inadequate: attempts to disarm the USSR at a time when capitalist agriculture was renewing its technology must be rejected in favour of 'a gigantic, simply frantic rate of mechanisation'.[60]

The November plenum of the central committee accordingly announced that 40,000 tractors (in 10 h.p. units) would be supplied to agriculture in 1929/30, and approved a decision of the Politburo of November 5 to construct and bring into full use by 1931/32 two additional tractor factories each capable of producing 50,000 caterpillar tractors, and two combine-harvester factories.[61] In the following month Mezhlauk, reporting to TsIK on the tractor industry in the light of his own visit to the United States, was able to

[58] *Soch.* xii, 156.

[59] P, September 5, 1929.

[60] EZh, October 22, 1929.

[61] *KPSS v rez.*, ii (1954), 627, 645; Nemakov (1966), 80; *Industrializatsiya SSSR, 1929–1932 gg.* (1970), 586; P, November 16, 1929; the latter source gives the capacity of the tractor factories as 40,000.

claim that as a result of the revision of the five-year plan Soviet production of tractors and agricultural engineering products generally would exceed that of the United States by the year 1932/33.[62] A few weeks later, a comparative survey of the utilisation of tractors in the USA and the USSR showed that tractors were used for far fewer hours per year in the USA than in the USSR; as a result, although the USSR would have a smaller stock of tractors than the United States in 1932/33, it would already be using more tractor horse-power hours per year.[63] In terms of mechanisation, the production of tractors planned in December 1929 for the year 1932/33 would enable 55–60 per cent of the total Soviet sown area to be ploughed by tractor, and during the first two or three years of the following five-year plan 'all animal draught power' would be 'fully driven out of the processes of agricultural production'.[64]

The increase in the supply of tractors during the course of the economic year 1929/30 provided some grounds for belief in the feasibility of these plans. In 1928/29, both home production and imports were substantially increased; and the total number of tractors supplied to agriculture was nearly three times as large as in the previous year, and larger than in any previous year except 1925/26. In December 1929 the Politburo commission on collectivisation recommended that 20,000 tractors should be imported in the course of 1929/30;[65] and, in the event, imports more than trebled in terms of numbers of tractors, and more than quadrupled in terms of horse-power, while home production trebled as a result of the successful launching of full-scale production in the tractor shop of the Putilov works.[66] As a result of this expansion, the stock of tractors in the USSR (in terms of horse-power) increased by 173 per cent between October 1, 1929, and October 1, 1930. According to official estimates, the draught power of tractors amounted to 7·7 per cent of all draught power by the end of 1930, as compared with only 2·8 per cent a year previously. In sovkhozy tractors overwhelmingly predominated, and had increased in importance since the previous

[62] *TsIK 2/V* (1929), No. 16, 9–11.

[63] B, 10, May 31, 1930, 81–3 (S. Uzhanskii); according to this article tractors in Iowa were used on average for only 200 hours a year in 1924, while the equivalent figure for the RSFSR in 1928 was 1,203. *Encyclopaedia Britannica*, xxii (Chicago, 1946), 343, article on 'Tractors', gives the average use in USA as 300–400 hours.

[64] NAF, 1, 1930, 62–3.

[65] VIK, 1, 1964, 39; for the commission see pp. 185–94 above.

[66] For these figures see Table 20 and (for 1925/26) Carr and Davies (1969), 945.

year; the rate of expansion of kolkhozy, however, outstripped the supply of tractors, and their tractor draught power fell from 62·3 to 20·1 per cent (see Table 20).

Looking to the future, further substantial increases in imports of tractors could not be hoped for. But the Stalingrad tractor factory was now beginning to operate, and the Khar'kov and Chelyabinsk factories were under construction. If their production programmes could be realised, and the further factories approved in November 1929 were also completed, there seemed to be adequate grounds for the view that the proletarian revolution, by combining collective agriculture with the new high level of world agricultural technology, had created for the first time in history conditions for 'a grandiose development of the productive forces' in which agriculture would overtake industry.[67] In the spring of 1929 Markevich had emphasised the necessity, in view of the economic backwardness of the Soviet Union, of using scarce and expensive capital more fully than in the United States, by employing more of the abundant rural labour force per unit of capital. In the practical prescriptions for the inculcation of the tractor at the end of 1930 this necessity was still firmly recognised: everywhere on kolkhoz lands the tractor was to be generously supported with the use of peasant labour and the horse. But this continued to be seen as merely an expedient for a brief transitional period. At the VI congress of soviets in March 1931, after reviewing the progress of mechanisation in agriculture in 1930, Markevich felt able to discard his earlier caution when considering future prospects. No doubt influenced by the growing contrast between the expanding economy of the Soviet Union and the economic crisis in the West, he compared the favourable conditions for the use of machinery in Soviet agriculture with capitalist countries in which it was often not profitable to use a machine in conditions of low wages. While in pre-revolutionary Russia machines had often been kept in sheds and brought out for a day or two when workers asked for higher wages, in the Soviet Union all this had been swept aside:

> I am deeply convinced that in two or three years the USSR will become the only classical country in the sphere of the application

[67] PKh, 5, 1930, 61 (Kraev).

> of advanced technology . . . Only in our country does the machine have unlimited application in agriculture.[68]

[68] *6 s''ezd sovetov* (1931), No. 17, 38–9. In the next three years, progress in the introduction of machinery into agriculture, though extremely rapid, fell far short of the hopes of 1930. Tractor output, planned to reach 5,220,000 h.p. in 1932/33 (*TsIK 2/V* (1929), No. 16, 10), in fact reached only 756,000 h.p. in 1932, 1,220,000 in 1933 and 1,751,000 in 1934 (*Sots. str.* (1935), 55). According to a decree of TsIK of December 8, 1929, the Soviet industry was to produce tractors with a total capacity of 9·5 million h.p. during the five-year plan (*Resheniya*, ii (1967), 145–9); according to more modest Gosplan calculations a few months later, the total stock of tractors (which would include imports) was planned to reach 'at least' 4 million h.p. in 1932/33 and 8 million in 1933/34 (PKh, 5, 1930, 15 (Grin'ko)); in fact the stock reached 2·2 million h.p. on December 31, 1932, 3·2 on December 31, 1933 and 4·5 on December 31, 1934 (*Sots. str.* (1935), 302).

CHAPTER ELEVEN

CONCLUSIONS

The decision in the autumn of 1929 to embark on forcible collectivisation was shaped by two major preceding sets of events. First, the victory of the Bolshevik revolution of 1917 and its consolidation during the Civil War excluded the possibility of more than a limited development of capitalist agriculture in Soviet Russia. The major industries were transferred to public ownership within a year of the revolution, and the restoration of private ownership of industry was thereafter never seriously contemplated. Individual peasant agriculture remained, but no group of Bolsheviks at any time displayed any propensity to contemplate the re-emergence of large-scale entrepreneurial private farming, or even of well-to-do peasant farms which employed more than a very small number of agricultural labourers; and all Bolsheviks believed that in the long term collective forms of agriculture must predominate. In 1919 and 1920, the Bolshevik victory seemed also to imply that collective agriculture would predominate within a few years, and that in the transition period the market would be replaced by non-monetary product-exchange between the state sector and private agriculture. But this perspective was abandoned in face of economic disorder, and of unrest among the working class and the peasantry. In sharp contrast to the vision of the future of 1919–20, the New Economic Policy offered the prospect of a non-coercive relationship through the market between the state sector and the peasantry lasting decades, and of the slow transformation of individual peasant agriculture into socialist cooperative agriculture. It is evident, then, that while the victory of Bolshevism meant that the state would prevent the rebirth of capitalist agriculture, it did not of itself determine the road to socialism.

The second major set of events which preceded the forcible collectivisation of agriculture was the breakdown of the market relation between the regime and the peasantry in the winter of 1927–8. Before this, the section of the party majority headed by

Stalin had come to share the view of the Left opposition that industrialisation must be accelerated. Simultaneously, administrative methods of planning had become much more widespread, fostered by the strengthening of the centralised monolithic regime in the party and by the growing influence at every level of party members who were disposed to favour blunt administrative methods in preference to delicate manoeuvring on the market. These were men with limited formal education, certainly with little knowledge of economics, whose previous experience of crisis was acquired during the bitter class battles of the Civil War, when military discipline was severe and the enforcement of administrative planning by forcible requisitioning of food from the peasants was essential to survival. The successful resolution of the grain crisis of the autumn of 1927 by administrative methods quickly consolidated the commitment of this section of the party to the use of coercion against the peasants, and to an ambitious programme of rapid industrialisation which would have been unrealisable within the framework of NEP.

At the beginning of 1928 Stalin drew two further conclusions from the grain crisis. First, the power of the kulak must be broken; according to Stalin, as the 'economic authority in the countryside' the kulak could persuade the middle peasant to follow him. Secondly, 'partial collectivisation', so that the socialised sector provided at least one-third of the grain required by the towns and the army, must be achieved within three or four years; and in the longer run individual peasant agriculture could not continue to exist, and must give way to the socialisation of the whole of agriculture.[1] This was not a call for immediate, still less for forcible, collectivisation. But collectivisation was now seen as a much more urgent task.

During 1928 and 1929 dramatic further shifts in policy took place. At the beginning of 1928 the section of the party leadership associated with Stalin was already committed to the continued use of coercion, if it proved necessary, to secure essential supplies of grain, and to an accelerated but still protracted programme of voluntary collectivisation. But in the second half of 1929 they were

[1] *Soch.*, xi, 6, 12 (speeches and circular of January–February 1928, first published 1949).

much bolder. In the summer the party launched an all-out drive to collect more grain more rapidly than in any previous year; and in November Molotov authoritatively called for the comprehensive collectivisation of the main grain-surplus areas within five months. How did these policy changes come about?

The political background was the defeat of the Right wing in the party, headed by Bukharin, Rykov and Tomsky. This was a complex and difficult struggle. Bukharin's approach, with its insistence on continuing to work within the framework of NEP, was supported by a substantial group of senior party officials and by virtually all the leading non-party experts in the major government departments; and it found ready sympathy among one section of the party rank and file, and among most peasants and many workers—when they had the opportunity to hear about it. But the new approach of Stalin and his group was welcomed enthusiastically by an influential group of party intellectuals, by some of the party rank and file, by many young communists and students, and by an unknown number of industrial workers. Above all support for the new policy from most members of the party central committee, and from many local party officials, provided the basis for Stalin and his group to prevail over the Right in the course of a protracted struggle between July 1928 and April 1929.[2]

This victory, together with the simultaneous campaign against the bourgeois specialists, considerably strengthened the position of the supporters of forced industrialisation and administrative planning both in the party and in the state administration. The senior economic advisers of Narkomfin and Narkomzem, including Kondratiev and Vainshtein, were removed from office. The views of 'teleological' planners such as Strumilin became overwhelmingly predominant in Gosplan, and the more moderate Groman and Bazarov were thrust aside. And Gosplan itself was then outflanked from the Left by the more ambitious plans of the predominant group in Vesenkha under Kuibyshev. Throughout 1928 and 1929 Rabkrin became increasingly important as policy-maker in agriculture, industry and planning. Rabkrin, dominated by party members to a greater extent than any other Commissariat, and headed by Stalin's close associate Ordzhonikidze, was both an instrument of

[2] For accounts of this struggle, which attempt to assess the balance of forces in the party and in the country at this time, see Carr (1971), 75–99; Cohen (1974), 270–336.

Stalin and his colleagues within the state administration and a means of concentrating the views and desires of the section of the party rank and file on which Stalin and his colleagues relied for support, and expressing them in specific proposals. Rabkrin consistently argued for more ambitious plans. The central staff of Rabkrin was joint with that of the party central control commission, also headed by Ordzhonikidze, and responsible for the enforcement of party discipline; and in its exposures of the bourgeois specialists Rabkrin worked more and more closely with the investigating agencies of the OGPU. The expression of disagreements with official policy in the party and in government departments still occurred, but became increasingly difficult, particularly in the case of disagreements which could be labelled as Right-wing. Thus the defeat of the Right wing was accompanied by the further consolidation of the monolithic central control over the party which had steadily become stronger throughout the 1920s.

In the course of the struggle against the Right, Stalin and his group consolidated—or expressed more openly—their programme for the construction in the USSR of what they believed would be a fully socialist society. The resistance of the peasants to the extraordinary measures at the beginning of 1928 was attributed to the strength of the kulaks in the countryside; and Stalin believed that 'the reconstruction of the economy on the basis of socialism' must take the form of 'the offensive of socialism against the capitalist elements of the economy along the whole front'. In Stalin's view, the class struggle would necessarily be intensified in the course of this offensive, as the kulaks and the Nepmen were bound to resist the socialist offensive.[3] The effort of the state to adapt the peasant economy to the imperative needs of industrialisation was seen, in effect, as a war against capitalist elements in the countryside, in which the victory of socialism would be assured through the power of the socialist state and through a Bolshevik approach, and Bolshevik organisation. Stalin told two famous anecdotes to the plenum of the central committee in April 1929 which dramatically expressed the essentials of the new approach. The first presented an image of correct Bolshevik leadership as compared with Rightist pusillanimity:

Have you seen fishermen before a storm on a great river like the

[3] *Soch.*, xi, 171 (July 9, 1928), xii, 13–15, 34–9 (April 22, 1929).

> Yenisei? I have seen them often. Faced with an oncoming storm, one group of fishermen will mobilise all their forces, encourage their men and boldly turn the boat to meet the storm: 'Hold on, lads, hold tight to the tiller, cut through the waves, we'll make it!'
>
> But there is another type of fisherman; they sense a storm and lose heart, and begin to snivel and demoralise their own ranks: 'Here's trouble, a storm is coming, lie down on the bottom of the boat, lads, close your eyes; perhaps it will get to the shore somehow'. (*Loud laughter.*)[4]

The second anecdote presented those who resisted the socialist offensive in terms of implacable hostility:

> One of our agitators, in Kazakhstan for example, tried for two hours to persuade the holders of grain to hand over grain to supply our country, and a kulak stepped forward with a pipe in his mouth and said: 'You do a little dance, boy, and then I'll give you half-a-hundredweight of grain'.
>
> *Voices*: Swine!
>
> *Stalin*: Just try to persuade such people.
>
> Yes, comrades, class is class. You can't avoid that truth.[5]

During the period from January 1928 to the middle of 1929 significant changes also took place in general economic policy, and in the economy itself. Industry developed rapidly: according to official figures, the production of large-scale industry increased by 21·6 per cent in October 1928–June 1929 as compared with the same period in 1927/28, the productivity of labour (output per man-month) increased by 12·3 per cent,[6] and production costs fell by about 3½ per cent.[7] These increases, though less than planned, were far more rapid than was anticipated a few years earlier: there was little sign so far of the declining rate of increase in output which all economists had expected to accompany the full absorption of pre-war capacity into production. Capital investment in industry also increased substantially during 1928, and was expected to be twice as large in the economic year 1928/29 as in 1925/26, when it already

[4] *Soch.*, xii, 18–19.

[5] *Soch.*, xii, 90.

[6] Calculated from data in EO, 3, 1930, 178–9; the underlying figures are in 1926/27 prices.

[7] EZh, August 9, 1929.

equalled the pre-war level.[8] In spite of the considerable deterioration in the quality of production which resulted from pressure to increase output and reduce costs,[9] these seemed to the leadership to be solid achievements, and greatly increased their confidence in the correctness of the course they had been following since the grain crisis.

Progress in industry was accompanied by the authorisation of increasingly ambitious industrial plans. After the approval of the higher optimum variant of the first five-year plan, already very ambitious, by the V congress of soviets in May 1929, the upward revision of targets began almost immediately. Soviet industry stood on the threshold of a fundamental transformation unparalleled in depth and rapidity. The conviction of the leaders that this transformation was urgently necessary in view of the international isolation of the Soviet Union did not diminish in 1928 and 1929. Soviet relations with the capitalist world had certainly been improving since the tense summer of 1927; the success of the British Labour party in the April 1929 elections removed the most hostile of the capitalist governments. Voroshilov is reported to have told a group of Soviet miners in May 1929 that 'war will not occur in the course of the next two years'.[10] But the new Comintern diagnosis of the international situation, vigorously promoted by Stalin and his supporters, was that the capitalist countries had entered a 'third period' in which the temporary stabilisation of capitalism was coming to an end, and a new epoch of wars and proletarian revolutions had begun.[11] The improvement in Soviet foreign relations was thus seen as a purely temporary respite. 'It is difficult to say now which capitalist countries will attack us', Voroshilov is reported to have said in May 1929, 'but the time is coming when they will certainly attack'.[12] A few months later Molotov asserted that 'messrs. the imperialists have not so far decided to attack us directly', and argued that in consequence 'we must utilise this moment for a decisive advance' (see p. 164 above). The new Comintern policy greatly overestimated the immediate potential for proletarian revolution in advanced capitalist countries, and

[8] See Carr and Davies (1969), 952–3.

[9] See, for example, the report in EZh, August 9, 1929 (Zeilinger).

[10] Yu. Zhukov, *Lyudy 30-kh godov* (1966), 92–3; these are reminiscences of a young Soviet journalist prepared 35 years after the event, and hence may not be reliable.

[11] See, for example, Stalin, *Soch.*, xii, 16 (speech of April 22, 1929).

[12] Zhukov (1966), 93.

underestimated the potential for technical progress within capitalism, and the extent to which capitalist economies could be managed by the state. On both these issues Bukharin was more realistic. But while neither the Comintern nor Bukharin anticipated that the capitalist world was about to plunge into its most profound economic crisis, the new Comintern leadership in 1929 showed a greater awareness than the 'Right wing' of the instability of capitalism, and of the potential for military aggression which lurked in some of the advanced capitalist countries, and was to dominate world politics after the triumph of Nazism in Germany four years later. To that extent the strategy of all-out industrialisation and military preparation was solidly based.

The rapid expansion of capital investment in industry in 1928 and 1929 was the most important factor in the disruption of the Soviet internal market, in the growing tension between the state and the peasantry, and in the deterioration of agricultural production. It was abundantly clear by the summer of 1929 (though never publicly admitted) that the plan to finance investment in industry primarily from costs' savings within industry itself, enshrined in all the successive drafts of the five-year plan, could not succeed. Even the level of industrial investment achieved in 1928, moderate by later standards, resulted in inflationary currency issues. In June 1929 the retail prices of agricultural goods on the private market were 114 per cent above those of June 1927, while those in socialised trade increased by only 16 per cent.[13] In the same period retail prices of industrial goods remained almost stable, but shortages became much more severe. The peasants were even more reluctant than during the grain crisis of 1927 to supply grain to the state at low fixed prices. After the 1928 harvest, however, with the Right wing in the party not yet defeated, the grain campaign was at first relatively mild; in consequence, even after coercion was again extensively used in the spring of 1929, the total amount of grain collected was substantially lower in the agricultural year 1928/29 than in the previous year (see pp. 56–60 above).

For the party leadership, the conclusion to be drawn was obvious. There could be no going back to the market relation with the peasantry; only inadequate control of the peasant economy by the state blocked the road to the achievement of the five-year plan. Experience seemed to have shown that the grain would be made

[13] Mendel'son, ed. (1930), 101–6.

available if strong action was taken against the 'kulaks'. The 'Ural–Siberian method' of grain collections, in which the authorities endeavoured to win the support of the mass of the peasants at the village assembly (skhod) for the grain quotas, and to isolate the kulaks, provided a quasi-democratic framework for legitimising the campaign. 'In those places where we broke kulak resistance', Syrtsov reported from Siberia, 'a strong flow of grain immediately began, as if a cork had been removed' (see pp. 57, 63 above). In June 1929, Mikoyan and his advisers, in contemplating the forthcoming harvest, continued a tradition already established by Gosplan in the middle 1920s, and swept aside the realistic estimates of the non-party experts that the harvest would be fairly low, concluding instead that in 1929 the harvest would be 6 million tons higher than in 1928. They were now liberated from the need to look back over their shoulders at the objections of the Right wing, and could mount a well-organised and militant campaign to collect in the grain rapidly, before it could be sold on the market, and to break the power of the kulaks. In these circumstances they easily convinced themselves that it was reasonable to increase the official grain collections by a mere 4 million tons (30 per cent) in 1929, especially as the socialised sector and contracts with individual peasants would alone supply 4 million tons more than in the previous year.

In June 1929, when this decision was taken, collectivisation was still envisaged in all the statements of the party leaders as a process which, even in the major grain areas, would take a decade or more. During this time, the massive supply of agricultural machinery to the kolkhozy would provide the technical basis for modern farming, and offer an adequate inducement to individual peasants to join the kolkhozy voluntarily. The party leaders were clearly not happy with this prospect. It meant that for many years rapidly growing state industry, the industrial working class, and the urban population generally, would depend on the individual peasants for a large part of their supplies of raw materials and food. In spite of their enthusiastic official campaign for increasing grain yields by 35 per cent during the five-year plan, the party leaders were sceptical about the ability of individual peasant households to increase their production and regarded supplies from them as inherently unreliable (in view of the lack of incentives available to peasants generally, and the squeeze on the well-to-do peasant, this scepticism was certainly justified). And they were very confident that the shift to large-scale mechanised socialist agriculture would result in a rapid increase in production.

In the spring and summer of 1929, a series of events, or preliminary decisions, paved the way for forced collectivisation at breakneck speed. First, a definite strategy for collectivisation was endorsed. The typical kolkhoz until 1929 included some poor peasant and one or two middle peasant households, while most households in the village continued individual farming. This was rejected as unsatisfactory: these kolkhozy were believed to be too small, and, unless generously financed by the state, also too poor, for efficient farming. At the XVI party conference in April 1929, many speakers argued that 'comprehensive collectivisation' of all, or nearly all, the peasants in a village would provide a much sounder basis for collectivisation. The assumption of 'comprehensive collectivisation' was thus that kolkhozy would include middle as well as poor peasants; while membership in theory remained voluntary, all, or nearly all, the peasants in the village would be persuaded to join by a systematic campaign. In May and June 1929 Kolkhoztsentr took a further step along the road to forced collectivisation when it designated a few favoured administrative districts as 'districts of comprehensive collectivisation' (RSKs), which would be provided with ample machinery and systematically collectivised. In July, the North Caucasus region decided that the collectivisation programme throughout the region would be based on the collectivisation of whole villages. In August, a model scheme was prepared in Kolkhoztsentr for collectivisation campaigns based on the Ural–Siberian method.

Secondly, in the course of 1928 and 1929, comprehensive collectivisation was tested out in several important areas, before any policy decision had been taken by Kolkhoztsentr or the party central committee. Stalin once wrote that 'sometimes the party . . . thinks it expedient to carry out a test action, to test the forces of its opponent, to check the preparedness of its forces for battle; and such a trial of strength is either undertaken consciously by the party, by its own choice . . . or is brought about by circumstances'.[14] It is not clear how far the 'trials of strength' for collectivisation were 'undertaken consciously' on orders from the centre and how far they emerged from local organisations in response to general directives to pay more attention to collectivisation. Markevich's Machine-Tractor Station, which pro-

[14] *Soch.*, v, 75–6 (draft pamphlet on strategy and tactics, July 1921).

vided machinery to the peasants while retaining central control, was almost certainly a local initiative in the autumn of 1927, though soon taken up by Stalin.[15] The formation in the spring of 1929 of the Gigant kolkhoz, or group of kolkhozy, in the Urals, which showed that rapid collectivisation could be achieved in a whole district, also seems to have been a spontaneous response by local officials to general exhortations from the centre. Collectivisation in Khoper okrug in the Lower Volga region, on the other hand, was apparently much more closely controlled by the central party authorities; this was a large grain area of 100,000 households in which only a small percentage of households was collectivised, typical of areas in which the collectivisation drive might meet with most resistance. The comprehensive collectivisation of Khoper okrug took place, apparently successfully, in the course of a couple of months in September and October 1929.

All these developments encouraged the view that rapid collectivisation was feasible. The successful collectivisation of the Gigant group of kolkhozy in the Urals and of Khoper okrug also seemed to demonstrate that the strongly held belief that comprehensive collectivisation required modern machinery was too pessimistic. The local organisers of the kolkhozy claimed that a considerable increase in efficiency was obtained through the use of peasant horses and implements in such kolkhozy. Perhaps, then, kolkhozy generally could, for a transitional period, be established without mechanisation, particularly as the revised draft of the five-year plan for agricultural machinery confidently predicted that ample supplies of tractors and combine harvesters would be available within a few years. While some prominent party leaders still seem to have been committed to immediate mechanisation as a condition for comprehensive collectivisation, by October 1929 the very brief experience of collectivisation without mechanisation of some districts and even a whole okrug greatly strengthened the growing conviction of Stalin and many of his supporters that collectivisation on a national scale could be pushed through forthwith.

The third major event which immediately preceded the full-scale launching of collectivisation was the great success of the first stage of the grain campaign. In July–September 1929, official grain collections amounted to over 6 million tons; and in the following

[15] See Carr and Davies (1969), 210.

month, October 1929, a further 5 million tons were collected. In the same four months of 1928/29, collections amounted to only 4 million tons; and in the whole of 1928/29 less grain was collected than in July–October 1929 alone (see Tables 8(a) and 8(d)). The collections were carried out, as in previous years, by a large *ad hoc* organisation of 'plenipotentiaries' sent in from the towns, but with a much more systematic effort to use the Ural–Siberian method to secure the support of the mass of the peasants and to isolate the kulaks. The village was subordinated to the will of the state quickly and effectively during the grain campaign. The 'quasi-democratic' features of the Ural–Siberian method were seen as an essential device for legitimising collectivisation; and, as no local administrative machinery for handling a mass collectivisation drive yet existed, the plenipotentiary system provided the required instrument for enforcing it. The decision to collectivise with the personnel of the grain campaign, many of them temporarily removed from their jobs, none of them permanently resident in the countryside, in itself dictated that the collectivisation drive, like the grain campaign, would, in the areas in which it was carried out, be fitted into a few months rather than protracted over many years.

A fourth factor, of a negative kind, added further urgency to the collectivisation drive. Reports from many different parts of the country revealed that 'self-dekulakisation' by the more prosperous peasants, who sold up their property and moved to the towns, had greatly accelerated in view of rumours of forthcoming collectivisation, even in places where comprehensive collectivisation had not yet occurred. Moreover, not only kulaks, but many middle peasants, in areas where some collectivisation had already taken place, were selling up their livestock and even their horses in preparation for joining the kolkhoz. This could have been prevented by calling a halt to forcible collectivisation, and limited by a firm announcement that members of kolkhozy were entitled to retain their own livestock. But no-one was prepared to call a halt to collectivisation; and many officials regarded the socialisation of livestock as essential to agricultural progress. In these circumstances many party leaders argued that collectivisation should be pressed ahead in order to take over the property of the well-to-do before it was disposed of, and the animals of the middle peasants before they were killed. On the slaughter of animals and the socialisation of livestock, as on most other issues, Stalin remained silent; but at the height of the collectivisation campaign, on February 9, 1930, he too declared 'there is only one way of resisting the "squandering" of kulak property—strengthen the work on collectivisation in districts without comprehensive collectivisation'.

These developments in the spring and summer of 1929 provided the immediate background to the decision to launch an all-out collectivisation drive, evidently taken by the party leaders sometime in October and announced in the reports of Molotov and Kaminsky at the November plenum of the central committee (though not fully expressed in its resolutions). At the plenum, some regional party leaders (notably Andreev) tried to restrain somewhat the proposed pace of collectivisation in their own region, but apparently Syrtsov was alone in expressing doubts about the general decision to accelerate greatly the pace of collectivisation. Any pressure for moderation would undoubtedly have been denounced as a Right deviation. A campaign against the Bukharin group began openly in the press in August 1929, and the early sittings of the plenum were dominated by vociferous denunciations of the Right. All this provided an atmosphere in which sweeping changes of policy could be pushed through without resistance. Most of the principal party leaders at the centre—Molotov, Kaganovich, Kuibyshev, Mikoyan and Rudzutak—and many of the major republican and regional party secretaries—including Sheboldaev, Khataevich, Eikhe, Bauman and Kosior—certainly gave every impression in their speeches at this time of active and enthusiastic commitment to the new line. But Stalin no doubt authorised the sharp denunciations of the Right at the November plenum, he was certainly extremely active in pushing through the plenum decisions, and he had undoubtedly approved the terms of Molotov's speech. Whether Stalin's personal authority was decisive at this crucial moment in Soviet history remains uncertain. The decision once taken, the successful outcome of the struggle for collectivisation seemed so essential to the future of Soviet communism that former oppositionists of both Right and Left—including even Shlyapnikov, head of the Workers' Opposition in 1920–1—rallied to the support of Stalin and the party leadership.

The important problem of the kulak remained unresolved at the November plenum. Both comprehensive collectivisation in selected areas and the grain campaign aroused bitter and often active hostility among the peasants, and this hostility was attributed in almost all party statements to the kulaks and their 'henchmen'. Kulaks and well-to-do peasants certainly handed over a higher proportion of their grain to the state than other peasants, and also stood to lose more as a result of collectivisation. No doubt the more prosperous peasants also tended to dominate the skhod, which would be swept aside by comprehensive collectivisation. But the more prosperous peasants were rarely kulaks in an exploitative sense; and they were seen by many peasants as solid citizens whose lead should be followed. All peasants were under pressure to hand over grain. The less prosperous peasants sold a higher proportion of their grain in the market and less to the state in 1927 and 1928 than the kulaks and the well-to-do, and may have particularly suffered from the 1929 collections, which greatly reduced market sales. The view of the authorities that the hostility in the village came from the kulaks was analogous to the view of some Vice-Chancellors and businessmen in present-day Britain that student unrest and workers' strikes, however widespread, are solely due to the machinations of a few Left-wing agitators and will be brought to an end if the agitators are isolated and handled firmly.

Comprehensive collectivisation posed the problem of the kulaks in an acute form: when all the poor and middle peasants in a village joined the kolkhoz, what was to be done with the kulaks? If they were admitted to the kolkhoz, they would bring into it their petty capitalist attitudes and their hostility. If they remained in the village at all, even on the outskirts, they would be a permanent source of friction, and permanently remind the collective farmers that individual farming offered an alternative to collectivisation. As early as the autumn of 1928, a small number of *bai* in Kazakhstan, who were much richer than kulaks in the rest of the USSR, were exiled by methods eventually used to deal with kulaks as a whole; it is not known whether this 'trial of strength' was initiated locally or centrally. There is, however, a great deal of evidence that many local party officials in areas in which comprehensive collectivisation was far advanced were pressing strongly, from the spring of 1929 onwards, for an outright ban on admission of kulaks to kolkhozy and, in some cases, for their expulsion from their villages. These harsh demands, which throw a great deal of light on the outlook of the section of the party which supported forced collectivisation, were resisted by the rural department of the central committee in Moscow. But at the November plenum Molotov firmly declared, and this undoubtedly reflected Stalin's own view, that the kulak should be treated as 'a most cunning and still undefeated enemy'. Andreev, Mikoyan and Khataevich still envisaged that kulaks would eventually be admitted to the kolkhozy; and a few weeks later the Politburo subcommission on the kulaks, under the chairmanship of Bauman, recommended that while recalcitrant kulaks should be treated very harshly, the majority of kulaks should be admitted to kolkhozy as probationary members. At this point Stalin's intervention was undoubtedly crucial: he declared at the end of December that kulaks should not be admitted to the kolkhozy under any circumstances, and that the time was ripe for eliminating them as a class; his harsh language paved the way for the elaborate decisions on the mass exile of kulaks prepared by a new Politburo commission headed by Molotov. This is an instructive example of the way in which Stalin based himself on, responded to and manipulated the outlook of one section of party officials.

After the November plenum, the central committee decree of January 5 laid down a rough time-table for collectivisation, but no brake was applied by the central authorities to those who moved faster than this time-table; and party and state officials at all other levels, afraid of being accused of Right deviation, were unwilling to apply any restraint to their more enthusiastic subordinates. As the Politburo evidently intended, the campaign escalated, and by the end of February 1930 over 50 per cent of peasant households were nominally enrolled in the kolkhozy.

The decision at the end of February to reaffirm the voluntary principle in collectivisation was primarily due to nervousness by the leaders at the widespread discontent, unrest and even rebellion among the peasants, which, if it continued, was certain to endanger the spring sowings and might have threatened the continued existence of the regime. The decision seems to have been made collectively by the Politburo after some of its members returned from the countryside; Stalin evidently published his article 'Dizzy with Success' in order to claim credit for this decision and cover up his responsibility for the 'excesses'. The form of the decision marked a further step towards the enforcement of the convention that the central committee and the Politburo were infallible. In February 1928 Stalin had declared that responsibility for the mistakes which resulted in the grain crisis 'obviously rests primarily with the central committee, and not only on local organisations';[16]

[16] *Soch.*, xi, 14; this was a circular to all party organisations dated February 13; it was not published until 1949.

in March and April 1930, however, he attributed all responsibility for excesses in collectivisation to the unfortunate local organisations. The consequences of the reaffirmation of the voluntary principle were unexpected to the Politburo, which evidently did not fully appreciate the extent of peasant hostility to collectivisation, and certainly did not anticipate that more than half the members would leave the kolkhozy within a few weeks.

The stormy collectivisation drive of 1929–30 brought immense changes in the Soviet countryside. In the summer of 1930, even after the mass withdrawals of peasants in March and April, 6 million peasant households, 24·6 per cent of the total number, belonged to 86,000 kolkhozy, as compared with less than 4 per cent in June 1929. The kolkhozy were much more viable agricultural units than in the previous year: the size of the average kolkhoz increased from 18 to 70 households. And while the kolkhozy still consisted for the most part of previously poor peasant households, and possessed on average only 40 horses, they owned, or used via MTS and tractor columns, a considerable number of tractors: it was estimated that kolkhozy covering a quarter of the area sown by kolkhozy were partly serviced by MTS or tractor columns. The prospect of full mechanisation within three or four years seemed bright, in view of the ambitious programme to produce 130,000 tractors a year in 1931/32. The kolkhozy were also in a strong position because they had acquired a considerable amount of land in the course of collectivisation. This came partly from the expropriated kulaks, whose land was transferred to the kolkhozy, and partly from individual peasants, whose land allotments were reduced during the collectivisation drive and the subsequent exodus. The kolkhozy also added a little more to their sown area by ploughing over the land which separated the strips and by bringing previously unused land into cultivation. In 1930, the 24·6 per cent of households in the kolkhozy controlled 35 per cent of the spring-sown area. Most kolkhozy included only some of the households in their village, or in a group of villages: typically, this was not yet comprehensive collectivisation. But, although the land allocations in the villages were very confused after the upheaval of the previous winter, the kolkhoz was usually in a commanding position, occupying the fields, or parts of fields, closest to the peasant cottages and the household plots.

The position of individual farming was thus greately weakened in all those villages in which the kolkhozy included a substantial proportion of households. The traditional pattern of peasant agriculture, and traditional peasant organisation, were in large part destroyed. Even in the main grain-surplus regions (except the North Caucasus) individual peasant households still amounted to more than 60 per cent of the total, but they now had much less land to cultivate, and this land was often inconveniently placed placed on the outskirts of the village, and its quality was below average. The mir, and the institution of the elected village elder, ceased to exist, or were greatly weakened, throughout the USSR; and in many villages the church was closed, and its priest had fled or been arrested. The most dangerous and bitter opponents of the kolkhozy, kulaks, or those labelled as such in Categories I and II, had been expelled from their villages to remote parts of their region or of the USSR; some 100,000 households were expelled by the end of 1930, or more than half-a-million people, mainly in the grain-surplus areas. A further 250,000 families, perhaps 1½ million people, were resettled on the outskirts of their village or elsewhere in their district and region; and an unknown number of households fled—at least 100,000. So in this first wave over 2½ million people were 'dekulakised', and half of these were driven altogether from their villages.

The destruction of the traditional village community was accompanied by a considerable strengthening of Soviet power within the village. The authority of the village soviet was enhanced; and it was bound closer to the central authorities by 'cleansing' it of unreliable members. The substantial influx of reliable party members into the kolkhozy from the towns also greatly strengthened control over the village by the central authorities (or, to be more accurate, it appeared to do so). The machinery for political and economic control of the kolkhozy and the villages was still very confused, and *ad hoc* plenipotentiaries abounded; but, with the abolition of the okrugs in the summer of 1930, the immediate authority for communicating with and controlling the village, the district, was greatly strengthened.

These major inroads into the strength of individual peasant agriculture in the winter of 1929–30 were achieved at a great price. The collectivisation drive resulted in a immense reduction of livestock numbers: by May 1930, the total number of animals in the USSR had fallen by 25 per cent in a single year, a greater loss than in the whole of the Civil War. These losses were partly due to the removal by the official collection agencies of grain which would otherwise have been available for fodder, and to that extent they were a price paid for rapid industrialisation; but in large part they were due to the unwillingness of the peasants to hand over their animals to the kolkhozy without compensation. The tractor power made available to the kolkhozy in 1930 was less than the animal power destroyed during the upheaval; and losses of cows, pigs and sheep were so great that, even on an optimistic assessment, meat and dairy production could not recover to its 1929 level for at least two years. Soviet agriculture escaped even greater disaster by a narrow margin. In the confusion of the retreat from collectivisation in spring of 1930, sowing, particularly by individual households, was greatly delayed; and only the good fortune of exceptionally favourable weather in the late spring, and of good weather in the summer, enabled a record grain harvest to be achieved. In 1930, as in previous years, Bolshevik policy gambled on good weather, and achieved a spectacular victory; but this triumph was to prove illusory.

For the moment, however, the harvest of 1930 encouraged great complacency on the part of the party leaders and an even more determined effort to compel agriculture to serve the interests of industrialisation. The record harvest was followed by record grain collections, amounting to 22 million tons, six million tons more than in 1929/30, and more than double the 1928/29 collections. This seemed to be a convincing demonstration of the success of the first phase of collectivisation: 40 per cent of the collections came from the socialised sector (see Table 8(c)), which contained only about a quarter of the households working in agriculture. As a result of the increase in the collections, grain supplies to the population by the state greatly increased. But this increase exaggerated the extent to which grain was diverted from the countryside to the towns. With the breakdown of the grain market, the state was forced to extend the range of consumers to whom it supplied grain. Small towns and timber areas, which were supplied largely from the market before 1929, now received most of their grain from the state; and the amount of grain supplied to the major industrial areas in the grain-deficit zone increased only slightly between 1928/29 and 1930/31.

The effects of the decline in livestock farming partly undermined the satisfactory outcome of the grain collections. Smaller quantities of livestock products were available for export, and, after the brief improvement due to the slaughter of animals in the winter of 1929–30, the amount of meat and dairy products available to the urban population on the market greatly declined. As with grain, the increase in official meat collections did not compensate for this. The total amount of food available per head of the urban population almost certainly declined in 1930.

While the crisis in food production and distribution did not lessen as a result of the first collectivisation drive, the generous supplies of grain made available to the producers of industrial crops, and the relatively high prices offered by the collection agencies, resulted in a substantial increase in the production of cotton, flax and tobacco. In 1930, as a result of this improvement in internal cotton supplies and of a reduction in cotton imports, significant progress was made towards the objective of self-sufficiency in cotton production. Moreover, sufficient grain was collected to make possible large grain exports, which covered the cost of substantial imports of machinery.

The retreat from collectivisation was described by Stalin, as early as April 3, 1930, as not a retreat but a temporary consolidation. The ambitious revised programme for industrial development was confirmed at the XVI congress in July and, in spite of severe economic difficulties, was maintained in the autumn. In the major public trial of the 'Industrial Party' in November 1930 leading non-party specialists were accused of conspiracy to overthrow the Soviet government. Many other 'bourgeois specialists' were arrested, and some, including an important group concerned with the meat and dairy industry, were summarily executed. The Right deviation within the party was again vigorously attacked, and objections by Syrtsov and Lominadze to the lack of realism of the programme for economic development were strongly condemned in a bitter press campaign. Within this uncompromising framework the grain collection campaign, as we have seen, was even more ambitious than that of 1929. The edge of the collections was turned against the individual peasants, who were already weakened by loss of much of their land to the kolkhozy in the previous spring. All this provided a basis for the further collectivisation drive, announced in the autumn of 1930, which was again to be accompanied by the expulsion of all kulaks from their farms in areas of comprehensive collectivisation, and by exiling a large minority of them to remote parts of the USSR.

In the autumn of 1930, the first phase of the collectivisation drive was completed, and the second was about to begin.

The basis for further collectivisation was considerably weaker than the strength of the kolkhozy in the summer of 1930 seemed to indicate. The kolkhozy in 1930 enjoyed a very favourable land allotment, which enabled them to achieve a reasonable harvest in that year; the individual peasants were greatly weakened. But the planned influx of the remaining households into the kolkhozy would necessarily reduce the sown area per household, and the level of mechanisation, and dilute the state resources which were now concentrated on the minority of the households which belonged to the kolkhozy. The kolkhozy, once they embraced the whole of the village, would have to manage without special privileges. And the countryside now lacked those peasants who had been most successful economically; the hastily trained townsmen sent into the countryside were keen but ignorant. Moreover, even knowledge of existing methods of peasant farming was of limited value. Comprehensive collectivisation necessarily involved a complete restructuring of the arrangements for farming grain and industrial crops, in terms both of farm organisation and of agricultural techniques; and for this no-one in the villages was prepared.

All these difficulties, however, were overshadowed by the inability of the kolkhozy to provide economic incentives to their members which might overcome the problems of the new collective agriculture. The kolkhozy were compelled to disgorge their grain and other products to the state; and the arbitrariness of the grain quota in practice meant that a kolkhoz which produced more grain tended to find that it had to deliver its additional production to be collection agencies. The money payments to kolkhoz members for collective work in 1930 were insignificant; far more was earned from the sale of non-grain products from the household plots. In 1930, grain payments in kind were usually distributed in equal amounts per head. The collective farmer therefore lacked any economic incentive to work on the collective land. The lack of incentive to the farmer, plus the low level of capital available as a result of the destruction of horses and oxen, augured ill for future grain production. These difficulties were not likely to lessen with the inclusion of the majority of individual households within the kolkhozy. While the number of horses per household might increase—if the horses survived the transition to collective ownership—the full brunt of the grain collections would in future fall on the kolkhozy. Unless the planned supplies of machinery and expertise to the countryside were forthcoming, and resulted in a substantial increase in agricultural production, comprehensive collectivisation would not overcome the weaknesses already present in the kolkhoz system in 1930. These dangers were partly concealed by the luck of a good harvest in 1930; they emerged all the more strongly in the next three years.

TABLES

Table 1. Agricultural production in physical terms, 1913–1930

	1909–1913	*1913*	*1925*	*1926*	*1927*	*1928*	*1929*	*1930*
Grain (m.t.)	65–80[1]	77–94[1]	72·5[2]	76·8[2]	72·3[2a]	73·3[2a]	71·7[2]	83·5[1,2]/77·2[3]
Potatoes (m.t.)	22·4[4]	29·9[5]/23·3[4]	38·9[5]	43·3[5]	41·5[5]	46·4[6]	45·6[6]	49·4[6]
Oil seeds (th.t.)[b]		2554[5]	3446[5]	2726[5]	3324[7]	3452[7]/3399[8]	3008[8]	2775[8]
Sugar beet (m.t.)		10·90[7]	9·07[7]	6·37[7]	10·41[7]	10·14[7]	6·25[2]	14·02[2]
Raw cotton (th.t.)	675[4]	744[4,7]	540[2]	540[2]	720[2]	820[2]	860[2]	1110[2]
Flax fibre (th.t.)[c]	260[4]	454[7]/330[4]	362[7]/300[2]	310[7]/270[2]	276[7]/240[2]	352[2]/320[2]	360[2]	440[2]

Sources: [1] See SS, xxvi (1974), 157–80 (Wheatcroft).
[2] *Sots. str.* (1935), 361–2.
[3] In grain-fodder balance reproduced from archives in Moshkov (1966), 230–1; see p. 349 above.
[4] *Sel. kh.* (1960), 199, 201.
[5] *KTs . . . na 1928/29* (1929), 408–9.
[6] *Sel. kh. 1935* (1936), 447.
[7] *KTs . . . na 1929/30* (1930), 440–1, 532–3.
[8] *Nar. kh.* (1932), 178–9.

Notes: [a] According to *KTs . . . na 1929/30* (1930), 532–3, production fell from 73·6 million tons in 1927 to 72·7 millions in 1928.
[b] All the years include sunflower, flax, hemp and 'other' oil seeds (excluding cotton seeds). The 1913 figure and those for 1925–7 and 1928 (source 7) seem to be comparable; the 1928–30 figures seem to have a somewhat smaller coverage of 'other oil seeds'.
[c] Note that the series from source 7 is high in relation to the series from source 2 and the alternative pre-war figures from source 4; the reason for the difference has not been ascertained.

Table 2. Number of animals, 1914–1930 (millions)

	1914 'Eve of war'[1a]	*1916*[2]	*1925* *Spring*[3]	*1926* *Spring*[3]	*1927* *Spring*[3]	*1928* *Spring*[3]	*1928* *July*[4]	*1929* *July*[4]	*1930* *July*[4]
Horses	38·5	35·5	26·2	28·4	31·2	33·2	33·5	34·6	30·2
Cattle	64·9	60·3	59·8	63·3	67·3	69·8	70·5	67·1	52·5
Sheep and goats	112·8[a]	121·0	115·4	123·5	137·4	145	146·7	147	108·8
Pigs	23·2	20·3	21·1	21·0	22·6	25·6	26·0	20	13·6

Sources: [1] *Ocherki po istorii statistiki SSSR* (1960), 115 (A. Vainshtein).
[2] *KTs . . . na 1928/29* (1929), 408–9.
[3] *KTs . . . na 1929/30* (1930), 530–1.
[4] *Sel. kh. 1935* (1936), 511.

Note: [a] Minimum figures; see p. 4, n. 10 above. The figure for sheep and goats does not seem to be comparable with that for 1916 (and possibly also with the figures for the 1920s?); according to *Ocherki po istorii statistiki SSSR* (1960), 113, their number declined by at least 1·8 per cent between 1914 and 1916.

Table 3. Gross agricultural production by branch of agriculture, 1929 and 1930 (million rubles at 1926/27 prices)

	1929	*1930*
1. Crop production		
Grain	3348	3741
Industrial crops	876	1059
Potatoes and vegetables	1866	2231
Fruit and wine	392	342
Other crops	2577	2229
Total	9059	9602
2. Livestock production		
Whole milk	2050	1857
Meat and fat: all kinds	2376	1723
Raw hides: all kinds	457	389
Sheep and camel wool	184	142
Other livestock production	619	295
Total	5686	4406
Total gross production	14745	14008

Source: *Sel. kh. 1935* (1936), 221.

Note: For a discussion of Soviet estimates of gross agricultural production see Jasny (1949), 657–66. The above figures include estimated increases in 'unfinished production' of crops and livestock (i.e. in crops not yet harvested, and in weight and numbers of live animals). Excluding these figures, gross production falls to 14,340 million rubles in 1929 and increases to 14,078 million rubles in 1930 (*Sots. str.* (1935), 282), but the difference seems much too small in view of the large decline in livestock numbers in 1929 and 1930. For alternative figures for gross production, in both 1928 prices and current prices, see *Materialy po balansu* (1932), 139, 142.

Table 4. Sown area by social sector for 1929 and 1930 harvests (million hectares)

	A. Autumn-sown grain[a]			B. Spring grain			C. Other spring-sown crops			Total spring crops (B+C)			Total crops (A+B+C)		
	1929	1930 (July 1930 estimate)	1930 (1932 estimate)	1929	1930 (July 1930 estimate)	1930 (1932 estimate)	1929	1930 (July 1930 estimate)	1930 (1932 estimate)	1929	1930 (July 1930 estimate)	1930 (1932 estimate)	1929	1930 (July 1932 estimate)	1930 (1932 estimate)
Sovkhozy[b]	0·40	0·77	0·85	1·14	2·15	2·66	0·74	1·00	1·13	1·87	3·15	3·78	2·27	3·93	4·64
Kolkhozy	0·62	5·43	5·20	2·77	24·26	22·67	0·76	8·39	6·97	3·54	32·65	29·63	4·15	38·08	34·84
Individual sowings of collective farmers[c]	0·42	2·10	31·36	0·77	0·32	35·81	0·32	0·95	15·55	1·09	1·27	51·37	1·51	3·37	82·73
Individual peasants	29·96	30·58		59·93	36·14		20·22	15·12		80·15	51·26		110·11	81·84	
Total	31·40	38·89	37·41	64·61	62·87	61·14	22·04	25·46	23·65	86·65	88·33	84·79	118·05	127·22	122·20

Sources: 1929 and 1930 (July 1930 estimate): *Sots. Str.* (1936), 282–7.
1930 (1932 estimate): *Nar. kh.* (1932), 152–3.
For the basis on which the Soviet statistical agencies made these estimates, see p. 307, n. 151, above.

Notes: [a] 1929 figure is for grain sown in the autumn of 1928; 1930 figure is for grain sown in the autumn of 1929. All figures are net of 'winter killings' of autumn-sown grain.
[b] 1929 and 1930 (July 1930 estimate) are stated to include 'sovkhozy, koopkhozy and other agricultural enterprises'; 1930 (1932 estimate) is sovkhozy 'including sowings by institutions and organisations'; the coverage of the 1932 estimate may be somewhat wider than the earlier estimates.
[c] This is sowings on household plots, but 'partly including autumn sowings in fields, not socialised by the spring, of new members of kolkhozy'.

… for marketed production of grain by social sector, 1931–1933 (million tons)

	May 1928 (Stalin)[1b]				April 1929 (Optimum variant of five-year plan)[2d]			
	1926/27		1931 or 1932 (Plan)[c]		1932/33		1932/33	
	Amount	%	Amount	%	Gross production	%	Marketed production	%
Sovkhozy	0·6 (Sovkhozy and Kolkhozy together)	6·0	1·3–1·6	c.10	4·4	4·1	3·4[e]	17·3
Kolkhozy			<1·6	c.10	12·0	11·3	5·0[e]	25·5
Individual peasants								
(a) Kulaks	2·06	20·0	2·1?	c.14	89·6 ((a) and (b) together)	84·6	11·3 ((a) and (b) together)	57·7
(b) Middle and poor peasants	7·63	74·0	9·3	60–65				
Total	10·32	100·0	14·4–15·2	100	105·9	100·0	19·6	100·0

Sources: [1] Stalin, *Soch.*, xi, 85, 88–92 (speech of May 28, 1928, originally published in P, June 2, 1928).
[2] *Pyatiletnii plan* (1930), ii, i, 328–9.

Notes: [a] Extra-rural marketings in the narrower sense, with peasant 'purchases back' deducted, hence not directly comparable with extra-rural marketings in the wider sense of Table 6.
[b] Stalin's figures were given in puds and have been converted into tons.
[c] These figures are all approximate: Stalin started that 'in three or four years 250–300 million puds [4·1–4·9 million tons] more marketed grain could be placed at the disposal of the state', including 80–100 million puds (1·3–1·6 million tons) from sovkhozy, 'up to 100 million puds' (1·6 million tons) for kolkhozy and 'at least 100 million puds [1·6 million tons] new marketed grain from small and middle individual peasant economies'; he gave no figure for future marketed grain from kulak households, which was presumably to remain stable.
[d] The plan stated that gross grain production by the three sectors in 1933/34 (i.e. from the 1933 harvest) would be 5·4, 19·1 and 91·9 million tons, 116·4 million tons in all, but gave no plan for marketed grain production in that year.
[e] These figures were specifically approved by a resolution of the XVI party conference, which also stated that 15·5 per cent of gross grain production and 43 per cent of marketed grain production from the 1932 harvest would be from the socialised sector (*KPSS v rez.*, ii (1954), 571).

Table 6. Production, marketings and collections by type of product, 1928–1930

(a) Crops (thousand tons)

	Gross production[1] from harvest of:			Extra-rural marketed production[2] for calendar years:			Collections[3] for agricultural years:					
							1928/29		1929/30		1930/31	
	1928	1929	1930	1928	1929	1930	Amount	% of gross production	Amount	% of gross production	Amount	% of gross production
Grain	73320	71740	83540/77200	15742	19502	22647	10789	14·7	16081	22·4	22139	26·5/28·7
Potatoes	46441	45630	49448	4139	5454	8810	n.a.		3253	7·1	5722	11.6
Vegetables	10498[4]	10624[4]	17550[4a]	1138	1456	2465	—	—	—	—	1491	8.4
Oil seeds[b]	3290[4]	2887[4]	2633[4]	1912	1693	1172	1343	40.8	1193	41·3	989	37.6
Flax fibre	320	360	440	159	254	185	172	53.8	227	63.1	180	40.9

Sources: [1] As for Table 1, except where otherwise stated.
[2] Barsov (1969), table facing p. 112.
[3] *Nar. kh.* (1932), 332–43.
[4] *Ibid.* 178–9.

Notes:
General note: The figures for gross production and collections are directly comparable, as collections for the agricultural year come from the annual harvest at the beginning of the year; marketed production, however, came partly from the harvest of the previous year. Extra-rural marketed production is all sales outside the village, including products purchased by peasants and returned to the village.
[a] An alternative figure of 13,854 is given in *Tekhnicheskie kul'tury: kartofel', ovoshchi* (1936), 85.
[b] Sunflower, flax and hemp seeds only, so not comparable with figures in Table 1.

Table 6 *(contd.)*

(b) Meat and dairy products

	Gross production			Extra-rural marketed production[4c]			Collections		
	1928	*1929*	*1930*	*1928*	*1929*	*1930*	*1928*	*1929*	*1930*
Livestock (carcass weight in th. t.)	3940[1a]	4473[1a]	2861[1a]	1651	1714	1187	954[5a]	1067[5a, d]	1039[5a, d]
Eggs (millions)	10770[2]	10109[2]	7193[2]	4731	4067	2785	2580[6]	1847[7]	886[7]
Wool[b]	178[3]	179[3]	139[3]	41	45	52	41[3]	46[3]	51[3]

Sources: [1] Nifontov (1937), 69.
[2] *Materialy po balansu* (1932), 328–9.
[3] Nifontov (1937), 76, 87.
[4] Barsov (1969), table facing p. 112.
[5] Nifontov (1937), 81.
[6] See Jasny (1949), 228.
[7] *Nar. kh.* (1932), 346–7, converted at rate of 1,440 eggs per box (see Jasny (1949), 228).

Notes: [a] Agricultural years 1928/29, 1929/30, 1930/31.
[b] Sheep, camel and goats' wool in original form (Nifontov (1937), 76).
[c] These figures include all sales outside the village, including products purchased by peasants and returned to the village.
[d] Cattle, sheep, goats and pigs; includes collections not for meat but for addition to herd of socialist sector, which in terms of live weight amounted to about 25 per cent of the collections in the calendar years 1930 and 1931 (see Table 10, note a).

Table 7. Peasant extra-rural money income and expenditure, 1928/29–1930 (million rubles at current prices)

Income

	1928/29 (preliminary)[1]	*1930 (preliminary)*[2]
Sale of farm products:	3210	7324
from planned collections	n.a.	4000
from non-planned sales	n.a.	3324
Timber, fishing and hunting	296	300
Hiring-out of labour, animals, implements, land	96	n.a.
Non-farming income	2800	3418
Production loans	217	737
Total	6619	11779

Expenditure

Purchase of goods:	(5307)	8022
industrial goods	}	6305
means of production	}4561	929
agricultural	} 746	788
Non-material expenditure	n.a.	350
Public catering	n.a.	260
Other expenditure	(396)	—
Payments and exactions	741	2140
Total	6444	10772
Net increase in balance in hand	175	1002

Sources: [1] *KTs . . . na 1929/30* (1930), 478–81.
[2] FP, 3–4, 1931, 23.

Note: The total stock of money in hand in the countryside was reported as 1,600–1,700 million rubles on October 1, 1929, and 'over 2,600–over 2,700' million rubles on October 1, 1930 (ZI, September 24, 1930 (Dukor)).

Table 8. Grain collections, 1926/27–1930/31 (thousand tons of grain-equivalent units, except where otherwise stated)

(a) By type of collection

	1926/27	*1927/28*	*1928/29*	*1929/30*	*1930/31*
Centralised collections	10610[1a]	10115[1a]	8300[3]	13160[4f]	—
Decentralised collections	1034[b]	934[d]	1050[3]	611[4f]	—
Total general collections	11644[2c]	11049[2c]	9350[2]	13781[2]	19916[2]
Milling levy:					
grain-surplus areas	—	—	1270[3e]	1729[5g]	
grain-deficit areas	—	—	160[3e]	501[b]	
Total milling levy	—	—	1440[2]	2300[2]	2224[2h]
Total collections	11644[2]	11049[2]	10789[2]	16081[2]	22139[2]

Sources: [1] *Ezhegodnik khlebooborota*, ii (1929), ii, 15–17.
[2] *Ibid.* iv–v (1932), i, 25.
[3] *Ibid.* iii (1931), i, p. xvii.
[4] *Ibid.*, iv–v (1932), ii, 80.
[5] *Spravochnik po khlebnomu delu* (1932), 46.

Notes: [a] Original data adjusted in original source for comparability with 1928/29; these figures at this stage were described as for planned organisations, and did not include decentralised (local) collections (cf. note f below).
[b] Residual.
[c] *Spravochnik po khlebnomu delu* (1932), 32–5, gives 11,622 for 1926/27 and 11,015 for 1927/28.
[d] Residual: given as 776 in source 3 above, which gives centralised collections as 10,273, and the same figure for total collections.
[e] Source 3 gives total milling levy as 1,430.
[f] Both centralised and decentralised collections are now described as from planned organisations (cf. note a above).
[g] 'Centralised part'.
[h] According to *Ezhegodnik khlebooborota*, iv–v (1932), ii, 95, an additional 96,000 tons was left in cooperatives, giving a total of 2,320,000 tons.

Table 8 *(contd.)*

(b) By type of grain

	1926/27	*1927/28*	*1928/29*	*1929/30*	*1930/31*
Food grains (rye and wheat)	8950	8648	6931	8881	14708
Other grains	2694	2401	3849	7200	7431
Total	11644	11049	10780	16081	22139

Source: *Ezhegodnik khlebooborota*, iv–v (1932), i, 25.

(c) Production and collections by social sector, 1929/30–1930/31 (million tons, excluding milling levy)

	1929/30		*1930/31*	
	Production[1]	*Collections*[2]	*Production*[3e]	*Collections*[4]
Sovkhozy	1·33[a]	0·39[c]	3·26[a]	1·27
Kolkhozy: including individual sowings	2·71[b]	1·51[d]	27·4	6·71
Individual peasants	67·71[b]	11·88[d]	52·9	11·93
Total	71·74	13·78	83·5	19·92

Sources: [1] *Nar. kh.* (1932), 162–3.
[2] *Ezhegodnik khlebooborota*, iv–v (1932), ii, 90.
[3] See Table 11.
[4] *Ezhegodnik khlebooborota*, iv–v (1932), i, 25, ii, 103.

Notes: [a] Sovkhozy, koopkhozy, ORSy and other farming enterprises.
[b] Production from individual sowings of collective farmers is not included with kolkhozy but with individual peasants, so these figures are not exactly comparable with collections.
[c] This figure is given in a variety of sources, but is almost certainly misleading. According to *Sdvigi* (1931), 157, sovkhozy with a production of only 1·08 million tons marketed 0·73 million tons, while *Nar. kh.* (1932), 124, reported that sovkhozy producing 1·33 million tons marketed about 0·69 millions. It is unlikely that much of the sovkhoz 'marketing' found its way to the free market, but for some reason it was not all included in the official collection figures.
[d] See note b. According to *Sdvigi* (1931), 157, total marketings by kolkhozy from their collective sowings amounted to 1·22 million tons; this was probably roughly equal to the collections figure.
[e] The production figures for 1930 are almost certainly too high; total production was probably 77·2 million tons (see p. 349 above).

Table 8 *(contd.)*

(d) By months

	1926/27[1a]	*1927/28*[1a]	*1928/29*[2b]	*1929/30*[3b]	*1930/31*[4b]
July	242	285	136	289	425
August	771	995	625	1921	2915
September	1435	1377	1602	3911	4944
First quarter	2448	2657	2363	6121	8284
October	1600	1066	2007	5096	6522
November	1610	690	1223	2304	3916
December	1504	680	1351	1124	1553
Second quarter	4714	2437	4581	8524	11991
Total July–December	7162	5094	6944	14646	20275
Total January–June	3678	5179	3847	1434	1864
Total for year	10841	10273	10790	16081	22139

Sources: [1] *Spravochnik po khlebnomu delu* (1932), 46.
[2] *Ezhegodnik khleboborota*, iii (1931), ii, 12, 17.
[3] *Ibid*. iv–v (1932), ii, 82, 84.
[4] *Ibid*. iv–v (1932), ii, 92, 96.

Notes: [a] Centralised collections.
[b] All general collections and whole of milling levy.

Table 8 *(contd.)*

(e) Production and collections, by area supplying grain, 1928/29–1930/31

	1928/29					
	Production	*General collection*	*Milling levy*	*Total collections*	*Total collections as % of production*	*Production*
1. RSFSR,						
Grain-deficit zone[a]	12471	215	110	325	2·6	12881
Central Black-Earth	5876	587	96	683	11·6	7043
Urals	4936	781	107	888	18·0	3627
Central Volga	5288	1043	102	1145	21·7	3402
Lower Volga	3777	874	98	972	25·7	3267
North Caucasus[b]	5128	918	169	1087	21·2	5441
Siberia[c]	8618	1770	167	1937	22·5	6481
Kazakhstan ASSR	3670	955	53	1008	27·5	2025
Other grain-surplus regions[d]	4135	538	57	595	14·4	3248
Total RSFSR	53899	7681	959	8640	16·0	47415
2. Ukrainian SSR	13886	1445	440	1885	13·6	18702
3. Belorussian SSR	1769	23	40	63	3·6	1894
4. Transcaucasian SSR	1824	28	—	28	1·5	1714
5. Central Asia (incl. Kirgiz ASSR)	1975	173	—	173	8·8	2018
Total for USSR	73320	9350	1440	10789	14·7	71742

Source: *Nar. kh.* (1932), 172–3, 332–9.

Notes: [a] Northern, Leningrad, Western, Moscow, Ivanovo and Nizhnii Novgorod regions.

[b] Includes Dagestan ASSR.

[c] Includes Far Eastern region, and (except in 1930/31, for which figures are not available) Buryat-Mongolian ASSR.

[d] Bashkiria, Tatar and Crimean ASSRs.

[e] These harvest figures for 1930/31 are believed to be overestimates in comparison with the previous years (see p. 349 above).

[f] The slight discrepancy from the total in the other tables is not explained.

1929/30				*1930/31*				
General collection	*Milling levy*	*Total collections*	*Total collections as % of production*	*Production*[e]	*General collection*	*Milling levy*	*Total collections*	*Total collections as % of production*
764	327	1091	8·5	13013	1125	305	1430	11·0
1600	205	1805	25·6	7568	1804	209	2013	26·6
570	138	708	19·5	4295	1180	133	1313	30·6
666	114	780	22·9	4318	1286	133	1419	32·6
1019	126	1145	35·0	3952	1468	146	1614	40·8
1537	234	1771	32·5	6676	2061	249	2310	34·6
1383	181	1564	24·1	7799	1769	164	1924	24·7
589	35	624	30·8	2300	735	28	763	33·2
576	99	675	20·8	4311	946	114	1071	24·8
8704	1459	10163	21·4	54232	12373	1481	13854	25·5
4564	736	5300	28·3	23172	6921	754	7675	33·1
106	75	181	9·6	2016	126	60	186	9·2
80	16	96	5·6	1952	119	10	129	6·6
328	14	342	16·9	2174	376	15	391	18·0
13781	2300	16081	22·4	83545	19916	2320	22236[f]	26·6

Table 9. Grain allocation, 1926/27–1930/31 (thousand tons of grain equivalent)

(a) All planned turnover by main uses

	1926/27	*1927/28*	*1928/29*	*1929/30*	*1930/31*
1. Supply of population (including fodder)					
General supply				7466[7]	9085[10]
Special-purpose supplies				2080[7h]	2929[9]
Deductions from milling levy				201[7]	126[9]
Total	6988[1]	8966[1]	7331[5d]	9747[7]	12141[10]
2. Army, industry, seeds, etc.					
Army, etc.	508[2]	465[2]	591[e]	n.a.	n.a.
Industry	249[3]	298[2c]	283[6f]	823[7]	1239[10]
Seeds	341[a]	437[e]	810[6]	1263[7]	452[10]
Total	898[1]	1200[1]	1684[5]	2086	1791
Total on internal market (1+2)	7886[1]	10166[1]	9015[5]	11831[7]	13832[10]
3. Net exports	2488[1]	426[1]	−184[5g]	1343[8i]	5832[8i]
4. Additions to stocks	−73[4]	−282[4]	300[4]	1298[4]	248[4]
Total allocation	10301[b]	10310[b]	9131[b]	14472[b]	19912[b]

Sources: [1] Moshkov (1966), 118 (calculated from *10 let na khlebnom fronte* (1932)).
[2] Konyukhov (1951), app. 2.
[3] *Ezhegodnik khlebooborota*, i (1928), ii, 52.
[4] Calculated from data *ibid.* iv–v (1932), i, 31.
[5] *Ibid.* iii (1931), i, p. xix.
[6] *Ibid.* iii (1931), ii, 30–1.
[7] *Ibid.* iv–v (1932), ii, 146–7.
[8] *Ibid.* iv–v (1932), ii, 144–5.
[9] *Ibid.* iv–v (1932), i, 27–8.
[10] *Ibid.* iv–v (1932), ii, 186–7.

Notes: [a] Residual.
[b] Calculated by present author; no allowance for losses.
[c] 326,000 tons if allocations to industry from general supplies are included (*Ezhegodnik khlebooborota*, ii (1929), ii, 31).
[d] Given as 8,033,000 tons in *Ezhegodnik khlebooborota*, iv–v (1932), i, 27; this figure, which also appears in *ibid.* iii (1931), ii, 123, apparently includes sales from local (decentralised) collections, and may therefore be a better figure for comparison with 1929/30 and 1930/31; the inclusion of this figure would give a total allocation on internal market (including Army) of 9,730,000 and a total allocation (including exports and stocks) of 9,846,000.

Table 9 *(contd.)*

[e] Residual.
[f] Given as 313,000 tons, *ibid.* iv–v (1932), i, 30; this presumably includes allocations to industry from general supplies (as in note c above), and is probably therefore the comparable figure with those for 1929/30 and 1930/31.
[g] Imports were 268,000, exports 84,000 tons.
[h] Given as 2,003,000, *ibid.* iv–v (1932), i, 27.
[i] Grain despatched to ports for export (otgruzka); includes unplanned exports in physical terms. Actual exports were about 94,000 tons less in 1929/30 and 323,000 tons less in 1930/31.

(b) Allocations to population by type of allocation, 1929/30–1930/31

	1929/30[1]	*1930/31*[2]
General supply	7242	8754
Deduction from milling levy	200	126
Lumber industry[a]	1030	1264
Fodder for animals and poultry[a]	158	336
Flax and hemp[a]	159	153
Fats and milk[a]	70	62
Cotton (excluding Central Asia)[a]	56	91
Other special allocations[a]	160	202
Soyuzzoloto (gold industry)[a]	—	115
Central Asia: population (urban)	223[b]	331[b]
: cotton[a]	447	637
: other uses[a]	—	69
Total	9746	12141

Sources: [1] *Ezhegodnik khlebooborota*, iv–v (1932), ii, 146–7.
[2] *Ibid.* 186–7.

Notes: [a] These items, allocated to particular industries or to encourage certain types of agriculture, form part of special-purpose supplies in Table 9(a).
[b] Included with general supply in Table 9(a).

Table 9 *(contd.)*

(c) Allocation to industry by type of industry, 1928/29–1930/31

	1928/29[1]	*1929/30*[2]	*1930/31*[3]
Macaroni and biscuit	57	145	314
Alcohol	124	509	733
Beer and yeast	72[a]	85	88
Starch and molasses	27	83	68
Other	33	—	27
Total	313	823	1239

Sources: [1] *Ezhegodnik khlebooborota*, iv–v (1932), i, 30.
[2] *Ibid.*, iv–v (1932), ii, 146–7.
[3] *Ibid.*, iv–v (1932), ii, 186–7.

Notes: [a] Misprinted as 12 in original source.

(d) Centralised stocks by main types of grain, July 1, 1927–July 1, 1931 (thousand tons)

	July 1, 1927	*July 1, 1928*	*July 1, 1929*	*July 1, 1930*	*July 1, 1931*
Food grains	644	415	479	1252	1422
Fodder grains	64	33	204	630	638
Meal, beans and other grains	60	38	103	202	272
Total stocks	768	486	786	2084	2332

Source: *Ezhegodnik khlebooborota*, iv–v (1932), i, 31.

Table 10. Quarterly livestock collections,[a] 1928/29–1930/31 (thousand tons)

	Meat and fat in terms of carcass weight	*Animals and meat in terms of live weight*
July–September 1928	204[1b]	
October–December 1928	284[1b]	
January–March 1929	219[1b]	
April–June 1929	246[1b]	
July–September 1929		615[2]
October–December 1929		881[2]
January–March 1930		462[2]
April–June 1930		238[2]
July–September 1930		460[2]

Table 10. *(contd.)*

	Meat and fat in terms of carcass weight	*Animals and meat in terms of live weight*
October–December 1930		567[2]
January–March 1931		955[2]
April–June 1931		360[2]
Agricultural year 1928/29	954[3]	1821[2]
Agricultural year 1929/30	1067[3]	2196[2]
Agricultural year 1930/31	1039[3]	2343[2]
Calendar year 1930		1739[2]
Calendar year 1931		2819[2]

Source: [1] Nifontov (1932), 290–1.
[2] *Ibid*. 298–9.
[3] *Ibid*. 288–9.

Notes: [a] These figures include collections not for meat but for adding to herd of socialist sector; these were certainly small until the autumn of 1929. They were estimated, in terms of live weight, at 434,000 out of 1,739,000 tons in 1930 and 705,000 out of 2,819,000 tons in 1931 (Nifontov (1932), 298–9).
[b] 'Approximate figures'.

Table 11. Households penalised for failure to deliver grain, Autumn 1929

	No. of households fined	*No. of households of which property partly or fully confiscated*
Central Volga[1a]	20000	6000
North Caucasus[2]	n.a.	30–35000
Siberia[2]	13000	6000[b]
Kazakhstan[3]	n.a.[c]	52000[d]
Ukraine[4]	n.a.	33000[e]

Sources: [1] IZ, lxxx (1967), 89.
[2] Ivnitskii (1972), 115.
[3] *Kollektivizatsiya*, i (Alma-Ata, 1967), 361.
[4] IZ, lxxix (1967), 43.

Notes: [a] These figures refer to the autumn of 1929 up to and including December.
[b] Number 'sentenced' (osuzhdeno).
[c] A value of nearly 24 million rubles was imposed in fines and confiscations of property, including 53,000 head of cattle (Ivnitskii (1972), 115, mistakenly gives a figure of 'nearly 14 million rubles').
[d] This figure is stated to be those 'put on trial' *in addition to* the fines and confiscations (see note c).
[e] This refers to spring and autumn 1929, so it includes some actions undertaken at the end of the 1928/29 campaign.

Table 12. Grain production by social sector: plan and result, 1930 harvest (million tons)

	June 1930 (Stalin)	*July 1930 plan*	*As %*	*August 1930 estimate*	*September 1930 estimate*	*As %*	*November 1930 estimate*	*1931 estimate*[6]	*1932 estimate*[7]	*1932 estimate adjusted*
Sovkhozy	2·8[1]	}			[3·0[c]]	3·4[4]		3·1[i]	3·3[g]	3·3[g]
Kolkhozy: excluding individual sowings	25·6[1]	} [34·7[a]]	39[2]				[24·3[5d]]	25·3	23·2	—
Kolkhozy: including individual sowings					[31·8[c]]	36·1[4]	—	—	—	27·4[h]
Individual poor and middle peasants		[51·6[a]]	58[2]		[53·2[c]]	} 60·5[4]	} [59·2[5e]]	} 59·1	} 57·1	} 52·9[h]
Kulaks		[2·7[a]]	3[2]			}	}	}	}	}
Total		[88·9]	100[2]	[87·9[3b]]	[88·0[c]]	100·0	87[f]	87·4	83·5	83·5

Sources: [1] Stalin, *Soch.*, xii, 284, 288 (report to XVI congress, June 27, 1930).
[2] PKh, 6, 1930, 12–13 (Chernov).
[3] P, August 17, 1930 (Chernov).
[4] EZh, September 27, 1930 (K. Bagdasarov).
[5] EZh, November 7, 1930 (Chernov).
[6] *Sdvigi* (1931), 200.
[7] *Nar. kh.* (1932), 162–3.

Notes: [a] Calculated by applying percentages to plan of 88·9 million tons (*KTs . . . na 1929/30* (1930), 533).
[b] Autumn and spring sowings for 1930 harvest reported as 9 per cent greater than for 1929 harvest, yield as 12 per cent greater. Hence output is 72 million tons (figure accepted for 1929) × 1·09 × 1·12 = 87·9.
[c] These figures assume a total harvest estimate of 88 million tons (given in P, October 24, 1930). The figure of 31·8 million tons for kolkhozy includes harvest from individual autumn sowings of collective farmers who joined the kolkhozy after these sowings. Gosplan figure for kolkhoz production, which excluded these sowings, was 30·6 per cent of all grain production (i.e. 26·9 million tons) (PKh, 7–8, 1930, 52 (Minaev)).
[d] Approximate: 4·26 tons per household × 5·7 million households.
[e] Approximate: 2·89 tons per household × 20·5 million households.
[f] If calculations in notes d and e are correct and sovkhoz harvest was 3 million tons.
[g] Sovkhozy include 'output of agricultural enterprises of government departments and establishments in rural localities'.
[h] 18 per cent has been added to kolkhoz harvest (4·2 million tons) to include grain from individual winter sowings of collective farmers, and 4·2 millions has been deducted from individual peasants; 18 per cent is the difference between the earlier Gosplan and Bagdasarov figures (see note c).
[i] Sovkhozy include 'sovkhozy, in trusts and not in trusts, and agricultural enterprises of establishments'; coverage may be wider than in 1931 estimate, which only includes those enterprises of establishments which are located in the countryside.

Table 13. Grain collections: plan and result, 1930 harvest (million tons)

	June 1930 (Stalin)	*As %*	*July 1930 Plan*	*As %*	*July 1930 (Mikoyan)*	*As %*	*August 1930 Plan*	*As %*	*September 1930 Plan*	*As %*	*October 1930 Plan*	*Final Plan*[7]	*Fulfil-ment*[8]
Sovkhozy	1·8[1]		} [12·8[c]] (Sovkhozy and Kolkhozy)	} 52[2] (Sovkhozy and Kolkhozy)		} 60[3] (Sovkhozy and Kolkhozy)	[1·8]	8	[1·8[h]]	8·0[5]		1·37	1·37
Kolkhozy (including individual sowings by collective farmers)	8·2[1]	>50[1a]					[10·1[g]]	44[4]	[9·5[h]]	42·1[5]	10·4[6]	6·75[i]	6·71[i]
Individual peasants:													
contracted			[6·2[c]]	25[2]			[5·8[g]]	25[4]	[5·5[h]]	24·4[5]		} 11·97 (Individual peasants)	11·93
not contracted			[4·9[c]]	20[2]			[4·6[g]]	20[4]	[2·7[h]]	12·1[5]			
kulaks			[0·7[c]]	3[2]			[0·7[g]]	3[4]					
Milling levy			[2·5[c]]						[2·5[h]]	11·1[5]		2·61	2·22
Return of seed loan									[0·5[h]]	2·3[5]		0·50	?
Total	[<16·4[b]]		[24·6[d]]	100[2]	[21·3[c]]		[22·5[f]]	100[4]	[22·5]	100·0[5]		23·20	22·14

Sources: [1] Stalin, *Soch.*, xii, 284, 288, 289 (report to XVI party congress on June 27, 1930); marketable production.
[2] PKh, 6, 1930 12–13, 19 (Chernov); marketable production.
[3] P, July 29, 1930; collections.
[4] P, August 17, 1930 (Chernov).
[5] EZh, September 27, 1930 (K. Bagdasarov).
[6] *Kollektivist*, 19, October 15, 1930, 2.
[7] *Ezhegodnik khleboobrota*, iv–v (1932), i, 25.
[8] *Ibid.* iv–v (1932), ii, 103.

Notes: [a] Stalin stated 'we have the possibility of receiving this year *more than half* of all marketed production of grain in the country from the kolkhozy'. In SZe, June 3, 1930, Mikoyan stated that the proportion of grain collections from sovkhozy and kolkhozy would be over 60 per cent; this is compatible with Stalin's statement.

[b] Calculated from Stalin's figures for kolkhozy; refers to 'marketed production' of grain, not to grain collections as such, but this was now often used as a synonym for collections.

[c] These figures are based on percentages for 'marketable production' (tovarnost'), and calculated as follows:

(1) Sovkhozy and kolkhozy. In July 1930 it was estimated that they would produce 39 per cent of grain production (PKh, 6, 1930, 12–13; article by Chernov, which from its context was written at the same time as his article in SZe, July 19, 1930). Grain production was planned at 88·9 million tons (*KTs . . . na 1929/30* (1930), 53; plan of November 1929, not revised later); so sovkhoz and kolkhoz production was planned at 39 per cent of this, about 34·7 million tons. This figure evidently includes the individual autumn sowings of collective farmers, as EZh, September 27, 1930, in giving sovkhozy plus kolkhozy as 39·5 per cent of the harvest, explicitly states that this includes these sowings.

Marketed production of sovkhozy was planned at 37 per cent of their harvest, which, applied to 34·7, gives 12·8 million tons.

(2) Individual peasants: calculated from percentages, on assumption that sovkhozy and kolkhozy were 12·8 million tons.

(3) Milling levy: calculated as residual.

[d] Approximate figure, calculated on assumption that 12·8 million tons is 52 per cent of marketable grain; as our calculations are based on rounded percentages, this figure could well be somewhat higher or somewhat lower; the true July plan could have been identical to the August plan of about 22·5 million tons. The figure of 24·6 million tons is given in BP (Prague), xcv (March 1932), 3, but without source or date.

[e] Approximate figure, calculated on assumption that grain collections from sovkhozy and kolkhozy equalled their marketed production.

[f] Approximate figure, calculated from statement that 8 per cent would come from sovkhozy, on assumption that 1·8 million ton figure for sovkhozy was unchanged from June ($\frac{100}{8} \times 1{\cdot}8 = 22{\cdot}5$); Chernov also stated in P, August 27, 1930, that 'marketability' of grain in 1930 was 26 per cent (i.e. 23 million tons) as compared with 19 per cent (i.e. 14 millions) in 1929.

[g] Calculated from percentages, on assumption that total is 22·5 million tons. A decree of Kolkhoztsentr gave the total collection plan from kolkhozy as 9·59 million tons, including 2·11 million tons from the individual sowings of collective farmers (see p. 348, n. 49 above); these figures evidently excluded the milling levy.

[h] Calculated from percentages, on assumption that total was still above 22·5 million tons, as in August.

[i] These and and other sources do not specifically state that collections from the individual sowings of collectives farmers are included with collections from kolkhozy, but this seems very likely. According to Chernov, collective farmers 'were entitled to hand over grain in accordance with the contracts they had signed' as individual peasants, but, as this would have resulted in very complicated accounts, the authorities endeavoured to persuade them to hand over grain at the rate of the kolkhoz delivery norm (*Ezhegodnik khlebooborota*, iv–v (1932), i, 21); this implies that these collections were put together with the collections from the socialised harvest of kolkhozy. But the possibility is not excluded that some part of the 2·1 million tons planned for collection from individual sowings (see note g) may have been included with collections from individual peasants.

Table 14. Grain yields by social sector, 1930 (tons per hectare)

	First estimate: August–September 1930	*Revised estimate: 1932*		
	All sowings	*Autumn sowings*	*Spring sowings*	*All sowings*
Sovkhozy	1·03	1·33	0·78	0·94
Kolkhozy (socialised sown area)	0·91	1·02	0·79	0·83
Individual peasant households (including individual sowings of collective farmers)	0·84	0·87	0·83	0·85

Sources: First estimate:

Assumes sown area as in Table 4 (July 1930 estimate, and production as in Table 12 (September 1930 estimate) (see note c for production on socialised sown area of kolkhozy).

Revised estimate:

Assumes sown area as in Table 4 (1932 estimate) and production as in Table 12 (1932 estimate) and *Nar. kh.* (1932), 162–3. This estimate covers a wider range of agricultural enterprises under sovkhozy than the first estimate (see Table 12, note i).

Table 15. Grain production and collections per household and per hectare, by social sector, 1930 (tons)

	Per household		Per hectare	
	Individual peasant	*Collective farmer*	*Individual peasant*	*Collective farmer*
1. Original plan, July–September 1930				
Grain production	2·69	5·51	0·80	0·99
Grain collections	0·53	1·77	0·17	0·31
Grain remaining	2·16	3·74	0·64	0·68
2. Result of campaign (assuming grain production 83·5 million tons)				
Grain production	2·61	4·81	0·82	0·90
Grain collections	0·66	1·32	0·21	0·25
Grain remaining	1·95	3·49	0·61	0·65

Sources: Original plan:

per household: from EZh, September 27, 1930.

per hectare:

(1) Sown area from Table 4 (July 1930 estimate) and then adjusted to include individual sowings by collective farmers under kolkhozy.

(2) Production and grain collections: see Table 12 (September 1930 estimate) and Table 13 (August 1930 plan).

Result of campaign:

per household:

(1) Production from Table 12 (adjusted 1932 estimate); Collections from Table 13 (fulfilment), with 0·8 million tons added to the collections from the kolkhozy, i.e. 7·5 million tons, and 1·4 million tons added to the collections from the individual peasants i.e. 13·3 million tons (milling levy, estimated as roughly proportionate to grain production).

(2) Number of households: kolkhoz households taken as 5·7 millions (the figure for July 1930—see Table 16); individual households 20·3 millions in spring 1930 (*Ezhegodnik po sel. kh. 1931* (1933), 233); the latter figure may be somewhat too high (see Table 17, sources).

per hectare:

(1) Sown area derived from Table 4 (1932 estimate) on assumption that individual sowing of collective farmers in this estimate were reduced by the same proportion in relation to the July 1930 estimate as were sowings by individual peasants;

(2) Production, collections and number of households: as for 'result of campaign: per household', above.

Note: All figures include individual sowings by collective farmers in autumn of 1930, and resulting production in 1930, under kolkhozy. It is not certain that all collections from these individual sowings appear in the figure for collections from kolkhozy used for my calculations of the result of the campaign (7·5 million tons). An alternative calculation, making the most unlikely assumption that the total collections from kolkhozy (including those from individual sowings) were 8·9 million tons (assuming that collections from individual sowings were obtained at the kolkhoz rate, and that none of them were included in the figure of 7·5 million tons), still leaves kolkhozy and collective farmers with 3·24 tons per household and individual peasants with only 2·02 tons.

Table 15 *(contd.)*

All the per hectare calculations have a margin of error in them, also associated with the knotty problem of the individual sowings of collective farmers. This area is evidently considerably underestimated in the July 1930 estimate, as a sown area of 2·42 million hectares (see Table 4) and a production of 4·2 million tons implies a yield of 1·74 tons per hectare, almost twice as large as the yield achieved by individual peasants. It is the apparently high yield from the area individually sown by collective farmers that reverses the relationship between kolkhoz and individual peasant yield in this table as compared with Table 14.

Table 16. Number of households collectivised, 1928–1931 (thousands)

June 1, 1928	417
June 1, 1929	1008
October 1, 1929	1919
January 1, 1930	4627[a]
February 1, 1930	8077
March 1, 1930	14597
March 10, 1930	14980[1]
April 1, 1930	9837
May 1, 1930	7131
May 1930	6000[2]
June 1, 1930	6332
July 1, 1930	5736
August 1, 1930	5581
September 1, 1930	5495
October 1, 1930	5563
November 1, 1930	5746
December 1, 1930	6162
January 1, 1931	6609

Sources: Except where otherwise stated, *Ezhegodnik po sel. kh. 1931* (1931), 440–3 (monthly returns from kolkhozy to Kolkhoztsentr; excludes Yakut ASSR until July 1, 1930, and Kara-Kalpak ASSR).

[1] SO, 3–4, 1930, 109.

[2] *Kolkhozy v 1930 g.* (1931), 7 (kolkhoz census; excludes Yakut ASSR).

Note: [a] This figure appears to be an error, and should probably be over 5,000,000 households (see Table 17, note a).

Table 17. Percentage of peasant households collectivised in selected regions, June 1928–January 1931

	1928	1929		1930			
Region or republic	June 1	June 1	October 1	January 1	February 1	March 1	April 1
USSR	1·7	3·9	7·5	18·1[a]	31·7	57·2	38·6
RSFSR	1·6	3·7	7·3	20·1	34·7	58·6	38·4
Including:							
Western	0·5	1·0	1·8	5·2	12·6	41·2	15·7
Moscow	0·7	1·8	3·3	14·3	37·1	74·2	12·5
Ivanovo-Industrial	0·4	1·0	1·5	4·9	10·2	30·7	9·5
Central Black-Earth	1·3	3·2	5·9	40·5	51·0	83·3	39·6
Ural	1·6	5·2	9·9	38·9	52·1	75·6	57·8
Central Volga	2·3	3·9	8·9	41·7	51·8	60·3	43·8
Lower Volga	2·1	5·9	18·1	56–70[b]	61·1	70·1	54·0
North Caucasus	5·2	7·3	19·1	48·1	62·7	79·4	67·0
Siberia	1·7	4·6	6·8	5·0?[c]	18·8	47·0	43·0
Ukraine	2·5	5·6	10·4	15·9	30·5	60·8	46·5
Uzbekistan	1·2	2·6	3·5	3·5[d]	3·5[d]	28·3	31·2

Sources: These percentages were obtained by dividing the number of households collectivised by the total number of households, except in the case of June 1, 1928, and June 1, 1929, where the percentages are reproduced from *Nar. kh.* (1932), 130–1.

The number of households collectivised in each month is given in *Ezhegodnik po sel. kh. 1931* (1933), 441–7; these are monthly returns from the kolkhozy via Kolkhoztsentr to Narkomzem.

The total number of households in the spring of 1929, taken as 25·5 millions, was calculated by adding 1·0 million households collectivised on June 1 to 24·5 million non-collectivised individual households (*ibid.* 233); sovkhozy are excluded. The number in each region was calculated approximately from the data on the number and percentage of households collectivised on June 1, 1929, in *ibid.* 448–50 and in *Nar. kh.* (1932), 130–1; the figures obtained were only approximate, as the percentages were available to only one decimal place, and they had to be reduced slightly, as the percentages for the USSR in this source implied that the total number of households was 25·8 not 25·5.

The number and percentage of households for June 1, 1930 in *Ezhegodnik po sel. kh. 1931* (1933), 448–50, imply a total number of households amounting to only 24·4 millions. This may be because kulak households are omitted: *Ezhegodnik po sel. kh. 1931* (1933) elsewhere (p. 233) states that the total number of individual households in the spring of 1930 was 20·25 millions, and even if the total of kolkhoz households was taken as only 5·5 millions, this would give a total of 25·75. For consistency, the calculations in the above table therefore assume that the number of households was 25.5 millions throughout; this gives slightly lower percentages than in some other sources. The kolkhoz census of May 1930 also used the number of households in the spring of 1929 for its 1930 calculations (see *Kolkhozy v 1930 g.* (1931), 149).

1930 May 1	June 1	July 1	August 1	September 1	October 1	November 1	December 1	*1931* January 1
28·0	24·8	22·5	21·9	21·5	21·8	22·5	24·2	25·9
25·3	22·4	20·5	20·3	20·0	20·4	21·1	22·8	24·4
8·2	7·4	7·4	6·5	7·2	7·2	7·5	7·8	8·6
7·5	7·3	7·3	7·1	7·1	7·4	7·5	7·8	8·2
5·9	5·5	5·4	5·4	5·4	5·6	5·6	5·7	6·8
18·2	16·0	15·4	15·3	15·0	15·8	17·4	19·9	?
31·9	29·1	27·0	27·8	26·9	27·0	27·7	30·9	33·3
30·1	27·0	27·0	27·0	24·3	24·4	24·6	24·8	26·7
41·4	39·4	36·1	35·4	36·1	37·9	45·2	50·8	57·5
63·2	58·0	50·2	53·1	51·1	52·4	54·2	57·5	60·0
25·6	22·4	21·4	20·1	21·6	21·6	21·9	22·4	23·0
41·5	36·3	31·5	29·6	28·8	28·8	28·8	30·6	33·1
27·0	27·2	27·2	27·4	27·5	27·5	28·8	34·9	37·5

Notes: [a] If adjusted to take account of the underestimates for the Lower Volga region, Siberia and Uzbekistan (see b, c and d), this percentage would increase to at least 19·6 (5 million households, as compared with 4·627 million in the original source). According to Ivnitskii (1972), 189, only 21·6 per cent of households were collectivised by January 20.

[b] The figure of 201·8 thousand households in the original source is evidently a clerical error; it would give only 21·0 per cent collectivised households. According to I, January 5, 1930, 70 per cent of households were reported to be collectivised on January 1; I, January 12, 1930, gives 72 per cent (684, 000 households); I, April 19, 1930, gives 62·5 per cent of households (608,000) for December 15, and states that 'no precise data are available for January 1'. According to Ivnitskii (1972), 189–90, however, citing the archives, the correct percentage was 56·0 (538,000).

[c] This figure, representing a decrease as compared with October 1, 1929, may be a clerical error.

[d] The source repeats the figure for collectivised households already given on October 1, 1929 (29·1 thousand); presumably figures were not available for January 1 and February 1, 1930, but they may be expected to have been substantially higher than 29·1 thousand.

Note on variation in figures for number of households collectivised. The figures for collectivisation from different sources varied considerably. The current returns from regional party committees were evidently often not much more than guesses based on partial information, and tended to be exaggerated. The monthly returns from Kolkhoztsentr on which the above table is based were derived from reports of decisions by general meetings of peasants and therefore also tended to be exaggerated (IA, 2, 1962, 192). Other Narkomzem returns referred to kolkhozy

Table 17 *(contd.)*

which had registered their Statutes, while Narkomfin collected data based on taxation censuses, and the agricultural cooperatives collected data on kolkhozy which had joined the cooperatives; all these sources tended to underestimate the number of households collectivised (IA, 2, 1962, 192). The most reliable data were provided by the censuses of kolkhozy taken in the spring of each year (*Kolkhozy v 1929 godu* (1931), etc.), but these of course lack information on the changes within a particular year, except where it is derived from other sources. The following table of percentage of households collectivised illustrates variations in the statistics for the main grain regions:

	Lower Volga	*Central Volga*	*North Caucasus*
January 1, 1930:			
Current reports	68·2,[1] 72[2]	52[3]	40[4]
Kolkhoztsentr returns	—	41·7[5]	48·1[5]
March 1, 1930			
Narkomzem current report	67·8[6]	56·4[6]	76·8[6]
Kolkhoztsentr returns	70·1[5]	60·3[5]	79·4[5]
May 1930			
Kolkhoztsentr returns: May 1	41·4[5]	30·1[5]	63·2[5]
Kolkhoztsentr returns: June 1	39·4[5]	27·0[5]	58·0[5]
Kolkhoz census: May	37·5[7]	20·5[7]	58·1[7]

Sources: [1] *Nizhnee Povol'zhe*, 2–3, 1930, 184.
[2] EZh, January 12, 1930.
[3] I, January 11, 1930.
[4] P, January 14, 1930.
[5] See Table 17.
[6] I, March 9, 1930.
[7] *Kolkhozy v 1930 g.* (1931), 3.

Table 18. Planned districts of comprehensive collectivisation in RSFSR, summer 1929

Region (1)	*Okrug* (2)	*District(s)* (3)	*Total area of district (thousand hectares)*[1] (4)	*Arable land already collectivised (thousand hectares)* (5)	*Number of households collectivised (thousands)* (6)	*Percentage of total households* (7)	*No. of tractors* (8)	*No. of horses* (9)
Western	Vyazma	Sezhskii	8(19)	0·3	0·6	30·0	12	30
Western	Smolensk	'Svitskii mokh'	(119)					
Ural	Irbit	Yelan', Znamenskii and Baikalovo	135(135)	27·2[2]	3·8[2]	54·4[2]	80	3700
Ural	Ishim	Armizon	90(160)	23·0	2·6	71·0	7	5100
Ural	Shadrinsk	Mekhonskii	(94)	16·8	2·3	37·0		2600
Central Volga	Samara	Chapaev	(210)	67·6	4·4	42·4[a]	139	
Lower Volga	Balashov	Samoilov	80(276)	29·8[b]	2·9	20·0	36	1900
Lower Volga	Volga German ASSR	Krasnyi Kut	90(336)			15·0		
North Caucasus	Terek	Mineral'nye Vody	40(88)	21·0[3]	3·1[3]	50·0[3]	20	
Central Industrial	Tula	Volovo	90(92)		1·2	8·0[c]	10	400
Northern	Vologda	Tiginsk	14(14)	1·1	0·4	48·0[c]	3	270
Total			597[1543]	[186·8]	[21·3]	[32·3]	148[d]	11400[d]

In addition to the above, the following districts gave reports to the July conference which indicated that they considered themselves RSKs (those asterisked also appeared in the list in the report of September 7, 1929, which also included an additional seven districts, or 25 in all: among the additional districts was Novo-Nikolaevskaya in Khoper okrug, the first 'okrug of comprehensive collectivisation' (see p. 130 above):

Table 18 (*contd.*)

(1)	(2)	(3)	(4)	(5)	(6)	(7)	(8)	(9)
* Central Black-Earth[4]	Tambov	Kirsanov	80				40	
Central Black-Earth[4]	Tambov	Inzhavino				20		
* Central Black-Earth[5]	Orel	Sverdlov	125	20·7	3·4	22·7	30	1900
* Bashkiria[4]		Myasogutovskii				26		
* Ural[5]		Shchuch'e(?)		13				
* Kazakhstan[6]	Petropavlovsk	Bulaevo	110	7·7	0·9	14.0	70	
* Central Volga[7]	Samara	Kinel'-Cherkasskii						

Sources: Except where otherwise stated, from an appendix to the report of the July 1929 conference of RSKs in ZKK (1929), 478, and from the Kolkhoztsentr report to the party central committee dated September 7, 1929 (*Materialy*, vii (1959), 232–4); the figures in the latter source are generally consistent with the information already supplied by delegates to the July conference of RSKs.

[1] The figures in brackets are given in the report of September 7, 1929, and demonstrate the unreliability of figures for total area.
[2] ZKK (1929), 28–9.
[3] Derived from ZKK (1929), 425.
[4] *Ibid*. 426.
[5] *Ibid*. 424–5; figures from *Materialy*, vii (1959), 232–3.
[6] ZKK (1929), 422; figures from *Materialy*, vii (1959), 232–3.
[7] ZKK (1929), 427.

Notes: [a] ZKK (1929), 427, gives 25 per cent.
[b] Only 15·2 thousand hectares were actually in agricultural use (osvoeno).
[c] ZKK (1929), 80, gives 6·5 per cent of arable land collectivised.
[d] Our total for six districts for which numbers of both horses and tractors are available.
[e] Percentage of arable land collectivised.

Table 19. Elimination of kulak households, 1929–1931 (thousands)

	Politburo commission, January 1930 (Plan)	'Borisov' series 1929–30	'Borisov' series 1931	'Borisov' series 1929–1931 Total	'Vyltsan' series 1930	'Vyltsan' series 1931	'Vyltsan' series 1930–1931 Total	'Abramov' series 1930	'Abramov' series 1931	'Abramov' series 1930–1931 Total	Other figures 1930	Other figures 1931	Other figures 1929–1931 Total
Category I	63[1]	80[1]	160[1]	[240]	77·98[2c]	162·96[2d]	[240·94]	115·2[3e]	265·8[3e]	381·0[4e]			318·0[6h]
Category II	150[1]												
Category III	(396)[1a] or (852)[a]	250[1]	200[1]	[450]									
Total	(609)[1a] or (1065)[a]	330[1]	370[1]	[700]							320+[5f]	200[6]	568·3[7i]
Self-dekulakised				200[1b]									

Sources: [1] Danilov *et al*., eds. (1970), 239 (Yu. S. Borisov).
[2] VI, 3, 1965, 19 (Vyltsan, Ivnitskii and Polyakov).
[3] *Leninskii kooperativnyi plan* (1969), 108, 121.
[4] VIK, 5, 1975, 140 (Abramov and Kocharli).
[5] *Voprosy agrarnoi istorii* (Vologda, 1968), 50 (Ivnitskii).
[6] Ivnitskii (1972), 292; Trifonov (1975), 376–7.
[7] VI, 7, 1968, 34 (Sidorov).

Notes: Square brackets [ ] indicate calculation by present author based on figures in Soviet source.
[a] See p. 236, n. 153 above for the basis of these alternative figures.
[b] 1929–32.
[c] Category II: exiled from RSKs; but see above, p. 248.
[d] Total exiled in 1931; this figure also appears in *Istoriya KPSS* (1972), 420, where it is said to refer only to exiling from RSKs in March 20–April 25 and May 10–September 18, 1931.
[e] For the dispute about these figures between Ivnitskii, on the one hand, and Abramov and Kocharli, see p. 248, n. 200 above.
[f] Preliminary data of Narkomzem, to July 1930 only.
[g] Towards end of 1931.
[h] Number of former kulak families which have been resettled, and are planned in Narkomzem control figures of September 1931 to receive land (245·4 thousand working in industry, 72·6 thousand in sovkhozy and artels without Statutes); actual number was substantially in excess of 328,000 by end-1931 (see figures in Ivnitskii (1972), 304–18, and Trifonov (1975), 379).
[i] 1930–1.

Table 20. Tractors supplied to agriculture, 1928/29–1930

(a) Annual supply

	Numbers			*Horse-power*		
	Home production	*Imports*	*Total*	*Home production*	*Imports*	*Total*
1928/29	2800	6666	9466	29540	96505	126405
1929/30	10050	23017	33067	103000	445900	548900
October–December 1930	4058	2117	6175	43705	42315	86020

Source of table (a): *Sots. str.* (1935), 303.

(b) Tractor draught-power as percentage of tractor and animal draught-power, by social sector, 1929–1930

	Sovkhozy	*Kolkhozy and MTS etc.*	*All sectors including individual peasants*
October 1, 1929	60·0	62·3	2·8
December 31, 1930	66·2	20·1	7·7

(c) Total mechanical and animal draught-power, 1929–1930 (thousand live h.p. equivalent)

	Animal power	*Mechanised power*	*Total power*
October 1, 1929	27176	782	27958
December 31, 1930	24056	2008	26064

Source of tables (b) and (c): Calculated from *Sots. str.* (1935), 302.

Note: The figures in Tables (b) and (c) exclude vehicles, and assume 1 horse = ½ of a mechanical h.p. According to the source, the second rows in Tables (b) and (c) refer to October 1, 1930, but it is clear from the figures in *Nar. kh.* (1932), 145, that this is an error.

An alternative calculation in Jasny (1949), 453, includes lorries and combines but assumes 1 horse = 0·75 h.p., and concludes that mechanical power was 2 per cent of the total in 1929, 6 per cent in 1930 and 12 per cent in 1931. According to this calculation, horse-power in terms of horses declined from 29·7 million in 1929 to 27·0 in 1930 and 24·2 in 1931.

GLOSSARY OF RUSSIAN TERMS AND ABBREVIATIONS USED IN TEXT

AIK	agro-industrial'nyi kombinat (agro-industrial combine)
aktiv	activists (politically-active members of a community)
art.	article
ASSR	Avtonomnaya Sovetskaya Sotsialisticheskaya Respublika (Autonomous Soviet Socialist Republic)
bai	rich peasants (in Kazakhstan)
batrak	rural labourer
CC	Central Committee [of Communist Party] (Tsentral'nyi komitet)
Cheka	Chrezvychainaya Komissiya (Extraordinary Commission [political police]), *later* GPU or OGPU
CP(b)T	Communist Party (Bolsheviks) of Turkmenia
CPSU(b)	Communist Party of the Soviet Union (Bolsheviks)
disk. listok	diskussionyi listok (discussion sheet)
Gosbank	Gosudarstvennyi Bank (State Bank)
Gosplan	Gosudarstvennaya Planovaya Komissiya (State Planning Commission)
GPU	*see* OGPU
Khlebotsentr	Vserossiskii Soyuz Sel'skokhozyaistvennykh Kooperativov po Proizvodstvu, Pererabotke i Sbytu Zernovykh i Maslichnykh Kul'tur (All-Russian Union of Agricultural Cooperatives for the Production, Processing and Sale of Grains and Oil Seeds)
khutor	peasant farm with fields and cottage enclosed

kolkhoz	kollektivnoe khozyaistvo (collective farm)
kolkhozkoopsoyuz	soyuz sel'skokhozyaistvennykh kollektivov i kooperativnykh obschchestv (union of agricultural collectives and agricultural cooperative societies)
kolkhozsoyuz	soyuz sel'skokhozyaistvennykh kollektivov (union of agricultural collectives)
Kolkhoztsentr	Vserossiskii (*from November 1929* Vsesoyuznyi) Soyuz Sel'skokhozyaistvennykh Kollektivov (All-Russian (*from November 1929* All-Union) Union of Agricultural Collectives)
komsod	komissiya po sodeistviyu khlebozagotovkam (commission to assist the grain collections)
Komsomol	Kommunisticheskii soyuz molodezhi (Communist League of Youth)
koopsoyuz	soyuz kooperativnykh obshchestv (union of [agricultural] cooperative societies)
kopek	1/100 ruble
mir	peasant commune (= zemel'noe obshchestvo (land society), obshchina)
MTS	Mashinno-traktornaya stantsiya (Machine-Tractor Station)
Narkomtorg	Narodnyi Komissariat Vneshnei i Vnutrennoi Torgovli (People's Commissariat of External and Internal Trade)
Narkomput'	Narodnyi Komissariat Putei Soobshcheniya (People's Commissariat of Ways of Communication [i.e. of Transport])
Narkomyust	Narodnyi Komissariat Yustitsii (People's Commissariat of Justice [of RSFSR])
Narkomzem	Narodnyi Komissariat Zemledeliya (People's Commissariat of Agriculture [of RSFSR up to December 1929, then of USSR])
NEP	Novaya ekonomicheskaya politika (New Economic Policy)
NKVD	Narodnyi Komissariat Vnutrennykh Del (People's Commissariat of Internal Affairs)
obshchina	peasant commune (= zemel'noe obshchestvo (land society), mir)
OGPU (GPU)	Ob"edinennoe Gosudarstvennoe Politich-

	eskoe Upravlenie (Unified State Political Administration [Political Police])
okrug	administrative unit between region and district (see p. xx above)
orgraspred	organizatsionno-raspredelitel'nyi otdel (Organisation and Distribution Department [personnel department of party central committee])
ORS	otdel rabochego snabzheniya (department of workers' supply [of food in factories, etc.])
otkhodnichestvo	'going away' to seasonal work outside one's own village or volost'.
otkhodnik	peasant who goes away from village or volost' for seasonal work.
otrub	peasant farm with fields only enclosed
pud	0·01638 tons[1]
pyatikratka	fine up to five times value of grain not delivered
Rabkrin	Narodnyi Komissariat Raboche-Krest'yanskoi Inspektsii (People's Commissariat of Workers' and Peasants' Inspection)
RSFSR	Rossiiskaya Sovetskaya Federativnaya Sotsialisticheskaya Respublika (Russian Soviet Federative Socialist Republic)
RSK	raion sploshnoi kollektivizatsii (district of comprehensive collectivisation)
ruble (rubl')	unit of currency, at par = £0·106 or $0·515
samotek	spontaneous flow [of grain]
skhod	gathering or general assembly of mir
sovkhoz	sovetskoe khozyaistvo (Soviet [i.e. state] farm)
Sovnarkom	Sovet Narodnykh Komissarov (Council of People's Commissars)
Soyuzkhleb	'Union Grain' (All-Union association (ob''edinenie) of Narkomtorg)
Soyuzmyaso	'Union Meat' (All-Union association (ob''edinenie) of Narkomtorg)
SR	Sotsialist-revolyutsioner (Socialist Revolutionary)

[1] Metric tons are used throughout this volume.

SSR	Sovetskaya Sotsialisticheskaya Respublika (Soviet Socialist Republic)
stanitsa	large village in North Caucasus
STO	Sovet Truda i Oborony (Council of Labour and Defence [Economic subcommittee of Sovnarkom])
TOZ	tovarishchestvo po sovmestnoi (*or* obshchestvennoi) obrabotke zemli (association for the joint cultivation of land [simplest form of kolkhoz])
Traktorotsentr	Vsesoyuznyi tsentr mashinno-traktornykh stantsii (All-Union Centre of Machine-Tractor Stations)
troika	committee or group of three persons
tsentner	0·1 tons
Tsentrosoyuz	Vsesoyuznyi tsentral'nyi soyuz potrebitel'skikh obshchestv (All-Union Central Union of Consumers' Societies)
TsIK	Tsentral'nyi Ispolnitel'nyi Komitet (Central Executive Committee [of Soviets of USSR])
volost'	rural district (before 1930, intermediate between village and uezd)
VTsIK	Vserossiskii Tsentral'nyi Ispolnitel'nyi Komitet (All-Russian Central Executive Committee of Soviets)
Zernotrest	Vsesoyuznyi trest zernovykh sovkhozov (All-Union Trust of [New] Grain Sovkhozy)

ABBREVIATIONS OF TITLES OF BOOKS AND PERIODICAL PUBLICATIONS USED IN FOOTNOTES

(For full titles, see appropriate section of Bibliography; items listed below are periodical publications unless otherwise stated.)

B	*Bol'shevik*
BO	*Byulleten' Oppozitsii*
BP	*Byulleten' ekonomicheskogo kabineta prof. S. N. Prokopovicha*
BU NKZ RSFSR	*Byulleten' uzakonenii . . . NKZ RSFSR*
DK	*Derevenskii kommunist*
EO	*Ekonomicheskoe obozrenie*
EZh	*Ekonomicheskaya zhizn'*
FP	*Finansovye problemy planovogo khozyaistva*
I	*Izvestiya*
IA	*Istoricheskii arkhiv*
IISO	*Istochnikovedenie istorii sovetskogo obshchestva*
IS	*Istoriya SSSR*
IZ	*Istoricheskie zapiski*
Izv. TsK	*Izvestiya Tsentral'nogo Komiteta*
KG	*Krest'yanskaya gazeta*
KGN	*Krest'yanskaya gazeta: izdanie dlya nizhne-vol'zhskogo kraya*
KTs . . . na . . .	*Kontrol'nye tsifry narodnogo khozyaistva SSSR na . . .* (books)
NAF	*Na agrarnom fronte*
NFK	*Na fronte kollektivizatsii*
NPF	*Na planovom fronte*
P	*Pravda*
PE	*Problemy ekonomiki*

PKh	*Planovoe khozyaistvo*
PS	*Partiinoe stroitel'stvo*
SKhG	*Sel'skokhozyastvennaya gazeta*
SKhIB	*Sel'skokhozyaistvennyi informatsionnyi byulleten'*
SO	*Statisticheskoe obozrenie*
SRSKh	*Sotsialisticheskaya rekonstruktsiya sel'skogo khozyaistva*
SS	*Soviet Studies*
ST	*Sovetskaya torgovlya*
St. spr. 1928	*Statisticheskii spravochnik SSSR za 1928* (book)
SU	*Sobranie uzakonenii*
SZ	*Sobranie zakonov*
SZe	*Sotsialisticheskoe zemledelie*
SZo	*Sotsialisticheskoe zemleustroistvo*
TPG	*Torgovo-promyshlennaya gazeta*
TsIK 2/V	*2 [Vtoraya] sessiya Tsentral'nogo Ispolnitel'nogo Komiteta* (book)
VF	*Vestnik finansov*
VI	*Voprosy istorii*
VIK	*Voprosy istorii KPSS*
VKA	*Vestnik Kommunisticheskoi Akademii*
VT	*Voprosy torgovli*
VTr	*Voprosy truda*
ZI	*Za industrializatsiyu*
ZKK	*Za krupnye kolkhozy* (book)

BIBLIOGRAPHY

Letters used as abbreviations for items in the bibliography are listed on pp. 453–4. All other books are referred to in the text footnotes either by their author or editor, or by an abbreviated title (always including the first word or syllable) when there is no author or editor, and by date of publication.

Place of publication is Moscow or Moscow–Leningrad, unless otherwise stated.

Only items referred to in the text are included in the bibliography.

SECTION I NEWSPAPERS, JOURNALS AND OTHER PERIODICAL PUBLICATIONS

Bol'shevik

Byulleten' ekonomicheskogo kabineta prof. S. N. Prokopovicha (Prague)

Byulleten' Kon''yunkturnogo Instituta

Byulleten' Oppozitsii (bol'shevikov-lenintsev) (Paris)

Byulleten' uzakonenii i rasporyazhenii po sel'skomu i lesnomu khozyaistvu: ezhenedel'nyi offitsial'nyi organ NKZ RSFSR

Derevenskii kommunist

Economic Development and Cultural Change (Chicago)

Economic Journal (London)

Ekonomicheskaya zhizn'

Ekonomicheskii vestnik (Berlin)

Ekonomicheskoe obozrenie

Ezhegodnik khlebooborota

Finansovye problemy planovogo khozyaistva (*Vestnik finansov* until no. 2, 1930)

Finansy i sotsialisticheskoe khozyaistvo

Istoricheskii arkhiv

Istoricheskie zapiski

Istochnikovedenie istorii sovetskogo obshchestva

Istoriya SSSR

Izvestiya
Izvestiya Tsentral'nogo Komiteta Vsesoyuznoi Kommunisticheskoi partii (b) (*Partiinoe stroitel'stvo* from November 1929)
Khlebotsentr
Kollektivist
Krasnaya zvezda
Krasnyi Khoper (Uryupinsk)
Krest'yanskaya gazeta
Krest'yanskaya gazeta: izdanie dlya nizhne-vol'zhskogo kraya
Materialy po istorii SSSR
Na agrarnom fronte
Na fronte kollektivizatsii
Na planovom fronte
Nizhnee povol'zhe (Saratov)
Partiinoe stroitel'stvo (*Izvestiya Tsentral'nogo Komiteta* until October 10, 1929)
Planovoe khozyaistvo
Povol'zhskaya pravda (Stalingrad)
Pravda
Problemy ekonomiki
Puti sel'skogo khozyaistva
Russkii ekonomicheskii sbornik (Berlin)
Sel'skokhozyaistvennaya gazeta (*Sotsialisticheskoe zemledelie* from January 29, 1930)
Sel'skokhozyaistvennyi informatsionnyi byulleten'
Slavic Review (Urbana-Champaign)
Sobranie uzakonenii i rasporyazhenii RSFSR
Sobranie zakonov i rasporyazhenii SSSR
Sotsialisticheskaya rekonstruktsiya sel'skogo khozyaistva
Sotsialisticheskii vestnik (Berlin)
Sotsialisticheskoe zemledelie (*Sel'skokhozyaistvennaya gazeta* until January 28, 1929)
Sotsialisticheskoe zemleustroistvo
Sovetskaya torgovlya
Soviet Studies (Oxford to xix, 1967–8, then Glasgow)
Statisticheskoe obozrenie
Statistika i narodnoe khozyaistvo
Torgovo-promyshlennaya gazeta (*Za industrializatsiyu* from beginning of 1930)
Vestnik finansov (*Finansovye problemy planovogo khozyaistva* from no. 3, 1930)

Vestnik Kommunisticheskoi Akademii
Vestnik krest'yanskoi Rossii (Prague)
Vlast' sovetov
Vneshnyaya torgovlya
Voprosy istorii
Voprosy istorii KPSS
Voprosy torgovli
Voprosy truda
Voprosy vneshnei torgovli
Za industrializatsiyu (*Torgovo-promyshlennaya gazeta* until end of 1929)

SECTION II BOOKS IN RUSSIAN

Andreev, A. A., *Uspekhi i nedostatki kolkhoznogo stroitel'stva, rech' na Rostovskom partaktive 18 marta 1930 goda* (Rostov, 1930)
Anfimov, A. M., *Krupnoe pomeshchich'e khozyaistvo Evropeiskoi Rossii (konets XIX-nachalo XX veka)* (1969)
Anfimov, A. M., *Rossiiskaya derevnya v gody pervoi mirovoi voiny (1914 fevral' 1917 g.)* (1962)
Arina, A. E., Kotov, G. G., Loseva, K. V., *Sotsial'no – ekonomicheskie izmeneniya v derevne: Melitopol'skii raion (1885–1938 gg.)* (1939)
Arkheograficheskli ezhegodnik za 1968 god (1970)
Barsov, A. A., *Balans stoimostnykh obmenov mezhdu gorodom i derevnei* (1969)
Bogdenko, M. L., *Stroitel'stvo zernovykh sovkhozov v 1928–1932 gg.* (1958)
Bukharin, N. I., *Put' k sotsializmu v Rossii: izbrannye proizvedeniya* (New York, 1967)
Chernopitskii, P. G., *Na velikom perelome: Sel'skie Sovety Dona v period podgotovki i provedeniya massovoi kollektivizatsii (1928–1931 gg.)* (Rostov, 1965)
Chigrinov, G. A., *Bor'ba KPSS za organizatsionno-khozyaistvennoe ukreplenie kolkhozov v dovoennye gody* (1970)
Danilov, V. P., *Sozdanie material'no-tekhnicheskikh predposylok kollektivizatsii sel'skogo khozyaistva v SSSR* (1957)
Danilov, V. P., *Sovetskaya dokolkhoznaya derevnya: naselenie, zemlepol'zovanie, khozyaistvo* (1977)
Danilov, V. P., ed., *Ocherki istorii sel'skogo khozyaistva v soyuznykh respublikakh* (1963)
Danilov, V. P., Kim, M. P., and Tropkina, N. V., eds., *Sovetskoe*

krest'yanstvo: Kratkii ocherk istorii (1917–1969) (1970)

Direktivy KPSS i sovetskogo pravitel'stva po khozyaistvennym voprosam: sbornik dokumentov, vol. I, *1917–1928 gody* (1957)

Dmitrenko, V. P., *Torgovaya politika sovetskogo gosudarstva posle perekhoda k nepu, 1921–1924 gg.* (1971)

Eikhe, R. I., *Likvidatsiya kulaka kak klassa* (Novosibirsk, 1930)

Ezhegodnik po sel'skomu khozyaistvu Sovetskogo Soyuza za 1931 god (1933)

Gaister, A. I., ed., *Kollektivizatsiya sovetskoi derevni: predvaritel'nye itogi sploshnykh obsledovanii, 1928 i 1929 gg.* (1929)

Gaister, A. I., ed., *Zhivotnovodstvo SSSR: dinamika skotovodstva, kormovaya baza, myasnoi balans* (1930)

Gershberg, S., *Rabota u nas takaya: zapiski zhurnalista-pravdista tridtsatykh godov* (1971)

Industrializatsiya SSSR, 1926–1928 gg.: dokumenty i materialy (1969)

Industrializatsiya SSSR, 1929–1932 gg.: dokumenty i materialy (1970)

Istoriya Kommunisticheskoi partii Sovetskogo Soyuza, 2nd edn (1962)

Istoriya Kommunisticheskoi partii Sovetskogo Soyuza, vol. IV (i) (1970)

Istoriya sovetskogo krest'yanstva i kolkhoznogo stroitel'stva v SSSR: materialy nauchnoi sessii, sostoyavsheisya 18–21 aprelya 1961 g. v Moskve (1963)

Itogi desyatiletiya Sovetskoi vlasti v tsifrakh, 1917–1927 (n.d. [?1928])

Itogi vypolneniya pervogo pyatiletnego plana razvitiya narodnogo khozyaistva SSSR (1933)

Ivnitskii, N. A., *Klassovaya bor'ba v derevne i likvidatsiya kulachestva kak klassa (1929–1932 gg.)* (1972)

Kalinin, M. I., *Izbrannye proizvedeniya*, vol. II, *1926–1932 gg.* (1960)

Khozyaistvennye itogi v 1923–1924 g. (1925)

Kolkhozy v 1929 godu: itogi sploshnogo obsledovaniya kolkhozov (1931)

Kolkhozy v 1930 g.: itogi raportov kolkhozov XVI s''ezdu VKP (b) (1931)

Kollektivizatsiya sel'skogo khozyaistva Kazakhstana (1926-iyun' 1941 gg.), vol. I (Alma-Ata, 1967)

Kollektivizatsiya sel'skogo khozyaistva na Severnom Kavkaze (1927–1937 gg.) (Krasnodar, 1972)

Kollektivizatsiya sel'skogo khozyaistva Tatarskoi ASSR, 1927–1937 (Kazan', 1968)

Kollektivizatsiya sel'skogo khozyaistva Tsentral'nogo promyshlennogo raiona (1927–1937 gg.) (Ryazan', 1971)

Kollektivizatsiya sel'skogo khozyaistva: vazhneishie postanovleniya Kommunisticheskoi partii i Sovetskogo pravitel'stva, 1927–1935 (1957)

Kollektivizatsiya sel'skogo khozyaistva v Severnom raione (1927–1937 gg.) (Vologda, 1964)

Kollektivizatsiya sel'skogo khozyaistva v Srednem povolzh'e (1927–1937 gg.) (Kuibyshev, 1970)

Kollektivizatsiya sel'skogo khozyaistva v Zapadnom raione RSFSR (1927–1937 gg.) (Smolensk, 1968)

Kommunisticheskaya partiya Sovetskogo Soyuza v rezolyutsiyakh i resheniyakh s''ezdov, konferentsii i plenumov TsK, 2nd edn, vol. II, *1924–1930*, vol. III, *1930–1954* (1954)

Kontrol'nye tsifry narodnogo khozyaistva SSSR na 1927/1928 god (1928)

Kontrol'nye tsifry narodnogo khozyaistva SSSR na 1928/1929 god (1929)

Kontrol'nye tsifry narodnogo khozyaistva SSSR na 1929/30 god, odobrennye Sovetom Narodnykh Komissarov SSSR (1930)

Konyukhov, G. A., *Bor'ba za khleb v 1928 g.* (1951)

Kozlova, L., *K pobede kolkhoznogo stroya: bor'ba Moskovskoi partiinoi organizatsii za podgotovku i provedenie kollektivizatsii* (1971)

Krasnikov, S., *Sergei Mironovich Kirov: zhizn' i deyatel'nost'* (1964)

Kritsman, L., *Geroicheskii period Russkoi revolyutsii* (n.d., [?1924])

Krzhizhanovskii, G. M., Kviring, E. I., and Kovalevskii, N. A., *Problemy postroeniya general'nogo plana* (1930)

Kukushkin, Yu. S., *Sel'skie sovety i klassovaya bor'ba v derevne (1921–1932 gg.)* (1968)

Latsis, M. I., and Litvinov, I. I., eds., *Puti pod''ema i sotsialisticheskoi rekonstruktsii sel'skogo khozyaistva: sbornik statei* (1929)

Lenin, V. I., *Sochineniya*, 4th edn, vols. III (1941), XVIII (1948), XXIV (1949), XXVII (1950), XXIX (1950), XXXI (1950)

Leninskii kooperativnyi plan i bor'ba partii za ego osushchestvlenie (1969)

Malafeev, A. N., *Istoriya tsenoobrazovaniya v SSSR (1917–1963 gg.)* (1964)

Markevich, A. M., *Mezhselennye mashinno-traktornye stantsii*, 2nd edn (1929)

Materialy po balansu narodnogo khozyaistva SSSR za 1928, 1929 i 1930 gg. (1932)

Materialy po istorii SSSR, i (1955), vii (1959)

Medvedev, V., *Krutoi perevorot (Iz istorii kollektivizatsii sel'skogo khozyaistva Nizhnego Povolzh'ya)* (Saratov, 1961)

Mendel'son, A. S.,ed., *Pokazateli kon''yunktury narodnogo khozyaistva SSSR za 1923/24–1928/29 gg.* (1930)

Mikoyan, A., *Rezul'taty kampanii po snizheniyu tsen* (1927)

Minaev, S. V., ed., *Sotsialisticheskoe pereustroistvo sel'skogo khozyaistva SSSR mezhdu XV i XVI s''ezdami VKP (b)* (1930)

Moshkov, Yu. A., *Zernovaya problema v gody sploshnoi kollektivizatsii sel'skogo khozyaistva SSSR (1929–1932 gg.)* (1966)

Na novom etape sotsialisticheskogo stroitel'stva: sbornik statei, vols. I–II (1930)

Narodno-khozyaistvennyi plan SSSR na 1931 god (1931)

Narodnoe khozyaistvo SSSR: statisticheskii spravochnik 1932 (1932)

Neizvedannymi putyami: vospominaniya uchastnikov sotsialisticheskogo stroitel'stva (Leningrad, 1967)

Nemakov, N. I., *Kommunisticheskaya partiya—organizator massovogo kolkhoznogo dvizheniya (1929–1932 gg.): po materialam nekotorykh oblastei i kraev RSFSR* (1966)

Nemchinov, V. S., *Izbrannye proizvedeniya*, vol. I (1967)

Neposredstvennaya podgotovka massovoi kollektivizatsii sel'skogo khozyaistva Turkmenskoi SSR (1927–1929 gg.), vol. I of *Kollektivizatsiya sel'skogo khozyaistva Turkmenskoi SSR (1927–1937 gg.): sbornik dokumentov* (Ashkhabad, 1972)

Nifontov, V. P. *Zhivotnovodstvo SSSR v tsifrakh* (1932)

Nifontov, V. P., *Produktsiya zhivotnovodstva SSSR* (1937)

Ocherki istorii Kommunisticheskoi partii Ukrainy, 2nd edn (Kiev, 1964)

Ocherki po istorii statistike SSSR (1960)

Ordzhonikidze, G. K., *Stat'i i rechi*, vol. II, *1926–1937 gg.* (1957)

Perspektivy razvitiya sel'skokhozyaistvennoi kooperatsii v SSSR: pyatiletnii plan na 1928/29–1932/33 gg. (1929)

Plan kollektivizatsii v vesennyuyu sel'skokhozyaistvennuyu kampaniyu 1930 g. (1930)

Pobeda kolkhoznogo stroya v Turkmenistane (1930–1937 gg.), vol. II of *Kollektivizatsiya sel'skogo khozyaistva Turkmenskoi SSR (1927–1937 gg.): sbornik dokumentov* (Ashkhabad, 1968)

Pogudin, V. I., *Put' sovetskogo krest'yanstva k sotsializmu: Istoriograficheskii ocherk* (1975)

Polyakov, Yu. A., *Perekhod k nepu i sovetskoe krest'yanstvo* (1967)

Popov, P. I., ed., *Balans narodnogo khozyaistva Soyuza SSR 1923/24 g.* (*Trudy TsSU, xxix*), i, ii (1926)

Posevnye ploshchadi SSSR i itogi ucheta posevnykh ploshchadei letom 1935 g., vol. I (1935)

Pyatiletnii plan narodno-khozyaistvennogo stroitel'stva SSSR, 3rd edn, vols. I, II(i), II(ii), III(1930)

[XV] *Pyatnadtsatyi s''ezd VKP(b): dekabr' 1927 goda: stenograficheskii otchet*, vol. II (1962)

Rashin, A. G., *Formirovanie rabochego klassa v Rossii* (1958)

Resheniya partii i pravitel'stva po khozyaistvennym voprosam, vol. II, *1929–1940 gody* (1967)

Saratovskaya partiinaya organizatsiya v gody sotsialisticheskoi industrializ-

atsii strany i podgotovki sploshnoi kollektivizatsii sel'skogo khozyaistva: dokumenty i materialy, 1926–1929 gg. (Saratov, 1960)

Saratovskaya partiinaya organizatsiya v period nastupleniya sotsializma po vsemu frontu. Sozdanie kolkhoznogo stroya: dokumenty i materialy 1930–1932 gg. (Saratov, 1961)

Sdvigi v sel'skom khozyaistve SSSR mezhdu XV i XVI partiinymi s''ezdami: statisticheskie svedeniya po sel'skomu khozyaistvu za 1927–1930 gg., 1st edn (1930), 2nd edn (1931)

Sel'skoe khozyaistvo SSSR: ezhegodnik 1935 (1936)

Sel'skoe khozyaistvo SSSR: statisticheskii sbornik (1960)

Selunskaya, V. M., *Rabochie-dvadtsatipyatitysyachniki* (1964)

Sharapov, G. *Razreshenie agrarnogo voprosa v Rossii posle pobedy oktyabr'skoi revolyutsii* (1961)

Sharova, P. N., *Kollektivizatsiya sel'skogo khozyaistva v Tsentral'-nochernozemnoi oblasti 1928–1932 gg.* (1963)

[*XVI*] *Shestnadtsataya konferentsiya VKP (b): aprel' 1929 goda: stenograficheskii otchet* (1962)

XVI [*Shestnadtsatyi*] *s''ezd Vsesoyuznoi Kommunisticheskoi partii (b): stenograficheskii otchet*, 2nd edn (1931)

6 [*Shestoi*] *s''ezd sovetov Soyuza SSR: stenograficheskii otchet*(1931)

Shuvaev, K. M., *Staraya i novaya derevnya: materialy issledovaniya s Novo-Zhitovinnogo i der. Mokhovatki Berezovskogo raiona, Voronezhskoi oblasti, za 1901 i 1907, 1926 i 1937 gg* (1937)

Slin'ko, I. I., *Sotsialistichna perebudova i tekhnichna rekonstruktsiya sil'skogo gospodarstva Ukraini (1927–1932 rr.)* (Kiev, 1961). (In Ukrainian)

Sotsialisticheskoe stroitel'stvo SSSR: statisticheskii ezhegodnik (1934)

Sotsialisticheskoe stroitel'stvo SSSR: statisticheskii ezhegodnik (1935)

Sotsialisticheskoe stroitel'stvo SSSR: statisticheskii ezhegodnik (1936)

Sotsial'naya struktura naseleniya Sibiri (Novosibirsk, 1970)

Spravochnik po khlebnomu delu (1932)

Stalin, I. V., *Sochineniya*, vols. V (1947), VII (1947), VIII (1948), XI (1949), XII (1949)

Statisticheskii spravochnik SSSR za 1928 (1929)

Stepichev, I. S., *Pobeda leninskogo kooperativnogo plana v vostochnosibir-skoi derevne* (Irkutsk, 1966)

Strumilin, S. G., *Na planovom fronte, 1920–1930 gg.* (1958)

Tekhnicheskie kul'tury; kartofel', ovoshchi (1936)

Trapeznikov, S. P., *Leninizm i agrarno-krest'yanskii vopros*, vol. II (1967)

Trifonov, I. Ya., *Likvidatsiya ekspluatatorskikh klassov v SSSR* (1975)

Trud i byt v kolkhozakh, vols. I–II (Leningrad, 1931)
Trudy pervoi Vsesoyuznoi konferentsii agrarnikov-marksistov, 20. xii–27. xii. 1930 [*sic*, 1929], vols. I, II(i) and II(ii) (1930)
Turchaninova, E. I., *Podgotovka i provedenie sploshnoi kollektivizatsii sel'skogo khozyaistva v Stavropol'e* (Dushanbe, 1963)
Umanskii, S. A., ed., *Mirovoe khozyaistvo: sbornik statisticheskikh materialov za 1913–1927 gg.* (1928)
Vaganov, F. M., *Pravyi uklon v VKP(b) i ego razgrom, 1928–1930 gg.* (1970)
Valentinov, N., *Novaya ekonomicheskaya politika posle smerti Lenina: gody raboty v VSNKh vo vremya NEP: vospominaniya* (Stanford, 1971)
Vneshnyaya torgovlya SSSR za 1918–1940 gg.: statisticheskii obzor (1960)
Voprosy agrarnoi istorii: materialy nauchnoi konferentsii po istorii sel'skogo khozyaistva i krest'yanstva Evropeiskogo Severa SSSR, gor. Vologda, 15–17. vi. 67 (Vologda, 1968)
Vsesoyuznaya perepis' naseleniya 1926 goda, vol. XXXIV (1930)
2 [*Vtoraya*] *sessiya Tsentral'nogo Ispolnitel'nogo Komiteta Soyuza SSR 5 Sozyva: stenograficheskii otchet* [November 29–December 8, 1929] (1929)
Yurovskii, L., *Denezhnaya politika sovetskoi vlasti (1917–1927)* (1928)
Zadachi i perspektivy kolkhoznogo stroitel'stva: proekt pyatiletnego plana (1929)
Za krupnye kolkhozy: materialy 1-go Vserossiiskogo soveshchaniya krupnykh kolkhozov (1929)
Zhukov, Y., *Lyudy 30-kh godov* (1966)

SECTION III BOOKS, THESES, ETC. IN OTHER LANGUAGES

Avtorkhanov, A., *Stalin and the Soviet Communist Party: a Study in the Technology of Power* (Munich, 1959)
Campbell, T. D., *Russia: Market or Menace?* (London, 1932)
Carr, E. H., *The Bolshevik Revolution, 1917–1923*, vol. II (London, 1952)
Carr, E. H., *The Interregnum, 1923–1924* (London, 1954)
Carr, E. H., *Socialism in One Country, 1924–1926*, vol. I (London, 1958), vol. II (London, 1959)
Carr, E. H., *Foundations of a Planned Economy, 1926–1929*, vol. II (London, 1971), vol. III (London, 1976–8)
Carr, E. H., and Davies, R. W., *Foundations of a Planned Economy, 1926–1929*, vol. I (London, 1969)

Chayanov, A. V., *The Theory of Peasant Economy* (Homewood, Illinois, 1966)
Ciliga, A., *The Russian Enigma* (London, 1940)
Cohen, S., *Bukharin and the Bolshevik Revolution: a Political Biography, 1888–1938* (London, 1974)
Deutscher, I., *The Prophet Outcast, Trotsky: 1929–1940* (London, 1963)
An Economic Profile of Mainland China: Studies Prepared for the Joint Economic Committee, Congress of the United States, vol. I (Washington, D.C., 1967)
Engels, F., *Herr Eugen Dühring's Revolution in Science (Anti-Dühring)* (London, n.d. [? 1939])
Fainsod, M., *Smolensk under Soviet Rule* (London, 1958)
Fitzpatrick, S., ed., *Cultural Revolution in Russia* (Bloomington, Indiana, 1978)
Grosskopf, S., *L'alliance ouvrière et paysanne en u.r.s.s. (1921–1928): le problème du blé* (Paris, 1976)
Halpern, I. P., 'Stalin's Revolution: the Struggle to Collectivize Rural Russia, 1927–1933', unpublished Ph.D. thesis (Columbia University, New York, 1965)
Harrison, R. M., 'Soviet Peasants and Soviet Price Policy in the 1920s', unpublished Discussion Papers SIPS 10 (Centre for Russian and East European Studies (CREES), University of Birmingham, 1977)
Harrison, R. M., 'Theories of Peasant Economy', unpublished D. Phil. thesis (University of Oxford, 1974)
Hindus, M., *Red Bread* (London, 1934; first published 1931)
History of the Communist Party of the Soviet Union (Bolsheviks): Short Course (Moscow, 1945; first published in 1938)
Hoover, C. B., *The Economic Life of Soviet Russia* (London, 1931)
Jasny, N., *The Socialized Agriculture of the USSR: Plans and Performance* (Stanford, 1949)
Jasny, N., *Soviet Economists of the Twenties: Names to be Remembered* (Cambridge, 1972)
Kaufman, A., *Small-scale Industry in the Soviet Union* (Washington, D.C., 1962)
Khrushchev Remembers, [vol. I] (London, 1971)
Knickerbocker, H. R., *The Soviet Five-Year Plan and its Effect on World Trade* (London, 1931)
Lewin, M., *Russian Peasants and Soviet Power: a Study of Collectivization* (London, 1968)

Lyons, E., *Assignment in Utopia* (London, 1938)
Male, D. J., *Russian Peasant Organisation before Collectivisation: a Study of Commune and Gathering, 1925–1930* (Cambridge, 1971)
Miller, R., *One Hundred Thousand Tractors: the MTS and the Development of Controls in Soviet Agriculture* (Cambridge, Mass., 1970)
Preobrazhensky, E., *The New Economics* (Oxford, 1965)
Reswick, W., *I Dreamt Revolution* (Chicago, 1952)
Scheffer, P., *Seven Years in Soviet Russia* (New York, 1932)
Serge, V., *Memoirs of a Revolutionary, 1901–1941* (London, 1967)
Shanin, T., *The Awkward Class: Political Sociology of Peasantry in a Developing Society: Russia, 1910–1925* (Oxford, 1972)
Tucker, R. C., *Stalin as Revolutionary, 1879–1929: a Study in History and Personality* (New York, 1973)
Tucker, R. C., ed., *Stalinism: Essays in Historical Perspective* (New York, 1977)
Van Bath, B. H. S., *The Agrarian History of Western Europe, A.D. 500–1850* (London, 1963)
Wheatcroft, S. G., 'The Population Dynamic and Factors Affecting It in the Soviet Union in the 1920s and 1930s', unpublished Discussion Papers SIPS 1–2 (Centre for Russian and East European Studies (CREES), University of Birmingham, 1976)
Wheatcroft, S. G., 'The Significance of Climatic and Weather Change on Soviet Agriculture (with Particular Reference to the 1920s and 1930s)', unpublished Discussion Papers SIPS 11 (Centre for Russian and East European Studies (CREES), University of Birmingham, 1977) (referred to in present volume as Wheatcroft (1977(1)).
Wheatcroft, S. G., 'Soviet Grain Production Statistics for the 1920s and the 1930s', unpublished Discussion Papers SIPS 13 (Centre for Russian and East European Studies (CREES), University of Birmingham, 1977) (referred to in present volume as Wheatcroft (1977(2))
Wheatcroft, S. G., 'Views on Grain Output, Agricultural Reality and Planning in the Soviet Union in the 1920s', unpublished M.Soc. Sc. thesis (Centre for Russian and East European Studies (CREES), University of Birmingham, 1974)
Wolfe, B., *Three Who Made a Revolution* (London, 1955)
Woodward, E. L., and Butler, R., *Documents on British Foreign Policy 1919–1939*, 2nd series, vol. VII *1929–32* (London, 1958)
Writings of Leon Trotsky (1930) (New York, 1975)

Wronski, H., *Rémunération et niveau de vie dans les kolkhoz; le troudoden* (Paris, 1957)
Zaleski, E., *Planning for Economic Growth in the Soviet Union, 1919–1932* (Chapel Hill, 1971)

NAME INDEX

SUBJECT INDEX

THE SOVIET COLLECTIVE FARM, 1929–1930

By the same author

THE INDUSTRIALISATION OF SOVIET RUSSIA 1: THE SOCIALIST OFFENSIVE, 1929–1930

THE INDUSTRIALISATION OF SOVIET RUSSIA 3: THE SOVIET ECONOMY IN TURMOIL, 1929–1930

THE DEVELOPMENT OF THE SOVIET BUDGETARY SYSTEM

FOUNDATIONS OF A PLANNED ECONOMY, 1926–1929 Volume One (with E. H. Carr)

SCIENCE POLICY IN THE USSR (with E. Zaleski and others)

THE SOVIET UNION (editor)

THE TECHNOLOGICAL LEVEL OF SOVIET INDUSTRY (editor with R. Amann and J. M. Cooper)

THE INDUSTRIALISATION OF SOVIET RUSSIA 2

THE SOVIET COLLECTIVE FARM, 1929–1930

R. W. DAVIES

Professor of Soviet Economic Studies
University of Birmingham

M

MACMILLAN
PRESS

First edition 1980
Reprinted 1989

Published by
THE MACMILLAN PRESS LTD
Houndmills, Basingstoke, Hampshire RG21 2XS
and London
Companies and representatives
throughout the world

Printed in China

British Library Cataloguing in Publication Data
Davies, Robert William
The industrialisation of Soviet Russia
2: The Soviet collective farm, 1929–1930
1. Russia–Industries–History
2. Russia–Economic conditions–1918–1945
I. Title. II. Soviet collective farm, 1929–1930
338.0947 HC335.2
ISBN 0–333–26172–0 (hardcover)
ISBN 0–333–46594–6 (paperback)

CONTENTS

LIST OF TABLES

LIST OF TABLES

PREFACE

During 1929–30 the collective farms (kolkhozy) achieved a commanding position in the Soviet countryside, although they still included only a minority of households. The present volume discusses in some detail the emergence of the kolkhoz as an economic unit. During the heady months of the first collectivisation drive in the winter of 1929–30, the kolkhozy were planned as giant, fully socialised enterprises modelled on the state-owned factories, and employing wage labour. Such schemes soon proved both impracticable and too costly, and aroused much peasant hostility. By the summer of 1930, a compromise system had been introduced. The kolkhoz henceforth roughly coincided with the boundaries of the settlement or village, or of a natural part of the village. Within this smaller kolkhoz, collective farmers were permitted to retain a personal household plot and their own animals, while arable land was collectivised, and was cultivated in common. A free market was reintroduced side by side with state planning. The collective farmers were remunerated for their work on the collective lands—in principle, though not yet in practice—in 'labour days'; these were proportionate to the quantity and quality of work, though they were paid only after the harvest, by sharing out what remained after state and collective needs were satisfied. In this compromise between state and peasant interests, the state predominated, by its power and its material advantages. The collective product was firmly controlled by state collection agencies, and, after a lengthy controversy, available tractors and other modern machinery were transferred to state-owned Machine-Tractor Stations, each of which served and controlled a number of kolkhozy.

The main features of the kolkhoz, as they emerged in the summer of 1930, continued throughout rapid industrialisation; the kolkhoz became an integral and major unit of Stalinist economic organisation, and many of the arrangements made in 1930 continue in the Soviet Union today. The emergence of the kolkhoz in 1929–30 was thus a crucial stage in the formation of the Soviet system.

The present volume, like the others in this series on *The Industrialisation of Soviet Russia*, has been written so that it can be read independently, and it has its own bibliography and index. Thanks for advice and assistance from many colleagues and organisations were expressed in the Preface to volume 1, and need not be repeated here. The reader's attention is also drawn to the 'Technical Note' in that volume, which briefly describes the organisation of Soviet central and local government, and sets out various conventions used throughout the series.

July 1979 R. W. DAVIES

CHAPTER ONE
THE STATE AND THE KOLKHOZ

(A) THE BACKGROUND

In 1929–30, much closer central control was established over agricultural production; and in the main grain-surplus regions most agricultural land and a large minority of peasant households were collectivised. Simultaneously several hundred thousand 'kulak' households were expropriated. The Soviet leaders carried out this 'revolution from above' with such violence and haste because they were convinced that it would provide the solution to the crisis in agricultural marketings which had developed since 1927, and was becoming more acute as they pressed forward and enlarged their industrialisation programme. They were confident that the consolidation of the planned state collections, and the replacement of individual peasant farms by kolkhozy, would immediately increase food supplies for the urban population, agricultural raw materials for industry, and agricultural exports generally.

The collectivisation of agriculture, and its planned control, were thus seen as conditions for industrialisation. But they were not undertaken with narrowly economic objectives. This was proclaimed to be a 'socialist offensive', a decisive stage in the construction of the first socialist society in the world. And, on the Soviet—or rather Stalinist—analysis, it was bound to be resisted, for both economic and political reasons, by the petty-capitalist peasant class, the kulaks who, together with their 'henchmen', had to be treated as irreconcilable enemies. According to Soviet theory, always stubbornly maintained in public, this battle of the regime against the petty-capitalist peasants was supported by the poor and middle peasants, who voluntarily participated in the collectivisation drive; but there is no doubt that the Soviet leaders were privately well aware that many ordinary peasants behaved like their image of petty capitalists when faced with low state collection prices for their products, and when invited to relinquish the family farming they knew for the unknown and alien kolkhoz. Moreover, the grain collections of the autumn of 1929 already amply demonstrated—and this was officially and publicly recognised at the time—that even the kolkhozy, themselves influenced, in the party view, by the kulaks, could not be relied upon automatically to submit themselves to commands and requisitions from the socialist state. For all these reasons, the Soviet authorities were determined to establish firm state political and administrative controls over the whole of agriculture, including its socialist sector, so that 'market spontaneity' would be replaced by central planning, and the peasant community would be subordinated to the state.

The socialist transformation of agriculture was, however, never seen by the Soviet authorities merely as an instrument for the exploitation of the peasantry. While an increased flow of agricultural products to the state was confidently expected, efforts were also made to provide definite quantities of industrial goods in return for agricultural products; 'market spontaneity' was to give way not simply to planned collections but also to 'product-exchange'. Even more important, in the Soviet view of future state–kolkhoz economic relations, was the supply by the state of tractors and agricultural machines in large numbers. The Soviet authorities cherished great hopes that mechanisation would bring about a rapid technical revolution in agriculture, and they believed that the replacement of the petty economies of the individual peasants by large-scale socialist agricultural economies was essential if this revolution was to succeed. The 'metal link' between the state and the kolkhoz would thus come to predominate over the 'textile link' between the state and the individual peasant. The political and administrative controls over the kolkhoz must therefore incorporate agencies and methods not only for exacting grain and other products from the peasants but also for coping with the reverse flow of products and assistance from the state and with the inculcation of mechanised agriculture.

Within this framework of state controls, an appropriate internal structure for the kolkhoz needed to be established. This was a new environment and a new system of agriculture; and the past experience of small market-oriented kolkhozy was of limited relevance. The type of kolkhoz now being established must simultaneously respond to the new and daunting requirements of state planning, and replace the deep-rooted family economy of the individual peasantry. If it were to work effectively, its size and structure should be such as to enable the efficient organisation of agricultural production, and its system of income distribution should promote adequate investment in the collective economy while providing economic incentives to collective farmers more powerful than the market incentives which stimulated the individual peasants.

In the summer of 1929, the Soviet political leaders had no clear idea either of the future pattern of controls over the kolkhoz, or of the shape and functioning of its economy. But they were strongly biased towards industry in their ideology and organisation, and, in an atmosphere of mounting enthusiasm for industrialisation, industrial experience and factory methods came to be seen as fully applicable in agriculture, and capable of greatly improving its efficiency. In September 1929, an editorial in *Pravda*, insisting that the example of the United States had 'compelled bourgeois economists to admit that in 10–15 years agriculture will have reached the level of an extractive industry', roundly asserted:

> All the most recent developments in agriculture, especially in technically more developed capitalist countries, have revealed that attempts to find methods and laws of development of agriculture different from the methods and laws of industry are completely groundless and stupid.[1]

Markevich, head of Traktorotsentr, declared in the same month that 'there is no difference in principle between agriculture and urban industry'.[2] The November 1929 plenum of the central committee argued that large kolkhozy and comprehensive collectivisation 'require the establishment of unity in the management of agricultural production on the basis of the utilisation of the experience of the management of Soviet industry'.[3] At the plenum, Molotov succinctly summed up the approach of the leadership to agricultural organisation with the slogan:

> Kolkhozy, in organising social production, model yourselves on the sovkhozy![4]

1 P, September 5, 1929.
2 EZh, September 10, 1929.
3 *KPSS v rez.*, ii (1954), 654.
4 B, 22, November 30, 1929, 20.

The sovkhozy, in their turn, were closely copying the experience of large industrial plants; it was not accidental that the new large grain sovkhozy were always described as 'grain factories'.

Uncritical enthusiasm for the application of industrial methods in kolkhoz affairs did not survive the winter of 1929–30. It soon became clear to the party leaders that the industrial model was too costly to apply immediately to peasant agriculture as a whole, and that the peasants were not ready for it. In July 1930, a resolution of the XVI party congress implicitly refuted Molotov's dictum of November 1929:

> All attempts to transfer the organisational system of management of the sovkhozy to the kolkhozy are anti-Leninist, because *unlike the sovkhoz*, which is a *state* enterprise, created by state resources, the kolkhoz is a voluntary social association of peasants, *created by the resources of the peasants themselves*, with all the ensuing consequences.[5]

This tactical retreat did not, however, change the fundamental assumption that the kolkhoz would eventually become an enterprise controlled and organised on factory lines. The resolution of the XVI congress also envisaged that the kolkhozy would create a 'new social discipline' in the peasants, who would, under party guidance, abandon their 'petty-bourgeois psychology and thirst for private accumulation'; to this end a large-scale mechanised economy would be provided for the kolkhozy, skilled collective farmers would be trained and the cultural level of the mass of collective farmers would be fundamentally improved. But it was now much more strongly emphasised that all this would require 'years of stubborn effort' by the party.[6]

(B) STATE CONTROL OF THE KOLKHOZ

On the eve of collectivisation, Soviet power in the villages was weak and ineffective (see vol. 1, pp. 51–5). Party membership was small, party members often unreliable; the village soviet commanded less respect, and had less influence on the peasants, than the mir and the

[5] *KPSS v rez.*, iii (1954), 53.
[6] *Ibid.* 61.

skhod, the traditional agencies of peasant self-government. The vast majority of the peasants were unsympathetic to the new policies of the party leadership. The extension of state control over agriculture in 1929–30 therefore required the invasion of the countryside by large numbers of temporary plenipotentiaries and brigades from the towns, supported as required by the militia, the army and the OGPU. The major instruments of state control in the villages were not the party cell, which did not exist in most villages, or the village soviet, but the plenipotentiaries; and agriculture was not controlled primarily by ordered and regular plans but by successive grain, livestock and sowing campaigns, above all by the drive for collectivisation and dekulakisation.

For more than a quarter of a century, campaigns by urban plenipotentiaries, backed by the power of the state, would remain a crucial element in state control of the countryside. But already in 1929–30 the outlines began to emerge, at the centre and in the localities, of a regular system of administration and control, which in part took over management of the campaigns, in part coexisted uneasily beside them.

At the centre, the most important development was the establishment at the end of 1929 of a Narkomzem and a Kolkhoztsentr for the whole USSR (see vol. 1, p. 169). The Narkomzem of the RSFSR had been dominated, until the end of 1927, by 'bourgeois specialists' strongly committed to the preservation of small-scale peasant agriculture; even after the expulsion of Kondratiev and his colleagues from its staff early in 1928 it continued to be a centre of resistance to the new agricultural policies. In contrast, the new Narkomzem of the USSR was dominated by party members whose loyalty to the Politburo was not in doubt. Yakovlev, the People's Commissar for Agriculture of the USSR, was the former deputy head of the People's Commissariat for Workers' and Peasants' Inspection, Rabkrin, which, as well as watching over government institutions and their bourgeois specialists on behalf of the party, was by this time the principal agency advising the Politburo about both policy and administration. A number of senior officials of Rabkrin were also transferred to the staff of both Narkomzem of the USSR and Kolkhoztsentr of the USSR at the end of 1929. A few weeks later, the rural department of the party central committee was abolished, one of the main arguments for this being that the establishment of a USSR Narkomzem made it redundant (see vol. 1, p. 216). All this seemed to indicate that strong and loyal governmental institutions were emerging in agriculture, responsible for transmitting party policy to the kolkhozy and the individual peasants, and in charge of the new kolkhoz system throughout the USSR; their control over agriculture was intended to correspond to the control of Vesenkha over industry.

From the beginning of 1930 Narkomzem and Kolkhoztsentr immediately plunged into the work of administering the kolkhozy, supplementing and continuing the work of their republican equivalents. But the changes in agriculture were so novel, so vast and so important to the regime that the Politburo and the party apparatus intervened more frequently and extensively than in industry; in practice Narkomzem and Kolkhoztsentr were of relatively minor importance in comparison with Vesenkha. Moreover, the executive responsibility for the grain, livestock and vegetable collections rested not with Yakovlev and Narkomzem but with Mikoyan and Narkomtorg. Appropriately, perhaps, Yakovlev was a second-rank political figure, and, unlike Mikoyan or Kuibyshev, the chairman of Vesenkha, he was not a member or even a candidate member of the Politburo.

Narkomzem and Kolkhoztsentr were also weaker than Vesenkha in another important respect. In industry, the major factories throughout the country were directly subordinate to powerful departments of Vesenkha located in Moscow. This imposed strict limits on the influence on industrial affairs of local party and soviet organisations, and of the local industrial committees, the sovnarkhozy, and strengthened the position of Vesenkha, which the Politburo and the central party apparatus found it difficult to bypass. In agriculture, however, the kolkhozy formed part of the local 'kolkhoz unions', the kolkhozsoyuzy, at district, okrug, regional and republican level. While the kolkhozsoyuzy were formally subordinate to their republican Kolkhoztsentr (which was identical with the USSR Kolkhoztsentr in the case of the RSFSR), they were much weaker organisations than the departments of Vesenkha. Designed for a small voluntary kolkhoz movement, they were suddenly confronted with the immense tasks imposed by mass collectivisation. They did not, even formally, acquire executive authority in relation to their kolkhozy until June 1929 (see vol. 1, p. 120). Soon after, they were plunged into a confusing series of reforms which continued throughout 1929 and 1930, and were intended to rationalise the control of the kolkhozy and the agricultural cooperatives. An attempt was first made to coordinate the work of the kolkhozsoyuzy and the koopsoyuzy (the local agencies of the various agricultural cooperatives), and then to fuse them; subsequently, in the summer of 1930, their functions were again divided (see vol. 1, pp. 301–2, 351–2). These reforms failed to strengthen the kolkhozsoyuzy. In October 1930, Yurkin, after touring nine districts in the Central Black-Earth region and the Ukraine, complained that 'most districts, it seems, only "plan" and are not directly leading the production work of the kolkhozy'; the kolkhozsoyuzy even lacked detailed information about kolkhoz activities:

> It is surprising how the kolkhozy, left to their own devices, and deprived of live leadership by the system, manage to cope with tremendous production tasks.[7]

A month later, a deputy chairman of Kolkhoztsentr reported that in the Lower Volga region the district kolkhozsoyuzy 'in essence are doing nothing'.[8] A district kolkhozsoyuz was supposed to have a full-time staff of ten, but a Narkomzem investigation at the end of 1930 reported that 'the extent of understaffing presents a threatening picture'; in many districts with a low percentage of collectivisation kolkhozsoyuzy separate from the koopsoyuzy had not even been established.[9]

The enforcement of the major agricultural campaigns, which required the recruitment of large numbers of townsmen for temporary work in the countryside, and often also involved a show of force, clearly lay far beyond the capacities of the local kolkhozsoyuzy, or of the well-established but conservative local departments of Narkomzem (the *zemotdely*). During 1929 and 1930, the secretaries of the local party organisations, supported by the chairman of the soviets, together with their respective committees and 'bureaux', became the effective local controllers of agriculture and the kolkhozy, intermediaries between the kolkhozy and the central party apparatus. The party leadership, attaching supreme importance to the subordination of agriculture to the will of the state, and to the transformation of its structure, bombarded its local organisations with instructions and appeals, and agricultural and

7 SZe, October 14, 1930 (report to board of Kolkhoztsentr); *Kollektivist*, 20, October 31, 1930, 3; see also I, September 4, 1930; Yurkin see pp. 135–6 below.

8 SZe, November 11, 1930 (Tataev's report to board of Kolkhoztsentr).

9 NFK, 24, [December?] 1930, 52, 54–5, 57.

kolkhoz affairs soon came to predominate in the activities of the local party and soviet authorities, particularly in view of the relative insignificance of their role in relation to industry.

During the collectivisation drive of the winter of 1929–30 the party and soviet apparatus at the level of the administrative district (raion) gradually emerged as the main focus of administration in the countryside. With the abolition of the okrugs in the summer of 1930, the 3,000 districts, each including an average of 8,000 households, became the sole administrative level between the large administrative regions (oblasti or krai), each with a million households or more, and the 70,000 village soviets. The district, already the main executive agency of Soviet power for the collection of grain and other foodstuffs, became the main planning and reporting unit for the second phase of comprehensive collectivisation which began in the autumn of 1930. The gap between region and district soon proved to be too large. It was closed in the course of the 1930s not by increasing the average size of the district, which remained more or less constant, but by greatly increasing the number of regions.[10] From 1930 onwards, then, the district was a stable unit of control in the countryside.

Much remained uncertain at the village level in 1930. Collectivisation and dekulakisation greatly weakened the mir and the skhod throughout the USSR, particularly in villages where the kolkhozy included a high proportion of the population. Comprehensive collectivisation also, for a time, threatened the village soviet; many officials argued that the kolkhoz could itself act as the primary unit of Soviet power, now that it was planned to correspond in size with the village (see vol. 1, p. 226n.). At one moment, comprehensive collectivisation even threatened the district soviet, when influential officials and publicists proposed that a single giant kolkhoz should be formed in each district (see pp. 41–7 below). But the principle that Soviet power in the village should be separate from the kolkhoz, even when their boundaries coincided, was strongly reaffirmed by the Soviet government as early as January 1930 (see vol. 1, pp. 225–6). By the end of 1930, there were already 113,000 kolkhozy,[11] as compared with 70,000 village soviets; henceforth, particularly in villages containing more than one settlement, a single village soviet frequently contained several kolkhozy. The village soviet emerged from the first collectivisation

[10] See *Nar. kh. 1958* (1959), 37.
[11] *Ezhegodnik po sel. kh. 1931* (1933), 442.

drive with strengthened authority: it was now the unchallengeable primary unit of Soviet government, responsible for taxation and policing, and for various minor public services, with its own separate sources of finance. But the functions of village soviet and kolkhoz board remained in many respects confused and overlapping.

Within this structure of authority, the arrangements for the collection of grain and other foodstuffs from the kolkhozy and the individual peasantry were relatively clear-cut by the summer of 1930. The collections, while carried out by campaign methods in which party organisations and plenipotentiaries were decisive, were planned and organised by Narkomtorg, using the grain cooperatives as its agents. Agricultural cooperation, in its traditional meaning of a voluntary organisation to assist peasant agriculture, was in a state of collapse; the agricultural cooperatives, instead of marketing peasant products, now acted as agents of the state in the collection of grain, livestock and vegetables from kolkhozy and individual peasants. For this purpose the district koopsoyuzy were both simplified and strengthened; significantly, in the autumn of 1930 the permanent establishment of staff was 50 per cent higher for the average district koopsoyuz than for the kolkhozsoyuz.[12]

The contracts signed by kolkhozy and groups of individual peasants with the agricultural cooperatives provided both for the supply of grain and other products by the peasants to the state and, in return, for the supply of industrial consumer goods, agrotechnical assistance and machinery by the state to the peasants. But the arrangements for the supply of industrial consumer goods, unlike the arrangements for the collections, were weak and ineffective. This was not entirely due to the shortage of industrial goods. Arrangements to cope with the shortage by earmarking supplies of goods to the value of 20–40 per cent of the value of the collections were tried out in the autumn of 1929, and revived in the autumn of 1930, and seem to have been viable in principle. But they rarely worked in practice (see vol. 1, pp. 80, 253). This failure was mainly due to the priorities imposed by the authorities, who concentrated their manpower, their decrees and their punishments on the drive for the collections, and failed to provide adequate support for the systematic distribution of industrial goods. Social policy also came into it; the authorities hesitated about enforcing

12 NFK, 24, [December?] 1930, 54–5.

the exchange of industrial goods for grain because they feared that too many of them would go to the well-to-do middle peasants who supplied much of the grain. But even here devices were available to correct this danger (see vol. 1, p. 80). Significantly, the authorities overcame social scruples and supply difficulties only in the case of industrial crops, particularly cotton, where they were convinced from experience that 'special-purpose supplies' in return for crops were essential to the urgently needed expansion of production. But here, ironically, the main product supplied efficiently by the state was not an industrial good, but grain, which had been collected from peasants in the grain-surplus areas without an adequate return.

With tractors and agricultural machinery, the authorities soon resolved that only the socialised sector should receive supplies, and henceforth they were not available to stimulate individual peasants to meet the grain quotas. Another element thus disappeared from the 'product-exchange' equation. Even in the case of the kolkhozy, while supplies of tractors were often used as a spur to further collectivisation (see vol. 1, pp. 383–4), they were rarely offered as an incentive to deliver grain.

Substantial resources, including foreign currency, were, however, devoted to increasing the present and future supplies of machinery in 1929 and 1930; mechanisation was genuinely regarded as the key to future success. Much effort was devoted to finding the best way of organising the tractor economy, culminating in the decision in September 1930 to concentrate all tractors used by the kolkhozy in state-owned Machine-Tractor Stations (MTS). The MTS thus became the principal embodiment of the main economic benefits provided by the state to the kolkhozy, and, in those districts in which they operated, a parallel centre of control to the kolkhozsoyuz. Chapter 2 deals with the story of their rise to a monopoly position. It should be borne in mind that the decisions about the tractor economy and internal kolkhoz organisation were inter-related. If the kolkhozy were to be giants incorporating many villages, they could manage and repair their own tractors; if the kolkhoz-village and the kolkhoz-settlement were the norm, then, particularly when few tractors were available, the tractor economy must be separately organised, whether by agricultural cooperatives, by the kolkhozsoyuzy or by the state. *Per contra*, if the state decided to establish its own multi-village MTS—whether to enhance its own control over the kolkhozy or to take advantage of economies of scale—then the main argument in favour of multi-village kolkhozy would collapse. The discussion of the rise of the MTS in chapter 2 is thus closely related to the discussion of the size of the kolkhoz in chapter 3.

(C) THE STATE AND KOLKHOZ INTERNAL ORGANISATION

In the months preceding the collectivisation drive, it was a platitude in official circles that almost nothing was known about how to organise the kolkhoz, and that the attention devoted to this crucial subject was woefully inadequate. At the XVI party conference in April, Kubyak, People's Commissar for Agriculture of the RSFSR, complained that 'we have been discussing collectivisation and the kolkhozy for two days and no-one has so far mentioned that it is necessary to organise farming properly in the kolkhozy'.[13] At the conference of large kolkhozy in July, one of the rapporteurs in the organisation section declared that 'questions of the organisation of labour in kolkhozy are little studied, and have been still less studied in large kolkhozy'.[14] At the November plenum, Vladimirsky, chairman of the Union of Unions of agricultural cooperatives, strongly emphasised the lack of information:

> I have read all the publications about the kolkhoz movement. They can almost be put in one pocket, and there is almost nothing there about the organisation of labour in kolkhozy.[15]

These criticisms were somewhat exaggerated. Vladimirsky would have needed a capacious pocket; the relevant items in the bibliography of the present volume contain over 1,000 pages, and are a small selection from a large literature. Much of the information about the organisation of small kolkhozy which was assembled and published in the early and mid-1920s was evidently not known to the party leaders. Some of it was known, but curtly discarded in the ambitious attempt to introduce industrial methods into kolkhoz management in the winter of 1929–30, only to be taken up again in the spring of 1930. Much of the experience of the small

[13] *XVI konf.* (1962), 421.
[14] ZKK (1929), 145.
[15] Chigrinov (1970), 50.

kolkhoz of the 1920s was, however, irrelevant to the typical kolkhoz of 1930, containing dozens of households.

During the collectivisation drive, the Soviet leaders refrained from prescribing the structure and *modus operandi* of the kolkhoz except in a rough outline; on the face of it, this was a sound approach, given their ignorance and lack of experience. When the November plenum insisted on 'unity in the management of agricultural production', this was a unity in which much was deliberately left to local initiative. Even Molotov, while reproaching the central kolkhoz administration for an insufficiently serious approach to kolkhoz organisation, left the door open for independent action:

> Kolkhozy can learn much from the well-organised Soviet factory, but the variety of conditions and the differences in the stages of development reached by the kolkhoz movement in particular [geographical] areas makes necessary an exceptional degree of flexibility in the forms and methods of kolkhoz construction.[16]

Symptomatic of the unwillingness of the party leaders to undertake the resolution of these questions at the centre, or of their indifference to them, was the failure to include a subcommission on kolkhoz organisation among the eight subcommissions of the Politburo commission on the kolkhoz movement of December 1929. The subcommission on organisational questions under M. Katsenelenbogen, who was on the staff of the central committee rural department, appears to have dealt only with the relations between kolkhozy and higher authorities.[17] At the conference of marxist agrarians in the same month, an agronomist from a Ural RSK reproached the central authorities with having no theory which could provide guidance about 'what to do, how to do it, and where to do it' with the result that 'there is complete chaos in the planned organisation of the land area, in the socialist organisation of the masses and of genuinely large-scale production'. 'Why don't you provide anything from the localities?,' called out someone in the audience. 'We do a bit,' the speaker replied, 'but we are practical officials.'[18] At a

[16] B, 22, November 30, 1929, 14–15.

[17] IISO, [i] (1964), 265–7. For Katsenelenbogen see *Trudy . . . agrarnikov-marksistov* (1930), i, 430.

[18] *Trudy . . . agrarnikov-marksistov* (1930), i, 146–7.

kolkhoz conference, also held in December, representatives of local organisations were said to be 'swimming on the waves of an unknown sea, improvising, talking in general terms rather than on the real theme'.[19] The central authorities continued, however, to abstain from any detailed prescriptions, and on February 20, 1930, Syrtsov complained of the 'organisational muddle and lack of commonsense' which had left the peasant without leadership.[20] Even at the XVI party congress in July 1930, after all the upheavals of the previous six months, Yakovlev told critics that, apart from its ruling on the proportion of the crop which should go to the state, the central committee did not propose to make specific provisions about the way in which the harvest should be divided up between the kolkhoz and its members:

> *Such bureaucratic castles in the air should not be permitted; in future instead of issuing new instructions one should be making sure that questions about the distribution of the harvest are decided not behind the backs of the collective farmers in some office but, as is laid down by the directives of the party central committee, by the collective farmers themselves, by the general meeting of collective farmers, with the approval of the general meeting of collective farmers.* That will be the best guarantee against mistakes.[21]

In August, in the course of his critical speech about the organisation of the economy, Syrtsov called for the 'standardisation of organisational forms and production methods' in the kolkhozy, but was condemned for his bureaucratic approach; 'this proposal', said one of his critics, 'would get first prize at a competition of Soviet bureaucrats'.[22]

The complicated questions of kolkhoz organisation were not, however, decided by a kind of Benthamite self-acting democracy. In each kolkhoz, in each district, okrug and region, decisions were reached within a definite framework of national policy; and local decisions on matters of organisation were pushed in different directions by the changes in policy at the centre. This was a learning process on a vast scale, and in an extremely brief period of time, in

[19] EZh, December 27, 1929; this conference is discussed further on pp. 44–5 below.

[20] B, 5, March 15, 1930, 48; for Syrtsov see vol. 1, p. 375, n. 10.

[21] *XVI s"ezd* (1931), 643–4.

[22] NAF, 11–12, 1930, p. xiii (Tal'); for this speech see vol. 1, pp. 375–6.

which party leaders and their advisers, local party officials, the peasants and economic regularities all contributed to the outcome. Out of the chaos and the brutality of the winter and spring of 1929–30, important features of the kolkhoz system gradually emerged, in the course of the failure of impossible solutions and the rejection of solutions unacceptable to the central authorities, or intolerable to the peasants. Major features of the kolkhoz system established in 1929–30 endured until Stalin's death, and for some time after it.

CHAPTER TWO

THE MACHINE-TRACTOR STATIONS

In the spring of 1929, new forms of organisation of the tractor economy were distinguished more by their potential than by their achievement. A couple of state-owned Machine-Tractor Stations attached to sovkhozy, with about a hundred tractors,[1] and some fifty 'tractor columns' of the grain cooperatives with over 1,000 tractors ploughed between them a mere 90,000 hectares or so of the 4 million hectares sown by the kolkhozy in the spring of 1929 (see Table 2(b)). In addition, several thousand tractors belonging to agricultural cooperatives were available for loan to kolkhozy through hiring points. A further 800 tractors were owned by 147 large kolkhozy (see vol. 1, p. 122, n. 60). But the vast majority of the 20,000 tractors serving the kolkhozy in the spring of 1929 were scattered among 57,000 small kolkhozy. Almost all tractors had been removed from individual owners; according to official statistics, none remained in their possession by October 1, 1929 (see Table 1).

In the rancorous and protracted discussions about the organisational forms through which tractors should be made available to kolkhozy, no objection was raised to the proposition that the small kolkhozy of 10–15 households were not capable of using a tractor efficiently. Their land area was insufficient—the sown area of the average kolkhoz in June 1929 was 73 hectares, but a 10 h.p. tractor, if fully used, would plough at least 200 hectares is a season. In a substantial minority of kolkhozy, in which the land was not consolidated, conditions for using tractors were particularly difficult. Facilities for maintenance and repair were also usually lacking. While large kolkhozy, covering a whole village or several villages, were able to make full use of their tractors, maintenance

[1] Carr and Davies (1969), 213, list three such MTS as in existence in the spring of 1929, but other accounts state that only one or two state MTS existed throughout 1929 (see Table 2(b), and SZe, February 11, 1930, which reports that only two state MTS existed on February 1, 1930).

was difficult except in the few kolkhozy large enough to use several tractors. The cooperative columns, with an average of 25–30 tractors each (see Table 2), were in principle sufficiently large to make reasonable maintenance feasible. But the state-owned Machine-Tractor Station, modelled on the successful experience of the Shevchenko sovkhoz in the Ukraine, seemed to offer considerable additional advantages. Markevich, the founder of the Shevchenko MTS, in his widely distributed booklet (the second edition alone was printed in 10,000 copies), claimed that in Soviet conditions by far the most efficient arrangement was to concentrate some 200 tractors, serving an arable area of 40,000–50,000 hectares, in a single station. Owing to the scarcity and expensiveness of capital, tractors must be used for longer periods in each year, and for a longer period altogether, than in the United States. Adequate maintenance was therefore essential and would carry with it higher productivity and fuel economies.[2] But this required a well-equipped repair shop, including for preference a casting shop, so that work need not be put out. Such a shop would not be economical for a small number of tractors. With a large number of tractors, it would also be possible to keep some spare tractors for emergencies. Markevich presented calculations of capital and current costs for different sizes of MTS, and claimed that total tractor costs per hectare fell steadily with the growth of the area served by the MTS.[3] Costs continued to fall for areas larger than 50,000 hectares, but Markevich argued that until technology improved and experience accumulated, a larger MTS was not justified in view of 'the complexity and difficulties of organisation'.[4]

Markevich's conclusions suffered from the important weakness that a few minor adjustments to the data made it possible to show that an MTS of 10,000 hectares was as efficient as one of 50,000 hectares.[5] But the viability of his general concept did not depend on

[2] Markevich (1929), 92–3.

[3] *Ibid.* 163–7. Total costs per hectare fell from 30 rubles 46 kopeks for 500 hectares to 15r 36k for 5,000 hectares, 13r 20k for 10,000 and 11r 10k for 50,000. These figures include (a) capital outlay, depreciation charge and interest at 6 per cent, on workshops, housing, staff, tractors and vehicles, (b) wages for the central staff of the MTS and its repair shop, and (c) running costs (materials, spare parts and fuel but *not* the wages of the drivers, which were to come from the village itself).

[4] *Ibid.* 169.

[5] A critic argued, on the assumption that the MTS acted as a grain collection point, that Markevich ignored the rising cost of transporting the marketed harvest

such calculations. He tried to combine in the MTS what he saw as two essential requirements for the advance of Soviet agriculture. The first was that agricultural technology should be managed by a '*unified organisational centre*' for the whole USSR. The unified centre would select the priority districts and okrugs for development, survey world technology to find the best systems and types of machinery for Soviet conditions, and then impose its requirements on Soviet industry; huge economies of scale could be obtained from standardisation and centralised supply.[6] Markevich regarded it as highly desirable, though not absolutely essential, that the MTS should be owned by this unified centre rather than by the group of villages served by the MTS; ownership by a group of villages would 'inevitably involve an artisan approach'. He rejected, on rather flimsy grounds, proposals resuscitated by Khrushchev 30 years later that each kolkhoz-village should possess its own tractors, but be served by the MTS as a repair base; this scheme would have been at least as profitable in terms of Markevich's own calculations.[7] But he did not insist that the unified centre should be a state enterprise; it could equally well be owned by the cooperatives or by a mixed joint-stock company.[8]

According to Markevich, the second requirement, if advanced technology were to be successfully introduced, was that it should be palatable to the peasants, while simultaneously leading them towards collectivisation. Markevich took it for granted that the existing village, or part of a village, must be the basic unit with which the MTS dealt; he made the obvious point that it would be much too expensive to rearrange the villages so that each had the same area.[9] According to Markevich, the minimum condition for economical use of the tractor was that all boundaries between strips within each village should be removed, and that all work should be carried out under the guidance of an agronomist and a mechanic from the MTS; the village would supply and pay all the labour, including tractor drivers trained by the MTS. The harvest would, at first, be distributed among the peasants according to the land

to the MTS; if this were taken into account the optimum size was 50,000 hectares *total* area (SZo, ix, October–November 1930, 21–3; see also SZo, vi, July 1930, 51–66).

6 Markevich (1929), 274–7, 288.

7 *Ibid*. 288–92.

8 *Ibid*. 280.

9 *Ibid*. 67.

each household contributed.[10] The peasants need not join formally into a kolkhoz, and, if they did, the best form in the first instance would be the simplest type of kolkhoz, the TOZ, in which each household kept its own animals, and only arable farming was undertaken in common.[11] Finally, whether the village became a kolkhoz or not, its payments to the MTS must be such as to provide a '*clear gain obvious to the peasantry*'. In Shevchenko the village handed over to the MTS a quarter or a third of its harvest, an arrangement which provided an incentive for both the MTS and the peasant to produce more; the alternative of a fixed charge per hectare would provide no incentive for the MTS and would cause the peasant insupportable losses in a bad year.[12]

In the spring of 1929, Markevich's call for centralised state control and his intention of separating the tractors physically and organisationally from the kolkhoz were strongly criticised. In the opinion of the agricultural cooperatives, state-managed MTS would inevitably be isolated from the kolkhozy and would not be able to take advantage of the contacts established over the years by the cooperatives.[13] At the XVI party conference in April 1929, considerable enthusiasm was shown for the Shevchenko experiment, but the conference resolution, adhering to the course strongly advocated by Kaminsky in the debate (see vol. 1, p. 115), impartially recommended the development of 'state and cooperative' MTS and tractor columns, and of large kolkhozy at the level of modern technology.[14]

After the XVI conference, events moved fast. On May 8, STO decided to establish an 'all-Union centre' to manage the Machine-Tractor Stations, and during the next few weeks inter-departmental meetings convened by Rabkrin, and a special commission of STO, prepared the appropriate legislation. The rival merits of kolkhoz and state ownership were much debated; the majority of the commission agreed that the development of the MTS should be concentrated in the hands of the state. Some members of the majority wanted the 'all-Union centre' to be a state trust; others proposed that it should be a 'joint-stock' enterprise. The draft

[10] *Ibid.* 298–301.
[11] *Ibid.* 18–19.
[12] *Ibid.* 182–5.
[13] For an account of the arguments advanced by the cooperatives see Lewin (1968), 365–7; Miller (1970), 72–8.
[14] *XVI konf.* (1962), 393–4; *KPSS v rez.*, ii (1954), 580, 587.

decree by Rabkrin supported the 'joint-stock' form, with state capital predominating; this would ensure that the kolkhoz and cooperative organisations were fully involved, and make it possible to collect peasant funds for the construction of MTS.[15] This proposal was accepted by STO in a decree of June 5, 1929, which established 'VTsMTS', the All-Union Centre of Machine-Tractor Stations, as a state joint-stock company in which the main government and cooperative organisations concerned with agriculture participated. VTsMTS, which soon became known as Traktorotsentr, was allocated 5,000 tractors 'as a minimum' for the year 1929/30, to begin the establishment of a network of MTS, the structure of which, as outlined in the decree, closely resembled that proposed by Markevich. A provision that sovkhoz MTS which were mainly cultivating peasant land should be transferred to the new centre enabled Shevchenko to be incorporated as the first unit in the new system.[16] The legal constitution of Traktorotsentr was thus a concession to fears of too much central control; it was later described as 'a special semi-state, semi-cooperative organisation'.[17] But, as with the other state joint-stock companies which existed at this time, this was almost entirely a legal fiction. All the property of Traktorotsentr and its MTS remained firmly in state ownership, even though peasant contributions were solicited for their establishment; and the whole operation was directed in detail by the central authorities.

The promised allocation of 5,000 tractors was substantial: in 1928/29 the total stock of tractors in the kolkhozy and the agricultural cooperatives increased by only 8,000 (see Table 1). At the conference of large kolkhozy in July 1929 one delegate complained that it was likely that as a result of the allocation to the new MTS no tractors would be left for the large kolkhozy.[18] But most existing tractors belonged to agricultural cooperatives, or to the kolkhozy themselves, and no hint was given in the decree of June 5 that Traktorotsentr would have any control over these tractors, or over the cooperative MTS and tractor columns; the establishment of MTS was described merely as 'one of the basic paths' to collectivisation.

The relation between the tractor and the kolkhoz was further

[15] IS, 2, 1978, 68 (Vyltsan); this account is based on the archives.
[16] *Kollektivizatsiya . . . 1927–1935* (1957), 179–80; SZ, 1929, art. 353.
[17] NAF, 11–12, 1929, 142.
[18] ZKK (1929), 302.

discussed at the conference of large kolkhozy, and the course of the discussion made it abundantly clear that the decree of June 5 had not settled the problem. Kaminsky, departing from his earlier impartial support for different forms of tractorisation, urged that the tractor columns of the agricultural cooperatives, at this time quantitatively much more important than the MTS, should be transformed into group holdings (kusty) of the kolkhozy, and that collective farmers should acquire resources to buy up the state-owned MTS.[19] Another official spokesman of Kolkhoztsentr, however, wanted Kolkhoztsentr itself to take over those tractor columns which served the kolkhozy.[20] In the debate at the conference, the common thread was the resistance by the kolkhozy to MTS or tractor columns which were independent of the kolkhoz system. Many delegates criticised Kaminsky for his conciliatory attitude to the cooperative tractor columns, and urged that they should be brought under the direct control of the kolkhoz system or preferably of the kolkhozy themselves. 'The instruments of production', one speaker declared, 'cannot be in someone else's hands', and a Kolkhoztsentr official complained that the main allocation of tractors had been made to tractor columns rather than to the kolkhozy themselves until Kolkhoztsentr got the decision reversed.[21] The resolution of the conference called for the eventual 'transfer by sale' of the tractor columns to the 'population of the kolkhoz'.[22]

During the summer, Traktorotsentr approved the locations of 100 MTS, each with 50 tractors in the first instance, which were to be set up in the spring of 1930; most of them were to be situated in RSKs.[23] In the meantime the agricultural cooperatives greatly expanded their tractor columns, which were now also frequently and confusingly described as 'MTS'; they contained 2,000 tractors by September 1929 (see Table 2(b)). This expansion was achieved not by acquiring new tractors but by removing existing ones from hiring points, small kolkhozy and producers' associations within the cooperative system.[24]

[19] ZKK (1929), 284–5.

[20] ZKK (1929), 292–3.

[21] ZKK (1929), 295, 298–301, 314–15.

[22] ZKK (1929), 318–20.

[23] P, September 12, 1929; *Krasnyi Khoper*, September 5, 1929 (referring to a Traktorotsentr plan dated August 28).

[24] There were 6,673 tractors in the agricultural cooperatives on October 1, 1928,

In August 1929 Rabkrin issued a highly critical report about the cooperative MTS and columns, criticising the absence of careful planning, the lack of preliminary preparation of the population, by either propaganda or technical training, the use of old tractors, the absence of repair shops, the frequent stoppages (amounting to 40 per cent of the working time) and the failure to involve the peasants in the provision of finance. The report castigated the whole operation of setting up the columns for 'hastiness', and for aiming at 'looking good from outside'.[25] In its report to the party central committee of September 7, 1929, Kolkhoztsentr, following up a further point in the Rabkrin report, criticised 'tractor columns outside the kolkhoz' because they failed to stimulate socialisation except in arable farming, and resulted in peasants transferring their activities to the development of other branches of farming on an individual basis. It also reproved both the tractor columns and Shevchenko for failing to attract peasant resources to their construction.[26] The inability of state MTS and cooperative columns to persuade the peasants to contribute to the cost of the tractors was frequently stressed by those who argued that the kolkhozy themselves should own the tractors; this must have been an important consideration for the authorities.

The November plenum of the central committee showed no disposition to favour any particular form of organisation for the tractor economy. At the plenum Molotov reproved Traktorotsentr for planning 102 MTS for the next spring and failing to notice that about 100 already existed; some were known as tractor columns, but this was a purely organisational distinction:

> In the last resort this is one and the same thing. Who has found in reality, or can find, a difference in principle between tractor stations and tractor columns?[27]

---

but only 3,769 in the cooperatives and 2,387 in 'MTS' (at this stage this must refer to cooperative columns), 6,156 in all, on October 1, 1929 (see Table 1). On the removal of tractors from kolkhozy by the cooperatives, see *XVI konf.* (1962), 422 (Kubyak).

25 P, August 2, 1929; the similar criticisms cited by Lewin (1968), 422–4, also all refer to the cooperative columns—Tsil'ko's article in NAF, 11–12, 1929, was presumably a version of the report cited above (Tsil'ko was at this time an official of Rabkrin).

26 *Materialy*, vii (1959), 228, 267.

27 B, 22, November 30, 1929, p. 12.

The resolution of the plenum again commended both MTS, as future 'centres of comprehensive collectivisation of whole districts', and the 'large mechanised kolkhozy'.[28] But it also made clear its anxiety to obtain finance from agriculture itself for the production of agricultural machinery: it recommended that kolkhozy ordering new tractors and other machinery should pay a deposit amounting to 20 per cent of their value, to be used to finance the construction of new tractor factories.[29]

With the reorganisation of the kolkhoz and cooperative system announced at this time (see vol. 1, pp. 301–2), which aimed at bringing together agricultural cooperatives and kolkhozsoyuzy into a common organisation at the regional, okrug and district level, the cooperative MTS and columns appeared to fall naturally into place as the tractor agency of the single district organisation. At the height of the collectivisation drive, the agricultural cooperatives supported attempts to establish giant kolkhozy each embracing a whole district, or a substantial part of a whole district, and running their own tractors and other machinery. On January 18, 1930, in a telegram to the Central Black-Earth region, Khlebotsentr ruled that every column or MTS which owned more than 20 tractors should set up a giant kolkhoz.[30] In the following month Belenky, a senior official of Khlebotsentr, announced that it had already organised 185 MTS and columns with over 5,000 tractors, and planned to set up a total of 490 with 18,000 tractors by the end of 1930 (see Table 2(b)).

Schemes to obtain payments for tractors from the kolkhozy were promoted during the collectivisation drive as part of the general campaign to obtain more money from the peasants (see pp. 120–4 below). The Politburo commission of December 1929 recommended in its draft resolution on collectivisation that deposits should be increased during 1930 to 60 per cent of the value of the tractors and 40 per cent of the value of agricultural machines; in addition tractor 'obligations' covering 120,000 tractors should be issued to the kolkhozy and paid in three instalments.[31] On December 30, a Sovnarkom decree ruled that in the case of MTS and tractor columns the peasants served by them must pay at least 25 per cent of

[28] *KPSS v rez.*, ii (1954), 646.
[29] *KPSS v rez.*, ii (1954), 645–6; Nemakov (1966), 80.
[30] IS, 4, 1969, 33; according to IZ, lxxiv (1963), 21, a decree of January 21, 1930, ordered the transfer of all grain cooperative MTS and tractor columns to giant kolkhozy before the spring sowing, or at the latest by the end of 1930.
[31] VIK, 1, 1964, 38.

their cost before construction began; payments were to be made via kolkhozy at the rate of 3–5 rubles per hectare of arable land.[32] In January and February 1930, the agricultural cooperatives collected substantial advance payments of 60 million rubles from the kolkhozy for the purchase of 25,000 tractors,[33] and in the course of 1930 the state-owned MTS collected 24 million rubles as compared with a capital investment in 1930 of 110–113 million rubles.[34]

Meanwhile, a cloud loomed over Traktorotsentr. At the beginning of December 1929, after the formation of Narkomzem and Kolkhoztsentr of the USSR, a Kolkhoztsentr conference proposed that as well as Traktorotsentr becoming an 'autonomous centre' within Kolkhoztsentr, as already proposed by the November plenum, the local agencies of Traktorotsentr should be placed under the leadership of the regional or okrug kolkhozsoyuz.[35] This recommendation was not immediately accepted, and both Kolkhoztsentr and Traktorotsentr continued to be autonomous organisations not formally subordinate to the new Narkomzem of the USSR (see vol. 1, p. 169, n. 95). But, significantly, Markevich, in spite of his status and popularity, was made neither a deputy People's Commissar nor a member of the collegium of Narkomzem of the USSR, unlike, for example, the chairman of the sovkhoz grain trust Zernotrest or the chairman of Kolkhoztsentr.[36] In December 1929, the ideas of Markevich, which had seemed very advanced six months before (see pp. 18–20 above), were sharply criticised for their moderation. At the conference of marxist agrarians a report on the MTS rebuked him for allegedly believing that 'motive power' as such would automatically lead to socialism; in the discussion, a speaker from the Lower Volga region, while conceding that the 'energy theory' or 'energy approach' of Markevich and Krzhizhanovsky had played a positive role, suggested that the failure to link it in practice with social problems

[32] SZ, 1930, arts. 16, 130; see also Danilov (1957), 380–1.

[33] P, May 22, 1930, disk. listok 1; SO, 3–4, 1930, 109, reported that 61·2 million rubles were collected for tractors by March 10, 1930.

[34] Danilov (1957), 381; IS, 2, 1978, 69, states that peasant contributions in 1930 amounted to 55 million rubles and capital investment in MTS to 99·3 million rubles, but does not make it clear whether the former figure includes contributions to cooperative MTS and columns.

[35] SKhG, December 4, 1929.

[36] SZ, 1929, ii, arts. 292, 299.

had 'a menshevik odour (*Voice*: Very interesting)'.[37] In this context, several delegates objected to Markevich's insistence that socialisation within the kolkhozy should at first be confined to arable farming. At a time when giant kolkhozy were increasingly popular, the reluctance of Traktorotsentr to deal with organisations larger than the village also gave rise to grave doubts.[38]

In his speech at the end of the conference, however, Stalin referred impartially to the benefits the kolkhozy would obtain from Machine-Tractor Stations, tractor columns and the acquisition of tractors by the kolkhozy themselves (see vol. 1, p. 393). The central committee resolution of January 5, 1930, was also cautious, merely instructing the MTS under Traktorotsentr, 'in view of the changed conditions' in RSKs, to

> reconstruct their work on the basis of (a) contracts mainly, if not exclusively, with collectives; (b) peasant obligations to cover the cost of the stations within three years.[39]

This ambiguous instruction conveyed no more than a hint of disapproval of the activities of Traktorotsentr. It did not refer to the admissibility or otherwise of the amalgamation of each MTS into a giant kolkhoz embracing a district, and left open the question of whether the MTS, after being paid for by the peasants, would be transferred to the kolkhozy.[40] On February 1, 1930, a decree of STO, announcing that the number of MTS in 1930 was to be increased from 106 to 219, called for the socialisation not only of draught animals and implements, but also of all 'commodity

[37] *Trudy . . . agrarnikov-marksistov* (1930), ii, 67, 105 (the report was by A. Lozovoi; the speaker from the Lower Volga was A. Gavrilov).

[38] *Ibid.* ii, 108, 160–1, 165–6. In a notorious telegram to the Khoper okrug kolkhozsoyuz signed by Markevich, Traktorotsentr refused to permit MTS to sign contracts with inter-village kolkhozy—the telegram read 'organisation of station precludes inter-settlement kolkhozy[;] must sign contracts with village production unions' (*ibid.* 161; SKhG, December 13, 1929). Some of the criticisms made at the conference were developed at length by M. Golendo, a member of the collegium of Narkomzem, in NAF, 2, 1930, 9–21, and by Karpinsky in SZe, February 11, 1930.

[39] *KPSS v rez.*, ii (1954), 666; clause(b) was clearly a truncated version of the proposal in the draft resolution prepared by the Politburo commission (see p. 22 above).

[40] Later statements (e.g. by Sarkis of the agricultural cooperatives, in P, May 22, 1930, disk. listok 1) to the effect that the resolution involved the *sale* of the MTS to the kolkhozy within three years go beyond its wording.

branches of agriculture' in the area of the MTS, and declared that the state MTS must be a 'fully mechanised large-scale economy, capable of being a model and a school for large-scale collective agricultural construction'; it also again insisted that the construction of an MTS must not begin until 25 per cent of its full cost had been paid in by the peasants.[41] Shortly afterwards, Markevich, conceding that 'basic changes' were needed in the MTS arrangements as compared with Shevchenko, emphasised that MTS must not be treated as a 'tractor hiring point' but as a means of organising 'unified inter-village collective production'; the term MTS should refer to the 'whole kolkhoz-production combine (kombinat)'.[42] This was the farthest point in concessions by Traktorotsentr to the fashionable trend towards kolkhozy much larger than a single village.

While the state MTS were still in process of formation, the abrupt change of policy at the end of February 1930 resulted in a mass exodus from the kolkhozy and the restoration of the viewpoint that the kolkhoz-village should be the basic agricultural unit (see pp. 51–4 below). This change in policy was not always advantageous to MTS operations: tractors now had sometimes to be sent long distances in order to be fully utilised.[43] But on the whole it greatly strengthened the position of Markevich and Traktorotsentr. The scheme of a centrally-managed state network of MTS could now remain intact, modified only by the elimination of the envisaged transitional period in which contracts by the MTS were signed with non-collectivised villages. Markevich's strongly-held opinions that the kolkhoz must be based on the existing village, and that socialisation should not go further than arable farming in the first stage of collectivisation, were now fully restored to party doctrine, supported by the disastrous experience of the excesses of the previous months.[44]

The arguments for keeping the tractor economy in MTS, separate from the individual kolkhozy, now seemed overwhelming. The

[41] SZ, 1930, art. 130; a recommendation of the collegium of Narkomzem of the USSR dated December 31, 1929, using similar wording, is cited from the archives in IS, 4, 1969, 33, and is interpreted as a proposal to establish giant kolkhozy on the basis of the MTS.

[42] P, February 13, 1930.

[43] See IS, 4, 1969, 34.

[44] See his strongly-worded article, or cry of triumph, in P, April 8, 1930 (and see p. 52 below).

break-up of the giant kolkhozy and the drastic reduction in the membership of all kolkhozy had eliminated almost all those which were of sufficient size to control a group of tractors effectively, and the decline in the number of horses and the shortage of tractors in any case made it desirable that each kolkhoz using tractors should be only partially mechanised at first. Moreover, the relaxation in the spring of 1930 of earlier financial pressures on the countryside (see pp. 124–5 below) made it impossible to collect more than a minor part of the cost of the tractors either from kolkhozy or from the peasants direct; this weakened the criticism of the state MTS for failing to persuade peasants to subscribe to tractor obligations.

The case for separating all MTS and tractor columns from the agricultural cooperatives was also now very strong. The agricultural cooperatives continued to form MTS and tractor columns at a remarkable pace in the spring of 1930 (see Table 2(b)); as well as converting existing hiring-points into columns, they must also have received a substantial allocation of new tractors. But, unlike the state MTS, the agricultural cooperatives emerged from the gigantic exertions of the first few weeks of 1930 much weakened, having merged most of their primary organisations with the kolkhozy (see vol. 1, pp. 299–300). The decision in July 1930 to separate the kolkhoz and agricultural cooperative system at every level (see vol. 1, pp. 351–2) deprived the cooperatives of most of their functions in relation to the kolkhozy, and removed the basis of their argument that the existence of Traktorotsentr and the MTS brought confusion to the administrative arrangements by providing a separate line of control over the kolkhozy.

While the separation of local kolkhoz administration from the agricultural cooperatives undermined the position of the cooperatives in relation to the MTS, it left intact the view widely held in the kolkhoz movement that the MTS should be subordinated not to a separate centralised network but to the district kolkhozsoyuzy, so that control over the activities of the kolkhozy was unified. At the party congress in June 1930, some talk took place behind the scenes about transferring the MTS to the kolkhoz system; Khataevich reported that 'comrade Yakovlev told me in a personal conversation that we shall hand over tractors, hand over the whole tractor economy, to the kolkhoz system; but I think that's not enough'.[45] Markevich confidently reported on the activities of

[45] *XVI s"ezd* (1931), 623; the reference here is to a transfer to district kolkhozsoyuzy, not to individual kolkhozy, *pace* IS, 4, 1969, 35. The latter source

'several hundred MTS' with 'twenty thousand tractors', as if the MTS of the agricultural cooperatives as well as those of Traktorotsentr were already under his control.[46] The reports by Stalin and Yakovlev, and the congress resolutions, however, again ignored the question of the relationship between the MTS, the tractor columns and the kolkhozy, and the resolution of the central control commission and Rabkrin of July 9, 1930, on kolkhoz organisation, prepared while the congress was in session, merely recommended the agricultural cooperatives and Traktorotsentr to 'coordinate with the local organisations the plans for the construction of MTS, and their work.'[47]

But matters were now soon resolved in favour of Markevich and the state network of MTS. A month after the party congress, on August 11, a central committee resolution on the Shevchenko MTS claimed that it had 'fully justified the role of the MTS as a powerful lever of the socialist reconstruction and advance of agriculture'.[48] On August 23, Traktorotsentr, which until then had formally retained an autonomous status, was attached to Kolkhoztsentr,[49] presumably in order to allay the strong anxieties within the kolkhoz system that an MTS network independent of Kolkhoztsentr would make control of the kolkhozy difficult and confusing. A few weeks later, on September 10, 1930, apparently without further public discussion, a brief resolution of the party central committee announced that 'all construction and management of MTS must be concentrated in Traktorotsentr'; Traktorotsentr would take over all the cooperative MTS and repair shops, assume responsibility for technical assistance to all tractors belonging to kolkhozy, and, 'on conditions agreed with the kolkhozy', also take over, both from individual kolkhozy and from groups of kolkhozy, all tractor columns capable of being reorganised into inter-village MTS.[50] This resolution greatly strengthened the position of Traktorotsentr, and, in spite of its caution about tractors owned by kolkhozy, effectively cleared the way for their removal to the MTS: the stock of tractors in kolkhozy fell by one-third in the next three months (see

---

reports from the archives that in the Central Volga region in August 1930 tractors were transferred to some kolkhozy big enough to use at least ten tractors.

[46] *XVI s"ezd* (1931), 640. [47] I, July 15, 1930.

[48] *Kollektivizatsiya . . . 1927–1935* (1957), 316–19.

[49] Miller (1970), 141.

[50] *Kollektivizatsiya . . . 1917–1935* (1957), 322; the decision was first published in I, September 13, 1930.

Table 1), and was again halved in the following year.[51] The resolution of September 10 did not propose any change in the status of Traktorotsentr as a 'joint-stock company', and it said nothing about the all-important question of the relation between the MTS and the district kolkhozsoyuzy. But some recognition was soon given to the need to integrate the MTS system and the kolkhoz system by the appointment of Yurkin, the chairman of Kolkhoztsentr, as chairman of Traktorotsentr as well, with Markevich as his deputy.[52] This was not in any but a formal sense a demotion for Markevich. He continued to act as the effective chairman of Traktorotsentr and as its public spokesman, and at this time he was at last appointed to the collegium of Narkomzem.[53]

In the autumn of 1930, with the resumption of the drive for collectivisation, the MTS were regarded as a major means of attracting individual peasants to kolkhozy, and became an even greater object of public attention. In the various congresses, meetings and publications where the work of the MTS was reviewed, Markevich and his colleagues looked back on 1930 with a considerable sense of achievement. By the spring of 1930, all the MTS planned in the previous autumn had been established, and with a larger stock of tractors, though with a somewhat lower horse-power, than originally planned (see Table 2). In the spring, the MTS cultivated a sown area of 2,000,000 hectares, 510,000 more than the plan (see Table 2) though only eight per cent of the total spring-sown area of the kolkhozy. In the districts served by MTS, 62 per cent of the peasants remained in the kolkhozy, a substantially higher proportion than in neighbouring non-MTS districts.[54] A large harvest was reported from kolkhozy served by MTS. The grain collection plan for these kolkhozy was exceeded by 22 per cent by the end of October and, in all, over half their grain harvest was handed over to the collection agencies; nevertheless, according to Yakovlev, the harvest was so successful in these kolkhozy that their collective farmers still received a larger amount of grain for their own needs than those in other kolkhozy.[55] The autumn sowing plan

[51] *Nar. kh.* (1932), 145.

[52] SZe, December 20, 1930, describes them in this way; I have not traced the announcement of the appointment.

[53] SZ, 1930, ii, art. 392 (dated November 1).

[54] NAF, 6, 1930, 112; SZe, October 23, 1930.

[55] *6 s"ezd sovetov* (1931), No. 16, p. 21, No. 17, p. 27; the grain recorded as handed

was also completed successfully.[56] The system of payment in kind, whereby the MTS took part of the harvest (one-quarter in 1930) to cover its expenses, was reported to have provided adequate incentives for both MTS and kolkhoz.[57] Good progress in the training of labour was also claimed. Traktorotsentr established its own network of vuzy, technical colleges and courses; 25,000 tractor drivers were trained during 1930, the vast majority of them collective farmers, and, according to Markevich, a considerable number worked 'not badly'.[58]

While the establishment of the first few state MTS was undoubtedly a solid achievement, the cost was high, and the claims made for them were overdrawn. No systematic investigation was ever published of the operation of the MTS in 1930. But a survey of groups of kolkhozy in North Caucasus and Leningrad regions revealed that, contrary to earlier claims, the gross income per household for a group of kolkhozy served by MTS was in fact slightly lower in 1930 than for a second group, those not served by MTS, though much higher than for a third group of kolkhozy 'with a weak technical base'. Moreover, in the kolkhozy served by MTS, the income distributed to the collective farmers was substantially lower than in the second group. This was also true of the income

---

over to the collection agencies presumably included the payments in grain for the work of the MTS.

56 SZe, December 30, 1930.

57 *6 s''ezd sovetov* (1931), No. 17, 23, 25. In cotton, flax and sugar-beet areas, where the harvest was automatically all handed to the state, the MTS charged a fixed amount in rubles per hectare depending on the type of work (*ibid.* No. 17, 23).

58 *Ibid.* No. 17, 35–6; according to Vyltsan (1959), 22, however, only 17,420 drivers and 2,070 senior drivers were trained by Traktorotsentr in 1930. The decision to send tractor drivers to Central Asia from the central regions was unsuccessful, as 'practice has shown that a European tractor driver on the cotton fields of Central Asia tries to give up the work and leave', so here too members of kolkhozy served by the MTS were to be trained as drivers (*6 s''ezd sovetov* (1931), No. 17, 36; SZe, December 20, 1930). According to a report in NAF, 6, 1930, 122–3, in the spring of 1930, of 322 'leading cadres', 75·1 per cent had been industrial workers, and only 5·9 per cent peasants; 52 per cent were party members; of 21,386 'middle and lower cadres', 5 per cent were party and 19.3 per cent Komsomol members; 15 per cent had been workers, 23·5 per cent batraks, 53·5 per cent poor peasants, and only 21·5 per cent middle peasants; only 5·7 per cent were women. The typical tractor driver was thus a male former batrak or poor peasant. A much higher proportion of the middle and lower cadres than of the collective farmers as a whole were in the party or Komsomol.

distributed in kind: in the North Caucasus the collective farmers served by MTS received 0·7 tons of grain per household, while other collective farmers received as much as 1·1 tons, and had grain to spare to sell on the free market. The lower level of distribution of grain, certainly displeasing to the peasants, was, however, regarded by the authorities as demonstrating the ability of the MTS system to provide better control over the economic activity of the kolkhozy.[59]

In their review of the first experience of the MTS, Soviet officials combined enthusiasm with a fairly frank recognition that they still worked badly in many respects. The MTS, as their opponents had warned, were remote from the kolkhozy. In his survey of the achievements of 1930 at the VI congress of soviets in March 1931, Markevich admitted that the MTS played little part in the work of the kolkhozy as such, sometimes being prevented from doing so by the local authorities.[60] The collective farmers who operated the tractors treated them with indifference:

> In most cases we still have a *barbarous* treatment of the machines not only through ignorance of the machine and inability to deal with it, but also through lack of willingness, carelessness, lack of understanding of the great importance of the machine for the collective farmer in the improvement of his well-being.

Ploughs squeaked through lack of oil, but the tractor driver and the ploughman paid no attention; and in 'hundreds of cases' deliberate damage was done by such acts as putting lumps of metal in the threshers.[61] The MTS, in common with the rest of the economy, suffered from the shortages and low quality of production endemic in the first stages of the industrialisation drive. Yurkin complained of the tradition of supplying sand with the oil, and as far as the kerosene used for fuel was concerned:

> Groznyi kerosene is such that it is capable of crippling a tractor of any system in a single spring, with the exception of the 'International' tractor, which will survive anything.[62]

59 SRSKh, 8, 1931, 158–9.
60 *6 s''ezd sovetov* (1931), No. 17, 24.
61 *Ibid.* No. 17, 37.
62 SZe, December 20, 1930.

Spare parts were always very scarce; and it took some time for industry to switch from horse-drawn to tractor-drawn implements, so that at the end of 1930 the production of ploughs and seeders was lagging behind the supply of tractors.[63] While tractors were imported in large numbers, lorries and cars were not, and Soviet production was negligible: at the end of 1930 the 158 MTS had in all only 200 lorries and 17 cars.[64] Perhaps the shortage of building materials was the most serious: as a result, new repair shops had been constructed in only half the MTS by December 1930;[65] the rest were presumably using makeshift buildings.

The plans for 1931, debated during the autumn of 1930, envisaged a further vast expansion. With the 13,000 tractors of the cooperatives, and some thousands of tractors transferred from the kolkhozy, the unified MTS system controlled 31,114 tractors by the end of 1930 (see Table 2(b)). The plan for 1931 stipulated that all tractors earmarked for the kolkhoz system were to be allocated to MTS, and none to individual kolkhozy. As a result, MTS were to receive 51·5 per cent of the tractor horse-power allocated, the rest going to the sovkhoz system,[66] and the number of tractors in MTS would rise to over 60,000 in the course of 1931.[67] The number of MTS was to rise to 1,000 in the main grain regions, which would make it possible for 80 per cent of their districts to have at least one MTS, and 405 MTS were to be established elsewhere. This would mean that each MTS would have only enough tractors, in the first year, to work an area of 25,000–30,000 hectares, and even in this area only the heavy work would be carried out by tractors, about 65–70 per cent still being done by horses. This gradual take-over by the tractor was in conflict with Markevich's original proposals of 1929, but would enable the new complement of tractors to provide 'partial tractorisation' of 18 million hectares over a large part of the USSR in the spring of 1931, whereas the alternative scheme would have provided 'full tractorisation' for only 5–6 million hectares.[68]

[63] SZe, December 20, 1930.

[64] SZe, December 20, 1930; *Sots. str.* (1935), 296.

[65] SZe, December 20, 1930.

[66] SZe, December 31, 1930; in addition to the 596,000 h.p. allocated to Traktorosentr, 35,000 h.p. were allocated to 'machine-tractor brigades' and 525,000 to sovkhozy, making a total of 1,157,000 h.p.

[67] P, October 22, 1930.

[68] Markevich's reports on the 1931 plan to the Ekoso of the RSFSR in October 1930, the collegium of Narkomzem in December 1930 and the VI congress of

The resources for this vast programme were to be provided mainly by the state, but in his report to the VI congress of soviets Markevich reminded his listeners that Traktorotsentr was a joint 'state–kolkhoz' organisation, insisted that 160 million of the 540 million rubles required for capital investment must come from the kolkhozy, and sternly warned that when kolkhozy did not pay up new MTS would be re-located to other districts.[69] The planned expansion made it necessary to train a further large number of new workers: the final plan proposed that 200,000 people should be put through courses by the spring of 1931, including 150,000 tractor drivers.[70]

In 1930, 139 of the 158 MTS were 'grain' MTS, and only 17 'cotton' and two 'sugar beet'; the attention of the MTS was heavily concentrated on the grain areas, and they were described at a session of Narkomzem as suffering from a '"rye and oats" psychology'.[71] In the plans for 1931, a sharp change occurred. Priority was to be given to mechanisation of cotton growing in Central Asia. Markevich claimed that the first experiments with MTS in the cotton areas in 1930 had given 'splendid results', but the task was truly heroic: in some areas 'fuel has to be carried hundreds of kilometres by water and camels', and according to Markevich the MTS created 'scissors' between the technology introduced into agriculture and the general cultural level of the population.[72] In flax areas, marshes would be dried and cleared of roots with the aid of caterpillar tractors, and the 'Stolypin khutors' scattered among the marshes would be 'uprooted with the forests and the bushes'. In these areas other crops would also be mechanised so as to release workers and thus eliminate the 'annual labour crisis' caused by

soviets in March 1931 are in SZe, October 23, December 20, 1930; *6 s''ezd sovetov* (1931), No. 17, 27–41. At the session of Ekoso, some speakers suggested that the number of tractors per MTS should be further reduced so as to enable additional MTS to be established.

69 *Ibid.* No. 17, 41; the original figure for kolkhoz contributions was 200 million rubles (SZe, December 20, 1930).

70 *6 s''ezd sovetov* (1931), No. 17, 35. A thousand or so directors were to be trained in 1931 for MTS to be set up in 1932; these potential directors were to spend a probationary period as assistant directors at an existing MTS (SZe, December 20, 1930).

71 *Sots. str.* (1935), 310; SZe, December 20, 1930.

72 SZe, December 20, 1930; *6 s''ezd sovetov* (1931), No. 17, 36; Markevich called for the gap to be closed by the general education system giving priority to areas served by the MTS.

labour-intensive flax preparation. With sugar beet, the intention was to spread beet cultivation over a wider area, including other crops in the rotation, and then to transport the beet on tractors or horses to single-line narrow-gauge railways leading to the factories. This would enable the factories to be spread out, and thus reduce the shortage of labour and horses in their vicinity.[73] All these proposals, like Markevich's original scheme, were informed with technical competence and ingenuity. But, as with the original scheme, the problem was whether resources and the competent staff would be available in sufficient quantities to gain the enthusiasm of the peasants.[74] And a further trouble menaced the grain regions: grain payments to the MTS were additional to the grain collections required from all kolkhozy. Would the MTS come to seem to the collective farmers not so much a centre of modernisation as an additional agency for exploitation?

[73] SZe, December 20, 1930.

[74] In 1931 the net increase in tractor horse-power in the MTS was 386,000 (*Nar. kh.* (1932), 145), as compared with the 596,000 planned, the main cause of the lag being the failure of the Stalingrad tractor factory to reach its planned level of production. Of the 1,228 MTS established by June 1, 1931, 688 were grain, 153 cotton, 137 flax, 154 sugar beet, and 83 vegetable and potato.

CHAPTER THREE

THE SIZE OF THE KOLKHOZ

(A) THE RURAL SETTLEMENT, THE KOLKHOZ AND THE TRACTOR, MID-1929

The mir was the basic unit of rural economic organisation in the USSR until the end of the 1920s (see vol. 1, p. 6) and was controlled by meetings of all adults in the village, under an elected elder. One or more rural settlements (seleniya) formed a mir, which was legally known as a 'land society', and one or more mirs together formed an administrative village (selo), the lowest unit in the hierarchy of soviets. In the USSR at the end of the 1920s there were approximately 600,000 rural settlements, 319,000 mirs and 72,000 village soviets, so there were on average 1·9 settlements per mir and 4·4 mirs per village soviet.[1] The size of these units varied considerably from one part of the country to another. The basic difference was between the small settlement of Central Industrial, North–Western and Western Russia and Belorussia, with an average of 16–20 households, and the larger settlement of South–Eastern Russia and the Ukraine, with an average of 100–150 households. In the main grain-surplus regions the average settlement was relatively large (100 or more households); the settlements of the Ural and Siberian regions, although somewhat smaller, still contained more households than the grain-deficit areas.[2] The village soviet was an official rather than an economic unit, and its boundaries were changed frequently during the 1920s.

The settlement and the mir were natural units when the horse-drawn plough was the basic agricultural implement: the peasant needed to be able to walk from his cottage and his household plot to his land allotments in the fields of the settlement. But the advent of the tractor challenged this arrangement. At first some efforts were

[1] For the figure for mirs, which may refer to the RSFSR, see SS, xiv (1962/63), 247 (Male) and Male (1971), 11–12; for settlements (approximately equal to 'other inhabited points') and soviets (referring to January 1, 1929) see *Administrativno-*

made to incorporate mechanised farming within the existing land structure, and in the middle 1920s a small minority of peasant households purchased their own tractors. But even at this time most tractors were allocated to sovkhozy and kolkhozy. This immediately raised the question of the size of the kolkhoz. The existing kolkhoz, generally consisting of only part of a settlement, was believed to be too small to cope with mechanised agriculture (see p. 15 above). The study of agricultural developments in the United States, and the energetic experiments and calculations of Markevich, led to the acceptance of a new optimum area for mechanised agriculture, 40,000–50,000 hectares of arable land (see p. 16 above). It was not, however, at first supposed that the unit appropriate for tractor maintenance was also appropriate for field work and other farming activities. Traktorotsentr treated the village as the largest unit of agricultural organisation, even in

---

territorial'noe selenie Soyuza SSR i spisok vazhneishikh naselennykh punktov (8th edn, 1929), 12.

2 The following table sums up the situation (derived from *ibid.* 24–31):

	No. of settlements per village soviet	*No. of persons per village soviet*	*No. of persons per settlement*
RSFSR	9	1540	180
of which:			
Leningrad region (excluding Murmansk okrug)	24	1930	80
Lower Volga region	3	1879	576
North Caucasus region	7	4145	564
Central Volga region	2	1666	747
Siberian region (excluding Krasnoyarsk okrug)	4	1468	405
Ural region (excluding Tobol'sk okrug)	8	2163	257
Central Black-Earth region	5	2312	462
Ukrainian SSR	5	2300	c.500
Belorussian SSR	27	2900	110
Transcaucasian SSR	5	1876	368
Uzbek SSR	6	2000	340
Turkmen SSR	6	2427	440

There is an unexplained discrepancy between the first two columns and the third. There were approximately five persons in each household. For more detailed figures see Male (1971), 92–3.

conditions of comprehensive collectivisation (see p. 24 above).

At the conference of large kolkhozy in July 1929, attended by delegates strongly identified with the need to increase the size of the kolkhoz, a sectional meeting on organisation resolved that 'the size of large kolkhozy is completely adequate for the rational organisation of collective production with high-productivity power and machine bases'.[3] At this time the average number of households in kolkhozy officially classified as 'large' was about 180, equivalent to the population of four or five rural settlements, and about half the size of the average village soviet. The largest kolkhoz then in existence, the Digorskii 'combine (kombinat)', North Caucasus region, included 13 settlements and 1,781 households.[4] At the conference the German expert Püschel argued that the basic unit should have an area of 1,500–2,000 hectares served by 10–15 tractors, which would provide the best possibility of precise supervision and would obviate unnecessary tractor journeys; this was about the size of the average village soviet. He proposed that the larger units which would be required in order to maintain a cultural centre and industrial enterprises could be established either by setting up larger kolkhozy divided into units, or by grouping smaller kolkhozy for common purposes.[5] All this was consistent with the assumption that a village or a larger settlement provided the natural limit for the maximum size of the larger kolkhoz.

Some excitement was caused at the conference by reports that several 'giant' kolkhozy had already been established. The term 'giant kolkhoz (kolkhoz-gigant)' was previously rarely used, and then referred to kolkhozy which embraced a whole village or a whole settlement.[6] These were now designated 'large' kolkhozy, and the term 'giant' henceforth referred to kolkhozy which included a substantial number of villages or even an entire administrative district of thousands of peasant households.[7] The establishment of giant kolkhozy was a startling new development and implied that

[3] ZKK (1929), 141.

[4] ZKK (1929), 91–5, 141, 470–7. For the debate about the definition of the 'large' kolkhoz, see vol. 1, pp. 121–2.

[5] ZKK (1929), 99–100.

[6] See, for example, *Kollektivizatsiya* (Kuibyshev, 1970), 52, 636–7 (a document of September 1928).

[7] The figures given for what is translated as 'giant' kolkhozy in Lewin (1968), 409, refer to 'large (krupnye)' kolkhozy in the wider definition of 2,000 hectares total area and above.

existing rural settlements need no longer be taken as a basis for the agricultural economy. But the giant kolkhozy were still rare exceptions to the general pattern. The movement for large kolkhozy continued to assume that the establishment of both large and giant kolkhozy could be justified only by a substantial degree of mechanisation, and that most kolkhozy would remain small. In July 1929 no-one anticipated the drastic new policies about the size of the kolkhoz which would become more or less orthodox early in 1930.

(B) THE DRIVE FOR GIANT KOLKHOZY, JULY–DECEMBER 1929

From the middle of 1929 onwards, the optimum size of kolkhozy was constantly under discussion, and by the end of the year the assumptions which still prevailed at the July conference of large kolkhozy were swept aside. The view temporarily became dominant that the mechanised kolkhoz must not be a 'large' kolkhoz but a 'giant'. Agricultural policy at this time was strongly influenced by the view that the methods of industry must prevail in agriculture, and industrial policy was increasingly directed towards the implanting of very large new factories using the most advanced United States technology. In this context, two circumstances were of particular importance in encouraging confidence in the viability of very large agricultural units.

First, the new giant sovkhozy set an example. With the support of its American advisers, Zernotrest decided early in 1929 that the optimum sovkhoz should have a sown area of 20,000–50,000 hectares, later raised to 40,000–50,000 hectares; these figures were consistent with Markevich's proposals for the optimum size of an MTS.[8] In the summer of 1929, the first harvest of Gigant sovkhoz in the Sal'sk okrug was thought satisfactory in quantity and yield (see vol. 1, p. 148), and this practical success further encouraged the supporters of giant sovkhozy. Kalmanovich reported that he had found only ten farms in the United States 'which on our understanding could be called large', and announced that the minimum sown area for a sovkhoz should be 30,000 hectares.[9] In his article of

[8] Bogdenko (1958), 62.

[9] EZh, October 3, 13, 1929; Kalmanovich was chairman of Zernotrest.

November 7, 1929, Stalin, a strong defender of the new grain sovkhozy during the discussions of 1928, now felt able to declare:

> The objections of 'science' to the possibility and expediency of organising large grain factories of 50,000–100,000 hectares have been exploded and turned into ashes.[10]

At the conference of marxist agrarians in December 1929, the rapporteur on sovkhozy argued that the criterion for deciding their size should be the 'most rational organisation of the main means of production, which in grain farming are the internal combustion engine, the tractor and all the appropriate attachments, and the repair shops', and concluded that the correct size would be 500 tractors and 100,000–150,000 hectares (this evidently referred to sown area or arable land);[11] this was already something like twice the size recommended by Markevich for the MTS.

Even if these vast areas were sensible in the case of the new grain sovkhozy, they should not have been regarded as necessarily appropriate for the kolkhoz movement: unlike the kolkhozy, the new sovkhozy were being established on virgin territory, and with the aid of very substantial supplies of imported large tractors and combine-harvesters. During the summer and autumn of 1929, however, the plans for the sovkhozy created a certain atmosphere in which the really successful agricultural unit was presumed to be a huge farm, larger than the biggest in the United States, and worked with modern machines and a small number of skilled technicians. In a mood of exuberance and thoughtlessness, the existing settlements and land structure were often seen as a mere obstacle to the technical revolution in agriculture; this was already the view taken of them when they got in the way of providing the sovkhozy with a continuous land area. At the conference of marxist agrarians, one speaker argued on the basis of the experience of the sovkhozy that the agrarian economist Chayanov was advocating a 'biological and in a sense a private capitalist orientation' when he suggested that the structure and organisation of the farms should be determined by the

[10] P, November 7, 1929. In the version of the speech published in Stalin, *Soch.*, xii (1949), 129, '50,000–100,000' is replaced by '40–50,000'. He did not indicate in either version whether he was referring to total land area, arable land, or sown area.

[11] *Trudy . . . agrarnikov-marksistov* (1930), ii, [i], 201–3 (Anisimov).

territory and type of crop rather than by the needs of the most up-to-date means of production.[12]

The second circumstance encouraging the formation of very large kolkhozy was the belief, vigorously advocated at all levels of the kolkhoz system, that tractors and agricultural machinery should be brought under the control of the kolkhozy themselves, or at least of the kolkhoz system, rather than being managed by a separate state agency such as Traktorotsentr or by the agricultural cooperatives (see p. 20 above). Existing small kolkhozy were at best large enough only for a single tractor, maintenance of which was difficult, and the kolkhozsoyuzy were weak and ineffective. The belief that tractors should not be managed by an agency external to the kolkhoz system thus encouraged the view that tractor and other farm operations should be fused under the unified management of a giant kolkhoz.

In September 1929, giant kolkhozy were still a very minor strand in plans for collectivisation. The grain cooperative organisation Khlebotsentr made a first tentative move towards bringing together tractor and other farm operations under a single management for an entire district. It arranged with Kolkhoztsentr that three districts of the Black-Earth region should be comprehensively collectivised in 1929/30 by extending the facilities of their MTS, which were part of the agricultural cooperative network, to cater for the whole population; in these districts the existing kolkhozy would retain their individual identities, but 'the transfer of the MTS to direct management by the collectivised population' would be accomplished through the establishment of a 'group cooperative union' of the kolkhozy of the district.[13] This plan would have resulted in the establishment of an organisation at the district level intermediate between a giant kolkhoz such as the Ural Gigant, and the district MTS surrounded by kolkhoz villages proposed by Markevich. But Markevich and Traktorotsentr remained sceptical about the prospects for giant kolkhozy. At an all-Union conference of the local officials of Traktorotsentr in September 1929, Markevich envisaged a future stage in which the optimum size of a kolkhoz, so as to enable the 'cheapest, most rational and most exact use of machinery' would

[12] *Ibid.* 229–30; Chayanov was working at this time on sovkhoz problems, and was criticised at the conference for being guided by the norms of the American Campbell's capitalist farm (*ibid.* 221); see also pp. 40–1 below.

[13] IS, 4, 1969, p. 32, citing the archives.

be 'thousands or tens of thousands of hectares'; but he continued to presume that in the 'first period' of kolkhoz development, which was evidently to be a lengthy one, the villages served by an MTS would remain separate economic units, with their own economy and crop rotation.[14]

A major shift in attitude followed the central committee plenum in November 1929. The resolutions of the plenum did not specifically refer to the size of kolkhozy or their relation with the MTS, and Molotov appears to have ignored the question in his wide-ranging reports. But Kaminsky in his unpublished report boldly declared that 'life itself is pressing for unification and grouping around the stronger collectives and for a further development via group associations (kustovye ob"edineniya) to large-scale production', and proposed the establishment of kolkhozy which included whole districts, claiming that only kolkhozy of this size could solve the grain and livestock problem by 1930/31.[15] Kaganovich, in his report on the plenum to party activists in Moscow region, pointed out that the land area of ten kolkhozy in the Urals amounted to a million hectares in all, and chose the famous Gigant kolkhoz as his principal example of successful kolkhoz development; this was the largest kolkhoz in the USSR, though so far equipped with relatively few tractors. He depicted—and predicted—in glowing phrases the setting up of a telephone network and a bakery for the whole kolkhoz and of communal kitchens which would deliver food straight to the fields.[16]

The impression that the party leadership was not averse to the establishment of giant kolkhozy equal in size to an administrative district, and that such kolkhozy need not await the arrival of large numbers of tractors, was reinforced by the vigorous campaign conducted at this time against the once powerful group of economists, mainly former Socialist Revolutionaries, who had persistently defended small-scale agriculture as economically more viable. The pressure exercised on these men by the campaign was such that in September 1929 their leading theoretician Chayanov repudiated his earlier defence of the peasant family unit as inappropriate to an age of technical revolution and vigorously advocated large-scale farming and the socialist reconstruction of

[14] EZh, September 10, 1929.
[15] Chigrinov (1970), 48.
[16] P, November 26, 1929 (report of November 21).

agriculture.[17] This change of heart was criticised by official writers as insincere,[18] and the adherents or former adherents of small-scale agriculture were abused on all sides. At the conference of marxist agrarians in December 1929, a work on agricultural settlements was denounced as propaganda for 'Belorussian national-democracy'. Particular scorn was directed at its argument that in the conditions of the Belorussian republic 'everything that is technically and economically progressive finds its maximum expression in settlements of 75–200 hectares' (some 8–20 households), put forward primarily on the grounds that all fields should be easily accessible on foot from the peasant's household plot.[19] A 'bourgeois specialist' who had recently recommended that the optimum area of a kolkhoz should be 1,600 hectares, so that the fields should not be more than two kilometres away from the peasant households, was equally repudiated.[20]

The corollary of this criticism of small kolkhozy was taken to be that the very large kolkhoz had great advantages. Larin, a strong critic of Chayanov, firmly declared at the conference that a single MTS and kolkhoz should be established in each district, and the district soviet executive committee should replace the land society; and he looked forward to a future in which electric vehicles and ploughs would have replaced petrol lorries and tractors, the kolkhozy would become sovkhozy or 'obkhozy' (obshchestvennye khozyaistva—public farms) and the peasants would move into agrotowns.[21] Shlikhter, People's Commissar for Agriculture of the Ukraine, objected to the 'almost dwarf character' of 80–90 per cent

[17] EO, 9, 1929, 39–51, 12, 1929, 95–101; in a letter published in the agricultural newspaper (SKhG, December 12, 1929), he criticised his past defence of individual agriculture as a 'crude reactionary mistake' and announced that a substantial work was now in press on *Organisation of the Large Economy in the Epoch of the Socialist Reconstruction of Agriculture* (his classical defence of the small farm was entitled *The Organisation of the Peasant Economy*).

[18] See for example O. Targul'yan in EZh, December 21, 1929; Milyutin and Gordeev in *Trudy . . . agrarnikov-marksistov* (1930), i, 38, 99–100.

[19] *Ibid.* 176; the work in question was N. Kislyakov, *Poselki* (1928) (100 hectares = 1 sq. km).

[20] *Trudy . . . agrarnikov-marksistov* (1930), i, 185 (1,600 hectares = an area of 4 × 4 km).

[21] *Trudy . . . agrarnikov-marksistov* (1930), i, 65–72; he developed these thoughts in an article in EO, 1, 1930, 41–50. Larin was a former Menshevik who throughout the 1920s consistently advocated more vigorous measures to curb kulaks and private capital.

of kolkhozy, and called for the establishment of inter-village kolkhozy of 50,000–60,000 hectares; these would be appropriate to 'the optimum set or system of machines', would enable land utilisation to be adjusted to the needs of the MTS, and would carry the corollary that the land society (the mir) could be abolished. As alternatives to the giant kolkhoz, Shlikhter also advocated the establishment of 'large integrated agro-industrial combines' (AIKs), and of 'sovkhoz–kolkhoz combines'; the latter would be more appropriate when sovkhozy already existed, or were being established, in places where an MTS was being set up. Both types of combine, according to Shlikhter, should, like the giant kolkhoz, cover an area of 50,000–60,000 hectares.[22]

The brakes were not quite off. In his report to the conference, the agrarian economist Lyashchenko called for central management in the kolkhoz to be 'differentiated' rather than 'integrated', so that the MTS, the processing plant, and so on, would each have different spans of control. He also warned that the transfer of the peasants' household plots into new population centres, which was being 'inexpediently attempted' in some places, involved 'colossal difficulties' and would take a number of years.[23] But the general attitude to the size of the kolkhoz in party circles was now radically different from that prevalent at the conference of large kolkhozy five months before.

(C) GIGANTOMANIA AT ITS PEAK, DECEMBER 1929–FEBRUARY 1930

(i) Policy

In the last weeks of 1929 and the first few weeks of 1930 the campaign in favour of giant kolkhozy was at its most intense, and seemed to form an integral part of the all-out drive for collectivisation. It is true that some directives and statements from the centre continued to assume that giant kolkhozy should be formed only when at least some degree of mechanisation was present. Thus

[22] *Trudy . . . agrarnikov-marksistov* (1930), i, 85–7. For these combines see p. 44, n. 32, below. Sovkhoz–kolkhoz combines (kombinaty) were sometimes known as 'associations' (ob''edineniya): the terms appear to have been interchangeable.
[23] *Ibid.* ii, [i], 56.

in its telegram of January 18, 1930, Khlebotsentr ruled that giant kolkhozy with 50,000–60,000 hectares of arable land should be formed on the basis of its MTS and tractor columns when these held more than 20 tractors (i.e. about 8–10 per cent of the full complement of tractors for an area of this size) (see p. 22 above). In the following month the chairman of Khlebotsentr, on the basis of a proposal by the party central committee in its resolution of January 5, 1930,[24] called for the establishment of 3,790 MKS (Mashinno-konnye stantsii—machine-horse stations) within kolkhozy, stipulating that the area of each kolkhoz should be a minimum of 3,000 hectares;[25] this, though much larger than the average kolkhoz, was very roughly equal in area to the group of rural settlements covered by an average village soviet. The All-Russian Land Consolidation Conference, which met from February 12 to 18, 1930, was also cautious. In his report Shuleikin condemned the widespread proposals to destroy existing rural settlements and to establish agrotowns, and the conference resolved:

> Considering the fact that a whole number of important issues have not yet been worked out, and bearing in mind the need to use capital already invested, elimination of existing settlements should be approached with special care.[26]

But these notes of caution were unusual. In January and February 1930, the central authorities did not commit themselves to specific recommendations about the size of the kolkhozy. But throughout these weeks, the central press and many leading officials made clamorous noises in condemnation of small kolkhozy, and in favour of giant kolkhozy. Thus M. Golendo condemned Markevich in an article in the agricultural journal for his insistence that the size of each agricultural unit was 'determined by the historically established dimensions of the villages', and claimed that, while existing buildings would continue to be used, the sections (uchastki) of most of the giant kolkhozy would not correspond to the boundaries of existing settlements.[27] On January 26, a Sovnarkom decree stated that in 1930 each of the new sovkhozy must undertake a full cycle of work on peasant land with an area of at least 100,000

[24] *KPSS v rez.*, (1954), 665.
[25] SZe, February 13, 1930.
[26] SZo, i–ii, January–February 1930, 92–4, 144.
[27] NAF, 2, 1930, 11–12.

hectares.[28] A survey article in *Pravda* reported the formation of giant kolkhozy covering thousands of hectares, and commented 'this is nothing to get cold feet about'.[29] Bukharin, in his enthusiastic defence of collectivisation published on February 19, praised the emergence of kolkhozy embracing a whole administrative district, 'district-kolkhozy', envisaging that each would ultimately be served by an industrial combine.[30] On the same day, Kalinin reported in a speech in Voronezh that the average kolkhoz in the Central Black-Earth region included 20,000 hectares and 20,000 people, but made no criticism of the size of these giant kolkhozy.[31] The view that giant kolkhozy must await mechanisation was now completely abandoned, though it was hopefully assumed that vast quantities of tractors would be available to them within a couple of years.

In this heady atmosphere, far-reaching schemes for establishing giant kolkhozy received much publicity and official acquiescence, and some official support. At the end of December 1929, while the conference of marxist agrarians was in progress, a conference to discuss the AIKs was held under the auspices of the All-Union Council of Kolkhozy. The AIKs were intended as a grandiose development of the association between farming and industrial activities, on a district scale, which had already been attempted by the Tiginskii combine.[32] Ten reports were heard from districts with widely different agricultural profiles, and the chairman asserted that all RSKs were tending to become AIKs. The conference was reported to have looked with disfavour on AIKs of a mere 30,000–40,000 hectares, and to have given its preference to what were described as 'future agricultural Dnieprostrois', evidently on a multi-district basis, of 500,000 hectares. These would include 'dozens of dairy

[28] SZ, 1930, art. 101.

[29] P, February 16, 1930 (V. Feigin).

[30] P, February 19, 1930.

[31] P, March 3, 1930; for the date of this speech see vol. 1, p. 255, n. 232.

[32] See NAF, 1, 1930, 40. The establishment of 'combine enterprises' or units 'of an agro-industrial type' was proposed by Professor V. R. Batyushkov in 1926, and was presented as a partial alternative to industrialisation via large-scale urban factory industry. He envisaged them as involving the collectivisation of agriculture and a considerable degree of mechanisation; they would vary in size from a few hundred to 30,000 hectares of arable land according to the type of production, with an average of 15,000 hectares and 3,000 households, so that there would be 8,000 in the USSR as a whole (PKh, 5, 1926, 107–27; he also published a pamphlet *Postroenie agroindustrial'nykh kombinatov* (1929), which I have not seen; see also article by Oganovsky in SKhG, November 19, 1929).

farms, oil seed and cheese factories, factories to process all other agricultural products, cattlesheds for a thousand animals, electric ploughs, power stations, cultured settlements' and were expected to increase marketed output to 10–15 times its existing level. Most resources for these vast developments were to be provided by the peasants themselves, and the economic newspaper suggested that 'with insignificant help from the state the land in these districts will become a factory'. But even on the wildly optimistic calculations presented at the conference, the cost of establishing these combines would evidently have been some tens of milliards of rubles a year, a substantial proportion of this being borne by the state.[33]

Proposals of this kind continued to appear for some weeks. The famous Khoper okrug in the Lower Volga announced that, with the aid of the Sovkhoz and Kolkhoz Faculty of the Timiryazev Agricultural Academy in Moscow, working all out for three days and three nights, a plan had been prepared for a grain–livestock combine with a single population centre, a 'socialist agrotown', of 44,000 persons, divided into 22 blocks of flats, with communal eating as in the best flats in Europe, not to mention a reading room, library, studies, gymnasium and solarium in each block. This would replace the present situation in which families were isolated from their neighbours and suffered 'boring loneliness under the dark smoky oil lamp in the long snowy winter evenings':

> Eight thousand separate, scattered economic cells, almost defenceless from fire, mass epidemics and other social evils. How much unnecessary waste of energy just to service and light the stoves, prepare eight thousand family dinners, heat water for baths, do the washing, etc.

The agricultural newspaper claimed that this plan was inspired by the spontaneous decision of a group of peasants, previously scattered over a radius of 15–20 km, to move to the centre of their kolkhoz, and commented that the 'local party and soviet agencies, as in the whole development of the process of comprehensive collectivisation, have proved far ahead of our centres, and this time have been the forerunners of a big revolution'.[34] In an article published in January

[33] EZh, December 26, 27, 1929; after a brief notice on December 26, *Pravda* did not apparently report the conference further. For a list of estimates made for particular AIKs, see Abramsky, ed. (1974), 278, n. 45 (Davies).

[34] SKhG, January 9, 1930.

1930, Nikulikhin boldly declared that 'all our agriculture will gradually be reorganised along the lines of an AIK'. 'Some comrades', he reported, 'believe it fully possible to have only 50,000 agricultural enterprises by the end of the present five-year plan'; and he envisaged that towards the end of the proposed 'general plan' (i.e. in 10–15 years) the whole of agriculture would be organised into some 5,000 AIKs of 100,000 hectares each.[35] In an address to the Communist Academy on February 22 Larin envisaged the future establishment, once electricity had become the main motive-power for agriculture, of agrotowns with several tens of thousands of inhabitants serving an area of 200,000 hectares; the present villages would become stores on the outskirts of the kolkhoz.[36] The historian sympathetic to industrialisation is almost tempted, as he turns these yellowing pages, to forget elementary economics and commonsense, and identify himself for a moment with these inexperienced urban enthusiasts in those grim January days of 1930, boldly dreaming about rapid progress towards giant mechanised factory farms, cajoling reluctant peasants into kolkhozy, denouncing recalcitrants and driving them out of the villages into the endless snow.

These fanciful programmes were only one strand, though a significant one, in the proposals about the optimum size of kolkhoz prepared in the last few weeks of 1929 and the first few weeks of 1930. In the absence of firm recommendations from the centre, the plans of different regions, or even of different okrugs within the same region, varied considerably. In the Ukraine, as we have seen, there was a general commitment to a kolkhoz–MTS unit of 50,000 hectares. In the Lower Volga region, plans varied from okrug to okrug. Some okrugs, such as Balashov, appear to have favoured giant kolkhozy each covering a whole district: in the Lower Volga, each of these would have been several times as large as the MTS optimum of 50,000 hectares. Others favoured smaller units: in Khoper okrug, the fantastic grain–livestock combine was planned as an experimental exception to the general pattern; for the okrug as a whole, it was proposed to set up 100 kolkhozy each with an area of 12,000 hectares. Gusti, a secretary of the regional party committee in the Lower Volga, argued that a kolkhoz covering a whole district

[35] NAF, 1, 1930, 39, 44; cf. Batyushkov's proposal in 1926 that 8,000 combines should be established with 15,000 hectares of arable land each (see p. 44, n. 32, above).

[36] EO, 3, 1930, 65–6.

would 'at present be almost impossible to manage': in districts served by an MTS, Markevich's optimum was appropriate; for the others districts (which were of course the majority), the regional party committee did not apparently go further than stipulating that each kolkhoz should include at least one village.[37] In the Central Black-Earth region, the regional soviet executive committee approved in one case the establishment of an AIK which included over 11,000 households; this presumably covered a whole district.[38] In the Tambov okrug of the same region, the Kirsanov district endeavoured to establish a single giant commune for the whole district of 198,000 hectares and 23,700 households, explicitly on the model of the Gigant sovkhoz in the North Caucasus; the okrug authorities insisted, however, that the district should limit itself in 1930 to establishing a number of large kolkhozy, and postpone unification until an adequate technical basis was available.[39] In the North Caucasus itself, the authorities appear to have decided to establish one kolkhoz in each *stanitsa*.[40]

At the beginning of 1930, then, policy—or rather policies—towards the size of the kolkhoz fall into the following pattern. It was generally accepted that with the replacement of the horse by the tractor the criterion for determining the size of the kolkhoz should not be the existing land configuration and practices of the peasants but the needs of the machine; and these needs were held to involve the organisation of units of 50,000 hectares of arable land or more. There was also a definite tendency to argue that in districts which were not yet mechanised, the size of kolkhoz should be determined not by the present but by the future level of mechanisation, though this tendency was resisted by some important local authorities. These policy decisions were made in an atmosphere, strongly encouraged by leading members of the Politburo, of 'big means best'; in this atmosphere arguments against giant units were rarely heard, at any rate in public, and wild schemes were rarely publicly rebuffed.

(ii) Practice

Much less was accomplished in practice than might be inferred from

37 KG, 104, December 30, 1929; SKhG, January 4, 1930.

38 Decision of January 4, 1930, *cit*, VI, 3, 1965, 14.

39 SZe, February 23, 1930.

40 SZe, March 26, 1930, describing the situation in the early part of February; the *stanitsa* was a large Cossack village, usually with a population of several thousands.

these discussions and decisions. Certainly a number of giant kolkhozy were established. The famous Gigant kolkhoz in the Urals was extended to embrace five administrative districts with a population of some 13,000 households and a total area of 275,000 hectares. Land consolidation was said to have been carried out over the whole territory. All animals, farm buildings and even dwellings were declared to have been socialised and transferred to indivisible capital; substantial numbers of cattle were driven into temporary cattlesheds, and an unknown number of peasant households—in addition to those classified as kulaks—were resettled in the course of the effort to establish a single commune over the whole territory. However, even in the case of the highly publicised Gigant the process of forming a single commune was far from complete. The 160 kolkhozy continued their separate existence until the end of January or beginning of February, when they were merged and their elected boards were replaced by 'production sections (uchastki)' of the commune with appointed managers.[41] Elsewhere in the Urals, the kolkhoz for the Shatrovskii district included 215,000 hectares before the end of 1929.[42] Kolkhozy of 354,000 and 259,000 hectares were reported from the Lower Volga region.[43] In Votsk region in the far north, although tractors were very rare, dozens of giant kolkhozy were established, sometimes embracing as many as 300 settlements.[44]

In addition to kolkhozy as large as a district, there were smaller giants which included a substantial number of villages: Kolkhozy including over 30,000 hectares were reported from the North Caucasus and the Central Black-Earth region.[45] In Khoper okrug, a total of 423 kolkhozy established by December 1929, with a total collectivised population of 52,000 households, were replaced early in 1930 by 81 kolkhozy covering 91,760 households, 90 per cent of the rural population of the okrug, as compared with the 100 kolkhozy planned in December 1929.[46]

Some AIKs and sovkhoz–kolkhoz combines were also established. The maximum figure I have found for the number of AIKs is

[41] P, January 12, 1930; SKhG, January 21, 1930; NAF, 5, 1930, 31, 36–7, and 7–8, 1930, 86–7, 92, 95.

[42] I, January 13, 1930.

[43] SKhG, January 4, 1930.

[44] NAF, 5, 1930, 35.

[45] P, December 13, 1929; SZe, February 23, March 9, 1930.

[46] KGN, 98, December 10, 1929, and 32, April 23, 1930.

that early in 1930 some 300 AIKs were 'in the course of being set up (voznikshie)'; in the RSFSR 36 of these were recognised as model combines.[47] Attempts to establish sovkhoz–kolkhoz combines were encouraged by a cautious paragraph in the central committee resolution of January 5, 1930, which welcomed experiments, in areas with a considerable number of sovkhozy, in establishing 'a type of combined economy' based on a sovkhoz and supplying tractor ploughing, machine harvesting and other services to kolkhozy by contract for payment.[48] A combine established round the 'Khutorok' sovkhoz in the North Caucasus included a total area of 150,000–200,000 hectares; a sovkhoz in the Lower Volga region in effect completely absorbed the kolkhozy in its area.[49] But no more than 10 or 20 combines of this kind existed by March 1930;[50] a later Soviet commentator drily commented that 'in practice the directive on setting up kolkhoz–sovkhoz combines was hardly carried out at all'.[51]

In sum, then, giant kolkhozy, varying in size from a whole district to a few villages, and the two kinds of combine were exceptions, even at the height of the collectivisation campaign. Over most of Soviet territory, the general pattern seems to have been that some existing kolkhozy amalgamated, others expanded to include many more members of their settlement or their village, and many new kolkhozy were formed. In the USSR as a whole, the average number of households per kolkhoz rose from 18 to 133 between June 1, 1929, and March 1, 1930 (see Table 3). The figures for households collectivised on March 1, 1930, are certainly overestimates, so the size of the average kolkhoz is also likely to be overestimated. But even accepting these figures as accurate, the 'average' kolkhoz had a population somewhere between that of a settlement and that of a village. The population of the average kolkhoz was larger than that of the average village only in the Lower Volga region, where there were 481 households per kolkhoz and only about 380 households per village (see p. 35, n. 2, above and Table 3). Even in the Ukraine, where the formation of giant

[47] NAF, 1, 1930, 39, 41; NAF, 3, 1930, 47. In SZe, February 5, 1930, Nikulikhin made the extravagant claim that AIKs already included an area of over 30 million hectares.

[48] *KPSS v rez.*, ii (1954), 666.

[49] *Materialy*, vii (1959), 311–21.

[50] NAF, 3, 1930, 49.

[51] *Materialy*, vii (1959), 316n. (Bogdenko).

kolkhozy had explicit official approval, there were 25,000 kolkhozy for 12,000 village soviets.[52] These figures leave out of account the various arrangements for the grouping (kustovanie) of kolkhozy. In the groups the constituent kolkhozy continued to retain their separate identity. Precise figures do not appear to be available, but in the Ukraine at least a substantial proportion of the kolkhozy were members of groups.[53] In some cases the groups controlled tractors and other farm machinery, more rarely some horses as well, in others they were responsible for joint industrial enterprises, dairy farms, silos and so on. But many of the groups were a mere formality.[54]

(D) GIGANTOMANIA IN RETREAT, MARCH–DECEMBER 1930

The size of the kolkhoz was not mentioned in Stalin's article of March 2, or in the party central committee resolution of March 14, and early in March some measures were adopted which seemed to give further encouragement to the formation of large units. On March 4, Sovkhoztsentr announced that it intended to form 12 sovkhoz–kolkhoz associations (ob"edineniya) in 12 regions, varying in area from 30,000 to 500,000 hectares, 1·5 million hectares in all.[55] A week later, a report on collectivisation in the Ukraine treated the village as the basic kolkhoz unit for the time being, but still argued that the village-kolkhozy should be unified, as the MTS developed, into 700–1,000 groups (i.e. one or two groups per district) which would themselves in future become kolkhozy: Markevich's optimum for the MTS thus still remained a goal for the size of kolkhoz.[56] In two long articles on the AIKs published in March, Nikulikhin recognised that the schemes for the immediate establishment of agrotowns were not feasible, but argued that AIKs could be immediately effective if they concentrated on expanding production rather than services for the next four or five years. He claimed that the immense waste of labour resulting from the highly

[52] SZe, March 12, 1930, and source cited in Table 3.

[53] 484 groups had apparently been formed in 22 of the 40 okrugs by the beginning of March, and in 15 of these more than half the kolkhozy belonged to groups (SZe, March 12, 1930).

[54] Minaev, ed. (1930), 239–41.

[55] SZe, March 4, 1930. For these associations or combines see p. 42 above.

[56] SZe, March 12, 1930.

seasonal nature of Russian agriculture could be avoided by establishing a single AIK in each district which would combine agriculture, seasonal industries such as peat and lumber, and simple local factories in which collective farmers would work in the winter months.[57] In this simpler form the proposed AIKs would have resembled the Chinese communes of the 1960s. In the USSR, schemes to handle the seasonality of agricultural labour through the establishment of AIKs were more or less forgotten in the turmoil of the 1930s, but were revived 47 years later.

Simultaneously with the attempts to save the giant kolkhozy strong criticisms of them began to appear in the press. As early as February 26, Odintsev, a deputy chairman of Kolkhoztsentr, criticised the establishment, without proper preparation, of giant kolkhozy of 50,000–70,000 hectares in Kursk okrug in the Central Black-Earth region.[58] On March 9, 1930, a further article by Odintsev was much sharper in tone. He strongly criticised the hasty formation of giant kolkhozy, giving an example, again from Kursk okrug, of a giant with only one telephone in its 16 villages:

> Giants are often thought up from above without preliminary work among the masses and without taking into account organisational, technical and economic prerequisites.

He still exempted from criticism, however, both carefully-prepared and long-established kolkhozy such as the Urals Gigant, even though they lacked tractors, and large inter-village kolkhozy in which each sub-unit corresponded to an existing settlement.[59] On March 13, an article in *Pravda* by Khataevich complained that 'super-giant' kolkhozy had been formed in the Central Volga region simply on the basis of instructions from the district kolkhozsoyuzy, endorsed by the boards of the kolkhozy, without the collective farmers knowing anything about it. A few days later, a telegram was published from Narkomzem of the USSR and Kolkhoztsentr which asked local authorities what steps they had taken both to cease further amalgamation and to 'divide up kolkhozy larger than justified by existing machinery'.[60] On the following day, Andreev condemned attempts in the North Caucasus to establish only 100

[57] NAF, 3, 1930, 39–50; B, 6, March 31, 1930, 31–45.
[58] EZh, February 26, 1930.
[59] SZe, March 9, 1930.
[60] I, March 17, 1930.

kolkhozy in each okrug, and pointed out that even a kolkhoz based on a single *stanitsa* containing 3,000 or 4,000 households could be more complicated to manage than any industrial enterprise.[61] On March 24, a conference held under the auspices of the agricultural newspaper 'decisively repudiated' uncritical or exclusive reliance either on giant kolkhozy which were tens and hundreds of thousands of hectares in area, or on small kolkhozy no bigger than a single settlement.[62]

The criticism of giant kolkhozy was now taken up at the highest level. In his article of April 3, Stalin criticised the concentration of attention on 'so-called "giants", which often developed into top-heavy headquarters on paper, lacking economic roots'; if kolkhoz officials turned their attention to 'the work of kolkhoz economic organisation in hamlets and villages', and were successful, giants would 'appear of their own accord'.[63] A few days later, Markevich bounced back into prominence with a scathing article 'On "Inter-Village Giants"'. He pointed out that a 'large' kolkhoz used to be one with 500 or 600 hectares sown to grain, but 'now a kolkhoz of 20,000–30,000 hectares in no way satisfies the "giant" appetites of our kolkhoz organisers'; one district had even proposed a kolkhoz of 500,000 hectares. This was 'bureaucratic "gigantomania"', in which the collective farmer played 'the passive role of a working unit'. Such giant kolkhozy had no positive side, as they did not result in any new association of labour and implements, and they should be replaced by one kolkhoz corresponding to each village; in such a kolkhoz the peasants knew the work, the animals, and each other, and would understand that the future depended on themselves. No optimum size of kolkhoz could be laid down, as villages varied greatly in size—the search for a standard optimum size was mere '"optimum" ignorance, "optimum" bureaucratisation, and "optimum" lack of comprehension, or lack of desire to comprehend the requirements of kolkhoz construction'.[64] A circular from Narkomzem of the RSFSR on breaking up the giants was also issued at about this time.[65]

Giant kolkhozy were now universally condemned. Astonishing tales were told of the ignorance of their organisers. In one giant

[61] Andreev (Rostov, 1930), 17; speech of March 18.
[62] SZe, March 26, 1930.
[63] *Soch.*, xii, 226.
[64] P, April 8, 1930.
[65] IZ, lxxvi (1965), 35.

kolkhoz each settlement became a field in the crop rotation: Settlement A, rye; B, potatoes; C, grass; D, a year off![66]

Long before the publication of these criticisms, most of the giant kolkhozy had been broken up 'from below'. As early as March 14, *Pravda* reported that in the Borisogleb okrug 'all the "giants" created by proclamation in the past 6–8 weeks are cracking up and disintegrating'. Even the Urals Gigant broke up into separate kolkhozy in the course of March; a district kolkhoz combine (raikolkhozkombinat) was established to handle some common activities, including sales and supplies.[67] During March and April 1930, most of the giant kolkhozy were subdivided or fell apart. Some smaller giants containing several settlements still remained: in May there were still some 200 kolkhozy without tractors and with a sown area in excess of 5,110 hectares,[68] and as late as the summer of 1930 some 'super-giants' of 100,000–200,000 hectares continued to exist.[69] The total number of kolkhozy fell from an estimated 110,000 on March 1, 1930, to 84,000 in May, and the number of households per kolkhoz fell from 127 to 70; in the Lower Volga region, the number of households per kolkhoz fell particularly rapidly, from 481 to 247 (see Table 3 and source there cited). Throughout the USSR the population of the average kolkhoz was now the equivalent of one or two settlements. But the departure of large numbers of peasants from the kolkhozy in a vast number of settlements brought a new problem: the typical kolkhoz now tended to include *part* of the population of each of a number of settlements.[70] Some kolkhozy which contained part of the population of only one settlement now contained only a few households; such very small kolkhozy were condemned by Kindeev as 'an anti-Leninist excess in the opposite direction'.[71] The disadvantages of small size were partly overcome by continuing 'group associations' of kol-

[66] SZe, May 30, 1930. Other attacks on giant kolkhozy appeared in I, May 6, 1930 (Khataevich); SZo, June 1, 1930 (A. Lisitsyn); NAF, 3, 1930, 10–11 (Gaister), 30–1 (Vareikis); Minaev, ed. (1930), 237–8.

[67] NAF, 7–8, 1930, 88, 100.

[68] Minaev, ed. (1930), 238.

[69] PKh, 7–8, 1930, 100 (Kindeev).

[70] 54·5 per cent of all kolkhozy contained 35 households or less (*Kolkhozy v 1930 g.* (1931), 78–9).

[71] PKh, 7–8, 1930, 100; he was a Rabkrin specialist on kolkhozy. For 'dwarf' kolkhozy of a few households formed at this time, see also SZe, June 1, 1930 (Lisitsyn).

khozy (see p. 40 above) for the joint use of tractors, horses and other services; 20,219 kolkhozy belonged to the associations in May 1930, most of them in the Ukraine.[72]

In July 1930, the more modest approach to the size of kolkhoz was endorsed by the XVI party congress, which roundly condemned 'the creation as so-called "giant" kolkhozy of lifeless bureaucratic organisations, designed on the principles of orders from above'.[73] The kolkhoz-village was now treated everywhere as the basic unit for further development.[74] The Rabkrin report on the kolkhozy, completed at the time of the congress, warned that 'even now some kolkhozy are too large, although they formally include only one village, and some are too small'. The report attributed such mistakes to the 'absence of precise directives (ustanovki)' on kolkhoz size, and called upon Kolkhoztsentr to prepare 'model sizes' for different regions.[75]

Much remained unresolved. In districts where agricultural machinery was relatively unimportant, the village would certainly remain the basic economic unit. But what would be the effect of mechanisation? How were the tractor and the existing land structure to be reconciled? Was the sole criterion for organisation to be the needs of the tractor and the machine, as was generally believed between the end of 1929 and the middle of 1930? Considerable differences of opinion remained. An article published in the planning journal immediately before the XVI party congress continued to assume that giant kolkhozy of 50,000–60,000 hectares would be formed when enough modern machinery was available; on the other hand Grin'ko, writing in the same journal, looked forward to the establishment of as many as 50,000 MTS (which would mean 10 or 15 per administrative district) and several hundred thousand kolkhozy (which would presumably mean one per settlement rather than one per village).[76]

The issue was resolved by the sudden decision in September 1930 to concentrate tractors in large state-owned MTS, each of which served a substantial group of kolkhozy (see p. 27 above). This

[72] *Kolkhozy v 1930 g.* (1931), 260.

[73] *KPSS v rez.*, iii (1954), 53.

[74] See the control figures for the economic year 1930/31, published in SZe, July 27, 1930.

[75] SZe, July 13, 1930 (resolution of presidium of central control commission and collegium of Rabkrin, dated July 9).

[76] PKh, 5, 1930, 79 (Kraev), 16; for Grin'ko see vol. 1, p. 169.

almost automatically set broad limits to the size of the kolkhoz. In conformity with Markevich's original scheme, the problem of the efficient unit for the management, maintenance and use of the tractor was separated, at least in part, from the problem of the efficient management of the farm. The needs of both management and production now pointed in the direction of keeping the order of magnitude of the production unit the same as that of the traditional rural settlement. Moreover, though this point was rarely mentioned, the kolkhoz based on the rural settlement or village was a workable unit, close to the peasant, for the collection of grain and other state exactions. The lure of giant agricultural units did not completely lose its savour in the summer and autumn of 1930; the existence of kolkhozy with over 1,000 households was reported in the last few months of 1930.[77] But such attempts to retain kolkhozy which included more than one village were now dogmatically criticised. While intermittent attempts were made to establish giant kolkhozy during the next quarter of a century, the compromise solution that the MTS should serve many kolkhozy while the kolkhoz was based on the traditional rural settlement or village remained more or less intact for a period of nearly 28 years between the summer of 1930 and the abolition of the MTS in 1958.

[77] SZe, August 3 (Yelan', Urals), December 16 (Far East), 1930.

CHAPTER FOUR
THE STRUCTURE OF THE KOLKHOZ

Like the mir, the typical small kolkhoz of the 1920s was a self-governing association both legally and to a large extent in practice. According to successive model Statutes, in all three types of kolkhoz the supreme organ was the general meeting of members—equivalent to the skhod. In the kolkhoz, unlike the mir, the model Statutes usually provided that the general meeting should elect a small executive council(sovet) or board(pravlenie) to run its affairs, but for many of the small kolkhozy in the 1920s such boards were hardly necessary, and they were often not established. In nearly all kolkhozy, as in mirs, the general meeting elected one of its members as its head. The head of the kolkhoz—at first known as the 'elder (starosta)' as in the mir, and later as the 'chairman'—in practice shared power with the general assembly. He (it was almost invariably a man and not a woman) sometimes possessed great powers. An authoritative textbook of the mid-1920s stated that 'he alone is in charge in the farm, allocates labour and manages the work'.[1] Model internal rules for artels adopted in 1929 also made the chairman responsible for all executive work, including the allocation of labour.[2] But he could always be replaced by the decision of the general meeting.

Before the revolution, the constituent members of the mir were the peasant households, represented at the skhod by the head of the household, normally the oldest man in the family. In the post-revolutionary mir, all the adults in the household, male and female, were supposed to be full members, and this principle was naturally followed in the kolkhozy. In practice, however, the household for many purposes remained the main economic and social unit, in the kolkhoz as well as in the mir. The main non-collectivised agricultural activities of collective farmers were carried out by the

[1] Bauer *et al.* (1925), 54; see also Wesson (1963), 135–8.

[2] *Pravila vnutrennego rasporyadka sel'skokhozyaistvennoi arteli* (8th edn, 1929), clauses 1–3, 30; these rules were a development of the model Statute prepared by Kolkhoztsentr in 1928.

household on the household plot; and in TOZy and artels the household, using its own horses and implements, often remained the basic unit of labour for a substantial part of collectivised farming. Women played only a minor role in kolkhoz management: only 6·8 per cent of the members of the administrative organs in the kolkhozy on June 1, 1929, were women.[3]

During the mass collectivisation drive of the winter of 1929–30, many millions of peasant households were forced into the kolkhozy against their will. Nevertheless, strenuous efforts to win the support of the peasantry were an integral part of the collectivisation process, and official propaganda loudly proclaimed that this support had in fact been secured. Against this background, both the February 6 and the March 1 versions of the model Statute of the artel fully retained the principles of self-government:

> Clause 19. The general meeting (or the meeting of plenipotentiaries) shall be the supreme organ of administration of the artel, shall decide the most important questions on the activity of the artel, shall elect a board and a commission of inspection and shall adopt an instruction about their work.[4]

The Statute did not formally provide for the election of a kolkhoz chairman; this omission seems to have been without significance, as the post of chairman was universally regarded as the senior position in the kolkhoz.[5]

Not surprisingly, the principles of self-government were frequently ignored. During the retreat from collectivisation the giant kolkhozy were strongly criticised on the grounds that their boards and their principal officials were not elected, but appointed from above.[6] The more flexible kolkhoz organisation established (or re-established) in the spring of 1930 did not avoid the crucial conflict between the rival principles of self-government and subordination to the state. In the winter of 1929–30 many of the traditional leaders

[3] *Kolkhozy v 1929 godu* (1931), 154–5.

[4] P, February 7, March 2, 1930; *Kollektivizatsiya . . . 1927–1935* (1957), 286–7. 'Plenipotentiaries' in this context had no connection with the urban workers sent in to the villages in support of collectivisation; they were peasant representatives elected by each settlement in the case of artels which hád many members or were territorially scattered (clause 18); see p. 61 below.

[5] In the model Statute of February 17, 1935, clause 20(b) stated that the chairman as well as the board should be elected by the general meeting.

[6] See, for example, NAF, 1930, 39–40 (Tsil'ko).

of the village community fled or were exiled as kulaks or 'kulak henchmen'. The general meetings of the kolkhozy were now expected to elect boards or chairmen who were acceptable to the state and prepared to bend the kolkhoz to its will. The 'elected' officials included many workers and others sent from the towns to take up leading positions in the kolkhozy. By the summer of 1930, 44·4 per cent of the 25,000-ers, all previously unknown to the collective farmers, had been 'elected' as chairmen of kolkhozy, and a further 15·3 per cent as members of their boards.[7] Some workers sent into the kolkhozy were no doubt welcomed by those collective farmers who remained after the exodus, themselves primarily batraks and poor peasants. But this cannot have been general. Nevertheless, the traditions of rural self-government were not extinguished, and the tension between the powerful state and party authorities and the residual democracy of the kolkhoz general meetings became a permanent if secondary feature of kolkhoz organisation throughout the Stalinist period.

The mass kolkhozy of 1930 continued the traditions of the 1920s in another important respect: the peasant household as a unit continued to be an integral part of the kolkhoz. The household was nowhere mentioned in the model Statute of February 6, prepared at the height of the campaign for socialisation. But the Statute of March 1 recognised the right of the members of the artel to their own livestock, minor agricultural implements, and *usad'ba*. All this implied the organisation of the non-collectivised sector of the kolkhoz on a household basis. The term '*usad'ba*' is translated in the present book as 'household plot', and although the word 'household' (dvor or khozyaistvo) was not used in connection with the *usad'ba* in the Statute, all the discussion about *usad'ba* lands assumed that they would be allocated to households and not to individuals. And the Statute formally recognised that households and not individuals would own non-socialised livestock, stating that 'in one-cow households(khozyaistva) dairy cattle shall not be socialised'.[8]

In the discussions and experiments in 1929–30 relating to the internal structure of the kolkhoz the crucial question was the

[7] Selunskaya (1964), 78; the percentages are based on records of the posts occupied by 17,888 of the 25,000-ers.

[8] *Kollektivizatsiya . . . 1927–1935* (1957), 283 (clause 4).

relation of collective farmer—yesterday's individual peasant—and kolkhoz administration. During NEP the individual peasant household, with help or hindrance from the arrangements made by the mir, was directly responsible for its own production, and sold its own crop on the market or through an intermediary. But the collective farmer of 1930 worked on the collective lands under the instructions of the kolkhoz, which also undertook the sale of the collective product. Management of the work of the collective farmer by the kolkhoz, and the associated rewards and penalties provided, now replaced joint work as a family and the stimulus of the market. Efficient labour organisation was recognised by all concerned to be essential to the success of the kolkhoz.

While internal organisation was not a serious problem for the average kolkhoz in the middle of 1929, with its membership of only 18 households, it was a major issue for the large kolkhozy. By July 1929 it was already normal practice for the large kolkhoz of 200–400 households to be subdivided into temporary or permanent work units of 15–30 households, variously referred to as 'brigades', 'departments (otdeleniya)', 'operational groups', etc. The term 'brigade', which soon became the standard expression for the basic kolkhoz work unit, was regularly and widely used in Siberian communes in the 1920s.[9] In one kolkhoz in the North Caucasus, the brigades were further subdivided into groups.[10] A brigade was sometimes formed on an *ad hoc* basis, but at first more often consisted of all the collective farmers living in a particular settlement; when the large kolkhoz was an amalgamation of smaller ones, each of the smaller kolkhozy, usually the whole or part of a particular settlement, was formed into a brigade. Brigades based on neighbourhood were frequently required to undertake additional field work elsewhere in the kolkhoz, or to send some of their members on other jobs; the brigade thus acted as a kind of bridge between the old and the new rural organisation. The brigade leaders met regularly with the chairman and senior administrators of the kolkhoz to receive work-orders (naryady), and this group in many cases acted as the council or working leadership of the kolkhoz.[11] Summing up

[9] For these terms and for reports on the organisation of large kolkhozy, see ZKK (1929), 22, 51–2, 55; SZe, April 2, 1930.

[10] ZKK (1929), 54.

[11] The above account is based on reports to the conference from representatives of large kolkhozy in the Siberian, Lower Volga and North Caucasus regions (ZKK (1929), 19–25, 48–55, 62–3).

this experience, the organisation section of the conference of large kolkhozy recommended that 'the cultivated land mass of a large kolkhoz should be divided into sections (uchastki) depending on the land relief, the quality of the soil, the crop rotation etc.' and that 'the cultivation of each section (or part of a section) should be entrusted to a brigade'; among examples cited were a field brigade with 23–28 members (including 20–24 men) and a nursery garden brigade with 25 members (including 23 women).[12] In the discussion, the rapporteur drew attention to an 'issue of principle': should field brigades be responsible for all the work in a particular area (ploughing, sowing, harvesting) or instead be separately organised for each agricultural process? He recommended the former arrangement for the time being, as it was less complicated.[13]

In the upheavals of the next 12 months, little further progress was made towards devising a rational kolkhoz structure. In the absence of a firm lead from the central authorities, a Kolkhoztsentr official complained that 'every kolkhoz is organising its administration as seems best'.[14] The giant kolkhozy which emerged between October 1929 and March 1930 were confronted with acute problems of internal organisation. Their large size made it necessary for them to be subdivided into a three- or four-stage hierarchy.[15] A kolkhoz group in the Central Black-Earth region, effectively organised as a single kolkhoz, was divided into ten 'economies (khozyaistva)'; each 'economy' had 120–200 households, and was in turn divided into brigades of 20 households, each headed by an appointed brigade leader (brigadir), generally known as the 'administrator of the link (admzveno)'.[16] In his vigorous criticism of giant kolkhozy, Markevich summarised their organisational complexity: typically the kolkhoz would be divided into 'economies (ekonomii)' of 5,000–10,000 hectares which were in turn divided into fields and sections (uchastki) without regard to the existing villages—the aim was to achieve a 'fully depersonalised optimum land area', and, as people, animals and implements were located randomly and unevenly, some 'economies' had two or three populated points and others had none.[17] On the industrial or military analogy, the subdivisions of the

[12] ZKK (1929), 161.
[13] ZKK (1929), 147.
[14] SZe, March 26, 1930.
[15] SZe, March 26, 1930; for an example see SZe, February 3, 1930.
[16] SZe, February 3, 1930.
[17] P, April 8, 1930; for this article see p. 52 above.

kolkhoz were even called 'shops' or 'detachments'; a party secretary of a North Caucasian kolkhoz suggested it should be divided into 'battle sectors' and 'battle columns' headed by 'commanders'.[18] The number of members, and the distances involved, also made general meetings impossible, so special delegate meetings were introduced, such as the 'institution of plenipotentiaries' in the North Caucasus region.[19]

Beneath these artificial structures, the settlement or the village remained the basic unit, except in those few cases where the population was transferred into a makeshift central 'agrotown' (see p. 48 above); and, even at the peak of the all-out drive, the average kolkhoz was in any case no larger than two or three settlements (see pp. 49–50 above). Both in the large and in the small kolkhoz, the neighbourhood or 'territorial' brigade, consisting of a group of neighbouring households (brigada-dvorka) tended at this time to be the primary unit of agricultural organisation.[20]

When the all-out collectivisation drive was put into reverse in March 1930, and the village or group of settlements emerged as the basis for the non-mechanised kolkhoz, the brigade of 15–35 households, or an equivalent number of individuals, was soon recognised as the basic unit within the kolkhoz (the brigades were in some cases grouped into sections of the kolkhoz concerned with particular activities, usually called 'ekonomii'). Much was uncertain: the membership of the kolkhoz was unstable, and its boundaries were often unclear; the division of the land between individual peasants and kolkhozy was not settled until the eve of the spring sowing (see vol. 1, pp. 291–3). These confusions and complexities made stable work units difficult to establish. Nevertheless, brigades were widely introduced as the main work unit in the course of the spring sowing,[21] and they become the main form of organisation everywhere by the time of the harvest.[22] It was often claimed that the brigade system had become so popular that individual peasant households very frequently copied them by combining in work teams (supryagi) to bring in the harvest;[23] it is more likely, however, that these *supryagi* were merely a resumption

[18] See, for example, B, 5, March 15, 1930, 48–9.
[19] SZe, March 26, 1930.
[20] Anisimov, ed. (1931), 29; P, February 25, 1930 (Lower Volga).
[21] P, April 18, 1930.
[22] VTr, 7–8, 1930, 37.
[23] VTr, 7–8, 1930, 37; SZe, June 22, 1930.

of the arrangements which were widespread among individual peasants in the 1920s.

Agreement was soon reached that the primary work unit should not be very large. The autumn ploughing in 1929 had already shown the disadvantages of large glamorous columns ploughing the whole field simultaneously: if one plough broke down the others were held up or had to go round, leaving gaps in the ploughing.[24] In large brigades record-keeping was complicated and supervision difficult. Brigades with 10, 12 or at most 25 ploughs or harrows were said to be more efficient than those with 70.[25]

While it was agreed in the spring of 1930 that the brigade, as a sub-unit within the kolkhoz, was an essential element in labour organisation, the way in which the brigades should be organised was quite unclear. As we have seen, the 'territorial' (neighbourhood) brigade seems to have predominated in the large kolkhozy in 1929. The main rival to the territorial brigade to emerge in the winter of 1929–30 was the 'production' brigade, a term which apparently covered all varieties of brigade in which the needs of agriculture rather than the territorial location of the workforce were the guiding principle of organisation. Production brigades were either permanent or temporary. Some permanent production brigades were, like the territorial brigades, responsible for all the agricultural work on a particular land area, and differed from the territorial brigades only in not drawing their membership from neighbouring households; they were known as 'mixed' or 'combined' brigades. Other permanent production brigades were 'specialised', dealing with, say, nursery gardening or livestock farming. Temporary production brigades, on the other hand, were usually formed to deal with a particular agricultural process or sub-process, such as sowing or reaping; they were thus specialised by function, though they did not necessarily include highly skilled personnel.[26]

Discussions about the best form of brigade continued throughout 1930 and after. The case for the territorial brigade rested on the natural or traditional character of a unit based on neighbours with the habit of working together. But it soon fell into disfavour. Its opponents argued that with such an arrangement the number of horses and the amount of land per household varied enormously in

[24] P, March 1, 1930; for later criticisms of so-called 'ploughing in one furrow' see *6 s''ezd sovetov* (1931), No. 17, 5–6 (Yurkin) and P, May 18, 1931.

[25] P, March 1, 1930; *6 s''ezd sovetov* (1931), No. 16, 13 (Yakovlev).

[26] VTr, 7–8, 1930, 37; P, February 25, April 5, 1930.

different parts of the same kolkhoz, depending on historical accident;[27] in the North Caucasus territorial brigades tended to turn into 'dwarf kolkhozy', a 'kolkhoz within the kolkhoz'.[28] Behind these objections lurked the fear that work units organised on a territorial basis would preserve or acquire the strength of the mir, and a potential source of resistance to the policies of the state would be re-established. In the spring of 1930, territorial brigades predominated in the North Caucasus, where the traditional village, the *stanitsa*, contained a large number of settlements, and the average kolkhoz contained some 200 households (see Table 3). Here the brigade normally consisted of 35, 50 or 100 households: the brigade was responsible for all the farming activities on the land allocated to it, and was itself divided into small work groups.[29]

In most other regions, the various forms of production brigade apparently predominated;[30] and from the spring of 1930 onwards the discussion focused on which type of production brigade should be preferred. Combined production brigades shared important advantages with the territorial brigades without their disadvantages. Handling the whole of the agricultural process on a particular land area from sowing to threshing, they could be held responsible for deficiencies and rewarded for successes; they could also take permanent charge of specific working animals and implements. They were compatible with a substantial measure of decentralisation of kolkhoz management: the work-orders from the kolkhoz board could be fairly simple and cover a substantial period of time. They could be divided into specialised groups, the nature of which could vary according to the stage of the work. Their principal disadvantage was their inflexibility. The amount of work on a particular land area varied considerably during the agricultural season, but the number of members of the brigade remained constant: it was difficult to transfer members of the brigade temporarily to jobs elsewhere in the kolkhoz. At the same time it was feared that in those parts of the country where labour was in surplus the establishment of permanent combined brigades would permanently exclude many collective farmers from agricultural work.

The alternative argument in favour of permanent specialised

27 *6 s''ezd sovetov* (1931), No. 17, 6.

28 SZe, December 13, 1930, January 19, 1931.

29 SZe, April 2, 1930; *6 s''ezd sovetov* (1931), No. 17, 6; P, May 18, 1931; Anisimov, ed. (1931), 26–8.

30 SZe, June 22, 1930 (Kudinov).

brigades was strong in the case of clear-cut and independent functions such as livestock breeding. But, within field work, brigades specialising in particular processes obviously had to be temporary in nature. Specialised temporary production brigades set up to undertake particular jobs made it possible to allocate labour more flexibly within the kolkhoz, and enabled collective farmers to develop special skills. On the other hand, their grave disadvantage was that responsibility for the final product was divided, with the consequence that the kolkhoz board had to issue its work-orders in great detail, sometimes on a daily basis.[31]

At the beginning of 1932 it was finally agreed that in field work the advantages of the permanent combined brigade outweighed the disadvantages. In 1930, the central kolkhoz authorities were concerned to emphasise their own lack of experience, and the importance of experiment, in the organisation of kolkhoz labour, and did not issue binding regulations. At first they indicated a definite preference for the establishment of combined brigades. A Kolkhoztsentr instruction published in February 1930 proposed that all collective farmers should be attached to definite work for at least a whole season as part of brigades for field work, livestock, etc.[32] At the end of May 1930 the instruction approved by Kolkhoztsentr proposed that brigades should each have responsibility for a certain area, though it assumed that new brigades would be formed at each main stage of agricultural work (harvesting, sowing of winter grains, and so on); this was a kind of temporary combined brigade.[33] But after the 1930 harvest the kolkhoz authorities, as well as taking a firmer line in opposition to the territorial brigade, now tended to favour the establishment of specialised brigades. At the kolkhoz conference in January 1931, Tataev, a deputy chairman of Kolkhoztsentr, argued that while permanent brigades could exist in special branches of farming, the brigade in general should be a 'mobile working nucleus'.[34] The resolution of the conference on labour in kolkhozy in January 1931 called rather

[31] For discussion of various types of production brigade see P, April 5, 1930, May 9, 1931; SZe, April 2, June 22, 1930; VTr, 7–8, 1930, 37–41; Anisimov, ed. (1931), 51–9.

[32] SZe, February 14, 1930.

[33] SZe, May 31, 1930; Jasny (1949), 335, is thus mistaken in supposing that 'the brigade itself appeared in a resolution of a central agency for the first time in the Party decision of February 4, 1932'.

[34] SZe, January 19, 1931.

unhelpfully for the establishment in field work of brigades of 40–60 members, divided into groups, which could be combined or specialised, permanent, seasonal or temporary.[35] At the VI congress of soviets in March 1931 Yurkin suggested that in the spring sowing combined brigades for all types of work, with 40–50 members, and specialised brigades for separate processes such as ploughing, were both possible forms of organisation; but he favoured the establishment of separate specialised brigades during the harvest period for each of the major processes of stacking (skirdometanie) and threshing.[36] The resolution of the congress failed to mention the brigade at all: flexibility was evidently still the order of the day.

Much also remained unclear about the relation between the brigade and the kolkhoz of which it formed a part. Should the brigade, like the kolkhoz, be a self-governing organisation, the leader of the brigade being elected by those who worked in it? One of the main objections to the giant kolkhozy was that those in charge of the work units were appointed by a remote board, not elected by the peasants.[37] A meeting convened by the agricultural newspaper proposed that all responsible officials of the kolkhozy, presumably including the brigade leaders, should be elected, not appointed (except for agricultural specialists): production conferences of the brigades, similar to general meetings, could propose several candidates, and the kolkhoz board could make the final choice.[38] This Utopian scheme had no practical outcome. From the point of view of the authorities, the election of brigade leaders may have appeared, like the establishment of territorial brigades, to encourage the infiltration of the principle of the mir into kolkhoz organisation, and was certainly incompatible with the notion of brigades which changed frequently in size and composition in response to agricultural needs. At the end of May 1930, without explanation, but presumably with these considerations in mind, an instruction endorsed by Kolkhoztsentr ruled that brigade leaders were to be appointed by the 'field-work organiser (polevod)', who was in charge of them all.[39] How far the instruction was carried out

35 SZe, February 8, 1931; this resolution was endorsed by Kolkhoztsentr.

36 *6 s"ezd sovetov* (1931), No. 17, 6–7.

37 NAF, 3, 1930, 9–11.

38 SZe, March 26, 1930; the meeting was held on March 24.

39 SZe, May 31, 1930; the instruction was prepared by the grain cooperative organisation Khlebotsentr, but apparently applied to all kolkhozy.

in practice is not known. But the issue was not yet quite settled. In the autumn of 1930 an article in the Narkomtrud journal proposed that brigade leaders should be elected by the collective farmers and approved by the kolkhoz board; this would avoid the appearance of 'ordering about' and inspire confidence.[40]

Another bone of contention was whether the brigade leader should simply be a supervisor, like the charge-hand in a factory (the Russian term—*brigadir*—was the same), and not take part in agricultural work himself. The party agricultural journal reported in the summer of 1930 that in the Central Volga region collective farmers complained to the brigade leaders:

> You just give us instructions, order us about and shout at us—you should come and work with us.[41]

On this issue the authorities sympathised with the collective farmers; Yurkin argued that large brigades, in which the brigade leader did not work, should be reduced in size.[42]

Behind all these discussions lay the uncomfortable fact that the post of brigade leader was a strange novelty in almost all Soviet villages. In the summer of 1930, trained brigade leaders were completely lacking. At the XVI party congress in July 1930, Yakovlev, characteristically comparing the brigade leader with the foreman in a factory, reported that about 1½ million needed to be trained, together with a million tractor drivers, and half a million agronomists with secondary education and 90,000 with higher education.[43] The shortage was made more acute by the tendency of the authorities to promote poor peasants and batraks, who were less agriculturally competent but presumed to be more reliable. At the party congress, Yakovlev complained that middle peasants were frequently removed even from positions such as group leader (zvenevoi) or head of the cattle yard, and were rarely admitted to membership of the kolkhoz board. The resolution of the congress urged 'the systematic involvement of *middle peasants in kolkhoz management*'. But the ambiguity of official attitudes was reflected in the support by the congress for continuation of the practice of

[40] VTr, 7–8, 1930, 38 (Reznikov).
[41] NAF, 7–8, 1930, 110.
[42] P, May 12, 1931.
[43] *XVI s''ezd* (1931), 596.

organising poor peasant groups in the kolkhozy, and in Yakovlev's assurance to the congress that while the middle peasant should participate in management, 'management will of course be in the hands of (budet za) the working class, the poor peasant and the batrak'.[44]

[44] *XVI s"ezd* (1931), 590; *KPSS v rez.*, iii (1954), 53, 60.

CHAPTER FIVE

SOCIALISATION WITHIN THE KOLKHOZ

(A) THE BACKGROUND

The three major types of kolkhoz—the commune, the artel and the association for joint cultivation of land (the TOZ or SOZ)—were defined primarily by the extent to which their means of production were socialised. In the commune, all land was supposed to be worked in common and all animals, implements and production buildings were collectively owned; in many communes members also shared living quarters and prepared and ate their food together. In the intermediate type of kolkhoz, the artel, arable farming was socialised: thus land was worked in common, except for the household plot (usad'ba), and draught animals and agricultural implements were owned collectively. Other branches of agriculture, however, remained partly or wholly private. In the TOZ, some land was worked in common, and major agricultural machines, if any, were owned collectively, but all animals, including draught animals, and most implements, remained in private possession.

No detailed official definition of the different types of kolkhoz was prescribed at an all-Union level; and the definitions adopted at different stages of kolkhoz development and in different regions varied considerably.[1] Frequently kolkhozy did not correspond to their official registration, or failed to change their registration when their degree of socialisation changed. In some communes only part of the land was cultivated in common. This was also true of artels, and in artels the proportion of implements and animals owned collectively also varied considerably. Societies for the joint use of machines and land-improvement societies were also sometimes

[1] A kolkhoz handbook in 1925, for example, stated that in artels the household plot and all means of production, including all animals, were held in common, and that 'all labour is devoted to the general economy' (Bauer *et al.* (1925), 11–12, 19); this was not the case either in principle or practice in the later 1920s.

classified as kolkhozy, though they appear in the official statistics as cooperatives.[2] At the XVI party conference in April 1929, Gusti, a secretary of the Lower Volga regional party committee, drew attention to an important factor which added to the prevailing confusion:

> Incentives are incentives, but they are given in collective farms simply on the basis of their name, and not according to the actual content of their work. Associations for joint cultivation of land get one level of tax reduction, artels another, and communes a third. But we all know that there are communes which are operating like associations for joint cultivation of land.[3]

Such arrangements obviously encouraged kolkhozy to register in a higher category than that to which they were entitled. The Central Statistical Administration, in a well-meaning attempt to make the record more realistic, confused matters further in some of its publications by disregarding the category in which kolkhozy were legally registered, instead classifying a kolkhoz as a TOZ, artel or commune according to the degree of socialisation of its means of production and its sown area.[4] But, in spite of all the exceptions, means of production were generally more socialised in communes than in artels, in artels than in TOZy.

In the official view, the movement from TOZ to artel and from artel to commune was a progression from 'lower' to 'higher' forms of production and distribution. The rise of the TOZy and the decline of the communes and artels between 1921 and the summer of 1928 thus indicated a persistent movement away from 'higher' towards 'lower' forms of collectivisation (see Table 4). The increase in the number of TOZy was nevertheless accepted and even encouraged by the authorities as a useful temporary concession to peasant psychology in the conditions of NEP, though this was regarded as a purely tactical requirement. Higher forms of production were believed to be much more efficient as well as socially desirable. In particular, the socialisation of livestock would make it possible to

[2] For the varied definitions and practices in 1921–8 see Lewin (1968), 109–12, 530, 533–4; Carr (1958), 219; and Carr and Davies (1969), 160–1.

[3] *XVI konf.* (1962), 419.

[4] NAF, 4, 1929, 95; kolkhozy were deemed to be artels if 90·1–100 per cent of their sown area and 60·1–95 per cent of means of production were socialised (NAF, 10, 1929, 117; see also Wronski (Paris, 1957), 16).

build adequate cattlesheds, employ specialists and organise a modern kolkhoz dairy industry.[5]

The trend towards lower forms of kolkhozy was reversed during the rapid expansion of the kolkhozy between October 1928 and June 1929. The proportion of artels and communes increased.[6] This was not simply a change in formal arrangements: draught animals in collective ownership increased from 27·7 to 44·0 per cent of the total number in the kolkhozy, and cows from 16·8 to 24·0 per cent.[7] Whether this remarkable new trend was brought about by direct pressure from the central authorities is not known. But it certainly corresponded to a change in official attitude. In the autumn of 1928, the long-standing tactical support for the TOZ and the prevalent toleration of a low level of socialisation in all types of kolkhozy were discarded. The plenum of the central committee in November 1928 criticised the 'inadequate growth of socialised means of production and capital' in the kolkhozy of the North Caucasus;[8] and the XVI party conference in April 1929 drew the attention of party organisations to the need for increased socialisation in TOZy, and for their transformation into artels and communes.[9] A month later the V congress of soviets added two further strands to the proposed pattern of development. It specifically approved the proposal in the final draft of the first five-year plan that 85 per cent of peasant households should become members of simple production cooperatives during the course of the five-year plan; and it looked forward to 'undeviating transformation' of associations of simple cooperatives into large kolkhozy.[10] Thus in the spring of 1929 the agreed strategy was to recruit the vast majority of peasant households into simple production associations during the next few years; a

[5] See for example Krot-Krival' (1926), 7–14; this is a typical pamphlet on collective farming.

[6] See Carr and Davies (1969), 945; these figures are evidently calculated on a different basis from those in Table 4 below.

[7] *Kolkhozy v 1928 g.* (1932), 48–51; *Kolkhozy v 1929 godu* (1931), 116–17; *Nar. kh.* (1932), 130–1; the figures for both 1928 and 1929 refer to June 1.

[8] *Kollektivizatsiya* (Krasnodar, 1972), 123.

[9] *KPSS v rez.*, ii (1954), 587. A version of the first five-year plan drawn up by the cooperative movement assumed, however, that 3·5 of the 4·4 million households in kolkhozy in 1932/33 would be in TOZy (Lewin (1968), 354).

[10] *Resheniya*, ii (1967), 71; the final draft of the five-year plan completed a month previously proposed that 85 per cent of households should be in *all* types of cooperatives and only 25 per cent in simple production associations (*Pyatiletnii plan*, ii, i (1930), 281).

substantial minority of these would be transformed into kolkhozy; existing small kolkhozy would be amalgamated; and the degree of socialisation in them would steadily increase.

By encouraging the artel at the expense of the TOZ the authorities hoped to bring about the socialisation of horses and implements, and thus provide the basis for collective production of grain. The socialisation of livestock apart from draught animals was rarely mentioned, and, when it was considered at all, was envisaged as a further stage subsequent to the consolidation of socialised arable farming. The authorities were aware that the general livestock situation had deteriorated,[11] but they were preoccupied with the far more urgent, and less intractable, grain problem. At the XVI party conference in April 1929, Eikhe complained that the five-year plan contained no precise recommendations about the development of collective livestock, and that current policy was 'murderous for livestock in the kolkhoz sector'.[12] During the next few months no change in policy took place as far as the mass of small kolkhozy was concerned. Mikoyan and Kalinin referred to the livestock shortage in major speeches, and attributed it to the absence of large-scale farming, but did not offer a practical solution.[13] The campaign for large kolkhozy, however, assumed that they would be advanced in organisation as well as technology, and among the first large kolkhozy the proportion of artels and particularly of communes was relatively high.[14] At the conference on large kolkhozy in July 1929, Kaminsky declared in his opening statement:

> *The large kolkhoz—and this is entirely clear to everyone—must in its* type be a production economy similar to *our socialist factories and state farms*.[15]

[11] See Carr and Davies (1969), 100.

[12] *XVI konf.* (1962), 90.

[13] P, June 27, 1929 (Mikoyan); P, July 19, 1929 (Kalinin).

[14] According to the report to the organisation section of the conference of large kolkhozy in July 1929 only one-third of the 147 large kolkhozy which then existed were TOZy as compared with 53 per cent of all kolkhozy (ZKK (1929), 124); the Kolkhoztsentr report to the central committee in September 1929, probably using information from the same date, reported that the 147 large kolkhozy included 48 TOZy, 37 artels and 15 groups with common arable farming, and as many as 47 communes—a much higher proportion than in the case of the ordinary kolkhozy (*Materialy*, vii (1959), 22).

[15] ZKK (1929), 7.

At the organisation section of the conference, the Kolkhoztsentr representative argued that the process of socialisation should be rapid and complete in the large kolkhozy, and that they should accordingly have a special unified Statute, thus obviating the need to re-register them whenever their degree of socialisation increased. He was, however, vigorously opposed by speakers from the grain areas, who were not persuaded that the mass of the middle peasantry would be prepared to accept a high degree of socialisation. Some speakers even challenged the view that horses should be socialised in all large kolkhozy, arguing that this might antagonise the middle peasants.[16] The socialisation of livestock other than draught animals was not specifically mentioned by Kaminsky in his main report, and little was said about it at the conference. Some speakers called for the socialisation of livestock in more advanced kolkhozy,[17] and Kolkhoztsentr endorsed an announcement from the Ural Gigant kolkhoz that its productive animals would be socialised by January 1, 1930.[18] But the Urals, with long-established communes, was recognised to be an exceptional area; the central kolkhoz authorities, in spite of their support for socialised arable farming, continued to believe that, except in specialised livestock-farming areas, and in the minority of communes, collective farm households should continue to work their own household plot, and to own a modest number of cows, pigs, sheep and poultry. The theses presented to the conference did not go beyond the proposal that land, agricultural machines, draught animals and means of transport should be socialised in large kolkhozy. Moreover, the conference did not take any decision about the proposed unified Statute for large kolkhozy, and it was not mentioned in the subsequent decree of Kolkhoztsentr.[19] For the moment, a cautious attitude to advanced forms of socialisation prevailed in official circles, even in relation to the large kolkhozy.

(B) THE FIRST PHASE, JULY–SEPTEMBER 1929

During the next few months, a significant increase took place in the socialisation of some large kolkhozy and areas of comprehensive collectivisation which were the objects of special attention from the

[16] ZKK (1929), 133–5, 152. [17] ZKK (1929), 145–52.
[18] ZKK (1929), 38, 437.
[19] ZKK (1929), 160–3, 465; the decree was dated July 25, 1929.

central authorities. The Gigant kolkhoz in the Urals already included 25 communes and 34 artels as against only 25 TOZy in July 1929;[20] by September there were 31 communes, 44 artels and only 17 TOZy—this was a far smaller proportion of TOZy, and a far higher proportion of communes, than in the country as a whole.[21] Khoper okrug in the Lower Volga region, which in September 1929 became the first 'okrug of comprehensive collectivisation' (see vol. 1, p. 131), announced as early as June that 100 per cent of draught animals and 35 per cent of cattle in the kolkhozy would be socialised,[22] and the local press reported that existing kolkhozy were being re-registered as communes, usually after amalgamation.[23] On August 27 the okrug party bureau resolved that all the large kolkhozy in the okrug should achieve 'full socialisation' of their means of production by November 1, and that all existing large kolkhozy should be re-registered as artels or communes by the time of the spring sowing.[24] In September, an inter-departmental okrug conference described in enthusiastic if rhetorical terms the transformation of Khoper into an 'okrug-commune of gigantic dimensions'. A survey carried out in the okrug in October or November reported that 95 per cent of draught animals, 40 per cent of cows, 57 per cent of sheep and 16 per cent of pigs were already socialised; socialisation was incomplete, however, as the animals were left with their former owners owing to the lack of common cowsheds and pigsties.[25] It is uncertain how far the upsurge of socialisation in these special areas was due to the spontaneous enthusiasm of the local officials, and how far it was inspired from Moscow.[26] But certainly it was not resisted by the central party authorities, and the activities of Gigant, abundantly publicised in *Pravda*, were presented as if they were of more general relevance.[27]

20 ZKK (1929), 433.

21 KG, 74, September 24, 1929.

22 *Krasnyi Khoper*, June 6, 1929.

23 *Povol'zhskaya pravda*, July 24, August 21, 1929; *Krasnyi Khoper*, August 13, 29, September 15, 1929; SKhG, August 31, September 4, 1929.

24 *Krasnyi Khoper*, September 17, 1929; for the date of this resolution see vol. 1, p. 130, n. 83.

25 In *Krasnyi Khoper*, December 12, 1929, the survey is said to be dated November 1 and to refer to 23 kolkhozy with 8,000 households; in P, January 13, 1930, the survey is said to have been general and to have taken place in October.

26 For a general discussion of this question see vol. 1, pp. 124–31.

27 Favourable reports appeared in the issues of August 22, September 12 and

In the mass of small kolkhozy the situation was quite different. Between June 1 and October 1, 1929, the new trends of the previous eight months were again reversed, and the TOZy increased more rapidly in numbers than the artels (see Table 4). But in view of the rapid expansion of the membership of kolkhozy, which almost doubled during these four months, this switch to the TOZ was not incompatible with the systematic but gradual progress from lower to higher types of kolkhoz which was envisaged by Kolkhoztsentr.

In extensive publicity in *Pravda* during August in favour of mass collectivisation and RSKs, little was said about the type of kolkhoz, or about socialisation generally, except in the case of the large kolkhozy.[28] Figures for the socialisation of draught animals and livestock in this period do not appear to be available. The continued decline in total livestock numbers gave rise to much anxiety, however, and was reported at length.[29] On August 22, a significant editorial in the economic newspaper, entitled 'For Large-scale Socialised Livestock Farming', attacked the Narkomzem five-year plan, which proposed that only seven per cent of all meat output should come from the socialised sector, for its 'completely obvious underestimation of the importance of livestock'. The editorial attributed the decline in livestock to the predominance of individual peasant farming, and condemned 'archaic ideas' that livestock breeding required 'careful individual handling', citing West European and American experience to demonstrate the superiority of large-scale mechanised livestock farming. It recommended the use 'in the main of the methods with which the grain problem was solved': large livestock sovkhozy should be established and livestock farming in the kolkhozy should undergo 'energetic socialisation'.[30]

For the moment this striking change of approach did not command general support. Throughout September the authorities remained cautious about proposals to extend socialisation beyond arable farming, except in the case of large kolkhozy. The Kolkhozsentr report to the central committee of September 7, 1929, called for increased socialisation in large kolkhozy, and provided information about the socialisation of cows in the kolkhozy of the RSKs, but on

October 1, 1929; at this time publicity in the central daily press for developments in Khoper seems to have been confined to the agricultural newspaper.

[28] See for example the editorials on August 7, 16, 23.

[29] See, for example, EZh, August 14, 1929 (A. Lositskii); for the decline in livestock in 1928/29 see vol. 1, pp. 44–6.

[30] EZh, August 22, 1929.

the whole it paid little attention to the question.[31] In a simultaneous article in *Pravda* Kaminsky specifically mentioned livestock only in relation to the non-grain areas, and in reiterating the earlier proposal that a unified Statute should be adopted for the large kolkhozy (see p. 72 above) he was careful to suggest that the maximum requirement was the socialisation of arable farming.[32] Later in the same month, at a Moscow regional soviet congress, Syrtsov drew attention to the lag of livestock behind grain, attributing it to the situation in which the kolkhozy owned 165,000 and the sovkhozy 82,000 cows as against the 30 million owned by the individual peasants, and called for the introduction of a 'zoominimum' to supplement the 'agrominimum'; but he also stopped short of making specific proposals for the socialisation of livestock.[33] Moreover, the assumption still persisted at this time that collective farmers would be compensated for relinquishing their livestock. The kolkhozy would purchase some animals from them outright, with the assistance of state loans and grants, and others would be transferred to the kolkhoz on the understanding that the state would support livestock farming in the kolkhoz by loans to construct collective cattlesheds, or by the allocation of breeding animals.[34] In the mass of small kolkhozy, the socialisation of livestock was to be cautious and relatively painless.

(C) THE DRIVE FOR SOCIALISATION, OCTOBER 1929–FEBRUARY 1930

From the beginning of October, the central kolkhoz authorities rapidly drifted into new waters. On October 6, 1929, *Pravda* published an appeal signed by Kaminsky as chairman of the All-Union Council of Kolkhozy in connection with the forthcoming Day of Harvest and Collectivisation (see vol. 1, p. 132), which made a significant favourable reference, applying to all the kolkhozy, to 'full socialisation':

> In the kolkhozy there are still strong groups which fasten on the remnants of their individual economy, and struggle against truly-

[31] *Materialy*, vii (1959), 230–5.
[32] P, September 12, 1929.
[33] P, September 25, 1929.
[34] EO, 9, 1929, 33 (I. Gershman); this issue was published in September 1929.

> kolkhoz strivings for full socialisation and real socialist reconstruction of the whole village.

This was intended as more than a conventional exhortation. A few days later, the plans of Kolkhoztsentr for the economic year 1929/30 were revealed, and included the socialisation of 60 per cent of draught animals and 50 per cent of productive animals in the kolkhozy by October 1, 1930; the corresponding percentages for the large kolkhozy were 80–100 and 80, and in respect of the large kolkhozy this was stated to be a government directive.[35]

In the same month in which these ambitious plans were published, a report submitted to the presidium of Gosplan strongly criticised the practice of providing loans from state funds to kolkhozy to enable them to purchase animals from collective farmers:

> If we followed this path, in the next few years we would have to spend hundreds and thousands of millions of rubles and hand them over to collective farmers who are socialising their sown areas, thus increasing the monetary resources of the countryside without being able to supply a corresponding quantity of consumer goods.[36]

The published volume of control figures took the same line, and also insisted that kolkhozy should carry out 'a huge amount of work' to

[35] P, October 13, 1929. The published volume on the control figures, prepared in the early autumn and eventually approved by Sovnarkom, gives somewhat lower figures (horses 55, cows 50, sheep 41 and pigs 40 per cent) (*KTs . . . na 1929/30* (1930), 124). NAF, 10, 1929, 64, reported that in large kolkhozy in the RSFSR and the Ukraine 80 per cent of cows, sheep and pigs were to be socialised, and in the Belorussian SSR 90 per cent.

[36] EO, 10, 1929, 51 (M. Golendo); the report stated that at most 120,000 out of the more than 1·5 million additional cattle planned for the socialised sector of the kolkhozy in 1929/30 would be paid for by the state. Golendo previously took a moderate line on agricultural problems (see Wheatcroft (1974), 166). Golendo, born in 1894 in a poor peasant family, joined the party in 1917 and became a political commissar in the Red Army; he was appointed deputy chairman of the agricultural section of Gosplan in 1924 (SKhG, December 19, 1929). According to Larin, the budget commission of TsIK, at its session in November 1929, discovered that kolkhozy had been spending state credits on the purchase of livestock and equipment from their members; he argued that all such expenditure within the boundaries of an RSK was impermissible (*Trudy . . . agrarnikov-marksistov* (1930), i, 65).

build cattlesheds, again primarily using their own labour, money and materials.[37] The peasant newspaper, in a special page devoted to the importance of livestock, argued that even TOZy should begin to establish collective cattlesheds, and that over the next two years all peasant dairy cooperative associations should build collective cattlesheds and turn into large dairy kolkhozy.[38] Thus the increasing pressure of industrialisation on state finance was believed to rule out the provision of economic incentives to socialisation in the kolkhozy by the injection of resources from outside. Instead the collective farmers themselves were expected to provide resources for their own kolkhozy and move them forward by their own efforts. How they were to be persuaded to accept these new arrangements was hardly mentioned and never satisfactorily explained. This was a further move towards a system based on exhortation and administrative order.

It was not yet, however, a commitment to the all-out drive for socialisation which was to take control at the end of 1929. In October 1929, it was still assumed that the proposed increase in socialisation within the kolkhozy should be only a fairly small element in the total livestock programme. The kolkhozy were expected to include 10 per cent of all households by October 1, 1930, so that by that date, even if the ambitious plans of Kolkhoztsentr were realised, only 1.6 million of the 31 million cows in the USSR would be in the socialised sector of the kolkhozy. Livestock development would thus still primarily depend on the individual peasants.[39] Moreover, opinions continued to be divided about the wisdom of the immediate socialisation of livestock. An official of Kolkhoztsentr called for a two or three year programme in the RSKs which would be marked by 'gradualness and a systematic approach in socialising means of production in conformity with the new technical base'.[40] In Khoper okrug, the local party newspaper strongly defended the artel and the TOZ against the commune, evidently encouraged by the caution of the visiting commission of Kolkhoztsentr:

[37] *KTs . . . na 1929/30* (1930), 124; the text of the volume was drafted in about October 1929.

[38] KG, 84, October 22, 1929; a *Pravda* journalist visiting Odessa okrug praised local party and soviet organisations which put pressure on a TOZ to establish a socialised cattleshed (P, October 10, 1929).

[39] *KTs . . . na 1929/30* (1930), 124.

[40] EZh, October 13, 1929.

> Our officials and the masses, not having measured their forces, not testing the ground under their feet, not strengthening the foundations enough, often in a burst of creative ecstasy decide to adopt the Statute of the commune.[41]

A few days later, in a letter to *Pravda* Sheboldaev, while defending the rapid pace of collectivisation in Khoper okrug, at the same time conceded that TOZy and artels rather than communes should predominate.[42]

The November plenum of the party central committee paid little attention to the question of socialisation within the kolkhoz. A few days before the plenum Stalin, in his article of November 3, conferred his approval impartially on 'joint cultivation of land, machine-tractor stations, artels and kolkhozy based on new technology, and giant sovkhozy equipped with hundreds of tractors and combine-harvesters'. He did not mention the commune in this list, and the only reference to it in his article was in his quotation of Lenin's famous statement that the middle peasant would say he was 'for the commune (i.e. for communism)' if provided with 100,000 first-class tractors.[43] At the plenum Kaminsky was more enthusiastic about socialisation; he recommended that preparation should be made for the transformation of large TOZy into communes and called for the solution of the livestock as well as the grain problem as early as 1930/31 through the establishment of large kolkhozy.[44] In contrast Molotov made no reference to different types of kolkhoz, and ignored the socialisation of livestock. But he stressed the need to increase the 'socialised Funds' in the kolkhozy, primarily by 'mobilisation' of the physical resources of the peasantry such as their implements. According to Molotov, these 'Funds' were particularly important because the state, 'in view of our poverty', was unable to provide much financial support for the kolkhozy.[45] This section of Molotov's speech was influential; it was henceforth abundantly clear that kolkhozy must depend on their members for their capital, and would get little help from the state.

The resolutions of the plenum were cautious about socialisation. The resolution on Kaminsky's report drew attention to the

[41] *Krasnyi Khoper*, October 17, 1929; for the commission, see vol. 1, pp. 152–3.
[42] P, October 22, 1929; for other aspects of this letter see vol. 1, p. 154.
[43] *Soch.*, xii, 125.
[44] VIK, 1, 1964, 36; Chigrinov (1965), 48.
[45] B, 22, November 30, 1929, 15–17.

importance of the socialised Funds of the kolkhoz, and sternly warned that animals and implements must not be sold by peasants before joining the kolkhozy, but it made no other reference to the livestock issue. And although the resolution on Ukrainian agriculture stressed that large kolkhozy as well as sovkhozy must organise livestock production, it merely mildly referred to the necessity of 'socialising in SOZy and artels the main instruments of production and animal draught power', and failed to mention other kinds of livestock.[46]

In spite of all this public caution by the central committee and by leading members of the Politburo, the effect of the plenum, with its atmosphere of urgency and self-confidence, was to foster the movement towards socialisation; and at the time of the plenum and during the following weeks a vigorous campaign was mounted in favour of higher types of kolkhozy and the immediate socialisation of livestock. In the campaign, increasing attention was paid to the problem of social inequality in the lower forms of kolkhozy, and the risk of kulak influence which this entailed. While the November plenum was in session, *Pravda* published an article by Azizyan, head of its department of agricultural affairs, which argued that kolkhozy with a small degree of socialisation provided 'conditions for the emergence and preservation of economic inequality'; this could be avoided only by further socialisation. According to Azizyan, the 'tendencies of small proprietors to develop individual accumulation' would remain even if the kulaks were driven out of the kolkhozy; such tendencies were strongly supported by the kulaks, who wanted the kolkhoz to become a 'joint-stock capitalist enterprise':

> *The ossification of the kolkhoz in the lower stages of socialisation is a fundamental element in all the tactics of the kulak within the kolkhoz.*[47]

This argument, far-fetched as it seems in the light of later developments, was obviously taken very seriously at the time. Trotsky, observing collectivisation from exile, argued a few weeks later that even when kulaks were expelled from the villages, 'preventing the re-emergence of the kulak within the kolkhoz is

[46] *KPSS v rez.*, ii (1954), 642–53, 658–9.

[47] P, November 11, 1929; he enlarged upon this view in B, 21, November 15, 1929, 53–8, and 22, November 30, 1929, 56–64 (for other aspects of these articles see vol. 1, pp. 183–4).

much more difficult'; the kolkhozy could become '*a new form of social and political disguise for the kulak*'. But Trotsky, unlike Azizyan, argued that only 'an industrial and cultural revolution' could avoid this danger.[48]

The more practical motive for intensifying the campaign for socialisation was the rapidly worsening livestock crisis in the autumn of 1929. The events of the previous autumn and winter were repeated on a larger scale. Much more grain was collected by the state, and this limited the availability to the peasants of a major source of fodder; part of the pasture was sown for grain; the harvest of hay and other fodder was poor; and the price of fodder rose.[49] And the enormous new complication was that peasants everywhere were selling their horses and other livestock before joining the kolkhoz. As early as August 1929 dozens of messages were sent from local soviets in the Black-Earth region urging livestock cooperatives to buy up animals to prevent their destruction, and in Stavropol' okrug in the North Caucasus 'kulaks drove herds of oxen, dairy cows, horses and sheep from district to district'.[50] At the November plenum, Petrovsky sounded a note of alarm:

> From all sides information is received that peasants write to their acquaintances and relatives: 'I am going into the collective, I have sold the cow, sold the horse, etc. . . . ' This is very dangerous and it is necessary for us to guard against it in advance, in order not to find ourselves in a very difficult position.[51]

By this time the market was flooded. A year later Mikoyan told a plenum of the party central committee that between October 1929 and March 1930 'the supply of animals was huge', so that delivery agencies had not needed to exert any effort in order to fulfil their plan.[52] The price of animals fell; and the peasants, instead of selling their cattle, pigs and sheep, now killed them in large numbers for home consumption or for sale as meat. In the Lower Volga region the meat collection agencies could not cope with the increased

[48] BO (Paris), ix (February–March 1930), 4–5 (article dated February 13, 1930).

[49] The alternative series for fodder production by Bryanskii and Nifontov both show a marked decline in 1929/30 (Gaister, ed. (1930), 58; Nifontov (1932), 127). See also NAF, 2, 1930, 5 (Vol'f); SO, 6, 1930, 16 (Gosplan survey); PKh, 9, 1930, 121–4 (Kindeev).

[50] SZe, February 1, 1930.

[51] Chigrinov (1965), 49.

[52] B, 1, January 15, 1931, 15.

numbers, the bazaar price of a milk cow fell from 93 rubles in September to 74 rubles in November 1929, and animals were 'driven from the bazaars unsold and killed at home, the meat being sold at bazaars or salted down'. The fall in the number of animals in the region between the spring of 1929 and the end of the year was estimated at 18 per cent, being as high as 25 per cent in Khoper okrug.[53] The price of meat also fell: in some places in the North Caucasus, it was cheaper than bread.[54] And rumours of imminent collectivisation led peasants to sell up their animals even in areas in which collectivisation was not taking place, or was taking place on a modest scale.

The crisis was an urgent one, and the anxiety of the peasants could have been brought to an end only by a very firm statement from the highest authorities that livestock would not be socialised in the kolkhozy. Instead, the authorities tried to gather livestock into the socialised sector of the economy as rapidly as possible, and became much more sympathetic to grandiose plans for the immediate establishment of giant communes. In an article published while the November plenum was in progress, Shlikhter, People's Commissar for Agriculture in the Ukraine, declared that a '*revolution in livestock farming*' was required, but was hindered because 'young animals in considerable quantities are going under the knife':

> Saving young animals from the knife, we must concentrate them exclusively in the socialist sector, in large sovkhozy and kolkhozy.[55]

He was soon followed by Ryskulov, who declared during his visit to Khoper okrug that the TOZ was out of date: higher types of kolkhozy should be organised immediately and the model Statutes should be re-examined. The crucial issue was livestock: 'We must immediately engage in the socialisation of product livestock, which are being sold right and left'.[56] On November 21, Kaganovich, in his report on the plenum to Moscow regional activists, included a

[53] *Nizhnee Povol'zhe*, 1, 1930, 32–4.

[54] SZe, February 1, 1930.

[55] P, November 16, 1929; in P, November 11, 1929, Shlikhter published another article, perhaps written before the plenum, which much more modestly set out a four-year socialisation programme for three Ukrainian RSKs.

[56] *Krasnyi Khoper*, November 19, 21, 1929; he visited some 20 kolkhozy on

long passage in praise of the Ural Gigant kolkhoz, though, like Stalin, Molotov and Mikoyan in these months, he made no specific mention of the socialisation of livestock in his published statements.[57] At a joint meeting of Sovnarkom and Ekoso of the USSR on November 27, Syrtsov was much more explicit:

> We cannot in this sphere leave to the will of fate the spontaneity which we can observe at present. *We must now, at once embark on the collectivisation of livestock*.[58]

An editorial in *Pravda*, while calling for the encouragement of livestock breeding by the individual peasant, placed its main emphasis on '*large-scale livestock farming in kolkhozy and sovkhozy*'; 'the stormy rate of growth of collectivisation' made it possible to embark on the rapid socialisation of livestock in kolkhozy.[59] At an all-Union conference of kolkhoz and cooperative officials under the auspices of Kolkhoztsentr of the USSR, the rapporteur returned to the theme that the livestock problem must be approached 'with the tempos and the methods used for work on the solution of the grain problem'.[60] At the session of TsIK which met at the beginning of December, the chairman of the Lower Volga regional soviet reported that most kolkhozy in his region were 'artels with socialised productive labour', but urged delegates not to fear higher forms of collectivisation: in the conflict within each peasant between his role as individual property owner and his role as master of the new collective economy, victory for the latter was assured: 'The general formula "aim for communes (itti na kommuny)" is completely correct'.[61] A delegate from Siberia, optimistically describing collectivisation as 'a more or less well-trodden path', and merely an 'initial stage', urged that it should be followed by socialisation of all means of production.[62] At a conference on collectivisation of members of TsIK held at this time Ryskulov, reporting on his visit to the Lower Volga, again urged a movement towards the artel and

---

November 16 and 17, and gave his report on November 19. For the term 'product livestock', see p. 89 below; for Ryskulov, see vol. 1, pp. 178–9, 187, 199.

[57] P, November 26, 1929; see also p. 40 above.

[58] SKhG, November 29, 1929.

[59] P, November 29, 1929.

[60] SKhG, December 1, 3, 1929.

[61] *TsIK 2/V* (1929), No. 6, 3.

[62] *Ibid.* No. 6, 19.

the commune.[63] Andreev, in an interview in *Pravda*, claimed to have observed in the North Caucasus a 'direct transition to purely kolkhoz forms, more complex and with a greater degree of socialisation than earlier in the kolkhoz movement'.[64] More ambitious plans for socialisation were now prepared in the localities. Tyumen' okrug in the Urals, for example, planned to socialise all animals by the end of 1930, and reported that in one district of the okrug 56 per cent of cows were already socialised.[65]

The plans for the spring sowing campaign prepared at this time were strongly influenced by the growing pressure for socialisation. At the beginning of December 1929, the plan of Narkomzem and Kolkhoztsentr proposed that by the end of the spring sowing 25 per cent of kolkhozy in the RSFSR should be TOZy, 50 per cent artels and 25 per cent communes. This proposal involved a very big change from the proportions actually prevailing on October 1, 1929 (62·3, 30·8, 6·9), a return, for a far higher level of collectivisation, to the kind of proportions which had prevailed at the end of war communism in 1921 (15, 65, 20) (see Table 4). The plan also proposed that 80 per cent of productive cattle, pigs and sheep should be socialised in RSKs, and 60 per cent in small kolkhozy.[66] These percentages were not much different from those in the plan for 1929/30 prepared in October, but they were now to be reached in six months instead of a year, and referred to kolkhozy which would include 37 per cent of households instead of the 10 per cent planned in October. In the October plan, 1·6 out of 31 million cows in the USSR were to be socialised by September 1930; in the December plan, 4·24 out of 23 million in the RSFSR were to be socialised by the spring of 1930. On December 11, a decree of Sovnarkom of the RSFSR endorsed the plan; it specificially approved the proposal that 'at least 70 per cent' of kolkhozy should be artels and communes, and declared January 1930 to be a 'Livestock Month'.[67] Meanwhile, on December 10, a telegram from Kolkhoztsentr of the USSR to its local organisations proposed similarly high figures for

63 EZh, December 6, 1929.

64 P, December 13, 1929.

65 P, December 24, 1929.

66 *Plan kollektivizatsii v vesennyuyu sel'skokhozyaistvennuyu kampaniyu 1930 g.* (1930), 16–17; Nemakov (1966), 89–90; the plan may be dated by an unsigned article in P, December 6, 1929, which gave the planned percentages of TOZy, artels and communes.

67 SU, 1929, art. 910; the Narkomzem plan in fact proposed 75 per cent.

the socialisation of livestock in RSKs and large kolkhozy.[68] Not to be outdone, a conference called by the grain cooperative organisation Khlebotsentr proposed that 88 per cent of cows should be socialised in kolkhozy by the spring.[69]

While these detailed instructions were prejudging the issue, socialisation within the kolkhozy was a major preoccupation of the Politburo commission on collectivisation; one of the eight subcommissions set up at its first meeting on December 8, 1929, dealt with 'the type of economy of collectivised districts' under the chairmanship of Grin'ko.[70] Before the subcommission could meet, Ryskulov, in an article in *Pravda*, again insisted that the new kolkhozy must mainly be artels and communes: 'The higher the form of the kolkhoz, the better its economy is managed'. He added that the charters of artels and communes should be revised so as to bring about an increased degree of socialisation. Thus the Indivisible Fund should be increased (see p. 120 below), and productive animals should be socialised in both artels and communes; the attention of the collective farmer would then no longer be divided between collective and individual interests.[71] The Grin'ko subcommission took a similar line. In a report to the meeting of chairmen of subcommissions held on December 14 and 15, it proposed that 'the artel type should be the minimum, with obligatory collectivisation of all arable land, all implements, all draught animals, all cattle, at least three-quarters of the pigs, at least half the sheep, etc., taking into account local circumstances', and that kolkhozy should be transformed into communes as soon as possible.[72] But these proposals were resisted in the main commission. Yakovlev stated:

> We have events, although they are not so many, when attempts are made to construct a directly Evangelical socialism in which everything to the last hen is socialised, and an immediate transition is made to the commune Statute without a sufficient base for it.[73]

[68] Danilov, ed. (1963), 41; Kolkhoztsentr proposed that 100 per cent of cows, 80 per cent of pigs and 60 per cent of sheep should be socialised in RSKs and large kolkhozy, and a further decree of December 24 proposed that 73–74 per cent of productive livestock in *all* kolkhozy in the RSFSR should be socialised.

[69] P, December 20, 1929.

[70] IISO, [i] (1964), 266–7, 274; for Grin'ko see vol. 1, p. 169.

[71] P, December 9, 1929.

[72] IISO, [i] (1964), 274–5.

[73] Nemakov (1966), 92; the date of the statement is not given, but it was

At this point in the proceedings, an editorial in *Pravda* insisted that the 'kolkhoz public and especially the kolkhoz activists' in RSKs were collectivising draught animals and productive livestock 'on their *own initiative*', and that the 'broad masses of poor and middle peasants' were striving for 'maximum socialisation of draught animals and productive livestock'; to cope with this, peasant buildings should be adapted as cattlesheds and pigsties.[74] In spite of this rallying-cry, in the draft decree forwarded to the Politburo on December 22 the main commission proposed that in view of the 'hesitations' of the middle peasants, who constituted the majority of collective farmers in okrugs of comprehensive collectivisation, the artel should be the 'main form of organisation at the present stage', and that in the artel the main means of production, including land, implements, working animals and 'commodity production animals' should be collectivised but there should be '*private property of the peasant in minor implements, small animals, milk cows, etc. where they serve the consumer needs of the peasant family*'.[75] The draft also warned:

> Each further step towards socialisation on the road to the commune must rely on the direct experience of the peasant collective farmers, on the growth of their belief in the stability, profitability and advantage of collective forms of management of the economy. Special care must be taken in the sphere of everyday life (byt), where the prejudices of the ordinary peasant are most profound.[76]

At this point in the deliberations, the conference of marxist agrarians, which met from December 20 to December 27, 1929, provided an opportunity for reflection on the nature of the kolkhoz and its place in the Soviet economy. Larin defined 'socialist economy in the true meaning of this concept' as one in which 'the economy is not the property of a particular group of individual owner-shareholders working in it, but of the state', and members of society work for the whole society and not for themselves. Hence kolkhozy, even in RSKs, were not socialist but transitional types of

---

presumably made either at the meeting of December 14 and 15 or at the meeting of the main commission on December 16 and 17.

74 P, December 17, 1929.

75 IISO, [i] (1964), 276; VIK, 1, 1964, 36; in the first source the phrase is italicised, in the second source it is not.

76 VI, 3, 1965, 12.

economy, in which some features assisted the movement to socialism and others were a basis for struggle against it.[77] In the kolkhozy, peasant families had no personal connections with a particular piece of land, plough or horse, but the means of production and farm output belonged to them collectively as 'a group of private persons'; a clash of interests was therefore possible between the kolkhoz and the state, both over state prices, which could lead the kolkhoz to try to sell its production on the private market, and over the type of crops grown. Kolkhozy would become a 'consistently-socialist type of economy' only when they were transformed into sovkhozy, though Larin conceded that 'in conditions of the dictatorship of the proletariat the transformation of *all means of production* into the indivisible capital of the kolkhoz would approach close to this'.[78] Larin's analysis supported his call for the conversion of kolkhozy, within a few years, into state enterprises, and for a rapid advance of socialisation.[79]

In the debate, Kalinin, while ignoring the theoretical issue, agreed that 'the kolkhoz, *taken by itself*, at the present stage still does not save us from the fact that it may carry on a capitalist policy', and contrasted the 'two souls' of the peasant, 'the soul of the proprietor and the soul of the labourer'; it was accordingly necessary to 'sharpen to a certain stage the struggle between the socialist and private capitalist tendencies inside the kolkhoz'. Collectivisation should be spread to 'fruit, eggs, milk and meat' as well as grain farming, appropriate forms of organisation being set up for each branch of farming.[80] Other speakers at the conference also called for more socialisation: a Moscow delegate presciently warned that a delay in socialisation would lead the peasant to settle into the kolkhoz with his cow and garden.[81] Larin's discussion of the nature of the kolkhoz was a major theme of the debate. Most speakers, while conceding to Larin that the kolkhozy were not yet economies of a 'consistently socialist' type, insisted that they were already 'socialist'

[77] *Trudy . . . agrarnikov-marksistov*, i (1930), 70, 63; according to a later speaker at the conference (*ibid.* i (1930), 107) and to P, December 25, 1929, Larin described comprehensive collectivisation as 'large-scale cooperative private economy production', but these words do not appear in his report as printed.

[78] *Trudy . . . agrarnikov-marksistov*, i (1930), 64, 70.

[79] For other aspects of Larin's report, see p. 4 above and vol. 1, pp. 195–7.

[80] *Trudy . . . agrarnikov-marksistov*, i (1930), 95–7; the divided interests of the peasant were a familiar theme at this time (see p. 79 above and p. 94 below).

[81] *Ibid.* ii (1930), 163–4 (G. Chernyi).

or 'transitional-socialist'. No agreement was reached on whether kolkhozy would become 'consistently socialist' with tractorisation, or only when they transferred their means of production to the state and thus became sovkhozy.[82]

On the last day of the conference, December 27, Stalin, in a dramatic intervention, vigorously attacked 'one of the speakers' (he did not deign to name Larin) who had 'uncrowned the kolkhozy'; the view that kolkhozy had 'nothing in common with the socialist form of economy' had 'nothing in common with Leninism'.[83] According to Stalin, the kolkhoz was 'a form of socialist economy' because its main instruments of production were socialised, land belonged to the state, and there were no exploiting and exploited classes within the kolkhoz. There were 'contradictions' within the kolkhozy, and 'individualistic and even kulak survivals', but these would 'fall away' as the kolkhozy grew stronger and were mechanised. Stalin admitted that 'elements of the class struggle' existed within the kolkhozy, resulting from the 'survivals of individualistic or even kulak psychology', and from 'a certain inequality in material position which still remains'; but he vigorously attacked ' "Leftist" phrasemongers' who equated this with the class struggle outside the kolkhozy.[84] A notable feature of Stalin's speech, otherwise distinguished for the vigour of its support for the collectivisation drive and dekulakisation, was his failure to mention all practical questions of socialisation in the kolkhozy, and his stress on the 'considerable amount of work' which would be required to 'correct the individual psychology' of the peasant collective farmer.

During the last few days of December 1929, the draft central committee resolution prepared by the Politburo commission on collectivisation was considered by members of the Politburo. When the draft was sent to Molotov, he objected to its treatment of the degree of socialisation of peasant property.[85] Ryskulov, in his note on the draft (see vol. 1, p. 199) criticised the restriction of

[82] *Trudy . . . agrarnikov-marksistov*, i (1930), 107–8 (Lozovyi), 109, 111 (Karpinskii), 149, 151 (Nazimov).

[83] *Soch.*, xii (1949), 161, where the word 'Leninism' which appeared in the verbatim report is replaced by the word 'reality'; Stalin's speech was first published in P, December 29, 1929.

[84] *Soch.*, xii, 162–5; for Stalin's criticism of Larin's attitude to the kulaks see vol. 1, p. 198.

[85] VI, 3, 1965, 6; no archival source is given.

socialisation to 'commodity livestock', and attacked the proposal to make a firm statement that small implements and other livestock should remain in private ownership as 'a clearly incorrect slogan' which would 'drag events backwards', and help the 'strong' or 'upper' middle peasant in his struggle against the 'poor peasant and the poor middle peasant'.[86] According to a Soviet source, these criticisms were approved by Stalin and Molotov,[87] though, as has been shown, in his only published statement at this time Stalin made light of class antagonism within the kolkhozy and ignored the question of livestock. At all events, Stalin sent back the draft resolution and proposed that it should be much abbreviated by referring questions relating to the Statute of the kolkhoz for inclusion in the forthcoming model Statute.[88] The final resolution of January 5, 1930, appeared to be a compromise between the main commission and the Grin'ko subcommission:

> Insofar as, in place of the association for joint cultivation of the land, in which, together with the socialisation of labour, private property in the means of production is maintained, experience of comprehensive collectivisation at the present stage of kolkhoz development is promoting the agricultural artel, in which the *main* means of production (implements and draught animals, farm buildings and commodity-product animals (tovarno-produktovyi skot)) are collectivised, the Central Committee of the CPSU(b) instructs Narkomzem of the USSR to work out as quickly as possible, involving kolkhoz organisations on a broad scale, a model Statute of the agricultural artel, as a form of the kolkhoz transitional to the commune, bearing in mind that it is impermissible for kulaks to join the kolkhozy.[89]

The draft resolution of December 22 had described the artel as the 'main form of organisation' and did not include the phrase 'transitional to the commune'; thus the revised wording in the resolution of January 5 removed the implication of the draft that kolkhozy could remain artels indefinitely into the future, and

[86] VI, 3, 1965, 12–13; IISO, [i] (1964), 280–1.

[87] IISO, [i] (1964), 282–4.

[88] See vol. 1, p. 199, and n. 206; on December 23, the collegium of Narkomzem instructed Kolkhoztsentr to prepare a draft Statute; a draft was submitted on December 28, but rejected as unsatisfactory (Ivnitskii (1972), 177).

[89] *KPSS v rez.*, ii (1954), 666.

promoted the status of the commune.[90] The cause of socialisation was also promoted by the omission from the resolution of the explicit acknowledgement in the draft of December 22 of the existence in the artel of private property in small animals and milk cows for consumption purposes.[91] This increased the ambiguity inherent in the term 'commodity-product livestock', which was nowhere defined.[92]

The ambiguity remained unresolved during the next two months. A few days after the decree, the agricultural newspaper reported unhelpfully that a Statute for the artel, 'just approved and published' by Kolkhoztsentr of the RSFSR, stated that 'pro-

[90] For these changes see VI, 3, 1965, 13.

[91] See p. 85 above. All these changes were already incorporated in Yakovlev's revised second draft submitted to the Politburo on January 3. As compared with the resolution of January 5, the draft of January 3 did not mention the TOZ, and stated that '*so far only* the main means of production . . . are collectivised' (my italics—RWD) in the artel (Ivnitskii (1972), 175–6). These changes appear to be editorial in character; 'so far only' was redundant when 'transitional to the commune' was added.

[92] The term was an unusual one. In the normal terminology, animals were officially divided into *rabochii skot* (working or draught animals, i.e. grown horses and oxen) and *pol'zovatel'skii skot* (all other animals). In the statistics, horses, *krupnyi rogatyi skot* (literally, 'large horned livestock'—i.e. oxen, bulls and cows) and *melkii skot* (literally, 'small livestock'—i.e. sheep, goats and pigs) were shown separately (EO, 10, 1929, 46). *Produktivnyi skot* (productive livestock) was a very frequently used term which sometimes appears to have referred to all 'large horned' and 'small' livestock except oxen, and sometimes only to cows: Kalinin later referred to 'dairy cattle (molochnyi skot) or, as they call it, productive livestock (produktivnyi skot)' (P, March 3, 1930). *Tovarno-produktivnyi skot* (commodity-productive livestock), a term often used at this time, presumably referred to that part of the dairy cattle, or of all the livestock, which was sold on the market, or whose products were sold on the market. But the term in the resolution of January 5 was *tovarno-produktovyi skot* (commodity-product livestock) which taken literally would mean all livestock sold on the market as a commodity or transferred to the state as a product: the term 'product livestock' reappeared in Yakovlev's speech published on January 24, where it was simply used to mean 'large horned' but not 'small' livestock (see p. 90 below; it was also used by Ryskulov on November 19 (see p. 81 above). It was replaced in the Statutes of February 6 and March 1 by the familiar term 'commodity-productive livestock'. Perhaps the term was simply a typing error. But whatever its nuances may have been, it certainly implied that the collective farmer could not retain in his own possession livestock, particularly cattle, for the primary purpose of selling them or their products, whether to the state or on the market. Any sale of meat or dairy produce by a collective farmer was thereby in jeopardy. It was, however, quite unclear how far the term covered, for example, cows in households which owned a single cow, sold a small part of the milk, and consumed the rest.

ductive animals (all or part)' were to be socialised.[93] A few days later, Yakovlev, addressing Moscow workers who were leaving to work in the kolkhozy, appeared to revert to the position of the Politburo main commission about the socialisation of livestock, while simultaneously encouraging the growth of communes:

> Last year the overwhelming majority of newly-organised collectives were associations for joint cultivation of land . . . From the summer and autumn of 1929, the collective movement has proposed as the main type of kolkhoz for the present moment the agricultural artel, *in which not only labour but all the main means of production and commodity-product animals are socialised. This is not yet a commune*, because socialisation does not yet include that part of product livestock which is kept for consumption, part of the small livestock, and the sphere of everyday living, *but it is undoubtedly a gigantic step towards the commune, a transitional stage to the commune.*
>
> This determines the main features of the new model Statute of the agricultural kolkhoz artel worked out by Narkomzem of the USSR in accordance with the directives of the party central committee of January 5, 1930.
>
> The Statute, envisaging the immediate socialisation only of the commodity part of the product herd, and the socialisation of household plots only to the extent of and in conformity with the creation of socialised vegetable gardens which are able to satisfy both the needs of the collective farmers and give commodities for the market, *warns against any excessive haste*, rushing ahead, warns in others words against forcing the transition from the agricultural artel to the next higher stage, the commune, artificially and by administrative means.[94]

However, the model Statute of the artel which was approved on February 6, 1930, did nothing to resolve the controversial issues. While insisting on the collective use of all the land allotments (nadel), it did not mention the household plot (usad'ba) and said

[93] SKhG, January 11, 1930. The model Statute of February 6, 1930, contained no such statement (see p. 91 below); it was approved by the new Narkomzem of the USSR and by Kolkhoztsentr of the USSR, and the latter had a common staff and a common chairman with the Kolkhoztsentr of the RSFSR. A draft model Statute, submitted by Kolkhoztsentr of the USSR on January 13, was 'approved in the main' (Ivnitskii (1972), 177); the Statute was referred to in an editorial in P, January 19, 1930.

[94] I, January 24, 1930.

nothing about excessive haste. In the clause on the means of production Yakovlev's qualification that 'only' commodity animals should be socialised was omitted; the clause hardly departed from the resolution of January 5, apart from the use of the word 'productive' instead of 'product':

> There shall be socialised all draught animals, agricultural implements, all commodity-productive animals, all stocks of seed, fodder resources in the amount needed to maintain the socialised animals, all farm buildings necessary for managing the economy of the artel, and all enterprises for reworking agricultural products.[95]

According to a contemporary Soviet source, secretaries of regional party committees, after the publication of the model Statute, appealed to the central committee and to Stalin to give a ruling on the extent to which livestock, small implements and household plots should be socialised, but received no answer; Vareikis commented that they had to act 'at their own risk and fear'.[96]

During the first six weeks of 1930, leading officials continued to demand the immediate socialisation of productive livestock. At the conference of RSKs which met from January 11 to January 14, 1930, Vrachev, a member of the board of Kolkhoztsentr, explained how the plan to socialise 80 per cent of the total number of cattle, pigs and sheep in each RSK during the spring campaign should be carried out. In higher forms of kolkhoz, all the animals would be socialised, but the more widespread arrangement would be to leave some of the animals with the collective farmers for consumption purposes, while using socialised fodder and common pastures. To house the socialised animals, existing buildings should be adapted and simple cattlesheds and pigsties should be constructed; socialised poultry and rabbit farms should be established in the kolkhozy.[97] Vrachev's proposals were wildly extravagant in comparison with the most extreme notions of a few months before, and with what came to be regarded as realistic three months later. It was

[95] I, February 7, 1930 (for the date of the Statute, see VI, 3, 1965, 12); those concerned with the British Labour Party may like to note that this was clause four . . .

[96] IISO, [i] (1964), 282–3 Vareikis was Central Black-Earth region party secretary.

[97] P, January 14, 1930; a long article by Vrachev, evidently the advance text of his report, appeared in SKhG, January 11, 1930, and has also been used here.

characteristic of the feverish excitement of those weeks, however, that, according to the newspaper report, 'particularly many objections were raised' to Vrachev's proposal that only 80 per cent of livestock should be socialised; delegates to the conference argued that this would deepen inequality in the kolkhoz and restrict production for sale, and proposed instead that all livestock should be socialised by the spring of 1930, using the existing cattlesheds of households until new ones had been constructed.[98] A representative from the Central Black-Earth region who proposed that the model Statute should recognise that the collective farmer should have his own household plot, milk cows and small animals for family needs was a lone voice, and was not reported in the press.[99] On the day the conference ended, an editorial in the agricultural newspaper insisted that fewer animals were killed or sold up in areas where collective livestock farming was taken seriously and collective cattlesheds were under construction; it urged the okrug press to pay more attention to socialisation, and called for the immediate cancellation of local decrees which delayed it, such as the decision in the North Caucasus that collective herds should contain only certain varieties of cattle.[100]

Legislation adopted in the first six weeks of 1930 continued to support a high level of socialisation. Instructions from the all-Union authorities were primarily directed towards securing the socialisation of draught animals and the collection of seed, urgently required before the spring sowing. In January a letter from Narkomzem urged the formation of horse and mixed horse-tractor bases in all kolkhozy, and the transfer of all horses, including those of expropriated kulaks, to the kolkhozy, as well as implements and fodder; pressure was to be exerted on those who refused, including if necessary explusion from the kolkhoz.[101] In February, the authorities complained that the progress of the socialisation of draught animals was 'completely unsatisfactory' and must be completed everywhere by April 1, and called for buildings and fodder to be made available.[102] Further decrees called for the collection of 'seed funds' (see vol. 1, pp. 238–9, 252–3).

Other legislation insisted on the socialisation of productive

[98] P, January 14, 1930.
[99] IISO, [i] (1964), 285; VI, 3, 1965, 7.
[100] SKhG, January 14, 1930.
[101] SKhG, January 7, 1930.
[102] SZ, 1930, art. 127 (Sovnarkom decree of February 11); Kolkhoztsentr decree

livestock. As late as February 13, 1930, a decree of Sovnarkom stated that in the course of the economic year 1929/30 cattle in sovkhozy and kolkhozy must reach 30 per cent and sheep and pigs 20 per cent of the total in the USSR, with the number of dairy cattle in kolkhozy reaching 11 million during the year, and again called for the organisation of socialised cattlesheds to accommodate them, and for the collective production of fodder.[103] This implied no reduction of the rate of socialisation proposed in December 1929, even though the expected level of collectivisation had more than doubled since December. In the RSFSR, a decree of Sovnarkom, whose chairman Syrtsov and vice-chairman Ryskulov were keen protagonists of the socialisation of livestock, planned to double the total number of hens by 1933, and to increase the proportion in the socialised sector to 70–80 per cent of all hens, with 60–70 per cent in the kolkhozy, and 10 per cent in the sovkhozy.[104] On February 11, a further decree of Sovnarkom of the RSFSR complained that Livestock Month had been 'completely unsatisfactory' in most regions, and instructed that it should be extended to March 1 in grain-surplus areas and March 15 in grain-deficit areas, by which time the slaughter must end and the 'necessary degree of socialisation' be achieved.[105]

In the middle of February the party central committee made its one published pronouncement since January 5 relevant to the socialisation of livestock. In its resolution about the Central Volga region of February 15, it urged the regional party organisation to improve 'production indicators and quality' in kolkhozy by 'more and more socialisation of means of production and processes of production in kolkhozy, more and more growth and strengthening in them of socialised indivisible capital'.[106] The Central Volga region was by no means backward at this time in its efforts to socialise livestock (see p. 100 below), so the Politburo had evidently not yet wavered in its enthusiasm about socialisation.

The flow of instructions was supplemented by visits from authoritative officials. Alarmed by the failure of the seed collections to keep pace with the growth of the kolkhozy, the Politburo

of February 11, in SZe, February 13, 1930 (the completion date given in the latter is April 30, but this must be a misprint).

103 SZ, 1930, art. 141.

104 SKhG, January 28, 1930.

105 SZe, February 20, 1930.

106 PS, 3–4 (5–6), 1930, 91–3.

sometime early in February despatched a number of members of the central committee to the provinces for ten days to enforce its decisions.[107] Exhortatory visits from representatives of the commissariats were also frequent. A brigade from Narkomzem of the USSR, for example, after touring Stavropol' okrug in the North Caucasus, complained in strong terms that dairy cattle and draught animals were not being socialised.[108] A plenipotentiary of Kolkhoztsentr in the Western region complained that village soviets had failed to organise groups of batraks and poor peasants against the kulaks, with the result that the kulaks, using the women, had prevented the socialisation of animals and implements.[109]

Further measures sought to prevent the destruction of livestock by peasants joining the kolkhozy. On January 16, a decree of TsIK and Sovnarkom condemned the destruction of animals, which it admitted was taking place 'in a number of places', as due to 'kulak wrecking'; kulaks who maliciously destroyed animals, or inspired others to do so, could be banned from all use of land, their animals and implements could be confiscated, and they could be sentenced to up to two years' deprivation of liberty with or without exile. The decree also endorsed the ruling of Kolkhoztsentr that peasants who destroyed or sold their animals should not be admitted to kolkhozy, and instructed local soviets to ban the killing of young animals.[110] As the expropriation of the kulaks was already taking place in many places, the penalties added little to their plight, and to be effective needed to be used against middle peasants as well as kulaks. On the day after the publication of the decree, a *Pravda* editorial returned in connection with the slaughter of livestock to the theme of the two peasant souls. It distinguished the kulak, who had only the soul of a proprietor, from two types of middle peasant. The middle peasant in whom the soul of a proprietor predominated killed and salted down his calves and piglets before joining the kolkhoz, but there was also another type of middle peasant whose prime motive was to join the kolkhoz and for whom selling his livestock was a 'tribute paid by the "soul" of the labourer to the "soul" of the proprietor'.[111] Within a few days the legislation was widened to cope with poor and middle

107 P, June 3, 1930 (Mikoyan).

108 SZe, February 1, 1930.

109 SZe, February 5, 1930.

110 SZ, 1930, art. 66; the draft prepared by Narkomzem did not include the provision about deprivation of liberty (SZe, January 16, 1930).

111 P, January 18, 1930 (see also p. 86 above).

peasants whose proprietorial souls led them to behave like kulaks. A new sub-clause added to the criminal code of the RSFSR, unlike the decree of January 16, made no mention of kulaks, merely stating that 'malicious slaughter of livestock, deliberate damage to it and inciting others to do this', were criminal offences punishable with deprivation of liberty if they were undertaken 'with the objective of disruption of the collectivisation of agriculture and preventing its advance.'[112] At the XVI party congress in June 1930, Krylenko complained that in practice this clause was applied to middle peasants, and referred to 'strict party directives' that it should be applied only to the kulak; he also objected to the practice of applying it retrospectively to animals sold months before.[113]

Financial penalties and incentives were also introduced in the hope of encouraging socialisation. A new decree on the agricultural tax, dated February 23, 1930, relating to the tax to be collected in the following autumn, imposed a much higher rate of taxation on the income of the collective farmer from his 'personal economy' than on kolkhoz income; the rate was even higher than on individual peasant households. The decree also increased the discrimination in favour of the commune as against other types of kolkhoz.[114]

Thus pressure from the centre for increased socialisation was extremely strong, though the ambiguities of the central committee resolution of January 5 and the model Statute of February 6, the silence of Stalin and his close political associates, and the cautionary remarks of Yakovlev all provided some room for manoeuvre. The extent to which this pressure was reflected in local instructions varied considerably, and practice varied still more. Such key areas as the Ural Gigant and Khoper okrug were already committed to a full-blooded socialisation policy (see p. 73 above). By January, all the 100 or so kolkhozy in the Ural Gigant had been converted into communes, and in that month they were formally merged into a single commune. Enthusiastic reports improbably claimed that the peasants, formerly 'conservative and immobile', now looked on their houses as living quarters provided by the commune, and willingly moved house, or even village, to improve their conditions or in the interests of farm management. In one commune, everything was socialised except the hens.[115] In Khoper okrug, all

112 I, January 24, 1930; the new sub-clause was 79^1.

113 *XVI s"ezd* (1931), 352.

114 SZ, 1930, arts. 143–4.

115 SKhG, January 21, 1930.

TOZy were abolished, 82 per cent of the kolkhozy were 'artels with a higher Statute' (i.e. with a greater degree of socialisation), and 18 per cent, including some of the largest, were communes.[116] In Khoper, the fanciful plans for establishing an agrogorod envisaged the conversion of a whole district into a giant commune (see p. 45 above). The campaign for agro-industrial combines (AIKs) was now at its height (see p. 46 above); its adherents saw them as a move towards '*unified large-scale agriculture of a higher type*', in which all branches of agriculture were fully socialised. This was seen as the only way to 'eliminate all petty-proprietorial incentives': with the introduction of AIKs, all animals, gardens and vegetable plots could be 'completely depersonalised'.[117] Giant communes were established in many places, even in national minority areas. In Votsk autonomous region, giant kolkhozy 'normally absorbed everything in their huge territory, turning into a kind of Great Universal Stores'; their Statutes were later said to be 'closer to a commune than to an artel'.[118]

Some regional authorities enthusiastically endorsed the socialisation of livestock. In the Central Volga region, Khataevich responded to the encouragement provided by the central committee resolution of February 15 (see p. 93 above) by declaring that 43 per cent socialisation of productive livestock was not enough.[119] In Belorussia, the party central committee called in January 1930 for a maximum switch to the commune, and for the socialisation of animals in general, without making it clear that animals kept for consumption purposes should not be socialised.[120]

Other regions were more modest. In the Lower Volga region, a secretary of the regional party committee recommended that the normal type of kolkhoz should be an 'artel of a higher type', which implied that all productive animals would be socialised, but added that the TOZ or the commune must be allowed if the artel was not accepted;[121] and Sheboldaev later claimed that the regional party bureau recommended on January 11, 1930, that not more than 40 per cent of milk cows should be socialised.[122] In the Central Black-

[116] SKhG, January 3, 1930; KGN, 2, January 7, 1930.
[117] SZe, February 5, 1930 (Nikulikhin).
[118] NAF, 5, 1930, 30, 35.
[119] P, February 16, 1930.
[120] P, May 19, 1930.
[121] SKhG, January 4, 1930 (Gusti).
[122] P, April 27, 1930.

Earth region collectivisation was undertaken at a frantic pace, but pressure for socialisation was less intense. In a series of articles in *Pravda* at the end of 1929, Vareikis did not go further than calling for the socialisation of draught animals.[123] At the conference of RSKs in January, a representative of the region called for the retention in the personal possession of the collective farmers of milk cows and small livestock (see p. 92 above). The instructions issued by the rural department of the Tambov okrug party committee in this region in January 1930 to workers involved in mass collectivisation merely told them to arrange for the socialisation of seeds, implements and draught animals, and stated that all means of production would not be socialised at first.[124] In the North Caucasus, in a report to a congress of comprehensive collectivisation on January 9, Andreev, while calling for the immediate socialisation of 'animals and large implements' argued that communes could not be established in the initial stage: 'for a certain period some elements of individual farming will remain within the framework of the kolkhoz—the household plot, the nursery garden, small livestock, poultry and various other branches of the economy'.[125] This left unclear what was to be done with the peasants' cows, but did at least set certain limits to socialisation; and in practice there does not seem to have been any pressure from the North Caucasus authorities for the establishment of communes or AIKs. The situation in the Ukraine seems to have been similar. Ukrainian officials later claimed that they had permitted the establishment of a much higher proportion of TOZy than elsewhere in the USSR.[126] However, there was strong pressure in the Ukraine to socialise livestock including, in a number of districts, small domestic animals and birds.[127]

During the all-out drive, changes in the definitions of different types of kolkhozy also encouraged further socialisation. New model Statutes for the TOZ were introduced in the Ukraine and in the RSFSR. In the Ukraine, the model Statute proposed that productive animals and poultry should be socialised;[128] in the RSFSR,

[123] P, December 28, 31, 1929. [124] *Materialy*, vii (1959), 341.

[125] P, January 10, 15, 1930.

[126] *XVI s"ezd* (1931), 603 (N. Demchenko); the proportion of TOZy in the Ukraine on June 1, 1930, was 42.5 per cent as compared with 17.3 per cent for the whole USSR (*Sots. str.* (1935), 320–1). [127] SZe, February 23, 1930 (Tsil'ko).

[128] Slin'ko (Kiev, 1961), 202 (Statute dated December 7, approved by Narkomzem and Kolkhoztsentr of the Ukraine).

the Statute more vaguely favoured 'all measures to develop kolkhoz livestock and socialise the livestock of the members'.[129] Similar changes were made in the regions. In the Lower Volga, the party committee called for the revision of the regional Statutes so that in the TOZ draught animals, seeds, fodder and breeding cattle should be socialised; in the artel, all productive animals; and in the commune, all property, living arrangements and feeding, with all property transferred to the Indivisible Fund. The Statute for the artel approved by the regional kolkhozsoyuz required the socialisation of '*all* productive and dairy animals'.[130] Such shifts in definition were widespread. An agricultural journal later complained:

> Frequently the association for joint cultivation of land became in essence what was called an agricultural artel a year ago, and the agricultural artel, in the form in which it was introduced in the localities, was in essence something close to a commune.[131]

(D) RESULTS OF THE DRIVE, SPRING 1930

No general picture of the relative importance of the different types of kolkhozy during these months of rapid change can now be reconstructed. Figures showing the proportion of TOZy, artels and communes nominally or actually established during January and February 1930 were rarely published for particular regions, and not published at all for the USSR as a whole; they may not have been collected. In the confusion and haste of the whole process, in many villages peasants were simply nominally inscribed in a kolkhoz without an up-to-date Statute being available: the model Statute for the artel was not published until February 7, when over 8 million households were officially supposed to belong to the kolkhozy (see vol. 1, Table 16).

Socialisation was taken furthest in the case of draught animals and seed. Here the intentions of the central authorities were unambiguous, and the urgency of completing the campaign in time for the spring sowing was obvious to all concerned. Between

[129] *Ustav tovarishchestva po obshchestvennoi obrabotke zemli* (16th edn, 1930, clauses 2–3 (Statute dated December 21).

[130] I, April 19, 1930 (A. Kiselev).

[131] NAF, 5, 1930, 30.

January 1 and March 1, socialised draught animals increased from 17·4 to 78·3 per cent of the total number in kolkhozy.[132] The tendency of the first phase of mass collectivisation in the summer of 1929 was thus dramatically reversed. Great efforts were made to collect socialised horses into common stables, for which purpose existing stables, particularly those previously belonging to kulaks, were taken over and converted.[133] The scheme to establish a central machine-horse station in each kolkhoz did not prove viable. Available stables were too small, and experience of managing large stables was completely lacking. With central stables, the journey from peasant cottage to stable to field was lengthened, and personal responsibility diminished.[134] In the Ukraine, only 85,000 of more than 1 million socialised horses were located in machine-horse stations on February 10.[135] A delay often occurred between formal socialisation and the transfer of the horse to a common stable.[136] But evidently most horses were transferred: in later discussions it was taken for granted that horses had already been removed from the household of their former owner.[137]

The seed campaign was at first less successful, and gave rise to much anxiety among the authorities (see vol. 1, p. 239). But by March 10 enough seed was collected to enable sowing to take place on 80 per cent of the land nominally collectivised at this peak moment in the collectivisation drive (see vol. 1, p. 253); this was more than adequate for the land which remained in the kolkhozy after the huge exodus of peasants in March and April.

[132] The following figures for draught animals were reported in I, March 9, 1930 (millions):

	January 20 [*?January 1*]	*February 1*	*February 10*	*February 20*	*March 1*
Total in kolkhozy	2·11	5·16	8·43	10·53	11·93
Total socialised	0·37	2·76	5·67	8·55	9·35

[133] See, for example, P, January 13, 1930 (Khoper okrug).

[134] See SZe, June 22, 1930 (I. Kudinov).

[135] P, February 22, 1930.

[136] See for example Shatskin in P, March 1, 1930 (referring to Lower Volga region); at this point he was still calling for complete transfer to common stables four weeks before field work began.

[137] See for example SZe, March 30, 1930, in which Tsil'ko describes the temporary transfer of the horse to its former owner as 'a very dangerous experiment which might lead to the break up of the kolkhoz', and also I, April 19, 1930 (Kiselev); NAF, 6, 1930, 103, 107, 110.

No precise information is available about the extent to which socialisation of cattle and other livestock was actually carried out. The claims of some RSKs look very impressive: Shatrovo district in the Urals claimed that 56 per cent of cows were socialised as early as December 1929, and Khoper okrug reported that in seven large kolkhozy as many as 70 per cent of cows, 64 per cent of sheep and goats and 69 per cent of pigs aged more than one year were socialised.[138] These areas were certainly not representative: in the Central Volga region as a whole, 43 per cent of productive animals were reported to have been socialised by January 15;[139] in the Ukraine, percentages varied between 5 and 30 in different okrugs on February 10.[140] An even lower percentage was recorded by Khlebotsentr, which reported that in the kolkhozy which belonged to grain cooperatives, which included 3·3 million households, only 600,000 productive animals were socialised, a mere 11 per cent of the plan.[141] All these are far below the equivalent percentages for the socialisation of draught animals. Even so, like the figures published at this time for the number of households in kolkhozy (see vol. 1, pp. 443–4), they often record transactions which took place purely on paper. As in the case of draught animals, the central authorities encouraged collective farmers to construct common animal sheds,[142] and at first they also urged that all socialised animals should be transferred to such makeshift buildings (see p. 91 above). In view of the harm caused by hasty transfer, however, they eventually agreed that the former owners of the animals should keep them for the time being, and many animals were therefore simply listed as belonging to the kolkhoz without being transferred to collective buildings.[143] A spokesman for the Lower Volga region at the conference of RSKs in January 1930 reported that

> hundreds of thousands of horses, oxen, cows, pigs, and small animals have already been brought into collective stables,

[138] P, December 24, 1929, January 13, 1930.

[139] P, February 16, 1930 (Khataevich).

[140] SZe, February 23, 1930 (Tsil'ko).

[141] SZe, February 22, 1930.

[142] See for example the article by G. Krumin launching Livestock Month, P, January 1, 1930, the editorial in SKhG, January 1, 1930, and SKhG, January 11, 1930 (I. Vrachev).

[143] See, for Khoper okrug, *Krasnyi Khoper*, December 14, 1929, and P, January 13, 1930.

cowsheds, sheep farms and pigsties, and for hundreds of thousands of other animals retention notes (okhrannye zapiski) have been issued.[144]

Throughout these months, sale and destruction of livestock by the peasants continued, in spite of the legislation to prevent it. As the drive for socialisation intensified, so did the destruction of animals. At a meeting of members of TsIK in December 1929, Mikoyan spoke of animals being thrown on the market in masses.[145] On January 9 Andreev described 'really rapacious squandering (razbazarivanie)' in the North Caucasus of 'simply dangerous dimensions', from which it would take four or five years to recover.[146] Vol'f also admitted that 'the losses to our livestock from kulak agitation cannot be immediately cured'.[147] Those animals which survived often entered the kolkhozy in a pitiable state. A speaker at the first conference of women collective farmers in December 1929 acidly remarked:

> It is necessary to put pressure on collective farmers that animals should be fed as they were before entering the kolkhoz. Otherwise the several million horses which are to be socialised will go into the kolkhozy in a state in which they won't be able to drag their own legs, let alone a plough.[148]

After socialisation, problems and losses continued. In the makeshift collective stables, cattlesheds and pigsties, the animals were badly looked after.[149] Organisation was poor and incentives were inadequate.[150] Cows were shifted from one household to another when they were on the point of calving, and a considerable number died as a result.[151] After investigating the Lower Volga region in March, a senior government official reported:

[144] P, January 12, 1930.
[145] EZh, December 7, 1929.
[146] P, January 10, 15, 1930.
[147] NAF, 2, 1930, 5; all official plans, however, expected complete recovery within a year.
[148] P, December 24, 1929.
[149] PKh, 9, 1930, 120 (K. Kindeev).
[150] See for example I, January 24, 1930 (Yakovlev).
[151] B, 5, March 15, 1930, 51 (Syrtsov).

> The management of livestock in several kolkhozy is simply *repulsive*. Cows are almost up to their knees in dung, and horses are not looked after properly either, which in general is leading to a fairly considerable *death rate* of draught animals. Pigs and poultry are also perishing in some places.[152]

In those kolkhozy in which poultry were collectivised, they were often kept in insanitary conditions, and sometimes fatal epidemics broke out.[153] And when cows and other livestock were left with the household which originally owned them, the peasant had little interest in looking after them. Speaking in Voronezh on February 19, Kalinin argued that to leave collectivised cows with their former owners until the autumn would risk considerable losses.[154] The fodder situation, generally difficult in the winter of 1929–30 (see vol. 1, pp. 44–5), was worse for collectivised livestock. No measures similar to those used in the seed campaign were taken to obtain fodder. Kindeev claimed that the planned expansion of socialised livestock did not take the question of fodder into account: even the inadequate existing plans for grasses and root crops had not been met, plans to store fodder in silos had hardly been carried out at all, and the results had never been checked.[155] Socialised fodder was badly managed: owing to the absence of feeding standards socialised animals often at first 'stood up to their stomachs in hay', but by sowing time nothing was left to feed the horses.[156] Touring RSKs in March, Preobrazhensky reported that fodder was the main problem; if it was not solved by improving crop rotation in the spring of 1930, the towns would remain on hunger rations in 1931.[157]

(E) THE RETREAT FROM SOCIALISATION, FEBRUARY–JUNE 1930

Socialisation was one of the major issues in the radical reconsideration of policy which took place in the last three weeks of

[152] I, April 19, 1930 (Kiselev); in his reply on this point, Sheboldaev merely grumbled that this line of argument helped the Right wing (P, April 27, 1930).

[153] SZe, February 26, 1930.

[154] P, March 3, 1930; the date of this report is given in Kalinin, ii (1960), 628.

[155] PKh, 9, 1930, 121–2 (Kindeev).

[156] NAF, 5, 1930, 37 (Tsil'ko).

[157] P, March 18, 1930.

February 1930,[158] and vacillation and confusion were amply displayed in the press. The statements in favour of the socialisation of livestock in the Sovnarkom decree of February 13 and the central committee resolution of February 15 (see p. 93 above) were the last to be made at the highest level. But an article in *Pravda* on February 17, and an editorial on the following day, made no reservations in their references to further socialisation of 'commodity-productive' livestock, and as late as February 26 the agricultural newspaper still assumed in a small item in its columns that 60–80 per cent of poultry in kolkhozy would be collectivised in the spring of 1930.[159] During the previous fortnight, however, such a radical change in policy had taken place that this already seemed to be the extravagances of a far-off era. On February 11, Syrtsov, formerly an enthusiastic protagonist of socialisation (see p. 82 above), and now turning into an even more vigorous advocate of caution, recommended at the Sovnarkom of the RSFSR that cows, while remaining in kolkhozy in social ownership, should be left in the household if improved common cattlesheds were not available.[160] On February 14, Mikoyan published an article on the 'meat problem' which managed to avoid the whole question of the socialisation of peasant cows.[161] On the following day, the agricultural newspaper reported without comment that it was now planned to socialise 6 million milk cows, all of which must be provided with warm stalls and fodder, in the whole of 1930; this was a substantial reduction on the plan of 11 million announced only three days earlier.[162] By this time Kalinin, Ordzhonikidze and Kaganovich were in the provinces investigating the situation on behalf of the Politburo (see vol. 1, p. 267). On February 16, Kalinin told collective farmers in the Central Black-Earth region that in his opinion they could be allowed to retain their own pigs and poultry, temporarily and as an exception, but did not apparently mention cows.[163] Three days later, on February 19, he reported his meetings with collective farmers to the regional soviet executive committee and the Voronezh soviet:

158 For other aspects of this reconsideration see p. 51 above and vol. 1, pp. 261–7.

159 SZe, February 26, 1930.

160 SZe, February 11, 1930; this recommendation was embodied in the decree of the Sovnarkom of the RSFSR dated February 11 (SZe, February 12, 1930).

161 SZe, February 14, 1930.

162 SZe, February 15, 1930 (A. Demchenko); for the earlier figure see p. 93 above.

163 IISO, [i] (1964), 283.

> If comrade Birn and I had not expressed our opinion and had relied on the natural development of the debate, then most probably collective farmers in all cases would have resolved to collectivise hens and piglets.

According to Kalinin, this enthusiasm came primarily not from the peasants but from party members, who were afraid of being accused of Right deviation. Kalinin now mentioned the socialisation of dairy cattle, arguing that it called for 'tremendous tact', and that it was necessary to move more slowly for reasons of expediency.[164] The following day, February 20, *Pravda* carried an article by Milyutin stressing the importance of socialisation, but arguing that '*to do it in a hurry, or only for show*' was '*completely impermissible*'; in the first stage kolkhozy specialising in grain and not livestock should not attempt to socialise cows. This seems to have been the first published statement at this time to urge moderation in the socialisation of cows. While no Politburo decision on this matter has been reported, this article obviously had the backing of higher party authorities: Milyutin was not the kind of man who would act independently on such an issue. The views of Yakovlev, who persistently resisted excessive socialisation, had now begun to prevail: the shift in policy was made easier because Stalin had never publicly endorsed the immediate socialisation of animals. On the same day Syrtsov, in a strongly-worded speech to the party cell of the Institute of Red Professors, which was not published until nearly a month later, anticipated many of the major points in Stalin's article of March 2 and in the central committee resolution of March 14. He described the 'reduction of the forces of production' in such sectors as livestock as 'very serious', though partly 'the inevitable overheads of revolution', and he attacked hasty efforts to turn kolkhozy into communes, which sometimes 'even' involved the socialisation of poultry and small animals:

> *The main issue now is not to drag as many cows and hens as possible into the kolkhozy but to organise people and horses correctly for work in the kolkhoz.*[165]

[164] P, March 3, 1930; for the date of this speech see vol. 1, p. 255, n. 232. This text of the speech was published after Stalin's article of March 2 and the new Statute of March 1, and may therefore have been tampered with.

[165] B, 5, March 15, 1930, 47, 51; this speech was not published until after Stalin's article and the resolution of March 14, and may also have been tampered with.

On February 21, on Ordzhonikidze's recommendation, the party central committee in the Ukraine resolved that the socialisation of 'small productive livestock' (i.e. sheep and pigs) should cease; cows were apparently not mentioned.[166] Thus far emphasis was placed on ceasing the socialisation of pigs and sheep and on reducing, but for the time being only, the rate of socialisation of cows. On February 21, however, a *Pravda* editorial, presumably prompted by the Politburo meeting of the previous day, went much further: it condemned the socialisation of any animals, including cows as well as pigs, sheep and poultry, which were not 'commodity in character', coolly reminding its readers that the Statute of February 6 had required the socialisation 'only' (the word does not appear in the Statute) of draught animals and productive livestock:

> Peasant livestock which is not commodity-productive in character, and dairy cattle, the socialisation of which will not help to increase marketed production (tovarnost') must remain in the personal use of collective farmers.

Numerous articles on these lines now followed. The need for caution in the socialisation of livestock was one of the major themes of Stalin's article of March 2. Stalin insisted that the grain problem was the '*main link of the kolkhoz movement*', the solution of which was a prerequisite for the solution of the problems of livestock and industrial crops. The artel was the best type of kolkhoz for solving the grain problem, and therefore must predominate at present. Stalin restored the original definitions of the three types of kolkhoz. In the TOZ, now a 'past stage', means of production were not yet socialised; in the commune, for which 'conditions are not yet ripe', distribution was socialised as well as production. In the artel:

> The main means of production are socialised, mainly those for grain farming: labour, land utilisation, machines and other implements, draught animals, farm buildings. The following *are not socialised*: the lands of the household plot (small nursery gardens, orchards), dwellings, a certain part of the dairy cattle, small livestock, poultry, etc.

Socialisation of small livestock and poultry was being carried out by

[166] IZ, lxxvi (1965), 26.

'the issuing of bureaucratic decrees on paper' when conditions were not ripe; this was 'stupid and harmful rushing ahead'.[167] The new version of the model Statute, also published on March 2, followed the same lines. It recommended that one cow should be retained per household; sheep and pigs should be socialised only in areas of 'developed industrial farming of small livestock', and even then collective farmers should retain some animals. Poultry should not be socialised at all. The Statute also recommended that households should retain implements with which to work their household plot.[168] The resolution of March 14 added that artels could in future be re-registered as communes only with the approval of the okrug soviet or kolkhozsoyuz,[169] and on the same day Narkomzem ordered that such re-registrations must cease immediately.[170] Finally, on April 2 Stalin further undermined the position of the communes by declaring that while a number of long-established communes were 'splendid', they should nevertheless be turned into artels; he added for good measure that it would be a long time before conditions were ripe for the transformation of existing artels into communes.[171] The reasons for these more cautious policies were stated fairly frankly. First, the middle peasants were not ready for this degree of socialisation, and were antagonised by it. Forced socialisation was treated in Stalin's article of March 2 as a major cause of peasant dissatisfaction 'useful only to our accursed enemies'.[172] An editorial in *Pravda* claimed that socialisation of livestock kept by peasants for consumption purposes had been used by kulaks to stir up anti-Soviet agitation.[173] An article on the role of women in the kolkhozy frankly admitted that those who 'strive to socialise everything straightaway' were 'ignoring the feelings of what is sometimes a significant part of the population', and reported that 'anti-Soviet demonstrations of peasant women' had occurred 'in a number of places'; in a village in Khoper okrug an illegal meeting called by kulaks had resolved 'not to give hens, cows and children to the kolkhoz'.[174] Peasant destruction of livestock was

[167] *Soch.*, xii, 195–8.
[168] P, March 2, 1930 (clause four, as in the previous Statute—see p. 91, n. 95 above).
[169] *Resheniya*, ii (1967), 196.
[170] SZe, March 14, 1930.
[171] *Soch.*, xii, 223–4.
[172] *Ibid.* 197–8.
[173] P, February 21, 1930.
[174] P, February 22, 1930.

usually attributed not to forced socialisation but to the influence of the deliberate campaign sponsored by the kulaks.

Secondly, forced socialisation was criticised for distracting attention from the grain problem, and in particular from preparations for the spring sowing:

> One might think [Stalin wrote] that the grain problem is already solved in the kolkhozy, that it is already a past stage, that the main task at the present moment is not the solution of the grain problem, but the solution of the problem of livestock breeding and poultry raising.[175]

Thirdly, socialisation, and the removal of the market regulators of the economic activity of the peasantry, was said to have encouraged 'an explosion of consumptionist tendencies'.[176] *Pravda* now admitted that hasty socialisation resulted in a fall in productivity, and pointed out that this did not make animals 'commodity-productive', but merely eliminated commodity production, including the supply of milk to the market.[177]

In March and April 1930, 8 million households left the kolkhozy, taking with them some 7 million draught animals (see Table 5), and an unknown number of socialised livestock. Within the kolkhozy which remained, a dual process occurred: the socialisation of draught animals continued and was almost completed, but the collective farmers removed from socialisation a large number of other animals which were previously socialised either nominally or in fact. The census of May 1930 revealed that as many as 95·1 per cent of draught animals were socialised, as compared with 78·3 per cent on March 1 and only 44·1 per cent on June 1, 1929 (see Table 5). Socialised draught animals in kolkhozy amounted to 16 per cent of the total number of draught animals in the USSR, as against only 1 per cent on June 1, 1929.[178] A far smaller percentage of cattle and other livestock was socialised by May 1930. But the absolute increase as compared with June 1, 1929 was impressive;[179] and, in spite of all the fluctuations in policy, the proportion of kol-

175 *Soch.*, xii, 197; see also P, February 22, 1930.

176 B, 5, March 15, 1930, 47 (Syrtsov).

177 P, February 21, 1930.

178 Calculated from Table 5 and vol. 1, Table 2.

179 The following are the percentages of total numbers in the USSR socialised in kolkhozy in May 1930 (percentages for June 1, 1929 in brackets): cattle 5 (0.6), sheep and goats 5 (0.5), pigs 6 (0.6) (for the statistics on which these percentages are based see Table 6 and vol.1, Table 2).

khoz animals which were socialised increased substantially: the percentage of socialisation increased from 24·0 per cent of all cows in kolkhozy on June 1, 1929, to 33·9 per cent in May 1930.[180] The main type of kolkhoz was now the artel: in May 1930 73·7 per cent of kolkhozy were in artels, and only 17·3 per cent in TOZy, as compared with 33·6 and 60·2 per cent on June 1, 1929 (see Table 4).

The increase in socialisation took place against the sombre background of a decline in the total number of draught animals and of all kinds of livestock. In less than twelve months all the increases of 1925–8 had been wiped out (see vol. 1, Table 2); and the decline was particularly substantial in the case of animals less than one year old. At least in the case of horses and cows it was physically impossible for the losses to be replaced for at least the next 18 months.

The new arrangements announced during March cleared up some of the most obvious ambiguities in official policy, but left lesser ones unresolved. First, while the right of the kolkhoz household to own a cow, sheep, pigs and poultry, and to work its own plot, was assured, a certain vagueness remained. The size of the household plot was not regulated. The right to own calves as well as a cow was not mentioned in the model Statute, and peasants continued to kill off their calves until this point was cleared up.[181] The boundary between 'commodity' and 'consumption' livestock remained somewhat indefinite. Although the model Statute permitted only one cow per household, Vareikis held that collective farmers had a complete right to keep their own cows unless they were of a '*purely commodity-industrial* character'; in his opinion, only the surplus sheep and pigs of the richer part of the peasantry should be socialised, and even then compensation should normally be paid.[182] Others were less prepared to return completely to past practices, and much discussion took place on the familiar question of the relationship between the size of the family, the number of animals and the size of the household plot. The prevailing view was that households with more than four or five members should be permitted to retain more

[180] *Nar. kh.* (1932), 130–1; 300,000 of the 1,400,000 cows in the socialised sector of the kolkhozy, or some 7 per cent of all cows in kolkhozy, were stated to have been expropriated from kulaks (PKh, 7–8, 1930, 66).

[181] Chigrinov (1970), 55–6.

[182] P, March 4, 1930; a writer in the agricultural newspaper wanted cows to be socialised only in areas of '*developed commodity-productive* livestock' (SZe, June 10, 1930).

than one cow, and should be allocated a larger household plot.[183]

Secondly, while collective farmers had an unrestricted right to take their products to market (see p. 160 below), it remained unclear whether they were required to sell part of the products of the household plot to the state. This was to remain a sensitive issue for the next 40 years. In March and April 1930, however, it was mentioned only cursorily.[184]

Thirdly, the official endorsement of the continued existence of a 'dual economy', the individual and socialised sectors of the kolkhoz, gave rise to new problems. A survey in the North Caucasus revealed that the socialisation of arable farming encroached drastically on the normal functioning of the individual household. The peasant customarily used his horse to fetch water, to take grain to the mill, to go to the hospital and the bazaar, to visit relatives and to go fishing. Now some kolkhozy required their members to give notice a day or two in advance, and to queue, before they could borrow a horse. Some peasants, with influence with the groom, got an unfair advantage; others, who did not use the horses much, still had to contribute to their maintenance; keen collective farmers did not have time to queue.[185] Nor was it clear whether the collective farmer was entitled to use kolkhoz horses on his household plot. An article in the agricultural newspaper insisted that for the collective farmer to take his horse home until the harvest would be 'a very dangerous experiment which might lead to the break-up of the kolkhoz'; on the other hand, it would annoy the collective farmer to observe his former horse standing idle.[186] Eventually it was agreed that horses and implements should be made available for the household plot; a small charge for this was to be arranged by the general meeting or meeting of plenipotentiaries of the kolkhoz, to be deducted from earnings at the end of the economic year.[187]

Equally contentious problems arose with livestock in individual possession. In some kolkhozy, cows were deprived of pasture, all the

183 SZe, April 11, June 10, 1930 (N. Nikol'skii, I. Urmanskii); P. July 10, 1930, disk. listok 30.

184 According to Vareikis, in P, March 4, 1930, sales would be 'at the personal discretion' of the collective farmer; according to SZe, April 11, 1930, the disposal of the 'marketable surplus' from the household plot should be determined by the kolkhoz board and general meeting, which would make contracts with the agricultural cooperatives.

185 B, 11–12, June 30, 1930, 108–9 (survey of Eisk district).

186 SZe, March 30, 1930 (Tsil'ko).

187 SZe, April 11, 1930.

land surrounding the village being sown to grain, and the distant land, occasionally 20 or 30 kilometres away, lacked a well. Frequently collective farmers, accustomed to taking their poultry with them into the steppe to feed, could do so no longer, and therefore killed and ate them.[188] The problem of fodder for both socialised and individually-owned animals in the autumn and winter of 1930–1 loomed before the collective farmer. A writer in *Pravda*, reporting that the newspaper had received numerous queries on this subject, suggested that the kolkhozy should make contracts for products from the individual economy of their members, including manure, in return for supplying them with fodder.[189]

The household plot and the individual ownership of livestock undoubtedly fostered inequality within the artel. Poor peasants had relinquished their only means of production, their horse and plough, and depended entirely on the socialised sector for their income, while middle peasants still retained one or more cows and various other animals; in the Central Volga region, some batraks and poor peasants left the kolkhozy as a result.[190] Long-standing members of kolkhozy also had no cows of their own, and had to buy milk.[191] More generally, those who worked diligently for the kolkhoz did not have enough time to cultivate their household plot, and their income declined as a result: in the spring of 1930 reports already appeared of collective farmers who neglected the kolkhoz fields, or left them after a morning's work, in order to cultivate their own plots [192] The tension between household plot and collective work remained a permanent feature of the kolkhoz, usually resolved by the collective farmer in favour of his own plot.

Yakovlev's theses to the XVI party congress, published on May 19, 1930 (see vol. 1, p. 323) provided an occasion for a general review of the disastrous experience of the previous nine months. Past practices in socialisation were again bluntly condemned:

> To require peasants, when they enter the artel, to renounce immediately all individualistic habits and interests, the possibility of carrying on, in addition to the social, a personal economy

[188] B, 11–12, June 30, 1930, 107, 109.
[189] P, May 9 (O. Popova), 31, 1930.
[190] *XVI s"ezd* (1931), 619.
[191] Hindus (1934), 151; P, May 31, 1930.
[192] P, May 1, 31, 1930.

(a cow, sheep, poultry, the vegetable garden of the household plot) and the possibility of themselves using earnings on the side, etc.—this is to forget the ABC of marxism – leninism.[193]

The theses further confirmed that the establishment of communes must await the further development of technology and experience, and commended the establishment of TOZy, as a transitional stage, in certain non-grain areas and in the national republics of the East. But they did not propose a return to the individual peasant economy, whether within or outside the kolkhoz, as the primary, or even the major, means of solving the livestock problem. While admitting the existence of a 'crisis of livestock farming', they also stressed the bright prospects opening up after the success of the spring sowing campaign: the solution of the grain problem would in itself result in an improvement in industrial crops and livestock, and demonstrated that other branches of agriculture could, like grain farming, be developed through collectivisation and state farming. Particular emphasis was placed on the establishment of livestock sovkhozy modelled on the grain sovkhozy, and the 'mass establishment of special farms (fermy) with a high degree of marketability' within the kolkhozy.[194]

In the pre-congress discussions of the next few weeks, the unease felt by many party members was reflected only in a few outbursts by bold critics. Mamaev, in the course of his indictment of the party authorities, firmly blamed them for 'repressive measures' in consequence of which the middle peasants had 'barbarously destroyed' marketable and breeding animals and a food crisis had resulted.[195] From the opposite extreme, another contributor to the discussion urged that without the immediate socialisation of all means of production, including cows and pigs, the kolkhozy would remain 'weak and pitiful'; while the individual economy remained, the collective farmer would continue to devote more attention to it.[196] Both deviations were vigorously condemned by other contributors, as was a more modest proposal that in the national areas collectivisation, even in the form of TOZy, should not be embarked upon until land consolidation was complete.[197]

193 *KPSS v rez.*, ii (1954), 52.

194 *Ibid.* 55–6.

195 P, June 10, 1930, disk. listok 9; for other aspects of this article see vol. 1, p. 325.

196 P, June 2, 1930, disk. listok 6 (P. Medvedskii).

197 A. Avtorkhanov in P, June 22, 1930, disk. listok 17. Avtorkhanov was

The livestock problem, and the wider question of the degree of socialisation in kolkhozy, were both prominent themes in the proceedings of the party congress, which met from June 26 to July 13, 1930. The official speakers, while continuing to condemn excessive socialisation, emphasised the universal advantages of large-scale economy. In the political report, Stalin recited statistics of the decline in livestock and in marketed meat output and attributed the decline to 'the instability and economic unreliability of small-scale economy and of economy with a low level of marketability'; the way forward was to 'follow the road which we followed in solving the grain problem', namely to organise sovkhozy and kolkhozy.[198] Yakovlev, in his report on the kolkhoz movement and the development of agriculture, also stressed the importance of large-scale socialised special livestock farms within the kolkhozy, claiming that large-scale pig breeding and the improved feeding of cattle would enable the consumption of meat and milk to be doubled during the five-year plan. In a sub-section on 'Inequality among Members of the Artel', he turned to a theme which underlay many of the anxieties expressed in previous discussions. While rejecting any notion that class antagonism between the poor peasant and the middle peasant was a feature of the kolkhoz, he admitted that 'inequality of property' resulted from the continued existence of an individual peasant economy within the kolkhoz:

> The inequality which subsists between factory workers in the USSR is in the main a result of the varying quantity and quality of labour, the varying skills of the workers. But in the artel, in which the output of the socialised economy is in the main distributed according to the quantity and quality of labour, there is this inequality and also an additional inequality, resulting from the varying property position, the varying dimensions of the supplementary individual economy of the middle and the poor peasant.

---

denounced in P, June 26, 1930, disk. listok 21 (K. Tabolov) and June 30, 1930, disk. listok 25 (L. Gotfrid), and recanted in P, July 4, 1930; he reported after emigrating that he had been threatened with expulsion from the party because of his article, and was eventually removed from the Institute of Red Professors and sent to work in the press bureau of the central committee (Avtorkhanov (Munich, 1959), 167–75).

[198] *Soch.*, xii, 275–6, 333.

The solution was to increase the socialised income of the kolkhoz systematically, thus reducing the proportion of this income which the collective farmer received from the individual sector, 'not hurrying unnecessarily or getting nervous'.[199]

A temperate but definite emphasis on the paramount importance of the socialised sector in solving the livestock problem also pervaded the congress debates. A speaker from the Northern region contended that in the North, Siberia, Kazakhstan and elsewhere socialised cattlesheds and fodder should be the central feature of the artel.[200] Lominadze, asserting that class distinctions and political differences would continue as long as private property remained within the kolkhozy, urged that their poor peasant groups should continue and that the elimination of economic inequality should 'not proceed all that slowly'.[201] Only Kalinin stressed that a successful pig-breeding programme must involve the individual economy of the collective farmer, and warned that the arguments about the need to eliminate petty-bourgeois tendencies might result in a harmful reduction in the size of the individual economy within the kolkhoz.[202]

(F) SOCIALISATION RESURGENT, JULY–DECEMBER 1930

In the course of the next few months, the rival themes of the expediency of providing proper facilities for the individual economy of the collective farmer, and the desirability of encouraging the socialised sector, continued in uneasy harness. While the party congress was still in session, a resolution of the central control commission and Rabkrin called upon the kolkhozy to provide enough animal power and implements to enable non-socialised vegetable gardens, melon plots and orchards to be cultivated, and, at least in principle, settled the conflict about the provision of kolkhoz fodder to non-socialised productive animals by ruling that it should be provided, but as part of payment for work on the kolkhoz.[203] A few weeks later, an explanatory note of Narkomzem and Kolkhoztsentr declared that the model Statute did not limit the

199 *XVI s''ezd* (1931), 579–80, 591–2.
200 *Ibid.* 171.
201 *Ibid.* 195–6.
202 *Ibid.* 635.
203 SZe, July 13, 1930.

right of collective farmers to rear calves or to buy and breed cattle and other livestock; it thus in effect extended the permitted size of the personal economy.[204] Simultaneously, however, plans were announced for a steady increase in the socialisation of kolkhoz animals. By the spring of 1931, the socialised dairy herd in kolkhozy was to expand from 1·5 million to 3·3 million, 1·5 million of these being located in special livestock farms within the kolkhozy. In the same period, the number of collective farmers was planned to double, so the proportion of socialised cows was to increase; other socialised livestock was planned to expand even more rapidly.[205] At a conference of planning officials in September 1930 Vol'f stressed the urgency of carrying out socialisation so that additional meat and dairy supplies were available by the spring of 1931.[206]

During the autumn of 1930, the authorities, in preparing for the further collectivisation drive, frequently stressed the importance of socialised livestock in kolkhozy and the inadequacy of the preparations for it. After a tour of the Central Black-Earth region and the Ukraine, Yurkin, the head of Kolkhoztsentr, condemned the 'complete inactivity' of the kolkhozy in this respect.[207] Andreev, in a report to the Politburo at the end of November 1930, claimed that in the North Caucasus socialised cattlesheds and poultry farms were being constructed on a substantial scale, and emphasised that kolkhozy should increase the socialised sector of the non-grain branches of their economy generally; all this would reduce the role of the individual economy, and 'eliminate duality'.[208] At this time the central agencies acquired greater powers to purchase livestock from all sectors of the economy, and a centralised system for vegetable deliveries was introduced (see vol. 1, pp. 362–8). With these levers of control, even if the personal economy of the collective farmer and the individual peasant could not be socialised immediately, it would be brought under stricter state control. At the same time, part of the livestock purchased by the state from peasants and collective farmers would be sold to kolkhozy to build up their socialised farms. Of the credit to kolkhozy of 1,000 million rubles planned for 1931, at least 400 millions were earmarked for livestock farming;[209] and Andreev urged kolkhozy to raise money from their

[204] SZ, 1930, art. 446 (dated August 25).

[205] SZe, July 27, 1930.

[206] PKh, 7–8, 1930, 58; he was the chief agricultural planner in Gosplan.

[207] SZe, October 15, 1930.

[208] Andreev (Rostov, 1931), 17, 22.

[209] SZ, 1930, art. 442 (Sovnarkom decree of August 11).

members for the purchase of livestock for their socialised sector.[210]

The joint plenum of the party central committee and central control commission in December 1930 heard a report from Mikoyan on the meat question. Attributing the difficulties of the past year to the 'kulak manoeuvre' which resulted in the destruction of large numbers of animals in the spring, he urged the development of specialised livestock kolkhozy in association with the large livestock sovkhozy; this, together with the establishment of 100–200 'livestock MTS', would make livestock farming as advanced as grain farming. Rejecting all suggestions that the pressure of the new system of official livestock collections would lead the peasants to reduce their livestock still further, he confidently predicted that the meat problem would be solved in 1932.[211] Although the authorities temporarily permitted the establishment of a clearly defined individual sector within the kolkhozy, and now intended to eliminate it gradually by example rather than immediately by persuasion, they were fully persuaded that the economic advantages of large-scale mechanised farming were so considerable that the individual sector would rapidly dwindle into insignificance. They had no conception of the magnitude of the further livestock crisis which would develop during the next two years.

[210] Andreev (Rostov, 1931), 22.

[211] B, 1, January 15, 1930, 14, 21–3; this is described as the 'shortened stenogram of the report'.

CHAPTER SIX

KOLKHOZ INCOME AND CAPITAL

The kolkhoz, like the individual peasant economy, was to a considerable extent a subsistence farm: part of the gross production of its socialised sector was used in kind to feed its members and its livestock, to provide seed and so on. This part of production thus became an income in kind, which did not involve a monetary transaction. The rest of kolkhoz production was sold to the state or on the market, and provided the major part of kolkhoz money income. Income in kind and money income were frequently combined and confused in the statistics, which did not always distinguish clearly between the *money* income of the kolkhoz, and the substantially larger total income *in money terms*, which included an estimate of the value of the kolkhoz income in kind.

The main sources of kolkhoz income in this wider sense were as follows:

(1) Membership fees in money and in kind, paid by peasants when joining the kolkhoz.
(2) Agricultural and other production retained in kind within the kolkhoz.
(3) Kolkhoz production sold to the state or on the market.
(4) Other payments by the peasants to the kolkhoz—e.g. a proportion of their money income from otkhodnichestvo.
(5) Money grants and loans from the state.

Kolkhoz expenditure in the wider sense similarly consisted of two major parts: the utilisation or expenditure within the kolkhoz of its income in kind, and the expenditure of its money income.

Income in kind was allocated in two principal directions:

(1) Collective requirements. These included working capital for further production—e.g. fodder for animals, which might be set aside in a Fodder Fund. Similarly some products might be allocated to a Fund to maintain the sick and elderly, etc.

(2) Individual requirements. Production was distributed in kind to collective farmers as remuneration for their work, for use as food, or as fodder for their personally owned animals (part of the distributed production might subsequently be sold by the collective farmer on the market).

Money income was allocated as follows:

(1) To pay taxes and repay loans.
(2) To various Funds for investment and other purposes.
(3) To collective farmers as remuneration for their work.

The fixed capital of the kolkhoz also included both capital in kind—its collectively owned equipment, animals and buildings—and capital held as money in its collective Funds (when it had any).

The pattern of kolkhoz income and expenditure was affected by two major issues, or decisions. The first, discussed in chapter 5, was the extent of socialisation within the kolkhoz. The shifts in the degree of socialisation affected the proportion of the total economic activity of the kolkhoz which formed part of its collectively managed, or socialised, income and expenditure, both in kind and in money.

The second major issue was the division of the income of the kolkhoz between collective and individual needs. The longer-term collective interest in investment and the immediate personal interest in consumption were perpetually in conflict. In the weak kolkhozy with low incomes characteristic of the 1920s the collective interest suffered.

Initially, most of the land and much of the capital equipment of the kolkhozy were obtained, via the state, from private estates confiscated after the revolution which were not divided up among the peasantry. This land and equipment was legally state property. In 1927 it was formally placed at the disposal of the kolkhozy 'in perpetuity'; on transfer, it was valued, and its value was treated as a 'permanent interest-free loan to the fixed (indivisible) capital of the agricultural collective'.[1] The term 'indivisible' implied that the property or money concerned could not be returned to members if they left the kolkhoz. As early as 1925, a system had already been established whereby members of kolkhozy paid small non-returnable 'membership fees (vstupitel'nye vznosy)', contributed

[1] Vlasov and Nazimov (1930), 17; SU, 1927, art. 605 (decree of August 22, 1927).

part of their property to the kolkhoz as 'share payments (pai)', and loaned another part of it to the kolkhoz as a 'deposit (vklad)' on which they were paid interest. By this time some kolkhozy were also already paying a regular share of their income or profits into their indivisible capital.[2] From 1926 onwards, the kolkhoz authorities made much greater efforts to encourage kolkhozy to establish their own 'indivisible capital' for investment purposes by setting aside part of their current money income.[3]

The injunctions to the kolkhozy to establish collective Funds were at first couched in very general terms: a report in 1929 complained that the kolkhozy 'received almost no specific instructions from leading agencies, and therefore have so far groped their way, sometimes simply thinking up different devices out of their heads'.[4] In the spring of 1929 the collective Funds of the kolkhozy were still very weak. Only 48·2 per cent of kolkhozy had formally established Funds of 'indivisible capital', and only 39·4 per cent of this capital was derived from kolkhoz income, almost all the rest being capital loaned by the state in perpetuity. In many kolkhozy, Funds of divisible capital in fees and deposits were also lacking: 67·6 per cent of kolkhozy had established a Fund of membership fees and fees levied on members by the kolkhoz general meeting, but a Fund of returnable 'deposits' of implements, animals, products or money loaned by members existed in only 30·9 per cent of kolkhozy.[5] No information has been traced about the extent to which either indivisible or divisible capital were money savings for future investment rather than merely an evaluation in money terms of property owned or used collectively, but money savings are likely to have been very small. The weak development of collective capital in the spring of 1929 is shown by the fact that, taking all the capital Funds together, in both money and kind, they were smaller than

[2] Bauer *et al.* (1925), 20–1. A model Statute current at the time provided that this should be not less than one-fifth of profits (*ibid.* 61); how profits were to be calculated was not stated.

[3] Vlasov and Nazimov (1930), 18–19.

[4] *Ibid.* 27.

[5] *Kolkhozy v 1929 godu* (1931), 136–7; 'deposits' and 'fees' were not always distinguished, and the compilers of the kolkhoz census pointed out that 'owing to the poor development of accounting in many kolkhozy the data on collective funds suffer from a certain incompleteness' (*ibid.* p. xlvi). 'Fees' presumably include 'share payments'. Other sources stated that membership fees, as distinct from other fees and share payments, were not returnable.

outstanding kolkhoz debts.[6] Collective Funds were of course much more strongly developed in artels and in communes than in TOZy: 83·5 per cent of communes, 55·2 per cent of artels and only 39·2 per cent of TOZy possessed indivisible capital, and the amount per kolkhoz was much higher in the communes and artels (see Table 7).

On the eve of comprehensive collectivisation, opinions about the feasibility of substantially enlarging the indivisible capital or Funds of the kolkhozy were divided.[7] At a seminar held in the Communist Academy in the summer or autumn of 1929 an official of the Kolkhoz Council of the USSR reported that proposals to incorporate all the savings of the kolkhozy in their Indivisible Funds had 'very many' supporters in the kolkhoz movement,[8] and at the seminar some speakers proposed that the size of deductions to Funds from kolkhoz income be fixed by central regulations, and not left to the whim of kolkhoz general meetings.[9] But the prevailing mood among the assembled officials was one of caution. An official of the Kolkhoztsentr of the RSFSR pointed out that any increase in the level of the Indivisible Fund could be obtained only by reducing personal income; with an excessive Indivisible Fund 'the economy grows, means of production increase—and members go hungry and have no trousers'.[10] Speakers from the Kolkhoz Council, Gosplan and the agricultural newspaper all recommended caution. One speaker pointed out that 'deductions to these Funds are far from evoking feelings of tenderness and delight among kolkhoz members', while another reported that some artels admitted that

[6] The figures are as follows (million rubles):

Indivisible capital	72·0
Deposits	24·6
Fees	38·1
Total collective Funds	134·7
Total outstanding debts	152·9

(*Kolkhozy v 1929 godu* (1931), 126–7); debts were almost all outstanding loans from the state and the cooperatives.

[7] In 1929 the term 'capital' began to be regarded as inappropriate for collective or state property, and to be replaced by the term 'Fund'.

[8] Vlasov and Nazimov (1930), 167; the date of the seminar is not given, but from internal evidence it seems to have taken place before the November plenum.

[9] *Ibid.* 146, 154.

[10] *Ibid.* 132.

payment into the Funds was like a 'sickle cutting the heart'.[11] The spokesman for the Kolkhoz Council of the USSR described a Ukrainian Kolkhoztsentr proposal to increase the size of the Indivisible Fund at the expense of the divisible Funds as 'simple, but not always good politics'.[12] Even the representative of Rabkrin, while insisting on the importance of the Indivisible Fund, agreed that 'it is wrong to force its creation'.[13]

The widespread hesitations were swept aside after the November plenum, at which Molotov strongly insisted that kolkhozy must rely on their own resources and not expect much help from the state (see p. 78 above). In December 1929 the Politburo commission on collectivisation recommended that monetary membership fees for kolkhozy should be fixed at between 5 and 50 rubles for most peasants, while well-to-do middle peasants should pay 100 rubles; the commission calculated that this would yield at least 80–100 million rubles in 1929/30.[14] In addition, at least 10 per cent of the assessed value of the socialised property of members should be allocated to the Indivisible Fund.[15] Ryskulov himself proposed that as much as 50 per cent of socialised capital in artels and 60 per cent in communes should be designated as part of the Indivisible Fund, and therefore not returnable on leaving;[16] it is not known whether the commission made any recommendations on this point.

The model Statute for the artel of February 6, 1930, went much further than the commission in respect of membership fees. It provided that between 2 and 10 per cent of the value of the socialised and non-socialised property of the peasant, except domestic goods and goods for personal use, should be paid into the Indivisible Fund as a 'monetary membership fee'; batraks, however, would pay only five rubles.[17] Membership fees on this scale could be expected to contribute a substantial sum: the value of fixed capital in the autumn of 1929 was about 660 rubles per household, excluding housing, so with fees of 2–10 per cent of property, the 6½ million households which joined kolkhozy in February 1930 were

[11] *Ibid.* 136–7, 148–9, 152–3, 158.
[12] *Ibid.* 167.
[13] *Ibid.* 195 (Kindeev); for Rabkrin see p. 5 above.
[14] VI, 1, 1964, 38; according to this source, entry fees were to be used for *working* capital.
[15] VI, 1, 1964, 38.
[16] P, December 9, 1929.
[17] I, February 7, 1930 (clause 8).

due to pay between 85 and 450 million rubles.[18] The Statute also went some way to meet Ryskulov's proposal by a provision that 25–50 per cent of the socialised property of collective farmers should be allocated to the Indivisible Fund, the higher percentage being applicable to wealthier households. The remaining 50–75 per cent of socialised property would be designated a returnable 'share fee (paevoi vznos)', but would be returnable 'as a rule only after the end of the economic year'. These allocations of socialised property between Indivisible Fund and share fees were of course, unlike the membership fees, transactions in kind; the lumping-together of socialised property and money accumulation in the Funds resulted in much confusion, both for the collective farmers and for future historians.

A further clause of the Statute, clause 11, concerned the proportion of kolkhoz income which was to be allocated to the various Funds, and evidently also covered income both in kind and in money. It read as follows:

> 11. Expenses for economic purposes and those related to the economy shall be covered from the incomes of the artel received by the end of the economic year, as shall expenditure to maintain those not capable of work; deductions shall be paid into the Indivisible and social Funds (from 10 to 30 per cent into the Indivisible Fund, from 5 to 15 per cent into other social Funds) and due payments to labour (raschety po oplate truda) shall be made.[19]

The wording of clause 11 seemed to imply that the deductions should be made from gross income even before products or money had been set aside for seeds, fodder and other necessary economic expenditure.[20] This would have been an impossibly crippling burden. But even if made from net income these deductions, like the membership fees, were very large, and reflected the extent to which the authorities were committed to socialisation and to forcing the kolkhozy to expand their own investment at their own expense.[21]

[18] For fixed capital in individual agriculture see *KTs . . . 1929/30* (1930), 446–9.
[19] P, February 7, 1930.
[20] This interpretation of the model Statute was accepted by Gei, a member of the board of Kolkhoztsentr (SZe, June 24, 1930), but rejected in NFK, 6, 1930, 39.
[21] The model Statute of the commune, approved on December 21, 1929, and still in force throughout the spring of 1930, proposed that 20 per cent of income should

The eagerness of the authorities to introduce a high level of monetary membership fees and deductions from current kolkhoz income was partly due to the large amount of money held by the peasants. Their cash holdings had been increasing relentlessly since the autumn of 1927: rural purchasing power rose rapidly, owing partly to increases in the market prices of agricultural products, and partly to increased rural earnings for seasonal work; and the supply of industrial consumer goods fell far short of the increase in demand (see vol. 1, p. 81). The middle peasants who joined the kolkhozy in the autumn of 1929 certainly held several hundred million rubles in cash, and added to the hoard by selling their animals before joining (see pp. 80–1, 101 above).

The authorities, as well as attempting to increase the Indivisible Funds and working capital of the kolkhozy, also conducted a vigorous campaign to 'mobilise the resources of the countryside' for the general purposes of industrialisation. At first sight, the kolkhozy were treated generously. In accordance with the central committee resolution of January 5, 1930, the plan for agricultural loans to kolkhozy in 1929/30 was increased from 275 to 500 million rubles, primarily by transferring credits originally intended for individual peasant households.[22] But simultaneously the issue of loans was made conditional on the contribution of a proportion of the required resources by the kolkhozy themselves; 'compulsory returnable contributions' to the agricultural credit system were introduced, payable on the same basis as self-taxation.[23] Other measures were also directed towards transferring money from the peasants to the state. On January 8, 1930, a decree called for compulsory collection prior to the due date of loans received by

---

be deducted to the Indivisible Fund and 10 per cent to the Cultural and Welfare, Bonus and other Funds; this Statute did provide that 'income' was what remained after depreciation and taxes had been deducted and economic needs covered, so communes were in a less ambiguous position than artels (NAF, 6, 1930, 39). The model Statute of the TOZ, adopted on the same date, provided that 30 per cent of income, again after economic expenditure had been met, should be allocated to Funds: a minimum of 60 per cent of the total was to be allocated to the Indivisible Fund, 10 per cent to the Cultural Fund, 10 per cent to reserves and 5 per cent to bonuses. This Statute stipulated that membership fees should be 5–100 rubles, and that at least 10 per cent of socialised means of production should be allocated to the Indivisible Fund (*Ustav tovarishchestva po obshchestvennoi obrabotke zemli* (16th edn, 1930), clauses 23–4, 29, 48–9). These Statutes both applied only in the RSFSR.

[22] SKhG, January 7, 1930.

[23] The relevant decrees are summarised in FP, 7–8, 1930, 67.

kulaks from the agricultural credit system.[24] This was followed on February 4, 1930, by a stringently worded decree of Sovnarkom which insisted that all loans to individual peasants which were due for repayment must be paid back to the bank when the peasant joined the kolkhoz, using compulsory procedures if necessary; loans due for repayment after the date of joining would be the responsibility of the kolkhoz itself.[25] During February a vigorous campaign for the immediate elimination of these debts was conducted in the press,[26] and the issue of new loans was made subject to the settlement of past debts in full.[27] Later in February, the collegium of Narkomfin, after a report from the workers' brigade of the electrical engineering works Elektrozavod, resolved to undertake a one-month campaign jointly with Elektrozavod to recover overdue debts in RSKs.[28] Fees to the consumer and agricultural credit cooperatives, and the number of contributors, were also planned to increase substantially. Finally, the kolkhozy were expected to persuade their members to subscribe to the Third Industrialisation Loan, to increase their deposits in the savings banks and to buy 'obligations' for the future purchase of tractors.[29]

No precise figures are available on the results of the campaign. Tractor obligations proved the most popular, and a sum of about 60 million rubles was subscribed (see p. 23 above). Subscriptions amounting to 205 million rubles were taken out for the Industrialisation Loan; only a small part of this sum was actually paid in, however, and payments were particularly sluggish in areas with a higher level of collectivisation. Some 25 million rubles were paid into the agricultural credit system in the form of compulsory deposits. But overdue debts to the agricultural credit system did not fall at all, fees to the cooperatives failed to reach the plan, and deposits in savings banks failed to increase. In most respects, therefore, the campaign was a failure.[30] In consequence, the authorities apparently carried out their threat to refuse loans to recalcitrant kolkhozy.[31]

[24] FP, 7–8, 1930, 67.
[25] SZ, 1930, art. 114.
[26] See, for example, SZe, February 14, 1930 (editorial).
[27] SZe, March 30, 1930.
[28] EZh, February 25, 1930.
[29] FP, 7–8, 1930, 66–7.
[30] For details see FP, 7–8, 1930, 65–71.
[31] Agricultural loans amounting to 235 million rubles were issued to kolkhozy

The financial campaign, reinforcing the natural reluctance of the peasants to hand over their cash to the kolkhozy, undoubtedly inhibited the accumulation of resources in the hands of the kolkhozy themselves. Only a small proportion of the new members actually paid the initial amounts due to the kolkhozy.[32] No precise figures about kolkhoz cash resources in February or March 1930 appear to be available. But there is no doubt that while the collective farmers personally continued to hold cash in large amounts, kolkhoz Funds remained very small, and the level of kolkhoz working capital in the spring of 1930 was described in the agricultural journal as 'almost catastrophic'.[33]

During the retreat from collectivisation the attempt of the state to exact large sums in cash from the peasants and the kolkhozy was called off. As early as February 27, 1930, Syrtsov, who had been extremely active in encouraging financial pressure on the peasantry in previous months, instructed the regional authorities to cease to collect deposits compulsorily, referring to 'difficulties connected with the present organisational period of kolkhoz construction'. He indicated, however, that other payments should be continued.[34] It was not until April 2, 1930, that a decree of TsIK and Sovnarkom withdrew the measures of December 1929 and January 1930: it postponed until November 1 repayment by the kolkhozy of loans to kolkhozy and their members which were overdue, freed them from debts due on property confiscated from the kulaks, cancelled the collection of fees and deposits due to cooperatives and postponed further payment of tractor obligations until the end of the economic year. Kolkhoz payments amounting to over 200 million rubles were cancelled for the economic year 1929/30 alone. At the same time the decree of April 2 emphasised that loans to kolkhozy should, in spite of this loss of state income, reach the figure of 500 million rubles in

and MTS in October 1929 – March 1930, which is in excess of what was required in terms of the original plan of 275 million rubles for the year 1929/30, and almost 50 per cent of the revised plan of 500 million rubles (for these plans see p. 122 above), but in January and February 1930 only 33 per cent of the loans planned for the January–March quarter were issued (SO, 3–4, 1930, 19; SO, 6, 1930, 22). This seems to indicate that substantial loans were issued in excess of the plan in October–December 1929 and March 1930, and much smaller amounts during the financial campaign.

[32] SZe, March 9, 1930; in the North Caucasus region, for example, only 7·9 per cent of planned payments had in fact been made by March 1.

[33] NAF, 5, 1930, 42.

[34] FP, 7–8, 1930, 68.

1929/30 which had been approved by the party central committee on January 5, 1930. The kolkhozy were also granted substantial exemptions from agricultural tax.[35] A further decree of April 23 abolished self-taxation of kolkhoz members in the year 1930/31, offered kolkhozy further exemptions from agricultural tax, and made available an additional loan for the spring sowing of 60 million rubles.[36]

All these measures improved the previously impossible financial position of kolkhozy. But they went only a small way towards providing them with adequate working capital. Moreover, the attempt to retain peasants in the kolkhozy on a voluntary basis led the authorities to relinquish in practice the high level of payments into the Indivisible Fund recommended by the model Statute of February 6. The revised model Statute of March 1, 1930, retained the relevant clauses without change. But this could not last. While kolkhozy continued to be urged to collect membership fees from their members in full in money or in easily saleable goods,[37] the 'explanatory note' of April 13, 1930, restricted them to a maximum fee, varying between 5 and 25 rubles according to the wealth of the household.[38] This was much lower than the fees proposed in the model Statute, lower even than the recommendations of the Politburo commission in December 1929 (see p. 120 above).

The proposed size of the Indivisible Fund for the moment remained intact, and this gave rise to much controversy. At a conference of kolkhoz officials in the middle of April, speakers urged that the maximum deduction to Funds of 45 per cent of income, plus a further deduction for those incapable of work, was 'very high', and 'frightened off the poor peasants as well as the middle peasants', because they feared that not enough would remain to feed their families.[39] Appropriate legislation followed during the next few months. On May 31, a circular from Narkomzem and Kolkhoztsentr admitted that most kolkhozy were not strong enough

35 SZ, 1930, art. 230; for the decrees of December 1929 and January 1930, see pp. 122–3 above. According to calculations by the Kolkhoz Bank, kolkhozy were freed from the following payments: share capital and fees due to other organisations, 96 million rubles; debts on land consolidation, 46 million rubles; debts on kulak property transferred to kolkhozy, 10 million rubles; exemption of socialised livestock from agricultural tax, 25 million rubles (IZ, lxxvi (1965), 33–4).

36 SZ, 1930, art. 261.

37 SKhIB, 1, April 10, 1930, 22.

38 SZ, 1930, art. 256.

39 SZe, April 15, 1930.

economically to carry out deductions even at the minimum level envisaged, and ruled that the deduction should be made not from gross income in money and kind but from income excluding the seed fund, fodder for socialised animals, and sums needed for agricultural tax and for insurance of kolkhoz property:[40] this was roughly equivalent to 'conditional net income' in the accepted terminology. At the XVI party congress in July, Yakovlev stated that only the 'necessary minimum deductions' should be made to kolkhoz Funds (i.e. 10 per cent to the Indivisible Fund and 5 per cent to other Funds) and that 'all the remainder should be distributed to the collective farmers'.[41] A further decree published on July 27, 1930, formally fixed deductions to Funds from income at this level and ruled that any additional deductions must be specifically authorised by a general meeting.[42]

The socialisation of arable farming, including the vast majority of the horses and ploughs of the collective farmers, necessarily involved a substantial increase in Indivisible Funds. The kolkhoz census of May 1930, carried out after the main exodus had already taken place, revealed that 79·0 per cent of kolkhozy had now formed Indivisible Funds, as compared with 48.2 per cent on June 1, 1929. According to the census figures, however, the average Indivisible Fund per household declined from 176 rubles in 1929 to 110 rubles in 1930.[43] Moreover, 34·4 per cent of all Indivisible Funds were acquired from expropriated kulaks, and the proportion was much higher in some kolkhozy, as only 50·1 per cent of kolkhozy possessed Indivisible Funds from this source. Outstanding debts were still large in relation to Indivisible Funds: 455 as compared with 510 million rubles (see Table 7). But the kolkhoz returns for Indivisible Funds were reported to be incomplete, so the size of debts as compared with Funds was exaggerated.[44]

All these figures for Indivisible Funds are certainly unreliable, and provide no more than a general indication of the size of that part of socialised property deemed to be permanently at the disposal of the kolkhozy. The state of kolkhoz accounts, where they existed at

[40] SKhIB, 18, 1930, 7.
[41] *XVI s"ezd* (1931), 642–3; see also Kindeev in PKh, 7–8, 1930, 110–11.
[42] SZe, July 27, 1930.
[43] Calculated from data in Table 7, on the assumption that kolkhozy with Indivisible Funds included the average number of kolkhoz households (18 in 1929 and 70 in 1930).
[44] *Ibid.* p. lv.

all, was chaotic. According to a leading Narkomtorg official, owing to the acute shortage of paper in the countryside, new figures were generally inserted on old tables, and 'in end everything is so confused that it makes the lower officials' heads spin'.[45] At best, accounts were kept on separate sheets of paper, as there were no account books in the kolkhozy.[46] There was an acute shortage of book-keepers. But there is no reason to doubt the general conclusions of an authoritative report based on returns from the kolkhozy, which showed that monetary working capital was very scarce, and complained that the state made no loans available to tide over the kolkhozy until their income flowed in from the new harvest, the result being that only 'miserly expenditure' was possible during the spring sowing.[47]

In the autumn of 1930, the economic and financial position of the kolkhozy improved considerably. They were more dependent on the harvest for their income than the individual peasants, as both their socialised livestock economy and their non-farming activities were very small: 91·3 per cent of their gross agricultural production came from crops.[48] The socialised sector of the kolkhozy was responsible for 18·2 per cent of all agricultural production, and as much as 25·6 per cent of crop production, and 29·0 per cent of grain.[49] If the production of collective farmers on their household plots is included, kolkhoz production amounted to as much as 23.9 per cent of all kolkhoz and peasant gross output.[50] In the second half of 1930 kolkhozy included some 22–24 per cent of all peasant households and 19–21 per cent of the peasant population.[51] The gross agricultural production per household of kolkhozy, including the household plots, was therefore somewhat higher than that of the

45 VT, 5, 1930, 13 (Chernov).

46 EZh, May 27, 1930.

47 Minaev, ed. (1930), 275–6; see also pp. 137–8 below.

48 *Materialy po balansu* (1932), 142 (measured in 1928 prices).

49 *Ibid.* 142; these figures exclude sovkhozy.

50 See Table 8; these figures are calculated on a slightly different basis from the series cited on p. 169, n. 146, below.

51 According to *Kolkhozy v 1930 g.* (1931), 8, in May 1930 23.6 per cent of peasant households and 21·0 per cent of the peasant population (or 26·86 million persons) were in kolkhozy; the figures for the number of kolkhoz households in the last few months of 1930 were on average about the same as in May (see vol. 1, Table 16). *Materialy po balansu* (1932), 112–14, 170, 212–13, however, assumes that the kolkhoz population in 1930 was only 23·35 millions, 19·8 per cent of the peasant population and 18·8 per cent of the total agricultural population.

individual peasants, and, as the number of persons per household was lower in kolkhozy, production per head was substantially higher. Kolkhoz income per head from production in 1930 was valued at 160 rubles as compared with 118 rubles for the individual peasant, but these figures may exaggerate the difference.[52] The *money* income of the kolkhozy in 1930 is not known. It is certain to have been low as compared with that of the individual peasants, as almost all the income of the kolkhozy from their collective production was obtained from sales to the official çollection agencies at fixed prices; their opportunities to sell products on the free market were far fewer than those of the individual peasants, or of the collective farmer in his personal capacity.

Considerable efforts were made by the authorities after the 1930 harvest to ensure that the stipulated minimum percentage of net kolkhoz income was allocated to the Indivisible Fund (10 per cent) and to the Social and Cultural Fund (5 per cent). Allocations from kolkhoz income to the Indivisible Fund were henceforth to be made in money and not in kind: a decree of Kolkhoztsentr ruled that products which had been allocated to the Fund must be sold to the official collection agencies at fixed prices, with the obvious intention of putting up the collections and further squeezing the kolkhozy.[53]

Only scattered information is available about the size of the Indivisible and other Funds actually formed by kolkhozy from their income after the harvest of 1930. In four groups of kolkhozy in the North Caucasus and the Central Black-Earth region where a survey was undertaken, the proportion of net income allocated to the Indivisible Fund varied from 6·7 to 17·3 per cent and allocations to Social and Cultural Funds varied from 4·3 to 5·4 per cent; the stipulated minima were 10 and 5 per cent respectively (see p. 126 above).[54]

After the 1930 harvest, the state also brought the financial relaxation of the spring and summer to an end. On September 2,

[52] Based on data in *Materialy po balansu* (1932), 212–13, for income from cooperative production and independent production, and for entrepreneurial income, of collective farmers, individual peasants and kulaks; these calculations assume that the kolkhoz population was only 23.35 millions (see n. 51 above); if the kolkhoz population was 26·9 millions, income per head becomes 140 rubles for collective farmers and 122 rubles for individual peasants.

[53] SZe, October 3, 9, 1930.

[54] SRSKh, 6, 1931, 226, 229; seed and fodder Funds, administrative expenditure and depreciation have been deducted from gross income.

1930, a decree of Narkomzem and Kolkhoztsentr sternly ruled that up to 50 per cent of the Indivisible Fund of each kolkhoz must be set aside to cover the outstanding debts; if this amount was insufficient, the percentage of kolkhoz income deducted to the Indivisible Fund must be increased. The remaining half of the Indivisible Fund was to be set aside to be used for capital investment during 1931. Those debts of members of kolkhozy which were not covered by the property they had transferred to the kolkhozy were to be paid from the share of the kolkhoz harvest due to the member concerned, or from his personal earnings.[55] A month later a further decree of Kolkhoztsentr, published on October 3, ordered all overdue debts to be paid at once in the case of the kolkhoz, and within five days in the case of the personal debt of a collective farmer, and announced firm dates for payment of agricultural tax and insurance. The same decree ruled that kolkhozy should transfer money to the village soviet to cover expenditure on economic and cultural needs.[56] The village budget in areas where a high proportion of households was collectivised lost a substantial part of its revenue through the reduction of taxes on the kolkhozy and the cancellation of self-taxation on collective farmers, and Narkomfin had already ruled in May that the kolkhoz must make up the loss.[57]

How far these various provisions were carried out by the kolkhozy in practice is not known. The stringent financial measures of the autumn of 1930 did not, however, completely cancel out the benefits resulting from the legislation of the spring of 1930. Although total income per head (in kind and in money) was higher for kolkhozy than for individual peasants, the taxes paid per collective farmer were much smaller. Direct taxes and compulsory state insurance paid from kolkhoz income amounted to only 1.9 per cent of gross income and 11.3 per cent of taxable income, as compared with 4.0 and 17.8 per cent in the case of individual peasants. Even if personal taxes and insurance paid by collective farmers are included, kolkhozy and individual collective farmers paid only 141 out of the 1,000 million rubles paid by the peasantry in 1930.[58] Moreover, in the economic year 1929/30, kolkhozy received the full sum in agricultural loans proposed in the revised

[55] SZe, September 2, 1930.

[56] SZe, October 3, 1930.

[57] EZh, May 11, 17, 1930.

[58] FP, 1–2, 1931, 29.

plan of January 1930, while loans to individual peasants were drastically reduced.[59] The financial policy of the state in the summer and autumn of 1930, like its grain collection policy (see vol. 1, pp. 355–9), was thus directed towards placing the collective farmer in a position where his remuneration was visibly higher than that of the individual peasant.

But the authorities were equally determined to insist that an increasing proportion of kolkhoz investment should be met by the resources of the kolkhozy themselves. The income side of the agricultural credit plan for the forthcoming economic year 1930/31 included no allocations from the state budget;[60] and the financial plan for the special quarter October–December 1930 allocated only 66 million rubles in agricultural loans to the kolkhozy as compared with 525 million rubles in the twelve months of 1929/30, while an expenditure of 177 million rubles was planned for this quarter from the Indivisible Funds and other resources of the kolkhozy.[61] Simultaneously, the financial viability of the kolkhozy was undermined by the firm ruling that all their 'marketable' products should be sold to the state at low fixed prices. At the end of 1930 the finances available to the kolkhozy were utterly inadequate to provide both for adequate investment and for adequate remuneration of their members. This fundamental defect remained throughout the period of rapid industrialisation.

[59] Gross agricultural loans to kolkhozy in 1929/30 amounted to 525 million rubles and net loans (new loans less past loans returned) to 424 million rubles, while individual peasants received gross agricultural loans amounting to only 50 million rubles, while paying back loans amounting to 125 million rubles (FP, 10–11, 1930, 72).

[60] FP, 10–11, 1930, 73.

[61] FP, 10–11, 1930, 74; PKh, 10–11, 1930, 353.

CHAPTER SEVEN

THE PERSONAL INCOME OF THE COLLECTIVE FARMER

(A) THE DISTRIBUTION OF COLLECTIVE INCOME

(i) The background

If the arrangements for distributing a share of the collective income of the kolkhoz to its members were to promote the kolkhoz economy, they would need to provide powerful incentives to collective work; but if they were to be palatable to the collective farmers, they could not depart too far from peasant traditions and experience. The Soviet authorities believed that proper incentives would be provided for kolkhoz labour if, like factory labour, it were remunerated according to its length, skill and intensity. Peasant traditions, on the other hand, suggested two further criteria, which were at variance both with each other and with the needs of an incentive system. On the one hand, the egalitarian tendencies of the mir, which provided land allotments related to the number of 'eaters' in the household, pointed to the need to relate remuneration to the size of the peasant family. On the other hand, if kolkhozy were to be attractive to middle peasants as well as to poor peasants and batraks, it seemed desirable that the past economic success of peasant households should be acknowledged by relating their earnings to the land, implements, animals and money which they brought into the kolkhoz as their share payment.

A major practical obstacle to the introduction of a wage system was that income from agricultural activities, unlike the income of most industrial enterprises, does not flow in evenly throughout the year. It reaches its peak in the months after the annual harvest, and the size of the harvest and of the income from it cannot be accurately assessed in the previous autumn and spring when much of the field work is undertaken. The peasants took this condition of life for granted, but it was obviously difficult to reconcile it with a wage system on factory lines. In the sovkhozy, short-term bank loans before the harvest, and government subsidies in the event of harvest failure, made a wage system possible. But with mass collectivisation, this kind of assistance was beyond the means and contrary to the intentions of a government determined to maximise capital investment in industry and to squeeze resources out of the peasant.

No national system of remuneration had ever been prescribed for the kolkhozy, and on the eve of mass collectivisation all three principles of payment were in use: labour; number of eaters; and land and capital contributed. A national survey of kolkhoz payment systems, and a more detailed study of kolkhozy in Kuban' okrug in the North Caucasus, both undertaken in 1928 (see Table 9), revealed that remuneration related to the collective capital contributed by the peasant was the least important: it affected only 11 per cent of kolkhozy, and even in these the capital was often contributed on a per family or per eater basis, or in proportion to the amount of labour on the kolkhoz undertaken by the household. In a larger number of kolkhozy, and particularly in TOZy, members worked on the collective land with their own horses and implements, and were paid accordingly. In others, the household was remunerated according to the land it held. This system was of major importance in TOZy in the Kuban'; however, here again the land held by each household to a considerable extent corresponded to the number of eaters in the family.[1] In the TOZy attached to the Shevchenko MTS the harvest was distributed according to the area of land held by each household when joining the TOZ, and each household was expected to contribute work in proportion: Markevich argued that this system, 'adapted from peasant thought', had the merit of simplicity, and that the distribution of the harvest in proportion to work would merely result in each household demanding more work.[2] But as a rule payment per eater and payment according to work were more prevalent in all types of kolkhozy, including the TOZy, than payment by capital or land contributed to the kolkhoz.[3] Payment per eater may have been even more

[1] Minaev, ed. (1930), 181.

[2] Markevich (1929), 44–8.

[3] According to one report, however, in the Ukraine one-third of income was distributed according to means of production contributed, one-third according to

important than Table 9 indicates: households with more dependants were frequently allocated more work per able-bodied person than those with fewer dependants.

The kolkhoz congress of June 1928 endeavoured to combine the advantages of payment per eater and payment according to work: it approved payment according to work as the best system, but also proposed that the amount of work made available to kolkhoz households should be related to the number of eaters. The congress also approved piece work and payment according to skill, providing that the differential between skills did not exceed 2:1.[4] Many different methods of payment according to work were used in practice.[5] In some kolkhozy the payment scale varied according to both skill and age;[6] others used a scale depending entirely on age.[7] Women were frequently paid less than men for a day's work.[8] Some attempts were made to devise piece-work payments, especially in Siberia. The more usual system, however, was time payment: kolkhozy simply recorded the number of days worked.[9] As early as 1926, these units were sometimes known as 'labour days (trudodni)'. At first no adjustment was made for skill, but early in 1929 the tractor column in Chapaev district worked out a system in which 0·75, 1, 1·25 or 1·5 'labour days' were credited for work in four grades from 'light simple' to 'responsible skilled'.[10] A publication of the All-Union Kolkhoz Council also recommended at this time that the labour days recorded for one day's work should vary from 0·5–1, according to the age of the worker.[11]

Little information is available about the methods by which the kolkhozy reconciled such schemes with their seasonal and uncertain

---

work, and one-third according to the number of eaters (B, 22, November 30, 1929, 22).

[4] *Kolkhozy . . . pervyi . . . s''ezd* (1929), 404–5.

[5] For examples see Kindeev (1929), 29–51.

[6] According to KG, 93, November 24, 1929, a commune in Zaporozh'e employed an eight-grade scale ranging from nine rubles per month (for children engaged in summer work) to 30 rubles a month for the kolkhoz chairman; the range of the adult scale was 2:1.

[7] 12–14-year-olds received one unit for a given period of work, 15–18: 1·5, 18–50: 2·0, 50 and over: 1·33 (Kindeev (1929), 81; *Trudy . . . agrarnikov-marksistov* (1930), i, 91).

[8] For examples see Kindeev (1929), 36–8.

[9] ZKK (1929), 148–9; SZe, June 20, 1930.

[10] Kindeev (1929), 109–10; SZe, June 20, 1930.

[11] Kindeev (1929), 80–1.

income. Many kolkhozy used a provisional payment scale, making advance payments when the work was carried out, and a final adjustment after the harvest; these arrangements were partly financed by advances from various state agencies to the kolkhozy on contracts for sale of their products. In the Central Volga region, a system of work units was used, and a value assigned to the unit after the harvest was sold; an advance payment was made of 50 per cent of the estimated income per unit.[12] The assignment of a firm value to a work unit *after* the harvest, coupled with the use as a unit of 'labour days' varying according to skill, eventually became the main system of remuneration in the kolkhozy (see pp. 142–3 below). Its main features thus dated back to practices already used in some kolkhozy before the mass collectivisation drive.

(ii) The drive for a wage system, summer 1929 – March 1930

At the conference of large kolkhozy in July 1929, the organisation section rejected payment per eater on the grounds that it did not provide incentives to work, and also expressed its disapproval of payment scales which were related to age or sex; instead it called for scales related to skill, and the introduction of work norms and piece work wherever possible. It also resolved that no more than 50 per cent of payments due to members for their work should be made before the end of the economic year.[13]

Propaganda in favour of payment according to work and of piece work continued intermittently during the next six months. At the plenum of the party central committee in November, Kaminsky criticised the 'equalising' and 'consumptionist' tendencies of most kolkhozy,[14] Molotov urged kolkhozy to model themselves on sovkhozy (see p. 3 above), and the plenum resolution stressed in general terms the need to create 'personal interest by every collective farmer in improved productivity of labour (piece work, norms of output, a bonus system, etc.)'.[15] A fortnight after the plenum, an article in the party journal dismissed the system of remuneration prevalent in the Ukraine (see p. 132, n. 3 above) as 'bourgeois', and hinted that it was part of the 'economic programme of the kulak'.[16] In the following month Kaminsky, echoing

[12] ZKK (1929), 153–5.
[13] ZKK (1929), 162.
[14] Cited in VIK, 4, 1962, 59–60.
[15] *KPSS v rez.*, ii (1954), 647.
[16] B, 22, November 30, 1929, 58.

Molotov, told a meeting of members of TsIK that the kolkhoz must base itself in matters of labour organisation on the large sovkhoz and the industrial enterprise.[17] In the same month the peasants' newspaper published a long report, the title of which speaks for itself: 'For Piece Work, For the Correct Organisation of Labour: Against Equalisation, Against the Parasitic Per-Eater System'.[18] But counsels were still to a certain extent divided. The tendency of the middle peasants to sell up their property before joining the kolkhoz called into question the viability of a system based entirely on remuneration for work. On December 15 Yakovlev proposed to the Politburo commission on collectivisation, or to one of its sub-commissions, that part of the remuneration of the collective farmer should be related to the size of his initial share capital and to his contribution to socialised property.[19] But this proposal was implicitly rejected. Early in January 1930, an order of Kolkhoztsentr of the RSFSR stated that payment should be based solely on the quantity and quality of work, with the exception of benefits for sickness or inability to work.[20] At the conference of RSKs a few days later, an official from the Ukrainian Kolkhoztsentr also firmly declared that '*the only measure in distribution must be the number of labour days worked by each collective farmer*', and the newspaper account of the conference reported that the 'overwhelming majority' of delegates opposed distribution per eater, and also rejected payment related to the amount of land contributed by the household to the kolkhoz.[21]

In the enthusiastic atmosphere of the next few weeks many proposals were made to introduce the continuous working week and the seven- or eight-hour day into the kolkhozy.[22] A number of RSKs began to introduce payment scales, the most favoured being a six-grade system with a 2:1 ratio between the top and bottom grades.[23] After the appointment of Yurkin, a former metal worker and sovkhoz director, as chairman of Kolkhoztsentr in the middle of

[17] EZh, December 6, 1929.

[18] KG, 102, December 24, 1929.

[19] Cited from the archives in IISO, [i] (1964), 275.

[20] SKhG, January 4, 1930.

[21] EZh, January 14, 1930.

[22] See for example P, December 24, 1929 (speech at women collective farmers' conference).

[23] For example, Samoilov district, Lower Volga region, and Samara okrug, Central Volga region; the Shevchenko okrug, however, was reported to be going over to a system of 'labour days', recording the hours and days worked, but without a firm payment scale (P, January 16, 1930).

January 1930, a vigorous effort was made to apply the industrial wage system in the kolkhozy; the treatment of the collective farmer as an industrial worker was later described as 'a general tendency which predominated in the *apparat* of the kolkhoz and cooperative system in the first stage of mass collectivisation'.[24] In February kolkhozy were instructed to organise 'labour bureaux' during the first 15 days of March; they should then prepare work norms in order to go over piece work, preference being given where possible to individual rather than group norms. At first no detailed instructions were issued about how the norms should be prepared, and kolkhozy bombarded the central authorities with telegrams demanding specific instructions.[25] On February 25, Kolkhoztsentr eventually issued instructions which were modelled closely on sovkhoz and industrial practices.[26] Details were also published of two proposed payment scales, in which work was graded according to skill and responsibility: mechanised kolkhozy were recommended to adopt a seven-grade scale with a spread of 3:1, and non-mechanised a five-grade scale with a spread of 2:1.[27] These instructions, though published a few days later than Stalin's article of March 2, marked the climax of the unsuccessful attempt by the authorities to introduce a wage system in the kolkhozy.

This system, in which all remuneration depended on the quantity and quality of work, was a complete break with peasant tradition. Payment per eater and payment related to the amount of land and capital contributed to the kolkhoz by the household were completely excluded in favour of a wage system in which earnings depended on payment scales related to work norms prepared by the kolkhozy along industrial lines. Quite apart from the break in

[24] VTr, 7–8, 1930, 33.

[25] SZe, February 27, 1930.

[26] SZe, March 5, 6, 1930. An example of a model norm (actual quantities to be inserted by the kolkhoz on the basis of local conditions): one day's sowing with an 11-row sower (ten-hour day) was normed at four hectares; the norm for the rate of pay for one day's sowing was one ruble; so the rate for sowing one hectare was 25 kopeks. Separate norms were suggested for animal and mechanical drawing power, based on a ten-hour and an eight-hour day respectively.

[27] SZe, March 5, 6, 1930; this scheme earlier appeared as a proposal in an article by a deputy chairman of Kolkhoztsentr, Ya. Terletskii, in SZe, February 8, 1930. Although the Kolkhoztsentr instructions were supposed to apply to the whole kolkhoz system, Khlebotsentr at this time recommended a nine-grade scale (SZe, February 27, 1930). A conference of Lower Volga kolkhozy recommended a six-grade and a four-grade scale, each with a spread of 2:1 (P, February 25, 1930).

peasant tradition which it represented, the attempt to prescribe an advance payment in rubles and kopeks for particular farm tasks was wishful thinking of an extreme kind. It assumed that the central authorities, and the board of each kolkhoz, were able to predict accurately the size and value of the forthcoming harvest. It also assumed that the kolkhoz held or could acquire enough working capital to pay its members in advance of the harvest. Many official documents and statements at the time assumed that a substantial part of his 'wage' would be handed over to the collective farmer immediately. The model Statute of February 6, 1930, repeating the proposal of the conference of large kolkhozy in the previous July (see p. 134 above), declared:

> Payment for the work of members of the artel shall be carried out by the following procedure: during the economic year, for food and other needs, members of the artel shall be paid in advance (in kind or in money) not more than 50 per cent of the amount accruing to them for the work. At the end of the economic year a final settlement of payment for work shall be carried out.[28]

Nothing was said in the Kolkhoztsentr instructions of February 25 about advance payments, but the discussions during the course of February at times went further than the 50 per cent maximum advance payment proposed in the Statute, and assumed that a collective farmer, like an industrial or sovkhoz worker, would be paid a full wage immediately.

In view of the acute shortage of financial resources in the kolkhozy (see p. 127 above), immediate payment of substantial sums for the spring field work was obviously impossible. In some areas, advances on contracts, which were made available to the kolkhozy in cash, were used to pay part of the wages due to the collective farmers.[29] But as a general rule payments to collective farmers were small, and even more frequently were not made at all. Vareikis' claim that the provision about advance payments 'is not applied anywhere in practice' was something of an exaggeration.[30]

[28] P, February 7, 1930 (clause 15).

[29] For example, in the Urals (FP, 5, 1930, 67); the extent of this practice has not been established. An untypical report from Rossoshanskii okrug, Central Black-Earth region, stated that 30 per cent advance payments were 'universally' made (I, April 19, 1930).

[30] NAF, 3, 1930, 32: this statement was made sometime in February.

But even kolkhozy which were particularly the object of official care and attention, such as the Ural Gigant, incurred large debts to their members.[31] Former batraks and poor peasants tended to rely on wages and casual earnings for a large part of their income, and were supposed to be given priority in wage payments by the kolkhoz. But many of them received nothing, and in consequence were among the first to leave the kolkhozy.[32]

The instructions from Kolkhoztsentr about methods of payments were almost completely disregarded. The regional authorities often failed to pass on the instructions from the centre, and issued numerous circulars and formulas of their own.[33] The labour departments of the kolkhoz system were often weak, even at the republican level: the labour department of the Ukrainian Kolkhoztsentr had only two members of staff, and regional kolkhozsoyuz labour departments were also inadequately staffed.[34] At the lower levels, according to one report, 'no work has been done on payment scales and norms'.[35] Narkomtrud was supposed to send 15,000 book-keepers and accountants to the kolkhozy by April 1, but even after a 'government mobilisation' in the Moscow region only 6,371 were sent.[36] In the kolkhozy, even simple work records were often lacking, though 'all literate people were mobilised' to act as clerks. Work norms were rarely prepared; and, even where records were kept, time payment predominated in the overwhelming majority of cases.[37]

In an endeavour to cope with their acute shortage of cash without antagonising their members, kolkhozy frequently resorted to the issue of what were variously known as 'bonds', 'receipts' or

[31] In Gigant unpaid wages amounted to 400,000 rubles, even though half the 'wages' were paid in kind (FP, 5, 1930, 67).

[32] NAF, 5, 1930, 42–3 (Tsil'ko). In the Lower Volga region a kolkhoz conference proposed that 50–60 per cent advance payments should eventually be made, but that new kolkhozy should make advance payments mainly to batraks and poor peasants, up to a maximum of 20 per cent of the estimated total remuneration (P, February 25, 1930); an investigation of the region undertaken in March revealed, however, that 'even batraks and poor peasants do not normally receive advance payments' (I, April 19, 1930).

[33] P, May 10, 1930 (referring to the okrugs in the Ukraine); SZe, April 2, 1930 (survey of kolkhozy in Urals, Siberia and North Caucasus).

[34] VTr, 7–8, 1930, 34.

[35] I, March 27, 1930.

[36] SZe, April 3, 1930; 'large numbers' of these failed to arrive.

[37] SZe, April 2, 1930 (survey of kolkhozy in Urals, Siberia and North Caucasus).

'coupons' (bony, raschetnye kvitantsii, raschetnye talony); these were a mixture between an internal currency, available for use within the kolkhoz for the purchase of goods, and a promissory note. At first the kolkhoz authorities argued that these devices were essential, and Narkomfin agreed to experiment with them in communes, but at the beginning of March Narkomfin condemned them as 'money surrogates'.[38]

Even after the publication of Stalin's famous article on March 2, the authorities showed little inclination or aptitude to cope with the practical problems of remuneration. The revised model Statute of March 1, 1930, merely repeated the provision of the previous Statute which permitted advance payments up to a maximum of 50 per cent of earnings.[39] Evidence of discontent among collective farmers about the failure to pay them appeared frequently in the press in March and April. The survey of kolkhozy carried out during March (see p. 138, n. 33, above) reported that collective farmers, believing that they were expected to work for nothing, exhibited a 'formal (kazennoe) indifferent attitude' to their work: no-one anywhere explained to them that '*payment cannot be a firm magnitude, guaranteed irrespectively of the financial and economic position of the kolkhoz*'.[40] In Khoper okrug, everyone tried to avoid agricultural work, and instead to do such things as cartage for which the kolkhoz received immediate payment and the collective farmer was accordingly paid in cash. In an *ekonomiya* (major sub-division) of one very large kolkhoz only 120 persons turned up for work out of 600 households; in the same kolkhoz some collective farmers had already been credited with wages amounting to 150–200 rubles, but no-one had thought about whether this debt could be honoured.[41] At the end of March, with the spring sowing under way in many regions, a senior agricultural official reported that questions of payment and distribution of the harvest '*are now disturbing every collective farmer*', and urged that a conference should be called within a month to sort matters out.[42] On April 2, perhaps in a moment of despair, Yurkin, in a letter written jointly with the deputy chairman of the agricultural cooperatives, announced an All-Union Competition to find out the best experience of labour organisation in

[38] EZh, March 1, 1930; FP, 5, 1930, 14–15.
[39] P, March 2, 1930.
[40] SZe, April 2, 1930.
[41] I, March 2, 1930.
[42] SZe, March 30, 1930 (Tsil'ko).

kolkhozy, with 100,000 rubles in prize money; Kalinin was appointed chairman of the jury.[43] But this was too late for the spring sowing. Perhaps the most remarkable feature of the spring of 1930 is that sowing took place quite successfully in the kolkhozy even though collective farmers were working on credit for an unknown amount of payment, often not knowing even the system by which they would be paid.

(iii) *The emergence of the labour-day system, April–July 1930*

In the middle of April 1930, a Conference of Officials of the Kolkhoz System met under the auspices of Narkomzem and Kolkhoztsentr specifically to discuss questions of labour organisation; and at the end of July 1930 a USSR Conference of Officials of the Kolkhoz System devoted much of its time to the same subject.[44] During this period, substantial progress was made towards designing a viable system for the remuneration of the collective farmer. Three main sets of decisions were adopted. First, the financial position of the kolkhozy was improved. Secondly, wage payments were replaced by payment according to 'labour days (trudodni)'. Thirdly, payment by capital contributed and payment per eater were again permitted in addition to payment according to work.

The financial position of the kolkhozy was improved both by reducing their obligations to the state (see pp. 124–5 above) and by a firm ruling that advance payments to members should not be permitted. The 'explanatory note' of April 13 insisted that payments for labour should be made only from the harvest or from other income.[45] The provision for advance payments in the model Statute was thus effectively rescinded; henceforth it was recognised that the collective farmer could not be treated like a factory worker, but must remain a peasant in the sense that his main income depended

[43] SZe, April 2, 1930.

[44] These conferences were reported in SZe, April 15, 17, and July 25, 27, 30, 1930; references to them in the following pages are taken from these newspaper accounts.

[45] SZ, 1930, art. 256. In practice the new harsher regulation was also applied to smiths, saddlers and other artisans, who were accustomed to be paid immediately, and to bargain over the price charged for a job rather than be paid on a fixed scale, and now had to await the harvest before receiving payment. According to I. Mezhlauk, their 'great dissatisfaction with the extremely sharp break with the traditional forms of payment' led them 'almost everywhere' to leave the kolkhozy (SZe, May 8, 1930).

upon and must await the results of the harvest, and must be received in kind, as well as in money. With the kolkhozy now free of their main financial obligations until after the harvest, Narkomfin again firmly banned their attempts to create 'money surrogates'.[46]

The second set of decisions in April–July 1930 replaced money wages by the 'labour-day' system, the main features of which continued until the 1960s. Under the labour-day system, a development of arrangements already in use in some kolkhozy before 1930 (see pp. 133–4 above), the number of units of work performed by a collective farmer are recorded, and after the harvest the available kolkhoz income, in money and in kind, is distributed among the collective farmers in proportion to the number of units recorded for each farmer. The 'labour day' is a unit of account; skilled work is allocated more 'labour days' for one actual day's labour than unskilled work, and piece work can be accommodated to the system by recording a 'labour day' for the achievement of a definite work norm rather than for working a certain number of hours. The system solved two central problems of remuneration in the kolkhoz: the income of the collective farmer was made to depend on the 'quantity and quality' of his or her labour, while at the same time the amount paid out depended on the income actually received by the kolkhoz as a whole during the year.

At the kolkhoz conference in April 1930, delegates from local kolkhozsoyuzy argued that firm money wages were impossible, and that all calculation should be made in terms of labour days. In his summing-up of the discussion, Gei, a member of the Kolkhoztsentr board, unwilling to forget the alluring dreams of previous weeks, still advocated the retention of a wage system in the largest fully-mechanised kolkhozy, but freely admitted that kolkhozy which did not come into this category (in fact virtually all kolkhozy at this time) must go over to labour days. Immediately after the conference a *Pravda* editorial sternly condemned the 'mechanical transfer of the

[46] EZh, May 17, June 12, 1930. At a conference on kolkhoz finance held on May 8, 1930, a speaker from the Urals reported that an 'investigating group' had found that while *bony* were 'not dangerous', they could cause great complications to currency issue in the long term, but several speakers cautiously defended the practice on the grounds that there was no other way of increasing the working capital of kolkhozy; it was attacked by Goldenberg and Vaisberg (EZh, May 11, 1930). The repetition of the ban in strong terms by Narkomfin on November 10, 1930 (*Finansy i sotsialisticheskoe khozyaistvo*, 5, February 20, 1931, 19) indicates that such substitutes continued to be issued.

system and methods of the large-scale industrial enterprise directly to the kolkhoz', and declared that all talk of a wages system must cease; instead, a system should be introduced which was simple and comprehensive, and took into account the number of days or hours worked by each collective farmer, as well as their level of skill, work norms and quality of work.[47] Neither the conference resolution nor the *Pravda* editorial specifically endorsed the labour-day system, however, and the editorial even declared that the introduction of a single system of remuneration in all kolkhozy was unnecessary.

On June 6, 1930, an instruction of Kolkhoztsentr officially endorsed the labour-day system, proclaiming that it would inculcate firmly in every collective farmer the knowledge that his income was determined by the total earnings of the kolkhoz and by his own work as a share in this total. The instruction announced that a model labour-day scheme would be sent out 'in the very near future',[48] but no such scheme appears to have been made available in the course of the summer of 1930. A long article in the agricultural newspaper described a possible scheme in some detail: collective farmers meeting work norms approved by the kolkhoz would be credited with 'normal labour units' or labour days according to a five-grade scale, the number of labour days credited increasing according to skill from one in grade 1 to two in grade 5. At the end of the year, the distributable income of the kolkhoz in kind and money would be divided by the total number of labour days earned by all kolkhoz members in order to establish what the collective farmer should receive per labour day.[49] But this proposal did not receive official endorsement, and on July 1, 1930, a lengthy decree of Kolkhoztsentr, while again supporting distribution according to the number of labour days, still made no detailed provisions.[50] A resolution of the presidium of the central control

[47] P, April 18, 1930.

[48] SKhIB, 15, 1930, 8; as far as is known, this is the first occasion on which remuneration by 'labour days' was approved in an official order. The 'explanatory note' of April 13, 1930, by insisting that payment should be in kind as well as in money (see pp. 140–1 above) in effect rejected the money-wage system, but it did not specifically mention labour days.

[49] SZe, June 20, 1930 (A. Deikin); the author also proposed that bonuses and fines for good and bad work should be imposed on a five-point scale.

[50] SKhIB, 19–20, 1930, 31. On June 29, 1930, a circular/instruction of Kolkhoztsentr ruled that administrative expenditure should not exceed 2–3 per cent of kolkhoz income, or 1–1½ per cent in the case of kolkhozy with total incomes in excess of 15,000 rubles a year; all administrative posts in kolkhozy should be paid

commission and the collegium of Rabkrin of July 9, 1930, called upon Kolkhoztsentr to issue directives on methods for distributing income in kolkhozy by July 15, and to study existing experience within a month,[51] but the resolution apparently remained without practical effect. In August, Narkomfin and Kolkhoztsentr further strengthened the status of the new system by ruling that all accounts with collective farmers were to be kept in labour days, and not switched to a monetary form until the end of the economic year.[52] But all detailed elaboration was left to the local kolkhozsoyuzy.

The third set of decisions in April–July 1930 made important concessions to the principles of payment by capital contributed and per eater. The 'explanatory note' of April 13, 1930, ruled that 5 per cent of the gross harvest, and of the income from socialised dairy cattle, should be set aside for distribution on the basis of the property transferred by the collective farmer or the household to the socialised funds.[53] This decision was surprising in view of the hostility of the central authorities to such arrangements in the past; like the decision to permit collective farmers to retain their own livestock, it was a bid to attract middle peasants to the kolkhozy, and was presented as such in the press.

The central authorities were less willing to reintroduce payment per eater. In this case they did not make a deliberate concession to the wishes of the majority of the peasants, but conducted a piecemeal retreat in the face of overwhelming pressures and difficulties. The explanatory note of April 13 ruled that payment was to be based on the quality and quantity of the work of the collective farmer or of the household, in accordance with the

---

not by a fixed salary or guaranteed wage but out of the results of the harvest, in money and in kind, on the same basis as collective farmers as a whole; the income received could not exceed the highest income received by a collective farmer, except that a mark-up of up to 40 per cent of basic pay could be awarded by decision of the general meeting; the instruction did not specifically mention labour days (SKhIB, 18, 1930, 12).

[51] I, July 15, 1930; the same resolution stated that 'the kolkhoz and cooperative system pays no attention to the norming of administrative expenditure, as a result of which cases occur of its excessive growth', and called upon Kolkhoztsentr to work out within a month a scale of general expenditure and standard schemes for administrative staff related to the size of the kolkhoz. A later decree of Narkomzem and Kolkhoztsentr merely reiterated the provision that administrative expenditure should not exceed a fixed proportion of total income (SZe, September 2, 1930).

[52] P, August 2, 1930.

[53] SZ, 1930, art. 256.

decisions of the general meeting of the kolkhoz; this seemed to exclude per-eater payments.[54] This was a very sensitive issue. In the mir, families with a small number of able-bodied adults traditionally received a separate land allotment for each eater, and those leaving the kolkhoz continued to do so; harder work by the adult members of the family could therefore partly compensate for the larger number of dependants. In the kolkhozy, many collective farmers strongly supported the allocation of part or all of the harvest per eater as more equitable than allocation solely in terms of work done. According to I. Mezhlauk, 'a fairly wide stratum of middle and poor peasants' found distribution solely by labour days so unacceptable that they would leave, or refuse to join, the kolkhoz,[55] while Kindeev argued that distribution per eater of part of the harvest in kind was 'more flexible and satisfactory in the eyes of the collective farmers'.[56] Reports from the provinces confirmed the strength of these feelings. In an RSK in the Urals a tendency was noted in favour of an 'egalitarian system';[57] at a conference of kolkhozy in the Lower Volga region 'strivings to equalisation' were expressed, especially in relation to payments to the kolkhoz management.[58] And while Yakovlev claimed that women were generally favourable to piece work because it was likely to achieve equality between the sexes more rapidly,[59] women in a German kolkhoz in the Crimea, supported by some of the men, argued that 'piece work puts us in the position of workers and puts the leading comrades we elect in the position of masters', and were not convinced by experience until the end of 1930.[60]

At the conference of kolkhoz officials in the middle of April 1930, Markevich, more attuned than most leading officials to peasant reactions, accordingly suggested that part of the harvest should be distributed per eater; the Kolkhoztsentr representative countered by the usual proposal that more work should be given to adult collective farmers in households with a large number of dependants.[61] The conference accepted the latter solution, and on this

[54] SZ, 1930, art. 256.
[55] SZe, May 8, 1930.
[56] PKh, 7–8, 1930, 111.
[57] P, January 16, 1930.
[58] P, February 25, 1930.
[59] *6 s"ezd sovetov* (1931), No. 16, p. 17.
[60] SZe, January 15, 1931.
[61] A discussion article in P, June 7, 1930, argued that only unskilled work should

basis resolved that the quantity and quality of labour should be the sole criterion for distribution. The argument continued during the next three months. In a discussion on the model kolkhoz Statute in the agricultural newspaper, I. Mezhlauk proposed that one-third to one-half of kolkhoz income should be distributed according to the number of eaters, and one-half to one-third according to labour days.[62] Most other contributors to the discussion were on the whole hostile to this suggestion, on the grounds that it would reduce work incentives: 'workers who earn identical wages', one writer argued, 'also live unequally because of the difference in their families'.[63] The instruction of June 6, 1930 (see p. 142 above) firmly stated that income must be distributed among collective farmers according to the quality and quantity of work, and the decree of July 1, 1930, reiterated this principle and suggested ways of allocating more work to larger families. Nevertheless, prominent officials in Kolkhoztsentr were careful to stress that each kolkhoz had the right to determine its own methods of remuneration: the right approach, according to a member of the board of Kolkhoztsentr, was to encourage kolkhozy to keep distribution per eater to a minimum, but not to prevent the introduction of a scheme such as I. Mezhlauk's if a kolkhoz were in favour of it.[64]

At the XVI party congress in July, several speakers advocated partial remuneration on a per-eater basis. Lominadze, now secretary of the Transcaucasian party committee, argued that some distribution per eater would in any case be required in 1930 as in some cases 'during the period of hesitations' 25–30 per cent of collective farmers refused to work.[65] A collective farm chairman, describing remuneration per eater as 'a matter very near to the hearts of the collective farmers', declared that without it 'family people would be unable to live in the kolkhoz'.[66] In face of such arguments, Yakovlev wavered in his reply to the discussion, and retreated to the principle that arrangements should not be re-

---

be allocated so as to even out income between families of different size: skilled collective farmers should be permanently and fully employed.

62 SZe, May 8, 1930.

63 SZe, June 10, 1930; some contributors argued that households with a large number of eaters should be allowed to retain two cows instead of one for their personal use.

64 SZe, June 24, 1930 (Gei).

65 *XVI s"ezd* (1931), 196.

66 *Ibid.* 619.

gulated in detail from the centre; he conceded that no objections would be raised if the kolkhoz 'set aside a certain part of its food products for members with large families', and that no special regulations were needed to enable them to do so.[67]

After the congress, the line that each kolkhoz should be allowed to take its own decision about the system of remuneration was treated as authoritative. An unsigned article in the agricultural newspaper, while claiming optimistically that the overwhelming majority of collective farmers preferred distribution by quality and quantity of work, insisted that 'we do not have the right to abstract outselves from the habits and customs of the peasant'; the system adopted in each case must be accepted by the peasant as 'the most suitable system from the point of view of *his conceptions* about the measures necessary to strengthen the kolkhoz and secure its further growth'.[68] A *Pravda* editorial a week later also argued that, while remuneration according to work was preferable, '*the collective farmer must decide himself*' about remuneration per eater and by capital contributed.[69] In the agricultural newspaper the Uzbek Narkomzem and Kolkhoztsentr were criticised for decreeing that only remuneration according to work was permissible, while the Central Volga region was equally criticised for its ruling that 50 per cent of the harvest should be distributed on a per-eater basis; the newspaper suggested that remuneration per eater should be introduced only 'on the initiative of the masses', and only up to a maximum of one-third of distributed income.[70] In the next few months, the authorities stuck more or less firmly to the position that they preferred a system of remuneration solely according to work, but would not prevent kolkhoz members from following the principle of partial distribution per eater if they chose to do so. A decree of Kolkhoztsentr stated that remuneration should be by quantity and quality of labour but added the significant phrase 'as a rule';[71] a later decree of Narkomzem and Kolkhoztsentr, by condemning distribution *solely* per eater as a '*direct distortion*', implied that *some* distribution per eater was permissible.[72] Meanwhile, further legislation (see p. 126

[67] *Ibid.* 644.
[68] SZe, July 16, 1930; Yakovlev's reply to the debate at the party congress was on July 10.
[69] P, July 23, 1930.
[70] SZe, July 18, 30, 1930.
[71] SZe, July 27, 1930.
[72] SZe, September 2, 1930.

above) sought to ensure that collective farmers would receive a substantial share of kolkhoz income.

(iv) The harvest of 1930

The decisions of April–July 1930 failed to eliminate the prevailing muddle; and, coming in the midst of the main agricultural season, the sharp changes in policy even confused matters further.

The previous official policy of encouraging wage systems along industrial lines continued to have repercussions. Wage systems were introduced in some kolkhozy, particularly in larger ones, and the decisions of the April kolkhoz conference were sufficiently ambiguous, or sufficiently lacking in authority, to allow kolkhozy and local authorities to continue their efforts to introduce a wage system, though always on the basis of 'promise to pay' after the harvest. In May a report from a large kolkhoz in the Kuban' described with approval the use of a nine-grade scale based on sovkhoz practice, with a wage rate of 80k – 2r 80k for a ten-hour day.[73] As late as May 30, 1930, a conference of chairmen of kolkhozy and village soviets in Vladimir district, Ivanovo region, resolved that 'piece payments shall be immediately introduced for basic activity, on the basis of work norms and the approved wage scale'.[74] Many local officials believed that a wage system was immediately feasible in the kolkhozy, and looked on the withdrawal of official support as pusillanimous and temporary. The wage system died hard. As late as the autumn of 1930, an article in an agricultural journal, based on experience in the North Caucasus, suggested that payments in money terms should be fixed in advance and adjusted in accordance with the results of the harvest.[75] In September 1930, a decree of Narkomzem and Kolkhoztsentr drew attention to the continuing practice of recording labour in the form of a money wage, and condemned it as 'contradicting the main principles of kolkhoz construction'.[76] In the autumn of 1930, many kolkhozy which persisted in fixing payments in money terms found themselves able to pay a mere 30 kopeks or less per 'ruble' recorded, while others became heavily indebted to their members.[77] At the VI congress of

[73] P, May 9, 1930.
[74] *Kollektivizatsiya* (Ryazan', 1971), 430.
[75] NAF, 9, 1930, 114.
[76] SZe, September 2, 1930.
[77] SRSKh, 8, 1931, 150.

soviets in March 1931, Yurkin still complained that piece work was 'often' valued in money terms, with 'very unfortunate results', and that 'kolkhozy are often confused with sovkhozy in the localities'; he criticised demands that collective farmers should get a guaranteed wage as 'a kulak slogan'.[78] In the discussion of Yurkin's report, a speaker from the Lower Volga region defended calculation in advance of the harvest of the amount of money and products to be distributed per labour day, but in his reply Yurkin repeated his warning that no promises or hints of promises should be made to collective farmers before the harvest.[79] This was evidently a point of tension between the regime and the peasants. According to a later account, 'kulaks' disrupted kolkhoz general meetings when the introduction of a labour-day system was proposed, arguing that 'collective farmers will get nothing if the kolkhozy go over to labour days, but if all work is calculated in money they will get something from the kolkhoz or the state, this year or next'.[80]

But the kolkhozy in which a wage system was introduced were certainly a small minority; and, with the adoption of the new legislation on labour days in June 1930, many of these abandoned the wage system with alacrity. But June was very late in the season; sowing was complete everywhere, and harvesting was soon to begin. At the kolkhoz conference in July, a representative of the board of Kolkhoztsentr reported that as late as the middle of July most kolkhozy had not yet discussed their arrangements for distributing the harvest, and claimed that the instructions issued by local kolkhozsoyuzy were complicated and incomprehensible.[81] The collective farmers lacked even an approximate idea of the grain and money they would personally receive. Vareikis pointed out:

> The absence of a clear perspective for the collective farmer, ignorance and lack of confidence about how the harvest will be divided and how the division of income between the individual members of the kolkhoz will in practice be arranged: all this has been a source of many misunderstandings, hesitations and disillusionments by the collective farmer.[82]

[78] *6 s"ezd sovetov* (1931), No. 17, 9–10.

[79] *Ibid.* No. 18, 11; No. 20, 53.

[80] SRSKh, 8, 1931, 150 (report of a kolkhoz conference held in the summer of 1931).

[81] SZe, July 30, 1930.

[82] B, 10, May 31, 1930, 41.

Records of the work performed by collective farmers were absent or chaotic. Their work during the spring period was very often not recorded at all (see p. 138 above). Though the elaborate proposals for record keeping made earlier in the year gave way to simpler methods from April onwards, it was not until late in the summer, if at all, that record books became generally available.[83] For most brigade leaders, keeping even simple records of the work performed by the collective farmers was a novel and difficult task; many reports bore witness both to their incompetence and to their hostility to the complexity of the system.[84] At the VI congress of soviets in March 1931, Yakovlev, declaring that '*where there are no records there is no large-scale economy*', cited many examples of inaccurate records.[85] Even when records were accurate, they were usually passed direct to the kolkhoz management, and the collective farmers had no note of the number of labour days they had worked or of the advances they received.[86] The first attempt to remedy this situation was made in a Statute of Narkomfin and Kolkhoztsentr, which ruled that every collective farmer should have an account book (raschetnaya kniga) showing the labour days credited, in addition to the personal account (litsevoi schet) recording the same information which was kept in the kolkhoz office.[87] But by this time much of the harvest work had already been done, and in most kolkhozy no account books (or labour books, as they were later called) were issued until 1931.[88]

[83] The new record forms worked out jointly by Kolkhoztsentr and Rabkrin were not available at the time of the harvest, so kolkhozy had to prepare their own forms (VTr, 7–8, 1930, 39); according to Kindeev, writing in August, 'in the overwhelming majority of the kolkhozy which have been surveyed, records of labour and accounts with members are only now being introduced' (PKh, 7–8, 1930, 111); a typical report from a district in the Lower Volga described the 'chaotic labour records', for which labour record books had not been introduced until August or September (P, October 27, 1930). Even the revised forms for recording work were said to be far too detailed (SZe, August 14, 1930).

[84] See for example P, October 27, 1930 (report from Lower Volga); SZe, January 16, 1931 (report from West Siberia).

[85] *6 s''ezd sovetov* (1931), No. 16, 6–7.

[86] VTr, 7–8, 1930, 39–40; kolkhozy in the Central Volga region issued individual receipts (tabeli) to their members, and elsewhere cheques, stamps or coupons were issued; sometimes different colours were used to indicate different grades of labour—but all these devices were said to be untypical.

[87] P, August 21, 1930.

[88] The decision to issue account books in addition to the personal accounts was made again at a kolkhoz conference in February 1931, and reported in a financial

Some progress was made towards recording the 'quantity and quality' of labour. The grade of work was often indicated: a great variety of systems was in use, with a spread varying between 1:2 and 1:5·75, though 1:3 was usually the maximum.[89] Otherwise records usually simply took the form of a note of the number of hours or days worked. Even this relatively simple operation was beset with difficulties. One 'day's' work might mean anything from 8–14 hours,[90] and there were cases in which one or two hours' work was recorded as one labour day.[91] It was certainly quite beyond the understanding or competence of most brigade leaders, and most members of the kolkhoz boards, to record the amount of work actually performed in a given period by each member, or even by a whole brigade. Just before the harvest, Sheboldaev, writing in the party journal, conceded that 'we shall succeed in going over to piece work only in the case of certain special jobs such as tractor drivers and blacksmiths'.[92] In the majority of kolkhozy, no piece-work system of any kind operated throughout 1930.[93] In most of the remainder, records of work performed were kept solely for groups of collective farmers, or for whole brigades, and not for the individual peasant. Group piece work was defended on the grounds that it was much simpler to record than individual piece work, an important consideration in view of the primitive state of kolkhoz records.[94] Some kolkhoz officials also argued that group piece work encouraged cooperation in small work groups.[95] But this was not the official view. At the VI congress of soviets in March 1931, Yakovlev admitted that brigades and groups were still the basis of piece work 'in most cases', but insisted that individual piece work was 'extremely desirable'.[96]

---

journal as if it were entirely new (*Finansy i sotsialisticheskoe khozyaistvo*, 6, February 28, 1931, 10).

[89] PKh, 7–8, 1930, 108 (Kindeev); according to this account, all the kolkhozy surveyed in the Central Black-Earth region used a grading system, 48 per cent of those in the North Caucasus and 43 per cent in the Lower Volga region.

[90] SZe, June 20, 1930.

[91] *6 s''ezd sovetov* (1931), No. 16, 16.

[92] B, 11–12, June 30, 1930, 59.

[93] According to a report in VTr, 7–8, 1930, 34, although the largest kolkhozy used work norms, in at least 50 per cent of the kolkhozy time work was the only method; a survey, reported by Kindeev in PKh, 7–8, 1930, 107, showed that work norms were used only in a minority of kolkhozy in all the regions surveyed.

[94] PKh, 7–8, 1930, 107.

[95] SZe, January 16, 1931.

[96] *6 s''ezd sovetov* (1931), No. 16, p. 13.

The problem of ensuring that work was performed properly received some attention. In February 1930, a Lower Volga kolkhoz conference recommended that a four-grade scale should be used to measure quality.[97] In March, a Kolkhoztsentr instruction ruled that the quality of all agricultural work must be evaluated, and work should be formally 'accepted' on completion;[98] this was a grandiose suggestion, as this was the term used to describe the act of transfer of completed capital construction projects from state building agencies to state customers. Proposals to introduce bonuses and penalties for good and bad work were made later in the year (see p. 142, n. 49 above). But in practice, with very rare exceptions, no attempt was made to record the quality of work. Rewards and sanctions for good or bad work were therefore not possible, although they were obviously particularly important when piece work was being introduced.

The confusion of the spring sowing period, when vast numbers of peasants were leaving the kolkhozy, the belatedness and inaccuracy of the records of the work of the collective farmer, and the failure of many collective farmers to work in the kolkhoz fields, made it inevitable that the income from the harvest should be distributed by simplified methods. Zealous local authorities frequently claimed that the majority of kolkhozy were distributing the harvest according to the quantity and quality of labour contributed.[99] But many reports to the contrary appeared in the press. In some cases, a monthly grain ration was issued to collective farmers;[100] in others, flour was issued instead of grain;[101] food was often issued on a per-head basis to collective farmers working in the fields.[102] All these arrangements were rejected by the authorities, whose elaborate instructions included a provision that food could be issued during field work only by a resolution of the kolkhoz general meeting, and that such food must be deducted from the amount due to the collective farmer concerned from the harvest.[103] But distribution per eater nevertheless predominated. A survey by Kindeev showed

97 P, February 25, 1930.

98 I, March 17, 1930.

99 See, for example, B, 14, July 31, 1930, 25; P, October 27, 1930; *6 s''ezd sovetov* (1931), No. 16, 6.

100 *Ibid.* No. 20, 3.

101 P, October 18, 1930.

102 SZe, September 2, 1930.

103 SZe, September 2, 1930.

that many kolkhozy distributed most of the harvest in kind on a per-household or per-eater basis: in these kolkhozy food grains were distributed solely per eater, and straw for fuel etc. were distributed per household; only fodder was distributed according to labour days, and even here the number of animals possessed by each household was taken into account.[104] At the VI congress of soviets, both Yakovlev and Yurkin reported that grain had been distributed per eater in the 'overwhelming majority' of kolkhozy.[105]

By the autumn of 1930, owing to the general shortage, the physical distribution of consumer goods was a crucial element in the real income of the peasants. But here, too, arrangements within the kolkhozy were apparently little influenced by the principle of remuneration according to work. Industrial consumer goods were distributed on a per-head basis in some places,[106] while in others they were simply made available at the discretion of the salesman in the village shop, and those who were not working tended to get there first.[107]

Thus the collective farmers received much of their share of the harvest, and their main supplies of industrial consumer goods, on a per-head basis. Only their collectively earned money income was distributed on the basis of labour days, and (see p. 156 below) this was a minor part of their total money income. In these circumstances, they could hardly have attached much importance to distribution on the basis of labour days.

While the authorities were temporarily compelled by force of circumstances to allow remuneration on a per-eater basis, the decision of April 13, 1930, to conciliate the middle peasant by distributing 5 per cent of the gross harvest in proportion to the property invested by the collective farmer in socialised Funds (see p. 143 above) was considerably modified in the course of 1930. A survey of a large number of kolkhozy by a group of instructors of Kolkhoztsentr concluded that 5 per cent was too high in areas in which MTS or former kulak property provided a substantial part of

[104] PKh, 7–8, 1930, 111.

[105] *6 s''ezd sovetov* (1931), No. 16, 6; No. 17, 14. Yakovlev's account was said to be based on direct enquiries to a large number of kolkhozy in face of contrary claims from many regional authorities.

[106] *6 s''ezd sovetov* (1931), No. 20, 3; SZe, October 12, 1930.

[107] SZe, October 12, 1930.

the capital used by the kolkhoz.[108] In June, a member of the board of Kolkhoztsentr accordingly proposed that property invested by collective farmers in socialised Funds should be deemed to include former kulak property, and that the appropriate proportion of 5 per cent of the harvest should be distributed to batraks and poor peasants.[109] Former kulak property constituted a substantial proportion of the Indivisible Funds of the kolkhozy (see p. 126 above), so this proposal, which was apparently widely put into practice, was a major modification of the original decision.[110] It was also proposed that in kolkhozy served by MTS the capital of the MTS should count in the allocation of the 5 per cent, the appropriate proportion being placed in the Indivisible Fund of the kolkhoz and used to purchase shares of Traktorotsentr, but this arrangement was not enforced in practice.[111] But the most important qualification to the original decision was that the 5 per cent deduction should not be paid in kind but in money made available by selling the products concerned to the collection agencies at fixed prices:[112] payment in rubles declining in value in conditions of goods shortage was obviously worth very much less in real terms than payment in kind. In the event, some payment was made: in groups of kolkhozy surveyed in the Central Black-Earth region and the North Caucasus, the percentage of gross income paid out under this head was reported to have varied from 3·5 to as much as 9·0 per cent.[113] But certainly the authorities reinterpreted their original decision in such a way as to diminish the amount paid in real terms to those collective farmers who had originally possessed more property.

At least 4 million of the 5 million peasant households which remained in the kolkhozy throughout 1930 joined after October 1, 1929, and for these 4 million households this was their first agricultural season as collective farmers. The traditional incentives

[108] SZe, October 9, 1930; the survey was presumably made in the spring, but its date was not given.

[109] SZe, June 24, 1930.

[110] Some discussion took place on whether the sums allocated should be set against their debts to the kolkhoz in the case of the numerous indebted poor peasants (SZe, August 6, 1930); I have not found out whether this was done.

[111] SZe, October 9, November 28, 1930.

[112] SZe, October 9, 1930.

[113] SRSKh, 6, 1931, 229.

of individual peasant agriculture had vanished for ever, with the important exception of their work on the household plot. The emergence of new incentives depended on the successful design and adoption of a new system of remuneration by the Soviet authorities; and on the accurate keeping of simple records for every collective farmer, and of more complex records for every collective farm, of a kind of which the Russian peasants had no experience. The authorities blundered in the first three months of 1930, introducing a system which was completely inappropriate to the conditions of its time. No new system emerged until the middle of 1930, and even then the barest outline of the new system was provided by the central authorities. Moreover, the new system, though ingenious and, given adequate resources, feasible, was complicated, and no mass training in the most elementary techniques had been provided for the hundreds of thousands of brigade leaders and tens of thousands of kolkhoz clerks or book-keepers who were required to operate it.

It is not surprising that, according to numerous reports published after the 1930 harvest, the confusion and incompleteness of the arrangements for reducing and remunerating the work of the collective farmer had very harmful effects on his performance. Without the exceptionally favourable weather conditions of 1930, disaster could hardly have been averted. At the VI congress of soviets in March 1931, Yakovlev, summing up the results of 1930, described the pernicious consequences of merely recording the number of days worked without any attention to the amount of work performed. Collective farmers got up at 8 a.m. in the busiest period of field work, and then chatted to their neighbours and prepared for work leisurely; when they were ready to go to the field, it was already by old peasant custom time for lunch (obed). Because no attention was paid in the remuneration system to quality, ploughing was rushed, leaving the soil in such a state that it damaged the machines; sowing was also hasty; grain was tied up badly so that some of it fell off the carts, and was left in the straw during threshing.[114] In a West Siberian kolkhoz 'brigade leaders had to go round and wake up members of the brigade in the mornings, and the meals were unduly prolonged'.[115] In a kolkhoz in central European Russia, the chairman had to kill a bull calf

[114] *6 s''ezd sovetov* (1931), No. 16, pp. 12, 15–16.
[115] SZe, January 16, 1931.

illegally and divide it up among a group of collective farmers in order to get them to cut hay in a remote part of the kolkhoz; 'the trouble is', a peasant remarked, 'that somehow people don't work on the *kolhoz* as they do for themselves. They are not as interested'.[116]

But even these troubles were relatively minor. Collective farmers were unclear about the remuneration they were to receive. They knew that most of the harvest was to be distributed on a per-eater basis irrespective of work done. They had alternative sources of income in their household plot and their animals. Money income was now of little value in view of the goods shortages. For all these reasons they were often very reluctant to work in the collective fields at all. In the Ukraine and the North Caucasus, for example, only young people turned up for work in the early stages of the harvest.[117] Elsewhere, peasants appeared for work belatedly when they discovered that remuneration was to be based on labour days,[118] or that the kolkhoz had decided to distribute grain per eater only to those households which had done a reasonable amount of work in the collective fields.[119] But on a kolkhoz in the Central Black-Earth region peasants who had not worked were permitted to pick cabbages, and were able to perform nearly as many labour days as those who had worked throughout the summer.[120] Yakovlev claimed that 'in every kolkhoz you can hear them saying "what's the use of working, you will get your share anyway"'.[121]

The situation varied, however, from kolkhoz to kolkhoz and from area to area. Other reports indicated something of a clamour to work for the kolkhoz, presumably in areas where agricultural labour was abundant and in kolkhozy where the peasant believed that the harvest would be distributed on the basis of labour days. In these cases, the adult members of families with large numbers of dependants were frequently allocated more work.[122] Where agricultural labour was abundant, kolkhozy often tended to allocate most of the work to former batraks and poor peasants, leaving the former middle peasants almost idle.[123] From this evidence of

116 Hindus (1934), 328. 117 VTr, 7–8, 1930, 35.
118 P, October 27, 1930 (Lower Volga).
119 P, October 27, 1930 (Lower Volga); *6 s"ezd sovetov* (1931), No. 18, 7.
120 *Ibid.* No. 18, 7.
121 *6 s"ezd sovetov* (1931), No. 16, 8.
122 *Ibid.* No. 16, 15.
123 VTr, 7–8, 1930, 35. The case for doing this was that the former middle

unwillingness to work in many places and an overabundance of labour in others, no firm conclusions can be drawn. On the basis of an extensive survey Yurkin claimed at the VI congress of soviets that only 40 per cent of collective farmers in all participated in harvest work in 1930;[124] this was misleading, however, as most of those not participating were women, who traditionally played a rather minor part in harvest work as such.

Firm figures about the income distributed to collective farmers by the kolkhozy in 1930 are almost completely lacking. By far the most important product distributed in kind was grain. If our calculations are correct, the kolkhozy retained about 3½ tons per household (see vol. 1, Table 15), and a substantial part of this was distributed to their members. They also received that part of the money income of the kolkhoz which remained after the payment of taxes and economic expenses, and allocations to the Indivisible and other Funds. But the money income of the kolkhoz was small, as it consisted almost entirely of payments by the collection agencies in fixed prices for grain and other agricultural products; a survey in eight areas of the USSR showed that in the agricultural year 1930/31 only approximately 17½ per cent of the money income of collective farmers came from the kolkhoz.[125]

The distribution of substantial quantities of grain to the collective farmers, at first encouraged by the authorities as a way of demonstrating to individual peasants that they would be better-off in the kolkhozy, had embarrassing consequences. Collective farmers sold some of their grain on the free market; this was not illegal, but was regarded as most improper.[126] Seeking to forestall such behaviour, some local authorities endeavoured to restrict grain distribution to the minimum needs of the collective farmer for personal consumption, and to maximise the distribution of money

---

peasant would tend to have more animals from which he could obtain products and income privately, and early in 1930 a Kolkhoztsentr decree had apparently ruled that priority in the allocation of work should be given to batraks and poor peasants; but at the kolkhoz conference in April 1930 Kolkhoztsentr recognised that this decree had 'forgotten the interests of the middle peasant' (SZe, April 15, 1930).

124 *6 s''ezd sovetov* (1931), No. 17, p. 15.

125 Unweighted average of percentages for two peasant social groups in eight areas, calculated from data in IISO, ii (1968), 334.

126 See SRSKh, 8, 1931, 151.

income. The Central Volga regional authorities stipulated that collective farmers who earned more than the permissible grain consumption norm in terms of labour days should simply be paid the money value of grain earned in excess of the norm, with the value calculated at the low official collection prices, while collective farmers who earned less than the norm should be permitted to buy grain at wholesale prices.[127] This system prevented grain sales on the free market, but at the price of greatly reducing the incentive to work on the collective lands.

(v) *The triumph of piece work and the labour day, end of 1930*

The Soviet authorities drew the lesson from this experience that the new system should be applied more consistently and more vigorously. After the successful completion of the harvest, and of the first stage of the grain collections, the attitude of the central press to remuneration per eater became far more critical.[128] The previous official view that the collective farmers must make their own decisions about the best system was abruptly modified. In July, distribution of the harvest on a per-eater basis was regarded as a traditional peasant attitude, to be handled with understanding and even sympathy. In October, an editorial in the agricultural newspaper castigated it as a 'kulak principle'.[129] The freedom of choice for the collective farmer was removed at a stroke. At the kolkhoz conference in January 1931, Yurkin, in his opening report, stressed the importance of work norms and piece work, and condemned hostility to them as due to '"eateristic" attitudes'; and he again firmly condemned the equal division of the results of labour as 'wrecking in character' and as advocated by kulaks.[130] In his concluding report to the conference on behalf of Kolkhoztsentr, Tataev declared: 'The eater principle, payment by the day, and so

127 *Kak raspredelyat'* (Samara, 1930), 7–8, 10–11, 15, 17–26.

128 See for example SZe, October 23, 1930.

129 SZe, October 26, 1930. The charge was incongruous, because per-eater distribution was simultaneously treated as a 'variant of consumptionist communism' (NAF, 10, 1930, 38). This was in connection with proposals made by Vareikis earlier in the year for a system of remuneration in which payments in kind from the harvest of grain, potatoes and fodder would be made on a per-head basis (NAF, 3, 1930, 32–3); these were now described as liable to 'disorganise the system of labour payment', and as 'depriving the kolkhoz of conditions enabling improved labour productivity' (NAF, 7–8, 1930, 103).

130 SZe, January 14, 1931.

on, are a joke, although they still exist'.[131] The kolkhoz conference again recommended that income should be distributed solely by labour days, and adopted a scheme for the division of kolkhoz labour into four grades, credited with 0·7–1·5 labour days.[132]

At the VI congress of soviets in March 1931 Yakovlev reported that Stalin, during the preliminary discussion of issues confronting the congress, had stated that distribution according to work, the securing of the interest of the collective farmer in the results of his work, and proper records were 'the cornerstone of our congress of soviets'.[133] Yakovlev's report provided an elaborate defence of distribution according to work, and presented numerous examples purporting to demonstrate that piece work substantially increased productivity. He still admitted, however, that large families had a good case for demanding a minimum allocation of work: 'I do not think the kulaks talked them into it, they are simply defending their own interests'.[134] In its resolution the congress condemned the per-eater principle as the first of two 'very important and most harmful faults in the work of the kolkhozy in 1930' (the other was the bad organisation of labour):

> In all cases it involved the disruption of the material interest of the collective farmer in the results of kolkhoz production, a sharp reduction in labour productivity and as a result the reduction of the income of the kolkhoz. In such kolkhozy some collective farmers, the best and most class-conscious, the most devoted to the common cause, worked honestly, but others shirked work and used the kolkhoz as a means of profiting from the labour of others, of grabbing more from common labour and working less. The distribution of income (both in money and in kind) not by the quantity and quality of labour contributed by the collective farmer but per head is very often advocated by kulaks and other enemies of the kolkhoz, trying to disrupt the kolkhoz system. Such adherents of living on other people's work must be most decisively rebuffed, even expelling them from the kolkhoz.

Instead the rule for all collective farmers and kolkhozy must be: 'he who works more and better, receives more; he who does not work,

131 SZe, January 19, 1931.

132 For this scheme see Wronski (Paris, 1957), 22–33.

133 *6 s"ezd sovetov* (1931), No. 16, pp. 17–18.

134 *Ibid.* No. 16, pp. 15, 17–18.

receives nothing'; 'piece work evaluated in labour days' must be applied on a mass scale for all the main agricultural activities'.[135] After the experience of the first year of mass collectivisation, piece work and the labour day were firmly enshrined as the instruments by which work for the kolkhozy by its members would be remunerated.

(B) EARNINGS FROM PRIVATE SALES

In the autumn and winter of 1929–30 it seemed obvious in party circles that work for the kolkhoz would soon embrace the whole economic activity of the collective farmer, and that he would no longer grow his own products for sale. During the grain collection campaign in the autumn of 1929, articles in economic journals and in the daily press stressed the virtues of the planned supply of industrial goods to the villages in return for agricultural products, and argued that the market relations of the 1920s were being replaced by planned commodity-exchange.[136] Soon even the somewhat market-oriented term 'commodity-exchange (tovaroobmen)' temporarily dropped out of use. At the plenum of November 1929, the party central committee castigated 'the panic-stricken demands of the Right-wing opportunists for the unleashing of "free turnover" for the capitalist elements' and declared that the party was 'preparing conditions for the development of planned product-exchange (produktoobmen) between town and country'.[137]

In the autumn of 1929, prices on the free market rose drastically,[138] while on the official market industrial goods were often unobtainable. The incentive for peasants and collective farmers to take their products to the free market was overwhelming. For the moment, however, the authorities were hesitant about the extent to which all private trade could be eliminated immediately. In December 1929, Mikoyan argued that 'the role of market spontaneity is gradually being folded up', and that meat and dairy

135 *Resheniya*, ii (1967), 289.

136 See for example VF, 5, 1929, 3–19 (L. Shanin); *KTs . . . na 1929/30* (1930), 222.

137 *KPSS v rez.*, ii (1954), 645.

138 According to the official Gosplan index of retail prices, by January 1930 the prices of agricultural goods were 60·3 per cent and the prices of industrial goods 46·2 per cent above the January 1929 level on the private market; the index stood at 475 and 358 (1913 = 100) as compared with 204 and 207 in socialised trade (SO, 3–4, 1930, 107).

products would be the next to be brought under control in the process of mastering the whole food chain 'systematically, and reconstructing it on a socialist foundation'. He conceded, however, that areas which had completed their grain collection plan should be allowed to 'go over to spontaneous flow (samotek)'.[139] Later in the same month Chernov argued even more strongly that the grain collection campaign had 'to a considerable extent *eliminated market relations between town and village*', though he also assumed that in 1930 'an insignificant part of marketed grain' would go to bazaars, and that 'non-organised intra-peasant turnover' would continue.[140]

In the new year, the abolition of unorganised trade was treated by leading officials as an urgent task. In February, at a conference on 'exchange and distribution', a Narkomtorg spokesman called for '100 per cent inclusion of the worker's budget in the socialised sector of trade'; to this end a 'unified plan of product-exchange between town and village' must replace collection plans for particular agricultural products in 1930.[141] In many areas, local markets and bazaars were closed in an endeavour to force all rural trade into official channels.

This policy was, soon repudiated. In his speech of February 20, 1930, Syrtsov declared that while relations with the kolkhozy would in the future move towards direct product-exchange they would at first remain 'within the formal framework of monetary deals'; two market systems existed, one controlled by the state and the other involving the private sector (the second market, according to Syrtsov, included both direct deals between state organisations and trade in food products by milk-women and on stalls).[142] The resolution of the party central committee on March 14, 1930, instructed party organisations: '*forbid* the closing of markets, *re-open* bazaars and *do not hinder* the sale of their products on the market by peasants, including collective farmers'.[143] At the XVI party congress, Stalin declared 'we are not yet abolishing NEP, for private trade and capitalist elements still remain, commodity turnover and the money economy still remain'.[144] Collective farmers were now

[139] P, December 7, 1929.

[140] *Torgovo-promyshlennaya gazeta*, December 29, 1929; he claimed that intra-peasant turnover was 'not marketed grain to the full extent'.

[141] EZh, February 14, 1930 (Vinogradskii).

[142] B, 5, March 15, 1930, 43–4.

[143] *Resheniya*, ii (1967), 196.

[144] *XVI s"ezd* (1931), 37.

entitled to possess their own farm animals and to the permanent use of a household plot (see pp. 105–6 above), and—for the moment—to dispose of the resulting production as they thought fit.[145]

The production from the non-socialised economies of collective farmers was a substantial proportion of the total production of the kolkhoz sector: collective farmers grew large quantities of fruit and vegetables on their household plots, and owned personally most of the livestock in the kolkhozy. According to Gosplan calculations, 30 per cent of the gross income of the kolkhoz sector from farming in money and kind came from the personal economies of the collective farmers (see Table 8).[146] How much of this production was sold on the free market is not known. Total rural incomes from free-market sales in 1930 have been variously estimated at 2,800 and 3,300 million rubles.[147] A survey of peasant money incomes in eight areas in the agricultural year 1930/31 disclosed that in almost every region collective farmers obtained a smaller proportion of their money income from sales on the market than individual peasants; the proportion was nevertheless substantial.[148]

As a result of the strengthening of the personal economy of the collective farmers, and the restoration of the free market, inequality between former poor peasants and former middle peasants persisted, as the supporters of socialisation had feared. In each of the eight areas surveyed former poor peasant households, whose individual economies were relatively weak, earned a substantially smaller proportion of their income from sales on the market than

[145] A special issue in 1930 was the land sown individually in the autumn of 1929 and transferred to the kolkhoz by new members when they joined. Land consolidation regulations had already warned against disturbing these sowings in the process of forming the kolkhoz fields from the strips (SZe, February 9, 1930), and the 'explanatory note' of April 13, 1930, ruled that the harvest from them was to belong to the collective farmer concerned (SZe, April 13, 1930).

[146] According to an alternative calculation 28·8 per cent of the 'production income' of kolkhozy in kind and money, valued at 1930 prices, came from 'independent' production (*Materialy po balansu* (1932), 212–13).

[147] Malafeev (1964), 131; FP, 3–4, 1931, 23.

[148] IISO, ii (1968), 334; 25 per cent of the money income of collective farmers and 33 per cent of the income of poor and middle individual peasants came from sales on the market (unweighted average of poor and middle peasant groups of collective farmers and individual peasants in eight areas; this rough calculation probably underestimates the difference, as it gives too much weight to ex-middle peasants in kolkhozy, where they were a minority, and to poor peasants among the individual peasants).

former middle peasants, and this was evidently a major reason why their total money incomes were also much lower.[149]

(C) EARNINGS FROM OTKHODNICHESTVO

The most urgent question for collective farmers before the harvest of 1930 was the immediate income they could earn from work outside the kolkhoz. At the end of the 1920s otkhodnichestvo was very substantial. In the summer of 1929, over 2 million people were employed on seasonal timber cutting and logging, and 1·5 million on seasonal building work, and a high proportion of these came from the countryside. In addition, more than 3 million people were employed in seasonal agricultural work in kolkhozy and sovkhozy, individual farms, and sugar-beet, cotton and tobacco plantations, and several hundred thousand others in seasonal industries, making a total approaching 7 million in all.[150] According to Narkomtrud surveys, 4·3 million of these came from the countryside.[151] In 1930, owing to the vast expansion of capital construction, the demand for building labour was expected to reach 2·16 million at the height of the season against 1·31 million in 1929;[152] labour shortages, and a consequent pressure on wages, were anticipated.

The enormous expansion of the kolkhozy at the end of 1929 and in the first two months of 1930 threatened to disrupt the traditional market arrangements through which seasonal labour had been recruited from the countryside. The number of collective farmers required for seasonal labour of all kinds during 1930 was first estimated at 1·5 million, and later at 2 million persons.[153] But the kolkhozy, anxious to retain as much labour as possible, sometimes endeavoured to prevent their members from leaving for seasonal work. According to one report, otkhodnichestvo ceased in RSKs;[154] according to another, collective farmers going to work in Baku

[149] *Ibid.* 332–5; unfortunately this summary by a Soviet historian of archival data is tantalisingly inadequate.

[150] *Industrializatsiya SSSR, 1929–1932 gg.* (1970), 359; for earlier figures, see vol. 1, pp. 12, 48.

[151] VTr, 2, 1930, 54, 58–60.

[152] *Industrializatsiya SSSR, 1929–1932 gg.* (1970), 386–7 (Narkomtrud report reprinted from the archives).

[153] SZe, February 12, March 11, 1930; these estimates were published before the exodus of peasants from the kolkhozy in March and April 1930.

[154] ZI, January 24, 1930.

without permission were treated as deserters.[155] When kolkhozy permitted their members to undertake seasonal work, they often made large deductions from their earnings. In the Lower Volga region, many kolkhozy tried to requisition all the wages their members earned on sovkhozy, and pay them at kolkhoz rates; elsewhere, deductions amounted to 40–50 per cent of earnings; the situation was described as '*complete anarchy*'.[156]

Confronted with these difficulties, Narkomtrud and Kolkhoztsentr proposed rival solutions. Uglanov, the People's Commissar for Labour, complaining of the great labour shortage in the lumber industry, in building, and in loading and unloading in transport, called for a decree instructing kolkhozy to release their seasonal workers.[157] Kolkhoztsentr, however, insisted that collective farmers must obtain permission from the board of their kolkhoz before taking part in seasonal work, and proposed that all recruitment of seasonal labour should be undertaken by contracts between labour agencies and the kolkhozy.[158] The standpoint of Kolkhoztsentr prevailed. A draft decree from Kolkhoztsentr was approved by the Politburo on February 25, 1930,[159] and on March 3 a circular of Narkomzem, Kolkhoztsentr, Vesenkha and Narkomtrud announced an elaborate system for the central planning of seasonal labour from the kolkhozy. 'Control figures for otkhodnichestvo' were to be prepared at the centre, and issued by Kolkhoztsentr of the USSR to the republican Kolkhoztsentry. On this basis, plans showing the number of collective farmers to be released from each kolkhoz should be prepared by the okrug labour departments and kolkhozsoyuzy, and the okrug labour departments of Narkomtrud, or the economic agencies concerned, should, before April 1, sign agreements with the individual kolkhoz boards. Work-orders (naryady) issued on the basis of these agreements were compulsory, both for the kolkhoz and for the collective farmer concerned. Collective farmers were permitted to undertake seasonal work only when issued with a work-order by the kolkhoz board; the work was to be carried out under a group leader who would carry a document informing the employing agency of the percentage of wages which

155 P, February 26, 1930; see also P, February 17, 1930; SZe, February 12, 1930.

156 P, February 26, 17, 1930; SZe, February 12, 1930, June 28, 1930 (referring to the period before the March legislation).

157 ZI, January 28, 1930.

158 SZe, February 12, 1930.

159 *Industrializatsiya SSSR, 1929–1932 gg.* (1970), 589.

was to be passed to the kolkhoz board.[160] These arrangements, if effective, would enable the central authorities to direct increasingly scarce seasonal labour to priority objectives, while at the same time ensuring that kolkhozy were not deprived of essential labour and did receive a share of the outside earnings of their members. But for the collective farmer they would represent a considerable restriction on his freedom to undertake seasonal work as compared with the position of the individual peasant.

The publication of this strongly-worded circular as late as the beginning of March reflected the confusion which prevailed at this time. Before it was published, the relaxation of the collectivisation drive at the end of February and the beginning of March had already affected otkhodnichestvo. While the model Statute of February 6 made no reference to otkhodnichestvo, the Statute of March 1, 1930, stipulated that deductions to kolkhoz income from outside earnings by collective farmers should be within the limits 3–10 per cent.[161] A fortnight later, on March 16, a Sovnarkom decree accused local soviets and kolkhoz organisations of causing 'great harm to the national economy' through their restrictions on the free departure of peasants to seasonal work, and instructed local authorities to prosecute those responsible.[162] The provisions of the model Statute and the decree did not abrogate the circular of March 3, but they by-passed it, for now a collective farmer was entitled to go freely to seasonal labour on his own initiative, as well as through the new contract system, providing he paid the stipulated proportion of his income to the kolkhoz.

In practice, the circular of March 3 was almost completely ineffective. In the Ukraine, only 5,307 of the 120,754 seasonal workers recruited were obtained through contracts;[163] in the Lower Volga, only a quarter of the kolkhozy followed official procedures; the situation was similar in other areas. Instead, 'spontaneity and lack of planning' prevailed.[164] From March onwards, substantial numbers of peasants went to work in the towns,[165] and frequent

[160] *Sbornik . . . prikazov po promyshlennosti, 1929/30*, No. 22, circular 41; ZI, March 4, 1930; see also SZe, March 11, 1930.

[161] I, February 7, March 2, 1930; the limits were repeated in categorical terms in later circulars of Kolkhoztsentr (SZe, April 4, 1930; SKhIB, 1, 1930, 18).

[162] SZ, 1930, art. 206.

[163] P, October 4, 1930.

[164] PKh, 7–8, 1930, 102 (Kindeev).

[165] P, June 29, 1930, disk. listok 24 (A. Golovanov).

reports appeared of disruption in the kolkhozy caused by the flow of labour to outside work. Kolkhozy were described in which families with many dependants were abandoned, and almost all the people remaining to work on the farm were schoolchildren.[166] Other reports, however, described continued restrictions by the kolkhozy: according to Vareikis, in the Central Black-Earth region the collective farmer was frequently subject to 'a considerable limitation of his personal freedom compared with his position before joining';[167] in the Central Volga region, only 5·5 per cent of all able-bodied collective farmers were released for seasonal work.[168]

Evidence about the extent to which the kolkhozy adhered to the stipulated limits on deductions from the incomes of their members from outside work also reveals great variations in kolkhoz practices. After the publication of the model Statute on March 2, some kolkhozy still deducted up to 50 per cent of these incomes, and even retained all the earnings of collective farmers who undertook casual outside work for a day or two.[169] A survey of 30 kolkhozy later in the summer showed that 21 made no deductions at all, while the other nine deducted amounts varying from 5 to 50 per cent.[170]

The extent of these personal and financial restrictions imposed by the kolkhozy on otkhodnichestvo in the summer of 1930 cannot now be established. The pressure on kolkhoz managements to retain labour was considerable: in many areas they were extremely short of labour at the peak of the agricultural season, both because their members were reluctant to work on the collective land (see pp. 154–5 above), and because their labour requirements were higher than in the individual peasant sector, owing to the larger cultivated area per household which the kolkhozy retained in the spring of 1930 (see vol. 1, pp. 308–9). All accounts agree that non-farming activities, and particularly otkhodnichestvo, were less important in the kolkhoz sector than in the individual sector. In 1930, the kolkhoz sector (including both the individual and the collective activities of collective farmers) earned only 18·6 per cent of non-farming gross rural income, as compared with 25.9 per cent of farming income (see Table 8). In all the eight areas covered by

[166] SZe, June 10, 1930; PKh, 7–8, 1930, 102, also reported that outside work 'often produced a critical situation for the whole economy of the kolkhoz'.

[167] B, 10, May 31, 1930, 40–1.

[168] NAF, 7–8, 1930, 111.

[169] SZe, March 30, April 2, 1930.

[170] PKh, 7–8, 1930, 102 (Kindeev).

the survey of rural money incomes in 1930/31, the percentage of money income received from non-farming earnings was higher for individual peasants than for collective farmers.[171] Another report showed that collective farmers, who constituted about 20 per cent of the peasant population, earned only 16.8 per cent of all peasant wage incomes.[172]

In a startling reversal of past trends, the total supply of seasonal labour to the towns fell considerably during the harvest period. The total number of building workers declined by 187,000 in August 1930, as compared with the previous month, while it increased in August 1929. The shortage of labour was partly due to the large increase in demand: the number of building workers in August 1930, estimated at 1·78 million, was as much as 56·6 per cent higher than in August 1929.[173] But in many reports the shortage was also attributed to the desire of kolkhoz managements to retain labour.[174]

With the acute labour shortage which resulted from the growing pressures of industrialisation, the authorities saw the flexible arrangements of 1930 as purely temporary. The availability of surplus labour in the kolkhoz, and the need to make use of it, was a persistent theme in the last few months of 1930. An article in the agricultural journal, envisaging an expansion of the seasonal labour force from 7 to 15 million in the course of two or three years, argued that it would become a second branch of collective production; it should be planned by the kolkhoz, and the kolkhoz should have the power to oblige its members to participate in it.[175] In August, Kolkhozsentr conducted a successful drive to recruit 20,000 collective farmers to work in the Donbass, where labour was extremely scarce; the collective farmers retained all the rights of members of kolkhozy, were awarded various privileges in relation to the harvest, and their wages were made subject only to the minimum deduction into kolkhoz income, but the kolkhoz was required to refuse to accept them back if they left the mines.[176] Reviewing this experience, a Narkomtrud official called for individual kolkhozy and particular areas to be attached to particular

[171] IISO, ii (1968), 335.

[172] *Materialy po balansu* (1932), 212–13; for the kolkhoz population see p. 127, n. 51, above.

[173] *Industrializatsiya SSSR, 1929–1932 gg.* (1970), 387.

[174] See for example *ibid.* 389, 392; this is a Narkomtrud report from the archives.

[175] NAF, 9, 1930, 67, 70–1.

[176] P, August 22, 1930; SZe, December 16, 1930.

economic agencies, so as to avoid all possibility of competition, and for the system of contracts with the kolkhozy to become the general rule.[177] At the conference on kolkhoz labour in January 1931, Barchuk, after reviewing the experience of 1930, announced that 9·6 million seasonal workers would be required in 1931, and called for the establishment of a system of control figures for otkhodnichestvo, based on labour balances, and broken down to districts and to obligatory plans for every kolkhoz; for the time being, unplanned otkhodnichestvo by individual collective farmers would also be permitted. To encourage the collective farmers to participate, the deduction to kolkhoz income from their earnings should be cut to from 3–10 to 2–3 per cent, they should be entitled to receive part of kolkhoz production in kind throughout their period of work, and their family should get a full share of products in kind even if they had not fulfilled their quota of labour days. At the same time, kolkhozy should develop artisan production in order to use up surplus female labour.[178] On these proposals, otkhodnichestvo, and non-agricultural production generally, would be an expanding element in the income of the collective farmers, and they would be subject to a comprehensive national plan for the training and allocation of seasonal labour.

(D) REMUNERATION AS A WHOLE

The main features of the arrangements for the remuneration of the collective farmer which were established by the autumn of 1930 persisted throughout the Stalin period and beyond. This was not a unified or even a coherent system, but a mixture of different systems and devices, traditional and new, introduced piecemeal in the course of the struggle to adapt the individual peasant to the new collective way of life.

Even after the retreat from collectivisation in the spring of 1930, the Soviet leaders took it for granted that the socialised sector of the kolkhoz would soon come to predominate overwhelmingly in the economic activity of the collective farmers, and provide the major source of their income. Over 90 per cent of the sown area of the

177 SZe, December 16, 1930; VTr, No. 12, 1930, 75–6 (both articles by I. Fominykh).

178 SZe, January 17, 1931.

kolkhoz was socialised, and the state allocated its machinery, money, manpower and advice almost exclusively to the socialised sector. While the household plot and privately-owned animals were officially permitted from the spring of 1930, the authorities confidently expected that these activities, and the income from them, would rapidly diminish with the strengthening of the socialised sector.

The products of the kolkhoz, like those of the individual peasant farm, were intended both for personal consumption by members and for sale, and collective farmers received their share of socialised income both in kind and in money. Income in kind was received mainly in grain, the principal product of the socialised sector of the kolkhoz. On average the collective farm household retained far more grain than the individual household, and this was a major factor impelling individual peasants to join, or rejoin, the kolkhozy in 1931.

But the arrangements for remunerating collective work did not offer adequate incentives to replace the stimulus provided to the individual peasants by the market, and by the need to produce food for their own consumption. The ingenious system of labour days successfully adjusted the level of payment of the peasants for their work before and during the harvest to the size of the income available for distribution after the harvest. But it proved very difficult to design work norms suitable for the immense variety of jobs and territory in the USSR, and still more difficult to penalise shoddy, and reward conscientious, work. In the autumn of 1930, the novel labour-day system was not yet much used in practice, and all these weaknesses seemed to be temporary administrative difficulties which would be overcome with experience; the authorities were confident that the system would work smoothly once it had fully replaced payment per eater. But in the ensuing decades these temporary administrative difficulties permanently haunted the kolkhoz.

The good harvest, and the high level of grain distribution in 1930, partly obscured an even more fundamental problem. The aim of the state was to remove as much production as possible from the kolkhoz through the official collections. In future years, with lower harvests, and with many more peasants in the kolkhozy, the grain collectors were more strict towards the kolkhozy, and they retained much less grain per household than in 1930; the unwillingness of the collective farmer to work on the collective lands became a permanent difficulty of the kolkhoz economy. Even in 1930, while grain distributions were high, the collective money income available for distribution was small; the kolkhozy received nearly all their money income from sales to the official collection agencies at fixed prices, now only a fraction of free-market prices. Because their money income from collective work was low, the collective farmers looked to their personal economies not only for food, apart from grain, but also for most of their money income, much of the rest of it being earned from otkhodnichestvo and other personal non-agricultural activities. Collective farmers received on the free market four or five times as many rubles for a product from their household plot than for the same product grown collectively and sold to the state. So even in 1930, the Indian summer of the kolkhoz system, their efforts and enthusiasm were directed to their personal economy; their work on the collective lands was less conscientious, and undertaken only for the minimum number of days required to obtain essential supplies of grain. A substantial increase in payment for collective work could change these priorities; but in the next quarter of a century this did not take place.

In 1930, the authorities were concerned to demonstrate unambiguously that it was more profitable to be a collective farmer than an individual peasant. It is not possible to assess accurately the income in 1930 of collective farm households in kind and in money in comparison with individual peasant households. Taking their total income in kind from the collective sector and their household plot together, their income in grain exceeded that of the individual peasant, but they undoubtedly consumed less meat and dairy products per head, as the total number of animals per household in the kolkhozy was lower than in the individual peasant sector (see vol. 1, p. 339). The average money income of a kolkhoz household in 1930/31 was estimated in a sample survey at only 591 rubles as compared with 605 rubles for an individual peasant household. Some monetary expenses which were paid by the individual peasant out of his income were, however, borne from the collective money income of the kolkhoz (for example, the purchase of fodder and harness for horses); when these expenses are taken into account, money income in 1930/31 could have been as high in the collective farm household as in the household of the individual peasant.[179] On the other hand, the cash held by the average collective farm

[179] IISO, ii (1968), 333.

household in the agricultural year 1930/31 was estimated at only 60 rubles as compared with 79 rubles held by the individual peasant.[180] Certainly the collective farmers did not have obviously larger money incomes than the individual peasants; and, in their total income in kind, the higher availability of grain must be set against the lower availability of meat and dairy products. In spite of the advantages of the kolkhozy in land allocation and state support, the average total income of the collective farm household did not substantially exceed that of the individual peasant. This was partly because most collective farmers were former batraks and middle peasants, who came into the kolkhozy with relatively little capital. For the peasants outside the kolkhoz, the advantages of membership were not overwhelmingly demonstrated by the outcome of the harvest of 1930.

[180] *Ibid.* 337.

CHAPTER EIGHT

CONCLUSIONS

Before the collectivisation drive of the winter of 1929–30, only a small minority of peasants belonged to kolkhozy, and most kolkhozy included only a minority of the households in the settlement of which they formed a part—on June 1, 1929, the average number of households per kolkhoz was only 17·7. Three-fifths of the 55,000 kolkhozy were TOZy, and the typical kolkhoz did not go beyond the partial socialisation of arable farming. Collective farmers were remunerated by a variety of payment systems, most prominent among which were payment for time devoted to collective work, and payment 'per eater', i.e. according to the number of members of the household. These small kolkhozy were simple in their structure and organisation. But in two important respects they were technically more advanced than the individual peasant economies which surrounded them. First, on most kolkhoz land, the fields of the crop rotation were not divided into strips, and this made for more efficient farming. Secondly, over one-third of all kolkhozy used or had access to a tractor. In consequence, yields were somewhat higher on kolkhoz lands than on comparable lands cultivated by individual peasants. But the economic advantages of the kolkhozy were not sufficient to persuade most individual peasants to relinquish voluntarily their traditional way of life.

For the party leaders, however, the kolkhozy had very obvious attractions. The proportion of grain production sold to the state was much higher for kolkhozy than for individual peasants. And the leaders were convinced that mechanisation and scientific farming on industrial lines would lead to a rapid expansion of agricultural production, and, together with the development of collective forms of agriculture, would resist and eventually eliminate petty capitalism in the countryside.

At the height of the collectivisation drive, comprehensive collectivisation came to imply that more advanced forms of kolkhoz organisation should prevail immediately. In December 1929–

February 1930, central and local kolkhoz authorities and local party organisations encouraged the immediate establishment of giant kolkhozy in which there was a high level of socialisation: the socialisation of all livestock was often advocated, and a large question mark appeared against the future of the personal household plots of collective farmers. Kolkhoztsentr approved a system for remunerating collective farmers which closely followed the industrial wage system. Trotsky commented acidly on these developments: 'An obvious contradiction: the wider the scale of forced collectivization, and consequently the lower its technical base, the higher is the type of social relations that the utopian-bureaucratic leadership wants to impose'.[1]

This precipitate shift towards higher forms of kolkhozy was not, however, a deliberate strategy planned in advance by Stalin and the Politburo. Stalin was silent or ambiguous about all these questions in his published pronouncements. In his speech of December 27, 1929, he even appeared to be unresponsive to the pressure for a high degree of socialisation, in marked contrast to his firm pronouncement in favour of the elimination of the kulaks and his insistence on the viability of collectivisation without mechanisation (see p. 87 above, and vol. 1, pp. 197–8, 391–2). No firm recommendations about kolkhoz organisation were made by the central committee. These matters were deliberately left to 'local initiative'. This was a time when, in all spheres of the economy, and of political, intellectual and cultural life, far-reaching plans and alternative sets of proposals were prepared and feverishly debated, with little detailed interference from the central party authorities.

But this 'system-building' was carried out within a definite political framework, in which the radical restructuring of society was regarded with approval, and traditional approaches were treated as manifestations of Right deviation. In these tumultuous months, it seemed to many party leaders and activists at every level that enthusiasm and improved organisation could solve all problems. Stalin and his associates evidently decided that this was a time of revolutionary break-through, in which manifestations of revolutionary élan, however extreme, should not for the moment be discouraged; and they were themselves captivated by this mood, and encouraged it, when only their own positive intervention could

[1] *Writings of Leon Trotsky (1930)* (New York, 1975), 112 (article of February 13, 1930).

have restrained the lower party organisations. Some statements by party leaders even supported more radical forms of kolkhoz organisation, though in rather general terms. Thus at the plenum of the central committee in November 1929 Molotov urged the kolkhozy to 'model yourselves on the sovkhozy', and shortly afterwards Kaganovich enthusiastically praised the Gigant kolkhoz in the Urals in a well-publicised report. There is also some evidence to suggest that behind the scenes Stalin encouraged the extravagant proposals about socialisation within the kolkhozy made by Ryskulov and others.

In the optimistic atmosphere of December 1929 – February 1930, the proposed forms of organisation seemed logical and coherent to enthusiastic adherents of rapid collectivisation. They argued that if the kolkhoz were to manage its own tractors, it must be a giant, approaching the size of an administrative district; otherwise its tractor economy would be small and inefficient. The district-kolkhoz would also enable the development of food-processing enterprises and industries using agricultural raw materials, which would be quite uneconomical on the scale of a single village. And, given that the experience of Khoper okrug had shown that large-scale farming could be conducted efficiently with horses and ploughs, it also seemed advantageous to establish giant kolkhozy in advance of mechanisation, and to replace the inefficient crop rotations of rural settlements, formed more or less accidentally in the course of history, by planned rotations on an inter-village basis. Such arguments in favour of the district-kolkhoz in 1930 rehearsed those in favour of the establishment of agricultural communes containing thousands of households in China in 1958.

The case for socialisation of livestock rested on similar premisses. Large-scale livestock farms within the kolkhozy would yield great economies of scale. And socialisation of livestock was made urgent by the widespread slaughter which began in the summer of 1929. Leading party officials insisted that livestock must be incorporated in the collective sector of the kolkhozy before it was destroyed. They also argued that, with middle peasants and even well-to-do middle peasants joining the kolkhozy in large numbers, the socialisation of livestock was essential to prevent social inequality; without socialisation, a kulak class might emerge within the kolkhozy on the basis of private livestock (this was a fear shared by Trotsky).

The decision to introduce a wage system within the kolkhoz based on payment for skill and quantity of work made it clear that the giant fully-socialised kolkhoz was not intended, at any rate by the central kolkhoz authorities, as a move towards communism, with payment according to need, but was instead modelled on the contemporary Soviet state factories, with their socialist system of payment according to work. But the notions of kolkhoz organisation which prevailed in the early weeks of 1930 were nevertheless wholly unrealistic. The farming skills and organisational experience required for the successful establishment of giant fully-socialised kolkhozy were completely lacking in the Soviet Union, and the state was quite unable, and unwilling, to make available even the minimum of resources required for such an immense reorganisation. When collectivisation was at its peak in March 1930, much of this ambitious programme remained without practical consequences. Giant kolkhozy were established only in a minority of cases. The payment of wages to collective farmers was usually impossible owing to the shortage of cash in the kolkhozy. Much livestock was socialised—with disastrous results—but even here the authorities paid most attention to the socialisation of seeds, horses and ploughs, essential to the success of the spring sowing.

The retreat from radical forms of kolkhoz organisation was an integral part of the retreat from collectivisation. It was shown in vol. 1 that the Politburo, fearing a catastrophic failure of the spring sowing, decided to call for a retreat when faced by widespread unrest among the peasants in many areas in February 1930. One of the major elements in this unrest was hostility to the attempts to introduce new forms of kolkhoz organisation. The giant kolkhozy lacked good communications and experienced organisers, and were remote from and alien to the collective farmers. The confusion of the arrangements for remuneration, and the universal absence of adequate payments, were further causes of resentment. The socialisation of livestock was the feature of kolkhoz organisation which aroused the greatest hostility, particularly among women collective farmers, who were responsible for tending the animals.

In the spring and summer of 1930 these schemes were all abandoned. The giant kolkhozy were dissolved, and the principle was restored that the boundaries of the kolkhozy should correspond to those of existing villages or settlements. The artel form of kolkhoz was henceforth strongly favoured in preference to the commune. The main fields, and the horses and ploughs of the collective farmers, were socialised, but most livestock remained in the ownership of the collective farm household, which was also guaranteed the right to its household plot for growing fruit and vegetables. The attempt to introduce a wage system was also abandoned, and replaced—in principle, though not yet in practice—by the ingenious 'labour-day' system: the collective farmer was rewarded according to work, but at the same time his or her earnings were treated as a residual or dividend, paid from what was left over from kolkhoz income in kind and in money after deliveries to the state had been completed and taxes paid, and after allocations had been made to the Indivisible and other Funds of the kolkhoz.

The resentment among the peasants aroused by the general process of collectivisation resulted in a purely temporary retreat by the authorities, *reculer pour mieux sauter*, and forcible collectivisation was resumed within less than a year (see vol. 1, ch. 9). But the 'kolkhoz compromise', the dual economy of socialised farming on collective lands (the former *nadel*), and private or personal farming on the household plot (the former *usad'ba*), has continued as a permanent feature of the kolkhoz economy; the kolkhoz has continued to be based on the traditional settlement or village; and the labour-day system began to give way to a wage system only in the 1960s.

In 1930, this was certainly not the intention. The authorities believed that the rapid growth of the socialised sector would soon make personal livestock and the household plot unprofitable and superflous, or at any rate quantitatively insignificant, and that the growing prosperity of the kolkhozy would soon make it possible to go over to a wage system.

These hopes rested on two false assumptions. First, it was supposed that within a few years Soviet agriculture would be the most technologically advanced in the world, with a higher level of production per head of population and per hectare than in the United States; this would rapidly reduce the household plots to insignificance. This was a false assumption about industry rather than agriculture; it accepted as feasible the over-optimistic revised five-year plans for the production of tractors and agricultural machinery, which were officially approved in the spring and summer of 1930 (these plans will be discussed in vol. 3). The second false assumption was that, with growing prosperity, the pressure of the state to acquire kolkhoz production at low prices would diminish, and collective farmers would receive an increasing flow of industrial consumer goods in return for the state collections; this would, it was supposed, make collective work far more attractive economically than work on the household plot. In fact after 1930 agricultural production declined, and the growing requirements of the capital goods' industries also led to a decline in the availability of industrial consumer goods. But state demands to acquire the production of kolkhozy at low prices did not diminish, and work on the collective lands was poorly remunerated. The household plot and private livestock therefore continued, as in 1930, to be far more rewarding than work on the collective lands, and remained a major source of urban and rural food supplies which the state did not try to eliminate by compulsion, and was unable to eliminate by competition. And the continuing poverty of the kolkhozy made the introduction of a wage system impossible.

The incorporation of private livestock in the kolkhoz system was primarily a victory for the former middle peasant households, and particularly for the female members of those households, as former middle peasant households possessed far more animals than former poor peasants and batraks. These inequalities were limited by the restrictions imposed on the number of animals which a kolkhoz household could own, but they remained a feature of the kolkhoz economy. They were soon overshadowed, however, by the emergence in the course of the early 1930s of new types of social and economic division within the kolkhoz, between the chairman and the other kolkhoz administrators, the brigade leaders and the rank-and-file collective farmers.

A further change completed the establishment of what continued to be the main features of kolkhoz organisation for over a quarter of a century. The decision in the spring of 1930 that each kolkhoz should be based on an existing settlement or village carried with it the consequence that tractors and other major items of agricultural machinery should not be owned by individual kolkhozy, which could not in the near future own enough machinery to be able to maintain and repair it efficiently. Whether the Machine-Tractor Stations should be managed by the state-owned Traktorotsentr, by the kolkhozsoyuzy or by the agricultural cooperatives still remained a matter of controversy. In September 1930, however, a central committee resolution gave clear priority to Traktorotsentr. Little is known about the circumstances of this decision. While it was obviously influenced by the decline of the cooperatives during the collectivisation drive, and by the weakness of the kolkhozsoyuzy, it proved to be a first major step towards the formal concentration of the management of the kolkhoz system in the hands of the state.

The kolkhoz, as it emerged in 1930, was thus in an ambiguous position. Formally it was owned and managed by its members as a cooperative organisation. In practice, while the influence of the members over its economic behaviour was not negligible, a large part of its production was appropriated by the state at nominal prices, and its economic activities were controlled by state officials and party activists acting under instructions from the state, and (where they existed) by the state or cooperative Machine-Tractor Stations. On the other hand, a substantial part of the production of collective farmers came from their household plots and could be sold by them at market prices; this was a wedge of personal or private economy built into the kolkhoz itself.

At the end of 1929, the social nature of the kolkhoz was the subject of intense debate. Larin argued that for an economic unit to be socialist it must be the property of the state and not of a particular group of individuals, and its members must work for the whole society; the kolkhoz was therefore not a socialist but a transitional type of economy, in which the collective interests of its members could result in a clash of interests with the state. Stalin, however, insisted that the kolkhoz was a form of socialist economy, in which the main instruments of production were socialised and land belonged to the state; the kolkhoz did not contain exploiting and exploited classes, and, although 'elements of class struggle' existed within the kolkhozy, these would soon die away. Nothing specific was said about the household plot or privately owned livestock, which were assumed to be of minor and diminishing significance, and they were not designated as 'socialist' (on the grounds that they formed part of the kolkhoz economy) until some years later. But ever since Stalin's pronouncement at the end of 1929 the kolkhoz has invariably been treated in Soviet publications as part of the socialist economy; even earlier, kolkhozy which resisted the demands of the state were castigated as 'bogus', as having, as it were, cast themselves out of the socialist economy.

With almost the whole of industry state- or cooperatively-owned, and with private trade (except bazaar trade by individuals) virtually eliminated, it followed, on the official Soviet definition, that after the completion of comprehensive collectivisation and the elimination of the individual peasant economies the whole Soviet economy would be socialist. In December 1930, the plenum of the party central committee accordingly announced that the successful completion of the plan to collectivise 50 per cent of all peasant households by the end of 1931 would result in 'an absolute predominance of socialist elements over the individual sector in the countryside', and would 'complete the construction of the foundation (fundament) of the socialist economy of the USSR', a 'victory of world-historical significance'.[2] Stalin's unambiguous definition of the kolkhoz as a 'form of socialist economy' had provided the basis for a speedy announcement of the triumph of socialism in one country.

[2] *KPSS v rez.*, iii (1954), 81.

TABLES

Table 1. Stock of tractors by social sector, October 1, 1928–January 1, 1931

(a) Number

	A. In sovkhozy	*B. In MTS, including cooperative columns*	*C. In agricultural cooperatives*	*D. In kolkhozy and their group associations*	*In MTS, kolkhozy and cooperatives (B+C+D)*	*E. In individual households*	*Total*
Stock on October 1, 1928	6719	—	6673	10854	17257	2487	26733
Net increase in 1928/29	2959	2387	−2904	8255	8008	−2487	8210
Stock on October 1, 1929	9678	2387	3769	19109	25265	—	34943
Net increase in 1929/30	15275	18414	−3769	1469	16114	—	31389
Stock on October 1, 1930	24953	20801	—	20578	41379	—	66332
Net increase in October–December 1930	2732	10313	—	−7299	3014	—	5746
Stock on January 1, 1931	27685	31114	—	13279	44393	—	72078

(b) Horse-power (thousands)

Stock on October 1, 1928	77·6	—	66·7	108·9	175·6	24·9	278·1
Net increase in 1928/29	45·8	23·9	−8·7	77·2	92·4	−24·9	113·3
Stock on October 1, 1929	123·4	23·9	58·0	186·1	268·0	—	391·4
Planned allocation for 1929/30	220	85·	—	57·	142·	—	362·
Net actual increase in 1929/30	322·1	233·2	−58·0	37·3	212·5	—	534·6
Stock on October 1, 1930	445·5	257·1	—	223·4	480·5	—	926·0
Net increase in October–December 1930	37·6	115·4	—	−75·5	39·9	—	77·5
Stock on January 1, 1931	483·1	372·5	—	147·9	—	—	1003·5

Sources: Calculated from *Nar. kh.* (1932), 145, except plan for 1929/30, which is calculated from *KTs . . . na 1929/30* (1930), 123, 131.

Table 2. Machine-Tractor Stations and tractor columns, 1929–1930

(a) Plans for 1929 and 1930

		System of Traktorotsentr				Cooperative system (Khlebotsentr)		
Date of plan	*Planned period*	*Number of MTS*	*Number of tractors*	*Tractor h.p. (thousands)*	*Sown area (thousand ha)*	*Number of MTS and columns*	*Number of tractors*	*Sown area (thousand ha)*
June 5, 1929[1]	1929/30		5000+	100	1000[a]			
December 16, 1929[2]	By spring 1930	104[b]	5200		520–624[c]			
February 1, 1930[3]	By spring 1930	159	5555[4]		1490[4d]			
	1929/30	214			1970[4e]			
February 13, 1930	1930					490[5f]	18000[5f]	

(b) Fulfilment in 1929 and 1930

Date								
Spring 1929		1[6]			24[6]	45[5fg]	1182[5fg]	70[7g]
September 1929						61[5f]	2045[5f]	
February 1930						185[5f]	5000+[5f]	
May–June 1930		158[8h]	7102[8h]	87[8h]	2000[4i]	465[9j]	12500[9j]	2200[9k]
December 31, 1930		360[10l]	31114[11l]	372·5[11l]				

Sources:
[1] SZ, 1929, art. 353.
[2] BU NKZ RSFSR, No. 52, 1930, p. 15.
[3] SZ, 1930, art. 130.
[4] NAF, 6, 1930, 121–3.
[5] P, February 13, 1930 (Belenky).
[6] Markevich (1929), 35.
[7] P, July 13, 1929.
[8] *Sots. str.* (1935), 310, 312.
[9] NFK, May 15, 1930, 13 (Belenky).
[10] PS, 3–4, 1931, 77–9 (decree of January 21, 1931).
[11] *Nar. kh.* (1932), 145.

Notes:
[a] Arable area.
[b] P, September 12, 1929, announced a Traktorotsentr plan to establish 100 new MTS in 1929/30 (see p. 20 above).
[c] 5,000–6,000 hectares per MTS.
[d] 1·31 million hectares grain plus 0·18 million hectares cotton.
[e] 1·75 grain arable plus 0·20 cotton, 0·01 sugar beet and 0·01 soya.
[f] This figure refers to the RSFSR; there were 36 columns and MTS in the Ukraine in the autumn of 1929 (Danilov (1957), 364).
[g] The number of cooperative MTS and columns is given as 58 and the number of their tractors as over 1,500 in P, July 13, 1929.
[h] June 1, 1930.
[i] By June 15, 1930; includes grain and cotton; this figure seems improbably high.
[j] Immediately before spring sowing.
[k] By May 1, 1930.
[l] Includes MTS and columns transferred from the cooperatives.

Table 3. Average number of households per kolkhoz, June 1, 1928–September 1, 1930

	June 1, 1928	*June 1, 1929*	*October 1, 1929*	*January 1, 1930*	*March 1, 1930*	*September 1, 1930*
USSR	12·5	17·7	28·5	63·5	132·7	58·0
RSFSR	12·5	16·9	28·0	71·4	136·5	56·3
Including:						
Western	10·0	11·3	14·9	26·4	47·3	30·1
Moscow	14·5	15·6	21·3	58·0	77·4	28·8
Ivanovo-Industrial	11·2	12·7	15·6	51·6	57·3	26·8
Central Black-Earth	14·5	20·6	32·7	141·8	253·4	54·4
Ural	11·0	20·3	33·1	101·1	226·6	45·7
Central Volga	15·5	17·9	31·5	45·7	196·4	68·5
Lower Volga	11·0	17·7	46·9	288·3[a]	480·6	108·4
North Caucasus	12·1	16·1	35·6	341·5	262·0	186·0
Siberia	12·9	20·4	27·9	26·5[a]	56·4	44·1
Ukraine	12·6	19·9	33·1	47·6	123·1	55·2
Uzbekistan	14·3	15·0	20·8	26·5[a]	96·6	68·2

Source: Calculated from data in *Ezhegodnik po sel. kh. 1931* (1933), 440–3.
Note: [a] Based on very low figures given in source for number of households collectivised (see vol. 1, Table 17, notes b, c and d).

Table 4. Kolkhozy by type of Statute,[a] 1927–1930

	Number				Percentage			
	Communes	*Artels*	*TOZy*	*Total*	*Communes*	*Artels*	*TOZy*	*Total*
1921	n.a.	n.a.	n.a.	n.a.	20[1]	65[1]	15[1]	100[1]
June 1, 1927[b]	1335[4]	7134[4]	6363[4]	14832[2]	9·0[3]	48·1[3]	42·9[3]	100
June 1, 1928[5c]	1847	11390	19694	32931	5·6	34.6	59·8	100
June 1, 1929[6c,d]	3416	18440	33043	54899	6·2	33·6	60·2	100
October 1, 1929[b]	4654[9]	20773[9]	42019[9]	67446[9]	6·9[8]	30·8[8]	62·3[8]	100
May 1930	7342[10]	62006[10]	14522[10]	84050[10e]	8·8[3]	73·7[3]	17·3[3]	99·8[3f]

Sources: [1] See Lewin (1968), 109–10.
[2] *Kolkhozy v 1930 g.* (1931), 6.
[3] *Ibid.* 12.
[4] Derived from sources 2 and 3 above.
[5] *Kolkhozy v 1928 g.* (1932), 2.
[6] *Kolkhozy v 1929 godu* (1931), 2.
[7] *Sdvigi* (1931), 22.
[8] *Ibid.* 30.
[9] Derived from sources 7 and 8 above.
[10] *Kolkhozy v 1930 g.* (1931), 78.

Notes: [a] All these figures refer to the Statute as which the kolkhoz was registered, not the 'economic type'.
[b] Excludes Yakut ASSR (17 kolkhozy on June 1, 1928).
[c] The number of kolkhozy 'by economic type' were:

	June 1, 1928	*June 1, 1929*
Communes	3335	3327
Artels	3796	17062
TOZy	16862	26661
Total	[23993]	[47050]

(*Kolkhozy v 1928 g.* (1932), pp. iv, 66; *Kolkhozy v 1929 godu* (1931), pp. xliv, 4). Kolkhozy by economic type exclude kolkhozy without collective sown area in 1928 and kolkhozy without a socialised branch of the economy in 1929 (in the 1929 figures, the Ural region is included by registered Statute and not by economic type).
[d] Excludes Yakut ASSR, Mari autonomous region and an okrug of Kirgiz ASSR. Total number of kolkhozy in the USSR on this date was 57045 (*Sdvigi* (1931), 22); oddly, the percentages of different types for the whole USSR given in *Sdvigi* (1931), 32, and elsewhere are identical with those given above for 54,899 kolkhozy; the above figures are more likely to be reliable.
[e] Total number of kolkhozy for this date is given as 85,950 in *Sdvigi* (1931), 22, and figures close to this are given in other sources; again, the percentages of different types of Statute given in this source (*ibid.* 30) are the same as those given for the lower number of kolkhozy in our source 10.
[f] Kolkhozy without a productive branch of agriculture are excluded from these percentages.

Table 5. Socialisation of draught animals in kolkhozy, 1929–1930 (thousands)

	Total number of draught animals in kolkhozy	*Number of socialised draught animals in kolkhozy*	*Socialised draught animals in kolkhozy as percentage of total*
June 1, 1929[1a]	703	312	44·4
January 1, 1930[2b]	2110	370	17·4
February 1, 1930[2]	5160	2760	51·8
February 10, 1930[2]	8430	5670	67·2
February 20, 1930[2]	10530	8550	81·2
March 1, 1930[2]	11930	9350[c]	78·3
May 1930[1d]	5020	4774	95·1

Sources: [1] *Kolkhozy v 1930 g.* (1931), 10–11.
[2] I, March 9, 1930; figures published during the campaign (e.g. in SZe, February 11, 21, 1930 referring to February 1 and 10) differ only slightly from these.

Notes: [a] Excluding Yakut ASSR.
[b] Given as January 20, 1930, in source.
[c] Number on March 10 was 10·3 million (SO, 3–4, 1930, 109).
[d] Excluding Tadzhik SSR, and Kirgiz and Yakut ASSRs.

Table 6. Socialised livestock, 1929–1930 (thousands)

(a) Socialised livestock in sovkhozy and kolkhozy

	May–June 1929			*May–June 1930*		
	Sovkhozy	*Kolkhozy*	*Total*	*Sovkhozy*	*Kolkhozy*	*Total*
Cattle	204	386	590	757	3620	4377
Sheep and goats	1203	695	1897	2754	5650	8605
Pigs	54	126	180	181	769	950

Source: *Nar. kh.* (1932), 188–9, 655–6; sovkhoz and kolkhoz figures for 1929 are from a complete census; method of collecting sovkhoz figures for 1930 is not stated; kolkhoz figures for 1930 are from tax returns sent via village soviets to Narkomfin.

(b) Socialisation of cows in kolkhozy

	Total number of cows in kolkhozy	*Number of socialised cows in kolkhozy*	*Socialised cows in kolkhozy as percentage of total*
June 1, 1929[a]	[704]	169	24·0
May 1930[b]	[4779]	1620	33·9

Source: *Kolkhozy v 1930 g.* (1931), 10–11; these figures are from the kolkhoz census of 1929 and 1930 and therefore differ slightly from those in Table 6(a); thus in the source for Table 6(a) the number of socialised cows in kolkhozy is given as 174,000 in 1929 and 1,413,000 in 1930.

Notes: [a] Excluding Yakut ASSR.
[b] Excluding Tadzhik SSR, and Kirgiz and Yakut ASSRs.

Table 7. Debts and Indivisible Funds (IFs) of kolkhozy, 1929–1930

	June 1, 1929					
	% of kolkhozy with outstanding debts	*Total of outstanding debts (mr)*	*Outstanding debt per kolkhoz with debts (r)*	*% of kolkhozy with IFs*	*Total value of IFs (mr)*	*IF per kolkhoz with IF (r)*
TOZy	92·0	55·4	2257	39·2	10·0	956
Artels	92·9	59·7	3769	55·5	31·3	3301
Communes	97·7	37·8	11623	83·5	30·8	11071
All kolkhozy	92·7	152·9	3504	48·2	72·0	3173

Source: [1] *Kolkhozy v 1929 godu* (1931), 126–7.
[2] *Kolkhozy v 1930 g.* (1931), 200–1.

Note: Indivisible Funds include the money value of permanently socialised buildings, animals, implements, etc.
For a further explanation of this table see pp. 118–19 and 126–7 above.

May 1930					
% of kolkhozy with outstanding debts	*Total of outstanding debts (mr)*	*Outstanding debt per kolkhoz (r)*	*% of kolkhozy with IFs*	*Total value of IFs (mr)*	*IF per kolkhoz with IF (r)*
79·0	29·6	2600	69·0	32·5	3200
85·4	306·7	5800	79·8	358·0	7200
92·1	118·1	17500	92·5	119·3	17600
84·8	454·6	6400	79·0	509·9	7700

Table 8. Peasant income in money and kind by social sector, 1930[a] (million rubles)

(a) Gross income (gross production)

	Farming Amount	Farming %	Non-farming Amount	Non-farming %	Total Amount	Total %
Kolkhozy	3691	18·1	536	7·0	4227	15·1
Collective farmers: individual sector	1587	7·8	886	11·6	2473	8·8
Individual peasants	15100	74·1	6197	81·3	21297	76·1
Total	20377	100·0	7619	100·0	27996	100·0

(b) Standard net income[b]

	Farming Amount	Farming %	Non-farming Amount	Non-farming %	Total Amount	Total %
Kolkhozy	2673	18·9	536	7·0	3209	14·7
Collective farmers: individual sector	1195	8·4	886	11·6	2081	9·6
Individual peasants	10293	72·7	6197	81·3	16490	75·7
Total	14160	100·0	7619	100·0	21780	100·0

Source: FP, 1–2, 1931, 26.

Notes: [a] Preliminary estimates by Gosplan; for details see original source, pp. 24–31. Includes most income in kind (money income was estimated at 11,779 million rubles (see vol. 1, Table 7)).

[b] Gross income less raw material inputs produced within the sector.

Table 9. Methods of remuneration in kolkhozy, 1928

(a) Kolkhozy by method of remuneration (percentage of all kolkhozy in group)

	TOZy	*Artels*	*Communes*	*All kolkhozy*
According to need	2·1	6·8	18·6	5·4
According to contribution to collective capital	9·8	13·6	11·2	11·0
According to labour force[a]	71·6	80·6	78·2	73·2
According to number of eaters	40·4	43·1	48·8	41·2
According to land	20·7	11·2	2·0	16·3
According to animals	7·2	5·6	1·3	5·7
According to work by means of production of members in kolkhozy	26·0	14·1	5·6	20·4

Source: *Kolkhozy v 1928 g.* (1932), 56–7, 136–7.

Notes: General note: the columns add up to more than 100 per cent, as kolkhozy reporting more than one method of remuneration are counted more than once.

[a] '*Po rabochei sile*'—according to labour force, or labour power; presumably this heading covers both payment by work done, and payment according to number of members of household working for the kolkhoz.

(b) Kolkhozy in Kuban' okrug by main method of remuneration (as % of total number of kolkhozy in okrug)

Payment for non-socialised means of production	6·7[a]
Per eater[b]	18·9[a]
Per family[b]	7·8[a]
For work done	14·4[c]
For work done (with a minimum payment per eater)	25·6[d]
For work done (with socially organised consumption)	13·3[e]
Other	13·3
Total	100·0

Source: Minaev, ed. (1930), 183–6.

Notes: [a] TOZy only.

[b] Eater or family provides a definite amount of labour, including non-socialised implements and animals.

[c] Artels and communes.

[d] TOZy with more than 50 per cent of sown land socialised, artels and communes.

[e] Communes only.

Table 9 *(contd.)*

(c) Collective production distributed in kolkhozy of Kuban' okrug by method of remuneration (as percentage of total distributed production)

Method of distribution	*In TOZy with 50 per cent or less of sown land collectivised*	*In TOZy with more than 50 per cent of sown land collectivised*	*In artels*	*In communes*	*In all kolkhozy*
For work done	22·4	14·6	50·6	45·5	35·7
Per person working	—	—	0·8	2·3	1·1
Per eater	3·4	17·8	22·5	17·6	17·3
Per family	5·6	2·4	5·2	0·4	2·2
Per kolkhoz member	9·1	9·4	0·2	—	3·5
For amount of land held	43·0	44·5	7·5	—	18·2
For amount of capital paid in	4·3	3·7	1·9	—	1·8
For means of production made available	8·6	4·0	—	—	1·9
For 'non-normed' needs (social services etc.)	3·6	3·6	11·3	34·2	18·3
Total	100.0	100.0	100.0	100.0	100.0

Source: Minaev, ed. (1930), 174.

(d) Kolkhozy in Kuban' okrug in which remuneration was based on capital paid in, 1928 (as percentage of total kolkhozy in the okrug)

	Kolkhozy with remuneration based on capital paid in	*Including: Kolkhozy in which capital paid in on per-eater basis*	*Kolkhozy in which capital paid in on per-family basis*	*Kolkhozy in which labour required is proportionate to capital paid in*	*Other kolkhozy with remuneration based on capital paid in*
TOZy	9·1	2·2	2·2	2·1	2·6
Artels	4·8	0·0	0·0	4·8	0·0

Source: Trudy . . . agrarnikov-marksistov, ii (1930), i, 31.

GLOSSARY OF RUSSIAN TERMS AND ABBREVIATIONS USED IN TEXT

AIK	agro-industrial'nyi kombinat (agro-industrial combine)
aktiv	activists (politically-active members of a community)
art.	article
ASSR	Avtonomnaya Sovetskaya Sotsialisticheskaya Respublika (Autonomous Soviet Socialist Republic)
bai	rich peasants (in Kazakhstan)
batrak	rural labourer
CC	Central Committee [of Communist Party] (Tsentral'nyi komitet)
CP(b)T	Communist Party (Bolsheviks) of Turkmenia
CPSU(b)	Communist Party of the Soviet Union (Bolsheviks)
disk. listok	diskussionyi listok (discussion sheet)
Ekoso	Ekonomicheskii Sovet (Economic Council [of the RSFSR; equivalent to STO for the USSR])
Gosbank	Gosudarstvennyi Bank (State Bank)
Gosplan	Gosudarstvennaya Planovaya Komissiya (State Planning Commission)
GPU	*see* OGPU
Khlebotsentr	Vserossiskii Soyuz Sel'skokhozyaistvennykh Kooperativov po Proizvodstvu, Pererabotke i Sbytu Zernovykh i Maslichnykh Kultur (All-Russian Union of Agricultural Cooperatives for the Production, Processing and Sale of Grains and Oil Seeds)
khutor	peasant farm with fields and cottage enclosed

KNS	komitet nezamozhnykh selyan (committee of poor pesants [in Ukraine])
kolkhoz	kollektivnoe khozyaistvo (collective farm)
kolkhozsoyuz	soyuz sel'skokhozyaistvennykh kollektivov (union of agricultural collectives)
Kolkhoztsentr	Vserossiskii (*from November 1929* Vsesoyuznyi) Soyuz Sel'skokhozyaistvennykh Kollektivov (All-Russian *from November 1929* All-Union) Union of Agricultural Collectives)
komsod	komissiya po sodeistviyu khlebozagotovkam (commission to assist the grain collections)
koopsoyuz	soyuz kooperativnykh obshchestv (union of [agricultural] cooperative societies)
kopek	1/100 ruble
mir	peasant commune (= zemel'noe obshchestvo (land society), obshchina)
MTS	Mashinno-traktornaya stantsiya (Machine-Tractor Station)
Narkomtorg	Narodnyi Komissariat Vneshnei i Vnutrennoi Torgovli (People's Commissariat of External and Internal Trade)
Narkomzem	Narodnyi Komissariat Zemledeliya (People's Commissariat of Agriculture [of RSFSR up to December 1929, then of USSR])
NEP	Novaya ekonomicheskaya politika (New Economic Policy)
obshchina	peasant commune (= zemel'noe obshchestvo (land society), mir)
OGPU (GPU)	Ob''edinennoe Gosudarstvennoe Politicheskoe Upravlenie (Unified State Political Administration [Political Police])
okrug	administrative unit between region and district (see Technical Note in Volume 1)
orgraspred	organizatsionno-raspredelitel'nyi otdel (Organisation and Distribution Department [personnel department of party central committee])
otkhodnichestvo	'going away' to seasonal work outside one's own village or volost'
otkhodnik	peasant who goes away from village or volost' for seasonal work

otrub	peasant farm with fields only enclosed
pud	0.01638 tons[1]
pyatikratka	fine up to five times value of grain not delivered
Rabkrin	Narodnyi Komissariat Raboche-Krest'yanskoi Inspektsii (People's Commissariat of Workers' and Peasants' Inspection)
RSFSR	Rossiiskaya Sovetskaya Federativnaya Sotsialisticheskaya Respublika (Russian Soviet Federative Socialist Republic)
RSK	raion sploshnoi kollektivizatsii (district of comprehensive collectivisation)
ruble (rubl')	unit of currency, at par = £0·106 or $0·515
skhod	gathering or general assembly of mir
sovkhoz	sovetskoe khozyaistvo (Soviet [i.e. state] farm)
Sovnarkom	Sovet Narodnykh Komissarov (Council of People's Commissars)
Soyuzkhleb	'Union Grain' (All-Union association (ob''edinenie) of Narkomtorg)
Soyuzmyaso	'Union Meat' (All-Union association (ob''edinenie) of Narkomtorg)
stanitsa	large village in North Caucasus
STO	Sovet Truda i Oborony (Council of Labour and Defence [Economic sub-committee of Sovnarkom])
TOZ	tovarishchestvo po sovmestnoi (*or* obshchestvennoi) obrabotke zemli (association for the joint cultivation of land [simplest form of kolkhoz])
Traktorotsentr	Vsesoyuznyi tsentr mashinno-traktornykh stantsii (All-Union Centre of Machine-Tractor Stations)
tsentner	0·1 tons
TsIK	Tsentral'nyi Ispolnitel'nyi Komitet (Central Executive Committee [of Soviets of USSR])
Vesenkha	Vysshii Sovet Narodnogo Khozyaistva (Supreme Council of National Economy [in charge of industry])

[1] Metric tons are used throughout this volume.

volost' rural district (before 1930, intermediate between village and uezd)

Zernotrest Vsesoyuznyi trest zernovykh sovkhozov (All-Union Trust of [New] Grain Sovkhozy)

ABBREVIATIONS OF TITLES OF BOOKS AND PERIODICAL PUBLICATIONS USED IN FOOTNOTES

(For full titles, see appropriate section of Bibliography; items listed below are periodical publications unless otherwise stated.)

B	*Bol'shevik*
BO	*Byulleten' Oppozitsii*
BP	*Byulleten' ekonomicheskogo kabineta prof. S. N. Prokopovicha*
BU NKZ RSFSR	*Byulleten' uzakonenii . . . NKZ RSFSR*
EO	*Ekonomicheskoe obozrenie*
EZh	*Ekonomicheskaya zhizn'*
FP	*Finansovye problemy planovogo khozyaistva*
I	*Izvestiya*
IISO	*Istochnikovedenie istorii sovetskogo obshchestva*
IS	*Istoriya SSSR*
IZ	*Istoricheskie zapiski*
KG	*Krest'yanskaya gazeta*
KGN	*Krest'yanskaya gazeta: izdanie dlya nizhne-vol'zhskogo kraya*
KTs . . . na . . .	*Kontrol'nye tsifry narodnogo khozyaistva SSSR na . . .* (books)
NAF	*Na agrarnom fronte*
NFK	*Na fronte kollektivizatsii*
P	*Pravda*
PKh	*Planovoe khozyaistvo*
PS	*Partiinoe stroitel'stvo*
SKhG	*Sel'skokhozyaistvennaya gazeta*
SKhIB	*Sel'skokhozyaistvennyi informatsionnyi byulleten'*
SO	*Statisticheskoe obozrenie*

SRSKh	*Sotsialisticheskaya rekonstruktsiya sel'skogo khozyaistva*
SU	*Sobranie uzakonenii*
SZ	*Sobranie zakonov*
SZe	*Sotsialisticheskoe zemledelie*
SZo	*Sotsialisticheskoe zemleustroistvo*
TsIK 2/V	*2 [Vtoraya] sessiya Tsentral'nogo Ispolnitel'nogo Komiteta* (book)
VI	*Voprosy istorii*
VIK	*Voprosy istorii KPSS*
VT	*Voprosy torgovli*
VTr	*Voprosy truda*
ZI	*Za industrializatsiyu*
ZKK	*Za krupnye kolkhozy* (book)

BIBLIOGRAPHY

Letters used as abbreviations for items in the bibliography are listed on pp. 197–8. All other books are referred to in the text footnotes either by their author or editor, or by an abbreviated title (always including the first word or syllable) when there is no author or editor, and by date of publication.

Place of publication is Moscow or Moscow–Leningrad, unless otherwise stated.

Only items referred to in the text are included in the bibliography.

SECTION I NEWSPAPERS, JOURNALS AND OTHER PERIODICAL PUBLICATIONS

Bol'shevik

Byulleten' ekonomicheskogo kabineta prof. S. N. Prokopovicha (Prague)

Byulleten' Oppozitsii (bol'shevikov-lenintsev) (Paris)

Byulleten' uzakonenii i rasporyazhenii po sel'skomu i lesnomu khozyaistvu: ezhenedel'nyi offitsial'nyi organ NKZ RSFSR

Ekonomicheskaya zhizn'

Ekonomicheskoe obozrenie

Finansovye problemy planovogo khozyaistva (*Vestnik finansov* until no. 2, 1930)

Finansy i sotsialisticheskoe khozyaistvo

Istoricheskie zapiski

Istochnikovedenie istorii sovetskogo obshchestva

Istoriya SSSR

Izvestiya

Kollektivist

Krasnyi Khoper (Uryupinsk)

Krest'yanskaya gazeta

Krest'yanskaya gazeta: izdanie dlya nizhne-vol'zhskogo kraya

Materialy po istorii SSSR

Na agrarnom fronte

Na fronte kollektivizatsii
Nizhnee Povol'zhe (Saratov)
Partiinoe stroitel'stvo
Planovoe khozyaistvo
Povol'zhskaya pravda (Stalingrad)
Pravda
Sbornik postanovlenii i prikazov po promyshlennosti
Sel'skokhozyaistvennaya gazeta (*Sotsialisticheskoe zemledelie* from January 29, 1930)
Sel'skokhozyaistvennyi informatsionnyi byulleten'
Sobranie uzakonenii i rasporyazhenii RSFSR
Sobranie zakonov i rasporyazhenii SSSR
Sotsialisticheskaya rekonstruktsiya sel'skogo khozyaistva
Sotsialisticheskoe zemledelie (*Sel'skokhozyaistvennaya gazeta* until January 28, 1929)
Sotsialisticheskoe zemleustroistvo
Statisticheskoe obozrenie
Statistika i narodnoe khozyaistvo
Torgovo-promyshlennaya gazeta (*Za industrializatsiyu* from beginning of 1930)
Voprosy istorii
Voprosy istorii KPSS
Voprosy torgovli
Voprosy truda
Za industrializatsiyu (*Torgovo-promyshlennaya gazeta* until end of 1929)

SECTION II BOOKS IN RUSSIAN

Administrativno-territorial'noe selenie Soyuza SSR i spisok vazhneishikh naselennykh punktov, 8th edn (1929)

Andreev, A. A., *Uspekhi i nedostatki kolkhoznogo stroitel'stva, rech' na Rostovskom partaktive 18 marta 1930 goda* (Rostov, 1930)

Andreev, A. A., *Uspekhi kollektivizatsii na Severnom Kavkaze: doklad v politbyuro TsK VKP (b) v kontse noyabrya 1930 g. i postanovlenie TsK VKP(b) ot 10–1–1931 g.* (Rostov, 1931)

Anisimov, N., ed. *Brigadnaya sistema organizatsii truda v kolkhozakh* (1931)

Bauer, A. A., Ioganzen, A. A., Khizhnyakov, V. V., and Khmelev, N. N., *Kollektivnoe zemledelie: spravochnaya kniga dlya zemledel'cheskikh artelei, kommun i tovarishchestv* (1925)

Bogdenko, M. L., *Stroitel'stvo zernovykh sovkhozov v 1928–1932 gg.* (1958)

Chigrinov, G. A., *Bor'ba KPSS za organizatsionno-khozyaistvennoe ukreplenie kolkhozov v dovoennye gody* (1970)

Danilov, V. P., *Sozdanie material'no-tekhnicheskikh predposylok kollektivizatsii sel'skogo khozyaistva v SSSR* (1957)

Danilov, V. P., ed. *Ocherki istorii sel'skogo khozyaistva v soyuznykh respublikakh* (1963)

Direktivy KPSS i sovetskogo pravitel'stva po khozyaistvennym voprosam: sbornik dokumentov, vol. I, *1917–1928 gody* (1957)

Drozdov, A., *Organizatsiya truda i raspredelenie dokhodov v kolkhoze* (1930)

Ezhegodnik po sel'skomu khozyaistvu Sovetskogo Soyuza za 1931 god (1933)

Gaister, A. I., ed., *Zhivotnovodstvo SSSR: dinamika skotovodstva, kormovaya baza, myasnoi balans* (1930)

Industrializatsiya SSSR, 1929–1932 gg.: dokumenty i materialy (1970)

Ivnitskii, N. A., *Klassovaya bor'ba v derevne i likvidatsiya kulachestva kak klassa (1929–1932 gg.)* (1972)

Kak raspredelyat' urozhai i dokhody v kolkhozakh (ukazaniya kraikolkhozsoyuza i kraizemupravleniya, utverzhdennye kraiispolkomom) (Samara, 1930)

Kalinin, M. I., *Izbrannye proizvedeniya*, vol. II, *1926–1932 gg.* (1960)

Kindeev, K. Ya., *Organizatsiya truda v kolkhozakh* (1929)

Kolkhozy: pervyi vsesoyuznyi s''ezd kolkhozov (1–6 iyunya 1928 g.) (1929)

Kolkhozy v 1928 g.: itogi obsledovaniya kolkhozov (1932)

Kolkhozy v 1929 godu: itogi sploshnogo obsledovaniya kolkhozov (1931)

Kolkhozy v 1930 g.: itogi raportov kolkhozov XVI s''ezdu VKP (b) (1931)

Kollektivizatsiya sel'skogo khozyaistva na Severnom Kavkaze (1927–1937 gg.) (Krasnodar, 1972)

Kollektivizatsiya sel'skogo khozyaistva Tsentral'nogo promyshlennogo raiona (1927–1937 gg) (Ryazan', 1971)

Kollektivizatsiya sel'skogo khozyaistva: vazhneishie postanovleniya Kommunisticheskoi partii i Sovetskogo pravitel'stva, 1927–1935 (1957)

Kollektivizatsiya sel'skogo khozyaistva v Srednem povol'zhe (1927–1937 gg.) (Kuibyshev, 1970)

Kommunisticheskaya partiya Sovetskogo Soyuza v rezolyutsiyakh i resheniyakh s''ezdov, konferentsii i plenumov TsK, 2nd edn, vol. II, *1924–1930*, vol. III, *1930–1954* (1954)

Kontrol'nye tsifry narodnogo khozyaistva SSSR na 1929/30 god, odobrennye Sovetom Narodnykh Komissarov SSSR (1930)

Krot-Krival', S. M., *Skotovodstvo i molochnoe khozyaistvo v sel. khoz. kollektivakh i ikh organizatsiya i vedenie* (1926)

Malafeev, A. N, *Istoriya tsenoobrazovaniya v SSSR (1917–1963 gg.)* (1964)

Markevich, A. M., *Mezhselennye mashinno-traktornye stantsii*, 2nd edn (1929)

Materialy po balansu narodnogo khozyaistva SSSR za 1928, 1929 i 1930 gg. (1932)

Minaev, S. V., ed., *Sotsialisticheskoe pereustroistvo sel'skogo khozyaistva SSSR mezhdu XV i XVI s''ezdami VKP(b)* (1930)

Narodnoe khozyaistvo SSSR v 1958 godu: statisticheskii ezhegodnik (1959)

Narodnoe khozyaistvo SSSR: statisticheskii spravochnik 1932 (1932)

Nemakov, N I., *Kommunisticheskaya partiya – organizator massovogo kolkhoznogo dvizheniya (1929–1932 gg.): po materialam nekotorykh oblastei i kraev RSFSR* (1966)

Nifontov, V. P., *Zhivotnovodstvo SSSR v tsifrakh* (1932)

Plan kollektivizatsii v vesennyuyu sel'kokhozyaistvennuyu kampaniyu 1930 g. (1930)

Pravila vnutrennego rasporyadka sel'skokhozyaistvennoi arteli, 8th edn (1929)

Pyatiletnii plan narodno-khozyaistvennogo stroitel'stva SSSR, 3rd edn, vols. I, II(i), II(ii), III (1930)

Resheniya partii i pravitel'stva po khozyaistvennym voprosam, vol. II, *1929–1940 gody* (1967)

Sdvigi v sel'skom khozyaistve SSSR mezhdu XV i XVI partiinymi s''ezdami: statisticheskie svedeniya po sel'skomu khozyaistvu za 1927–1930 gg., 1st edn (1930), 2nd edn (1931)

Selunskaya, V. M., *Rabochie-dvadtsatipyatitysyachniki* (1964)

Shestnadtsataya konferentsiya VKP(b): aprel' 1929 goda: stenograficheskii otchet (1962)

XVI [Shestnadtsatyi] s''ezd Vsesoyuznoi Kommunisticheskoi partii (b): stenograficheskii otchet, 2nd edn (1931)

6 [Shestoi] s''ezd sovetov Soyuza SSR: stenograficheskii otchet (1931)

Slin'ko, I. I. *Sotsialistichna perebudova i tekhnichna rekonstruktsiya sil'skogo gospodarstva Ukraini (1927–1932 rr.)* (Kiev, 1961). (In Ukrainian)

Sotsialisticheskoe stroitel'stvo SSSR: statisticheskii ezhegodnik (1935)

Stalin, I. V., *Sochineniya*, vols. XI, XII (1949)

Trudy pervoi Vsesoyuznoi konferentsii agrarnikov-marksistov, 20.xii–27.xii.1930 [*sic* 1929], vols. I, II(i) and II(ii) (1930)

Ustav tovarishchestva po obshchestvennoi obrabotke zemli, 16th edn (1930)

Vlasov, N. S., and Nazimov, I. N., *Nedelimye fondy i struktura sredstv v kolkhozakh* (1930)
2 *[Vtoraya] sessiya Tsentral'nogo Ispolnitel'nogo Komiteta Soyuza SSR 5 Sozyva: stenograficheskii otchet* [November 29 – December 8, 1929] (1929)
Vyltsan, M. A., *Ukreplenie material'no-tekhnicheskoi bazy kolkhoznogo stroya vo 2-i pyatiletke, 1933–1937 gg.* (1959)
Za krupnye kolkhozy: materialy 1-go Vserossiiskogo soveshchaniya krupnykh kolkhozov (1929)

SECTION III BOOKS, THESES, ETC. IN OTHER LANGUAGES

Abramsky, C., ed., *Essays in Honour of E. H. Carr* (London, 1974)
Avtorkhanov, A., *Stalin and the Soviet Communist Party: a Study in the Technology of Power* (Munich, 1959)
Carr, E. H., *Socialism in One Country, 1924–1926*, vol. I (London, 1958), vol. II (London, 1959)
Carr, E. H., and Davies, R. W., *Foundations of a Planned Economy, 1926–1929*, vol. 1 (London, 1969)
Jasny, N., *The Socialized Agriculture of the USSR: Plans and Performance* (Stanford, 1949)
Lewin, M., *Russian Peasants and Soviet Power: a Study of Collectivization* (London, 1968)
Male, D. J., *Russian Peasant Organisation before Collectivisation: a Study of Commune and Gathering, 1925–1930* (Cambridge, 1971)
Miller, R., *One Hundred Thousand Tractors: the MTS and the Development of Controls in Soviet Agriculture* (Cambridge, Mass., 1970)
Wesson, R. G., *Soviet Communes* (New Brunswick N. J., 1963)
Wheatcroft, S. G., 'Soviet Grain Production Statistics for the 1920s and the 1930s', unpublished Discussion Papers SIPS 13 (Centre for Russian and East European Studies (CREES), University of Birmingham, 1977)
Wheatcroft, S. G., 'Views on Grain Output, Agricultural Reality and Planning in the Soviet Union in the 1920s', unpublished M.Soc.Sc. thesis (Centre for Russian and East European Studies (CREES), University of Birmingham, 1974)
Wronski, H., *Rémunération et niveau de vie dans les kolkhoz: le troudoden* (Paris, 1957)

NAME INDEX

SUBJECT INDEX